300 Best Without a Four-Year Degree

Second Edition

Part of JIST's Best Jobs™ Series

Michael Farr
With Database Work by Laurence Shatkin, Ph.D.

Also in JIST's *Best Jobs* Series

- *Best Jobs for the 21st Century*
- *200 Best Jobs for College Graduates*
- *250 Best Jobs Through Apprenticeships*
- *50 Best Jobs for Your Personality*
- *40 Best Fields for Your Career*
- *225 Best Jobs for Baby Boomers*

JIST Works
America's Career Publisher

300 Best Jobs Without a Four-Year Degree, Second Edition

© 2006 by JIST Publishing, Inc.

Published by JIST Works, an imprint of JIST Publishing, Inc.
8902 Otis Avenue
Indianapolis, IN 46216-1033

Phone: 1-800-648-JIST   Fax: 1-800-JIST-FAX
E-mail: info@jist.com   Web site: www.jist.com

Some Other Books by the Authors

Michael Farr

The Quick Resume & Cover Letter Book

Getting the Job You Really Want

The Very Quick Job Search

Overnight Career Choice

Laurence Shatkin

Quick Guide to College Majors and Careers

Quick Guide to Career Training in Two Years or Less

Quantity discounts are available for JIST products. Please call 1-800-648-JIST or visit www.jist.com for a free catalog and more information.

Visit www.jist.com for information on JIST, free job search information, book excerpts, and ordering information on our many products. For free information on 14,000 job titles, visit www.careeroink.com.

Acquisitions Editor: Susan Pines
Development Editor: Stephanie Koutek
Cover and Interior Designer: Aleata Howard

Interior Layout: Carolyn J. Newland
Proofreaders: Paula Lowell, Jeanne Clark
Indexer: Kelly D. Henthorne

Printed in the United States of America

10 09 08 07 06 05   9 8 7 6 5 4 3 2 1

   Library of Congress Cataloging-in-Publication Data
Farr, J. Michael.
   300 best jobs without a four-year degree / Michael Farr ; with database work by
Laurence Shatkin.— 2nd ed.
         p. cm. — (Jist's best jobs series)
   Includes bibliographical references and index.
   ISBN 1-59357-242-5 (alk. paper)
   1. Vocational guidance. 2. Employment forecasting. 3. Job hunting. I. Shatkin, Laurence. II. Title. III. Farr, J. Michael.
   JIST's best jobs series.
   HF5381.F4562 2006
   331.702—dc22
                                                                    2005032561

This Is a Big Book, But It Is Very Easy to Use

This book is designed for people who want to move ahead in their careers and have or are considering getting on-the-job training, vocational training, or a two-year degree.

It helps you explore your career options in a variety of interesting ways. The nice thing about this book is that you don't have to read it all. Instead, we designed it to allow you to browse and find information that most interests you.

The table of contents will give you a good idea of what's inside and how to use the book, so we suggest you start there. The first part is made up of interesting lists that will help you explore jobs based on pay, interests, education or training level, personality type, and many other criteria. The second part provides descriptions for the 300 jobs that met our criteria for this book (high pay, fast growth, and large number of openings). Just find a job that interests you in one of the lists in Part I and look up its description in Part II. Simple.

Some Things You Can Do with This Book

- Identify more-interesting or better-paying jobs that don't require additional training or education.
- Develop long-term career plans that may require additional training, education, or experience.
- Explore and select a training or educational program that relates to a career objective.
- Find reliable earnings information to negotiate pay.
- Prepare for interviews.

These are a few of the many ways you can use this book. We hope you find it as interesting to browse as we did to put together. We have tried to make it easy to use and as interesting as occupational information can be.

When you are done with this book, pass it along or tell someone else about it. We wish you well in your career and in your life.

(continued)

(continued)

Credits and Acknowledgments: While the authors created this book, it is based on the work of many others. The occupational information is based on data obtained from the U.S. Department of Labor and the U.S. Census Bureau. These sources provide the most authoritative occupational information available. The job titles and their related descriptions are from the O*NET database, which was developed by researchers and developers under the direction of the U.S. Department of Labor. They, in turn, were assisted by thousands of employers who provided details on the nature of work in the many thousands of job samplings used in the database's development. We used the most recent version of the O*NET database, release 8.0. We appreciate and thank the staff of the U.S. Department of Labor for their efforts and expertise in providing such a rich source of data.

Table of Contents

Summary of Major Sections

Introduction. A short overview to help you better understand and use the book. *Starts on page 1.*

Part I. The Best Jobs Lists: Jobs That Don't Require a Four-Year Degree. Very useful for exploring career options! Lists are arranged into easy-to-use groups. The first group of lists presents the 300 jobs that do not require a four-year degree and that have the highest rankings based on earnings, projected growth, and number of openings. More-specialized lists follow, presenting the best jobs by age, gender, level of education or training, personality type, and interest. The column starting at right presents all the list titles. *Starts on page 11.*

Part II. The Job Descriptions. Provides complete descriptions of the jobs that met our criteria for a combination of high pay, fast growth, and large number of openings. Each description contains information on earnings, projected growth, job duties, skills, related job titles, education and training required, related knowledge and courses, and many other details. *Starts on page 111.*

Detailed Table of Contents

Introduction

We want to keep our introduction short to encourage you to actually read or at least scan it. For this reason, we don't provide many details on the technical issues we had to solve in order to create this book. Instead, we give you short explanations that will help you understand the information presented in the book and use it well as a career exploration or planning tool.

Why We Created This Book

Several years ago we wrote a book titled *Best Jobs for the 21st Century.* It was very well received and has since been revised. It covers all major jobs at all levels of education and training and includes only those with earnings, projected growth rate, and number of job openings over certain criteria that we set. It is a very good book for those who want to consider jobs at all levels of education and training, but over one-third of the jobs included require a four-year college degree or higher.

So we decided that the world needs a good book for the many people who want to get ahead or change jobs—but who do not have a four-year college degree and are not planning to obtain one in the next few years.

This is that book.

How We Selected the 300 Best Jobs for People Without a Four-Year Degree

Deciding on the "best" job is a choice that only you can make, but objective criteria can help you identify jobs that are, for example, better paying than other jobs with similar duties. We sorted through the data for all major jobs and selected only those jobs that meet the following criteria:

1. They do not require a four-year college degree. The U.S. Department of Labor assigns a minimum level of training or education for entry into each job it tracks. This book excludes all jobs that require a four-year college degree or above. We included jobs requiring up to but not more than a two-year associate's degree—including those

requiring short-term to long-term on-the-job training, work experience in a related field, and/or formal or informal training lasting from several weeks to several years. There were 695 jobs that met this criterion.

2. They have the highest combined scores for earnings, growth, and number of openings. For the 695 jobs that met our first criterion, we collected data from a variety of government sources and created three lists that organized the jobs from highest to lowest on three measures:

   - Annual earnings
   - Projected growth rate through 2012
   - Number of job openings per year

3. We then assigned a number to the relative rank of the 695 jobs on each list. We combined each job's ranks from the three lists and sorted the jobs by this total score. The 300 jobs with the best combined score for earnings, growth rate, and number of openings per year are included in this book. They comprise the lists in Part I, and descriptions for each are located in Part II.

We are not suggesting that all of these jobs are good ones for you to consider—some will not be. But the 300 jobs that met our criteria cover such a wide range that you are likely to find one or more that interest you. The jobs that met our criteria are more likely than average to have higher pay, faster projected growth, and a larger number of openings than other jobs at similar levels of education and training.

Where the Information Came From

The information we used in creating this book came from three major sources:

- The U.S. Department of Labor—We used a variety of data sources to construct the information in this book. Most came from various databases of information provided by the U.S. Department of Labor. We started with the jobs included in the Department of Labor's O*NET (Occupational Information Network) database. The O*NET includes data on more than 1,000 occupations and is now the primary source of detailed information on occupations. The Labor Department updates the O*NET on a regular basis, and we used the most recent one available—O*NET version 8.

- The U.S. Census Bureau—Because we wanted to include earnings, growth, number of openings, and other data not in the O*NET, we cross-referenced information on earnings developed by the U.S. Bureau of Labor Statistics (BLS) and the U.S. Census Bureau. This information on earnings is the most reliable data we could obtain. For data on projected growth and number of openings, the BLS uses a slightly different system of job titles than the O*NET uses. We were able to link the BLS data to many of the O*NET job titles in this book and tie growth and earnings information to the job titles in this book.

- US—That's "us," the authors. We did many things to help make all the data useful and present it to you in a way that is more understandable than any boring database format.

The "How We Selected the 300 Best Jobs for People Without a Four-Year Degree" section at the beginning of this introduction includes a brief description of how we selected the jobs we included in this book. Here are a few more details:

1. We began by creating our own database of information from the O*NET and the Census Bureau and other sources to include the information we wanted. This database covered more than 1,000 job titles at all levels of education and training.

2. We cut our initial list to include only those jobs requiring up to but not more than a two-year associate degree. We also excluded any job for which we had only limited information (for example, information on income or skills or work tasks was missing), and we excluded a few jobs that are expected to employ fewer than 500 workers per year and to shrink rather than grow in workforce size. A total of 695 jobs met our criteria: they require short- to long-term on-the-job training, apprenticeship, work experience, career or vocational school training, or a two-year associate degree, and we had the full range of information about them.

3. Next, we created three lists that ranked all 695 of these jobs based on three major criteria: annual earnings, projected growth through 2012, and number of job openings projected per year.

4. We then added the ranks for each job from all three lists to calculate its overall score.

5. To emphasize jobs that tend to pay more, are likely to grow more rapidly, and have more job openings, we selected the 300 job titles with the best numerical scores for our final list. These jobs are the focus of this book.

For example, Registered Nurses has the best combined score for earnings, growth, and number of job openings, so Registered Nurses is listed first in our "The 300 Best Jobs That Don't Require a Four-Year Degree" list even though it is not the best-paying job (which is Air Traffic Controllers), the fastest-growing job (which is Medical Assistants), or the job with the most openings (which is Cashiers).

Understand the Limits of the Data in This Book

In this book we use the most reliable and up-to-date information available on earnings, projected growth, number of openings, and other topics. Some came from the U.S. Department of Labor source known as Occupation and Employment Statistics, and others came from the Current Population Survey from the Census Bureau. As you look at the figures, keep in mind that they are estimates. They give you a general idea about the number of workers employed, annual earnings, rate of job growth, and annual job openings.

Understand that a problem with data is that it is true only on the average. Just as there is no precisely average person, there is no such thing as a statistically average example of a particular job. We say this because data, while helpful, can also be misleading.

Take, for example, the yearly earnings information in this book. This is highly reliable data obtained from a very large U.S. working population sample by the Bureau of Labor Statistics. It tells us the average annual pay received by people in various job titles (actually, it is the median annual pay, which means that half earned more and half less).

This sounds great, except that half of all people in that occupation earned less than that amount. For example, people entering the occupation or with a few years of work experience often earn much less than the average amount. People who live in rural areas or who work for smaller employers typically earn less than those who do similar work in cities (where the cost of living is higher) or for bigger employers. People in certain areas of the country earn less than those in others. Other factors also influence how much you are likely to earn in a given job in your area. For example, Lawn Service Managers have median earnings of $35,340, but those in cold climate areas would work only part of the year.

So, in reviewing the information in this book, please understand the limitations of data. You need to use common sense in career decision-making as in most other things in life. Even so, we hope that you find the information helpful and interesting.

The Data Complexities

For those of you who like details, we present some of the complexities inherent in our sources of information and what we did to make sense of them here. You don't need to know this to use the book, so jump to the next section of the Introduction if you are bored with details.

Earnings, Growth, and Number of Openings

We include information on earnings, projected growth, and number of job openings for each job throughout this book.

Earnings

The employment security agency of each state gathers information on earnings for various jobs and forwards it to the U.S. Bureau of Labor Statistics. This information is organized in standardized ways by a BLS program called Occupational Employment Statistics, or OES. To keep the earnings for the various jobs and regions comparable, the OES screens out certain types of earnings and includes others, so the OES earnings we use in this book represent straight-time gross pay exclusive of premium pay. More specifically, the OES earnings include the job's base rate; cost-of-living allowances; guaranteed pay; hazardous-duty pay; incentive pay, including commissions and production bonuses; on-call pay; and tips but do not include back pay, jury duty pay, overtime pay, severance pay, shift differentials, non-production bonuses, or tuition reimbursements. Also, self-employed workers are not included in the estimates, and they can be a significant segment in certain occupations. When data on earnings for an occupation is highly unreliable, OES does not report a figure, which meant that we reluctantly had to exclude from this book a few occupations such as Musicians and Singers. The average earnings for all workers in all occupations were $28,770 in May 2004.

The OES earnings data uses a system of job titles called the Standard Occupational Classification system, or SOC. We cross-referenced these titles to the O*NET job titles we use in this book, so we can rank the jobs by their earnings and include earnings information in the job descriptions. In some cases, an SOC title cross-references to more than one O*NET job title. For example, the O*NET has separate information for Heavy Truck Drivers and Tractor-Trailer Truck Drivers, but the SOC reports earnings for a single occupation called Truck Drivers, Heavy and Tractor-Trailer. Therefore you may notice that the salary we report for Heavy Truck Drivers ($33,520) is identical to the salary we report for Tractor-Trailer Truck Drivers. In reality there probably is a difference, but this is the best information that is available.

Projected Growth and Number of Job Openings

This information comes from the Office of Occupational Statistics and Employment Projections, a program within the Bureau of Labor Statistics that develops information about projected trends in the nation's labor market for the next ten years. The most recent projections available cover the years from 2002 to 2012. The projections are based on information about people moving into and out of occupations. The BLS uses data from various sources in projecting the growth and number of openings for each job title—some data comes from the Census Bureau's Current Population Survey and some comes from an OES survey. The projections assume that there will be no major war, depression, or other economic upheaval.

Like the earnings figures, the figures on projected growth and job openings are reported according to the SOC classification, so again you will find that some of the SOC jobs cross-walk to more than one O*NET job. To continue the example we used earlier, SOC reports growth (19.0%) and openings (299,000) for one occupation called Truck Drivers, Heavy and Tractor-Trailer, but in this book we report these figures separately for the occupation Heavy Truck Drivers and for the occupation Tractor-Trailer Truck Drivers. When you see Heavy Truck Drivers with 19.0% projected growth and 299,000 projected job openings, and Tractor-Trailer Truck Drivers with the same two numbers, you should realize that the 19.0% rate of projected growth represents the average of these two occupations—one may actually experience higher growth than the other—and that these two occupations will share the 299,000 projected openings.

While salary figures are fairly straightforward, you may not know what to make of job-growth figures. For example, is projected growth of 15% good or bad? You should keep in mind that the average (mean) growth projected for all occupations in the OES survey is 14.8%. One-quarter of the occupations have a growth projection of 4.7% or lower. Growth of 12.4% is the median, meaning that half of the occupations have more, half less. Only one-quarter of the occupations have growth projected at more than 19.4%.

Remember, however, that the jobs in this book were selected as "best" partly on the basis of high growth, so their mean growth is an impressive 17.5%. Among these 300 outstanding jobs, the job ranked 100th by projected growth has a figure of 19.3%, the job ranked 150th (the median) has a projected growth of 16.5%, and the job ranked 200th has a projected growth of 13.2%.

Part I. The Best Jobs Lists: Jobs That Don't Require a Four-Year Degree

Sixty-two lists are included in Part I of this book—look in the table of contents for a complete list of them. Although there are a lot of lists, they are not difficult to understand because they have clear titles and are organized into groupings of related lists.

Depending on your situation, some of the jobs lists in Part I will interest you more than others. For example, if you are young, you may be interested in finding out about the best-paying jobs that employ high percentages of young people. Other lists show jobs at various levels of training, experience, or education that you might consider in your career planning.

Whatever your situation, we suggest you use the lists that make sense for you to help explore career options. Following are the names of each group of lists along with short comments on each group. You will find additional information in a brief introduction provided at the beginning of each group of lists in Part I. Comments are also provided at the beginning of many of the lists.

Here is an overview of each major group of lists in Part I.

Best Jobs Overall: Jobs with the Highest Pay, Fastest Growth, and Most Openings

Four lists are in this group, and they are the ones that most people want to see first. The first list presents all 300 jobs that are included in this book in order of their combined scores for earnings, growth, and number of job openings. These jobs are used in the more-specialized lists that follow. Three more lists in this group present the 100 best-paying jobs, the 100 fastest-growing jobs, and the 100 jobs with the most openings.

Best Jobs with High Percentages of Workers Age 16–24, Workers Age 55 and Over, Part-Time Workers, Self-Employed Workers, Women, and Men

This group includes a total of 30 lists that are arranged into subgroups of five lists for each population covered. For example, the first subgroup presents five lists for workers age 16 to 24. The first list in this subgroup presents jobs with a high percentage of workers age 16 to 24. In this case, we set the criteria of 20 percent or higher of workers age 16 to 24, and 54 jobs met this criterion. This list is then followed by more specialized lists:

- Best Jobs Overall for Workers Age 16–24—This list includes the 25 jobs with the best combined scores for earnings, growth, and number of openings.

- Best-Paying Jobs for Workers Age 16–24—A list of the 25 jobs with the highest pay.

- Fastest-Growing Jobs for Workers Age 16–24—A list of 25 jobs that are projected to grow the fastest through 2012.

- Jobs with the Most Openings for Workers Age 16–24—A list of 25 jobs that are projected to have the most openings per year.

Best Jobs Based on Levels of Education, Training, and Experience

The six lists in this group present jobs that require different levels of education or training. The jobs are all from our list of 300 best jobs used throughout this book. One list is provided for each level of education and training up to and including a two-year associate degree.

The levels are those used by the U.S. Department of Labor, and they represent the minimum level of education or training typically required for entry to that job. The number of jobs in each list varies based on how many of the jobs in our top 300 require each of the levels. The lists cover jobs for the following levels: short-term on-the-job training, moderate-term on-the-job training, long-term on-the-job training, work experience in a related job, postsecondary vocational training, and associate degree. The introduction to this group of lists in Part I describes these levels and provides other information.

Best Jobs Based on Interests

There are 16 lists in this group, and they contain all of the jobs from our 300 best jobs list that fall within each of 16 major areas of interest. The number of jobs varies by list, and the lists are organized in order of combined score for earnings, growth, and number of openings.

Best Jobs Based on Personality Types

This group provides one list of jobs for each of six personality types, based on a system that is used in a variety of popular career exploration inventories. The lists present the jobs in order of their combined scores for earnings, growth, and number of openings. We explain the six personality types in the introduction to these lists.

Part II. The Job Descriptions

This part of the book provides a brief but information-packed description for each of the 300 best jobs that met our criteria for this book. The descriptions are presented in alphabetical order. This structure makes it easy to look up a job that you've identified in a list from Part I and you want to learn more about.

We used the most current information from a variety of government sources to create the descriptions. Although we've tried to make the descriptions easy to understand, the sample job description that follows—and the explanation of each of its parts—may help you better understand and use the descriptions.

Here are details on each of the major parts of the job descriptions you will find in Part II:

- ◎ **Job Title**—This is the job title for the job as defined by the U.S. Department of Labor and used in its O*NET database.

- ◎ **Data Elements**—This information comes from various government databases for this occupation, as explained elsewhere in this Introduction.

- ◎ **Summary Description and Tasks**—The bold sentences provide a summary description of the occupation. This is followed by a listing of tasks that are generally performed by people who work in the job.

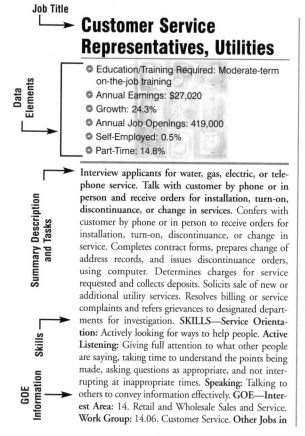

Job Title

Customer Service Representatives, Utilities

Data Elements

- ◎ Education/Training Required: Moderate-term on-the-job training
- ◎ Annual Earnings: $27,020
- ◎ Growth: 24.3%
- ◎ Annual Job Openings: 419,000
- ◎ Self-Employed: 0.5%
- ◎ Part-Time: 14.8%

Summary Description and Tasks

Interview applicants for water, gas, electric, or telephone service. Talk with customer by phone or in person and receive orders for installation, turn-on, discontinuance, or change in services. Confers with customer by phone or in person to receive orders for installation, turn-on, discontinuance, or change in service. Completes contract forms, prepares change of address records, and issues discontinuance orders, using computer. Determines charges for service requested and collects deposits. Solicits sale of new or additional utility services. Resolves billing or service complaints and refers grievances to designated departments for investigation. **SKILLS—Service Orientation:** Actively looking for ways to help people. **Active Listening:** Giving full attention to what other people are saying, taking time to understand the points being made, asking questions as appropriate, and not interrupting at inappropriate times. **Speaking:** Talking to others to convey information effectively. **GOE—Interest Area:** 14. Retail and Wholesale Sales and Service. **Work Group:** 14.06. Customer Service. **Other Jobs in**

GOE Information | **Skills**

This Work Group: Adjustment Clerks; Cashiers; Counter and Rental Clerks; Gaming Change Persons and Booth Cashiers; Order Clerks; Receptionists and Information Clerks. **PERSONALITY TYPE:** Conventional. Conventional occupations frequently involve following set procedures and routines. These occupations can include working with data and details more than with ideas. Usually there is a clear line of authority to follow.

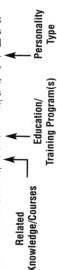

Personality Type

EDUCATION/TRAINING PROGRAM(S)—Customer Service Support/Call Center/Teleservice Operation; Receptionist. **RELATED KNOWLEDGE/COURSES—Sales and Marketing:** Knowledge of principles and methods for showing, promoting, and selling products or services. This includes marketing strategy and tactics, product demonstrations, sales techniques, and sales control systems. **Customer and Personal Service:** Knowledge of principles and processes for providing customer and personal services. This includes customer needs assessment, meeting quality standards for services, and evaluation of customer satisfaction. **Economics and Accounting:** Knowledge of economic and accounting principles and practices, the financial markets, banking, and the analysis and reporting of financial data. **Telecommunications:** Knowledge of transmission, broadcasting, switching, control, and operation of telecommunications systems. **Clerical Practices:** Knowledge of administrative and clerical procedures and systems such as word processing, managing files and records, stenography and transcription, designing forms, and other office procedures and terminology.

Education/Training Program(s)

Related Knowledge/Courses

- ◉ **Skills**—The government provides data on many skills; we decided to list only those that were most important for each job rather than list pages of unhelpful details. For each job, we identified any skill with a rating that was higher than the average rating for this skill for all jobs. We order the skills by the amount by which their ratings exceed the average rating for all occupations, from highest to lowest. If there are more than eight such skills, we include only those eight with the highest ratings. We include up to 10 skills if scores were tied for eighth place. If no skill has a rating higher than the average for all jobs, we say "None met the criteria." Each listed skill is followed by a brief description of that skill.

- ◉ **GOE Information**—This information cross-references the Guide for Occupational Exploration (or the GOE), a system developed by the U.S. Department of Labor that organizes jobs based on interests. We use the groups from the *New Guide for Occupational Exploration: Linking Interests, Learning, and Careers,* Fourth Edition, published by JIST. This edition of the GOE uses a set of interest fields based on the 16 career clusters developed by the U.S. Department of Education and used in a variety of career information systems. The description includes the major Interest Area the job fits into, its more-specific Work Group, and a list of related O*NET job titles that are in this same GOE Work Group. This information will help you identify other job titles that have similar interests or require similar skills. You can find more information on the GOE and its Interest Areas in the introduction to the lists of jobs based on interests in Part I.

- ◉ **Personality Type**—This part gives the name of the personality type that most closely matches each job as well as a brief definition of this personality type. You can find more information on the personality types in the introduction to the lists of jobs based on personality types in Part I.

- ◉ **Education/Training Program(s)**—This part of the job description provides the name of the educational or training program or programs for the job. It will help you identify sources of formal or informal training for a job that interests you. To get this information, we used a crosswalk created by the National Crosswalk Service Center to connect information in the Classification of Instruction Programs (CIP) to the O*NET job titles we use in this book. We made various changes to connect the O*NET job titles to the education or training programs related to them and also modified the names of some education and training programs so they would be more easily understood.

- ◉ **Related Knowledge/Courses**—This entry can help you understand the most important knowledge areas that are required for a job and the types of courses or programs you will likely need to take to prepare for it. We used information in the Department of Labor's O*NET database for this entry. We went through a process similar to the one we used for skills (earlier in this list) to determine which entries were most important for each job.

Sources of Additional Information

Hundreds of sources of career information are available; here are a few we consider most helpful for getting additional information on the jobs listed in this book.

Print References

◉ *O*NET Dictionary of Occupational Titles*—Revised on a regular basis, this book provides good descriptions for all jobs listed in the U.S. Department of Labor's O*NET database (more than 1,000 jobs at all levels of education and training), plus lists of related job titles in other major career information sources, educational programs, and other information. Published by JIST.

◉ *New Guide for Occupational Exploration: Linking Interests, Learning, and Careers,* **Fourth Edition**—This new edition of the GOE is cross-referenced in the descriptions provided in Part II. The *New GOE* provides helpful information to consider on each of the Interest Areas and Work Groups as well as descriptions of all O*NET jobs within each group, and it has many other features useful for exploring career options. Published by JIST.

◉ *Enhanced Occupational Outlook Handbook*—Updated regularly, this handbook provides thorough descriptions for more than 270 major jobs, descriptions for the O*NET jobs that are related to each, brief descriptions of thousands of more-specialized jobs, and other information. Published by JIST.

Internet Resources

◉ **The U.S. Department of Labor Web site**—The U.S. Department of Labor Web site (http://www.bls.gov) provides a lot of career information, including links to other pages that provide information on the jobs covered in this book. The site is a bit formal and, well, confusing, but it will take you to the major sources of government career information if you explore its options.

◉ **O*NET site**—Go to http://www.onetcenter.org for a variety of information on the O*NET database, including additional detailed information on the O*NET job titles presented in Part II of this book.

◉ **CareerOINK.com**—This site (at http://www.careeroink.com) is operated by JIST and includes lots of free information on all major jobs, easy-to-use crosswalks between major career information systems, links from military to civilian jobs, sample resumes, and many other features. A link at http://www.jist.com will also take you to the CareerOINK Web site.

Thanks

Thanks for reading this introduction. You are surely a more thorough person than someone who jumped into the book without reading it, and you will likely get more out of the book.

We wish you a satisfying career and, more importantly, a satisfying life.

PART I

The Best Jobs Lists: Jobs That Don't Require a Four-Year Degree

This part contains a lot of interesting lists, and it's a good place for you to start using the book. Here are some suggestions for using the lists to explore career options:

◎ The table of contents at the beginning of this book presents a complete listing of the list titles in this section. The lists are arranged in easy-to-use groups. You can browse the lists or use the table of contents to find those that interest you most.

◎ We organized the lists into sensible groups and gave them clear titles, so most require little explanation. We provide comments for each group of lists to inform you of the selection criteria we used or other details we think you may want to know.

◎ This part contains a large variety of lists to meet many different interests and needs. Some lists will help you identify jobs based on your interests or personality type; others provide information on jobs by education or training needed, jobs with high percentages of men or women, and many other criteria. The table of contents also provides page numbers for these lists.

◎ As you review the lists, one or more of the occupations may appeal to you enough that you want to seek additional information. As this happens, mark that occupation (or, if someone else will be using this book, write it on a separate sheet of paper) so that you can look up the description of that job in Part II.

◎ All data in this book comes from government sources, including the U.S. Department of Labor and the Census Bureau. The earnings figures are based on the average annual pay received by full-time workers. Some occupations have high percentages of part-time workers, and those workers would receive, of course, proportionately less pay on a weekly or annual basis. The earnings also represent the national averages, and actual pay rates can vary greatly by location, amount of previous work experience, and other factors.

Understand the Limitations of the Information

Many of the lists emphasize jobs with high pay, high growth, or large numbers of openings. Most people consider these factors important in selecting a desirable job, and they are also easily quantifiable. While these measures are important, we think you should also think about other factors in considering your career options. For example, location, liking the people you work with, having an opportunity to serve others, and enjoying your work are just a few of the many factors that may define the ideal job for you. These measures are difficult or impossible to objectively quantify and are not, therefore, presented in this book. For this reason, we suggest that you consider the importance of these issues yourself and that you thoroughly research any job before making a firm decision.

For example, of the 300 jobs in our Best Jobs Overall list, the last job is Photographers, Scientific. It has annual earnings of $26,080, a 13.6 percent growth rate, and 18,000 job openings per year. Is this a "bad" job, one you should avoid? No, of course not. It all depends on what you like or want to do. Another example is the job that had the very best overall score for earnings, growth, and number of openings, Registered Nurses. Is this job a great job to consider? Many people (the authors included) would not want to work in this job or may not have the skills or interest needed to do it well. It would be a great job for someone who was good at it and who would enjoy doing it, but it would simply not be right for someone else. On the other hand, the perfect job for some people would be Photographers, Scientific, because they enjoy it and are good at it.

So, as you look at the lists that follow, keep in mind that earnings, growth, and number of openings are just some things to consider. Also consider that half of all people in a given job earn more than the earnings you will see in this book—and half earn less. If a job really appeals to you, you should consider it even if it is not among the highest paying. And you should also consider jobs not among the fastest growing and jobs with few openings for similar reasons, because openings are always available, even for jobs with slow or negative growth projections or with small numbers of openings.

Some Details on the Lists

The sources of the information we used in constructing these lists are presented in this book's introduction. Here are some additional details on how we created the lists:

◎ **We excluded some jobs for which very little information is available.** In the full list of 1,167 jobs that are described in the U.S. Department of Labor's O*NET database, information on education required is not available for 42, so they could not be included in this book. Of the remaining occupations, 841 require less than four years of education, but 137 of these have no information beyond a definition and, in some cases, a list of tasks. These are either catchall titles (such as "Media and Communication Workers, All Other") that make the O*NET as comprehensive as possible or dummy occupations that help the O*NET match up better with occupational information from other government agencies. Census Bureau data is available for some of them, but little or no O*NET data is available for them, so we dropped them from consideration. We also reluctantly excluded five jobs because no wage information is available for them: Actors; Dancers; Hunters and Trappers; Musicians, Instrumental; and Singers. This left 699 occupations.

⚙ **We excluded some jobs that are shrinking and that offer very few opportunities.** Among the 699 jobs requiring less than four years and for which we have both O*NET and wage information, four are expected to employ fewer than 500 workers per year and to shrink rather than grow in workforce size: Bridge and Lock Tenders; Fabric Menders, Except Garment; Nuclear Power Reactor Operators; and Radio Operators. These jobs can't be considered "best jobs," so we excluded them from consideration for this book. Thus we sorted 695 jobs to determine the best 300 for this book.

⚙ **Some jobs have the same scores for one or more data elements.** For example, in the category of jobs with the most openings, three jobs (First-Line Supervisors/Managers of Food Preparation and Serving Workers; Personal and Home Care Aides; and Shipping, Receiving, and Traffic Clerks) are expected to have the same number of job openings per year, 154,000. Therefore we ordered these three jobs alphabetically, and their order has no other significance. There was no way to avoid these ties, so simply understand that the difference of several positions on a list may not mean as much as it seems.

We hope you find these lists both interesting and helpful. They can help you explore your career options in a variety of interesting ways. We suggest you find the ones that are most helpful to you and focus your attention on them. Enjoy!

Best Jobs Overall: Jobs with the Highest Pay, Fastest Growth, and Most Openings

We consider the four lists that follow to be our premier lists. They are the lists that are most often mentioned in the media and the ones that most readers want to see. The first list presents the jobs with the highest combined scores for pay, growth, and number of openings that do not require a four-year college degree. This is a very popular list because it represents jobs with the very highest quantifiable measures from our labor market. Three additional lists present jobs with the highest scores in each of three measures: annual earnings, projected percentage growth through 2012, and largest number of openings. As you review these lists, keep in mind that the lists include jobs with the highest measures from a database of jobs that included all major jobs that don't require a four-year degree in our economy. Jobs that did not make it onto the list of 300 best jobs are not included in the descriptions in Part II.

The 300 Best Jobs That Don't Require a Four-Year Degree

This is the list that most people want to know about. It includes the 300 jobs that don't require a four-year college degree that have the highest overall combined ratings for earnings, projected growth, and number of openings.

One job had the same score as the 300th job in the list. So, to be perfectly fair, this book title might have been a less memorable "301 Best Jobs Without a Four-Year Degree." To avoid this unnatural situation, we simply dropped the last job title from the 300 Best Jobs That Don't Require a Four-Year Degree list and the three lists of 100 jobs that follow. We did, however, include the additional job in the more-specialized lists you will find later in this section, and we included its description in Part II. The job tied for last place in the list is Professional Photographers; it is tied because the Department of Labor reports figures on earnings, growth, and openings for Photographers and does not distinguish between Photographers, Scientific and Professional Photographers.

A wide variety of jobs are on the list. Among the top 20 are jobs in sales, education, law enforcement, construction, administration, and transportation. The top 20 also include several management and supervisory jobs, proving that these kinds of jobs do exist for people without a college degree.

Registered Nurses was the occupation with the best combined score, and it is on the top of the list. The other occupations follow in descending order based on their combined scores. Many jobs had tied scores and were simply listed one after another, so there are often only very small or even no differences between the scores of jobs that are near each other on a list. All other jobs lists in this book use these jobs as their source list. You can find descriptions for each of these jobs beginning on page 111.

The 300 Best Jobs That Don't Require a Four-Year Degree

Job	Annual Earnings	Percent Growth	Annual Openings
1. Registered Nurses	$52,330	27.3%	215,000
2. Vocational Education Teachers, Postsecondary	$40,740	38.1%	216,000
3. Highway Patrol Pilots	$45,210	24.7%	67,000
4. Police Patrol Officers	$45,210	24.7%	67,000
5. Sheriffs and Deputy Sheriffs	$45,210	24.7%	67,000
6. Sales Representatives, Wholesale and Manufacturing, Except Technical and Scientific Products	$45,400	19.1%	160,000
7. Sales Representatives, Agricultural	$58,580	19.3%	44,000
8. Sales Representatives, Chemical and Pharmaceutical	$58,580	19.3%	44,000
9. Sales Representatives, Electrical/Electronic	$58,580	19.3%	44,000
10. Sales Representatives, Instruments	$58,580	19.3%	44,000

The 300 Best Jobs That Don't Require a Four-Year Degree

Job	Annual Earnings	Percent Growth	Annual Openings
11. Sales Representatives, Mechanical Equipment and Supplies	$58,580	19.3%	44,000
12. Sales Representatives, Medical	$58,580	19.3%	44,000
13. Computer Support Specialists	$40,430	30.3%	71,000
14. Electricians	$42,300	23.4%	65,000
15. Paralegals and Legal Assistants	$39,130	28.7%	29,000
16. Heating and Air Conditioning Mechanics	$36,260	31.8%	35,000
17. Refrigeration Mechanics	$36,260	31.8%	35,000
18. Pipe Fitters	$41,290	18.7%	56,000
19. Pipelaying Fitters	$41,290	18.7%	56,000
20. Plumbers	$41,290	18.7%	56,000
21. First-Line Supervisors and Manager/Supervisors—Construction Trades Workers	$50,450	14.1%	67,000
22. First-Line Supervisors and Manager/Supervisors—Extractive Workers	$50,450	14.1%	67,000
23. Dental Hygienists	$58,350	43.1%	9,000
24. First-Line Supervisors/Managers of Mechanics, Installers, and Repairers	$50,340	15.4%	42,000
25. Tractor-Trailer Truck Drivers	$33,520	19.0%	299,000
26. Truck Drivers, Heavy	$33,520	19.0%	299,000
27. Storage and Distribution Managers	$66,600	19.7%	13,000
28. Transportation Managers	$66,600	19.7%	13,000
29. Refractory Materials Repairers, Except Brickmasons	$37,640	16.3%	155,000
30. Licensed Practical and Licensed Vocational Nurses	$33,970	20.2%	105,000
31. Child Support, Missing Persons, and Unemployment Insurance Fraud Investigators	$53,990	22.4%	11,000
32. Criminal Investigators and Special Agents	$53,990	22.4%	11,000
33. Immigration and Customs Inspectors	$53,990	22.4%	11,000
34. Police Detectives	$53,990	22.4%	11,000
35. Police Identification and Records Officers	$53,990	22.4%	11,000
36. Radiologic Technicians	$43,350	22.9%	21,000
37. Radiologic Technologists	$43,350	22.9%	21,000
38. Correctional Officers and Jailers	$33,600	24.2%	49,000
39. Forest Fire Fighters	$38,330	20.7%	29,000
40. Municipal Fire Fighters	$38,330	20.7%	29,000
41. Legal Secretaries	$36,720	18.8%	39,000
42. Respiratory Therapists	$43,140	34.8%	10,000

(continued)

(continued)

The 300 Best Jobs That Don't Require a Four-Year Degree

Job	Annual Earnings	Percent Growth	Annual Openings
43. Self-Enrichment Education Teachers	$30,880	40.1%	39,000
44. Sheet Metal Workers	$35,560	19.8%	30,000
45. First-Line Supervisors/Managers of Police and Detectives	$64,430	15.3%	14,000
46. First-Line Supervisors/Managers of Non-Retail Sales Workers	$59,300	6.8%	72,000
47. Caption Writers	$44,350	16.1%	23,000
48. Talent Directors	$52,840	18.3%	10,000
49. Technical Directors/Managers	$52,840	18.3%	10,000
50. Claims Examiners, Property and Casualty Insurance	$44,220	14.2%	31,000
51. Insurance Adjusters, Examiners, and Investigators	$44,220	14.2%	31,000
52. Physical Therapist Assistants	$37,890	44.6%	10,000
53. Forest Fire Fighting and Prevention Supervisors	$58,920	18.7%	8,000
54. Municipal Fire Fighting and Prevention Supervisors	$58,920	18.7%	8,000
55. Flight Attendants	$43,440	15.9%	23,000
56. Adjustment Clerks	$27,020	24.3%	419,000
57. Customer Service Representatives, Utilities	$27,020	24.3%	419,000
58. First-Line Supervisors/Managers of Production and Operating Workers	$44,740	9.5%	66,000
59. Massage Therapists	$31,960	27.1%	24,000
60. Food Service Managers	$39,610	11.5%	58,000
61. Production, Planning, and Expediting Clerks	$36,340	14.1%	51,000
62. First-Line Supervisors and Manager/Supervisors—Landscaping Workers	$35,340	21.6%	18,000
63. Lawn Service Managers	$35,340	21.6%	18,000
64. Maintenance and Repair Workers, General	$30,710	16.3%	155,000
65. Cement Masons and Concrete Finishers	$31,400	26.1%	24,000
66. Telecommunications Line Installers and Repairers	$40,330	18.8%	13,000
67. Dental Assistants	$28,330	42.5%	35,000
68. Human Resources Assistants, Except Payroll and Timekeeping	$31,750	19.3%	36,000
69. Bill and Account Collectors	$27,450	24.5%	76,000
70. Surgical Technologists	$34,010	27.9%	13,000
71. Brazers	$30,620	17.0%	71,000
72. First-Line Supervisors/Managers of Transportation and Material-Moving Machine and Vehicle Operators	$44,810	12.1%	23,000
73. Solderers	$30,620	17.0%	71,000
74. Welder-Fitters	$30,620	17.0%	71,000
75. Welders and Cutters	$30,620	17.0%	71,000
76. Welders, Production	$30,620	17.0%	71,000

The 300 Best Jobs That Don't Require a Four-Year Degree

Job	Annual Earnings	Percent Growth	Annual Openings
77. Appraisers, Real Estate	$43,390	17.6%	11,000
78. Assessors	$43,390	17.6%	11,000
79. Diagnostic Medical Sonographers	$52,490	24.0%	4,000
80. Boat Builders and Shipwrights	$34,900	10.1%	193,000
81. Brattice Builders	$34,900	10.1%	193,000
82. Carpenter Assemblers and Repairers	$34,900	10.1%	193,000
83. Construction Carpenters	$34,900	10.1%	193,000
84. Rough Carpenters	$34,900	10.1%	193,000
85. Ship Carpenters and Joiners	$34,900	10.1%	193,000
86. Cardiovascular Technologists and Technicians	$38,690	33.5%	6,000
87. Medical Assistants	$24,610	58.9%	78,000
88. Brickmasons and Blockmasons	$41,740	14.2%	21,000
89. Ceiling Tile Installers	$34,030	21.4%	17,000
90. Drywall Installers	$34,030	21.4%	17,000
91. Advertising Sales Agents	$40,300	13.4%	24,000
92. Calibration and Instrumentation Technicians	$46,310	10.0%	24,000
93. Electrical Engineering Technicians	$46,310	10.0%	24,000
94. Electronics Engineering Technicians	$46,310	10.0%	24,000
95. First-Line Supervisors, Administrative Support	$41,030	6.6%	140,000
96. First-Line Supervisors, Customer Service	$41,030	6.6%	140,000
97. Roofers	$30,840	18.6%	38,000
98. Automotive Master Mechanics	$32,450	12.4%	100,000
99. Automotive Specialty Technicians	$32,450	12.4%	100,000
100. Truck Drivers, Light or Delivery Services	$24,540	23.2%	219,000
101. Bus and Truck Mechanics and Diesel Engine Specialists	$35,780	14.2%	28,000
102. Coroners	$47,390	9.8%	20,000
103. Environmental Compliance Inspectors	$47,390	9.8%	20,000
104. Equal Opportunity Representatives and Officers	$47,390	9.8%	20,000
105. Government Property Inspectors and Investigators	$47,390	9.8%	20,000
106. Licensing Examiners and Inspectors	$47,390	9.8%	20,000
107. Pressure Vessel Inspectors	$47,390	9.8%	20,000
108. Executive Secretaries and Administrative Assistants	$34,970	8.7%	210,000
109. Social and Human Service Assistants	$24,270	48.7%	63,000
110. City and Regional Planning Aides	$34,360	17.5%	18,000
111. Social Science Research Assistants	$34,360	17.5%	18,000
112. Receptionists and Information Clerks	$21,830	29.5%	296,000

(continued)

(continued)

The 300 Best Jobs That Don't Require a Four-Year Degree

Job	Annual Earnings	Percent Growth	Annual Openings
113. Costume Attendants	$25,050	27.8%	66,000
114. Fitness Trainers and Aerobics Instructors	$25,470	44.5%	38,000
115. Grader, Bulldozer, and Scraper Operators	$35,360	10.4%	45,000
116. Hazardous Materials Removal Workers	$33,320	43.1%	8,000
117. Irradiated-Fuel Handlers	$33,320	43.1%	8,000
118. Operating Engineers	$35,360	10.4%	45,000
119. First-Line Supervisors/Managers of Retail Sales Workers	$32,720	9.1%	251,000
120. Medical and Clinical Laboratory Technicians	$30,840	19.4%	21,000
121. Respiratory Therapy Technicians	$36,740	34.2%	5,000
122. Security Guards	$20,320	31.9%	228,000
123. Nuclear Medicine Technologists	$56,450	23.6%	2,000
124. Automatic Teller Machine Servicers	$35,150	15.1%	19,000
125. Data Processing Equipment Repairers	$35,150	15.1%	19,000
126. Office Machine and Cash Register Servicers	$35,150	15.1%	19,000
127. Nursing Aides, Orderlies, and Attendants	$20,980	24.9%	302,000
128. Radiation Therapists	$57,700	31.6%	1,000
129. First-Line Supervisors/Managers of Helpers, Laborers, and Material Movers, Hand	$38,280	14.0%	16,000
130. Structural Iron and Steel Workers	$42,430	15.9%	9,000
131. Chefs and Head Cooks	$30,680	15.8%	33,000
132. Aircraft Body and Bonded Structure Repairers	$45,290	11.0%	12,000
133. Aircraft Engine Specialists	$45,290	11.0%	12,000
134. Airframe-and-Power-Plant Mechanics	$45,290	11.0%	12,000
135. Emergency Medical Technicians and Paramedics	$25,310	33.1%	32,000
136. Construction and Building Inspectors	$43,670	13.8%	10,000
137. Elevator Installers and Repairers	$58,710	17.1%	3,000
138. First-Line Supervisors/Managers of Correctional Officers	$44,720	19.0%	4,000
139. Emergency Management Specialists	$45,390	28.2%	2,000
140. Agricultural Crop Farm Managers	$50,700	5.1%	25,000
141. Fish Hatchery Managers	$50,700	5.1%	25,000
142. Medical Records and Health Information Technicians	$25,590	46.8%	24,000
143. Nursery and Greenhouse Managers	$50,700	5.1%	25,000
144. Private Detectives and Investigators	$32,110	25.3%	9,000
145. Interviewers, Except Eligibility and Loan	$23,670	28.0%	46,000
146. Automotive Body and Related Repairers	$34,690	13.2%	23,000
147. Tapers	$39,070	20.8%	5,000

The 300 Best Jobs That Don't Require a Four-Year Degree

Job	Annual Earnings	Percent Growth	Annual Openings
148. Occupational Therapist Assistants	$38,430	39.2%	3,000
149. Athletes and Sports Competitors	$48,310	19.2%	3,000
150. Pharmacy Technicians	$23,650	28.8%	39,000
151. Home Health Aides	$18,330	48.1%	141,000
152. Environmental Science and Protection Technicians, Including Health	$35,340	36.8%	4,000
153. Painters, Construction and Maintenance	$30,260	11.6%	69,000
154. Environmental Engineering Technicians	$38,550	28.4%	3,000
155. Landscaping and Groundskeeping Workers	$20,420	22.0%	203,000
156. Bus Drivers, Transit and Intercity	$29,730	15.2%	33,000
157. Medical Transcriptionists	$28,380	22.6%	18,000
158. Dispatchers, Except Police, Fire, and Ambulance	$30,920	14.4%	28,000
159. Teacher Assistants	$19,410	23.0%	259,000
160. Painters, Transportation Equipment	$35,120	17.5%	9,000
161. Personal and Home Care Aides	$16,900	40.5%	154,000
162. Mapping Technicians	$30,380	23.1%	10,000
163. Surveying Technicians	$30,380	23.1%	10,000
164. Tile and Marble Setters	$35,410	26.5%	4,000
165. Security and Fire Alarm Systems Installers	$33,410	30.2%	5,000
166. Carpet Installers	$34,090	16.8%	10,000
167. Gaming Supervisors	$40,840	15.7%	6,000
168. Housekeeping Supervisors	$29,510	16.2%	28,000
169. Janitorial Supervisors	$29,510	16.2%	28,000
170. Medical Secretaries	$26,540	17.2%	50,000
171. First-Line Supervisors/Managers of Food Preparation and Serving Workers	$25,410	15.5%	154,000
172. Counter and Rental Clerks	$18,280	26.3%	144,000
173. Biological Technicians	$33,210	19.4%	7,000
174. Packaging and Filling Machine Operators and Tenders	$22,200	21.1%	69,000
175. Audio and Video Equipment Technicians	$32,570	26.7%	5,000
176. Combined Food Preparation and Serving Workers, Including Fast Food	$14,690	22.8%	734,000
177. Refuse and Recyclable Material Collectors	$25,760	17.6%	42,000
178. Electrical and Electronics Repairers, Commercial and Industrial Equipment	$42,600	10.3%	10,000
179. Water and Liquid Waste Treatment Plant and System Operators	$34,960	16.0%	9,000
180. Construction Laborers	$25,160	14.2%	166,000

(continued)

(continued)

The 300 Best Jobs That Don't Require a Four-Year Degree

Job	Annual Earnings	Percent Growth	Annual Openings
181. Machinists	$33,960	8.2%	30,000
182. Janitors and Cleaners, Except Maids and Housekeeping Cleaners	$18,790	18.3%	454,000
183. Desktop Publishers	$32,340	29.2%	4,000
184. Locker Room, Coatroom, and Dressing Room Attendants	$17,550	27.8%	66,000
185. Food Preparation Workers	$16,710	20.2%	267,000
186. Sound Engineering Technicians	$38,110	25.5%	2,000
187. Coaches and Scouts	$26,350	18.3%	26,000
188. Mobile Heavy Equipment Mechanics, Except Engines	$38,150	9.6%	12,000
189. Real Estate Sales Agents	$35,670	5.7%	34,000
190. Bus Drivers, School	$23,250	16.7%	76,000
191. Insulation Workers, Mechanical	$33,330	15.8%	9,000
192. Tax Preparers	$27,730	23.2%	11,000
193. Interpreters and Translators	$33,860	22.1%	4,000
194. Cargo and Freight Agents	$34,250	15.5%	8,000
195. Mechanical Engineering Technicians	$43,400	11.0%	6,000
196. Glaziers	$32,650	17.2%	7,000
197. Commercial Pilots	$53,870	14.9%	2,000
198. Amusement and Recreation Attendants	$15,550	27.8%	66,000
199. Veterinary Technologists and Technicians	$24,940	44.1%	11,000
200. Cartoonists	$38,060	16.5%	4,000
201. Painters and Illustrators	$38,060	16.5%	4,000
202. Sculptors	$38,060	16.5%	4,000
203. Sketch Artists	$38,060	16.5%	4,000
204. Electric Meter Installers and Repairers	$43,710	12.0%	5,000
205. Meter Mechanics	$43,710	12.0%	5,000
206. Valve and Regulator Repairers	$43,710	12.0%	5,000
207. Industrial Truck and Tractor Operators	$26,580	11.1%	94,000
208. Central Office and PBX Installers and Repairers	$49,840	−0.6%	23,000
209. Communication Equipment Mechanics, Installers, and Repairers	$49,840	−0.6%	23,000
210. Frame Wirers, Central Office	$49,840	−0.6%	23,000
211. Station Installers and Repairers, Telephone	$49,840	−0.6%	23,000
212. Telecommunications Facility Examiners	$49,840	−0.6%	23,000
213. Air Traffic Controllers	$102,030	12.6%	2,000
214. Industrial Machinery Mechanics	$39,060	5.5%	19,000

The 300 Best Jobs That Don't Require a Four-Year Degree

Job	Annual Earnings	Percent Growth	Annual Openings
215. Real Estate Brokers	$58,720	2.4%	11,000
216. Hotel, Motel, and Resort Desk Clerks	$17,700	23.9%	46,000
217. Waiters and Waitresses	$14,050	17.5%	721,000
218. Helpers—Installation, Maintenance, and Repair Workers	$21,310	20.3%	33,000
219. Reservation and Transportation Ticket Agents	$27,750	12.2%	35,000
220. Travel Clerks	$27,750	12.2%	35,000
221. Forensic Science Technicians	$44,010	18.9%	1,000
222. Cooks, Restaurant	$19,520	15.9%	211,000
223. Retail Salespersons	$18,680	14.6%	1,014,000
224. First-Line Supervisors/Managers of Personal Service Workers	$30,350	9.4%	26,000
225. Industrial Engineering Technicians	$43,590	8.7%	7,000
226. Highway Maintenance Workers	$29,550	10.4%	25,000
227. Aviation Inspectors	$50,380	7.7%	5,000
228. Freight Inspectors	$50,380	7.7%	5,000
229. Marine Cargo Inspectors	$50,380	7.7%	5,000
230. Motor Vehicle Inspectors	$50,380	7.7%	5,000
231. Public Transportation Inspectors	$50,380	7.7%	5,000
232. Railroad Inspectors	$50,380	7.7%	5,000
233. Office Clerks, General	$22,770	10.4%	550,000
234. Civil Engineering Technicians	$38,480	7.6%	10,000
235. Farmers and Ranchers	$40,440	−20.6%	118,000
236. Medical Equipment Repairers	$37,220	14.8%	4,000
237. Library Assistants, Clerical	$20,720	21.5%	27,000
238. Insulation Workers, Floor, Ceiling, and Wall	$30,310	15.8%	9,000
239. Postal Service Mail Carriers	$44,450	−0.5%	20,000
240. Loading Machine Operators, Underground Mining	$33,250	8.9%	14,000
241. First-Line Supervisors and Manager/Supervisors—Agricultural Crop Workers	$35,490	11.4%	6,000
242. First-Line Supervisors and Manager/Supervisors—Animal Care Workers, Except Livestock	$35,490	11.4%	6,000
243. First-Line Supervisors and Manager/Supervisors—Animal Husbandry Workers	$35,490	11.4%	6,000
244. First-Line Supervisors and Manager/Supervisors—Fishery Workers	$35,490	11.4%	6,000
245. First-Line Supervisors and Manager/Supervisors—Horticultural Workers	$35,490	11.4%	6,000
246. Opticians, Dispensing	$27,950	18.2%	10,000

(continued)

(continued)

The 300 Best Jobs That Don't Require a Four-Year Degree

Job	Annual Earnings	Percent Growth	Annual Openings
247. Subway and Streetcar Operators	$49,290	13.2%	2,000
248. Transit and Railroad Police	$45,430	15.9%	1,000
249. Counter Attendants, Cafeteria, Food Concession, and Coffee Shop	$15,660	16.7%	190,000
250. Library Technicians	$24,940	16.8%	22,000
251. Electro-Mechanical Technicians	$41,440	11.5%	4,000
252. Billing, Cost, and Rate Clerks	$27,040	7.9%	78,000
253. Billing, Posting, and Calculating Machine Operators	$27,040	7.9%	78,000
254. Plasterers and Stucco Masons	$32,440	13.5%	8,000
255. Statement Clerks	$27,040	7.9%	78,000
256. Nonfarm Animal Caretakers	$17,460	22.2%	32,000
257. Taxi Drivers and Chauffeurs	$19,570	21.7%	28,000
258. Camera Operators, Television, Video, and Motion Picture	$37,610	13.4%	4,000
259. Demonstrators and Product Promoters	$20,700	17.0%	38,000
260. Police, Fire, and Ambulance Dispatchers	$28,930	12.7%	15,000
261. Residential Advisors	$21,430	33.6%	12,000
262. Lodging Managers	$37,660	6.6%	10,000
263. Architectural Drafters	$39,190	4.2%	14,000
264. Civil Drafters	$39,190	4.2%	14,000
265. Dragline Operators	$31,970	8.9%	14,000
266. Excavating and Loading Machine Operators	$31,970	8.9%	14,000
267. Bookkeeping, Accounting, and Auditing Clerks	$28,570	3.0%	274,000
268. Tree Trimmers and Pruners	$26,150	18.6%	11,000
269. Packers and Packagers, Hand	$17,150	14.4%	198,000
270. Cashiers	$16,240	13.2%	1,221,000
271. Hosts and Hostesses, Restaurant, Lounge, and Coffee Shop	$15,630	16.4%	95,000
272. Court Clerks	$28,430	12.3%	14,000
273. Electrical and Electronic Inspectors and Testers	$28,410	4.7%	87,000
274. License Clerks	$28,430	12.3%	14,000
275. Materials Inspectors	$28,410	4.7%	87,000
276. Mechanical Inspectors	$28,410	4.7%	87,000
277. Municipal Clerks	$28,430	12.3%	14,000
278. Precision Devices Inspectors and Testers	$28,410	4.7%	87,000
279. Production Inspectors, Testers, Graders, Sorters, Samplers, Weighers	$28,410	4.7%	87,000
280. Crane and Tower Operators	$37,410	10.8%	5,000

The 300 Best Jobs That Don't Require a Four-Year Degree

Job	Annual Earnings	Percent Growth	Annual Openings
281. Gaming Dealers	$14,340	24.7%	26,000
282. Hairdressers, Hairstylists, and Cosmetologists	$19,800	14.7%	68,000
283. Insurance Appraisers, Auto Damage	$45,330	11.7%	2,000
284. Model Makers, Metal and Plastic	$44,250	14.6%	1,000
285. Electrical Power-Line Installers and Repairers	$49,100	1.6%	9,000
286. Pest Control Workers	$26,220	17.0%	11,000
287. Recreational Vehicle Service Technicians	$28,980	21.8%	4,000
288. Millwrights	$43,720	5.3%	7,000
289. Locksmiths and Safe Repairers	$30,360	21.0%	3,000
290. Slaughterers and Meat Packers	$20,860	18.1%	23,000
291. Dining Room and Cafeteria Attendants and Bartender Helpers	$14,770	14.9%	143,000
292. Helpers—Electricians	$23,420	17.9%	17,000
293. New Accounts Clerks	$26,860	11.2%	24,000
294. Court Reporters	$42,920	12.7%	2,000
295. Gaming Change Persons and Booth Cashiers	$20,530	24.1%	12,000
296. Riggers	$35,330	14.3%	3,000
297. Child Care Workers	$16,760	11.7%	406,000
298. Choreographers	$33,670	15.8%	3,000
299. Nannies	$16,760	11.7%	406,000
300. Photographers, Scientific	$26,080	13.6%	18,000

The 100 Best-Paying Jobs That Don't Require a Four-Year Degree

From the 300 jobs that met our criteria for this book, this list shows the 100 with the highest earnings. This is a very popular list for obvious reasons. It includes jobs at all levels of training, although many of the better-paying jobs do require technical training and/or work experience.

For example, the highest-paying job on the list is Air Traffic Controllers, a job that requires considerable training and on-the-job experience. Among the top 25, seven are in sales and others require management, supervision, or technical skills.

We mention in the introduction that earnings can vary considerably by region of the country, by amount of experience, and because of many other factors, so do keep this in mind as you review this and any other list. Entry-level workers, for example, would typically be paid considerably less than the amounts listed here.

The 100 Best-Paying Jobs That Don't Require a Four-Year Degree

Job	Annual Earnings
1. Air Traffic Controllers	$102,030
2. Storage and Distribution Managers	$66,600
3. Transportation Managers	$66,600
4. First-Line Supervisors/Managers of Police and Detectives	$64,430
5. First-Line Supervisors/Managers of Non-Retail Sales Workers	$59,300
6. Forest Fire Fighting and Prevention Supervisors	$58,920
7. Municipal Fire Fighting and Prevention Supervisors	$58,920
8. Real Estate Brokers	$58,720
9. Elevator Installers and Repairers	$58,710
10. Sales Representatives, Agricultural	$58,580
11. Sales Representatives, Chemical and Pharmaceutical	$58,580
12. Sales Representatives, Electrical/Electronic	$58,580
13. Sales Representatives, Instruments	$58,580
14. Sales Representatives, Mechanical Equipment and Supplies	$58,580
15. Sales Representatives, Medical	$58,580
16. Dental Hygienists	$58,350
17. Radiation Therapists	$57,700
18. Nuclear Medicine Technologists	$56,450
19. Child Support, Missing Persons, and Unemployment Insurance Fraud Investigators	$53,990
20. Criminal Investigators and Special Agents	$53,990
21. Immigration and Customs Inspectors	$53,990
22. Police Detectives	$53,990
23. Police Identification and Records Officers	$53,990
24. Commercial Pilots	$53,870
25. Talent Directors	$52,840
26. Technical Directors/Managers	$52,840
27. Diagnostic Medical Sonographers	$52,490
28. Registered Nurses	$52,330
29. Agricultural Crop Farm Managers	$50,700
30. Fish Hatchery Managers	$50,700
31. Nursery and Greenhouse Managers	$50,700
32. First-Line Supervisors and Manager/Supervisors—Construction Trades Workers	$50,450
33. First-Line Supervisors and Manager/Supervisors—Extractive Workers	$50,450
34. Aviation Inspectors	$50,380
35. Freight Inspectors	$50,380
36. Marine Cargo Inspectors	$50,380
37. Motor Vehicle Inspectors	$50,380

The 100 Best-Paying Jobs That Don't Require a Four-Year Degree

Job	Annual Earnings
38. Public Transportation Inspectors	$50,380
39. Railroad Inspectors	$50,380
40. First-Line Supervisors/Managers of Mechanics, Installers, and Repairers	$50,340
41. Central Office and PBX Installers and Repairers	$49,840
42. Communication Equipment Mechanics, Installers, and Repairers	$49,840
43. Frame Wirers, Central Office	$49,840
44. Station Installers and Repairers, Telephone	$49,840
45. Telecommunications Facility Examiners	$49,840
46. Subway and Streetcar Operators	$49,290
47. Electrical Power-Line Installers and Repairers	$49,100
48. Athletes and Sports Competitors	$48,310
49. Coroners	$47,390
50. Environmental Compliance Inspectors	$47,390
51. Equal Opportunity Representatives and Officers	$47,390
52. Government Property Inspectors and Investigators	$47,390
53. Licensing Examiners and Inspectors	$47,390
54. Pressure Vessel Inspectors	$47,390
55. Calibration and Instrumentation Technicians	$46,310
56. Electrical Engineering Technicians	$46,310
57. Electronics Engineering Technicians	$46,310
58. Transit and Railroad Police	$45,430
59. Sales Representatives, Wholesale and Manufacturing, Except Technical and Scientific Products	$45,400
60. Emergency Management Specialists	$45,390
61. Insurance Appraisers, Auto Damage	$45,330
62. Aircraft Body and Bonded Structure Repairers	$45,290
63. Aircraft Engine Specialists	$45,290
64. Airframe-and-Power-Plant Mechanics	$45,290
65. Highway Patrol Pilots	$45,210
66. Police Patrol Officers	$45,210
67. Sheriffs and Deputy Sheriffs	$45,210
68. First-Line Supervisors/Managers of Transportation and Material-Moving Machine and Vehicle Operators	$44,810
69. First-Line Supervisors/Managers of Production and Operating Workers	$44,740
70. First-Line Supervisors/Managers of Correctional Officers	$44,720
71. Postal Service Mail Carriers	$44,450

(continued)

(continued)

The 100 Best-Paying Jobs That Don't Require a Four-Year Degree

Job	Annual Earnings
72. Caption Writers	$44,350
73. Model Makers, Metal and Plastic	$44,250
74. Claims Examiners, Property and Casualty Insurance	$44,220
75. Insurance Adjusters, Examiners, and Investigators	$44,220
76. Forensic Science Technicians	$44,010
77. Millwrights	$43,720
78. Electric Meter Installers and Repairers	$43,710
79. Meter Mechanics	$43,710
80. Valve and Regulator Repairers	$43,710
81. Construction and Building Inspectors	$43,670
82. Industrial Engineering Technicians	$43,590
83. Flight Attendants	$43,440
84. Mechanical Engineering Technicians	$43,400
85. Appraisers, Real Estate	$43,390
86. Assessors	$43,390
87. Radiologic Technicians	$43,350
88. Radiologic Technologists	$43,350
89. Respiratory Therapists	$43,140
90. Court Reporters	$42,920
91. Electrical and Electronics Repairers, Commercial and Industrial Equipment	$42,600
92. Structural Iron and Steel Workers	$42,430
93. Electricians	$42,300
94. Brickmasons and Blockmasons	$41,740
95. Electro-Mechanical Technicians	$41,440
96. Pipe Fitters	$41,290
97. Pipelaying Fitters	$41,290
98. Plumbers	$41,290
99. First-Line Supervisors, Administrative Support	$41,030
100. First-Line Supervisors, Customer Service	$41,030

The 100 Fastest-Growing Jobs That Don't Require a Four-Year Degree

From the 300 jobs that met our criteria for this book, this list presents the 100 jobs that are projected to have the highest percentage increase in the numbers of people employed through 2012.

Fourteen of the top 25 jobs are in the health care field, an industry that is growing quickly and that will provide many opportunities. But you will see a variety of rapidly growing jobs in many different fields as you go through this list. Some of these jobs have average or lower earnings, but some have good earnings—and training requirements vary tremendously, from short-term on-the-job training to technical training that may require up to two years.

The 100 Fastest-Growing Jobs That Don't Require a Four-Year Degree

Job	Percent Growth
1. Medical Assistants	58.9%
2. Social and Human Service Assistants	48.7%
3. Home Health Aides	48.1%
4. Medical Records and Health Information Technicians	46.8%
5. Physical Therapist Assistants	44.6%
6. Fitness Trainers and Aerobics Instructors	44.5%
7. Veterinary Technologists and Technicians	44.1%
8. Dental Hygienists	43.1%
9. Hazardous Materials Removal Workers	43.1%
10. Irradiated-Fuel Handlers	43.1%
11. Dental Assistants	42.5%
12. Personal and Home Care Aides	40.5%
13. Self-Enrichment Education Teachers	40.1%
14. Occupational Therapist Assistants	39.2%
15. Vocational Education Teachers, Postsecondary	38.1%
16. Environmental Science and Protection Technicians, Including Health	36.8%
17. Respiratory Therapists	34.8%
18. Respiratory Therapy Technicians	34.2%
19. Residential Advisors	33.6%
20. Cardiovascular Technologists and Technicians	33.5%
21. Emergency Medical Technicians and Paramedics	33.1%
22. Security Guards	31.9%
23. Heating and Air Conditioning Mechanics	31.8%
24. Refrigeration Mechanics	31.8%
25. Radiation Therapists	31.6%
26. Computer Support Specialists	30.3%
27. Security and Fire Alarm Systems Installers	30.2%
28. Receptionists and Information Clerks	29.5%
29. Desktop Publishers	29.2%
30. Pharmacy Technicians	28.8%
31. Paralegals and Legal Assistants	28.7%

(continued)

(continued)

The 100 Fastest-Growing Jobs That Don't Require a Four-Year Degree

Job	Percent Growth
32. Environmental Engineering Technicians	28.4%
33. Emergency Management Specialists	28.2%
34. Interviewers, Except Eligibility and Loan	28.0%
35. Surgical Technologists	27.9%
36. Amusement and Recreation Attendants	27.8%
37. Costume Attendants	27.8%
38. Locker Room, Coatroom, and Dressing Room Attendants	27.8%
39. Registered Nurses	27.3%
40. Massage Therapists	27.1%
41. Audio and Video Equipment Technicians	26.7%
42. Tile and Marble Setters	26.5%
43. Counter and Rental Clerks	26.3%
44. Cement Masons and Concrete Finishers	26.1%
45. Sound Engineering Technicians	25.5%
46. Private Detectives and Investigators	25.3%
47. Nursing Aides, Orderlies, and Attendants	24.9%
48. Gaming Dealers	24.7%
49. Highway Patrol Pilots	24.7%
50. Police Patrol Officers	24.7%
51. Sheriffs and Deputy Sheriffs	24.7%
52. Bill and Account Collectors	24.5%
53. Adjustment Clerks	24.3%
54. Customer Service Representatives, Utilities	24.3%
55. Correctional Officers and Jailers	24.2%
56. Gaming Change Persons and Booth Cashiers	24.1%
57. Diagnostic Medical Sonographers	24.0%
58. Hotel, Motel, and Resort Desk Clerks	23.9%
59. Nuclear Medicine Technologists	23.6%
60. Electricians	23.4%
61. Tax Preparers	23.2%
62. Truck Drivers, Light or Delivery Services	23.2%
63. Mapping Technicians	23.1%
64. Surveying Technicians	23.1%
65. Teacher Assistants	23.0%
66. Radiologic Technicians	22.9%
67. Radiologic Technologists	22.9%

The 100 Fastest-Growing Jobs That Don't Require a Four-Year Degree

Job	Percent Growth
68. Combined Food Preparation and Serving Workers, Including Fast Food	22.8%
69. Medical Transcriptionists	22.6%
70. Child Support, Missing Persons, and Unemployment Insurance Fraud Investigators	22.4%
71. Criminal Investigators and Special Agents	22.4%
72. Immigration and Customs Inspectors	22.4%
73. Police Detectives	22.4%
74. Police Identification and Records Officers	22.4%
75. Nonfarm Animal Caretakers	22.2%
76. Interpreters and Translators	22.1%
77. Landscaping and Groundskeeping Workers	22.0%
78. Recreational Vehicle Service Technicians	21.8%
79. Taxi Drivers and Chauffeurs	21.7%
80. First-Line Supervisors and Manager/Supervisors—Landscaping Workers	21.6%
81. Lawn Service Managers	21.6%
82. Library Assistants, Clerical	21.5%
83. Ceiling Tile Installers	21.4%
84. Drywall Installers	21.4%
85. Packaging and Filling Machine Operators and Tenders	21.1%
86. Locksmiths and Safe Repairers	21.0%
87. Tapers	20.8%
88. Forest Fire Fighters	20.7%
89. Municipal Fire Fighters	20.7%
90. Helpers—Installation, Maintenance, and Repair Workers	20.3%
91. Food Preparation Workers	20.2%
92. Licensed Practical and Licensed Vocational Nurses	20.2%
93. Sheet Metal Workers	19.8%
94. Storage and Distribution Managers	19.7%
95. Transportation Managers	19.7%
96. Biological Technicians	19.4%
97. Medical and Clinical Laboratory Technicians	19.4%
98. Human Resources Assistants, Except Payroll and Timekeeping	19.3%
99. Sales Representatives, Agricultural	19.3%
100. Sales Representatives, Chemical and Pharmaceutical	19.3%

The 100 Jobs with the Most Openings That Don't Require a Four-Year Degree

From the 300 jobs that met our criteria for this book, this list presents the 100 jobs that are projected to have the largest number of job openings per year.

Jobs with many openings present several advantages that may be attractive to you. Because there are many openings, these jobs can be easier to obtain, particularly for those just entering the job market. These jobs may also offer more opportunities for part-time or short-term employment or the ability to move from one employer to another with relative ease. Though some of these jobs have average or below-average pay, some also pay quite well and can provide good long-term career opportunities or the ability to move up to more responsible roles.

The 100 Jobs with the Most Openings That Don't Require a Four-Year Degree

Job	Annual Openings
1. Cashiers	1,221,000
2. Retail Salespersons	1,014,000
3. Combined Food Preparation and Serving Workers, Including Fast Food	734,000
4. Waiters and Waitresses	721,000
5. Office Clerks, General	550,000
6. Janitors and Cleaners, Except Maids and Housekeeping Cleaners	454,000
7. Adjustment Clerks	419,000
8. Customer Service Representatives, Utilities	419,000
9. Child Care Workers	406,000
10. Nannies	406,000
11. Nursing Aides, Orderlies, and Attendants	302,000
12. Tractor-Trailer Truck Drivers	299,000
13. Truck Drivers, Heavy	299,000
14. Receptionists and Information Clerks	296,000
15. Bookkeeping, Accounting, and Auditing Clerks	274,000
16. Food Preparation Workers	267,000
17. Teacher Assistants	259,000
18. First-Line Supervisors/Managers of Retail Sales Workers	251,000
19. Security Guards	228,000
20. Truck Drivers, Light or Delivery Services	219,000
21. Vocational Education Teachers, Postsecondary	216,000
22. Registered Nurses	215,000

The 100 Jobs with the Most Openings That Don't Require a Four-Year Degree

Job	Annual Openings
23. Cooks, Restaurant	211,000
24. Executive Secretaries and Administrative Assistants	210,000
25. Landscaping and Groundskeeping Workers	203,000
26. Packers and Packagers, Hand	198,000
27. Boat Builders and Shipwrights	193,000
28. Brattice Builders	193,000
29. Carpenter Assemblers and Repairers	193,000
30. Construction Carpenters	193,000
31. Rough Carpenters	193,000
32. Ship Carpenters and Joiners	193,000
33. Counter Attendants, Cafeteria, Food Concession, and Coffee Shop	190,000
34. Construction Laborers	166,000
35. Sales Representatives, Wholesale and Manufacturing, Except Technical and Scientific Products	160,000
36. Maintenance and Repair Workers, General	155,000
37. Refractory Materials Repairers, Except Brickmasons	155,000
38. First-Line Supervisors/Managers of Food Preparation and Serving Workers	154,000
39. Personal and Home Care Aides	154,000
40. Counter and Rental Clerks	144,000
41. Dining Room and Cafeteria Attendants and Bartender Helpers	143,000
42. Home Health Aides	141,000
43. First-Line Supervisors, Administrative Support	140,000
44. First-Line Supervisors, Customer Service	140,000
45. Farmers and Ranchers	118,000
46. Licensed Practical and Licensed Vocational Nurses	105,000
47. Automotive Master Mechanics	100,000
48. Automotive Specialty Technicians	100,000
49. Hosts and Hostesses, Restaurant, Lounge, and Coffee Shop	95,000
50. Industrial Truck and Tractor Operators	94,000
51. Electrical and Electronic Inspectors and Testers	87,000
52. Materials Inspectors	87,000
53. Mechanical Inspectors	87,000
54. Precision Devices Inspectors and Testers	87,000
55. Production Inspectors, Testers, Graders, Sorters, Samplers, Weighers	87,000
56. Billing, Cost, and Rate Clerks	78,000

(continued)

(continued)

The 100 Jobs with the Most Openings That Don't Require a Four-Year Degree

Job	Annual Openings
57. Billing, Posting, and Calculating Machine Operators	78,000
58. Medical Assistants	78,000
59. Statement Clerks	78,000
60. Bill and Account Collectors	76,000
61. Bus Drivers, School	76,000
62. First-Line Supervisors/Managers of Non-Retail Sales Workers	72,000
63. Brazers	71,000
64. Computer Support Specialists	71,000
65. Solderers	71,000
66. Welder-Fitters	71,000
67. Welders and Cutters	71,000
68. Welders, Production	71,000
69. Packaging and Filling Machine Operators and Tenders	69,000
70. Painters, Construction and Maintenance	69,000
71. Hairdressers, Hairstylists, and Cosmetologists	68,000
72. First-Line Supervisors and Manager/Supervisors—Construction Trades Workers	67,000
73. First-Line Supervisors and Manager/Supervisors—Extractive Workers	67,000
74. Highway Patrol Pilots	67,000
75. Police Patrol Officers	67,000
76. Sheriffs and Deputy Sheriffs	67,000
77. Amusement and Recreation Attendants	66,000
78. Costume Attendants	66,000
79. First-Line Supervisors/Managers of Production and Operating Workers	66,000
80. Locker Room, Coatroom, and Dressing Room Attendants	66,000
81. Electricians	65,000
82. Social and Human Service Assistants	63,000
83. Food Service Managers	58,000
84. Pipe Fitters	56,000
85. Pipelaying Fitters	56,000
86. Plumbers	56,000
87. Production, Planning, and Expediting Clerks	51,000
88. Medical Secretaries	50,000
89. Correctional Officers and Jailers	49,000
90. Hotel, Motel, and Resort Desk Clerks	46,000
91. Interviewers, Except Eligibility and Loan	46,000

The 100 Jobs with the Most Openings That Don't Require a Four-Year Degree

Job	Annual Openings
92. Grader, Bulldozer, and Scraper Operators	45,000
93. Operating Engineers	45,000
94. Sales Representatives, Agricultural	44,000
95. Sales Representatives, Chemical and Pharmaceutical	44,000
96. Sales Representatives, Electrical/Electronic	44,000
97. Sales Representatives, Instruments	44,000
98. Sales Representatives, Mechanical Equipment and Supplies	44,000
99. Sales Representatives, Medical	44,000
100. First-Line Supervisors/Managers of Mechanics, Installers, and Repairers	42,000

Best Jobs with High Percentages of Workers Age 16–24, Workers Age 55 and Over, Part-Time Workers, Self-Employed Workers, Women, and Men

The data we used to create this book included information that allowed us to compile more-specialized sets of lists that include high percentages of younger workers, older workers, part-time workers, self-employed workers, women, and men. As with the other lists, these lists start with the jobs included in the list of 300 jobs with the highest overall scores that don't require a four-year college degree.

We have created five lists for each group. For example, the best jobs lists for younger workers include

- Jobs with the Highest Percentage of Workers Age 16–24
- Best Jobs Overall for Workers Age 16–24
- Best-Paying Jobs for Workers Age 16–24
- Fastest-Growing Jobs for Workers Age 16–24
- Jobs with the Most Openings for Workers Age 16–24

As in the previous groupings, the Best Jobs Overall list is based on the jobs' combined scores for pay, growth, and number of openings.

We hope you find these lists interesting and useful. Do note that we are not suggesting that you should use the lists to limit your choices. For example, many jobs with a high percentage of women would provide excellent opportunities for, and should be considered by, men who find them interesting.

Best Jobs with a High Percentage of Workers Age 16–24

Workers age 16–24 make up 14 percent of the workforce, but jobs in the lists that follow include at least 20 percent of these workers. A total of 54 occupations met this criterion.

While young workers are employed in virtually all major occupations, the ones with the highest percentage of workers age 16–24 tend to be in entry-level, part-time, seasonal, or service jobs. This makes sense in that many young workers have not yet settled into careers or are working while going to school. The jobs they get tend to be relatively easy to obtain but have relatively low wages.

Almost half (40 percent) of the jobs on these lists pay less than $10 an hour, while less than 17 percent pay more than $15 an hour and none pays more than $22 an hour. (For two of the jobs, no hourly wage figures are available.) These low-paying jobs are often referred to as entry-level jobs because they offer inexperienced workers an opportunity to enter the labor market. Many young people work in them to earn some money, gain basic job skills, and use their experience to move up to better-paying jobs.

Best Jobs with the Highest Percentage of Workers Age 16–24

Job	Percent Workers 16–24
1. Hosts and Hostesses, Restaurant, Lounge, and Coffee Shop	77.8%
2. Counter Attendants, Cafeteria, Food Concession, and Coffee Shop	75.4%
3. Waiters and Waitresses	53.1%
4. Amusement and Recreation Attendants	52.4%
5. Costume Attendants	52.4%
6. Locker Room, Coatroom, and Dressing Room Attendants	52.4%
7. Cashiers	49.1%
8. Gaming Change Persons and Booth Cashiers	49.1%
9. Combined Food Preparation and Serving Workers, Including Fast Food	49.0%
10. Choreographers	46.9%
11. Hotel, Motel, and Resort Desk Clerks	46.0%
12. Helpers—Electricians	44.7%
13. Dining Room and Cafeteria Attendants and Bartender Helpers	43.6%
14. Library Technicians	43.5%
15. Counter and Rental Clerks	42.2%
16. Food Preparation Workers	41.3%

Best Jobs with the Highest Percentage of Workers Age 16–24

Job	Percent Workers 16–24
17. Athletes and Sports Competitors	35.3%
18. Coaches and Scouts	35.3%
19. Residential Advisors	34.1%
20. Cooks, Restaurant	33.6%
21. Nonfarm Animal Caretakers	32.5%
22. City and Regional Planning Aides	30.8%
23. Environmental Science and Protection Technicians, Including Health	30.8%
24. Forensic Science Technicians	30.8%
25. Social Science Research Assistants	30.8%
26. Retail Salespersons	30.5%
27. Fitness Trainers and Aerobics Instructors	29.1%
28. Child Care Workers	27.9%
29. Nannies	27.9%
30. Receptionists and Information Clerks	27.6%
31. Recreational Vehicle Service Technicians	26.7%
32. Library Assistants, Clerical	26.7%
33. Landscaping and Groundskeeping Workers	26.6%
34. Tree Trimmers and Pruners	26.6%
35. Helpers—Installation, Maintenance, and Repair Workers	25.8%
36. Pharmacy Technicians	24.7%
37. Respiratory Therapy Technicians	24.7%
38. Surgical Technologists	24.7%
39. Veterinary Technologists and Technicians	24.7%
40. First-Line Supervisors/Managers of Food Preparation and Serving Workers	24.3%
41. Construction Laborers	23.7%
42. Office Clerks, General	23.3%
43. Roofers	22.7%
44. Medical Assistants	21.5%
45. Medical Transcriptionists	21.5%
46. Security Guards	20.6%
47. Interviewers, Except Eligibility and Loan	20.6%
48. Medical Records and Health Information Technicians	20.6%
49. Adjustment Clerks	20.5%
50. Customer Service Representatives, Utilities	20.5%
51. Insulation Workers, Floor, Ceiling, and Wall	20.5%
52. Insulation Workers, Mechanical	20.5%
53. Gaming Dealers	20.0%
54. Security and Fire Alarm Systems Installers	20.0%

Best Jobs Overall with a High Percentage of Workers Age 16–24

Job	Percent Workers 16–24	Annual Earnings	Percent Growth	Annual Openings
1. Adjustment Clerks	20.5%	$27,020	24.3%	419,000
2. Customer Service Representatives, Utilities	20.5%	$27,020	24.3%	419,000
3. Medical Assistants	21.5%	$24,610	58.9%	78,000
4. Fitness Trainers and Aerobics Instructors	29.1%	$25,470	44.5%	38,000
5. Receptionists and Information Clerks	27.6%	$21,830	29.5%	296,000
6. Medical Records and Health Information Technicians	20.6%	$25,590	46.8%	24,000
7. Respiratory Therapy Technicians	24.7%	$36,740	34.2%	5,000
8. Security Guards	20.6%	$20,320	31.9%	228,000
9. Costume Attendants	52.4%	$25,050	27.8%	66,000
10. Environmental Science and Protection Technicians, Including Health	30.8%	$35,340	36.8%	4,000
11. Surgical Technologists	24.7%	$34,010	27.9%	13,000
12. Interviewers, Except Eligibility and Loan	20.6%	$23,670	28.0%	46,000
13. Pharmacy Technicians	24.7%	$23,650	28.8%	39,000
14. Security and Fire Alarm Systems Installers	20.0%	$33,410	30.2%	5,000
15. Roofers	22.7%	$30,840	18.6%	38,000
16. Veterinary Technologists and Technicians	24.7%	$24,940	44.1%	11,000
17. Counter and Rental Clerks	42.2%	$18,280	26.3%	144,000
18. Medical Transcriptionists	21.5%	$28,380	22.6%	18,000
19. Landscaping and Groundskeeping Workers	26.6%	$20,420	22.0%	203,000
20. Combined Food Preparation and Serving Workers, Including Fast Food	49.0%	$14,690	22.8%	734,000
21. Locker Room, Coatroom, and Dressing Room Attendants	52.4%	$17,550	27.8%	66,000
22. City and Regional Planning Aides	30.8%	$34,360	17.5%	18,000
23. Social Science Research Assistants	30.8%	$34,360	17.5%	18,000
24. Residential Advisors	34.1%	$21,430	33.6%	12,000
25. Athletes and Sports Competitors	35.3%	$48,310	19.2%	3,000

Best-Paying Jobs with a High Percentage of Workers Age 16–24

Job	Percent Workers 16–24	Annual Earnings
1. Athletes and Sports Competitors	35.3%	$48,310
2. Forensic Science Technicians	30.8%	$44,010
3. Respiratory Therapy Technicians	24.7%	$36,740
4. Environmental Science and Protection Technicians, Including Health	30.8%	$35,340
5. City and Regional Planning Aides	30.8%	$34,360
6. Social Science Research Assistants	30.8%	$34,360
7. Surgical Technologists	24.7%	$34,010
8. Choreographers	46.9%	$33,670
9. Security and Fire Alarm Systems Installers	20.0%	$33,410
10. Insulation Workers, Mechanical	20.5%	$33,330
11. Roofers	22.7%	$30,840
12. Insulation Workers, Floor, Ceiling, and Wall	20.5%	$30,310
13. Recreational Vehicle Service Technicians	26.7%	$28,980
14. Medical Transcriptionists	21.5%	$28,380
15. Adjustment Clerks	20.5%	$27,020
16. Customer Service Representatives, Utilities	20.5%	$27,020
17. Coaches and Scouts	35.3%	$26,350
18. Tree Trimmers and Pruners	26.6%	$26,150
19. Medical Records and Health Information Technicians	20.6%	$25,590
20. Fitness Trainers and Aerobics Instructors	29.1%	$25,470
21. First-Line Supervisors/Managers of Food Preparation and Serving Workers	24.3%	$25,410
22. Construction Laborers	23.7%	$25,160
23. Costume Attendants	52.4%	$25,050
24. Library Technicians	43.5%	$24,940
25. Veterinary Technologists and Technicians	24.7%	$24,940

Fastest-Growing Jobs with a High Percentage of Workers Age 16–24

Job	Percent Workers 16–24	Percent Growth
1. Medical Assistants	21.5%	58.9%
2. Medical Records and Health Information Technicians	20.6%	46.8%
3. Fitness Trainers and Aerobics Instructors	29.1%	44.5%
4. Veterinary Technologists and Technicians	24.7%	44.1%
5. Environmental Science and Protection Technicians, Including Health	30.8%	36.8%

(continued)

(continued)

Fastest-Growing Jobs with a High Percentage of Workers Age 16–24

Job	Percent Workers 16–24	Percent Growth
6. Respiratory Therapy Technicians	24.7%	34.2%
7. Residential Advisors	34.1%	33.6%
8. Security Guards	20.6%	31.9%
9. Security and Fire Alarm Systems Installers	20.0%	30.2%
10. Receptionists and Information Clerks	27.6%	29.5%
11. Pharmacy Technicians	24.7%	28.8%
12. Interviewers, Except Eligibility and Loan	20.6%	28.0%
13. Surgical Technologists	24.7%	27.9%
14. Amusement and Recreation Attendants	52.4%	27.8%
15. Costume Attendants	52.4%	27.8%
16. Locker Room, Coatroom, and Dressing Room Attendants	52.4%	27.8%
17. Counter and Rental Clerks	42.2%	26.3%
18. Gaming Dealers	20.0%	24.7%
19. Adjustment Clerks	20.5%	24.3%
20. Customer Service Representatives, Utilities	20.5%	24.3%
21. Gaming Change Persons and Booth Cashiers	49.1%	24.1%
22. Hotel, Motel, and Resort Desk Clerks	46.0%	23.9%
23. Combined Food Preparation and Serving Workers, Including Fast Food	49.0%	22.8%
24. Medical Transcriptionists	21.5%	22.6%
25. Nonfarm Animal Caretakers	32.5%	22.2%

Jobs with the Most Openings with a High Percentage of Workers Age 16–24

Job	Percent Workers 16–24	Annual Openings
1. Cashiers	49.1%	1,221,000
2. Retail Salespersons	30.5%	1,014,000
3. Combined Food Preparation and Serving Workers, Including Fast Food	49.0%	734,000
4. Waiters and Waitresses	53.1%	721,000
5. Office Clerks, General	23.3%	550,000
6. Adjustment Clerks	20.5%	419,000
7. Customer Service Representatives, Utilities	20.5%	419,000
8. Child Care Workers	27.9%	406,000
9. Nannies	27.9%	406,000

Jobs with the Most Openings with a High Percentage of Workers Age 16–24

Job	Percent Workers 16–24	Annual Openings
10. Receptionists and Information Clerks	27.6%	296,000
11. Food Preparation Workers	41.3%	267,000
12. Security Guards	20.6%	228,000
13. Cooks, Restaurant	33.6%	211,000
14. Landscaping and Groundskeeping Workers	26.6%	203,000
15. Counter Attendants, Cafeteria, Food Concession, and Coffee Shop	75.4%	190,000
16. Construction Laborers	23.7%	166,000
17. First-Line Supervisors/Managers of Food Preparation and Serving Workers	24.3%	154,000
18. Counter and Rental Clerks	42.2%	144,000
19. Dining Room and Cafeteria Attendants and Bartender Helpers	43.6%	143,000
20. Hosts and Hostesses, Restaurant, Lounge, and Coffee Shop	77.8%	95,000
21. Medical Assistants	21.5%	78,000
22. Amusement and Recreation Attendants	52.4%	66,000
23. Costume Attendants	52.4%	66,000
24. Locker Room, Coatroom, and Dressing Room Attendants	52.4%	66,000
25. Hotel, Motel, and Resort Desk Clerks	46.0%	46,000

Best Jobs with a High Percentage of Workers Age 55 and Over

Workers age 55 and over make up about 17.2 percent of the labor market. We included occupations in this list if the percent of workers 55 and over was 15 percent or higher. A total of 118 jobs met this criterion and are included in this group of lists.

One use for these lists is to help you identify careers that might be interesting as you decide to change careers or approach retirement. Some occupations on the lists may be attractive to older workers wanting part-time work to supplement their retirement income. For example, we think that the job of Private Detectives and Investigators is appealing because the job pays pretty well, can be done less than full time and on a flexible schedule, and lends itself to self-employment. Other occupations on the lists (such as Sculptors) take many years of training and experience. After a person is established in that career, the person often works in that occupation until retirement.

Best Jobs with the Highest Percentage of Workers Age 55 and Over

Job	Percent Workers 55 and Over
1. Farmers and Ranchers	48.7%
2. Tax Preparers	35.2%
3. Demonstrators and Product Promoters	34.2%
4. Real Estate Brokers	33.4%
5. Real Estate Sales Agents	33.4%
6. Model Makers, Metal and Plastic	33.3%
7. Taxi Drivers and Chauffeurs	31.1%
8. Agricultural Crop Farm Managers	30.1%
9. Fish Hatchery Managers	30.1%
10. Nursery and Greenhouse Managers	30.1%
11. Bus Drivers, School	29.6%
12. Bus Drivers, Transit and Intercity	29.6%
13. Lodging Managers	26.9%
14. Personal and Home Care Aides	25.4%
15. Desktop Publishers	25.0%
16. Vocational Education Teachers, Postsecondary	24.5%
17. Appraisers, Real Estate	24.4%
18. Assessors	24.4%
19. Security Guards	24.3%
20. Construction and Building Inspectors	24.2%
21. Caption Writers	23.7%
22. Private Detectives and Investigators	23.4%
23. Bookkeeping, Accounting, and Auditing Clerks	23.2%
24. Cartoonists	22.6%
25. Painters and Illustrators	22.6%
26. Sculptors	22.6%
27. Sketch Artists	22.6%
28. Helpers—Installation, Maintenance, and Repair Workers	22.6%
29. Janitors and Cleaners, Except Maids and Housekeeping Cleaners	22.3%
30. First-Line Supervisors and Manager/Supervisors—Agricultural Crop Workers	21.5%
31. First-Line Supervisors and Manager/Supervisors—Animal Care Workers, Except Livestock	21.5%
32. First-Line Supervisors and Manager/Supervisors—Animal Husbandry Workers	21.5%
33. First-Line Supervisors and Manager/Supervisors—Fishery Workers	21.5%
34. First-Line Supervisors and Manager/Supervisors—Horticultural Workers	21.5%
35. First-Line Supervisors/Managers of Personal Service Workers	21.0%
36. Self-Enrichment Education Teachers	19.9%

Best Jobs with the Highest Percentage of Workers Age 55 and Over

Job	Percent Workers 55 and Over
37. Housekeeping Supervisors	19.9%
38. Janitorial Supervisors	19.9%
39. Library Assistants, Clerical	19.8%
40. Crane and Tower Operators	19.7%
41. Executive Secretaries and Administrative Assistants	19.5%
42. Legal Secretaries	19.5%
43. Medical Secretaries	19.5%
44. Medical Equipment Repairers	19.4%
45. Millwrights	19.2%
46. Emergency Management Specialists	19.1%
47. First-Line Supervisors/Managers of Non-Retail Sales Workers	19.0%
48. Air Traffic Controllers	18.4%
49. Postal Service Mail Carriers	18.3%
50. Residential Advisors	18.2%
51. Subway and Streetcar Operators	18.2%
52. Commercial Pilots	18.1%
53. Water and Liquid Waste Treatment Plant and System Operators	18.0%
54. Receptionists and Information Clerks	17.8%
55. Maintenance and Repair Workers, General	17.8%
56. Interpreters and Translators	17.7%
57. Gaming Supervisors	17.6%
58. Tractor-Trailer Truck Drivers	17.4%
59. Truck Drivers, Heavy	17.4%
60. Truck Drivers, Light or Delivery Services	17.4%
61. Aviation Inspectors	17.4%
62. Freight Inspectors	17.4%
63. Library Technicians	17.4%
64. Locksmiths and Safe Repairers	17.4%
65. Marine Cargo Inspectors	17.4%
66. Motor Vehicle Inspectors	17.4%
67. Public Transportation Inspectors	17.4%
68. Railroad Inspectors	17.4%
69. First-Line Supervisors, Administrative Support	17.3%
70. First-Line Supervisors, Customer Service	17.3%
71. First-Line Supervisors/Managers of Retail Sales Workers	17.2%
72. Electrical and Electronic Inspectors and Testers	17.2%

(continued)

(continued)

Best Jobs with the Highest Percentage of Workers Age 55 and Over

Job	Percent Workers 55 and Over
73. Materials Inspectors	17.2%
74. Mechanical Inspectors	17.2%
75. Precision Devices Inspectors and Testers	17.2%
76. Production Inspectors, Testers, Graders, Sorters, Samplers, Weighers	17.2%
77. Retail Salespersons	17.1%
78. Dragline Operators	17.0%
79. Excavating and Loading Machine Operators	17.0%
80. Loading Machine Operators, Underground Mining	17.0%
81. Interviewers, Except Eligibility and Loan	17.0%
82. Human Resources Assistants, Except Payroll and Timekeeping	16.9%
83. First-Line Supervisors/Managers of Mechanics, Installers, and Repairers	16.8%
84. Advertising Sales Agents	16.7%
85. Cargo and Freight Agents	16.7%
86. Riggers	16.7%
87. First-Line Supervisors/Managers of Production and Operating Workers	16.6%
88. Machinists	16.3%
89. Sales Representatives, Agricultural	16.2%
90. Sales Representatives, Chemical and Pharmaceutical	16.2%
91. Sales Representatives, Electrical/Electronic	16.2%
92. Sales Representatives, Instruments	16.2%
93. Sales Representatives, Mechanical Equipment and Supplies	16.2%
94. Sales Representatives, Medical	16.2%
95. Sales Representatives, Wholesale and Manufacturing, Except Technical and Scientific Products	16.2%
96. First-Line Supervisors/Managers of Correctional Officers	16.1%
97. Bus and Truck Mechanics and Diesel Engine Specialists	15.9%
98. Medical Records and Health Information Technicians	15.9%
99. Coroners	15.9%
100. Environmental Compliance Inspectors	15.9%
101. Equal Opportunity Representatives and Officers	15.9%
102. Government Property Inspectors and Investigators	15.9%
103. Licensing Examiners and Inspectors	15.9%
104. Pressure Vessel Inspectors	15.9%
105. Refuse and Recyclable Material Collectors	15.9%
106. Court Clerks	15.7%
107. License Clerks	15.7%

Best Jobs with the Highest Percentage of Workers Age 55 and Over

Job	Percent Workers 55 and Over
108. Municipal Clerks	15.7%
109. Licensed Practical and Licensed Vocational Nurses	15.6%
110. Claims Examiners, Property and Casualty Insurance	15.5%
111. Insurance Adjusters, Examiners, and Investigators	15.5%
112. Insurance Appraisers, Auto Damage	15.5%
113. Office Clerks, General	15.3%
114. Slaughterers and Meat Packers	15.1%
115. Mobile Heavy Equipment Mechanics, Except Engines	15.0%
116. Billing, Cost, and Rate Clerks	15.0%
117. Billing, Posting, and Calculating Machine Operators	15.0%
118. Statement Clerks	15.0%

Best Jobs Overall with a High Percentage of Workers Age 55 and Over

Job	Percent Workers 55 and Over	Annual Earnings	Percent Growth	Annual Openings
1. Sales Representatives, Agricultural	16.2%	$58,580	19.3%	44,000
2. Sales Representatives, Chemical and Pharmaceutical	16.2%	$58,580	19.3%	44,000
3. Sales Representatives, Electrical/Electronic	16.2%	$58,580	19.3%	44,000
4. Sales Representatives, Instruments	16.2%	$58,580	19.3%	44,000
5. Sales Representatives, Mechanical Equipment and Supplies	16.2%	$58,580	19.3%	44,000
6. Sales Representatives, Medical	16.2%	$58,580	19.3%	44,000
7. Vocational Education Teachers, Postsecondary	24.5%	$40,740	38.1%	216,000
8. Sales Representatives, Wholesale and Manufacturing, Except Technical and Scientific Products	16.2%	$45,400	19.1%	160,000
9. Tractor-Trailer Truck Drivers	17.4%	$33,520	19.0%	299,000
10. Truck Drivers, Heavy	17.4%	$33,520	19.0%	299,000
11. Licensed Practical and Licensed Vocational Nurses	15.6%	$33,970	20.2%	105,000
12. First-Line Supervisors/Managers of Mechanics, Installers, and Repairers	16.8%	$50,340	15.4%	42,000
13. Receptionists and Information Clerks	17.8%	$21,830	29.5%	296,000

(continued)

(continued)

Best Jobs Overall with a High Percentage of Workers Age 55 and Over

Job	Percent Workers 55 and Over	Annual Earnings	Percent Growth	Annual Openings
14. Self-Enrichment Education Teachers	19.9%	$30,880	40.1%	39,000
15. Truck Drivers, Light or Delivery Services	17.4%	$24,540	23.2%	219,000
16. Legal Secretaries	19.5%	$36,720	18.8%	39,000
17. Security Guards	24.3%	$20,320	31.9%	228,000
18. First-Line Supervisors/Managers of Non-Retail Sales Workers	19.0%	$59,300	6.8%	72,000
19. Personal and Home Care Aides	25.4%	$16,900	40.5%	154,000
20. Maintenance and Repair Workers, General	17.8%	$30,710	16.3%	155,000
21. Claims Examiners, Property and Casualty Insurance	15.5%	$44,220	14.2%	31,000
22. Human Resources Assistants, Except Payroll and Timekeeping	16.9%	$31,750	19.3%	36,000
23. Insurance Adjusters, Examiners, and Investigators	15.5%	$44,220	14.2%	31,000
24. Caption Writers	23.7%	$44,350	16.1%	23,000
25. First-Line Supervisors/Managers of Production and Operating Workers	16.6%	$44,740	9.5%	66,000

Best-Paying Jobs with a High Percentage of Workers Age 55 and Over

Job	Percent Workers 55 and Over	Annual Earnings
1. Air Traffic Controllers	18.4%	$102,030
2. First-Line Supervisors/Managers of Non-Retail Sales Workers	19.0%	$59,300
3. Real Estate Brokers	33.4%	$58,720
4. Sales Representatives, Agricultural	16.2%	$58,580
5. Sales Representatives, Chemical and Pharmaceutical	16.2%	$58,580
6. Sales Representatives, Electrical/Electronic	16.2%	$58,580
7. Sales Representatives, Instruments	16.2%	$58,580
8. Sales Representatives, Mechanical Equipment and Supplies	16.2%	$58,580
9. Sales Representatives, Medical	16.2%	$58,580
10. Commercial Pilots	18.1%	$53,870
11. Agricultural Crop Farm Managers	30.1%	$50,700
12. Fish Hatchery Managers	30.1%	$50,700
13. Nursery and Greenhouse Managers	30.1%	$50,700

Best-Paying Jobs with a High Percentage of Workers Age 55 and Over

Job	Percent Workers 55 and Over	Annual Earnings
14. Aviation Inspectors	17.4%	$50,380
15. Freight Inspectors	17.4%	$50,380
16. Marine Cargo Inspectors	17.4%	$50,380
17. Motor Vehicle Inspectors	17.4%	$50,380
18. Public Transportation Inspectors	17.4%	$50,380
19. Railroad Inspectors	17.4%	$50,380
20. First-Line Supervisors/Managers of Mechanics, Installers, and Repairers	16.8%	$50,340
21. Subway and Streetcar Operators	18.2%	$49,290
22. Coroners	15.9%	$47,390
23. Environmental Compliance Inspectors	15.9%	$47,390
24. Equal Opportunity Representatives and Officers	15.9%	$47,390
25. Government Property Inspectors and Investigators	15.9%	$47,390

Fastest-Growing Jobs with a High Percentage of Workers Age 55 and Over

Job	Percent Workers 55 and Over	Percent Growth
1. Medical Records and Health Information Technicians	15.9%	46.8%
2. Personal and Home Care Aides	25.4%	40.5%
3. Self-Enrichment Education Teachers	19.9%	40.1%
4. Vocational Education Teachers, Postsecondary	24.5%	38.1%
5. Residential Advisors	18.2%	33.6%
6. Security Guards	24.3%	31.9%
7. Receptionists and Information Clerks	17.8%	29.5%
8. Desktop Publishers	25.0%	29.2%
9. Emergency Management Specialists	19.1%	28.2%
10. Interviewers, Except Eligibility and Loan	17.0%	28.0%
11. Private Detectives and Investigators	23.4%	25.3%
12. Tax Preparers	35.2%	23.2%
13. Truck Drivers, Light or Delivery Services	17.4%	23.2%
14. Interpreters and Translators	17.7%	22.1%
15. Taxi Drivers and Chauffeurs	31.1%	21.7%
16. Library Assistants, Clerical	19.8%	21.5%

(continued)

(continued)

Fastest-Growing Jobs with a High Percentage of Workers Age 55 and Over

Job	Percent Workers 55 and Over	Percent Growth
17. Locksmiths and Safe Repairers	17.4%	21.0%
18. Helpers—Installation, Maintenance, and Repair Workers	22.6%	20.3%
19. Licensed Practical and Licensed Vocational Nurses	15.6%	20.2%
20. Human Resources Assistants, Except Payroll and Timekeeping	16.9%	19.3%
21. Sales Representatives, Agricultural	16.2%	19.3%
22. Sales Representatives, Chemical and Pharmaceutical	16.2%	19.3%
23. Sales Representatives, Electrical/Electronic	16.2%	19.3%
24. Sales Representatives, Instruments	16.2%	19.3%
25. Sales Representatives, Mechanical Equipment and Supplies	16.2%	19.3%

Jobs with the Most Openings with a High Percentage of Workers Age 55 and Over

Job	Percent Workers 55 and Over	Annual Openings
1. Retail Salespersons	17.1%	1,014,000
2. Office Clerks, General	15.3%	550,000
3. Janitors and Cleaners, Except Maids and Housekeeping Cleaners	22.3%	454,000
4. Tractor-Trailer Truck Drivers	17.4%	299,000
5. Truck Drivers, Heavy	17.4%	299,000
6. Receptionists and Information Clerks	17.8%	296,000
7. Bookkeeping, Accounting, and Auditing Clerks	23.2%	274,000
8. First-Line Supervisors/Managers of Retail Sales Workers	17.2%	251,000
9. Security Guards	24.3%	228,000
10. Truck Drivers, Light or Delivery Services	17.4%	219,000
11. Vocational Education Teachers, Postsecondary	24.5%	216,000
12. Executive Secretaries and Administrative Assistants	19.5%	210,000
13. Sales Representatives, Wholesale and Manufacturing, Except Technical and Scientific Products	16.2%	160,000
14. Maintenance and Repair Workers, General	17.8%	155,000
15. Personal and Home Care Aides	25.4%	154,000
16. First-Line Supervisors, Administrative Support	17.3%	140,000
17. First-Line Supervisors, Customer Service	17.3%	140,000
18. Farmers and Ranchers	48.7%	118,000

Jobs with the Most Openings with a High Percentage of Workers Age 55 and Over

Job	Percent Workers 55 and Over	Annual Openings
19. Licensed Practical and Licensed Vocational Nurses	15.6%	105,000
20. Electrical and Electronic Inspectors and Testers	17.2%	87,000
21. Materials Inspectors	17.2%	87,000
22. Mechanical Inspectors	17.2%	87,000
23. Precision Devices Inspectors and Testers	17.2%	87,000
24. Production Inspectors, Testers, Graders, Sorters, Samplers, Weighers	17.2%	87,000
25. Billing, Cost, and Rate Clerks	15.0%	78,000

Best Jobs with a High Percentage of Part-Time Workers

Starting with the 300 jobs that met our criteria for this book, we ran lists that included only those with 30 percent or more of part-time workers. A total of 35 jobs met this criterion and are included in this group of lists.

If you want to work part time, these lists will be helpful in identifying where most others are finding opportunities for this kind of work. Many people prefer to work less than full time. For example, people who are attending school or who have young children may prefer part-time work due to its flexibility. People also work part time for money-related reasons, such as supplementing income from a full-time job or working two or more part-time jobs because one desirable full-time job is not available.

Many of these jobs can be learned quickly, offer flexible work schedules, are easy to obtain, and offer other desirable advantages. Although many people think of part-time jobs as requiring low skills and providing low pay, this is not always the case. Some of these jobs pay quite well, require substantial training or experience, or are growing quickly.

Best Jobs with the Highest Percentage of Part-Time Workers

Job	Percent Part-Time Workers
1. Hosts and Hostesses, Restaurant, Lounge, and Coffee Shop	66.9%
2. Counter Attendants, Cafeteria, Food Concession, and Coffee Shop	65.8%
3. Dental Hygienists	57.8%
4. Dining Room and Cafeteria Attendants and Bartender Helpers	54.0%
5. Library Technicians	53.4%

(continued)

(continued)

Best Jobs with the Highest Percentage of Part-Time Workers

Job	Percent Part-Time Workers
6. Demonstrators and Product Promoters	52.5%
7. Amusement and Recreation Attendants	51.9%
8. Costume Attendants	51.9%
9. Locker Room, Coatroom, and Dressing Room Attendants	51.9%
10. Library Assistants, Clerical	50.4%
11. Waiters and Waitresses	49.9%
12. Cashiers	44.8%
13. Gaming Change Persons and Booth Cashiers	44.8%
14. Food Preparation Workers	41.9%
15. Massage Therapists	41.2%
16. Teacher Assistants	41.1%
17. Self-Enrichment Education Teachers	41.0%
18. Combined Food Preparation and Serving Workers, Including Fast Food	40.4%
19. Athletes and Sports Competitors	36.3%
20. Coaches and Scouts	36.3%
21. Counter and Rental Clerks	35.9%
22. Fitness Trainers and Aerobics Instructors	35.6%
23. Dental Assistants	35.6%
24. Bus Drivers, Transit and Intercity	35.6%
25. Bus Drivers, School	35.6%
26. Child Care Workers	35.2%
27. Nannies	35.2%
28. Personal and Home Care Aides	34.0%
29. Choreographers	33.8%
30. Retail Salespersons	32.6%
31. Nonfarm Animal Caretakers	31.7%
32. Cooks, Restaurant	31.6%
33. Receptionists and Information Clerks	31.5%
34. Hairdressers, Hairstylists, and Cosmetologists	31.1%
35. Interviewers, Except Eligibility and Loan	30.4%

Best Jobs Overall with a High Percentage of Part-Time Workers

Job	Percent Part-Time Workers	Annual Earnings	Percent Growth	Annual Openings
1. Receptionists and Information Clerks	31.5%	$21,830	29.5%	296,000
2. Self-Enrichment Education Teachers	41.0%	$30,880	40.1%	39,000
3. Fitness Trainers and Aerobics Instructors	35.6%	$25,470	44.5%	38,000
4. Dental Assistants	35.6%	$28,330	42.5%	35,000
5. Costume Attendants	51.9%	$25,050	27.8%	66,000
6. Dental Hygienists	57.8%	$58,350	43.1%	9,000
7. Interviewers, Except Eligibility and Loan	30.4%	$23,670	28.0%	46,000
8. Personal and Home Care Aides	34.0%	$16,900	40.5%	154,000
9. Teacher Assistants	41.1%	$19,410	23.0%	259,000
10. Massage Therapists	41.2%	$31,960	27.1%	24,000
11. Counter and Rental Clerks	35.9%	$18,280	26.3%	144,000
12. Locker Room, Coatroom, and Dressing Room Attendants	51.9%	$17,550	27.8%	66,000
13. Combined Food Preparation and Serving Workers, Including Fast Food	40.4%	$14,690	22.8%	734,000
14. Bus Drivers, School	35.6%	$23,250	16.7%	76,000
15. Food Preparation Workers	41.9%	$16,710	20.2%	267,000
16. Athletes and Sports Competitors	36.3%	$48,310	19.2%	3,000
17. Retail Salespersons	32.6%	$18,680	14.6%	1,014,000
18. Cooks, Restaurant	31.6%	$19,520	15.9%	211,000
19. Coaches and Scouts	36.3%	$26,350	18.3%	26,000
20. Amusement and Recreation Attendants	51.9%	$15,550	27.8%	66,000
21. Library Assistants, Clerical	50.4%	$20,720	21.5%	27,000
22. Waiters and Waitresses	49.9%	$14,050	17.5%	721,000
23. Bus Drivers, Transit and Intercity	35.6%	$29,730	15.2%	33,000
24. Demonstrators and Product Promoters	52.5%	$20,700	17.0%	38,000
25. Gaming Change Persons and Booth Cashiers	44.8%	$20,530	24.1%	12,000

Best-Paying Jobs with a High Percentage of Part-Time Workers

Job	Percent Part-Time Workers	Annual Earnings
1. Dental Hygienists	57.8%	$58,350
2. Athletes and Sports Competitors	36.3%	$48,310
3. Choreographers	33.8%	$33,670
4. Massage Therapists	41.2%	$31,960
5. Self-Enrichment Education Teachers	41.0%	$30,880
6. Bus Drivers, Transit and Intercity	35.6%	$29,730
7. Dental Assistants	35.6%	$28,330
8. Coaches and Scouts	36.3%	$26,350
9. Fitness Trainers and Aerobics Instructors	35.6%	$25,470
10. Costume Attendants	51.9%	$25,050
11. Library Technicians	53.4%	$24,940
12. Interviewers, Except Eligibility and Loan	30.4%	$23,670
13. Bus Drivers, School	35.6%	$23,250
14. Receptionists and Information Clerks	31.5%	$21,830
15. Library Assistants, Clerical	50.4%	$20,720
16. Demonstrators and Product Promoters	52.5%	$20,700
17. Gaming Change Persons and Booth Cashiers	44.8%	$20,530
18. Hairdressers, Hairstylists, and Cosmetologists	31.1%	$19,800
19. Cooks, Restaurant	31.6%	$19,520
20. Teacher Assistants	41.1%	$19,410
21. Retail Salespersons	32.6%	$18,680
22. Counter and Rental Clerks	35.9%	$18,280
23. Locker Room, Coatroom, and Dressing Room Attendants	51.9%	$17,550
24. Nonfarm Animal Caretakers	31.7%	$17,460
25. Personal and Home Care Aides	34.0%	$16,900

Fastest-Growing Jobs with a High Percentage of Part-Time Workers

Job	Percent Part-Time Workers	Percent Growth
1. Fitness Trainers and Aerobics Instructors	35.6%	44.5%
2. Dental Hygienists	57.8%	43.1%
3. Dental Assistants	35.6%	42.5%
4. Personal and Home Care Aides	34.0%	40.5%
5. Self-Enrichment Education Teachers	41.0%	40.1%
6. Receptionists and Information Clerks	31.5%	29.5%

Fastest-Growing Jobs with a High Percentage of Part-Time Workers

Job	Percent Part-Time Workers	Percent Growth
7. Interviewers, Except Eligibility and Loan	30.4%	28.0%
8. Amusement and Recreation Attendants	51.9%	27.8%
9. Costume Attendants	51.9%	27.8%
10. Locker Room, Coatroom, and Dressing Room Attendants	51.9%	27.8%
11. Massage Therapists	41.2%	27.1%
12. Counter and Rental Clerks	35.9%	26.3%
13. Gaming Change Persons and Booth Cashiers	44.8%	24.1%
14. Teacher Assistants	41.1%	23.0%
15. Combined Food Preparation and Serving Workers, Including Fast Food	40.4%	22.8%
16. Nonfarm Animal Caretakers	31.7%	22.2%
17. Library Assistants, Clerical	50.4%	21.5%
18. Food Preparation Workers	41.9%	20.2%
19. Athletes and Sports Competitors	36.3%	19.2%
20. Coaches and Scouts	36.3%	18.3%
21. Waiters and Waitresses	49.9%	17.5%
22. Demonstrators and Product Promoters	52.5%	17.0%
23. Library Technicians	53.4%	16.8%
24. Bus Drivers, School	35.6%	16.7%
25. Counter Attendants, Cafeteria, Food Concession, and Coffee Shop	65.8%	16.7%

Jobs with the Most Openings with a High Percentage of Part-Time Workers

Job	Percent Part-Time Workers	Annual Openings
1. Cashiers	44.8%	1,221,000
2. Retail Salespersons	32.6%	1,014,000
3. Combined Food Preparation and Serving Workers, Including Fast Food	40.4%	734,000
4. Waiters and Waitresses	49.9%	721,000
5. Child Care Workers	35.2%	406,000
6. Nannies	35.2%	406,000
7. Receptionists and Information Clerks	31.5%	296,000
8. Food Preparation Workers	41.9%	267,000
9. Teacher Assistants	41.1%	259,000
10. Cooks, Restaurant	31.6%	211,000

(continued)

(continued)

Jobs with the Most Openings with a High Percentage of Part-Time Workers

Job	Percent Part-Time Workers	Annual Openings
11. Counter Attendants, Cafeteria, Food Concession, and Coffee Shop	65.8%	190,000
12. Personal and Home Care Aides	34.0%	154,000
13. Counter and Rental Clerks	35.9%	144,000
14. Dining Room and Cafeteria Attendants and Bartender Helpers	54.0%	143,000
15. Hosts and Hostesses, Restaurant, Lounge, and Coffee Shop	66.9%	95,000
16. Bus Drivers, School	35.6%	76,000
17. Hairdressers, Hairstylists, and Cosmetologists	31.1%	68,000
18. Amusement and Recreation Attendants	51.9%	66,000
19. Costume Attendants	51.9%	66,000
20. Locker Room, Coatroom, and Dressing Room Attendants	51.9%	66,000
21. Interviewers, Except Eligibility and Loan	30.4%	46,000
22. Self-Enrichment Education Teachers	41.0%	39,000
23. Demonstrators and Product Promoters	52.5%	38,000
24. Fitness Trainers and Aerobics Instructors	35.6%	38,000
25. Dental Assistants	35.6%	35,000

Best Jobs with a High Percentage of Self-Employed Workers

About 7.5 percent of all working people are self-employed or own their own unincorporated business. This substantial part of our workforce gets little mention in most career books.

The jobs in the lists in this section all have 20 percent or more self-employed workers. Forty-eight jobs met this requirement. Many jobs in these lists, such as the various types of photographers or artists, are held by people who operate one- or two-person businesses and who may also do this work part time. Those in other occupations, such as Carpet Installers, often work on a per-job basis under the supervision of others.

As you will see from these lists, self-employed people hold a wide range of jobs at all levels of pay and skill. Many are in the construction trades, but many other fields are also represented. Also, while the lists do not include data on age and gender, older workers and women make up a rapidly growing part of the self-employed population. For example, some highly experienced older workers set up consulting and other small businesses following a layoff or as an alternative to full retirement. Large numbers of women are forming small businesses or creating self-employment opportunities as an alternative to traditional employment.

Best Jobs with the Highest Percentage of Self-Employed Workers

Job	Percent Self-Employed Workers
1. Farmers and Ranchers	99.3%
2. Massage Therapists	70.1%
3. Caption Writers	67.9%
4. Real Estate Brokers	59.1%
5. Real Estate Sales Agents	59.0%
6. Cartoonists	55.5%
7. Painters and Illustrators	55.5%
8. Sculptors	55.5%
9. Sketch Artists	55.5%
10. Carpet Installers	53.5%
11. Photographers, Scientific	52.5%
12. Professional Photographers	52.5%
13. Lodging Managers	50.3%
14. First-Line Supervisors/Managers of Personal Service Workers	49.4%
15. First-Line Supervisors/Managers of Non-Retail Sales Workers	44.7%
16. Hairdressers, Hairstylists, and Cosmetologists	44.3%
17. Child Care Workers	43.4%
18. Nannies	43.4%
19. Demonstrators and Product Promoters	42.1%
20. Painters, Construction and Maintenance	41.7%
21. Appraisers, Real Estate	34.8%
22. Assessors	34.8%
23. First-Line Supervisors and Manager/Supervisors—Landscaping Workers	34.7%
24. Food Service Managers	34.7%
25. Lawn Service Managers	34.7%
26. Private Detectives and Investigators	34.7%
27. Gaming Supervisors	33.8%
28. First-Line Supervisors/Managers of Retail Sales Workers	33.0%
29. Talent Directors	32.8%
30. Technical Directors/Managers	32.8%
31. Roofers	31.9%
32. Athletes and Sports Competitors	31.5%
33. Boat Builders and Shipwrights	29.7%
34. Brattice Builders	29.7%
35. Carpenter Assemblers and Repairers	29.7%

(continued)

(continued)

Best Jobs with the Highest Percentage of Self-Employed Workers

Job	Percent Self-Employed Workers
36. Construction Carpenters	29.7%
37. Rough Carpenters	29.7%
38. Ship Carpenters and Joiners	29.7%
39. Brickmasons and Blockmasons	27.9%
40. Nonfarm Animal Caretakers	27.3%
41. Coaches and Scouts	26.6%
42. Tax Preparers	26.2%
43. Tree Trimmers and Pruners	25.6%
44. Camera Operators, Television, Video, and Motion Picture	23.8%
45. Landscaping and Groundskeeping Workers	23.3%
46. Medical Equipment Repairers	23.2%
47. First-Line Supervisors and Manager/Supervisors—Construction Trades Workers	20.1%
48. First-Line Supervisors and Manager/Supervisors—Extractive Workers	20.1%

Best Jobs Overall with a High Percentage of Self-Employed Workers

Job	Percent Self-Employed Workers	Annual Earnings	Percent Growth	Annual Openings
1. First-Line Supervisors and Manager/Supervisors—Construction Trades Workers	20.1%	$50,450	14.1%	67,000
2. First-Line Supervisors and Manager/Supervisors—Extractive Workers	20.1%	$50,450	14.1%	67,000
3. Talent Directors	32.8%	$52,840	18.3%	10,000
4. Technical Directors/Managers	32.8%	$52,840	18.3%	10,000
5. Landscaping and Groundskeeping Workers	23.3%	$20,420	22.0%	203,000
6. Appraisers, Real Estate	34.8%	$43,390	17.6%	11,000
7. Assessors	34.8%	$43,390	17.6%	11,000
8. Caption Writers	67.9%	$44,350	16.1%	23,000
9. First-Line Supervisors and Manager/Supervisors—Landscaping Workers	34.7%	$35,340	21.6%	18,000
10. Lawn Service Managers	34.7%	$35,340	21.6%	18,000
11. First-Line Supervisors/Managers of Non-Retail Sales Workers	44.7%	$59,300	6.8%	72,000
12. Massage Therapists	70.1%	$31,960	27.1%	24,000
13. Athletes and Sports Competitors	31.5%	$48,310	19.2%	3,000

Best Jobs Overall with a High Percentage of Self-Employed Workers

Job	Percent Self-Employed Workers	Annual Earnings	Percent Growth	Annual Openings
14. Brickmasons and Blockmasons	27.9%	$41,740	14.2%	21,000
15. Roofers	31.9%	$30,840	18.6%	38,000
16. Boat Builders and Shipwrights	29.7%	$34,900	10.1%	193,000
17. Brattice Builders	29.7%	$34,900	10.1%	193,000
18. Carpenter Assemblers and Repairers	29.7%	$34,900	10.1%	193,000
19. Construction Carpenters	29.7%	$34,900	10.1%	193,000
20. Food Service Managers	34.7%	$39,610	11.5%	58,000
21. Rough Carpenters	29.7%	$34,900	10.1%	193,000
22. Ship Carpenters and Joiners	29.7%	$34,900	10.1%	193,000
23. Nonfarm Animal Caretakers	27.3%	$17,460	22.2%	32,000
24. Coaches and Scouts	26.6%	$26,350	18.3%	26,000
25. Farmers and Ranchers	99.3%	$40,440	−20.6%	118,000

Best-Paying Jobs with a High Percentage of Self-Employed Workers

Job	Percent Self-Employed Workers	Annual Earnings
1. First-Line Supervisors/Managers of Non-Retail Sales Workers	44.7%	$59,300
2. Real Estate Brokers	59.1%	$58,720
3. Talent Directors	32.8%	$52,840
4. Technical Directors/Managers	32.8%	$52,840
5. First-Line Supervisors and Manager/Supervisors—Construction Trades Workers	20.1%	$50,450
6. First-Line Supervisors and Manager/Supervisors—Extractive Workers	20.1%	$50,450
7. Athletes and Sports Competitors	31.5%	$48,310
8. Caption Writers	67.9%	$44,350
9. Appraisers, Real Estate	34.8%	$43,390
10. Assessors	34.8%	$43,390
11. Brickmasons and Blockmasons	27.9%	$41,740
12. Gaming Supervisors	33.8%	$40,840
13. Farmers and Ranchers	99.3%	$40,440
14. Food Service Managers	34.7%	$39,610
15. Cartoonists	55.5%	$38,060
16. Painters and Illustrators	55.5%	$38,060

(continued)

(continued)

Best-Paying Jobs with a High Percentage of Self-Employed Workers

Job	Percent Self-Employed Workers	Annual Earnings
17. Sculptors	55.5%	$38,060
18. Sketch Artists	55.5%	$38,060
19. Lodging Managers	50.3%	$37,660
20. Camera Operators, Television, Video, and Motion Picture	23.8%	$37,610
21. Medical Equipment Repairers	23.2%	$37,220
22. Real Estate Sales Agents	59.0%	$35,670
23. First-Line Supervisors and Manager/Supervisors—Landscaping Workers	34.7%	$35,340
24. Lawn Service Managers	34.7%	$35,340
25. Boat Builders and Shipwrights	29.7%	$34,900

Fastest-Growing Jobs with a High Percentage of Self-Employed Workers

Job	Percent Self-Employed Workers	Percent Growth
1. Massage Therapists	70.1%	27.1%
2. Private Detectives and Investigators	34.7%	25.3%
3. Tax Preparers	26.2%	23.2%
4. Nonfarm Animal Caretakers	27.3%	22.2%
5. Landscaping and Groundskeeping Workers	23.3%	22.0%
6. First-Line Supervisors and Manager/Supervisors—Landscaping Workers	34.7%	21.6%
7. Lawn Service Managers	34.7%	21.6%
8. Athletes and Sports Competitors	31.5%	19.2%
9. Roofers	31.9%	18.6%
10. Tree Trimmers and Pruners	25.6%	18.6%
11. Coaches and Scouts	26.6%	18.3%
12. Talent Directors	32.8%	18.3%
13. Technical Directors/Managers	32.8%	18.3%
14. Appraisers, Real Estate	34.8%	17.6%
15. Assessors	34.8%	17.6%
16. Demonstrators and Product Promoters	42.1%	17.0%
17. Carpet Installers	53.5%	16.8%
18. Cartoonists	55.5%	16.5%

Fastest-Growing Jobs with a High Percentage of Self-Employed Workers

Job	Percent Self-Employed Workers	Percent Growth
19. Painters and Illustrators	55.5%	16.5%
20. Sculptors	55.5%	16.5%
21. Sketch Artists	55.5%	16.5%
22. Caption Writers	67.9%	16.1%
23. Gaming Supervisors	33.8%	15.7%
24. Medical Equipment Repairers	23.2%	14.8%
25. Hairdressers, Hairstylists, and Cosmetologists	44.3%	14.7%

Jobs with the Most Openings with a High Percentage of Self-Employed Workers

Job	Percent Self-Employed Workers	Annual Openings
1. Child Care Workers	43.4%	406,000
2. Nannies	43.4%	406,000
3. First-Line Supervisors/Managers of Retail Sales Workers	33.0%	251,000
4. Landscaping and Groundskeeping Workers	23.3%	203,000
5. Boat Builders and Shipwrights	29.7%	193,000
6. Brattice Builders	29.7%	193,000
7. Carpenter Assemblers and Repairers	29.7%	193,000
8. Construction Carpenters	29.7%	193,000
9. Rough Carpenters	29.7%	193,000
10. Ship Carpenters and Joiners	29.7%	193,000
11. Farmers and Ranchers	99.3%	118,000
12. First-Line Supervisors/Managers of Non-Retail Sales Workers	44.7%	72,000
13. Painters, Construction and Maintenance	41.7%	69,000
14. Hairdressers, Hairstylists, and Cosmetologists	44.3%	68,000
15. First-Line Supervisors and Manager/Supervisors—Construction Trades Workers	20.1%	67,000
16. First-Line Supervisors and Manager/Supervisors—Extractive Workers	20.1%	67,000
17. Food Service Managers	34.7%	58,000
18. Demonstrators and Product Promoters	42.1%	38,000
19. Roofers	31.9%	38,000
20. Real Estate Sales Agents	59.0%	34,000

(continued)

(continued)

Jobs with the Most Openings with a High Percentage of Self-Employed Workers

Job	Percent Self-Employed Workers	Annual Openings
21. Nonfarm Animal Caretakers	27.3%	32,000
22. Coaches and Scouts	26.6%	26,000
23. First-Line Supervisors/Managers of Personal Service Workers	49.4%	26,000
24. Massage Therapists	70.1%	24,000
25. Caption Writers	67.9%	23,000

Best Jobs with a High Percentage of Women

We knew we would create some controversy when we first included the best jobs lists with high percentages of men and women. But these lists are not meant to restrict women or men from considering job options—our reason for including these lists is exactly the opposite. We hope the lists help people see possibilities that they might not otherwise have considered. For example, we suggest that women browse the lists of jobs that employ high percentages of men. Many of these occupations pay quite well, and women who want to do them and who have or obtain the necessary education and training should consider them.

We created the lists by sorting the jobs that met the criteria for this book and including only those employing 70 percent or more of men or women. Of the 300 best jobs, 54 jobs met this criteria for women and 161 jobs did so for men.

An interesting and unfortunate tidbit to bring up at your next party is that the average earnings for the 54 jobs (not requiring a four-year degree) with the highest percentage of women is $29,867, compared to average earnings of $40,267 for the 161 jobs with the highest percentage of men. But earnings don't tell the whole story. We computed the average growth and job openings of the 54 jobs with the highest percentage of women and found statistics of 23.3% growth and 119,815 openings, compared to 15.3% growth and 43,224 openings for the 161 jobs with the highest percentage of men. This discrepancy reinforces the idea that men have had more problems than women in adapting to an economy dominated by service and information-based jobs. Many women may simply be better prepared for these jobs, possessing more appropriate skills for the jobs that are now growing rapidly and have more job openings.

Perhaps you can come to other conclusions, but there is a variety of evidence that women equipped with skills in demand are doing quite well in the labor market. And it is increasingly true that people of either gender without these skills are less likely to find the best jobs.

Best Jobs Employing the Highest Percentage of Women

Job	Percent Women
1. Dental Hygienists	97.7%
2. Dental Assistants	97.1%
3. Executive Secretaries and Administrative Assistants	96.5%
4. Legal Secretaries	96.5%
5. Medical Secretaries	96.5%
6. Child Care Workers	94.7%
7. Nannies	94.7%
8. Licensed Practical and Licensed Vocational Nurses	93.0%
9. Receptionists and Information Clerks	92.7%
10. Registered Nurses	92.4%
11. Teacher Assistants	91.6%
12. Medical Records and Health Information Technicians	91.0%
13. Hairdressers, Hairstylists, and Cosmetologists	90.3%
14. Bookkeeping, Accounting, and Auditing Clerks	89.4%
15. Billing, Cost, and Rate Clerks	88.5%
16. Billing, Posting, and Calculating Machine Operators	88.5%
17. Statement Clerks	88.5%
18. Medical Assistants	88.0%
19. Medical Transcriptionists	88.0%
20. Home Health Aides	87.8%
21. Nursing Aides, Orderlies, and Attendants	87.8%
22. Hosts and Hostesses, Restaurant, Lounge, and Coffee Shop	87.3%
23. Personal and Home Care Aides	87.3%
24. Occupational Therapist Assistants	87.2%
25. Paralegals and Legal Assistants	86.1%
26. New Accounts Clerks	85.0%
27. Choreographers	84.2%
28. Office Clerks, General	83.9%
29. Library Assistants, Clerical	81.9%
30. Massage Therapists	81.2%
31. Human Resources Assistants, Except Payroll and Timekeeping	81.1%
32. Pharmacy Technicians	80.7%
33. Respiratory Therapy Technicians	80.7%
34. Surgical Technologists	80.7%
35. Veterinary Technologists and Technicians	80.7%
36. Flight Attendants	78.7%

(continued)

(continued)

Best Jobs Employing the Highest Percentage of Women

Job	Percent Women
37. Court Clerks	78.2%
38. License Clerks	78.2%
39. Municipal Clerks	78.2%
40. Demonstrators and Product Promoters	77.4%
41. Cashiers	76.0%
42. Gaming Change Persons and Booth Cashiers	76.0%
43. Physical Therapist Assistants	76.0%
44. Library Technicians	74.2%
45. Waiters and Waitresses	74.2%
46. Medical and Clinical Laboratory Technicians	73.9%
47. Court Reporters	73.3%
48. Cardiovascular Technologists and Technicians	71.7%
49. Diagnostic Medical Sonographers	71.7%
50. Nuclear Medicine Technologists	71.7%
51. Radiologic Technicians	71.7%
52. Radiologic Technologists	71.7%
53. Interviewers, Except Eligibility and Loan	71.4%
54. Bill and Account Collectors	71.0%

Best Jobs Overall Employing a High Percentage of Women

Job	Percent Women	Annual Earnings	Percent Growth	Annual Openings
1. Registered Nurses	92.4%	$52,330	27.3%	215,000
2. Paralegals and Legal Assistants	86.1%	$39,130	28.7%	29,000
3. Dental Hygienists	97.7%	$58,350	43.1%	9,000
4. Medical Assistants	88.0%	$24,610	58.9%	78,000
5. Licensed Practical and Licensed Vocational Nurses	93.0%	$33,970	20.2%	105,000
6. Receptionists and Information Clerks	92.7%	$21,830	29.5%	296,000
7. Dental Assistants	97.1%	$28,330	42.5%	35,000
8. Physical Therapist Assistants	76.0%	$37,890	44.6%	10,000
9. Home Health Aides	87.8%	$18,330	48.1%	141,000
10. Nursing Aides, Orderlies, and Attendants	87.8%	$20,980	24.9%	302,000
11. Radiologic Technicians	71.7%	$43,350	22.9%	21,000

Best Jobs Overall Employing a High Percentage of Women

Job	Percent Women	Annual Earnings	Percent Growth	Annual Openings
12. Radiologic Technologists	71.7%	$43,350	22.9%	21,000
13. Bill and Account Collectors	71.0%	$27,450	24.5%	76,000
14. Massage Therapists	81.2%	$31,960	27.1%	24,000
15. Medical Records and Health Information Technicians	91.0%	$25,590	46.8%	24,000
16. Cardiovascular Technologists and Technicians	71.7%	$38,690	33.5%	6,000
17. Personal and Home Care Aides	87.3%	$16,900	40.5%	154,000
18. Legal Secretaries	96.5%	$36,720	18.8%	39,000
19. Occupational Therapist Assistants	87.2%	$38,430	39.2%	3,000
20. Respiratory Therapy Technicians	80.7%	$36,740	34.2%	5,000
21. Diagnostic Medical Sonographers	71.7%	$52,490	24.0%	4,000
22. Surgical Technologists	80.7%	$34,010	27.9%	13,000
23. Executive Secretaries and Administrative Assistants	96.5%	$34,970	8.7%	210,000
24. Interviewers, Except Eligibility and Loan	71.4%	$23,670	28.0%	46,000
25. Pharmacy Technicians	80.7%	$23,650	28.8%	39,000

Best-Paying Jobs Employing a High Percentage of Women

Job	Percent Women	Annual Earnings
1. Dental Hygienists	97.7%	$58,350
2. Nuclear Medicine Technologists	71.7%	$56,450
3. Diagnostic Medical Sonographers	71.7%	$52,490
4. Registered Nurses	92.4%	$52,330
5. Flight Attendants	78.7%	$43,440
6. Radiologic Technicians	71.7%	$43,350
7. Radiologic Technologists	71.7%	$43,350
8. Court Reporters	73.3%	$42,920
9. Paralegals and Legal Assistants	86.1%	$39,130
10. Cardiovascular Technologists and Technicians	71.7%	$38,690
11. Occupational Therapist Assistants	87.2%	$38,430
12. Physical Therapist Assistants	76.0%	$37,890
13. Respiratory Therapy Technicians	80.7%	$36,740
14. Legal Secretaries	96.5%	$36,720

(continued)

(continued)

Best-Paying Jobs Employing a High Percentage of Women

Job	Percent Women	Annual Earnings
15. Executive Secretaries and Administrative Assistants	96.5%	$34,970
16. Surgical Technologists	80.7%	$34,010
17. Licensed Practical and Licensed Vocational Nurses	93.0%	$33,970
18. Choreographers	84.2%	$33,670
19. Massage Therapists	81.2%	$31,960
20. Human Resources Assistants, Except Payroll and Timekeeping	81.1%	$31,750
21. Medical and Clinical Laboratory Technicians	73.9%	$30,840
22. Bookkeeping, Accounting, and Auditing Clerks	89.4%	$28,570
23. Court Clerks	78.2%	$28,430
24. License Clerks	78.2%	$28,430
25. Municipal Clerks	78.2%	$28,430

Fastest-Growing Jobs Employing a High Percentage of Women

Job	Percent Women	Percent Growth
1. Medical Assistants	88.0%	58.9%
2. Home Health Aides	87.8%	48.1%
3. Medical Records and Health Information Technicians	91.0%	46.8%
4. Physical Therapist Assistants	76.0%	44.6%
5. Veterinary Technologists and Technicians	80.7%	44.1%
6. Dental Hygienists	97.7%	43.1%
7. Dental Assistants	97.1%	42.5%
8. Personal and Home Care Aides	87.3%	40.5%
9. Occupational Therapist Assistants	87.2%	39.2%
10. Respiratory Therapy Technicians	80.7%	34.2%
11. Cardiovascular Technologists and Technicians	71.7%	33.5%
12. Receptionists and Information Clerks	92.7%	29.5%
13. Pharmacy Technicians	80.7%	28.8%
14. Paralegals and Legal Assistants	86.1%	28.7%
15. Interviewers, Except Eligibility and Loan	71.4%	28.0%
16. Surgical Technologists	80.7%	27.9%
17. Registered Nurses	92.4%	27.3%
18. Massage Therapists	81.2%	27.1%
19. Nursing Aides, Orderlies, and Attendants	87.8%	24.9%

Fastest-Growing Jobs Employing a High Percentage of Women

Job	Percent Women	Percent Growth
20. Bill and Account Collectors	71.0%	24.5%
21. Gaming Change Persons and Booth Cashiers	76.0%	24.1%
22. Diagnostic Medical Sonographers	71.7%	24.0%
23. Nuclear Medicine Technologists	71.7%	23.6%
24. Teacher Assistants	91.6%	23.0%
25. Radiologic Technicians	71.7%	22.9%

Jobs with the Most Openings Employing a High Percentage of Women

Job	Percent Women	Annual Openings
1. Cashiers	76.0%	1,221,000
2. Waiters and Waitresses	74.2%	721,000
3. Office Clerks, General	83.9%	550,000
4. Child Care Workers	94.7%	406,000
5. Nannies	94.7%	406,000
6. Nursing Aides, Orderlies, and Attendants	87.8%	302,000
7. Receptionists and Information Clerks	92.7%	296,000
8. Bookkeeping, Accounting, and Auditing Clerks	89.4%	274,000
9. Teacher Assistants	91.6%	259,000
10. Registered Nurses	92.4%	215,000
11. Executive Secretaries and Administrative Assistants	96.5%	210,000
12. Personal and Home Care Aides	87.3%	154,000
13. Home Health Aides	87.8%	141,000
14. Licensed Practical and Licensed Vocational Nurses	93.0%	105,000
15. Hosts and Hostesses, Restaurant, Lounge, and Coffee Shop	87.3%	95,000
16. Billing, Cost, and Rate Clerks	88.5%	78,000
17. Billing, Posting, and Calculating Machine Operators	88.5%	78,000
18. Medical Assistants	88.0%	78,000
19. Statement Clerks	88.5%	78,000
20. Bill and Account Collectors	71.0%	76,000
21. Hairdressers, Hairstylists, and Cosmetologists	90.3%	68,000
22. Medical Secretaries	96.5%	50,000
23. Interviewers, Except Eligibility and Loan	71.4%	46,000
24. Legal Secretaries	96.5%	39,000
25. Pharmacy Technicians	80.7%	39,000

Best Jobs with a High Percentage of Men

We suggest you read the introductory material in the "Best Jobs with a High Percentage of Women" section to better understand the purpose of publishing the following lists. As we state in that section, we are not suggesting that the best jobs lists for men include the only jobs that men should consider.

For example, there is a strong demand for Registered Nurses, a job that employs a high percentage of women, so the few available are recruited aggressively and often find jobs quickly. Just as women should consider careers typically held by men, many men should consider career opportunities usually associated with women. This is particularly true now, since occupations with high percentages of women workers are growing more rapidly than occupations in our similar lists for men.

In the Best Jobs Overall list for men, note that 16 of the best jobs are in the construction, law enforcement, and repair fields, whereas 19 of the best jobs overall for women are in the health field. This difference confirms the concerns of many educators, counselors, and social advocates about sexual stereotyping of occupations. In many cases, both men and women would be well advised to consider occupations typically held by the opposite gender.

Another thing we noticed is that many jobs with high percentages of men have significantly higher earnings than jobs with high percentages of women. The average pay for all jobs in the list for women was only 74 percent of the average for men. This indicates that women interested in improving their earnings may want to seriously consider jobs traditionally dominated by men.

Best Jobs Employing the Highest Percentage of Men

Job	Percent Men
1. Mobile Heavy Equipment Mechanics, Except Engines	99.0%
2. Brickmasons and Blockmasons	98.9%
3. Bus and Truck Mechanics and Diesel Engine Specialists	98.8%
4. Plasterers and Stucco Masons	98.7%
5. Cement Masons and Concrete Finishers	98.6%
6. Elevator Installers and Repairers	98.6%
7. Recreational Vehicle Service Technicians	98.4%
8. Roofers	98.4%
9. Pipe Fitters	98.3%
10. Pipelaying Fitters	98.3%
11. Plumbers	98.3%
12. Riggers	98.3%
13. Dragline Operators	98.2%

Best Jobs Employing the Highest Percentage of Men

Job	Percent Men
14. Excavating and Loading Machine Operators	98.2%
15. Heating and Air Conditioning Mechanics	98.2%
16. Loading Machine Operators, Underground Mining	98.2%
17. Refrigeration Mechanics	98.2%
18. Automotive Master Mechanics	98.1%
19. Automotive Specialty Technicians	98.1%
20. Boat Builders and Shipwrights	98.1%
21. Brattice Builders	98.1%
22. Carpenter Assemblers and Repairers	98.1%
23. Construction Carpenters	98.1%
24. Rough Carpenters	98.1%
25. Ship Carpenters and Joiners	98.1%
26. Automotive Body and Related Repairers	97.9%
27. Grader, Bulldozer, and Scraper Operators	97.8%
28. Millwrights	97.8%
29. Operating Engineers	97.8%
30. Structural Iron and Steel Workers	97.6%
31. Carpet Installers	97.5%
32. Tile and Marble Setters	97.5%
33. Electricians	97.4%
34. Ceiling Tile Installers	97.3%
35. Drywall Installers	97.3%
36. Electrical Power-Line Installers and Repairers	97.3%
37. Tapers	97.3%
38. First-Line Supervisors and Manager/Supervisors—Construction Trades Workers	97.2%
39. First-Line Supervisors and Manager/Supervisors—Extractive Workers	97.2%
40. Forest Fire Fighting and Prevention Supervisors	97.1%
41. Municipal Fire Fighting and Prevention Supervisors	97.1%
42. Security and Fire Alarm Systems Installers	96.9%
43. Crane and Tower Operators	96.6%
44. Construction Laborers	96.5%
45. Forest Fire Fighters	96.4%
46. Municipal Fire Fighters	96.4%
47. Industrial Machinery Mechanics	96.2%
48. Refractory Materials Repairers, Except Brickmasons	96.2%
49. Commercial Pilots	96.0%

(continued)

(continued)

Best Jobs Employing the Highest Percentage of Men

Job	Percent Men
50. Highway Maintenance Workers	96.0%
51. Insulation Workers, Floor, Ceiling, and Wall	95.9%
52. Insulation Workers, Mechanical	95.9%
53. Maintenance and Repair Workers, General	95.9%
54. Sheet Metal Workers	95.9%
55. Glaziers	95.6%
56. Electric Meter Installers and Repairers	95.2%
57. Meter Mechanics	95.2%
58. Valve and Regulator Repairers	95.2%
59. Aircraft Body and Bonded Structure Repairers	95.1%
60. Aircraft Engine Specialists	95.1%
61. Airframe-and-Power-Plant Mechanics	95.1%
62. Helpers—Electricians	94.8%
63. Machinists	94.7%
64. Water and Liquid Waste Treatment Plant and System Operators	94.6%
65. Electrical and Electronics Repairers, Commercial and Industrial Equipment	94.1%
66. Tractor-Trailer Truck Drivers	94.1%
67. Truck Drivers, Heavy	94.1%
68. Truck Drivers, Light or Delivery Services	94.1%
69. Pest Control Workers	93.7%
70. Telecommunications Line Installers and Repairers	93.5%
71. First-Line Supervisors and Manager/Supervisors—Landscaping Workers	93.3%
72. Lawn Service Managers	93.3%
73. Locksmiths and Safe Repairers	93.0%
74. Brazers	92.6%
75. Painters, Construction and Maintenance	92.6%
76. Solderers	92.6%
77. Welder-Fitters	92.6%
78. Welders and Cutters	92.6%
79. Welders, Production	92.6%
80. Industrial Truck and Tractor Operators	92.4%
81. Landscaping and Groundskeeping Workers	92.4%
82. Tree Trimmers and Pruners	92.4%
83. First-Line Supervisors/Managers of Mechanics, Installers, and Repairers	91.8%
84. Mapping Technicians	91.1%
85. Subway and Streetcar Operators	91.1%
86. Surveying Technicians	91.1%
87. Hazardous Materials Removal Workers	90.8%

Best Jobs Employing the Highest Percentage of Men

Job	Percent Men
88. Irradiated-Fuel Handlers	90.8%
89. Refuse and Recyclable Material Collectors	90.8%
90. Helpers—Installation, Maintenance, and Repair Workers	90.7%
91. Construction and Building Inspectors	90.2%
92. Medical Equipment Repairers	87.9%
93. First-Line Supervisors/Managers of Police and Detectives	87.2%
94. Central Office and PBX Installers and Repairers	87.0%
95. Communication Equipment Mechanics, Installers, and Repairers	87.0%
96. Frame Wirers, Central Office	87.0%
97. Station Installers and Repairers, Telephone	87.0%
98. Telecommunications Facility Examiners	87.0%
99. Highway Patrol Pilots	86.9%
100. Police Patrol Officers	86.9%
101. Sheriffs and Deputy Sheriffs	86.9%
102. Transit and Railroad Police	86.9%
103. Taxi Drivers and Chauffeurs	86.7%
104. Automatic Teller Machine Servicers	86.5%
105. Data Processing Equipment Repairers	86.5%
106. Office Machine and Cash Register Servicers	86.5%
107. Audio and Video Equipment Technicians	85.8%
108. Sound Engineering Technicians	85.8%
109. Agricultural Crop Farm Managers	85.5%
110. Fish Hatchery Managers	85.5%
111. Nursery and Greenhouse Managers	85.5%
112. Farmers and Ranchers	85.4%
113. Model Makers, Metal and Plastic	85.2%
114. First-Line Supervisors and Manager/Supervisors—Agricultural Crop Workers	84.4%
115. First-Line Supervisors and Manager/Supervisors—Animal Care Workers, Except Livestock	84.4%
116. First-Line Supervisors and Manager/Supervisors—Animal Husbandry Workers	84.4%
117. First-Line Supervisors and Manager/Supervisors—Fishery Workers	84.4%
118. First-Line Supervisors and Manager/Supervisors—Horticultural Workers	84.4%
119. Aviation Inspectors	83.8%
120. Freight Inspectors	83.8%
121. Marine Cargo Inspectors	83.8%
122. Motor Vehicle Inspectors	83.8%
123. Public Transportation Inspectors	83.8%
124. Railroad Inspectors	83.8%

(continued)

(continued)

Best Jobs Employing the Highest Percentage of Men

Job	Percent Men
125. Painters, Transportation Equipment	83.2%
126. Storage and Distribution Managers	82.9%
127. Transportation Managers	82.9%
128. Air Traffic Controllers	81.6%
129. First-Line Supervisors/Managers of Helpers, Laborers, and Material Movers, Hand	81.2%
130. First-Line Supervisors/Managers of Transportation and Material-Moving Machine and Vehicle Operators	81.2%
131. Camera Operators, Television, Video, and Motion Picture	81.1%
132. Calibration and Instrumentation Technicians	80.9%
133. Civil Engineering Technicians	80.9%
134. Electrical Engineering Technicians	80.9%
135. Electro-Mechanical Technicians	80.9%
136. Electronics Engineering Technicians	80.9%
137. Environmental Engineering Technicians	80.9%
138. Industrial Engineering Technicians	80.9%
139. Mechanical Engineering Technicians	80.9%
140. Chefs and Head Cooks	80.8%
141. Architectural Drafters	80.1%
142. Civil Drafters	80.1%
143. First-Line Supervisors/Managers of Production and Operating Workers	79.1%
144. Child Support, Missing Persons, and Unemployment Insurance Fraud Investigators	79.0%
145. Criminal Investigators and Special Agents	79.0%
146. Immigration and Customs Inspectors	79.0%
147. Police Detectives	79.0%
148. Police Identification and Records Officers	79.0%
149. Security Guards	79.0%
150. Slaughterers and Meat Packers	76.3%
151. First-Line Supervisors/Managers of Correctional Officers	74.3%
152. Correctional Officers and Jailers	74.0%
153. Sales Representatives, Agricultural	73.9%
154. Sales Representatives, Chemical and Pharmaceutical	73.9%
155. Sales Representatives, Electrical/Electronic	73.9%
156. Sales Representatives, Instruments	73.9%
157. Sales Representatives, Mechanical Equipment and Supplies	73.9%
158. Sales Representatives, Medical	73.9%
159. Sales Representatives, Wholesale and Manufacturing, Except Technical and Scientific Products	73.9%
160. Cargo and Freight Agents	73.1%
161. Janitors and Cleaners, Except Maids and Housekeeping Cleaners	70.1%

Best Jobs Overall Employing a High Percentage of Men

Job	Percent Men	Annual Earnings	Percent Growth	Annual Openings
1. Highway Patrol Pilots	86.9%	$45,210	24.7%	67,000
2. Police Patrol Officers	86.9%	$45,210	24.7%	67,000
3. Sheriffs and Deputy Sheriffs	86.9%	$45,210	24.7%	67,000
4. Sales Representatives, Agricultural	73.9%	$58,580	19.3%	44,000
5. Sales Representatives, Chemical and Pharmaceutical	73.9%	$58,580	19.3%	44,000
6. Sales Representatives, Electrical/Electronic	73.9%	$58,580	19.3%	44,000
7. Sales Representatives, Instruments	73.9%	$58,580	19.3%	44,000
8. Sales Representatives, Mechanical Equipment and Supplies	73.9%	$58,580	19.3%	44,000
9. Sales Representatives, Medical	73.9%	$58,580	19.3%	44,000
10. Sales Representatives, Wholesale and Manufacturing, Except Technical and Scientific Products	73.9%	$45,400	19.1%	160,000
11. Electricians	97.4%	$42,300	23.4%	65,000
12. Storage and Distribution Managers	82.9%	$66,600	19.7%	13,000
13. Transportation Managers	82.9%	$66,600	19.7%	13,000
14. Child Support, Missing Persons, and Unemployment Insurance Fraud Investigators	79.0%	$53,990	22.4%	11,000
15. Criminal Investigators and Special Agents	79.0%	$53,990	22.4%	11,000
16. Immigration and Customs Inspectors	79.0%	$53,990	22.4%	11,000
17. Police Detectives	79.0%	$53,990	22.4%	11,000
18. Police Identification and Records Officers	79.0%	$53,990	22.4%	11,000
19. Heating and Air Conditioning Mechanics	98.2%	$36,260	31.8%	35,000
20. Refrigeration Mechanics	98.2%	$36,260	31.8%	35,000
21. First-Line Supervisors and Manager/Supervisors—Construction Trades Workers	97.2%	$50,450	14.1%	67,000
22. First-Line Supervisors and Manager/Supervisors—Extractive Workers	97.2%	$50,450	14.1%	67,000
23. Pipe Fitters	98.3%	$41,290	18.7%	56,000
24. Pipelaying Fitters	98.3%	$41,290	18.7%	56,000
25. Plumbers	98.3%	$41,290	18.7%	56,000

Best-Paying Jobs Employing a High Percentage of Men

Job	Percent Men	Annual Earnings
1. Air Traffic Controllers	81.6%	$102,030
2. Storage and Distribution Managers	82.9%	$66,600
3. Transportation Managers	82.9%	$66,600
4. First-Line Supervisors/Managers of Police and Detectives	87.2%	$64,430
5. Forest Fire Fighting and Prevention Supervisors	97.1%	$58,920
6. Municipal Fire Fighting and Prevention Supervisors	97.1%	$58,920
7. Elevator Installers and Repairers	98.6%	$58,710
8. Sales Representatives, Agricultural	73.9%	$58,580
9. Sales Representatives, Chemical and Pharmaceutical	73.9%	$58,580
10. Sales Representatives, Electrical/Electronic	73.9%	$58,580
11. Sales Representatives, Instruments	73.9%	$58,580
12. Sales Representatives, Mechanical Equipment and Supplies	73.9%	$58,580
13. Sales Representatives, Medical	73.9%	$58,580
14. Child Support, Missing Persons, and Unemployment Insurance Fraud Investigators	79.0%	$53,990
15. Criminal Investigators and Special Agents	79.0%	$53,990
16. Immigration and Customs Inspectors	79.0%	$53,990
17. Police Detectives	79.0%	$53,990
18. Police Identification and Records Officers	79.0%	$53,990
19. Commercial Pilots	96.0%	$53,870
20. Agricultural Crop Farm Managers	85.5%	$50,700
21. Fish Hatchery Managers	85.5%	$50,700
22. Nursery and Greenhouse Managers	85.5%	$50,700
23. First-Line Supervisors and Manager/Supervisors—Construction Trades Workers	97.2%	$50,450
24. First-Line Supervisors and Manager/Supervisors—Extractive Workers	97.2%	$50,450
25. Aviation Inspectors	83.8%	$50,380

Fastest-Growing Jobs Employing a High Percentage of Men

Job	Percent Men	Percent Growth
1. Hazardous Materials Removal Workers	90.8%	43.1%
2. Irradiated-Fuel Handlers	90.8%	43.1%
3. Security Guards	79.0%	31.9%
4. Heating and Air Conditioning Mechanics	98.2%	31.8%

Fastest-Growing Jobs Employing a High Percentage of Men

Job	Percent Men	Percent Growth
5. Refrigeration Mechanics	98.2%	31.8%
6. Security and Fire Alarm Systems Installers	96.9%	30.2%
7. Environmental Engineering Technicians	80.9%	28.4%
8. Audio and Video Equipment Technicians	85.8%	26.7%
9. Tile and Marble Setters	97.5%	26.5%
10. Cement Masons and Concrete Finishers	98.6%	26.1%
11. Sound Engineering Technicians	85.8%	25.5%
12. Highway Patrol Pilots	86.9%	24.7%
13. Police Patrol Officers	86.9%	24.7%
14. Sheriffs and Deputy Sheriffs	86.9%	24.7%
15. Correctional Officers and Jailers	74.0%	24.2%
16. Electricians	97.4%	23.4%
17. Truck Drivers, Light or Delivery Services	94.1%	23.2%
18. Mapping Technicians	91.1%	23.1%
19. Surveying Technicians	91.1%	23.1%
20. Child Support, Missing Persons, and Unemployment Insurance Fraud Investigators	79.0%	22.4%
21. Criminal Investigators and Special Agents	79.0%	22.4%
22. Immigration and Customs Inspectors	79.0%	22.4%
23. Police Detectives	79.0%	22.4%
24. Police Identification and Records Officers	79.0%	22.4%
25. Landscaping and Groundskeeping Workers	92.4%	22.0%

Jobs with the Most Openings Employing a High Percentage of Men

Job	Percent Men	Annual Openings
1. Janitors and Cleaners, Except Maids and Housekeeping Cleaners	70.1%	454,000
2. Tractor-Trailer Truck Drivers	94.1%	299,000
3. Truck Drivers, Heavy	94.1%	299,000
4. Security Guards	79.0%	228,000
5. Truck Drivers, Light or Delivery Services	94.1%	219,000
6. Landscaping and Groundskeeping Workers	92.4%	203,000
7. Boat Builders and Shipwrights	98.1%	193,000
8. Brattice Builders	98.1%	193,000

(continued)

(continued)

Jobs with the Most Openings Employing a High Percentage of Men

Job	Percent Men	Annual Openings
9. Carpenter Assemblers and Repairers	98.1%	193,000
10. Construction Carpenters	98.1%	193,000
11. Rough Carpenters	98.1%	193,000
12. Ship Carpenters and Joiners	98.1%	193,000
13. Construction Laborers	96.5%	166,000
14. Sales Representatives, Wholesale and Manufacturing, Except Technical and Scientific Products	73.9%	160,000
15. Maintenance and Repair Workers, General	95.9%	155,000
16. Refractory Materials Repairers, Except Brickmasons	96.2%	155,000
17. Farmers and Ranchers	85.4%	118,000
18. Automotive Master Mechanics	98.1%	100,000
19. Automotive Specialty Technicians	98.1%	100,000
20. Industrial Truck and Tractor Operators	92.4%	94,000
21. Brazers	92.6%	71,000
22. Solderers	92.6%	71,000
23. Welder-Fitters	92.6%	71,000
24. Welders and Cutters	92.6%	71,000
25. Welders, Production	92.6%	71,000

Best Jobs Based on Levels of Education, Training, and Experience

The lists in this section separate the 300 jobs that met our criteria for this book into lists based on the education or training typically required for entry. Unlike many of the other lists, we did not include separate lists for highest pay, growth, or number of openings. Instead, we provided one list that includes all the occupations in our database that fit into each of the education levels and ranked the occupations by their combined score (on earnings, growth, and job openings).

You can use these lists in a variety of ways. For example, they can help you identify a job with higher potential but with a similar level of education to the job you now hold.

You can also use these lists to figure out additional job possibilities that would open up if you were to get additional training, education, or work experience. For example, maybe you are a high school graduate working in the health care field. There are many jobs in this field at all levels of education. You can identify the job you're interested in and the related training you need so you can move ahead in the health care field.

The lists of jobs by education should also help you when you're planning your education. For example, you might be thinking about a job in the construction field, but you aren't sure what kind of work you want to do. The lists show that a job as a Drywall Installer requires moderate-term on-the-job training and pays $34,030, while a job as a Glazier requires long-term on-the-job training but pays $32,650. If you want higher earnings without lengthy training, this information might make a difference in your choice.

As you review these lists, keep in mind that they do not include jobs that typically require a four-year college degree or more. Many of the jobs in the lists that follow are related to and can help you prepare for jobs requiring a four-year degree. If you are considering jobs requiring education beyond an associate degree, we suggest you refer to the books and resources listed in the front of this book.

The Education Levels

Here are brief descriptions used by the U.S. Department of Labor for the training and education levels used in the lists that follow:

- **Short-term on-the-job training**—It is possible to work in these occupations and achieve an average level of performance within a few days or weeks through on-the-job training.

- **Moderate-term on-the-job training**—Occupations that require this type of training can be performed adequately after a 1- to 12-month period of combined on-the-job and informal training. Typically, untrained workers observe experienced workers performing tasks and are gradually moved into progressively more difficult assignments.

- **Long-term on-the-job training**—This type of job requires more than 12 months of on-the-job training or combined work experience and formal classroom instruction. This includes occupations that use formal apprenticeships for training workers that may take up to four years. It also includes intensive occupation-specific, employer-sponsored training like police academies. Furthermore, it includes occupations that require natural talent that must be developed over many years.

- **Work experience in a related occupation**—This type of job requires a worker to have experience—usually several years of experience—in a related occupation (such as Police Detectives, who are selected based on their experience as Police Patrol Officers).

- **Postsecondary vocational training**—This requirement involves training that lasts at least a few months but usually less than one year. In a few instances, there may be as many as four years of training.

- **Associate degree**—This degree typically requires two years of full-time academic work beyond high school.

Another Warning About the Data

We warned you in the introduction to use caution in interpreting the data we use, and we want to do it again here. The occupational data we use is the most accurate available anywhere, but it has its limitations. For example, the education or training requirements for entry into a job are those typically required as a minimum—but some people working in those jobs may have considerably more or different credentials. For example, most Registered Nurses now have a four-year bachelor's degree, although the two-year associate degree is the minimum level of training this job requires.

In a similar way, people with jobs that require long-term on-the-job training typically earn more than people with jobs that require short-term on-the-job training. However, some people with short-term on-the-job training do earn more than the average for the highest-paying occupations listed in this book. On the other hand, some people with long-term on-the-job training earn much less than the average shown in this book—this is particularly true early in a person's career.

So as you browse the lists that follow, please use them as a way to be encouraged rather than discouraged. Education and training are very important for success in the labor market of the future, but so are ability, drive, initiative, and, yes, luck.

Having said this, we encourage you to get as much education and training as you can. It used to be that you got your schooling and never went back, but this is not a good attitude to have now. You will probably need to continue learning new things throughout your working life. You can do so by going to school, and this is a good thing for many people to do. But there are also many other ways to learn, such as workshops, certification programs, employer training, professional conferences, Internet training, reading related books and magazines, and many others. Upgrading your computer and other technical skills is particularly important in our rapidly changing workplace, and you avoid doing so at your peril.

As one of our grandfathers used to say, "The harder you work, the luckier you get." It is just as true now as it was then.

Best Jobs Requiring Short-Term On-the-Job Training

It is possible to work in these occupations and achieve an average level of performance within a few days or weeks through on-the-job training. Fifty-seven jobs met this requirement. The average annual earnings for these jobs are $23,416, the average rate of growth is 18.5 percent, and the average number of openings annually is about 181,000. While there are exceptions, many of these jobs do not have higher-than-average earnings or are not projected to grow more rapidly than the average for all jobs. Even so, these jobs can have advantages that make them of interest to many people.

Best Jobs Requiring Short-Term On-the-Job Training

Job	Annual Earnings	Percent Growth	Annual Openings
1. Truck Drivers, Heavy	$33,520	19.0%	299,000
2. Receptionists and Information Clerks	$21,830	29.5%	296,000
3. Nursing Aides, Orderlies, and Attendants	$20,980	24.9%	302,000
4. Truck Drivers, Light or Delivery Services	$24,540	23.2%	219,000
5. Security Guards	$20,320	31.9%	228,000
6. Bill and Account Collectors	$27,450	24.5%	76,000
7. Refractory Materials Repairers, Except Brickmasons	$37,640	16.3%	155,000
8. Home Health Aides	$18,330	48.1%	141,000
9. Teacher Assistants	$19,410	23.0%	259,000
10. Landscaping and Groundskeeping Workers	$20,420	22.0%	203,000
11. Brazers	$30,620	17.0%	71,000
12. Interviewers, Except Eligibility and Loan	$23,670	28.0%	46,000
13. Personal and Home Care Aides	$16,900	40.5%	154,000
14. Solderers	$30,620	17.0%	71,000
15. Welders, Production	$30,620	17.0%	71,000
16. Counter and Rental Clerks	$18,280	26.3%	144,000
17. Human Resources Assistants, Except Payroll and Timekeeping	$31,750	19.3%	36,000
18. Janitors and Cleaners, Except Maids and Housekeeping Cleaners	$18,790	18.3%	454,000
19. Combined Food Preparation and Serving Workers, Including Fast Food	$14,690	22.8%	734,000
20. Retail Salespersons	$18,680	14.6%	1,014,000
21. Production, Planning, and Expediting Clerks	$36,340	14.1%	51,000
22. Food Preparation Workers	$16,710	20.2%	267,000
23. Packaging and Filling Machine Operators and Tenders	$22,200	21.1%	69,000
24. Office Clerks, General	$22,770	10.4%	550,000
25. Locker Room, Coatroom, and Dressing Room Attendants	$17,550	27.8%	66,000
26. Waiters and Waitresses	$14,050	17.5%	721,000
27. Bus Drivers, School	$23,250	16.7%	76,000
28. Refuse and Recyclable Material Collectors	$25,760	17.6%	42,000
29. Hotel, Motel, and Resort Desk Clerks	$17,700	23.9%	46,000
30. Cashiers	$16,240	13.2%	1,221,000
31. Production Inspectors, Testers, Graders, Sorters, Samplers, Weighers	$28,410	4.7%	87,000
32. Amusement and Recreation Attendants	$15,550	27.8%	66,000
33. Industrial Truck and Tractor Operators	$26,580	11.1%	94,000

(continued)

(continued)

Best Jobs Requiring Short-Term On-the-Job Training

Job	Annual Earnings	Percent Growth	Annual Openings
34. Billing, Cost, and Rate Clerks	$27,040	7.9%	78,000
35. Billing, Posting, and Calculating Machine Operators	$27,040	7.9%	78,000
36. Helpers—Installation, Maintenance, and Repair Workers	$21,310	20.3%	33,000
37. Statement Clerks	$27,040	7.9%	78,000
38. Gaming Change Persons and Booth Cashiers	$20,530	24.1%	12,000
39. Library Assistants, Clerical	$20,720	21.5%	27,000
40. Riggers	$35,330	14.3%	3,000
41. Taxi Drivers and Chauffeurs	$19,570	21.7%	28,000
42. Tree Trimmers and Pruners	$26,150	18.6%	11,000
43. Packers and Packagers, Hand	$17,150	14.4%	198,000
44. Child Care Workers	$16,760	11.7%	406,000
45. Counter Attendants, Cafeteria, Food Concession, and Coffee Shop	$15,660	16.7%	190,000
46. Helpers—Electricians	$23,420	17.9%	17,000
47. Nannies	$16,760	11.7%	406,000
48. Reservation and Transportation Ticket Agents	$27,750	12.2%	35,000
49. Travel Clerks	$27,750	12.2%	35,000
50. Library Technicians	$24,940	16.8%	22,000
51. Court Clerks	$28,430	12.3%	14,000
52. License Clerks	$28,430	12.3%	14,000
53. Municipal Clerks	$28,430	12.3%	14,000
54. Nonfarm Animal Caretakers	$17,460	22.2%	32,000
55. Postal Service Mail Carriers	$44,450	–0.5%	20,000
56. Hosts and Hostesses, Restaurant, Lounge, and Coffee Shop	$15,630	16.4%	95,000
57. Dining Room and Cafeteria Attendants and Bartender Helpers	$14,770	14.9%	143,000

Best Jobs Requiring Moderate-Term On-the-Job Training

Occupations that require this type of training can be performed adequately after one month to one year of combined on-the-job training and informal training. There were 66 jobs that met this requirement. The average annual earnings are $35,191. The average rate of growth is 18.2 percent, and the average number of openings annually is just under 65,000.

Best Jobs Requiring Moderate-Term On-the-Job Training

Job	Annual Earnings	Percent Growth	Annual Openings
1. Sales Representatives, Agricultural	$58,580	19.3%	44,000
2. Sales Representatives, Chemical and Pharmaceutical	$58,580	19.3%	44,000
3. Sales Representatives, Electrical/Electronic	$58,580	19.3%	44,000
4. Sales Representatives, Instruments	$58,580	19.3%	44,000
5. Sales Representatives, Mechanical Equipment and Supplies	$58,580	19.3%	44,000
6. Sales Representatives, Medical	$58,580	19.3%	44,000
7. Sales Representatives, Wholesale and Manufacturing, Except Technical and Scientific Products	$45,400	19.1%	160,000
8. Pipelaying Fitters	$41,290	18.7%	56,000
9. Tractor-Trailer Truck Drivers	$33,520	19.0%	299,000
10. Correctional Officers and Jailers	$33,600	24.2%	49,000
11. Adjustment Clerks	$27,020	24.3%	419,000
12. Customer Service Representatives, Utilities	$27,020	24.3%	419,000
13. Sheet Metal Workers	$35,560	19.8%	30,000
14. Medical Assistants	$24,610	58.9%	78,000
15. Caption Writers	$44,350	16.1%	23,000
16. Social and Human Service Assistants	$24,270	48.7%	63,000
17. Ceiling Tile Installers	$34,030	21.4%	17,000
18. Costume Attendants	$25,050	27.8%	66,000
19. Drywall Installers	$34,030	21.4%	17,000
20. Brattice Builders	$34,900	10.1%	193,000
21. Carpenter Assemblers and Repairers	$34,900	10.1%	193,000
22. Rough Carpenters	$34,900	10.1%	193,000
23. Ship Carpenters and Joiners	$34,900	10.1%	193,000
24. Tapers	$39,070	20.8%	5,000
25. Dental Assistants	$28,330	42.5%	35,000
26. Executive Secretaries and Administrative Assistants	$34,970	8.7%	210,000
27. Hazardous Materials Removal Workers	$33,320	43.1%	8,000
28. Irradiated-Fuel Handlers	$33,320	43.1%	8,000
29. Grader, Bulldozer, and Scraper Operators	$35,360	10.4%	45,000
30. Operating Engineers	$35,360	10.4%	45,000
31. Advertising Sales Agents	$40,300	13.4%	24,000
32. Pharmacy Technicians	$23,650	28.8%	39,000
33. Roofers	$30,840	18.6%	38,000
34. Painters, Transportation Equipment	$35,120	17.5%	9,000
35. Mapping Technicians	$30,380	23.1%	10,000

(continued)

(continued)

Best Jobs Requiring Moderate-Term On-the-Job Training

Job	Annual Earnings	Percent Growth	Annual Openings
36. Construction Laborers	$25,160	14.2%	166,000
37. Carpet Installers	$34,090	16.8%	10,000
38. Painters, Construction and Maintenance	$30,260	11.6%	69,000
39. Tax Preparers	$27,730	23.2%	11,000
40. Electric Meter Installers and Repairers	$43,710	12.0%	5,000
41. Meter Mechanics	$43,710	12.0%	5,000
42. Valve and Regulator Repairers	$43,710	12.0%	5,000
43. Model Makers, Metal and Plastic	$44,250	14.6%	1,000
44. Residential Advisors	$21,430	33.6%	12,000
45. Dispatchers, Except Police, Fire, and Ambulance	$30,920	14.4%	28,000
46. Subway and Streetcar Operators	$49,290	13.2%	2,000
47. Bus Drivers, Transit and Intercity	$29,730	15.2%	33,000
48. Bookkeeping, Accounting, and Auditing Clerks	$28,570	3.0%	274,000
49. Cargo and Freight Agents	$34,250	15.5%	8,000
50. Medical Equipment Repairers	$37,220	14.8%	4,000
51. Insulation Workers, Mechanical	$33,330	15.8%	9,000
52. Camera Operators, Television, Video, and Motion Picture	$37,610	13.4%	4,000
53. Locksmiths and Safe Repairers	$30,360	21.0%	3,000
54. Crane and Tower Operators	$37,410	10.8%	5,000
55. Electrical and Electronic Inspectors and Testers	$28,410	4.7%	87,000
56. Materials Inspectors	$28,410	4.7%	87,000
57. Precision Devices Inspectors and Testers	$28,410	4.7%	87,000
58. Demonstrators and Product Promoters	$20,700	17.0%	38,000
59. Insulation Workers, Floor, Ceiling, and Wall	$30,310	15.8%	9,000
60. Slaughterers and Meat Packers	$20,860	18.1%	23,000
61. Highway Maintenance Workers	$29,550	10.4%	25,000
62. Pest Control Workers	$26,220	17.0%	11,000
63. Police, Fire, and Ambulance Dispatchers	$28,930	12.7%	15,000
64. Loading Machine Operators, Underground Mining	$33,250	8.9%	14,000
65. Dragline Operators	$31,970	8.9%	14,000
66. Excavating and Loading Machine Operators	$31,970	8.9%	14,000

Best Jobs Requiring Long-Term On-the-Job Training

These jobs require a worker to have more than 12 months of on-the-job training or combined work experience and formal classroom instruction. The jobs also include occupations that use formal apprenticeships that may take up to four years and intensive occupation-specific, employer-sponsored training. There were 61 jobs that met this requirement. The average annual earnings are $39,847. The average rate of growth is 15.6 percent, and the average number of openings annually is about 36,000.

Best Jobs Requiring Long-Term On-the-Job Training

Job	Annual Earnings	Percent Growth	Annual Openings
1. Highway Patrol Pilots	$45,210	24.7%	67,000
2. Police Patrol Officers	$45,210	24.7%	67,000
3. Sheriffs and Deputy Sheriffs	$45,210	24.7%	67,000
4. Electricians	$42,300	23.4%	65,000
5. Heating and Air Conditioning Mechanics	$36,260	31.8%	35,000
6. Refrigeration Mechanics	$36,260	31.8%	35,000
7. Pipe Fitters	$41,290	18.7%	56,000
8. Plumbers	$41,290	18.7%	56,000
9. Talent Directors	$52,840	18.3%	10,000
10. Technical Directors/Managers	$52,840	18.3%	10,000
11. Forest Fire Fighters	$38,330	20.7%	29,000
12. Municipal Fire Fighters	$38,330	20.7%	29,000
13. Claims Examiners, Property and Casualty Insurance	$44,220	14.2%	31,000
14. Insurance Adjusters, Examiners, and Investigators	$44,220	14.2%	31,000
15. Cement Masons and Concrete Finishers	$31,400	26.1%	24,000
16. Athletes and Sports Competitors	$48,310	19.2%	3,000
17. Flight Attendants	$43,440	15.9%	23,000
18. Telecommunications Line Installers and Repairers	$40,330	18.8%	13,000
19. Elevator Installers and Repairers	$58,710	17.1%	3,000
20. Welder-Fitters	$30,620	17.0%	71,000
21. Welders and Cutters	$30,620	17.0%	71,000
22. Environmental Compliance Inspectors	$47,390	9.8%	20,000
23. Equal Opportunity Representatives and Officers	$47,390	9.8%	20,000
24. Government Property Inspectors and Investigators	$47,390	9.8%	20,000
25. Licensing Examiners and Inspectors	$47,390	9.8%	20,000
26. Maintenance and Repair Workers, General	$30,710	16.3%	155,000
27. Pressure Vessel Inspectors	$47,390	9.8%	20,000

(continued)

(continued)

Best Jobs Requiring Long-Term On-the-Job Training

Job	Annual Earnings	Percent Growth	Annual Openings
28. Telecommunications Facility Examiners	$49,840	–0.6%	23,000
29. Brickmasons and Blockmasons	$41,740	14.2%	21,000
30. Boat Builders and Shipwrights	$34,900	10.1%	193,000
31. Construction Carpenters	$34,900	10.1%	193,000
32. Tile and Marble Setters	$35,410	26.5%	4,000
33. Farmers and Ranchers	$40,440	–20.6%	118,000
34. Cooks, Restaurant	$19,520	15.9%	211,000
35. Coaches and Scouts	$26,350	18.3%	26,000
36. Audio and Video Equipment Technicians	$32,570	26.7%	5,000
37. Structural Iron and Steel Workers	$42,430	15.9%	9,000
38. Surveying Technicians	$30,380	23.1%	10,000
39. Air Traffic Controllers	$102,030	12.6%	2,000
40. Interpreters and Translators	$33,860	22.1%	4,000
41. Electrical Power-Line Installers and Repairers	$49,100	1.6%	9,000
42. Automatic Teller Machine Servicers	$35,150	15.1%	19,000
43. Cartoonists	$38,060	16.5%	4,000
44. Office Machine and Cash Register Servicers	$35,150	15.1%	19,000
45. Painters and Illustrators	$38,060	16.5%	4,000
46. Sculptors	$38,060	16.5%	4,000
47. Sketch Artists	$38,060	16.5%	4,000
48. Transit and Railroad Police	$45,430	15.9%	1,000
49. Automotive Body and Related Repairers	$34,690	13.2%	23,000
50. Water and Liquid Waste Treatment Plant and System Operators	$34,960	16.0%	9,000
51. Glaziers	$32,650	17.2%	7,000
52. Recreational Vehicle Service Technicians	$28,980	21.8%	4,000
53. Industrial Machinery Mechanics	$39,060	5.5%	19,000
54. Opticians, Dispensing	$27,950	18.2%	10,000
55. Machinists	$33,960	8.2%	30,000
56. Insurance Appraisers, Auto Damage	$45,330	11.7%	2,000
57. Mechanical Inspectors	$28,410	4.7%	87,000
58. Millwrights	$43,720	5.3%	7,000
59. Photographers, Scientific	$26,080	13.6%	18,000
60. Professional Photographers	$26,080	13.6%	18,000
61. Plasterers and Stucco Masons	$32,440	13.5%	8,000

Best Jobs Requiring Work Experience in a Related Occupation

Jobs in this list require a worker to have experience in a related occupation. An example is Police Detectives, who are selected based on their experience as Police Patrol Officers. Forty-seven jobs met this requirement. The average annual earnings are $45,954. The average rate of growth is almost 15 percent, and the average number of openings annually is just under 38,000.

Best Jobs Requiring Work Experience in a Related Occupation

Job	Annual Earnings	Percent Growth	Annual Openings
1. Vocational Education Teachers Postsecondary	$40,740	38.1%	216,000
2. Storage and Distribution Managers	$66,600	19.7%	13,000
3. Transportation Managers	$66,600	19.7%	13,000
4. Child Support, Missing Persons, and Unemployment Insurance Fraud Investigators	$53,990	22.4%	11,000
5. Criminal Investigators and Special Agents	$53,990	22.4%	11,000
6. Immigration and Customs Inspectors	$53,990	22.4%	11,000
7. Police Detectives	$53,990	22.4%	11,000
8. Police Identification and Records Officers	$53,990	22.4%	11,000
9. First-Line Supervisors and Manager/Supervisors— Construction Trades Workers	$50,450	14.1%	67,000
10. First-Line Supervisors and Manager/Supervisors— Extractive Workers	$50,450	14.1%	67,000
11. First-Line Supervisors/Managers of Non-Retail Sales Workers	$59,300	6.8%	72,000
12. First-Line Supervisors/Managers of Police and Detectives	$64,430	15.3%	14,000
13. Self-Enrichment Education Teachers	$30,880	40.1%	39,000
14. First-Line Supervisors/Managers of Mechanics, Installers, and Repairers	$50,340	15.4%	42,000
15. Forest Fire Fighting and Prevention Supervisors	$58,920	18.7%	8,000
16. Municipal Fire Fighting and Prevention Supervisors	$58,920	18.7%	8,000
17. First-Line Supervisors/Managers of Production and Operating Workers	$44,740	9.5%	66,000
18. First-Line Supervisors and Manager/Supervisors— Landscaping Workers	$35,340	21.6%	18,000
19. Lawn Service Managers	$35,340	21.6%	18,000
20. First-Line Supervisors/Managers of Food Preparation and Serving Workers	$25,410	15.5%	154,000
21. Food Service Managers	$39,610	11.5%	58,000

(continued)

(continued)

Best Jobs Requiring Work Experience in a Related Occupation

Job	Annual Earnings	Percent Growth	Annual Openings
22. Agricultural Crop Farm Managers	$50,700	5.1%	25,000
23. Fish Hatchery Managers	$50,700	5.1%	25,000
24. Nursery and Greenhouse Managers	$50,700	5.1%	25,000
25. First-Line Supervisors/Managers of Retail Sales Workers	$32,720	9.1%	251,000
26. First-Line Supervisors/Managers of Transportation and Material-Moving Machine and Vehicle Operators	$44,810	12.1%	23,000
27. Housekeeping Supervisors	$29,510	16.2%	28,000
28. Janitorial Supervisors	$29,510	16.2%	28,000
29. Coroners	$47,390	9.8%	20,000
30. Emergency Management Specialists	$45,390	28.2%	2,000
31. First-Line Supervisors, Administrative Support	$41,030	6.6%	140,000
32. First-Line Supervisors, Customer Service	$41,030	6.6%	140,000
33. Private Detectives and Investigators	$32,110	25.3%	9,000
34. Real Estate Brokers	$58,720	2.4%	11,000
35. First-Line Supervisors/Managers of Helpers, Laborers, and Material Movers, Hand	$38,280	14.0%	16,000
36. First-Line Supervisors/Managers of Correctional Officers	$44,720	19.0%	4,000
37. Construction and Building Inspectors	$43,670	13.8%	10,000
38. First-Line Supervisors/Managers of Personal Service Workers	$30,350	9.4%	26,000
39. Aviation Inspectors	$50,380	7.7%	5,000
40. Freight Inspectors	$50,380	7.7%	5,000
41. Marine Cargo Inspectors	$50,380	7.7%	5,000
42. Motor Vehicle Inspectors	$50,380	7.7%	5,000
43. Public Transportation Inspectors	$50,380	7.7%	5,000
44. Railroad Inspectors	$50,380	7.7%	5,000
45. New Accounts Clerks	$26,860	11.2%	24,000
46. Choreographers	$33,670	15.8%	3,000
47. Lodging Managers	$37,660	6.6%	10,000

Best Jobs Requiring Postsecondary Vocational Training

Postsecondary vocational training typically consists of a few months to a year of full-time academic work. There were 34 jobs that met this requirement. The average annual earnings are $37,367. The average rate of growth is 16.4 percent, and the average number of openings annually is about 27,000.

Best Jobs Requiring Postsecondary Vocational Training

Job	Annual Earnings	Percent Growth	Annual Openings
1. Licensed Practical and Licensed Vocational Nurses	$33,970	20.2%	105,000
2. Legal Secretaries	$36,720	18.8%	39,000
3. Fitness Trainers and Aerobics Instructors	$25,470	44.5%	38,000
4. Emergency Medical Technicians and Paramedics	$25,310	33.1%	32,000
5. Appraisers, Real Estate	$43,390	17.6%	11,000
6. Assessors	$43,390	17.6%	11,000
7. Central Office and PBX Installers and Repairers	$49,840	–0.6%	23,000
8. Communication Equipment Mechanics, Installers, and Repairers	$49,840	–0.6%	23,000
9. Frame Wirers, Central Office	$49,840	–0.6%	23,000
10. Station Installers and Repairers, Telephone	$49,840	–0.6%	23,000
11. Massage Therapists	$31,960	27.1%	24,000
12. Respiratory Therapy Technicians	$36,740	34.2%	5,000
13. Surgical Technologists	$34,010	27.9%	13,000
14. Automotive Master Mechanics	$32,450	12.4%	100,000
15. Automotive Specialty Technicians	$32,450	12.4%	100,000
16. Medical Secretaries	$26,540	17.2%	50,000
17. Bus and Truck Mechanics and Diesel Engine Specialists	$35,780	14.2%	28,000
18. Aircraft Body and Bonded Structure Repairers	$45,290	11.0%	12,000
19. Aircraft Engine Specialists	$45,290	11.0%	12,000
20. Airframe-and-Power-Plant Mechanics	$45,290	11.0%	12,000
21. Commercial Pilots	$53,870	14.9%	2,000
22. Chefs and Head Cooks	$30,680	15.8%	33,000
23. Gaming Dealers	$14,340	24.7%	26,000
24. Data Processing Equipment Repairers	$35,150	15.1%	19,000
25. Hairdressers, Hairstylists, and Cosmetologists	$19,800	14.7%	68,000
26. Sound Engineering Technicians	$38,110	25.5%	2,000
27. Gaming Supervisors	$40,840	15.7%	6,000
28. Real Estate Sales Agents	$35,670	5.7%	34,000
29. Security and Fire Alarm Systems Installers	$33,410	30.2%	5,000
30. Civil Drafters	$39,190	4.2%	14,000
31. Desktop Publishers	$32,340	29.2%	4,000
32. Court Reporters	$42,920	12.7%	2,000
33. Mobile Heavy Equipment Mechanics, Except Engines	$38,150	9.6%	12,000
34. Electrical and Electronics Repairers, Commercial and Industrial Equipment	$42,600	10.3%	10,000

Best Jobs Requiring an Associate Degree

An associate degree usually requires two years of full-time academic work. Thirty-six jobs met this requirement. The average annual earnings are $40,383. The average rate of growth is 22.4 percent, and the average number of openings annually is a little under 19,000.

Best Jobs Requiring an Associate Degree

Job	Annual Earnings	Percent Growth	Annual Openings
1. Registered Nurses	$52,330	27.3%	215,000
2. Dental Hygienists	$58,350	43.1%	9,000
3. Computer Support Specialists	$40,430	30.3%	71,000
4. Paralegals and Legal Assistants	$39,130	28.7%	29,000
5. Radiologic Technicians	$43,350	22.9%	21,000
6. Radiologic Technologists	$43,350	22.9%	21,000
7. Respiratory Therapists	$43,140	34.8%	10,000
8. Medical Records and Health Information Technicians	$25,590	46.8%	24,000
9. Calibration and Instrumentation Technicians	$46,310	10.0%	24,000
10. Electrical Engineering Technicians	$46,310	10.0%	24,000
11. Electronics Engineering Technicians	$46,310	10.0%	24,000
12. Physical Therapist Assistants	$37,890	44.6%	10,000
13. Radiation Therapists	$57,700	31.6%	1,000
14. Diagnostic Medical Sonographers	$52,490	24.0%	4,000
15. Cardiovascular Technologists and Technicians	$38,690	33.5%	6,000
16. Nuclear Medicine Technologists	$56,450	23.6%	2,000
17. Veterinary Technologists and Technicians	$24,940	44.1%	11,000
18. Occupational Therapist Assistants	$38,430	39.2%	3,000
19. Medical and Clinical Laboratory Technicians	$30,840	19.4%	21,000
20. City and Regional Planning Aides	$34,360	17.5%	18,000
21. Mechanical Engineering Technicians	$43,400	11.0%	6,000
22. Medical Transcriptionists	$28,380	22.6%	18,000
23. Social Science Research Assistants	$34,360	17.5%	18,000
24. Environmental Engineering Technicians	$38,550	28.4%	3,000
25. Environmental Science and Protection Technicians, Including Health	$35,340	36.8%	4,000
26. Industrial Engineering Technicians	$43,590	8.7%	7,000
27. Forensic Science Technicians	$44,010	18.9%	1,000
28. Architectural Drafters	$39,190	4.2%	14,000
29. Electro-Mechanical Technicians	$41,440	11.5%	4,000
30. Biological Technicians	$33,210	19.4%	7,000

Best Jobs Requiring an Associate Degree

Job	Annual Earnings	Percent Growth	Annual Openings
31. First-Line Supervisors and Manager/Supervisors—Agricultural Crop Workers	$35,490	11.4%	6,000
32. First-Line Supervisors and Manager/Supervisors—Animal Care Workers, Except Livestock	$35,490	11.4%	6,000
33. First-Line Supervisors and Manager/Supervisors—Animal Husbandry Workers	$35,490	11.4%	6,000
34. First-Line Supervisors and Manager/Supervisors—Fishery Workers	$35,490	11.4%	6,000
35. First-Line Supervisors and Manager/Supervisors—Horticultural Workers	$35,490	11.4%	6,000
36. Civil Engineering Technicians	$38,480	7.6%	10,000

Best Jobs Based on Interests

The lists that follow organize the 300 jobs that met the criteria for this book into 16 interest areas that are used in a variety of career exploration systems. The lists provide a very useful way to quickly identify jobs based on your interests.

The lists can help you identify jobs that are related to ones you have had in the past or that require similar skills to those you want to use in the future. Within each interest grouping, occupations are arranged in order of their combined scores based on earnings, growth, and number of openings.

The system of interest areas is called the Guide for Occupational Exploration, or GOE, and it was developed by the U.S. Department of Labor as an intuitive way to assist in career exploration. The lists that follow use the revised *GOE* groupings as presented in the *New Guide for Occupational Exploration: Linking Interests, Learning, and Careers,* Fourth Edition, published by JIST. The 16 interest areas used in the *New GOE* are based on the 16 career clusters that were developed by the U.S. Department of Education's Office of Vocational and Adult Education around 1999 and that presently are being used by many states to organize their career-oriented programs and career information.

Brief descriptions follow for each of the 16 interest areas used in the lists. Simply find the area or areas that interest you most and then use the lists in this section to identify jobs that are likely to interest you. Then, as with most of our lists, simply look up the job descriptions in Part II for the jobs that interest you most. Note that we put each of the 300 best jobs into only one interest area list, the one it fit into best. However, many jobs could be included in more than one list, so consider reviewing a variety of these interest areas to find jobs that you might otherwise overlook. Also note that the descriptions for each of the interest areas may use sample jobs that are not among those described in this book.

- **Agriculture and Natural Resources:** *An interest in working with plants, animals, forests, or mineral resources for agriculture, horticulture, conservation, extraction, and other purposes.* You can satisfy this interest by working in farming, landscaping, forestry, fishing, mining, and related fields. You may like doing physical work outdoors, such as on a farm or ranch, in a forest, or on a drilling rig. If you have scientific curiosity, you could study plants and animals or analyze biological or rock samples in a lab. If you have management ability, you could own, operate, or manage a fish hatchery, a landscaping business, or a greenhouse.

- **Architecture and Construction:** *An interest in designing, assembling, and maintaining components of buildings and other structures.* You may want to be part of the team of architects, drafters, and others who design buildings and render the plans. If construction interests you, you can find fulfillment in the many building projects that are being undertaken at all times. If you like to organize and plan, you can find careers in managing these projects. Or you can play a more direct role in putting up and finishing buildings by doing jobs such as plumbing, carpentry, masonry, painting, or roofing, either as a skilled craftsworker or as a helper. You can prepare the building site by operating heavy equipment or install, maintain, and repair vital building equipment and systems such as electricity and heating.

- **Arts and Communication:** *An interest in creatively expressing feelings or ideas, in communicating news or information, or in performing.* You can satisfy this interest in creative, verbal, or performing activities. For example, if you enjoy literature, perhaps writing or editing would appeal to you. Journalism and public relations are other fields for people who like to use their writing or speaking skills. Do you prefer to work in the performing arts? If so, you could direct or perform in drama, music, or dance. If you especially enjoy the visual arts, you could create paintings, sculpture, or ceramics or design products or visual displays. A flair for technology might lead you to specialize in photography, broadcast production, or dispatching.

- **Business and Administration:** *An interest in making a business organization or function run smoothly.* You can satisfy this interest by working in a position of leadership or by specializing in a function that contributes to the overall effort in a business, a nonprofit organization, or a government agency. If you especially enjoy working with people, you may find fulfillment from working in human resources. An interest in numbers may lead you to consider accounting, finance, budgeting, billing, or financial record-keeping. A job as an administrative assistant may interest you if you like a variety of work in a busy environment. If you are good with details and word processing, you may enjoy a job as a secretary or data entry keyer. Or perhaps you would do well as the manager of a business.

- **Education and Training:** *An interest in helping people learn.* You can satisfy this interest by teaching students, who may be preschoolers, retirees, or any age in between. You may specialize in a particular academic field or work with learners of a particular age, with a particular interest, or with a particular learning problem. Working in a library or museum may give you an opportunity to expand people's understanding of the world.

◉ **Finance and Insurance:** *An interest in helping businesses and people be assured of a financially secure future.* You can satisfy this interest by working in a financial or insurance business in a leadership or support role. If you like gathering and analyzing information, you may find fulfillment as an insurance adjuster or financial analyst. Or you may deal with information at the clerical level as a banking or insurance clerk or in person-to-person situations providing customer service. Another way to interact with people is to sell financial or insurance services that will meet their needs.

◉ **Government and Public Administration:** *An interest in helping a government agency serve the needs of the public.* You can satisfy this interest by working in a position of leadership or by specializing in a function that contributes to the role of government. You may help protect the public by working as an inspector or examiner to enforce standards. If you enjoy using clerical skills, you may work as a clerk in a law court or government office. Or perhaps you prefer the top-down perspective of a government executive or urban planner.

◉ **Health Science:** *An interest in helping people and animals be healthy.* You can satisfy this interest by working in a health care team as a doctor, therapist, or nurse. You might specialize in one of the many different parts of the body (such as the teeth or eyes) or in one of the many different types of care. Or you may want to be a generalist who deals with the whole patient. If you like technology, you might find satisfaction working with X rays or new methods of diagnosis. You might work with healthy people, helping them eat right. If you enjoy working with animals, you might care for them and keep them healthy.

◉ **Hospitality, Tourism, and Recreation:** *An interest in catering to the personal wishes and needs of others so that they may enjoy a clean environment, good food and drink, comfortable lodging away from home, and recreation.* You can satisfy this interest by providing services for the convenience, care, and pampering of others in hotels, restaurants, airplanes, beauty parlors, and so on. You may want to use your love of cooking as a chef. If you like working with people, you may want to provide personal services by being a travel guide, a flight attendant, a concierge, a hairdresser, or a waiter. You may want to work in cleaning and building services if you like a clean environment. If you enjoy sports or games, you may work for an athletic team or casino.

◉ **Human Service:** *An interest in improving people's social, mental, emotional, or spiritual well-being.* You can satisfy this interest as a counselor, social worker, or religious worker who helps people sort out their complicated lives or solve personal problems. You may work as a caretaker for very young people or the elderly. Or you may interview people to help identify the social services they need.

◉ **Information Technology:** *An interest in designing, developing, managing, and supporting information systems.* You can satisfy this interest by working with hardware, software, multimedia, or integrated systems. If you like to use your organizational skills, you might work as an administrator of a system or database. Or you can solve complex problems as a software engineer or systems analyst. If you enjoy getting your hands on the hardware, you might find work servicing computers, peripherals, and information-intense machines such as cash registers and ATMs.

◎ **Law and Public Safety:** *An interest in upholding people's rights or in protecting people and property by using authority, inspecting, or investigating.* You can satisfy this interest by working in law, law enforcement, fire fighting, the military, and related fields. For example, if you enjoy mental challenge and intrigue, you could investigate crimes or fires for a living. If you enjoy working with verbal skills and research skills, you may want to defend citizens in court or research deeds, wills, and other legal documents. If you want to help people in critical situations, you may want to fight fires, work as a police officer, or become a paramedic. Or, if you want more routine work in public safety, perhaps a job in guarding, patrolling, or inspecting would appeal to you. If you have management ability, you could seek a leadership position in law enforcement and the protective services. Work in the military gives you a chance to use technical and leadership skills while serving your country.

◎ **Manufacturing:** *An interest in processing materials into intermediate or final products or maintaining and repairing products by using machines or hand tools.* You can satisfy this interest by working in one of many industries that mass-produce goods or by working for a utility that distributes electric power or other resources. You may enjoy manual work, using your hands or hand tools in highly skilled jobs such as assembling engines or electronic equipment. If you enjoy making machines run efficiently or fixing them when they break down, you could seek a job installing or repairing such devices as copiers, aircraft engines, cars, or watches. Perhaps you prefer to set up or operate machines that are used to manufacture products made of food, glass, or paper. You may enjoy cutting and grinding metal and plastic parts to desired shapes and measurements. Or you may want to operate equipment in systems that provide water and process wastewater. You may like inspecting, sorting, counting, or weighing products. Another option is to work with your hands and machinery to move boxes and freight in a warehouse. If leadership appeals to you, you could manage people engaged in production and repair.

◎ **Retail and Wholesale Sales and Service:** *An interest in bringing others to a particular point of view by personal persuasion and by sales and promotional techniques.* You can satisfy this interest in a variety of jobs that involve persuasion and selling. If you like using your knowledge of science, you may enjoy selling pharmaceutical, medical, or electronic products or services. Real estate offers several kinds of sales jobs as well. If you like speaking on the phone, you could work as a telemarketer. Or you may enjoy selling apparel and other merchandise in a retail setting. If you prefer to help people, you may want a job in customer service.

◎ **Scientific Research, Engineering, and Mathematics:** *An interest in discovering, collecting, and analyzing information about the natural world; in applying scientific research findings to problems in medicine, the life sciences, human behavior, and the natural sciences; in imagining and manipulating quantitative data; and in applying technology to manufacturing, transportation, and other economic activities.* You can satisfy this interest by working with the knowledge and processes of the sciences. You may enjoy researching and developing new knowledge in mathematics, or perhaps solving problems in the physical, life, or social sciences would appeal to you. You may want to study engineering and help create new machines, processes, and structures. If you want to work with scientific equipment and procedures, you could seek a job in a research or testing laboratory.

◎ **Transportation, Distribution, and Logistics:** *An interest in operations that move people or materials.* You can satisfy this interest by managing a transportation service, by helping vehicles keep on their assigned schedules and routes, or by driving or piloting a vehicle. If you enjoy taking responsibility, perhaps managing a rail line would appeal to you. If you work well with details and can take pressure on the job, you might consider being an air traffic controller. Or would you rather get out on the highway, on the water, or up in the air? If so, then you could drive a truck from state to state, be employed on a ship, or fly a crop duster over a cornfield. If you prefer to stay closer to home, you could drive a delivery van, taxi, or school bus. You can use your physical strength to load freight and arrange it so it gets to its destination in one piece.

Best Jobs for People Interested in Agriculture and Natural Resources

Job	Annual Earnings	Percent Growth	Annual Openings
1. First-Line Supervisors and Manager/Supervisors—Extractive Workers	$50,450	14.1%	67,000
2. Agricultural Crop Farm Managers	$50,700	5.1%	25,000
3. Fish Hatchery Managers	$50,700	5.1%	25,000
4. Nursery and Greenhouse Managers	$50,700	5.1%	25,000
5. First-Line Supervisors and Manager/Supervisors—Landscaping Workers	$35,340	21.6%	18,000
6. Landscaping and Groundskeeping Workers	$20,420	22.0%	203,000
7. Lawn Service Managers	$35,340	21.6%	18,000
8. Farmers and Ranchers	$40,440	–20.6%	118,000
9. First-Line Supervisors and Manager/Supervisors—Agricultural Crop Workers	$35,490	11.4%	6,000
10. First-Line Supervisors and Manager/Supervisors—Animal Husbandry Workers	$35,490	11.4%	6,000
11. First-Line Supervisors and Manager/Supervisors—Fishery Workers	$35,490	11.4%	6,000
12. First-Line Supervisors and Manager/Supervisors—Horticultural Workers	$35,490	11.4%	6,000
13. Environmental Science and Protection Technicians, Including Health	$35,340	36.8%	4,000
14. Pest Control Workers	$26,220	17.0%	11,000
15. Tree Trimmers and Pruners	$26,150	18.6%	11,000
16. Loading Machine Operators, Underground Mining	$33,250	8.9%	14,000
17. Excavating and Loading Machine Operators	$31,970	8.9%	14,000

Best Jobs for People Interested in Architecture and Construction

Job	Annual Earnings	Percent Growth	Annual Openings
1. Electricians	$42,300	23.4%	65,000
2. Pipe Fitters	$41,290	18.7%	56,000
3. Pipelaying Fitters	$41,290	18.7%	56,000
4. Plumbers	$41,290	18.7%	56,000
5. First-Line Supervisors and Manager/Supervisors—Construction Trades Workers	$50,450	14.1%	67,000
6. Heating and Air Conditioning Mechanics	$36,260	31.8%	35,000
7. Refrigeration Mechanics	$36,260	31.8%	35,000
8. Refractory Materials Repairers, Except Brickmasons	$37,640	16.3%	155,000
9. Sheet Metal Workers	$35,560	19.8%	30,000
10. Telecommunications Line Installers and Repairers	$40,330	18.8%	13,000
11. Boat Builders and Shipwrights	$34,900	10.1%	193,000
12. Brattice Builders	$34,900	10.1%	193,000
13. Brickmasons and Blockmasons	$41,740	14.2%	21,000
14. Carpenter Assemblers and Repairers	$34,900	10.1%	193,000
15. Construction Carpenters	$34,900	10.1%	193,000
16. Rough Carpenters	$34,900	10.1%	193,000
17. Ship Carpenters and Joiners	$34,900	10.1%	193,000
18. Elevator Installers and Repairers	$58,710	17.1%	3,000
19. Cement Masons and Concrete Finishers	$31,400	26.1%	24,000
20. Structural Iron and Steel Workers	$42,430	15.9%	9,000
21. Ceiling Tile Installers	$34,030	21.4%	17,000
22. Drywall Installers	$34,030	21.4%	17,000
23. Central Office and PBX Installers and Repairers	$49,840	−0.6%	23,000
24. Communication Equipment Mechanics, Installers, and Repairers	$49,840	−0.6%	23,000
25. Frame Wirers, Central Office	$49,840	−0.6%	23,000
26. Maintenance and Repair Workers, General	$30,710	16.3%	155,000
27. Station Installers and Repairers, Telephone	$49,840	−0.6%	23,000
28. Tapers	$39,070	20.8%	5,000
29. Telecommunications Facility Examiners	$49,840	−0.6%	23,000
30. Construction and Building Inspectors	$43,670	13.8%	10,000
31. Grader, Bulldozer, and Scraper Operators	$35,360	10.4%	45,000
32. Operating Engineers	$35,360	10.4%	45,000
33. Roofers	$30,840	18.6%	38,000
34. Tile and Marble Setters	$35,410	26.5%	4,000
35. Helpers—Installation, Maintenance, and Repair Workers	$21,310	20.3%	33,000

Best Jobs for People Interested in Architecture and Construction

Job	Annual Earnings	Percent Growth	Annual Openings
36. Construction Laborers	$25,160	14.2%	166,000
37. Hazardous Materials Removal Workers	$33,320	43.1%	8,000
38. Electric Meter Installers and Repairers	$43,710	12.0%	5,000
39. Meter Mechanics	$43,710	12.0%	5,000
40. Security and Fire Alarm Systems Installers	$33,410	30.2%	5,000
41. Painters, Construction and Maintenance	$30,260	11.6%	69,000
42. Carpet Installers	$34,090	16.8%	10,000
43. Electrical Power-Line Installers and Repairers	$49,100	1.6%	9,000
44. Architectural Drafters	$39,190	4.2%	14,000
45. Civil Drafters	$39,190	4.2%	14,000
46. Helpers—Electricians	$23,420	17.9%	17,000
47. Crane and Tower Operators	$37,410	10.8%	5,000
48. Insulation Workers, Mechanical	$33,330	15.8%	9,000
49. Glaziers	$32,650	17.2%	7,000
50. Riggers	$35,330	14.3%	3,000
51. Highway Maintenance Workers	$29,550	10.4%	25,000
52. Insulation Workers, Floor, Ceiling, and Wall	$30,310	15.8%	9,000
53. Plasterers and Stucco Masons	$32,440	13.5%	8,000
54. Dragline Operators	$31,970	8.9%	14,000

Best Jobs for People Interested in Arts and Communication

Job	Annual Earnings	Percent Growth	Annual Openings
1. Talent Directors	$52,840	18.3%	10,000
2. Technical Directors/Managers	$52,840	18.3%	10,000
3. Caption Writers	$44,350	16.1%	23,000
4. Costume Attendants	$25,050	27.8%	66,000
5. Cartoonists	$38,060	16.5%	4,000
6. Painters and Illustrators	$38,060	16.5%	4,000
7. Sculptors	$38,060	16.5%	4,000
8. Sketch Artists	$38,060	16.5%	4,000
9. Audio and Video Equipment Technicians	$32,570	26.7%	5,000
10. Interpreters and Translators	$33,860	22.1%	4,000
11. Sound Engineering Technicians	$38,110	25.5%	2,000
12. Dispatchers, Except Police, Fire, and Ambulance	$30,920	14.4%	28,000

(continued)

(continued)

Best Jobs for People Interested in Arts and Communication

Job	Annual Earnings	Percent Growth	Annual Openings
13. Air Traffic Controllers	$102,030	12.6%	2,000
14. Camera Operators, Television, Video, and Motion Picture	$37,610	13.4%	4,000
15. Professional Photographers	$26,080	13.6%	18,000
16. Police, Fire, and Ambulance Dispatchers	$28,930	12.7%	15,000
17. Choreographers	$33,670	15.8%	3,000

Best Jobs for People Interested in Business and Administration

Job	Annual Earnings	Percent Growth	Annual Openings
1. Executive Secretaries and Administrative Assistants	$34,970	8.7%	210,000
2. Legal Secretaries	$36,720	18.8%	39,000
3. First-Line Supervisors, Administrative Support	$41,030	6.6%	140,000
4. First-Line Supervisors, Customer Service	$41,030	6.6%	140,000
5. Human Resources Assistants, Except Payroll and Timekeeping	$31,750	19.3%	36,000
6. Production, Planning, and Expediting Clerks	$36,340	14.1%	51,000
7. Office Clerks, General	$22,770	10.4%	550,000
8. Housekeeping Supervisors	$29,510	16.2%	28,000
9. Industrial Engineering Technicians	$43,590	8.7%	7,000
10. Janitorial Supervisors	$29,510	16.2%	28,000
11. Tax Preparers	$27,730	23.2%	11,000
12. Bookkeeping, Accounting, and Auditing Clerks	$28,570	3.0%	274,000
13. Billing, Cost, and Rate Clerks	$27,040	7.9%	78,000
14. Billing, Posting, and Calculating Machine Operators	$27,040	7.9%	78,000
15. Medical Secretaries	$26,540	17.2%	50,000
16. Statement Clerks	$27,040	7.9%	78,000

Best Jobs for People Interested in Education and Training

Job	Annual Earnings	Percent Growth	Annual Openings
1. Self-Enrichment Education Teachers	$30,880	40.1%	39,000
2. Fitness Trainers and Aerobics Instructors	$25,470	44.5%	38,000
3. Teacher Assistants	$19,410	23.0%	259,000
4. Library Assistants, Clerical	$20,720	21.5%	27,000
5. Library Technicians	$24,940	16.8%	22,000
6. Vocational Education Teachers, Postsecondary	$40,740	38.1%	216,000

Best Jobs for People Interested in Finance and Insurance

Job	Annual Earnings	Percent Growth	Annual Openings
1. Claims Examiners, Property and Casualty Insurance	$44,220	14.2%	31,000
2. Insurance Adjusters, Examiners, and Investigators	$44,220	14.2%	31,000
3. Bill and Account Collectors	$27,450	24.5%	76,000
4. Appraisers, Real Estate	$43,390	17.6%	11,000
5. Assessors	$43,390	17.6%	11,000
6. Advertising Sales Agents	$40,300	13.4%	24,000
7. Insurance Appraisers, Auto Damage	$45,330	11.7%	2,000
8. New Accounts Clerks	$26,860	11.2%	24,000

Best Jobs for People Interested in Government and Public Administration

Job	Annual Earnings	Percent Growth	Annual Openings
1. Child Support, Missing Persons, and Unemployment Insurance Fraud Investigators	$53,990	22.4%	11,000
2. Immigration and Customs Inspectors	$53,990	22.4%	11,000
3. Environmental Compliance Inspectors	$47,390	9.8%	20,000
4. Equal Opportunity Representatives and Officers	$47,390	9.8%	20,000
5. Government Property Inspectors and Investigators	$47,390	9.8%	20,000
6. Licensing Examiners and Inspectors	$47,390	9.8%	20,000
7. Pressure Vessel Inspectors	$47,390	9.8%	20,000
8. City and Regional Planning Aides	$34,360	17.5%	18,000
9. Court Clerks	$28,430	12.3%	14,000
10. License Clerks	$28,430	12.3%	14,000

(continued)

(continued)

Best Jobs for People Interested in Government and Public Administration

Job	Annual Earnings	Percent Growth	Annual Openings
11. Municipal Clerks	$28,430	12.3%	14,000
12. Aviation Inspectors	$50,380	7.7%	5,000
13. Marine Cargo Inspectors	$50,380	7.7%	5,000
14. Motor Vehicle Inspectors	$50,380	7.7%	5,000
15. Railroad Inspectors	$50,380	7.7%	5,000
16. Court Reporters	$42,920	12.7%	2,000
17. Mechanical Inspectors	$28,410	4.7%	87,000

Best Jobs for People Interested in Health Science

Job	Annual Earnings	Percent Growth	Annual Openings
1. Registered Nurses	$52,330	27.3%	215,000
2. Dental Hygienists	$58,350	43.1%	9,000
3. Medical Assistants	$24,610	58.9%	78,000
4. Home Health Aides	$18,330	48.1%	141,000
5. Physical Therapist Assistants	$37,890	44.6%	10,000
6. Dental Assistants	$28,330	42.5%	35,000
7. Medical Records and Health Information Technicians	$25,590	46.8%	24,000
8. Respiratory Therapists	$43,140	34.8%	10,000
9. Radiologic Technicians	$43,350	22.9%	21,000
10. Radiologic Technologists	$43,350	22.9%	21,000
11. Massage Therapists	$31,960	27.1%	24,000
12. Radiation Therapists	$57,700	31.6%	1,000
13. Cardiovascular Technologists and Technicians	$38,690	33.5%	6,000
14. Licensed Practical and Licensed Vocational Nurses	$33,970	20.2%	105,000
15. Nursing Aides, Orderlies, and Attendants	$20,980	24.9%	302,000
16. Pharmacy Technicians	$23,650	28.8%	39,000
17. Surgical Technologists	$34,010	27.9%	13,000
18. Occupational Therapist Assistants	$38,430	39.2%	3,000
19. Veterinary Technologists and Technicians	$24,940	44.1%	11,000
20. Diagnostic Medical Sonographers	$52,490	24.0%	4,000
21. Respiratory Therapy Technicians	$36,740	34.2%	5,000
22. Coroners	$47,390	9.8%	20,000
23. Nuclear Medicine Technologists	$56,450	23.6%	2,000
24. Medical and Clinical Laboratory Technicians	$30,840	19.4%	21,000

Best Jobs for People Interested in Health Science

Job	Annual Earnings	Percent Growth	Annual Openings
25. Medical Transcriptionists	$28,380	22.6%	18,000
26. Nonfarm Animal Caretakers	$17,460	22.2%	32,000
27. Biological Technicians	$33,210	19.4%	7,000
28. First-Line Supervisors and Manager/Supervisors—Animal Care Workers, Except Livestock	$35,490	11.4%	6,000
29. Opticians, Dispensing	$27,950	18.2%	10,000

Best Jobs for People Interested in Hospitality, Tourism, and Recreation

Job	Annual Earnings	Percent Growth	Annual Openings
1. Janitors and Cleaners, Except Maids and Housekeeping Cleaners	$18,790	18.3%	454,000
2. Food Preparation Workers	$16,710	20.2%	267,000
3. Locker Room, Coatroom, and Dressing Room Attendants	$17,550	27.8%	66,000
4. Combined Food Preparation and Serving Workers, Including Fast Food	$14,690	22.8%	734,000
5. Amusement and Recreation Attendants	$15,550	27.8%	66,000
6. Cooks, Restaurant	$19,520	15.9%	211,000
7. Athletes and Sports Competitors	$48,310	19.2%	3,000
8. Hotel, Motel, and Resort Desk Clerks	$17,700	23.9%	46,000
9. Counter Attendants, Cafeteria, Food Concession, and Coffee Shop	$15,660	16.7%	190,000
10. Coaches and Scouts	$26,350	18.3%	26,000
11. First-Line Supervisors/Managers of Food Preparation and Serving Workers	$25,410	15.5%	154,000
12. Flight Attendants	$43,440	15.9%	23,000
13. Waiters and Waitresses	$14,050	17.5%	721,000
14. Chefs and Head Cooks	$30,680	15.8%	33,000
15. Food Service Managers	$39,610	11.5%	58,000
16. Hosts and Hostesses, Restaurant, Lounge, and Coffee Shop	$15,630	16.4%	95,000
17. Hairdressers, Hairstylists, and Cosmetologists	$19,800	14.7%	68,000
18. Gaming Supervisors	$40,840	15.7%	6,000
19. Reservation and Transportation Ticket Agents	$27,750	12.2%	35,000
20. Travel Clerks	$27,750	12.2%	35,000
21. Gaming Dealers	$14,340	24.7%	26,000
22. Dining Room and Cafeteria Attendants and Bartender Helpers	$14,770	14.9%	143,000
23. First-Line Supervisors/Managers of Personal Service Workers	$30,350	9.4%	26,000
24. Lodging Managers	$37,660	6.6%	10,000

Best Jobs for People Interested in Human Service

Job	Annual Earnings	Percent Growth	Annual Openings
1. Social and Human Service Assistants	$24,270	48.7%	63,000
2. Personal and Home Care Aides	$16,900	40.5%	154,000
3. Child Care Workers	$16,760	11.7%	406,000
4. Interviewers, Except Eligibility and Loan	$23,670	28.0%	46,000
5. Nannies	$16,760	11.7%	406,000
6. Residential Advisors	$21,430	33.6%	12,000

Best Jobs for People Interested in Information Technology

Job	Annual Earnings	Percent Growth	Annual Openings
1. Computer Support Specialists	$40,430	30.3%	71,000
2. Automatic Teller Machine Servicers	$35,150	15.1%	19,000
3. Data Processing Equipment Repairers	$35,150	15.1%	19,000
4. Office Machine and Cash Register Servicers	$35,150	15.1%	19,000

Best Jobs for People Interested in Law and Public Safety

Job	Annual Earnings	Percent Growth	Annual Openings
1. Highway Patrol Pilots	$45,210	24.7%	67,000
2. Police Patrol Officers	$45,210	24.7%	67,000
3. Sheriffs and Deputy Sheriffs	$45,210	24.7%	67,000
4. Security Guards	$20,320	31.9%	228,000
5. Paralegals and Legal Assistants	$39,130	28.7%	29,000
6. Criminal Investigators and Special Agents	$53,990	22.4%	11,000
7. Police Detectives	$53,990	22.4%	11,000
8. Police Identification and Records Officers	$53,990	22.4%	11,000
9. Emergency Medical Technicians and Paramedics	$25,310	33.1%	32,000
10. Emergency Management Specialists	$45,390	28.2%	2,000
11. Correctional Officers and Jailers	$33,600	24.2%	49,000
12. First-Line Supervisors/Managers of Police and Detectives	$64,430	15.3%	14,000
13. Forest Fire Fighting and Prevention Supervisors	$58,920	18.7%	8,000
14. Municipal Fire Fighting and Prevention Supervisors	$58,920	18.7%	8,000
15. Forest Fire Fighters	$38,330	20.7%	29,000

Best Jobs for People Interested in Law and Public Safety

Job	Annual Earnings	Percent Growth	Annual Openings
16. Municipal Fire Fighters	$38,330	20.7%	29,000
17. Private Detectives and Investigators	$32,110	25.3%	9,000
18. First-Line Supervisors/Managers of Correctional Officers	$44,720	19.0%	4,000
19. Transit and Railroad Police	$45,430	15.9%	1,000
20. Forensic Science Technicians	$44,010	18.9%	1,000

Best Jobs for People Interested in Manufacturing

Job	Annual Earnings	Percent Growth	Annual Openings
1. First-Line Supervisors/Managers of Mechanics, Installers, and Repairers	$50,340	15.4%	42,000
2. Brazers	$30,620	17.0%	71,000
3. Solderers	$30,620	17.0%	71,000
4. Welder-Fitters	$30,620	17.0%	71,000
5. Welders and Cutters	$30,620	17.0%	71,000
6. Welders, Production	$30,620	17.0%	71,000
7. Automotive Master Mechanics	$32,450	12.4%	100,000
8. Automotive Specialty Technicians	$32,450	12.4%	100,000
9. First-Line Supervisors/Managers of Production and Operating Workers	$44,740	9.5%	66,000
10. Irradiated-Fuel Handlers	$33,320	43.1%	8,000
11. Aircraft Body and Bonded Structure Repairers	$45,290	11.0%	12,000
12. Aircraft Engine Specialists	$45,290	11.0%	12,000
13. Airframe-and-Power-Plant Mechanics	$45,290	11.0%	12,000
14. Bus and Truck Mechanics and Diesel Engine Specialists	$35,780	14.2%	28,000
15. Painters, Transportation Equipment	$35,120	17.5%	9,000
16. First-Line Supervisors/Managers of Helpers, Laborers, and Material Movers, Hand	$38,280	14.0%	16,000
17. Packaging and Filling Machine Operators and Tenders	$22,200	21.1%	69,000
18. Packers and Packagers, Hand	$17,150	14.4%	198,000
19. Automotive Body and Related Repairers	$34,690	13.2%	23,000
20. Desktop Publishers	$32,340	29.2%	4,000
21. Refuse and Recyclable Material Collectors	$25,760	17.6%	42,000
22. Water and Liquid Waste Treatment Plant and System Operators	$34,960	16.0%	9,000

(continued)

(continued)

Best Jobs for People Interested in Manufacturing

Job	Annual Earnings	Percent Growth	Annual Openings
23. Model Makers, Metal and Plastic	$44,250	14.6%	1,000
24. Industrial Truck and Tractor Operators	$26,580	11.1%	94,000
25. Medical Equipment Repairers	$37,220	14.8%	4,000
26. Slaughterers and Meat Packers	$20,860	18.1%	23,000
27. Industrial Machinery Mechanics	$39,060	5.5%	19,000
28. Valve and Regulator Repairers	$43,710	12.0%	5,000
29. Electrical and Electronics Repairers, Commercial and Industrial Equipment	$42,600	10.3%	10,000
30. Mobile Heavy Equipment Mechanics, Except Engines	$38,150	9.6%	12,000
31. Recreational Vehicle Service Technicians	$28,980	21.8%	4,000
32. Machinists	$33,960	8.2%	30,000
33. Electrical and Electronic Inspectors and Testers	$28,410	4.7%	87,000
34. Locksmiths and Safe Repairers	$30,360	21.0%	3,000
35. Materials Inspectors	$28,410	4.7%	87,000
36. Precision Devices Inspectors and Testers	$28,410	4.7%	87,000
37. Production Inspectors, Testers, Graders, Sorters, Samplers, Weighers	$28,410	4.7%	87,000
38. Millwrights	$43,720	5.3%	7,000

Best Jobs for People Interested in Retail and Wholesale Sales and Service

Job	Annual Earnings	Percent Growth	Annual Openings
1. Adjustment Clerks	$27,020	24.3%	419,000
2. Customer Service Representatives, Utilities	$27,020	24.3%	419,000
3. Receptionists and Information Clerks	$21,830	29.5%	296,000
4. Sales Representatives, Agricultural	$58,580	19.3%	44,000
5. Sales Representatives, Chemical and Pharmaceutical	$58,580	19.3%	44,000
6. Sales Representatives, Electrical/Electronic	$58,580	19.3%	44,000
7. Sales Representatives, Instruments	$58,580	19.3%	44,000
8. Sales Representatives, Mechanical Equipment and Supplies	$58,580	19.3%	44,000
9. Sales Representatives, Medical	$58,580	19.3%	44,000
10. First-Line Supervisors/Managers of Non-Retail Sales Workers	$59,300	6.8%	72,000

Best Jobs for People Interested in Retail and Wholesale Sales and Service

Job	Annual Earnings	Percent Growth	Annual Openings
11. Sales Representatives, Wholesale and Manufacturing, Except Technical and Scientific Products	$45,400	19.1%	160,000
12. Counter and Rental Clerks	$18,280	26.3%	144,000
13. First-Line Supervisors/Managers of Retail Sales Workers	$32,720	9.1%	251,000
14. Retail Salespersons	$18,680	14.6%	1,014,000
15. Cashiers	$16,240	13.2%	1,221,000
16. Gaming Change Persons and Booth Cashiers	$20,530	24.1%	12,000
17. Real Estate Brokers	$58,720	2.4%	11,000
18. Demonstrators and Product Promoters	$20,700	17.0%	38,000
19. Real Estate Sales Agents	$35,670	5.7%	34,000

Best Jobs for People Interested in Scientific Research, Engineering, and Mathematics

Job	Annual Earnings	Percent Growth	Annual Openings
1. Calibration and Instrumentation Technicians	$46,310	10.0%	24,000
2. Electrical Engineering Technicians	$46,310	10.0%	24,000
3. Electronics Engineering Technicians	$46,310	10.0%	24,000
4. Social Science Research Assistants	$34,360	17.5%	18,000
5. Mapping Technicians	$30,380	23.1%	10,000
6. Surveying Technicians	$30,380	23.1%	10,000
7. Environmental Engineering Technicians	$38,550	28.4%	3,000
8. Mechanical Engineering Technicians	$43,400	11.0%	6,000
9. Photographers, Scientific	$26,080	13.6%	18,000
10. Electro-Mechanical Technicians	$41,440	11.5%	4,000
11. Civil Engineering Technicians	$38,480	7.6%	10,000

Best Jobs for People Interested in Transportation, Distribution, and Logistics

Job	Annual Earnings	Percent Growth	Annual Openings
1. Storage and Distribution Managers	$66,600	19.7%	13,000
2. Transportation Managers	$66,600	19.7%	13,000
3. Tractor-Trailer Truck Drivers	$33,520	19.0%	299,000
4. Truck Drivers, Heavy	$33,520	19.0%	299,000
5. Truck Drivers, Light or Delivery Services	$24,540	23.2%	219,000
6. Taxi Drivers and Chauffeurs	$19,570	21.7%	28,000
7. Bus Drivers, School	$23,250	16.7%	76,000
8. Bus Drivers, Transit and Intercity	$29,730	15.2%	33,000
9. First-Line Supervisors/Managers of Transportation and Material-Moving Machine and Vehicle Operators	$44,810	12.1%	23,000
10. Commercial Pilots	$53,870	14.9%	2,000
11. Cargo and Freight Agents	$34,250	15.5%	8,000
12. Freight Inspectors	$50,380	7.7%	5,000
13. Public Transportation Inspectors	$50,380	7.7%	5,000
14. Postal Service Mail Carriers	$44,450	−0.5%	20,000
15. Subway and Streetcar Operators	$49,290	13.2%	2,000

Best Jobs Based on Personality Types

Several popular career assessment inventories organize jobs into groupings based on personality types. The most-used system is one that presents six personality types: Realistic, Investigative, Artistic, Social, Enterprising, and Conventional. This system is used in the *Self Directed Search (SDS)*, developed by John Holland, and many other inventories.

If you have used one of these career exploration systems, the following lists may help. Even if you have not, you may find the concept of personality types—and the jobs that are related to them—helpful to you.

We've ranked the jobs within each grouping based on their combined scores for earnings, growth, and annual openings. Like the job lists for education levels, there is only one list for each personality type. (Note that data on personality type is not available for 15 of the best 300 jobs, so you will not find them in this set of lists.)

Here are brief descriptions for each of the six personality types presented in these lists:

◎ **Realistic:** These occupations frequently involve work activities that include practical, hands-on problems and solutions. They often deal with plants, animals, and real-world materials like wood, tools, and machinery. Many of the occupations require working outside and do not involve a lot of paperwork or working closely with others.

- **Investigative:** These occupations frequently involve working with ideas and require an extensive amount of thinking. These occupations can involve searching for facts and figuring out problems mentally.

- **Artistic:** These occupations frequently involve working with forms, designs, and patterns. They often require self-expression, and the work can be done without following a clear set of rules.

- **Social:** These occupations frequently involve working with, communicating with, and teaching people. These occupations often involve helping or providing service to others.

- **Enterprising:** These occupations frequently involve starting up and carrying out projects. These occupations can involve leading people and making many decisions. They sometimes require risk taking and often deal with business.

- **Conventional:** These occupations frequently involve following set procedures and routines. These occupations can include working with data and details more than with ideas. Usually there is a clear line of authority to follow.

Best Jobs for People with a Realistic Personality Type

Job	Annual Earnings	Percent Growth	Annual Openings
1. Highway Patrol Pilots	$45,210	24.7%	67,000
2. Electricians	$42,300	23.4%	65,000
3. Heating and Air Conditioning Mechanics	$36,260	31.8%	35,000
4. Refrigeration Mechanics	$36,260	31.8%	35,000
5. Pipe Fitters	$41,290	18.7%	56,000
6. Pipelaying Fitters	$41,290	18.7%	56,000
7. Plumbers	$41,290	18.7%	56,000
8. Radiologic Technicians	$43,350	22.9%	21,000
9. Radiologic Technologists	$43,350	22.9%	21,000
10. Tractor-Trailer Truck Drivers	$33,520	19.0%	299,000
11. Truck Drivers, Heavy	$33,520	19.0%	299,000
12. Refractory Materials Repairers, Except Brickmasons	$37,640	16.3%	155,000
13. Forest Fire Fighters	$38,330	20.7%	29,000
14. Municipal Fire Fighters	$38,330	20.7%	29,000
15. Correctional Officers and Jailers	$33,600	24.2%	49,000
16. Sheet Metal Workers	$35,560	19.8%	30,000
17. Truck Drivers, Light or Delivery Services	$24,540	23.2%	219,000
18. Forest Fire Fighting and Prevention Supervisors	$58,920	18.7%	8,000
19. Municipal Fire Fighting and Prevention Supervisors	$58,920	18.7%	8,000
20. Technical Directors/Managers	$52,840	18.3%	10,000

(continued)

(continued)

Best Jobs for People with a Realistic Personality Type

Job	Annual Earnings	Percent Growth	Annual Openings
21. Combined Food Preparation and Serving Workers, Including Fast Food	$14,690	22.8%	734,000
22. Landscaping and Groundskeeping Workers	$20,420	22.0%	203,000
23. Cement Masons and Concrete Finishers	$31,400	26.1%	24,000
24. First-Line Supervisors and Manager/Supervisors— Landscaping Workers	$35,340	21.6%	18,000
25. Telecommunications Line Installers and Repairers	$40,330	18.8%	13,000
26. Food Preparation Workers	$16,710	20.2%	267,000
27. Surgical Technologists	$34,010	27.9%	13,000
28. Maintenance and Repair Workers, General	$30,710	16.3%	155,000
29. Janitors and Cleaners, Except Maids and Housekeeping Cleaners	$18,790	18.3%	454,000
30. Amusement and Recreation Attendants	$15,550	27.8%	66,000
31. Ceiling Tile Installers	$34,030	21.4%	17,000
32. Drywall Installers	$34,030	21.4%	17,000
33. Brazers	$30,620	17.0%	71,000
34. Brickmasons and Blockmasons	$41,740	14.2%	21,000
35. Solderers	$30,620	17.0%	71,000
36. Welder-Fitters	$30,620	17.0%	71,000
37. Welders and Cutters	$30,620	17.0%	71,000
38. Welders, Production	$30,620	17.0%	71,000
39. Boat Builders and Shipwrights	$34,900	10.1%	193,000
40. Brattice Builders	$34,900	10.1%	193,000
41. Carpenter Assemblers and Repairers	$34,900	10.1%	193,000
42. Construction Carpenters	$34,900	10.1%	193,000
43. Rough Carpenters	$34,900	10.1%	193,000
44. Ship Carpenters and Joiners	$34,900	10.1%	193,000
45. Packaging and Filling Machine Operators and Tenders	$22,200	21.1%	69,000
46. Calibration and Instrumentation Technicians	$46,310	10.0%	24,000
47. Electrical Engineering Technicians	$46,310	10.0%	24,000
48. Electronics Engineering Technicians	$46,310	10.0%	24,000
49. Elevator Installers and Repairers	$58,710	17.1%	3,000
50. Roofers	$30,840	18.6%	38,000
51. Tapers	$39,070	20.8%	5,000
52. Bus and Truck Mechanics and Diesel Engine Specialists	$35,780	14.2%	28,000
53. Sound Engineering Technicians	$38,110	25.5%	2,000

Best Jobs for People with a Realistic Personality Type

Job	Annual Earnings	Percent Growth	Annual Openings
54. Tile and Marble Setters	$35,410	26.5%	4,000
55. Automotive Master Mechanics	$32,450	12.4%	100,000
56. Automotive Specialty Technicians	$32,450	12.4%	100,000
57. Irradiated-Fuel Handlers	$33,320	43.1%	8,000
58. Farmers and Ranchers	$40,440	−20.6%	118,000
59. Structural Iron and Steel Workers	$42,430	15.9%	9,000
60. Cooks, Restaurant	$19,520	15.9%	211,000
61. Medical and Clinical Laboratory Technicians	$30,840	19.4%	21,000
62. Nonfarm Animal Caretakers	$17,460	22.2%	32,000
63. Pressure Vessel Inspectors	$47,390	9.8%	20,000
64. Aircraft Body and Bonded Structure Repairers	$45,290	11.0%	12,000
65. Aircraft Engine Specialists	$45,290	11.0%	12,000
66. Airframe-and-Power-Plant Mechanics	$45,290	11.0%	12,000
67. Central Office and PBX Installers and Repairers	$49,840	−0.6%	23,000
68. Communication Equipment Mechanics, Installers, and Repairers	$49,840	−0.6%	23,000
69. Frame Wirers, Central Office	$49,840	−0.6%	23,000
70. Grader, Bulldozer, and Scraper Operators	$35,360	10.4%	45,000
71. Operating Engineers	$35,360	10.4%	45,000
72. Station Installers and Repairers, Telephone	$49,840	−0.6%	23,000
73. Telecommunications Facility Examiners	$49,840	−0.6%	23,000
74. Helpers—Installation, Maintenance, and Repair Workers	$21,310	20.3%	33,000
75. Taxi Drivers and Chauffeurs	$19,570	21.7%	28,000
76. Automatic Teller Machine Servicers	$35,150	15.1%	19,000
77. Commercial Pilots	$53,870	14.9%	2,000
78. Data Processing Equipment Repairers	$35,150	15.1%	19,000
79. Office Machine and Cash Register Servicers	$35,150	15.1%	19,000
80. Bus Drivers, School	$23,250	16.7%	76,000
81. Construction Laborers	$25,160	14.2%	166,000
82. Refuse and Recyclable Material Collectors	$25,760	17.6%	42,000
83. Surveying Technicians	$30,380	23.1%	10,000
84. Packers and Packagers, Hand	$17,150	14.4%	198,000
85. Painters, Transportation Equipment	$35,120	17.5%	9,000
86. Automotive Body and Related Repairers	$34,690	13.2%	23,000
87. Desktop Publishers	$32,340	29.2%	4,000
88. Bus Drivers, Transit and Intercity	$29,730	15.2%	33,000

(continued)

(continued)

Best Jobs for People with a Realistic Personality Type

Job	Annual Earnings	Percent Growth	Annual Openings
89. Dining Room and Cafeteria Attendants and Bartender Helpers	$14,770	14.9%	143,000
90. Electric Meter Installers and Repairers	$43,710	12.0%	5,000
91. Meter Mechanics	$43,710	12.0%	5,000
92. Subway and Streetcar Operators	$49,290	13.2%	2,000
93. Valve and Regulator Repairers	$43,710	12.0%	5,000
94. Electrical and Electronics Repairers, Commercial and Industrial Equipment	$42,600	10.3%	10,000
95. Painters, Construction and Maintenance	$30,260	11.6%	69,000
96. Biological Technicians	$33,210	19.4%	7,000
97. Carpet Installers	$34,090	16.8%	10,000
98. Industrial Truck and Tractor Operators	$26,580	11.1%	94,000
99. Water and Liquid Waste Treatment Plant and System Operators	$34,960	16.0%	9,000
100. Model Makers, Metal and Plastic	$44,250	14.6%	1,000
101. Mechanical Engineering Technicians	$43,400	11.0%	6,000
102. Slaughterers and Meat Packers	$20,860	18.1%	23,000
103. Aviation Inspectors	$50,380	7.7%	5,000
104. Industrial Machinery Mechanics	$39,060	5.5%	19,000
105. Motor Vehicle Inspectors	$50,380	7.7%	5,000
106. Railroad Inspectors	$50,380	7.7%	5,000
107. Electrical Power-Line Installers and Repairers	$49,100	1.6%	9,000
108. Electro-Mechanical Technicians	$41,440	11.5%	4,000
109. Glaziers	$32,650	17.2%	7,000
110. Helpers—Electricians	$23,420	17.9%	17,000
111. Machinists	$33,960	8.2%	30,000
112. Insulation Workers, Mechanical	$33,330	15.8%	9,000
113. Medical Equipment Repairers	$37,220	14.8%	4,000
114. Mobile Heavy Equipment Mechanics, Except Engines	$38,150	9.6%	12,000
115. Architectural Drafters	$39,190	4.2%	14,000
116. Civil Drafters	$39,190	4.2%	14,000
117. Tree Trimmers and Pruners	$26,150	18.6%	11,000
118. Recreational Vehicle Service Technicians	$28,980	21.8%	4,000
119. Millwrights	$43,720	5.3%	7,000
120. Electrical and Electronic Inspectors and Testers	$28,410	4.7%	87,000
121. Materials Inspectors	$28,410	4.7%	87,000

Best Jobs for People with a Realistic Personality Type

Job	Annual Earnings	Percent Growth	Annual Openings
122. Mechanical Inspectors	$28,410	4.7%	87,000
123. Precision Devices Inspectors and Testers	$28,410	4.7%	87,000
124. Production Inspectors, Testers, Graders, Sorters, Samplers, Weighers	$28,410	4.7%	87,000
125. First-Line Supervisors and Manager/Supervisors— Animal Care Workers, Except Livestock	$35,490	11.4%	6,000
126. First-Line Supervisors and Manager/Supervisors— Fishery Workers	$35,490	11.4%	6,000
127. First-Line Supervisors and Manager/Supervisors— Horticultural Workers	$35,490	11.4%	6,000
128. Civil Engineering Technicians	$38,480	7.6%	10,000
129. Locksmiths and Safe Repairers	$30,360	21.0%	3,000
130. Pest Control Workers	$26,220	17.0%	11,000
131. Crane and Tower Operators	$37,410	10.8%	5,000
132. Highway Maintenance Workers	$29,550	10.4%	25,000
133. Riggers	$35,330	14.3%	3,000
134. Insulation Workers, Floor, Ceiling, and Wall	$30,310	15.8%	9,000
135. Plasterers and Stucco Masons	$32,440	13.5%	8,000
136. Loading Machine Operators, Underground Mining	$33,250	8.9%	14,000
137. Dragline Operators	$31,970	8.9%	14,000
138. Excavating and Loading Machine Operators	$31,970	8.9%	14,000

Best Jobs for People with an Investigative Personality Type

Job	Annual Earnings	Percent Growth	Annual Openings
1. Coroners	$47,390	9.8%	20,000
2. Environmental Compliance Inspectors	$47,390	9.8%	20,000
3. Computer Support Specialists	$40,430	30.3%	71,000
4. Respiratory Therapists	$43,140	34.8%	10,000
5. Nuclear Medicine Technologists	$56,450	23.6%	2,000
6. Cardiovascular Technologists and Technicians	$38,690	33.5%	6,000
7. Environmental Science and Protection Technicians, Including Health	$35,340	36.8%	4,000
8. Forensic Science Technicians	$44,010	18.9%	1,000
9. Industrial Engineering Technicians	$43,590	8.7%	7,000

Best Jobs for People with an Artistic Personality Type

Job	Annual Earnings	Percent Growth	Annual Openings
1. Talent Directors	$52,840	18.3%	10,000
2. Caption Writers	$44,350	16.1%	23,000
3. Cartoonists	$38,060	16.5%	4,000
4. Painters and Illustrators	$38,060	16.5%	4,000
5. Sculptors	$38,060	16.5%	4,000
6. Sketch Artists	$38,060	16.5%	4,000
7. Costume Attendants	$25,050	27.8%	66,000
8. Interpreters and Translators	$33,860	22.1%	4,000
9. Photographers, Scientific	$26,080	13.6%	18,000
10. Professional Photographers	$26,080	13.6%	18,000
11. Camera Operators, Television, Video, and Motion Picture	$37,610	13.4%	4,000
12. Choreographers	$33,670	15.8%	3,000

Best Jobs for People with a Social Personality Type

Job	Annual Earnings	Percent Growth	Annual Openings
1. Vocational Education Teachers Postsecondary	$40,740	38.1%	216,000
2. Registered Nurses	$52,330	27.3%	215,000
3. Medical Assistants	$24,610	58.9%	78,000
4. Dental Hygienists	$58,350	43.1%	9,000
5. Home Health Aides	$18,330	48.1%	141,000
6. Social and Human Service Assistants	$24,270	48.7%	63,000
7. Fitness Trainers and Aerobics Instructors	$25,470	44.5%	38,000
8. Physical Therapist Assistants	$37,890	44.6%	10,000
9. Police Patrol Officers	$45,210	24.7%	67,000
10. Self-Enrichment Education Teachers	$30,880	40.1%	39,000
11. Sheriffs and Deputy Sheriffs	$45,210	24.7%	67,000
12. Dental Assistants	$28,330	42.5%	35,000
13. Security Guards	$20,320	31.9%	228,000
14. Nursing Aides, Orderlies, and Attendants	$20,980	24.9%	302,000
15. Personal and Home Care Aides	$16,900	40.5%	154,000
16. Licensed Practical and Licensed Vocational Nurses	$33,970	20.2%	105,000
17. Occupational Therapist Assistants	$38,430	39.2%	3,000
18. Radiation Therapists	$57,700	31.6%	1,000

Best Jobs for People with a Social Personality Type

Job	Annual Earnings	Percent Growth	Annual Openings
19. Teacher Assistants	$19,410	23.0%	259,000
20. Emergency Medical Technicians and Paramedics	$25,310	33.1%	32,000
21. Waiters and Waitresses	$14,050	17.5%	721,000
22. Equal Opportunity Representatives and Officers	$47,390	9.8%	20,000
23. Child Care Workers	$16,760	11.7%	406,000
24. Residential Advisors	$21,430	33.6%	12,000
25. Locker Room, Coatroom, and Dressing Room Attendants	$17,550	27.8%	66,000
26. Counter Attendants, Cafeteria, Food Concession, and Coffee Shop	$15,660	16.7%	190,000
27. Police, Fire, and Ambulance Dispatchers	$28,930	12.7%	15,000

Best Jobs for People with an Enterprising Personality Type

Job	Annual Earnings	Percent Growth	Annual Openings
1. Sales Representatives, Agricultural	$58,580	19.3%	44,000
2. Sales Representatives, Chemical and Pharmaceutical	$58,580	19.3%	44,000
3. Sales Representatives, Electrical/Electronic	$58,580	19.3%	44,000
4. Sales Representatives, Instruments	$58,580	19.3%	44,000
5. Sales Representatives, Mechanical Equipment and Supplies	$58,580	19.3%	44,000
6. Sales Representatives, Medical	$58,580	19.3%	44,000
7. Sales Representatives, Wholesale and Manufacturing, Except Technical and Scientific Products	$45,400	19.1%	160,000
8. Storage and Distribution Managers	$66,600	19.7%	13,000
9. Transportation Managers	$66,600	19.7%	13,000
10. Child Support, Missing Persons, and Unemployment Insurance Fraud Investigators	$53,990	22.4%	11,000
11. Criminal Investigators and Special Agents	$53,990	22.4%	11,000
12. Police Detectives	$53,990	22.4%	11,000
13. First-Line Supervisors/Managers of Non-Retail Sales Workers	$59,300	6.8%	72,000
14. Paralegals and Legal Assistants	$39,130	28.7%	29,000
15. First-Line Supervisors and Manager/Supervisors— Construction Trades Workers	$50,450	14.1%	67,000
16. First-Line Supervisors and Manager/Supervisors— Extractive Workers	$50,450	14.1%	67,000

(continued)

(continued)

Best Jobs for People with an Enterprising Personality Type

Job	Annual Earnings	Percent Growth	Annual Openings
17. First-Line Supervisors/Managers of Mechanics, Installers, and Repairers	$50,340	15.4%	42,000
18. First-Line Supervisors/Managers of Police and Detectives	$64,430	15.3%	14,000
19. First-Line Supervisors/Managers of Production and Operating Workers	$44,740	9.5%	66,000
20. First-Line Supervisors/Managers of Food Preparation and Serving Workers	$25,410	15.5%	154,000
21. Hosts and Hostesses, Restaurant, Lounge, and Coffee Shop	$15,630	16.4%	95,000
22. First-Line Supervisors, Administrative Support	$41,030	6.6%	140,000
23. First-Line Supervisors, Customer Service	$41,030	6.6%	140,000
24. Insurance Adjusters, Examiners, and Investigators	$44,220	14.2%	31,000
25. Gaming Dealers	$14,340	24.7%	26,000
26. Lawn Service Managers	$35,340	21.6%	18,000
27. Food Service Managers	$39,610	11.5%	58,000
28. Retail Salespersons	$18,680	14.6%	1,014,000
29. Flight Attendants	$43,440	15.9%	23,000
30. First-Line Supervisors/Managers of Retail Sales Workers	$32,720	9.1%	251,000
31. Athletes and Sports Competitors	$48,310	19.2%	3,000
32. Appraisers, Real Estate	$43,390	17.6%	11,000
33. Demonstrators and Product Promoters	$20,700	17.0%	38,000
34. Hairdressers, Hairstylists, and Cosmetologists	$19,800	14.7%	68,000
35. Chefs and Head Cooks	$30,680	15.8%	33,000
36. Private Detectives and Investigators	$32,110	25.3%	9,000
37. Coaches and Scouts	$26,350	18.3%	26,000
38. Housekeeping Supervisors	$29,510	16.2%	28,000
39. Janitorial Supervisors	$29,510	16.2%	28,000
40. Agricultural Crop Farm Managers	$50,700	5.1%	25,000
41. Fish Hatchery Managers	$50,700	5.1%	25,000
42. Nursery and Greenhouse Managers	$50,700	5.1%	25,000
43. First-Line Supervisors/Managers of Transportation and Material-Moving Machine and Vehicle Operators	$44,810	12.1%	23,000
44. Government Property Inspectors and Investigators	$47,390	9.8%	20,000
45. Transit and Railroad Police	$45,430	15.9%	1,000
46. Advertising Sales Agents	$40,300	13.4%	24,000
47. Gaming Supervisors	$40,840	15.7%	6,000
48. First-Line Supervisors/Managers of Helpers, Laborers, and Material Movers, Hand	$38,280	14.0%	16,000

Best Jobs for People with an Enterprising Personality Type

Job	Annual Earnings	Percent Growth	Annual Openings
49. Real Estate Sales Agents	$35,670	5.7%	34,000
50. Opticians, Dispensing	$27,950	18.2%	10,000
51. First-Line Supervisors/Managers of Personal Service Workers	$30,350	9.4%	26,000
52. Public Transportation Inspectors	$50,380	7.7%	5,000
53. First-Line Supervisors and Manager/Supervisors—Agricultural Crop Workers	$35,490	11.4%	6,000
54. First-Line Supervisors and Manager/Supervisors—Animal Husbandry Workers	$35,490	11.4%	6,000
55. Lodging Managers	$37,660	6.6%	10,000

Best Jobs for People with a Conventional Personality Type

Job	Annual Earnings	Percent Growth	Annual Openings
1. Adjustment Clerks	$27,020	24.3%	419,000
2. Customer Service Representatives, Utilities	$27,020	24.3%	419,000
3. Legal Secretaries	$36,720	18.8%	39,000
4. Bill and Account Collectors	$27,450	24.5%	76,000
5. Receptionists and Information Clerks	$21,830	29.5%	296,000
6. Immigration and Customs Inspectors	$53,990	22.4%	11,000
7. Police Identification and Records Officers	$53,990	22.4%	11,000
8. Production, Planning, and Expediting Clerks	$36,340	14.1%	51,000
9. Human Resources Assistants, Except Payroll and Timekeeping	$31,750	19.3%	36,000
10. Claims Examiners, Property and Casualty Insurance	$44,220	14.2%	31,000
11. Counter and Rental Clerks	$18,280	26.3%	144,000
12. Interviewers, Except Eligibility and Loan	$23,670	28.0%	46,000
13. Executive Secretaries and Administrative Assistants	$34,970	8.7%	210,000
14. Pharmacy Technicians	$23,650	28.8%	39,000
15. Medical Records and Health Information Technicians	$25,590	46.8%	24,000
16. Assessors	$43,390	17.6%	11,000
17. Audio and Video Equipment Technicians	$32,570	26.7%	5,000
18. City and Regional Planning Aides	$34,360	17.5%	18,000
19. Dispatchers, Except Police, Fire, and Ambulance	$30,920	14.4%	28,000
20. Hotel, Motel, and Resort Desk Clerks	$17,700	23.9%	46,000

(continued)

(continued)

Best Jobs for People with a Conventional Personality Type

Job	Annual Earnings	Percent Growth	Annual Openings
21. Medical Secretaries	$26,540	17.2%	50,000
22. Mapping Technicians	$30,380	23.1%	10,000
23. Bookkeeping, Accounting, and Auditing Clerks	$28,570	3.0%	274,000
24. Licensing Examiners and Inspectors	$47,390	9.8%	20,000
25. Tax Preparers	$27,730	23.2%	11,000
26. Air Traffic Controllers	$102,030	12.6%	2,000
27. Cashiers	$16,240	13.2%	1,221,000
28. Construction and Building Inspectors	$43,670	13.8%	10,000
29. Billing, Cost, and Rate Clerks	$27,040	7.9%	78,000
30. Billing, Posting, and Calculating Machine Operators	$27,040	7.9%	78,000
31. Reservation and Transportation Ticket Agents	$27,750	12.2%	35,000
32. Statement Clerks	$27,040	7.9%	78,000
33. Travel Clerks	$27,750	12.2%	35,000
34. Cargo and Freight Agents	$34,250	15.5%	8,000
35. Office Clerks, General	$22,770	10.4%	550,000
36. Library Assistants, Clerical	$20,720	21.5%	27,000
37. Postal Service Mail Carriers	$44,450	−0.5%	20,000
38. Court Clerks	$28,430	12.3%	14,000
39. License Clerks	$28,430	12.3%	14,000
40. Municipal Clerks	$28,430	12.3%	14,000
41. Insurance Appraisers, Auto Damage	$45,330	11.7%	2,000
42. Library Technicians	$24,940	16.8%	22,000
43. Freight Inspectors	$50,380	7.7%	5,000
44. Marine Cargo Inspectors	$50,380	7.7%	5,000
45. New Accounts Clerks	$26,860	11.2%	24,000

PART II

The Job Descriptions

This part provides descriptions for all the jobs included in one or more of the lists in Part I. The book's introduction gives more details on how to use and interpret the job descriptions, but here are the highlights, along with some additional information:

- The job descriptions that follow met our criteria for inclusion in this book, as we describe in the introduction. The jobs in this book do not require a four-year college degree and have the 300 highest total combined scores for earnings, projected growth, and number of job openings. Many good jobs do not meet these criteria, but we think the jobs that do are the best ones to consider in your career planning.

- The job descriptions are arranged in alphabetical order by job title. This approach allows you to quickly find a description if you know its title from one of the lists in Part I. Part I features many interesting lists that will help you identify job titles to explore in more detail. If you have not browsed the lists in Part I, consider spending some time there. The lists are interesting and will help you identify job titles you can look up in the descriptions that follow.

- Refer to the introduction, beginning on page 1, for details on interpreting the job descriptions' content.

- The GOE job description section includes a subsection titled Other Job Titles in This Work Group to help you identify similar jobs. In some cases, the list of jobs here can be very long, and when this happens, we limit the number of job titles listed to a reasonable number followed by "others" as the last entry. If you want to see the complete list of job titles, consult the "Sources of Additional Information" section in the introduction for details on how to obtain them.

When reviewing the descriptions, keep in mind that the jobs meet our criteria for being among the top 300 jobs based on their total scores for earnings, growth, and number of openings—but one or more of these measures may not be among the highest. For example, an occupation that has high pay may be included, even though growth rate and number of job openings are below average.

"Well," you might ask, "doesn't this mean that at least some 'bad' jobs are described in this part?" Our answer is yes and no. Some jobs with high scores for all measures, such as Registered Nurses—the job with the highest total for pay, growth, and number of openings—would be very bad for people who dislike or are not good at that sort of work. On the other hand, many people love working as Child Care Workers even though that job has lower earnings, a lower projected growth rate, and fewer openings. Descriptions for both jobs are included in this book.

Most likely, somewhere an ex-registered nurse works as a child care worker and loves it. Some who do so may even have figured out how to make more money (say, by running a small child care center), have a more flexible schedule, have more fun, or have other advantages not available in their previous career.

The point is that each job is right for some people at the right time in their lives. We are all likely to change careers and jobs several times, and it's not always money that motivates us. So browse the job descriptions that follow and know that somewhere there is a good place for you. We hope you find it.

Adjustment Clerks

- Education/Training Required: Moderate-term on-the-job training
- Annual Earnings: $27,020
- Growth: 24.3%
- Annual Job Openings: 419,000
- Self-Employed: 0.5%
- Part-Time: 14.8%

Investigate and resolve customers' inquiries concerning merchandise, service, billing, or credit rating. Examine pertinent information to determine accuracy of customers' complaints and responsibility for errors. Notify customers and appropriate personnel of findings, adjustments, and recommendations, such as exchange of merchandise, refund of money, credit to customers' accounts, or adjustment to customers' bills. Notifies customer and designated personnel of findings and recommendations, such as exchanging merchandise, refunding money, or adjustment of bill. Examines weather conditions, calculates number of days in billing period, and reviews meter accounts for errors which might explain high utility charges. Writes work order. Prepares reports showing volume, types, and disposition of claims handled. Compares merchandise with original requisition and information on invoice and prepares invoice for returned goods. Orders tests to detect product malfunction and determines if defect resulted from faulty construction. Trains dealers or service personnel in construction of products, service operations, and customer service. Reviews claims adjustments with dealer, examines parts claimed to be defective, and approves or disapproves of dealer's claim. **SKILLS—Instructing:** Teaching others how to do something. **Speaking:** Talking to others to convey information effectively. **Writing:** Communicating effectively in writing as appropriate for the needs of the audience. **Active Listening:** Giving full attention to what other people are saying, taking time to understand the points being made, asking questions as appropriate, and not interrupting at inappropriate times. **Service Orientation:** Actively looking for ways to help people. **Persuasion:** Persuading others to change their minds or behavior. **Negotiation:** Bringing others together and trying to

reconcile differences. **GOE—Interest Area:** 14. Retail and Wholesale Sales and Service. **Work Group:** 14.06. Customer Service. **Other Jobs in This Work Group:** Cashiers; Counter and Rental Clerks; Customer Service Representatives, Utilities; Gaming Change Persons and Booth Cashiers; Order Clerks; Receptionists and Information Clerks. **PERSONALITY TYPE:** Conventional. Conventional occupations frequently involve following set procedures and routines. These occupations can include working with data and details more than with ideas. Usually there is a clear line of authority to follow.

EDUCATION/TRAINING PROGRAM(S)—Customer Service Support/Call Center/Teleservice Operation; Receptionist. **RELATED KNOWLEDGE/ COURSES—Economics and Accounting:** Knowledge of economic and accounting principles and practices, the financial markets, banking, and the analysis and reporting of financial data. **Clerical Practices:** Knowledge of administrative and clerical procedures and systems such as word processing, managing files and records, stenography and transcription, designing forms, and other office procedures and terminology. **Education and Training:** Knowledge of principles and methods for curriculum and training design, teaching and instruction for individuals and groups, and the measurement of training effects.

Advertising Sales Agents

- Education/Training Required: Moderate-term on-the-job training
- Annual Earnings: $40,300
- Growth: 13.4%
- Annual Job Openings: 24,000
- Self-Employed: 9.5%
- Part-Time: 11.2%

Sell or solicit advertising, including graphic art, advertising space in publications, custom-made signs, or TV and radio advertising time. May obtain leases for outdoor advertising sites or persuade retailer to use sales promotion display items. Prepare and deliver sales presentations to new and existing customers in order to sell new advertising programs and to protect and increase existing advertising. Explain to customers how specific types of advertising will help promote their products or services in the most effective way possible. Maintain assigned account bases while developing new accounts. Process all correspondence and paperwork related to accounts. Deliver advertising or illustration proofs to customers for approval. Draw up contracts for advertising work and collect payments due. Locate and contact potential clients in order to offer advertising services. Provide clients with estimates of the costs of advertising products or services. Recommend appropriate sizes and formats for advertising, depending on medium being used. Inform customers of available options for advertisement artwork and provide samples. Obtain and study information about clients' products, needs, problems, advertising history, and business practices in order to offer effective sales presentations and appropriate product assistance. Determine advertising medium to be used and prepare sample advertisements within the selected medium for presentation to customers. Consult with company officials, sales departments, and advertising agencies in order to develop promotional plans. Prepare promotional plans, sales literature, media kits, and sales contracts, using computer. Identify new advertising markets and propose products to serve them. Write copy as part of layout. Attend sales meetings, industry trade shows, and training seminars to gather information, promote products, expand network of contacts, and increase knowledge. Gather all relevant material for bid processes and coordinate bidding and contract approval. **SKILLS—Negotiation:** Bringing others together and trying to reconcile differences. **Social Perceptiveness:** Being aware of others' reactions and understanding why they react as they do. **Persuasion:** Persuading others to change their minds or behavior. **Service Orientation:** Actively looking for ways to help people. **Management of Financial Resources:** Determining how money will be spent to get the work done and accounting for these expenditures. **Speaking:** Talking to others to convey information effectively. **Instructing:** Teaching others how to do something. **Learning Strategies:** Selecting and using training/instructional methods and procedures appropriate for the situation when learning or teaching new things. **Complex Problem Solving:** Identifying complex problems and reviewing related information to

develop and evaluate options and implement solutions. **GOE—Interest Area:** 06. Finance and Insurance. **Work Group:** 06.05. Finance/Insurance Sales and Support. **Other Jobs in This Work Group:** Insurance Sales Agents; Personal Financial Advisors; Sales Agents, Financial Services; Sales Agents, Securities and Commodities. **PERSONALITY TYPE:** Enterprising. Enterprising occupations frequently involve starting up and carrying out projects. These occupations can involve leading people and making many decisions. They sometimes require risk taking and often deal with business.

EDUCATION/TRAINING PROGRAM(S)— Advertising. **RELATED KNOWLEDGE/COURSES—Sales and Marketing:** Knowledge of principles and methods for showing, promoting, and selling products or services. This includes marketing strategy and tactics, product demonstrations, sales techniques, and sales control systems. **Customer and Personal Service:** Knowledge of principles and processes for providing customer and personal services. This includes customer needs assessment, meeting quality standards for services, and evaluation of customer satisfaction. **Economics and Accounting:** Knowledge of economic and accounting principles and practices, the financial markets, banking, and the analysis and reporting of financial data. **Communications and Media:** Knowledge of media production, communication, and dissemination techniques and methods. This includes alternative ways to inform and entertain via written, oral, and visual media. **English Language:** Knowledge of the structure and content of the English language, including the meaning and spelling of words, rules of composition, and grammar. **Administration and Management:** Knowledge of business and management principles involved in strategic planning, resource allocation, human resources modeling, leadership technique, production methods, and coordination of people and resources.

Agricultural Crop Farm Managers

- Education/Training Required: Work experience in a related occupation
- Annual Earnings: $50,700
- Growth: 5.1%
- Annual Job Openings: 25,000
- Self-Employed: 0.9%
- Part-Time: 9.2%

Direct and coordinate, through subordinate supervisory personnel, activities of workers engaged in agricultural crop production for corporations, cooperatives, or other owners. Directs and coordinates worker activities, such as planting, irrigation, chemical application, harvesting, grading, payroll, and record-keeping. Contracts with farmers or independent owners for raising of crops or for management of crop production. Coordinates growing activities with those of engineering, equipment maintenance, packing houses, and other related departments. Analyzes market conditions to determine acreage allocations. Confers with purchasers and arranges for sale of crops. Records information such as production, farm management practices, and parent stock and prepares financial and operational reports. Determines procedural changes in drying, grading, storage, and shipment for greater efficiency and accuracy. Analyzes soil to determine type and quantity of fertilizer required for maximum production. Inspects equipment to ensure proper functioning. Inspects orchards and fields to determine maturity dates of crops or to estimate potential crop damage from weather. Plans and directs development and production of hybrid plant varieties with high yield or disease- and insect-resistant characteristics. Purchases machinery, equipment, and supplies, such as tractors, seed, fertilizer, and chemicals. Hires, discharges, transfers, and promotes workers; enforces safety regulations; and interprets policies. Negotiates with bank officials to obtain credit from bank. Evaluates financial statements and makes budget proposals. **SKILLS—Management of Financial Resources:** Determining how money will be spent to get the work done and accounting for these expenditures. **Management of Personnel Resources:** Motivating, developing, and directing people as they work, identifying the best people for the job. **Negotiation:** Bringing others together and trying to reconcile differences. **Management of Material Resources:** Obtaining and seeing to the appropriate use of equipment, facilities, and materials needed to do certain work. **Coordination:** Adjusting actions in relation to others' actions. **Systems Analysis:** Determining how a system should work and how changes in conditions, operations, and the environment will affect outcomes. **Writing:** Communicating effectively in writing as appropriate for the needs of the audience. **Speaking:** Talking to others to convey information effectively. **Systems Evaluation:** Identifying measures or indicators of system performance and the actions needed to improve or correct performance relative to the goals of the system. **GOE—Interest Area:** 01. Agriculture and Natural Resources. **Work Group:** 01.01. Managerial Work in Agriculture and Natural Resources. **Other Jobs in This Work Group:** Farmers and Ranchers; First-Line Supervisors and Manager/Supervisors—Agricultural Crop Workers; First-Line Supervisors and Manager/Supervisors—Animal Husbandry Workers; First-Line Supervisors and Manager/Supervisors—Extractive Workers; First-Line Supervisors and Manager/Supervisors—Fishery Workers; First-Line Supervisors and Manager/Supervisors—Horticultural Workers; First-Line Supervisors and Manager/Supervisors—Landscaping Workers; First-Line Supervisors and Manager/Supervisors—Logging Workers; Fish Hatchery Managers; Lawn Service Managers; Nursery and Greenhouse Managers; Park Naturalists; Purchasing Agents and Buyers, Farm Products. **PERSONALITY TYPE:** Enterprising. Enterprising occupations frequently involve starting up and carrying out projects. These occupations can involve leading people and making many decisions. They sometimes require risk taking and often deal with business.

EDUCATION/TRAINING PROGRAM(S)— Agribusiness/Agricultural Business Operations; Agricultural Business and Management, General; Agricultural Business and Management, Other; Agricultural Production Operations, General; Agricultural Production Operations, Other; Agronomy and Crop Science; Crop Production; Dairy Husbandry and Production; Farm/Farm and Ranch Management; Greenhouse Operations and Management; Horticultural

Science; Ornamental Horticulture; Plant Nursery Operations and Management; Plant Protection and Integrated Pest Management; Plant Sciences, General; Range Science and Management. **RELATED KNOWLEDGE/COURSES—Food Production:** Knowledge of techniques and equipment for planting, growing, and harvesting food products (both plant and animal) for consumption, including storage/handling techniques. **Economics and Accounting:** Knowledge of economic and accounting principles and practices, the financial markets, banking, and the analysis and reporting of financial data. **Administration and Management:** Knowledge of business and management principles involved in strategic planning, resource allocation, human resources modeling, leadership technique, production methods, and coordination of people and resources. **Production and Processing:** Knowledge of raw materials, production processes, quality control, costs, and other techniques for maximizing the effective manufacture and distribution of goods. **Personnel and Human Resources:** Knowledge of principles and procedures for personnel recruitment, selection, training, compensation and benefits, labor relations and negotiation, and personnel information systems. **Mathematics:** Knowledge of arithmetic, algebra, geometry, calculus, and statistics and their applications.

Air Traffic Controllers

- ◎ Education/Training Required: Long-term on-the-job training
- ◎ Annual Earnings: $102,030
- ◎ Growth: 12.6%
- ◎ Annual Job Openings: 2,000
- ◎ Self-Employed: 0%
- ◎ Part-Time: 3.6%

Control air traffic on and within vicinity of airport and movement of air traffic between altitude sectors and control centers according to established procedures and policies. Authorize, regulate, and control commercial airline flights according to government or company regulations to expedite and ensure flight safety. Monitor aircraft within a specific airspace, using radar, computer equipment, and visual references.

Monitor and direct the movement of aircraft within an assigned airspace and on the ground at airports to minimize delays and maximize safety. Organize flight plans and traffic management plans to prepare for planes about to enter assigned airspace. Provide flight path changes or directions to emergency landing fields for pilots traveling in bad weather or in emergency situations. Compile information about flights from flight plans, pilot reports, radar, and observations. Relay to control centers such air traffic information as courses, altitudes, and expected arrival times. Transfer control of departing flights to traffic control centers and accept control of arriving flights. Complete daily activity reports and keep records of messages from aircraft. Initiate and coordinate searches for missing aircraft. Inspect, adjust, and control radio equipment and airport lights. Review records and reports for clarity and completeness and maintain records and reports as required under federal law. Alert airport emergency services in cases of emergency and when aircraft are experiencing difficulties. Analyze factors such as weather reports, fuel requirements, and maps in order to determine air routes. Check conditions and traffic at different altitudes in response to pilots' requests for altitude changes. Conduct pre-flight briefings on weather conditions, suggested routes, altitudes, indications of turbulence, and other flight safety information. Contact pilots by radio to provide meteorological, navigational, and other information. Determine the timing and procedures for flight vector changes. Direct ground traffic, including taxiing aircraft, maintenance and baggage vehicles, and airport workers. Direct pilots to runways when space is available or direct them to maintain a traffic pattern until there is space for them to land. Inform pilots about nearby planes as well as potentially hazardous conditions such as weather, speed and direction of wind, and visibility problems. Issue landing and take-off authorizations and instructions. **SKILLS—Operation and Control:** Controlling operations of equipment or systems. **Operation Monitoring:** Watching gauges, dials, or other indicators to make sure a machine is working properly. **Active Listening:** Giving full attention to what other people are saying, taking time to understand the points being made, asking questions as appropriate, and not interrupting at inappropriate times. **Coordination:** Adjusting actions in relation to others' actions. **Critical Thinking:** Using logic and reasoning to identify the strengths and weaknesses of alternative solutions, conclusions, or approaches to problems. **Systems Analysis:** Determining how a system should work and how changes in conditions, operations, and the environment will affect outcomes. **Active Learning:** Understanding the implications of new information for both current and future problem-solving and decision-making. **Troubleshooting:** Determining causes of operating errors and deciding what to do about them. **Judgment and Decision Making:** Considering the relative costs and benefits of potential actions to choose the most appropriate one. **GOE— Interest Area:** 03. Arts and Communication. **Work Group:** 03.10. Communications Technology. **Other Jobs in This Work Group:** Airfield Operations Specialists; Central Office Operators; Directory Assistance Operators; Dispatchers, Except Police, Fire, and Ambulance; Police, Fire, and Ambulance Dispatchers. **PERSONALITY TYPE:** Conventional. Conventional occupations frequently involve following set procedures and routines. These occupations can include working with data and details more than with ideas. Usually there is a clear line of authority to follow.

EDUCATION/TRAINING PROGRAM(S)—Air Traffic Controller. **RELATED KNOWLEDGE/ COURSES—Transportation:** Knowledge of principles and methods for moving people or goods by air, rail, sea, or road, including the relative costs and benefits. **Physics:** Knowledge and prediction of physical principles and laws and their interrelationships and applications to understanding fluid, material, and atmospheric dynamics and mechanical, electrical, atomic, and subatomic structures and processes. **Telecommunications:** Knowledge of transmission, broadcasting, switching, control, and operation of telecommunications systems. **Geography:** Knowledge of principles and methods for describing the features of land, sea, and air masses, including their physical characteristics; locations; interrelationships; and distribution of plant, animal, and human life. **Computers and Electronics:** Knowledge of circuit boards, processors, chips, electronic equipment, and computer hardware and software, including applications and programming. **Engineering and Technology:** Knowledge of the practical application of engineering science and technology. This includes applying principles, tech-

niques, procedures, and equipment to the design and production of various goods and services.

Aircraft Body and Bonded Structure Repairers

- ◉ Education/Training Required: Postsecondary vocational training
- ◉ Annual Earnings: $45,290
- ◉ Growth: 11.0%
- ◉ Annual Job Openings: 12,000
- ◉ Self-Employed: 1.0%
- ◉ Part-Time: 1.2%

Repair body or structure of aircraft according to specifications. Locates and marks dimension and reference lines on defective or replacement part, using templates, scribes, compass, and steel rule. Trims and shapes replacement section to specified size and fits and secures section in place, using adhesives, hand tools, and power tools. Cleans, strips, primes, and sands structural surfaces and materials prior to bonding. Spreads plastic film over area to be repaired to prevent damage to surrounding area. Cures bonded structure, using portable or stationary curing equipment. Reinstalls repaired or replacement parts for subsequent riveting or welding, using clamps and wrenches. Repairs or fabricates defective section or part, using metal fabricating machines, saws, brakes, shears, and grinders. Reads work orders, blueprints, and specifications or examines sample or damaged part or structure to determine repair or fabrication procedures and sequence of operations. Communicates with other workers to fit and align heavy parts or expedite processing of repair parts. Removes or cuts out defective part or drills holes to gain access to internal defect or damage, using drill and punch. **SKILLS—Installation:** Installing equipment, machines, wiring, or programs to meet specifications. **Repairing:** Repairing machines or systems by using the needed tools. **Equipment Maintenance:** Performing routine maintenance on equipment and determining when and what kind of maintenance is needed. **Equipment Selection:** Determining the kind of tools and equipment needed to do a job. **Mathematics:** Using mathematics to solve problems. **Operation Monitoring:** Watching gauges, dials, or other indicators to make sure a machine is working properly. **Operation and Control:** Controlling operations of equipment or systems. **Troubleshooting:** Determining causes of operating errors and deciding what to do about them. **GOE—Interest Area:** 13. Manufacturing. **Work Group:** 13.14. Vehicle and Facility Mechanical Work. **Other Jobs in This Work Group:** Aircraft Engine Specialists; Aircraft Rigging Assemblers; Aircraft Structure Assemblers, Precision; Aircraft Systems Assemblers, Precision; Airframe-and-Power-Plant Mechanics; Automotive Body and Related Repairers; Automotive Glass Installers and Repairers; Automotive Master Mechanics; Automotive Specialty Technicians; Bus and Truck Mechanics and Diesel Engine Specialists; Farm Equipment Mechanics; Fiberglass Laminators and Fabricators; Mobile Heavy Equipment Mechanics, Except Engines; Motorboat Mechanics; Motorcycle Mechanics; Outdoor Power Equipment and Other Small Engine Mechanics; Rail Car Repairers; Recreational Vehicle Service Technicians; Tire Repairers and Changers. **PERSONALITY TYPE:** Realistic. Realistic occupations frequently involve work activities that include practical, hands-on problems and solutions. These occupations often deal with plants, animals, and real-world materials like wood, tools, and machinery. Many of the occupations require working outside and do not involve a lot of paperwork or working closely with others.

EDUCATION/TRAINING PROGRAM(S)—Agricultural Mechanics and Equipment/Machine Technology; Airframe Mechanics and Aircraft Maintenance Technology/Technician. **RELATED KNOWLEDGE/COURSES—Mechanical Devices:** Knowledge of machines and tools, including their designs, uses, repair, and maintenance. **Building and Construction:** Knowledge of the materials, methods, and tools involved in the construction or repair of houses, buildings, or other structures such as highways and roads. **Design:** Knowledge of design techniques, tools, and principles involved in production of precision technical plans, blueprints, drawings, and models. **Engineering and Technology:** Knowledge of the practical application of engineering science and technology. This includes applying principles, techniques, procedures, and equipment to the design and produc-

tion of various goods and services. **Production and Processing:** Knowledge of raw materials, production processes, quality control, costs, and other techniques for maximizing the effective manufacture and distribution of goods. **Physics:** Knowledge and prediction of physical principles and laws and their interrelationships and applications to understanding fluid, material, and atmospheric dynamics and mechanical, electrical, atomic, and subatomic structures and processes.

Aircraft Engine Specialists

◎ Education/Training Required: Postsecondary vocational training
◎ Annual Earnings: $45,290
◎ Growth: 11.0%
◎ Annual Job Openings: 12,000
◎ Self-Employed: 1.0%
◎ Part-Time: 1.2%

Repair and maintain the operating condition of aircraft engines. Includes helicopter engine mechanics. Replaces or repairs worn, defective, or damaged components, using hand tools, gauges, and testing equipment. Tests engine operation, using test equipment such as ignition analyzer, compression checker, distributor timer, and ammeter, to identify malfunction. Listens to operating engine to detect and diagnose malfunctions, such as sticking or burned valves. Reassembles engine and installs engine in aircraft. Disassembles and inspects engine parts, such as turbine blades and cylinders, for wear, warping, cracks, and leaks. Removes engine from aircraft, using hoist or forklift truck. Services, repairs, and rebuilds aircraft structures, such as wings, fuselage, rigging, and surface and hydraulic controls, using hand or power tools and equipment. Adjusts, repairs, or replaces electrical wiring system and aircraft accessories. Reads and interprets manufacturers' maintenance manuals, service bulletins, and other specifications to determine feasibility and methods of repair. Services and maintains aircraft and related apparatus by performing activities such as flushing crankcase, cleaning screens, and lubricating moving parts. **SKILLS—Equipment Maintenance:** Performing routine maintenance on equipment and determining when and what kind of maintenance is needed. **Repairing:** Repairing machines or systems by using the needed tools. **Installation:** Installing equipment, machines, wiring, or programs to meet specifications. **Troubleshooting:** Determining causes of operating errors and deciding what to do about them. **Operation Monitoring:** Watching gauges, dials, or other indicators to make sure a machine is working properly. **Quality Control Analysis:** Conducting tests and inspections of products, services, or processes to evaluate quality or performance. **Judgment and Decision Making:** Considering the relative costs and benefits of potential actions to choose the most appropriate one. **Systems Analysis:** Determining how a system should work and how changes in conditions, operations, and the environment will affect outcomes. **GOE—Interest Area:** 13. Manufacturing. **Work Group:** 13.14. Vehicle and Facility Mechanical Work. **Other Jobs in This Work Group:** Aircraft Body and Bonded Structure Repairers; Aircraft Rigging Assemblers; Aircraft Structure Assemblers, Precision; Aircraft Systems Assemblers, Precision; Airframe-and-Power-Plant Mechanics; Automotive Body and Related Repairers; Automotive Glass Installers and Repairers; Automotive Master Mechanics; Automotive Specialty Technicians; Bus and Truck Mechanics and Diesel Engine Specialists; Farm Equipment Mechanics; Fiberglass Laminators and Fabricators; Mobile Heavy Equipment Mechanics, Except Engines; Motorboat Mechanics; Motorcycle Mechanics; Outdoor Power Equipment and Other Small Engine Mechanics; Rail Car Repairers; Recreational Vehicle Service Technicians; Tire Repairers and Changers. **PERSONALITY TYPE:** Realistic. Realistic occupations frequently involve work activities that include practical, hands-on problems and solutions. These occupations often deal with plants, animals, and real-world materials like wood, tools, and machinery. Many of the occupations require working outside and do not involve a lot of paperwork or working closely with others.

EDUCATION/TRAINING PROGRAM(S)—Agricultural Mechanics and Equipment/Machine Technology; Aircraft Powerplant Technology/Technician. **RELATED KNOWLEDGE/COURSES—Mechanical Devices:** Knowledge of machines and tools, including their designs, uses, repair, and maintenance. **Engineering and Technology:** Knowledge of the prac-

tical application of engineering science and technology. This includes applying principles, techniques, procedures, and equipment to the design and production of various goods and services. **Physics:** Knowledge and prediction of physical principles and laws and their interrelationships and applications to understanding fluid, material, and atmospheric dynamics and mechanical, electrical, atomic, and subatomic structures and processes. **Building and Construction:** Knowledge of the materials, methods, and tools involved in the construction or repair of houses, buildings, or other structures such as highways and roads. **Design:** Knowledge of design techniques, tools, and principles involved in production of precision technical plans, blueprints, drawings, and models. **Mathematics:** Knowledge of arithmetic, algebra, geometry, calculus, and statistics and their applications.

Airframe-and-Power-Plant Mechanics

◎ Education/Training Required: Postsecondary vocational training
◎ Annual Earnings: $45,290
◎ Growth: 11.0%
◎ Annual Job Openings: 12,000
◎ Self-Employed: 1.0%
◎ Part-Time: 1.2%

Inspect, test, repair, maintain, and service aircraft. Adjusts, aligns, and calibrates aircraft systems, using hand tools, gauges, and test equipment. Examines and inspects engines or other components for cracks, breaks, or leaks. Disassembles and inspects parts for wear, warping, or other defects. Assembles and installs electrical, plumbing, mechanical, hydraulic, and structural components and accessories, using hand tools and power tools. Services and maintains aircraft systems by performing tasks such as flushing crankcase, cleaning screens, greasing moving parts, and checking brakes. Repairs, replaces, and rebuilds aircraft structures, functional components, and parts, such as wings and fuselage, rigging, and hydraulic units. Tests engine and system operations, using testing equipment, and listens to engine sounds to detect and diagnose malfunctions. Removes engine from aircraft or installs engine, using hoist or forklift truck. Modifies aircraft structures, space vehicles, systems, or components, following drawings, engineering orders, and technical publications. Reads and interprets aircraft maintenance manuals and specifications to determine feasibility and method of repairing or replacing malfunctioning or damaged components. **SKILLS— Equipment Maintenance:** Performing routine maintenance on equipment and determining when and what kind of maintenance is needed. **Installation:** Installing equipment, machines, wiring, or programs to meet specifications. **Repairing:** Repairing machines or systems by using the needed tools. **Troubleshooting:** Determining causes of operating errors and deciding what to do about them. **Operation Monitoring:** Watching gauges, dials, or other indicators to make sure a machine is working properly. **Quality Control Analysis:** Conducting tests and inspections of products, services, or processes to evaluate quality or performance. **Science:** Using scientific rules and methods to solve problems. **Equipment Selection:** Determining the kind of tools and equipment needed to do a job. **GOE—Interest Area:** 13. Manufacturing. **Work Group:** 13.14. Vehicle and Facility Mechanical Work. **Other Jobs in This Work Group:** Aircraft Body and Bonded Structure Repairers; Aircraft Engine Specialists; Aircraft Rigging Assemblers; Aircraft Structure Assemblers, Precision; Aircraft Systems Assemblers, Precision; Automotive Body and Related Repairers; Automotive Glass Installers and Repairers; Automotive Master Mechanics; Automotive Specialty Technicians; Bus and Truck Mechanics and Diesel Engine Specialists; Farm Equipment Mechanics; Fiberglass Laminators and Fabricators; Mobile Heavy Equipment Mechanics, Except Engines; Motorboat Mechanics; Motorcycle Mechanics; Outdoor Power Equipment and Other Small Engine Mechanics; Rail Car Repairers; Recreational Vehicle Service Technicians; Tire Repairers and Changers. **PERSONALITY TYPE:** Realistic. Realistic occupations frequently involve work activities that include practical, hands-on problems and solutions. These occupations often deal with plants, animals, and real-world materials like wood, tools, and machinery. Many of the occupations require working outside and do not involve a lot of paperwork or working closely with others.

EDUCATION/TRAINING PROGRAM(S)—Agricultural Mechanics and Equipment/Machine Technology; Aircraft Powerplant Technology/Technician; Airframe Mechanics and Aircraft Maintenance Technology/Technician. **RELATED KNOWLEDGE/ COURSES—Mechanical Devices:** Knowledge of machines and tools, including their designs, uses, repair, and maintenance. **Engineering and Technology:** Knowledge of the practical application of engineering science and technology. This includes applying principles, techniques, procedures, and equipment to the design and production of various goods and services. **Building and Construction:** Knowledge of the materials, methods, and tools involved in the construction or repair of houses, buildings, or other structures such as highways and roads. **Design:** Knowledge of design techniques, tools, and principles involved in production of precision technical plans, blueprints, drawings, and models. **Physics:** Knowledge and prediction of physical principles and laws and their interrelationships and applications to understanding fluid, material, and atmospheric dynamics and mechanical, electrical, atomic, and subatomic structures and processes. **Public Safety and Security:** Knowledge of relevant equipment, policies, procedures, and strategies to promote effective local, state, or national security operations for the protection of people, data, property, and institutions.

Amusement and Recreation Attendants

- Education/Training Required: Short-term on-the-job training
- Annual Earnings: $15,550
- Growth: 27.8%
- Annual Job Openings: 66,000
- Self-Employed: 0.4%
- Part-Time: 51.9%

Perform variety of attending duties at amusement or recreation facility. May schedule use of recreation facilities, maintain and provide equipment to participants of sporting events or recreational pursuits, or operate amusement concessions and rides. Provide

information about facilities, entertainment options, and rules and regulations. Record details of attendance, sales, receipts, reservations, and repair activities. Monitor activities to ensure adherence to rules and safety procedures and arrange for the removal of unruly patrons. Sell tickets and collect fees from customers. Keep informed of shut-down and emergency evacuation procedures. Clean sporting equipment, vehicles, rides, booths, facilities, and grounds. Operate machines to clean, smooth, and prepare the ice surfaces of rinks for activities such as skating, hockey, and curling. Announce and describe amusement park attractions to patrons in order to entice customers to games and other entertainment. Fasten safety devices for patrons or provide them with directions for fastening devices. Inspect equipment to detect wear and damage and perform minor repairs, adjustments, and maintenance tasks such as oiling parts. Operate, drive, or explain the use of mechanical riding devices or other automatic equipment in amusement parks, carnivals, or recreation areas. Rent, sell, or issue sporting equipment and supplies such as bowling shoes, golf balls, swimming suits, and beach chairs. Verify, collect, or punch tickets before admitting patrons to venues such as amusement parks and rides. Tend amusement booths in parks, carnivals, or stadiums, performing duties such as conducting games, photographing patrons, and awarding prizes. Direct patrons to rides, seats, or attractions. Provide assistance to patrons entering or exiting amusement rides, boats, or ski lifts or mounting or dismounting animals. Sell and serve refreshments to customers. Schedule the use of recreation facilities such as golf courses, tennis courts, bowling alleys, and softball diamonds. **SKILLS—Learning Strategies:** Selecting and using training/instructional methods and procedures appropriate for the situation when learning or teaching new things. **Social Perceptiveness:** Being aware of others' reactions and understanding why they react as they do. **Service Orientation:** Actively looking for ways to help people. **Active Listening:** Giving full attention to what other people are saying, taking time to understand the points being made, asking questions as appropriate, and not interrupting at inappropriate times. **Instructing:** Teaching others how to do something. **Reading Comprehension:** Understanding written sentences and paragraphs in work-related documents. **Speaking:** Talking to others to convey information effectively. **Critical Thinking:** Using logic and reasoning to identify the strengths and weaknesses of alternative solutions, conclusions, or approaches to problems. **GOE—Interest Area:** 09. Hospitality, Tourism, and Recreation. **Work Group:** 09.02. Recreational Services. **Other Jobs in This Work Group:** Gaming and Sports Book Writers and Runners; Gaming Dealers; Locker Room, Coatroom, and Dressing Room Attendants; Motion Picture Projectionists; Recreation Workers; Slot Key Persons; Ushers, Lobby Attendants, and Ticket Takers. **PERSONALITY TYPE:** Realistic. Realistic occupations frequently involve work activities that include practical, hands-on problems and solutions. These occupations often deal with plants, animals, and real-world materials like wood, tools, and machinery. Many of the occupations require working outside and do not involve a lot of paperwork or working closely with others.

EDUCATION/TRAINING PROGRAM(S)—No data available. **RELATED KNOWLEDGE/COURSES—Customer and Personal Service:** Knowledge of principles and processes for providing customer and personal services. This includes customer needs assessment, meeting quality standards for services, and evaluation of customer satisfaction. **Public Safety and Security:** Knowledge of relevant equipment, policies, procedures, and strategies to promote effective local, state, or national security operations for the protection of people, data, property, and institutions. **Medicine and Dentistry:** Knowledge of the information and techniques needed to diagnose and treat human injuries, diseases, and deformities. This includes symptoms, treatment alternatives, drug properties and interactions, and preventive health-care measures. **Sales and Marketing:** Knowledge of principles and methods for showing, promoting, and selling products or services. This includes marketing strategy and tactics, product demonstrations, sales techniques, and sales control systems. **Sociology and Anthropology:** Knowledge of group behavior and dynamics, societal trends and influences, human migrations, ethnicity, and cultures and their history and origins. **History and Archeology:** Knowledge of historical events and their causes, indicators, and effects on civilizations and cultures.

Appraisers, Real Estate

- Education/Training Required: Postsecondary vocational training
- Annual Earnings: $43,390
- Growth: 17.6%
- Annual Job Openings: 11,000
- Self-Employed: 34.8%
- Part-Time: 8.9%

Appraise real property to determine its value for purchase, sales, investment, mortgage, or loan purposes. Compute final estimation of property values, taking into account such factors as depreciation, replacement costs, value comparisons of similar properties, and income potential. Draw land diagrams that will be used in appraisal reports to support findings. Estimate building replacement costs, using building valuation manuals and professional cost estimators. Evaluate land and neighborhoods where properties are situated, considering locations and trends or impending changes that could influence future values. Examine the type and location of nearby services such as shopping centers, schools, parks, and other neighborhood features in order to evaluate their impact on property values. Inspect properties to evaluate construction, condition, special features, and functional design and to take property measurements. Obtain county land values and sales information about nearby properties in order to aid in establishment of property values. Photograph interiors and exteriors of properties in order to assist in estimating property value, substantiate findings, and complete appraisal reports. Prepare written reports that estimate property values, outline methods by which the estimations were made, and meet appraisal standards. Search public records for transactions such as sales, leases, and assessments. Verify legal descriptions of properties by comparing them to county records. Check building codes and zoning bylaws in order to determine any effects on the properties being appraised. Examine income records and operating costs of income properties. Interview persons familiar with properties and immediate surroundings, such as contractors, homeowners, and real estate agents, in order to obtain pertinent information. Testify in court as to the value of a piece of real estate property. **SKILLS—Writing:** Communicating effectively in writing as appropriate for the needs of the audience. **Mathematics:** Using mathematics to solve problems. **Management of Personnel Resources:** Motivating, developing, and directing people as they work, identifying the best people for the job. **Systems Analysis:** Determining how a system should work and how changes in conditions, operations, and the environment will affect outcomes. **Speaking:** Talking to others to convey information effectively. **Reading Comprehension:** Understanding written sentences and paragraphs in work-related documents. **Time Management:** Managing one's own time and the time of others. **Active Listening:** Giving full attention to what other people are saying, taking time to understand the points being made, asking questions as appropriate, and not interrupting at inappropriate times. **Management of Financial Resources:** Determining how money will be spent to get the work done and accounting for these expenditures. **GOE—Interest Area:** 06. Finance and Insurance. **Work Group:** 06.02. Finance/Insurance Investigation and Analysis. **Other Jobs in This Work Group:** Assessors; Claims Examiners, Property and Casualty Insurance; Cost Estimators; Credit Analysts; Financial Analysts; Insurance Adjusters, Examiners, and Investigators; Insurance Appraisers, Auto Damage; Insurance Underwriters; Loan Counselors; Loan Officers; Market Research Analysts; Survey Researchers. **PERSONALITY TYPE:** Enterprising. Enterprising occupations frequently involve starting up and carrying out projects. These occupations can involve leading people and making many decisions. They sometimes require risk taking and often deal with business.

EDUCATION/TRAINING PROGRAM(S)—Real Estate. **RELATED KNOWLEDGE/COURSES—Building and Construction:** Knowledge of the materials, methods, and tools involved in the construction or repair of houses, buildings, or other structures such as highways and roads. **Personnel and Human Resources:** Knowledge of principles and procedures for personnel recruitment, selection, training, compensation and benefits, labor relations and negotiation, and personnel information systems. **Economics and Accounting:** Knowledge of economic and accounting principles and practices, the financial markets, banking, and the analysis and reporting of financial data. **Law and Government:** Knowledge of laws, legal codes, court procedures, precedents, government regulations, executive orders, agency rules, and the democratic political process. **Geography:** Knowledge of principles and methods for describing the features of land, sea, and air masses, including their physical characteristics; locations; interrelationships; and distribution of plant, animal, and human life. **Administration and Management:** Knowledge of business and management principles involved in strategic planning, resource allocation, human resources modeling, leadership technique, production methods, and coordination of people and resources. **Communications and Media:** Knowledge of media production, communication, and dissemination techniques and methods. This includes alternative ways to inform and entertain via written, oral, and visual media.

Architectural Drafters

- Education/Training Required: Associate degree
- Annual Earnings: $39,190
- Growth: 4.2%
- Annual Job Openings: 14,000
- Self-Employed: 3.7%
- Part-Time: 5.1%

Prepare detailed drawings of architectural designs and plans for buildings and structures according to specifications provided by architect. Analyze building codes, bylaws, space and site requirements, and other technical documents and reports to determine their effect on architectural designs. Operate computer-aided drafting equipment or conventional drafting station to produce designs, working drawings, charts, forms, and records. Coordinate structural, electrical, and mechanical designs and determine a method of presentation in order to graphically represent building plans. Obtain and assemble data to complete architectural designs, visiting job sites to compile measurements as necessary. Draw rough and detailed scale plans for foundations, buildings, and structures based on preliminary concepts, sketches, engineering calculations, specification sheets, and other data. Lay out and plan interior room arrangements for commercial buildings, using computer-assisted drafting (CAD) equip-

ment and software. Supervise, coordinate, and inspect the work of draftspersons, technicians, and technologists on construction projects. Represent architect on construction site, ensuring builder compliance with design specifications and advising on design corrections under architect's supervision. Check dimensions of materials to be used and assign numbers to lists of materials. Determine procedures and instructions to be followed according to design specifications and quantity of required materials. Analyze technical implications of architect's design concept, calculating weights, volumes, and stress factors. Create freehand drawings and lettering to accompany drawings. Prepare colored drawings of landscape and interior designs for presentation to client. Reproduce drawings on copy machines or trace copies of plans and drawings, using transparent paper or cloth, ink, pencil, and standard drafting instruments. Prepare cost estimates, contracts, bidding documents, and technical reports for specific projects under an architect's supervision. Calculate heat loss and gain of buildings and structures to determine required equipment specifications, following standard procedures. **SKILLS—Coordination:** Adjusting actions in relation to others' actions. **Operations Analysis:** Analyzing needs and product requirements to create a design. **Active Learning:** Understanding the implications of new information for both current and future problem-solving and decision-making. **Technology Design:** Generating or adapting equipment and technology to serve user needs. **Persuasion:** Persuading others to change their minds or behavior. **Complex Problem Solving:** Identifying complex problems and reviewing related information to develop and evaluate options and implement solutions. **Mathematics:** Using mathematics to solve problems. **Critical Thinking:** Using logic and reasoning to identify the strengths and weaknesses of alternative solutions, conclusions, or approaches to problems. **Service Orientation:** Actively looking for ways to help people. **GOE—Interest Area:** 02. Architecture and Construction. **Work Group:** 02.03. Architecture/Construction Engineering Technologies. **Other Jobs in This Work Group:** Civil Drafters; Construction and Building Inspectors; Electrical Drafters; Surveyors. **PERSONALITY TYPE:** Realistic. Realistic occupations frequently involve work activities that include practical, hands-on problems and solutions. These occupations often deal with plants, animals, and real-world materials like wood, tools, and machinery. Many of the occupations require working outside and do not involve a lot of paperwork or working closely with others.

EDUCATION/TRAINING PROGRAM(S)— Architectural Drafting and Architectural CAD/CADD; Architectural Technology/Technician; CAD/CADD Drafting and/or Design Technology/Technician; Civil Drafting and Civil Engineering CAD/CADD; Drafting and Design Technology/Technician, General. **RELATED KNOWLEDGE/COURSES—Design:** Knowledge of design techniques, tools, and principles involved in production of precision technical plans, blueprints, drawings, and models. **Building and Construction:** Knowledge of the materials, methods, and tools involved in the construction or repair of houses, buildings, or other structures such as highways and roads. **Computers and Electronics:** Knowledge of circuit boards, processors, chips, electronic equipment, and computer hardware and software, including applications and programming. **Engineering and Technology:** Knowledge of the practical application of engineering science and technology. This includes applying principles, techniques, procedures, and equipment to the design and production of various goods and services. **Mathematics:** Knowledge of arithmetic, algebra, geometry, calculus, and statistics and their applications. **Public Safety and Security:** Knowledge of relevant equipment, policies, procedures, and strategies to promote effective local, state, or national security operations for the protection of people, data, property, and institutions.

Assessors

- ◎ Education/Training Required: Postsecondary vocational training
- ◎ Annual Earnings: $43,390
- ◎ Growth: 17.6%
- ◎ Annual Job Openings: 11,000
- ◎ Self-Employed: 34.8%
- ◎ Part-Time: 8.9%

Appraise real and personal property to determine its fair value. May assess taxes in accordance with pre-scribed schedules. Determine taxability and value of properties, using methods such as field inspection, structural measurement, calculation, sales analysis, market trend studies, and income and expense analysis. Inspect new construction and major improvements to existing structures in order to determine values. Explain assessed values to property owners and defend appealed assessments at public hearings. Inspect properties, considering factors such as market value, location, and building or replacement costs to determine appraisal value. Prepare and maintain current data on each parcel assessed, including maps of boundaries, inventories of land and structures, property characteristics, and any applicable exemptions. Identify the ownership of each piece of taxable property. Conduct regular reviews of property within jurisdictions in order to determine changes in property due to construction or demolition. Complete and maintain assessment rolls that show the assessed values and status of all property in a municipality. Issue notices of assessments and taxes. Review information about transfers of property to ensure its accuracy, checking basic information on buyers, sellers, and sales prices and making corrections as necessary. Maintain familiarity with aspects of local real estate markets. Analyze trends in sales prices, construction costs, and rents in order to assess property values and/or determine the accuracy of assessments. Approve applications for property tax exemptions or deductions. Establish uniform and equitable systems for assessing all classes and kinds of property. Write and submit appraisal and tax reports for public record. Serve on assessment review boards. Hire staff members. Provide sales analyses to be used for equalization of school aid. Calculate tax bills for properties by multiplying assessed values by jurisdiction tax rates. **SKILLS—Social Perceptiveness:** Being aware of others' reactions and understanding why they react as they do. **Mathematics:** Using mathematics to solve problems. **Negotiation:** Bringing others together and trying to reconcile differences. **Persuasion:** Persuading others to change their minds or behavior. **Active Listening:** Giving full attention to what other people are saying, taking time to understand the points being made, asking questions as appropriate, and not interrupting at inappropriate times. **Speaking:** Talking to others to convey information effectively. **Service Orientation:** Actively looking for ways to help people. **Instructing:** Teaching others how to do something. **Systems Analysis:** Determining how a system should work and how changes in conditions, operations, and the environment will affect outcomes. **GOE—Interest Area:** 06. Finance and Insurance. **Work Group:** 06.02. Finance/Insurance Investigation and Analysis. **Other Jobs in This Work Group:** Appraisers, Real Estate; Claims Examiners, Property and Casualty Insurance; Cost Estimators; Credit Analysts; Financial Analysts; Insurance Adjusters, Examiners, and Investigators; Insurance Appraisers, Auto Damage; Insurance Underwriters; Loan Counselors; Loan Officers; Market Research Analysts; Survey Researchers. **PERSONALITY TYPE:** Conventional. Conventional occupations frequently involve following set procedures and routines. These occupations can include working with data and details more than with ideas. Usually there is a clear line of authority to follow.

EDUCATION/TRAINING PROGRAM(S)—Real Estate. **RELATED KNOWLEDGE/COURSES**—**Customer and Personal Service:** Knowledge of principles and processes for providing customer and personal services. This includes customer needs assessment, meeting quality standards for services, and evaluation of customer satisfaction. **Building and Construction:** Knowledge of the materials, methods, and tools involved in the construction or repair of houses, buildings, or other structures such as highways and roads. **Clerical Practices:** Knowledge of administrative and clerical procedures and systems such as word processing, managing files and records, stenography and transcription, designing forms, and other office procedures and terminology. **Law and Government:** Knowledge of laws, legal codes, court procedures, precedents, government regulations, executive orders, agency rules, and the democratic political process. **Mathematics:** Knowledge of arithmetic, algebra, geometry, calculus, and statistics and their applications. **Computers and Electronics:** Knowledge of circuit boards, processors, chips, electronic equipment, and computer hardware and software, including applications and programming.

Athletes and Sports Competitors

- Education/Training Required: Long-term on-the-job training
- Annual Earnings: $48,310
- Growth: 19.2%
- Annual Job Openings: 3,000
- Self-Employed: 31.5%
- Part-Time: 36.3%

Compete in athletic events. Assess performance following athletic competition, identifying strengths and weaknesses and making adjustments to improve future performance. Attend scheduled practice and training sessions. Exercise and practice under the direction of athletic trainers or professional coaches in order to develop skills, improve physical condition, and prepare for competitions. Maintain optimum physical fitness levels by training regularly, following nutrition plans, and consulting with health professionals. Participate in athletic events and competitive sports according to established rules and regulations. Receive instructions from coaches and other sports staff prior to events and discuss their performance afterwards. Lead teams by serving as captains. Maintain equipment used in a particular sport. Represent teams or professional sports clubs, performing such activities as meeting with members of the media, making speeches, or participating in charity events. **SKILLS—Monitoring:** Monitoring or assessing your performance or that of other individuals or organizations to make improvements or take corrective action. **Coordination:** Adjusting actions in relation to others' actions. **Social Perceptiveness:** Being aware of others' reactions and understanding why they react as they do. **GOE—Interest Area:** 09. Hospitality, Tourism, and Recreation. **Work Group:** 09.06. Sports. **Other Jobs in This Work Group:** Coaches and Scouts; Umpires, Referees, and Other Sports Officials. **PERSONALITY TYPE:** Enterprising. Enterprising occupations frequently involve starting up and carrying out projects. These occupations can involve leading people and making many decisions. They sometimes require risk taking and often deal with business.

EDUCATION/TRAINING PROGRAM(S)— Health and Physical Education, General. **RELATED KNOWLEDGE/COURSES—Biology:** Knowledge of plant and animal organisms and their tissues, cells, functions, interdependencies, and interactions with each other and the environment. **Medicine and Dentistry:** Knowledge of the information and techniques needed to diagnose and treat human injuries, diseases, and deformities. This includes symptoms, treatment alternatives, drug properties and interactions, and preventive health-care measures. **Communications and Media:** Knowledge of media production, communication, and dissemination techniques and methods. This includes alternative ways to inform and entertain via written, oral, and visual media.

Audio and Video Equipment Technicians

- ◎ Education/Training Required: Long-term on-the-job training
- ◎ Annual Earnings: $32,570
- ◎ Growth: 26.7%
- ◎ Annual Job Openings: 5,000
- ◎ Self-Employed: 9.1%
- ◎ Part-Time: 12.5%

Set up or set up and operate audio and video equipment, including microphones, sound speakers, video screens, projectors, video monitors, recording equipment, connecting wires and cables, sound and mixing boards, and related electronic equipment, for concerts, sports events, meetings and conventions, presentations, and news conferences. May also set up and operate associated spotlights and other custom lighting systems. Notify supervisors when major equipment repairs are needed. Monitor incoming and outgoing pictures and sound feeds to ensure quality and notify directors of any possible problems. Mix and regulate sound inputs and feeds or coordinate audio feeds with television pictures. Install, adjust, and operate electronic equipment used to record, edit, and transmit radio and television programs, cable programs, and motion pictures. Design layouts of audio and video equipment and perform upgrades and main-tenance. Perform minor repairs and routine cleaning of audio and video equipment. Diagnose and resolve media system problems in classrooms. Switch sources of video input from one camera or studio to another, from film to live programming, or from network to local programming. Meet with directors and senior members of camera crews to discuss assignments and determine filming sequences, camera movements, and picture composition. Construct and position properties, sets, lighting equipment, and other equipment. Compress, digitize, duplicate, and store audio and video data. Obtain, set up, and load videotapes for scheduled productions or broadcasts. Edit videotapes by erasing and removing portions of programs and adding video and/or sound as required. Direct and coordinate activities of assistants and other personnel during production. Plan and develop pre-production ideas into outlines, scripts, storyboards, and graphics, using own ideas or specifications of assignments. Maintain inventories of audiotapes, videotapes, and related supplies. Determine formats, approaches, content, levels, and mediums to effectively meet objectives within budgetary constraints, utilizing research, knowledge, and training. Record and edit audio material such as movie soundtracks, using audio recording and editing equipment. Inform users of audiotaping and videotaping service policies and procedures. Obtain and preview musical performance programs prior to events in order to become familiar with the order and approximate times of pieces. Produce rough and finished graphics and graphic designs. Locate and secure settings, properties, effects, and other production necessities. **SKILLS—Troubleshooting:** Determining causes of operating errors and deciding what to do about them. **Installation:** Installing equipment, machines, wiring, or programs to meet specifications. **Equipment Maintenance:** Performing routine maintenance on equipment and determining when and what kind of maintenance is needed. **Operation and Control:** Controlling operations of equipment or systems. **Operation Monitoring:** Watching gauges, dials, or other indicators to make sure a machine is working properly. **Service Orientation:** Actively looking for ways to help people. **Repairing:** Repairing machines or systems by using the needed tools. **Technology Design:** Generating or adapting equipment and technology to serve user needs. **GOE—Interest Area:** 03.

Arts and Communication. **Work Group:** 03.09. Media Technology. **Other Jobs in This Work Group:** Broadcast Technicians; Camera Operators, Television, Video, and Motion Picture; Film and Video Editors; Multi-Media Artists and Animators; Photographic Hand Developers; Photographic Reproduction Technicians; Photographic Retouchers and Restorers; Professional Photographers; Radio Operators; Sound Engineering Technicians. **PERSONALITY TYPE:** Conventional. Conventional occupations frequently involve following set procedures and routines. These occupations can include working with data and details more than with ideas. Usually there is a clear line of authority to follow.

EDUCATION/TRAINING PROGRAM(S)—Agricultural Communication/Journalism; Photographic and Film/Video Technology/Technician and Assistant; Recording Arts Technology/Technician. **RELATED KNOWLEDGE/COURSES**—**Computers and Electronics:** Knowledge of circuit boards, processors, chips, electronic equipment, and computer hardware and software, including applications and programming. **Telecommunications:** Knowledge of transmission, broadcasting, switching, control, and operation of telecommunications systems. **Engineering and Technology:** Knowledge of the practical application of engineering science and technology. This includes applying principles, techniques, procedures, and equipment to the design and production of various goods and services. **Communications and Media:** Knowledge of media production, communication, and dissemination techniques and methods. This includes alternative ways to inform and entertain via written, oral, and visual media. **Mechanical Devices:** Knowledge of machines and tools, including their designs, uses, repair, and maintenance. **Design:** Knowledge of design techniques, tools, and principles involved in production of precision technical plans, blueprints, drawings, and models.

Automatic Teller Machine Servicers

- Education/Training Required: Long-term on-the-job training
- Annual Earnings: $35,150
- Growth: 15.1%
- Annual Job Openings: 19,000
- Self-Employed: 12.2%
- Part-Time: 8.2%

Collect deposits and replenish automatic teller machines with cash and supplies. Tests machine functions and balances machine cash account, using electronic keypad. Corrects malfunctions, such as jammed cash or paper, or calls repair personnel when ATM needs repair. Removes money canisters from ATM and replenishes machine supplies, such as deposit envelopes, receipt paper, and cash. Counts cash and items deposited by customers and compares to transactions indicated on transaction tape from ATM. Records transaction information on form or log and notifies designated personnel of discrepancies. **SKILLS**—**Repairing:** Repairing machines or systems by using the needed tools. **Programming:** Writing computer programs for various purposes. **Management of Financial Resources:** Determining how money will be spent to get the work done and accounting for these expenditures. **GOE—Interest Area:** 11. Information Technology. **Work Group:** 11.03. Digital Equipment Repair. **Other Jobs in This Work Group:** Coin, Vending, and Amusement Machine Servicers and Repairers; Data Processing Equipment Repairers; Office Machine and Cash Register Servicers. **PERSONALITY TYPE:** Realistic. Realistic occupations frequently involve work activities that include practical, hands-on problems and solutions. These occupations often deal with plants, animals, and real-world materials like wood, tools, and machinery. Many of the occupations require working outside and do not involve a lot of paperwork or working closely with others.

EDUCATION/TRAINING PROGRAM(S)—Business Machine Repair; Computer Installation and Repair Technology/Technician. **RELATED KNOWL-**

EDGE/COURSES—**Telecommunications:** Knowledge of transmission, broadcasting, switching, control, and operation of telecommunications systems. **Computers and Electronics:** Knowledge of circuit boards, processors, chips, electronic equipment, and computer hardware and software, including applications and programming.

Automotive Body and Related Repairers

- Education/Training Required: Long-term on-the-job training
- Annual Earnings: $34,690
- Growth: 13.2%
- Annual Job Openings: 23,000
- Self-Employed: 11.3%
- Part-Time: 3.3%

Repair and refinish automotive vehicle bodies and straighten vehicle frames. File, grind, sand, and smooth filled or repaired surfaces, using power tools and hand tools. Sand body areas to be painted and cover bumpers, windows, and trim with masking tape or paper to protect them from the paint. Follow supervisors' instructions as to which parts to restore or replace and how much time the job should take. Remove damaged sections of vehicles, using metal-cutting guns, air grinders, and wrenches, and install replacement parts, using wrenches or welding equipment. Cut and tape plastic separating film to outside repair areas in order to avoid damaging surrounding surfaces during repair procedure and remove tape and wash surfaces after repairs are complete. Prime and paint repaired surfaces, using paint spray guns and motorized sanders. Inspect repaired vehicles for dimensional accuracy and test drive them to ensure proper alignment and handling. Mix polyester resins and hardeners to be used in restoring damaged areas. Chain or clamp frames and sections to alignment machines that use hydraulic pressure to align damaged components. Fill small dents that cannot be worked out with plastic or solder. Fit and weld replacement parts into place, using wrenches and welding equipment, and grind down welds to smooth them, using power grinders and other tools. Position dolly blocks against surfaces of dented areas and beat opposite surfaces to remove dents, using hammers. Remove damaged panels and identify the family and properties of the plastic used on a vehicle. Review damage reports, prepare or review repair cost estimates, and plan work to be performed. Remove small pits and dimples in body metal, using pick hammers and punches. Remove upholstery, accessories, electrical window-and-seat-operating equipment, and trim in order to gain access to vehicle bodies and fenders. Clean work areas, using air hoses, in order to remove damaged material and discarded fiberglass strips used in repair procedures. Adjust or align headlights, wheels, and brake systems. Apply heat to plastic panels, using hot-air welding guns or immersion in hot water, and press the softened panels back into shape by hand. **SKILLS—Repairing:** Repairing machines or systems by using the needed tools. **Installation:** Installing equipment, machines, wiring, or programs to meet specifications. **Equipment Maintenance:** Performing routine maintenance on equipment and determining when and what kind of maintenance is needed. **Troubleshooting:** Determining causes of operating errors and deciding what to do about them. **Equipment Selection:** Determining the kind of tools and equipment needed to do a job. **Learning Strategies:** Selecting and using training/instructional methods and procedures appropriate for the situation when learning or teaching new things. **Negotiation:** Bringing others together and trying to reconcile differences. **Complex Problem Solving:** Identifying complex problems and reviewing related information to develop and evaluate options and implement solutions. **GOE—Interest Area:** 13. Manufacturing. **Work Group:** 13.14. Vehicle and Facility Mechanical Work. **Other Jobs in This Work Group:** Aircraft Body and Bonded Structure Repairers; Aircraft Engine Specialists; Aircraft Rigging Assemblers; Aircraft Structure Assemblers, Precision; Aircraft Systems Assemblers, Precision; Airframe-and-Power-Plant Mechanics; Automotive Glass Installers and Repairers; Automotive Master Mechanics; Automotive Specialty Technicians; Bus and Truck Mechanics and Diesel Engine Specialists; Farm Equipment Mechanics; Fiberglass Laminators and Fabricators; Mobile Heavy Equipment Mechanics, Except Engines; Motorboat Mechanics; Motorcycle Mechanics; Outdoor Power Equipment and Other Small Engine Mechanics; Rail Car Repairers; Recreational Vehicle Service Technicians; Tire Repairers and Changers. **PERSONALITY TYPE:** Realistic. Realistic occupations frequently involve work activities that include practical, hands-on problems and solutions. These occupations often deal with plants, animals, and real-world materials like wood, tools, and machinery. Many of the occupations require working outside and do not involve a lot of paperwork or working closely with others.

EDUCATION/TRAINING PROGRAM(S)— Autobody/Collision and Repair Technology/ Technician. **RELATED KNOWLEDGE/COURS-ES—Mechanical Devices:** Knowledge of machines and tools, including their designs, uses, repair, and maintenance. **Building and Construction:** Knowledge of the materials, methods, and tools involved in the construction or repair of houses, buildings, or other structures such as highways and roads. **Customer and Personal Service:** Knowledge of principles and processes for providing customer and personal services. This includes customer needs assessment, meeting quality standards for services, and evaluation of customer satisfaction. **Administration and Management:** Knowledge of business and management principles involved in strategic planning, resource allocation, human resources modeling, leadership technique, production methods, and coordination of people and resources. **Chemistry:** Knowledge of the chemical composition, structure, and properties of substances and of the chemical processes and transformations that they undergo. This includes uses of chemicals and their danger signs, production techniques, and disposal methods. **Transportation:** Knowledge of principles and methods for moving people or goods by air, rail, sea, or road, including the relative costs and benefits. **Production and Processing:** Knowledge of raw materials, production processes, quality control, costs, and other techniques for maximizing the effective manufacture and distribution of goods.

Automotive Master Mechanics

- Education/Training Required: Postsecondary vocational training
- Annual Earnings: $32,450
- Growth: 12.4%
- Annual Job Openings: 100,000
- Self-Employed: 15.5%
- Part-Time: 4.3%

Repair automobiles, trucks, buses, and other vehicles. Master mechanics repair virtually any part on the vehicle or specialize in the transmission system. Examine vehicles to determine extent of damage or malfunctions. Test drive vehicles and test components and systems, using equipment such as infrared engine analyzers, compression gauges, and computerized diagnostic devices. Repair, reline, replace, and adjust brakes. Review work orders and discuss work with supervisors. Follow checklists to ensure all important parts are examined, including belts, hoses, steering systems, spark plugs, brake and fuel systems, wheel bearings, and other potentially troublesome areas. Plan work procedures, using charts, technical manuals, and experience. Test and adjust repaired systems to meet manufacturers' performance specifications. Confer with customers to obtain descriptions of vehicle problems and to discuss work to be performed and future repair requirements. Perform routine and scheduled maintenance services such as oil changes, lubrications, and tune-ups. Disassemble units and inspect parts for wear, using micrometers, calipers, and gauges. Overhaul or replace carburetors, blowers, generators, distributors, starters, and pumps. Repair and service air conditioning, heating, engine-cooling, and electrical systems. Repair or replace parts such as pistons, rods, gears, valves, and bearings. Tear down, repair, and rebuild faulty assemblies such as power systems, steering systems, and linkages. Rewire ignition systems, lights, and instrument panels. Repair radiator leaks. Install and repair accessories such as radios, heaters, mirrors, and windshield wipers. Repair manual and automatic transmissions. Repair or replace shock absorbers. Align vehicles' front ends. Rebuild parts such as crankshafts and cylinder blocks. **SKILLS—**

Troubleshooting: Determining causes of operating errors and deciding what to do about them. **Repairing:** Repairing machines or systems by using the needed tools. **Installation:** Installing equipment, machines, wiring, or programs to meet specifications. **Equipment Maintenance:** Performing routine maintenance on equipment and determining when and what kind of maintenance is needed. **Active Learning:** Understanding the implications of new information for both current and future problem-solving and decision-making. **Complex Problem Solving:** Identifying complex problems and reviewing related information to develop and evaluate options and implement solutions. **Equipment Selection:** Determining the kind of tools and equipment needed to do a job. **Instructing:** Teaching others how to do something. **GOE—Interest Area:** 13. Manufacturing. **Work Group:** 13.14. Vehicle and Facility Mechanical Work. **Other Jobs in This Work Group:** Aircraft Body and Bonded Structure Repairers; Aircraft Engine Specialists; Aircraft Rigging Assemblers; Aircraft Structure Assemblers, Precision; Aircraft Systems Assemblers, Precision; Airframe-and-Power-Plant Mechanics; Automotive Body and Related Repairers; Automotive Glass Installers and Repairers; Automotive Specialty Technicians; Bus and Truck Mechanics and Diesel Engine Specialists; Farm Equipment Mechanics; Fiberglass Laminators and Fabricators; Mobile Heavy Equipment Mechanics, Except Engines; Motorboat Mechanics; Motorcycle Mechanics; Outdoor Power Equipment and Other Small Engine Mechanics; Rail Car Repairers; Recreational Vehicle Service Technicians; Tire Repairers and Changers. **PERSONALITY TYPE:** Realistic. Realistic occupations frequently involve work activities that include practical, hands-on problems and solutions. These occupations often deal with plants, animals, and real-world materials like wood, tools, and machinery. Many of the occupations require working outside and do not involve a lot of paperwork or working closely with others.

EDUCATION/TRAINING PROGRAM(S)— Alternative Fuel Vehicle Technology/Technician; Automobile/Automotive Mechanics Technology/Technician; Automotive Engineering Technology/Technician; Medium/Heavy Vehicle and Truck Technology/Technician; Vehicle Emissions Inspection and Maintenance Technology/Technician. **RELATED**

KNOWLEDGE/COURSES—Mechanical Devices: Knowledge of machines and tools, including their designs, uses, repair, and maintenance. **Computers and Electronics:** Knowledge of circuit boards, processors, chips, electronic equipment, and computer hardware and software, including applications and programming. **Physics:** Knowledge and prediction of physical principles and laws and their interrelationships and applications to understanding fluid, material, and atmospheric dynamics and mechanical, electrical, atomic, and subatomic structures and processes. **Engineering and Technology:** Knowledge of the practical application of engineering science and technology. This includes applying principles, techniques, procedures, and equipment to the design and production of various goods and services. **Education and Training:** Knowledge of principles and methods for curriculum and training design, teaching and instruction for individuals and groups, and the measurement of training effects. **Customer and Personal Service:** Knowledge of principles and processes for providing customer and personal services. This includes customer needs assessment, meeting quality standards for services, and evaluation of customer satisfaction.

Automotive Specialty Technicians

- Education/Training Required: Postsecondary vocational training
- Annual Earnings: $32,450
- Growth: 12.4%
- Annual Job Openings: 100,000
- Self-Employed: 15.5%
- Part-Time: 4.3%

Repair only one system or component on a vehicle, such as brakes, suspension, or radiator. Align and repair wheels, axles, frames, torsion bars, and steering mechanisms of automobiles, using special alignment equipment and wheel-balancing machines. Examine vehicles, compile estimates of repair costs, and secure customers' approval to perform repairs. Install and repair air conditioners and service components such as compressors, condensers, and controls. Rebuild, repair, and test automotive fuel injection units. Remove and replace defective mufflers and tailpipes. Repair and rebuild clutch systems. Repair and replace automobile leaf springs. Repair and replace defective ball joint suspensions, brake shoes, and wheel bearings. Repair, overhaul, and adjust automobile brake systems. Repair, replace, and adjust defective carburetor parts and gasoline filters. Test electronic computer components in automobiles to ensure that they are working properly. Tune automobile engines to ensure proper and efficient functioning. Use electronic test equipment to locate and correct malfunctions in fuel, ignition, and emissions control systems. Convert vehicle fuel systems from gasoline to butane gas operations and repair and service operating butane fuel units. Inspect and test new vehicles for damage and then record findings so that necessary repairs can be made. Repair, install, and adjust hydraulic and electromagnetic automatic lift mechanisms used to raise and lower automobile windows, seats, and tops. **SKILLS—Installation:** Installing equipment, machines, wiring, or programs to meet specifications. **Repairing:** Repairing machines or systems by using the needed tools. **Troubleshooting:** Determining causes of operating errors and deciding what to do about them. **Equipment Maintenance:** Performing routine maintenance on equipment and determining when and what kind of maintenance is needed. **Quality Control Analysis:** Conducting tests and inspections of products, services, or processes to evaluate quality or performance. **Operation Monitoring:** Watching gauges, dials, or other indicators to make sure a machine is working properly. **Technology Design:** Generating or adapting equipment and technology to serve user needs. **Management of Material Resources:** Obtaining and seeing to the appropriate use of equipment, facilities, and materials needed to do certain work. **GOE—Interest Area:** 13. Manufacturing. **Work Group:** 13.14. Vehicle and Facility Mechanical Work. **Other Jobs in This Work Group:** Aircraft Body and Bonded Structure Repairers; Aircraft Engine Specialists; Aircraft Rigging Assemblers; Aircraft Structure Assemblers, Precision; Aircraft Systems Assemblers, Precision; Airframe-and-Power-Plant Mechanics; Automotive Body and Related Repairers; Automotive Glass Installers and Repairers; Automotive Master Mechanics; Bus and Truck Mechanics and Diesel Engine Specialists; Farm Equipment Mechanics; Fiberglass Laminators and Fabricators; Mobile Heavy Equipment Mechanics, Except Engines; Motorboat Mechanics; Motorcycle Mechanics; Outdoor Power Equipment and Other Small Engine Mechanics; Rail Car Repairers; Recreational Vehicle Service Technicians; Tire Repairers and Changers. **PERSONALITY TYPE:** Realistic. Realistic occupations frequently involve work activities that include practical, hands-on problems and solutions. These occupations often deal with plants, animals, and real-world materials like wood, tools, and machinery. Many of the occupations require working outside and do not involve a lot of paperwork or working closely with others.

EDUCATION/TRAINING PROGRAM(S)— Alternative Fuel Vehicle Technology/Technician; Automobile/Automotive Mechanics Technology/Technician; Automotive Engineering Technology/Technician; Medium/Heavy Vehicle and Truck Technology/Technician; Vehicle Emissions Inspection and Maintenance Technology/Technician. **RELATED KNOWLEDGE/COURSES—Mechanical Devices:** Knowledge of machines and tools, including their designs, uses, repair, and maintenance. **Design:** Knowledge of design techniques, tools, and principles involved in production of precision technical plans, blueprints, drawings, and models. **Computers and Electronics:** Knowledge of circuit boards, processors, chips, electronic equipment, and computer hardware and software, including applications and programming. **Physics:** Knowledge and prediction of physical principles and laws and their interrelationships and applications to understanding fluid, material, and atmospheric dynamics and mechanical, electrical, atomic, and subatomic structures and processes. **Engineering and Technology:** Knowledge of the practical application of engineering science and technology. This includes applying principles, techniques, procedures, and equipment to the design and production of various goods and services. **Chemistry:** Knowledge of the chemical composition, structure, and properties of substances and of the chemical processes and transformations that they undergo. This includes uses of chemicals and their danger signs, production techniques, and disposal methods.

Aviation Inspectors

- Education/Training Required: Work experience in a related occupation
- Annual Earnings: $50,380
- Growth: 7.7%
- Annual Job Openings: 5,000
- Self-Employed: 0.4%
- Part-Time: 3.2%

Inspect aircraft, maintenance procedures, air navigational aids, air traffic controls, and communications equipment to ensure conformance with federal safety regulations. Analyze training programs and conduct oral and written examinations to ensure the competency of persons operating, installing, and repairing aircraft equipment. Approve or deny issuance of certificates of airworthiness. Conduct flight test programs to test equipment, instruments, and systems under a variety of conditions, using both manual and automatic controls. Examine landing gear; tires; and exteriors of fuselage, wings, and engines for evidence of damage or corrosion and to determine whether repairs are needed. Examine maintenance records and flight logs to determine if service and maintenance checks and overhauls were performed at prescribed intervals. Inspect new, repaired, or modified aircraft to identify damage or defects and to assess airworthiness and conformance to standards, using checklists, hand tools, and test instruments. Inspect work of aircraft mechanics performing maintenance, modification, or repair and overhaul of aircraft and aircraft mechanical systems in order to ensure adherence to standards and procedures. Prepare and maintain detailed repair, inspection, investigation, and certification records and reports. Recommend replacement, repair, or modification of aircraft equipment. Start aircraft and observe gauges, meters, and other instruments to detect evidence of malfunctions. Examine aircraft access plates and doors for security. Investigate air accidents and complaints to determine causes. Issue pilots' licenses to individuals meeting standards. Observe flight activities of pilots to assess flying skills and to ensure conformance to flight and safety regulations. Recommend changes in rules, policies, standards, and regulations based on knowledge of operating conditions, aircraft improvements, and other factors. Schedule and coordinate in-flight testing programs with ground crews and air traffic control to ensure availability of ground tracking, equipment monitoring, and related services. **SKILLS—Operation Monitoring:** Watching gauges, dials, or other indicators to make sure a machine is working properly. **Quality Control Analysis:** Conducting tests and inspections of products, services, or processes to evaluate quality or performance. **Science:** Using scientific rules and methods to solve problems. **Systems Analysis:** Determining how a system should work and how changes in conditions, operations, and the environment will affect outcomes. **Systems Evaluation:** Identifying measures or indicators of system performance and the actions needed to improve or correct performance relative to the goals of the system. **Writing:** Communicating effectively in writing as appropriate for the needs of the audience. **Critical Thinking:** Using logic and reasoning to identify the strengths and weaknesses of alternative solutions, conclusions, or approaches to problems. **Reading Comprehension:** Understanding written sentences and paragraphs in work-related documents. **GOE—Interest Area:** 07. Government and Public Administration. **Work Group:** 07.03. Regulations Enforcement. **Other Jobs in This Work Group:** Agricultural Inspectors; Child Support, Missing Persons, and Unemployment Insurance Fraud Investigators; Environmental Compliance Inspectors; Equal Opportunity Representatives and Officers; Financial Examiners; Fire Inspectors; Fish and Game Wardens; Forest Fire Inspectors and Prevention Specialists; Government Property Inspectors and Investigators; Immigration and Customs Inspectors; Licensing Examiners and Inspectors; Marine Cargo Inspectors; Mechanical Inspectors; Motor Vehicle Inspectors; Nuclear Monitoring Technicians; Occupational Health and Safety Specialists; Pressure Vessel Inspectors; Railroad Inspectors; Tax Examiners, Collectors, and Revenue Agents. **PERSONALITY TYPE:** Realistic. Realistic occupations frequently involve work activities that include practical, hands-on problems and solutions. These occupations often deal with plants, animals, and real-world materials like wood, tools, and machinery. Many of the occupations require working outside and do not involve a lot of paperwork or working closely with others.

EDUCATION/TRAINING PROGRAM(S)—No data available. **RELATED KNOWLEDGE/COURSES**—**Engineering and Technology:** Knowledge of the practical application of engineering science and technology. This includes applying principles, techniques, procedures, and equipment to the design and production of various goods and services. **Public Safety and Security:** Knowledge of relevant equipment, policies, procedures, and strategies to promote effective local, state, or national security operations for the protection of people, data, property, and institutions. **Mechanical Devices:** Knowledge of machines and tools, including their designs, uses, repair, and maintenance. **Physics:** Knowledge and prediction of physical principles and laws and their interrelationships and applications to understanding fluid, material, and atmospheric dynamics and mechanical, electrical, atomic, and subatomic structures and processes. **Law and Government:** Knowledge of laws, legal codes, court procedures, precedents, government regulations, executive orders, agency rules, and the democratic political process. **Transportation:** Knowledge of principles and methods for moving people or goods by air, rail, sea, or road, including the relative costs and benefits.

Bill and Account Collectors

- Education/Training Required: Short-term on-the-job training
- Annual Earnings: $27,450
- Growth: 24.5%
- Annual Job Openings: 76,000
- Self-Employed: 0.9%
- Part-Time: 11.3%

Locate and notify customers of delinquent accounts by mail, telephone, or personal visit to solicit payment. Duties include receiving payment and posting amount to customer's account, preparing statements to credit department if customer fails to respond, initiating repossession proceedings or service disconnection, and keeping records of collection and status of accounts. Receive payments and post amounts paid to customer accounts. Locate and monitor overdue accounts, using computers and a variety of automated systems. Record information about financial status of customers and status of collection efforts. Locate and notify customers of delinquent accounts by mail, telephone, or personal visits in order to solicit payment. Confer with customers by telephone or in person to determine reasons for overdue payments and to review the terms of sales, service, or credit contracts. Advise customers of necessary actions and strategies for debt repayment. Persuade customers to pay amounts due on credit accounts, damage claims, or nonpayable checks or to return merchandise. Sort and file correspondence and perform miscellaneous clerical duties such as answering correspondence and writing reports. Perform various administrative functions for assigned accounts, such as recording address changes and purging the records of deceased customers. Arrange for debt repayment or establish repayment schedules based on customers' financial situations. Negotiate credit extensions when necessary. Trace delinquent customers to new addresses by inquiring at post offices, telephone companies, or credit bureaus or through the questioning of neighbors. Notify credit departments, order merchandise repossession or service disconnection, and turn over account records to attorneys when customers fail to respond to collection attempts. **SKILLS**—**Social Perceptiveness:** Being aware of others' reactions and understanding why they react as they do. **Service Orientation:** Actively looking for ways to help people. **Time Management:** Managing one's own time and the time of others. **Management of Financial Resources:** Determining how money will be spent to get the work done and accounting for these expenditures. **Management of Personnel Resources:** Motivating, developing, and directing people as they work, identifying the best people for the job. **Persuasion:** Persuading others to change their minds or behavior. **Speaking:** Talking to others to convey information effectively. **Judgment and Decision Making:** Considering the relative costs and benefits of potential actions to choose the most appropriate one. **GOE—Interest Area:** 06. Finance and Insurance. **Work Group:** 06.04. Finance/Insurance Customer Service. **Other Jobs in This Work Group:** Loan Interviewers and Clerks; New Accounts Clerks; Tellers. **PERSONALITY TYPE:** Conventional. Conventional occupations frequently involve following set procedures and routines. These occupations can include working with data and details more than with ideas. Usually there is a clear line of authority to follow.

EDUCATION/TRAINING PROGRAM(S)— Banking and Financial Support Services. **RELATED KNOWLEDGE/COURSES—Clerical Practices:** Knowledge of administrative and clerical procedures and systems such as word processing, managing files and records, stenography and transcription, designing forms, and other office procedures and terminology. **Customer and Personal Service:** Knowledge of principles and processes for providing customer and personal services. This includes customer needs assessment, meeting quality standards for services, and evaluation of customer satisfaction. **Computers and Electronics:** Knowledge of circuit boards, processors, chips, electronic equipment, and computer hardware and software, including applications and programming. **Law and Government:** Knowledge of laws, legal codes, court procedures, precedents, government regulations, executive orders, agency rules, and the democratic political process. **Economics and Accounting:** Knowledge of economic and accounting principles and practices, the financial markets, banking, and the analysis and reporting of financial data. **Personnel and Human Resources:** Knowledge of principles and procedures for personnel recruitment, selection, training, compensation and benefits, labor relations and negotiation, and personnel information systems.

Billing, Cost, and Rate Clerks

- Education/Training Required: Short-term on-the-job training
- Annual Earnings: $27,040
- Growth: 7.9%
- Annual Job Openings: 78,000
- Self-Employed: 2.2%
- Part-Time: 16.1%

Compile data, compute fees and charges, and prepare invoices for billing purposes. Duties include computing costs and calculating rates for goods, services, and shipment of goods; posting data; and keeping other

relevant records. **May involve use of computer or typewriter, calculator, and adding and bookkeeping machines.** Verify accuracy of billing data and revise any errors. Operate typing, adding, calculating, and billing machines. Prepare itemized statements, bills, or invoices and record amounts due for items purchased or services rendered. Review documents such as purchase orders, sales tickets, charge slips, or hospital records in order to compute fees and charges due. Perform bookkeeping work, including posting data and keeping other records concerning costs of goods and services and the shipment of goods. Keep records of invoices and support documents. Resolve discrepancies in accounting records. Type billing documents, shipping labels, credit memorandums, and credit forms, using typewriters or computers. Contact customers in order to obtain or relay account information. Compute credit terms, discounts, shipment charges, and rates for goods and services in order to complete billing documents. Answer mail and telephone inquiries regarding rates, routing, and procedures. Track accumulated hours and dollar amounts charged to each client job in order to calculate client fees for professional services such as legal and accounting services. Review compiled data on operating costs and revenues in order to set rates. Compile reports of cost factors, such as labor, production, storage, and equipment. Consult sources such as rate books, manuals, and insurance company representatives in order to determine specific charges and information such as rules, regulations, and government tax and tariff information. Update manuals when rates, rules, or regulations are amended. Estimate market value of products or services. **SKILLS—Instructing:** Teaching others how to do something. **Service Orientation:** Actively looking for ways to help people. **Active Listening:** Giving full attention to what other people are saying, taking time to understand the points being made, asking questions as appropriate, and not interrupting at inappropriate times. **Social Perceptiveness:** Being aware of others' reactions and understanding why they react as they do. **Writing:** Communicating effectively in writing as appropriate for the needs of the audience. **Reading Comprehension:** Understanding written sentences and paragraphs in work-related documents. **Learning Strategies:** Selecting and using training/instructional methods and procedures appropriate for the situation when learning or teaching new things. **Speaking:** Talking to others to convey information effectively. **Negotiation:** Bringing others together and trying to reconcile differences. **GOE—Interest Area:** 04. Business and Administration. **Work Group:** 04.06. Mathematical Clerical Support. **Other Jobs in This Work Group:** Bookkeeping, Accounting, and Auditing Clerks; Brokerage Clerks; Payroll and Timekeeping Clerks; Statement Clerks; Tax Preparers. **PERSONALITY TYPE:** Conventional. Conventional occupations frequently involve following set procedures and routines. These occupations can include working with data and details more than with ideas. Usually there is a clear line of authority to follow.

EDUCATION/TRAINING PROGRAM(S)— Accounting Technology/Technician and Bookkeeping. **RELATED KNOWLEDGE/COURSES—Clerical Practices:** Knowledge of administrative and clerical procedures and systems such as word processing, managing files and records, stenography and transcription, designing forms, and other office procedures and terminology. **Computers and Electronics:** Knowledge of circuit boards, processors, chips, electronic equipment, and computer hardware and software, including applications and programming. **Customer and Personal Service:** Knowledge of principles and processes for providing customer and personal services. This includes customer needs assessment, meeting quality standards for services, and evaluation of customer satisfaction. **Economics and Accounting:** Knowledge of economic and accounting principles and practices, the financial markets, banking, and the analysis and reporting of financial data. **English Language:** Knowledge of the structure and content of the English language, including the meaning and spelling of words, rules of composition, and grammar. **Mathematics:** Knowledge of arithmetic, algebra, geometry, calculus, and statistics and their applications.

Billing, Posting, and Calculating Machine Operators

- Education/Training Required: Short-term on-the-job training
- Annual Earnings: $27,040
- Growth: 7.9%
- Annual Job Openings: 78,000
- Self-Employed: 2.2%
- Part-Time: 16.1%

Operate machines that automatically perform mathematical processes, such as addition, subtraction, multiplication, and division, to calculate and record billing, accounting, statistical, and other numerical data. Duties include operating special billing machines to prepare statements, bills, and invoices and operating bookkeeping machines to copy and post data, make computations, and compile records of transactions. Enter into machines all information needed for bill generation. Train other calculating machine operators and review their work. Operate special billing machines to prepare statements, bills, and invoices. Operate bookkeeping machines to copy and post data, make computations, and compile records of transactions. Reconcile and post receipts for cash received by various departments. Prepare transmittal reports for changes to assessment and tax rolls and redemption file changes and for warrants, deposits, and invoices. Encode and add amounts of transaction documents, such as checks or money orders, using encoding machines. Balance and reconcile batch control totals with source documents or computer listings in order to locate errors, encode correct amounts, or prepare correction records. Compute payroll and retirement amounts, applying knowledge of payroll deductions, actuarial tables, disability factors, and survivor allowances. Maintain ledgers and registers, posting charges and refunds to individual funds and computing and verifying balances. Compute monies due on personal and real property, inventories, redemption payments, and other amounts, applying specialized knowledge of tax rates, formulas, interest rates, and other relevant information. Verify and post to ledgers purchase orders, reports of goods received, invoices, paid vouchers, and other information. Assign purchase order numbers to invoices, requisitions, and formal and informal bids. Verify completeness and accuracy of original documents such as business property statements, tax rolls, invoices, bonds and coupons, and redemption certificates. Bundle sorted documents to prepare those drawn on other banks for collection. Transcribe data from office records, using specified forms, billing machines, and transcribing machines. Sort and list items for proof or collection. Send completed bills to billing clerks for information verification. Transfer data from machines, such as encoding machines, to computers. Sort and microfilm transaction documents, such as checks, using sorting machines. Observe operation of sorters to locate documents that machines cannot read and manually record amounts of these documents. **SKILLS—Active Listening:** Giving full attention to what other people are saying, taking time to understand the points being made, asking questions as appropriate, and not interrupting at inappropriate times. **Speaking:** Talking to others to convey information effectively. **Writing:** Communicating effectively in writing as appropriate for the needs of the audience. **Instructing:** Teaching others how to do something. **Management of Financial Resources:** Determining how money will be spent to get the work done and accounting for these expenditures. **Reading Comprehension:** Understanding written sentences and paragraphs in work-related documents. **Persuasion:** Persuading others to change their minds or behavior. **Critical Thinking:** Using logic and reasoning to identify the strengths and weaknesses of alternative solutions, conclusions, or approaches to problems. **Monitoring:** Monitoring or assessing your performance or that of other individuals or organizations to make improvements or take corrective action. **Negotiation:** Bringing others together and trying to reconcile differences. **GOE—Interest Area:** 04. Business and Administration. **Work Group:** 04.08. Clerical Machine Operation. **Other Jobs in This Work Group:** Data Entry Keyers; Duplicating Machine Operators; Mail Machine Operators, Preparation and Handling; Switchboard Operators, Including Answering Service; Word Processors and Typists. **PERSONALITY TYPE:** Conventional. Conventional occupations frequently involve following set procedures and routines.

These occupations can include working with data and details more than with ideas. Usually there is a clear line of authority to follow.

EDUCATION/TRAINING PROGRAM(S)— Accounting Technology/Technician and Bookkeeping. **RELATED KNOWLEDGE/COURSES—Economics and Accounting:** Knowledge of economic and accounting principles and practices, the financial markets, banking, and the analysis and reporting of financial data. **Clerical Practices:** Knowledge of administrative and clerical procedures and systems such as word processing, managing files and records, stenography and transcription, designing forms, and other office procedures and terminology. **Personnel and Human Resources:** Knowledge of principles and procedures for personnel recruitment, selection, training, compensation and benefits, labor relations and negotiation, and personnel information systems. **English Language:** Knowledge of the structure and content of the English language, including the meaning and spelling of words, rules of composition, and grammar. **Computers and Electronics:** Knowledge of circuit boards, processors, chips, electronic equipment, and computer hardware and software, including applications and programming. **Telecommunications:** Knowledge of transmission, broadcasting, switching, control, and operation of telecommunications systems.

Biological Technicians

◎ Education/Training Required: Associate degree

◎ Annual Earnings: $33,210

◎ Growth: 19.4%

◎ Annual Job Openings: 7,000

◎ Self-Employed: 0.1%

◎ Part-Time: 9.7%

Assist biological and medical scientists in laboratories. Set up, operate, and maintain laboratory instruments and equipment; monitor experiments; make observations; and calculate and record results. May analyze organic substances, such as blood, food, and drugs. Keep detailed logs of all work-related activities. Monitor laboratory work to ensure compliance with set standards. Isolate, identify, and prepare specimens for examination. Use computers, computer-interfaced equipment, robotics, and high-technology industrial applications to perform work duties. Conduct or assist in conducting research, including the collection of information and samples such as blood, water, soil, plants and animals. Set up, adjust, calibrate, clean, maintain, and troubleshoot laboratory and field equipment. Provide technical support and services for scientists and engineers working in fields such as agriculture, environmental science, resource management, biology, and health sciences. Clean, maintain, and prepare supplies and work areas. Participate in the research, development, and manufacturing of medicinal and pharmaceutical preparations. Conduct standardized biological, microbiological, and biochemical tests and laboratory analyses to evaluate the quantity or quality of physical or chemical substances in food and other products. Analyze experimental data and interpret results to write reports and summaries of findings. Measure or weigh compounds and solutions for use in testing or animal feed. Monitor and observe experiments, recording production and test data for evaluation by research personnel. Examine animals and specimens to detect the presence of disease or other problems. Conduct or supervise operational programs such as fish hatcheries, greenhouses, and livestock production programs. **SKILLS—Science:** Using scientific rules and methods to solve problems. **Learning Strategies:** Selecting and using training/instructional methods and procedures appropriate for the situation when learning or teaching new things. **Active Learning:** Understanding the implications of new information for both current and future problem-solving and decision-making. **Instructing:** Teaching others how to do something. **Equipment Maintenance:** Performing routine maintenance on equipment and determining when and what kind of maintenance is needed. **Troubleshooting:** Determining causes of operating errors and deciding what to do about them. **Technology Design:** Generating or adapting equipment and technology to serve user needs. **Quality Control Analysis:** Conducting tests and inspections of products, services, or processes to evaluate quality or performance. **GOE—Interest Area:** 08. Health Science. **Work Group:** 08.06. Medical Technology. **Other Jobs in This Work Group:** Cardiovascular Technologists and Technicians; Diagnostic Medical Sonographers; Medical and Clinical Laboratory Technicians; Medical and Clinical Laboratory Technologists; Medical Equipment Preparers; Medical Records and Health Information Technicians; Nuclear Medicine Technologists; Opticians, Dispensing; Orthotists and Prosthetists; Radiologic Technicians; Radiologic Technologists. **PERSONALITY TYPE:** Realistic. Realistic occupations frequently involve work activities that include practical, hands-on problems and solutions. These occupations often deal with plants, animals, and real-world materials like wood, tools, and machinery. Many of the occupations require working outside and do not involve a lot of paperwork or working closely with others.

EDUCATION/TRAINING PROGRAM(S)—Biology Technician/Biotechnology Laboratory Technician. **RELATED KNOWLEDGE/COURSES—Chemistry:** Knowledge of the chemical composition, structure, and properties of substances and of the chemical processes and transformations that they undergo. This includes uses of chemicals and their danger signs, production techniques, and disposal methods. **Biology:** Knowledge of plant and animal organisms and their tissues, cells, functions, interdependencies, and interactions with each other and the environment. **Mathematics:** Knowledge of arithmetic, algebra, geometry, calculus, and statistics and their applications. **English Language:** Knowledge of the structure and content of the English language, including the meaning and spelling of words, rules of composition, and grammar. **Production and Processing:** Knowledge of raw materials, production processes, quality control, costs, and other techniques for maximizing the effective manufacture and distribution of goods.

Boat Builders and Shipwrights

- ◎ Education/Training Required: Long-term on-the-job training
- ◎ Annual Earnings: $34,900
- ◎ Growth: 10.1%
- ◎ Annual Job Openings: 193,000
- ◎ Self-Employed: 29.7%
- ◎ Part-Time: 5.3%

Construct and repair ships or boats according to blueprints. Cuts and forms parts, such as keel, ribs, sidings, and support structures and blocks, using woodworking hand tools and power tools. Constructs and shapes wooden frames, structures, and other parts according to blueprint specifications, using hand tools, power tools, and measuring instruments. Attaches metal parts, such as fittings, plates, and bulkheads, to ship, using brace and bits, augers, and wrenches. Establishes dimensional reference points on layout and hull to make template of parts and locate machinery and equipment. Smoothes and finishes ship surfaces, using power sander, broadax, adz, and paint, and waxes and buffs surface to specified finish. Cuts out defect, using power tools and hand tools, and fits and secures replacement part, using caulking gun, adhesive, or hand tools. Assembles and installs hull timbers and other structures in ship, using adhesive, measuring instruments, and hand tools or power tools. Measures and marks dimensional lines on lumber, following template and using scriber. Consults with customer or supervisor and reads blueprint to determine necessary repairs. Attaches hoist to sections of hull and directs hoist operator to align parts over blocks according to layout of boat. Marks outline of boat on building dock, shipway, or mold loft according to blueprint specifications, using measuring instruments and crayon. Inspects boat to determine location and extent of defect. Positions and secures support structures on construction area. **SKILLS—Installation:** Installing equipment, machines, wiring, or programs to meet specifications. **Repairing:** Repairing machines or systems by using the needed tools. **Operations Analysis:** Analyzing needs and product requirements to create a design. **Technology Design:** Generating or adapting equipment and technology to serve user needs. **Equipment Selection:** Determining the kind of tools and equipment needed to do a job. **Equipment Maintenance:** Performing routine maintenance on equipment and determining when and what kind of maintenance is needed. **Mathematics:** Using mathematics to solve problems. **Quality Control Analysis:** Conducting tests and inspections of products, services, or processes to evaluate quality or performance. **GOE—Interest Area:** 02. Architecture and Construction. **Work Group:** 02.04. Construction Crafts. **Other Jobs in This Work Group:** Boilermakers; Brattice Builders; Brickmasons

and Blockmasons; Carpet Installers; Ceiling Tile Installers; Cement Masons and Concrete Finishers; Commercial Divers; Construction Carpenters; Crane and Tower Operators; Dragline Operators; Drywall Installers; Electricians; Fence Erectors; Floor Layers, Except Carpet, Wood, and Hard Tiles; Floor Sanders and Finishers; Glaziers; Grader, Bulldozer, and Scraper Operators; Hazardous Materials Removal Workers; Insulation Workers, Floor, Ceiling, and Wall; Insulation Workers, Mechanical; Manufactured Building and Mobile Home Installers; Operating Engineers; Painters, Construction and Maintenance; Paperhangers; Paving, Surfacing, and Tamping Equipment Operators; Pile-Driver Operators; Pipe Fitters; Pipelayers; Pipelaying Fitters; Plasterers and Stucco Masons; Plumbers; Rail-Track Laying and Maintenance Equipment Operators; Refractory Materials Repairers, Except Brickmasons; Reinforcing Iron and Rebar Workers; Riggers; Roofers; Rough Carpenters; Security and Fire Alarm Systems Installers; Segmental Pavers; Sheet Metal Workers; Ship Carpenters and Joiners; Stone Cutters and Carvers; Stonemasons; Structural Iron and Steel Workers; Tapers; Terrazzo Workers and Finishers; Tile and Marble Setters. **PERSONALITY TYPE:** Realistic. Realistic occupations frequently involve work activities that include practical, hands-on problems and solutions. These occupations often deal with plants, animals, and real-world materials like wood, tools, and machinery. Many of the occupations require working outside and do not involve a lot of paperwork or working closely with others.

EDUCATION/TRAINING PROGRAM(S)— Carpentry/Carpenter. **RELATED KNOWLEDGE/ COURSES—Building and Construction:** Knowledge of the materials, methods, and tools involved in the construction or repair of houses, buildings, or other structures such as highways and roads. **Design:** Knowledge of design techniques, tools, and principles involved in production of precision technical plans, blueprints, drawings, and models. **Mechanical Devices:** Knowledge of machines and tools, including their designs, uses, repair, and maintenance. **Engineering and Technology:** Knowledge of the practical application of engineering science and technology. This includes applying principles, techniques, procedures, and equipment to the design and production of various goods and services. **Production and Processing:**

Knowledge of raw materials, production processes, quality control, costs, and other techniques for maximizing the effective manufacture and distribution of goods. **Physics:** Knowledge and prediction of physical principles and laws and their interrelationships and applications to understanding fluid, material, and atmospheric dynamics and mechanical, electrical, atomic, and subatomic structures and processes.

Bookkeeping, Accounting, and Auditing Clerks

- ◉ Education/Training Required: Moderate-term on-the-job training
- ◉ Annual Earnings: $28,570
- ◉ Growth: 3.0%
- ◉ Annual Job Openings: 274,000
- ◉ Self-Employed: 7.9%
- ◉ Part-Time: 25.0%

Compute, classify, and record numerical data to keep financial records complete. Perform any combination of routine calculating, posting, and verifying duties to obtain primary financial data for use in maintaining accounting records. May also check the accuracy of figures, calculations, and postings pertaining to business transactions recorded by other workers. Check figures, postings, and documents for correct entry, mathematical accuracy, and proper codes. Operate computers programmed with accounting software to record, store, and analyze information. Comply with federal, state, and company policies, procedures, and regulations. Debit, credit, and total accounts on computer spreadsheets and databases, using specialized accounting software. Classify, record, and summarize numerical and financial data in order to compile and keep financial records, using journals and ledgers or computers. Calculate, prepare, and issue bills, invoices, account statements, and other financial statements according to established procedures. Compile statistical, financial, accounting, or auditing reports and tables pertaining to such matters as cash receipts, expenditures, accounts payable and receivable, and profits and losses. Code documents according to company procedures. Access computerized financial information to answer general questions as well as those related to specific accounts. Operate 10-key calculators, typewriters, and copy machines to perform calculations and produce documents. Reconcile or note and report discrepancies found in records. Perform financial calculations such as amounts due, interest charges, balances, discounts, equity, and principal. Perform general office duties such as filing, answering telephones, and handling routine correspondence. Prepare bank deposits by compiling data from cashiers; verifying and balancing receipts; and sending cash, checks, or other forms of payment to banks. Receive, record, and bank cash, checks, and vouchers. Calculate and prepare checks for utilities, taxes, and other payments. Compare computer printouts to manually maintained journals in order to determine if they match. Reconcile records of bank transactions. Prepare trial balances of books. Monitor status of loans and accounts to ensure that payments are up to date. Transfer details from separate journals to general ledgers and/or data processing sheets. Compile budget data and documents based on estimated revenues and expenses and previous budgets. **SKILLS—Management of Financial Resources:** Determining how money will be spent to get the work done and accounting for these expenditures. **Time Management:** Managing one's own time and the time of others. **Instructing:** Teaching others how to do something. **Critical Thinking:** Using logic and reasoning to identify the strengths and weaknesses of alternative solutions, conclusions, or approaches to problems. **Negotiation:** Bringing others together and trying to reconcile differences. **Active Learning:** Understanding the implications of new information for both current and future problem-solving and decision-making. **Learning Strategies:** Selecting and using training/instructional methods and procedures appropriate for the situation when learning or teaching new things. **Mathematics:** Using mathematics to solve problems. **Persuasion:** Persuading others to change their minds or behavior. **GOE—Interest Area:** 04. Business and Administration. **Work Group:** 04.06. Mathematical Clerical Support. **Other Jobs in This Work Group:** Billing, Cost, and Rate Clerks; Brokerage Clerks; Payroll and Timekeeping Clerks; Statement Clerks; Tax Preparers. **PERSONALITY TYPE:** Conventional. Conventional occupations frequently involve following set procedures and routines. These occupations can include working with data and details more than with ideas. Usually there is a clear line of authority to follow.

EDUCATION/TRAINING PROGRAM(S)—Accounting and Related Services, Other; Accounting Technology/Technician and Bookkeeping. **RELATED KNOWLEDGE/COURSES—Clerical Practices:** Knowledge of administrative and clerical procedures and systems such as word processing, managing files and records, stenography and transcription, designing forms, and other office procedures and terminology. **Economics and Accounting:** Knowledge of economic and accounting principles and practices, the financial markets, banking, and the analysis and reporting of financial data. **Mathematics:** Knowledge of arithmetic, algebra, geometry, calculus, and statistics and their applications. **Computers and Electronics:** Knowledge of circuit boards, processors, chips, electronic equipment, and computer hardware and software, including applications and programming. **Customer and Personal Service:** Knowledge of principles and processes for providing customer and personal services. This includes customer needs assessment, meeting quality standards for services, and evaluation of customer satisfaction. **English Language:** Knowledge of the structure and content of the English language, including the meaning and spelling of words, rules of composition, and grammar.

Brattice Builders

- ◉ Education/Training Required: Moderate-term on-the-job training
- ◉ Annual Earnings: $34,900
- ◉ Growth: 10.1%
- ◉ Annual Job Openings: 193,000
- ◉ Self-Employed: 29.7%
- ◉ Part-Time: 5.3%

Build doors or brattices (ventilation walls or partitions) in underground passageways to control the proper circulation of air through the passageways and to the working places. Installs rigid and flexible air ducts to transport air to work areas. Drills and blasts obstructing boulders to reopen ventilation shafts. Erects partitions to support roof in areas unsuited to

timbering or bolting. **SKILLS—Installation:** Installing equipment, machines, wiring, or programs to meet specifications. **Technology Design:** Generating or adapting equipment and technology to serve user needs. **Operations Analysis:** Analyzing needs and product requirements to create a design. **Equipment Selection:** Determining the kind of tools and equipment needed to do a job. **Quality Control Analysis:** Conducting tests and inspections of products, services, or processes to evaluate quality or performance. **GOE—Interest Area:** 02. Architecture and Construction. **Work Group:** 02.04. Construction Crafts. **Other Jobs in This Work Group:** Boat Builders and Shipwrights; Boilermakers; Brickmasons and Blockmasons; Carpet Installers; Ceiling Tile Installers; Cement Masons and Concrete Finishers; Commercial Divers; Construction Carpenters; Crane and Tower Operators; Dragline Operators; Drywall Installers; Electricians; Fence Erectors; Floor Layers, Except Carpet, Wood, and Hard Tiles; Floor Sanders and Finishers; Glaziers; Grader, Bulldozer, and Scraper Operators; Hazardous Materials Removal Workers; Insulation Workers, Floor, Ceiling, and Wall; Insulation Workers, Mechanical; Manufactured Building and Mobile Home Installers; Operating Engineers; Painters, Construction and Maintenance; Paperhangers; Paving, Surfacing, and Tamping Equipment Operators; Pile-Driver Operators; Pipe Fitters; Pipelayers; Pipelaying Fitters; Plasterers and Stucco Masons; Plumbers; Rail-Track Laying and Maintenance Equipment Operators; Refractory Materials Repairers, Except Brickmasons; Reinforcing Iron and Rebar Workers; Riggers; Roofers; Rough Carpenters; Security and Fire Alarm Systems Installers; Segmental Pavers; Sheet Metal Workers; Ship Carpenters and Joiners; Stone Cutters and Carvers; Stonemasons; Structural Iron and Steel Workers; Tapers; Terrazzo Workers and Finishers; Tile and Marble Setters. **PERSONALITY TYPE:** Realistic. Realistic occupations frequently involve work activities that include practical, hands-on problems and solutions. These occupations often deal with plants, animals, and real-world materials like wood, tools, and machinery. Many of the occupations require working outside and do not involve a lot of paperwork or working closely with others.

EDUCATION/TRAINING PROGRAM(S)—Carpentry/Carpenter. **RELATED KNOWLEDGE/**

COURSES—**Building and Construction:** Knowledge of the materials, methods, and tools involved in the construction or repair of houses, buildings, or other structures such as highways and roads. **Physics:** Knowledge and prediction of physical principles and laws and their interrelationships and applications to understanding fluid, material, and atmospheric dynamics and mechanical, electrical, atomic, and subatomic structures and processes. **Engineering and Technology:** Knowledge of the practical application of engineering science and technology. This includes applying principles, techniques, procedures, and equipment to the design and production of various goods and services. **Mechanical Devices:** Knowledge of machines and tools, including their designs, uses, repair, and maintenance.

Brazers

- ◎ Education/Training Required: Short-term on-the-job training
- ◎ Annual Earnings: $30,620
- ◎ Growth: 17.0%
- ◎ Annual Job Openings: 71,000
- ◎ Self-Employed: 5.6%
- ◎ Part-Time: 2.1%

Braze together components to assemble fabricated metal parts, using torch or welding machine and flux. Guides torch and rod along joint of workpieces to heat to brazing temperature, melt braze alloy, and bond workpieces together. Cuts carbon electrodes to specified size and shape, using cutoff saw. Removes workpiece from fixture, using tongs, and cools workpiece, using air or water. Cleans joints of workpieces by dipping them into cleaning solution or using wire brush. Examines seam and rebrazes defective joints or broken parts. Connects hoses from torch to regulator valves and cylinders of oxygen and specified fuel gas (acetylene or natural). Turns valves to start flow of gases, lights flame, and adjusts valves to obtain desired color and size of flame. Brushes flux onto joint of workpiece or dips braze rod into flux to prevent oxidation of metal. Aligns and secures workpieces in fixtures, jigs, or vise, using rule, square, or template. Melts and separates brazed joints to remove and straighten damaged

or misaligned components, using hand torch or furnace. Selects torch tip, flux, and brazing alloy from data charts or work order. Adjusts electric current and timing cycle of resistance welding machine to heat metal to bonding temperature. SKILLS—**Operation and Control:** Controlling operations of equipment or systems. **Operation Monitoring:** Watching gauges, dials, or other indicators to make sure a machine is working properly. **Installation:** Installing equipment, machines, wiring, or programs to meet specifications. **Equipment Selection:** Determining the kind of tools and equipment needed to do a job. **Science:** Using scientific rules and methods to solve problems. GOE—**Interest Area:** 13. Manufacturing. **Work Group:** 13.04. Welding, Brazing, and Soldering. **Other Jobs in This Work Group:** Fitters, Structural Metal—Precision; Metal Fabricators, Structural Metal Products; Solderers; Soldering and Brazing Machine Operators and Tenders; Welder-Fitters; Welders and Cutters; Welders, Production; Welding Machine Operators and Tenders; Welding Machine Setters and Set-Up Operators. **PERSONALITY TYPE:** Realistic. Realistic occupations frequently involve work activities that include practical, hands-on problems and solutions. These occupations often deal with plants, animals, and real-world materials like wood, tools, and machinery. Many of the occupations require working outside and do not involve a lot of paperwork or working closely with others.

EDUCATION/TRAINING PROGRAM(S)— Welding Technology/Welder. **RELATED KNOWLEDGE/COURSES—Engineering and Technology:** Knowledge of the practical application of engineering science and technology. This includes applying principles, techniques, procedures, and equipment to the design and production of various goods and services. **Building and Construction:** Knowledge of the materials, methods, and tools involved in the construction or repair of houses, buildings, or other structures such as highways and roads. **Mechanical Devices:** Knowledge of machines and tools, including their designs, uses, repair, and maintenance. **Chemistry:** Knowledge of the chemical composition, structure, and properties of substances and of the chemical processes and transformations that they undergo. This includes uses of chemicals and their danger signs, production techniques, and disposal methods.

Brickmasons and Blockmasons

- Education/Training Required: Long-term on-the-job training
- Annual Earnings: $41,740
- Growth: 14.2%
- Annual Job Openings: 21,000
- Self-Employed: 27.9%
- Part-Time: 5.3%

Lay and bind building materials, such as brick, structural tile, concrete block, cinder block, glass block, and terra-cotta block, with mortar and other substances to construct or repair walls, partitions, arches, sewers, and other structures. Construct corners by fastening in plumb position a corner pole or building a corner pyramid of bricks and then filling in between the corners, using a line from corner to corner to guide each course, or layer, of brick. Measure distance from reference points and mark guidelines to lay out work, using plumb bobs and levels. Calculate angles and courses and determine vertical and horizontal alignment of courses. Fasten or fuse brick or other building material to structure with wire clamps, anchor holes, torch, or cement. Break or cut bricks, tiles, or blocks to size, using trowel edge, hammer, or power saw. Remove excess mortar with trowels and hand tools and finish mortar joints with jointing tools for a sealed, uniform appearance. Interpret blueprints and drawings to determine specifications and to calculate the materials required. Apply and smooth mortar or other mixture over work surface. Mix specified amounts of sand, clay, dirt, or mortar powder with water to form refractory mixtures. Examine brickwork or structure to determine need for repair. Clean working surface to remove scale, dust, soot, or chips of brick and mortar, using broom, wire brush, or scraper. Lay and align bricks, blocks, or tiles to build or repair structures or high-temperature equipment, such as cupola, kilns, ovens, or furnaces. Remove burned or damaged brick or mortar, using sledgehammer, crowbar, chipping gun, or chisel. **SKILLS—Equipment Maintenance:** Performing routine maintenance on equipment and determining when and what kind of maintenance is needed. **Mathematics:** Using mathematics to solve problems. **Installation:** Installing equipment, machines, wiring, or programs to meet specifications. **Instructing:** Teaching others how to do something. **Coordination:** Adjusting actions in relation to others' actions. **Social Perceptiveness:** Being aware of others' reactions and understanding why they react as they do. **Technology Design:** Generating or adapting equipment and technology to serve user needs. **Management of Financial Resources:** Determining how money will be spent to get the work done and accounting for these expenditures. **GOE—Interest Area:** 02. Architecture and Construction. **Work Group:** 02.04. Construction Crafts. **Other Jobs in This Work Group:** Boat Builders and Shipwrights; Boilermakers; Brattice Builders; Carpet Installers; Ceiling Tile Installers; Cement Masons and Concrete Finishers; Commercial Divers; Construction Carpenters; Crane and Tower Operators; Dragline Operators; Drywall Installers; Electricians; Fence Erectors; Floor Layers, Except Carpet, Wood, and Hard Tiles; Floor Sanders and Finishers; Glaziers; Grader, Bulldozer, and Scraper Operators; Hazardous Materials Removal Workers; Insulation Workers, Floor, Ceiling, and Wall; Insulation Workers, Mechanical; Manufactured Building and Mobile Home Installers; Operating Engineers; Painters, Construction and Maintenance; Paperhangers; Paving, Surfacing, and Tamping Equipment Operators; Pile-Driver Operators; Pipe Fitters; Pipelayers; Pipelaying Fitters; Plasterers and Stucco Masons; Plumbers; Rail-Track Laying and Maintenance Equipment Operators; Refractory Materials Repairers, Except Brickmasons; Reinforcing Iron and Rebar Workers; Riggers; Roofers; Rough Carpenters; Security and Fire Alarm Systems Installers; Segmental Pavers; Sheet Metal Workers; Ship Carpenters and Joiners; Stone Cutters and Carvers; Stonemasons; Structural Iron and Steel Workers; Tapers; Terrazzo Workers and Finishers; Tile and Marble Setters. **PERSONALITY TYPE:** Realistic. Realistic occupations frequently involve work activities that include practical, hands-on problems and solutions. These occupations often deal with plants, animals, and real-world materials like wood, tools, and machinery. Many of the occupations require working outside and do not involve a lot of paperwork or working closely with others.

EDUCATION/TRAINING PROGRAM(S)— Mason/Masonry. **RELATED KNOWLEDGE/**

COURSES—**Building and Construction:** Knowledge of the materials, methods, and tools involved in the construction or repair of houses, buildings, or other structures such as highways and roads. **Design:** Knowledge of design techniques, tools, and principles involved in production of precision technical plans, blueprints, drawings, and models. **Public Safety and Security:** Knowledge of relevant equipment, policies, procedures, and strategies to promote effective local, state, or national security operations for the protection of people, data, property, and institutions. **Production and Processing:** Knowledge of raw materials, production processes, quality control, costs, and other techniques for maximizing the effective manufacture and distribution of goods. **Mathematics:** Knowledge of arithmetic, algebra, geometry, calculus, and statistics and their applications. **Mechanical Devices:** Knowledge of machines and tools, including their designs, uses, repair, and maintenance.

Bus and Truck Mechanics and Diesel Engine Specialists

- Education/Training Required: Postsecondary vocational training
- Annual Earnings: $35,780
- Growth: 14.2%
- Annual Job Openings: 28,000
- Self-Employed: 3.9%
- Part-Time: 2.5%

Diagnose, adjust, repair, or overhaul trucks, buses, and all types of diesel engines. Includes mechanics working primarily with automobile diesel engines. Use hand tools, such as screwdrivers, pliers, wrenches, pressure gauges, and precision instruments, as well as power tools, such as pneumatic wrenches, lathes, welding equipment, and jacks and hoists. Inspect brake systems, steering mechanisms, wheel bearings, and other important parts to ensure that they are in proper operating condition. Perform routine maintenance such as changing oil, checking batteries, and lubricating equipment and machinery. Adjust and reline brakes,

align wheels, tighten bolts and screws, and reassemble equipment. Raise trucks, buses, and heavy parts or equipment, using hydraulic jacks or hoists. Test-drive trucks and buses to diagnose malfunctions or to ensure that they are working properly. Inspect, test, and listen to defective equipment to diagnose malfunctions, using test instruments such as handheld computers, motor analyzers, chassis charts, and pressure gauges. Examine and adjust protective guards, loose bolts, and specified safety devices. Inspect and verify dimensions and clearances of parts to ensure conformance to factory specifications. Specialize in repairing and maintaining parts of the engine, such as fuel injection systems. Attach test instruments to equipment and read dials and gauges in order to diagnose malfunctions. Rewire ignition systems, lights, and instrument panels. Recondition and replace parts, pistons, bearings, gears, and valves. Repair and adjust seats, doors, and windows and install and repair accessories. Inspect, repair, and maintain automotive and mechanical equipment and machinery such as pumps and compressors. Disassemble and overhaul internal combustion engines, pumps, generators, transmissions, clutches, and differential units. Rebuild gas and/or diesel engines. Align front ends and suspension systems. SKILLS—**Equipment Maintenance:** Performing routine maintenance on equipment and determining when and what kind of maintenance is needed. **Repairing:** Repairing machines or systems by using the needed tools. **Troubleshooting:** Determining causes of operating errors and deciding what to do about them. **Installation:** Installing equipment, machines, wiring, or programs to meet specifications. **Learning Strategies:** Selecting and using training/instructional methods and procedures appropriate for the situation when learning or teaching new things. **Technology Design:** Generating or adapting equipment and technology to serve user needs. **Science:** Using scientific rules and methods to solve problems. **Social Perceptiveness:** Being aware of others' reactions and understanding why they react as they do. **Coordination:** Adjusting actions in relation to others' actions. **Instructing:** Teaching others how to do something. **GOE—Interest Area:** 13. Manufacturing. **Work Group:** 13.14. Vehicle and Facility Mechanical Work. **Other Jobs in This Work Group:** Aircraft Body and Bonded Structure Repairers; Aircraft Engine Specialists; Aircraft Rigging Assemblers; Aircraft Structure Assemblers, Precision; Aircraft Systems Assemblers, Precision; Airframe-and-Power-Plant Mechanics; Automotive Body and Related Repairers; Automotive Glass Installers and Repairers; Automotive Master Mechanics; Automotive Specialty Technicians; Farm Equipment Mechanics; Fiberglass Laminators and Fabricators; Mobile Heavy Equipment Mechanics, Except Engines; Motorboat Mechanics; Motorcycle Mechanics; Outdoor Power Equipment and Other Small Engine Mechanics; Rail Car Repairers; Recreational Vehicle Service Technicians; Tire Repairers and Changers. **PERSONALITY TYPE:** Realistic. Realistic occupations frequently involve work activities that include practical, hands-on problems and solutions. These occupations often deal with plants, animals, and real-world materials like wood, tools, and machinery. Many of the occupations require working outside and do not involve a lot of paperwork or working closely with others.

EDUCATION/TRAINING PROGRAM(S)— Diesel Mechanics Technology/Technician; Medium/Heavy Vehicle and Truck Technology/Technician. **RELATED KNOWLEDGE/COURSES—Mechanical Devices:** Knowledge of machines and tools, including their designs, uses, repair, and maintenance. **Transportation:** Knowledge of principles and methods for moving people or goods by air, rail, sea, or road, including the relative costs and benefits. **Public Safety and Security:** Knowledge of relevant equipment, policies, procedures, and strategies to promote effective local, state, or national security operations for the protection of people, data, property, and institutions. **Engineering and Technology:** Knowledge of the practical application of engineering science and technology. This includes applying principles, techniques, procedures, and equipment to the design and production of various goods and services. **Physics:** Knowledge and prediction of physical principles and laws and their interrelationships and applications to understanding fluid, material, and atmospheric dynamics and mechanical, electrical, atomic, and subatomic structures and processes. **Chemistry:** Knowledge of the chemical composition, structure, and properties of substances and of the chemical processes and transformations that they undergo. This includes uses of chemicals and their danger signs, production tech-

niques, and disposal methods. **Law and Government:** Knowledge of laws, legal codes, court procedures, precedents, government regulations, executive orders, agency rules, and the democratic political process.

Bus Drivers, School

- ◎ Education/Training Required: Short-term on-the-job training
- ◎ Annual Earnings: $23,250
- ◎ Growth: 16.7%
- ◎ Annual Job Openings: 76,000
- ◎ Self-Employed: 0.7%
- ◎ Part-Time: 35.6%

Transport students or special clients such as the elderly or persons with disabilities. Ensure adherence to safety rules. May assist passengers in boarding or exiting. Drive gasoline, diesel, or electrically powered multi-passenger vehicles to transport students between neighborhoods, schools, and school activities. Check the condition of a vehicle's tires, brakes, windshield wipers, lights, oil, fuel, water, and safety equipment to ensure that everything is in working order. Comply with traffic regulations in order to operate vehicles in a safe and courteous manner. Follow safety rules as students are boarding and exiting buses and as they cross streets near bus stops. Pick up and drop off students at regularly scheduled neighborhood locations, following strict time schedules. Read maps and follow written and verbal geographic directions. Regulate heating, lighting, and ventilation systems for passenger comfort. Escort small children across roads and highways. Keep bus interiors clean for passengers. Maintain knowledge of first-aid procedures. Maintain order among pupils during trips in order to ensure safety. Make minor repairs to vehicles. Prepare and submit reports that may include the number of passengers or trips, hours worked, mileage, fuel consumption, and/or fares received. Report any bus malfunctions or needed repairs. Report delays, accidents, or other traffic and transportation situations, using telephones or mobile two-way radios. **SKILLS—Repairing:** Repairing machines or systems by using the needed tools. **Operation and Control:** Controlling operations of equipment or systems. **Operation Monitoring:**

Watching gauges, dials, or other indicators to make sure a machine is working properly. **Equipment Maintenance:** Performing routine maintenance on equipment and determining when and what kind of maintenance is needed. **GOE—Interest Area:** 16. Transportation, Distribution, and Logistics. **Work Group:** 16.06. Other Services Requiring Driving. **Other Jobs in This Work Group:** Ambulance Drivers and Attendants, Except Emergency Medical Technicians; Bus Drivers, Transit and Intercity; Couriers and Messengers; Driver/Sales Workers; Parking Lot Attendants; Postal Service Mail Carriers; Taxi Drivers and Chauffeurs. **PERSONALITY TYPE:** Realistic. Realistic occupations frequently involve work activities that include practical, hands-on problems and solutions. These occupations often deal with plants, animals, and real-world materials like wood, tools, and machinery. Many of the occupations require working outside and do not involve a lot of paperwork or working closely with others.

EDUCATION/TRAINING PROGRAM(S)— Truck and Bus Driver/Commercial Vehicle Operation. **RELATED KNOWLEDGE/COURSES—Transportation:** Knowledge of principles and methods for moving people or goods by air, rail, sea, or road, including the relative costs and benefits. **Public Safety and Security:** Knowledge of relevant equipment, policies, procedures, and strategies to promote effective local, state, or national security operations for the protection of people, data, property, and institutions. **Customer and Personal Service:** Knowledge of principles and processes for providing customer and personal services. This includes customer needs assessment, meeting quality standards for services, and evaluation of customer satisfaction. **Mechanical Devices:** Knowledge of machines and tools, including their designs, uses, repair, and maintenance. **Geography:** Knowledge of principles and methods for describing the features of land, sea, and air masses, including their physical characteristics; locations; interrelationships; and distribution of plant, animal, and human life. **Law and Government:** Knowledge of laws, legal codes, court procedures, precedents, government regulations, executive orders, agency rules, and the democratic political process.

Bus Drivers, Transit and Intercity

- Education/Training Required: Moderate-term on-the-job training
- Annual Earnings: $29,730
- Growth: 15.2%
- Annual Job Openings: 33,000
- Self-Employed: 0.7%
- Part-Time: 35.6%

Drive bus or motor coach, including regular route operations, charters, and private carriage. May assist passengers with baggage. May collect fares or tickets. Inspect vehicles and check gas, oil, and water levels prior to departure. Drive vehicles over specified routes or to specified destinations according to time schedules in order to transport passengers, complying with traffic regulations. Park vehicles at loading areas so that passengers can board. Assist passengers with baggage and collect tickets or cash fares. Report delays or accidents. Advise passengers to be seated and orderly while on vehicles. Regulate heating, lighting, and ventilating systems for passenger comfort. Load and unload baggage in baggage compartments. Record cash receipts and ticket fares. Make minor repairs to vehicle and change tires. **SKILLS—Social Perceptiveness:** Being aware of others' reactions and understanding why they react as they do. **Equipment Maintenance:** Performing routine maintenance on equipment and determining when and what kind of maintenance is needed. **Operation and Control:** Controlling operations of equipment or systems. **Troubleshooting:** Determining causes of operating errors and deciding what to do about them. **Negotiation:** Bringing others together and trying to reconcile differences. **Operation Monitoring:** Watching gauges, dials, or other indicators to make sure a machine is working properly. **Service Orientation:** Actively looking for ways to help people. **Instructing:** Teaching others how to do something. **GOE—Interest Area:** 16. Transportation, Distribution, and Logistics. **Work Group:** 16.06. Other Services Requiring Driving. **Other Jobs in This Work Group:** Ambulance Drivers and Attendants, Except Emergency Medical Technicians; Bus Drivers, School; Couriers and Messengers; Driver/Sales Workers; Parking Lot Attendants; Postal Service Mail Carriers; Taxi Drivers and Chauffeurs. **PERSONALITY TYPE:** Realistic. Realistic occupations frequently involve work activities that include practical, hands-on problems and solutions. These occupations often deal with plants, animals, and real-world materials like wood, tools, and machinery. Many of the occupations require working outside and do not involve a lot of paperwork or working closely with others.

EDUCATION/TRAINING PROGRAM(S)— Truck and Bus Driver/Commercial Vehicle Operation. **RELATED KNOWLEDGE/COURSES—Transportation:** Knowledge of principles and methods for moving people or goods by air, rail, sea, or road, including the relative costs and benefits. **Customer and Personal Service:** Knowledge of principles and processes for providing customer and personal services. This includes customer needs assessment, meeting quality standards for services, and evaluation of customer satisfaction. **Geography:** Knowledge of principles and methods for describing the features of land, sea, and air masses, including their physical characteristics; locations; interrelationships; and distribution of plant, animal, and human life. **Public Safety and Security:** Knowledge of relevant equipment, policies, procedures, and strategies to promote effective local, state, or national security operations for the protection of people, data, property, and institutions. **Psychology:** Knowledge of human behavior and performance; individual differences in ability, personality, and interests; learning and motivation; psychological research methods; and the assessment and treatment of behavioral and affective disorders. **Law and Government:** Knowledge of laws, legal codes, court procedures, precedents, government regulations, executive orders, agency rules, and the democratic political process.

Calibration and Instrumentation Technicians

- Education/Training Required: Associate degree
- Annual Earnings: $46,310
- Growth: 10.0%
- Annual Job Openings: 24,000
- Self-Employed: 0.4%
- Part-Time: 5.0%

Develop, test, calibrate, operate, and repair electrical, mechanical, electromechanical, electrohydraulic, or electronic measuring and recording instruments, apparatus, and equipment. Plans sequence of testing and calibration program for instruments and equipment according to blueprints, schematics, technical manuals, and other specifications. Performs preventative and corrective maintenance of test apparatus and peripheral equipment. Confers with engineers, supervisor, and other technical workers to assist with equipment installation, maintenance, and repair techniques. Analyzes and converts test data, using mathematical formulas, and reports results and proposed modifications. Sets up test equipment and conducts tests on performance and reliability of mechanical, structural, or electromechanical equipment. Selects sensing, telemetering, and recording instrumentation and circuitry. Disassembles and reassembles instruments and equipment, using hand tools, and inspects instruments and equipment for defects. Sketches plans for developing jigs, fixtures, instruments, and related nonstandard apparatus. Modifies performance and operation of component parts and circuitry to specifications, using test equipment and precision instruments. **SKILLS— Technology Design:** Generating or adapting equipment and technology to serve user needs. **Equipment Maintenance:** Performing routine maintenance on equipment and determining when and what kind of maintenance is needed. **Quality Control Analysis:** Conducting tests and inspections of products, services, or processes to evaluate quality or performance. **Science:** Using scientific rules and methods to solve problems. **Equipment Selection:** Determining the kind of tools and equipment needed to do a job. **Troubleshooting:** Determining causes of operating errors and deciding what to do about them. **Installation:** Installing equipment, machines, wiring, or programs to meet specifications. **Operation Monitoring:** Watching gauges, dials, or other indicators to make sure a machine is working properly. **GOE—Interest Area:** 15. Scientific Research, Engineering, and Mathematics. **Work Group:** 15.09. Engineering Technology. **Other Jobs in This Work Group:** Aerospace Engineering and Operations Technicians; Cartographers and Photogrammetrists; Civil Engineering Technicians; Electrical Engineering Technicians; Electro-Mechanical Technicians; Electronic Drafters; Electronics Engineering Technicians; Environmental Engineering Technicians; Mapping Technicians; Mechanical Drafters; Mechanical Engineering Technicians; Surveying Technicians. **PERSONALITY TYPE:** Realistic. Realistic occupations frequently involve work activities that include practical, hands-on problems and solutions. These occupations often deal with plants, animals, and real-world materials like wood, tools, and machinery. Many of the occupations require working outside and do not involve a lot of paperwork or working closely with others.

EDUCATION/TRAINING PROGRAM(S)—Computer Engineering Technology/Technician; Computer Technology/Computer Systems Technology; Electrical and Electronic Engineering Technologies/Technicians, Other; Electrical, Electronic, and Communications Engineering Technology/Technician; Telecommunications Technology/Technician. RELATED KNOWLEDGE/COURSES—**Design:** Knowledge of design techniques, tools, and principles involved in production of precision technical plans, blueprints, drawings, and models. **Mathematics:** Knowledge of arithmetic, algebra, geometry, calculus, and statistics and their applications. **Engineering and Technology:** Knowledge of the practical application of engineering science and technology. This includes applying principles, techniques, procedures, and equipment to the design and production of various goods and services. **Computers and Electronics:** Knowledge of circuit boards, processors, chips, electronic equipment, and computer hardware and software, including applications and programming. **Mechanical Devices:** Knowledge of machines and

tools, including their designs, uses, repair, and maintenance. **Physics:** Knowledge and prediction of physical principles and laws and their interrelationships and applications to understanding fluid, material, and atmospheric dynamics and mechanical, electrical, atomic, and subatomic structures and processes.

Camera Operators, Television, Video, and Motion Picture

- ◎ Education/Training Required: Moderate-term on-the-job training
- ◎ Annual Earnings: $37,610
- ◎ Growth: 13.4%
- ◎ Annual Job Openings: 4,000
- ◎ Self-Employed: 23.8%
- ◎ Part-Time: 20.4%

Operate television, video, or motion picture camera to photograph images or scenes for various purposes, such as TV broadcasts, advertising, video production, or motion pictures. Operate television or motion picture cameras to record scenes for television broadcasts, advertising, or motion pictures. Compose and frame each shot, applying the technical aspects of light, lenses, film, filters, and camera settings in order to achieve the effects sought by directors. Operate zoom lenses, changing images according to specifications and rehearsal instructions. Use cameras in any of several different camera mounts, such as stationary, track-mounted, or crane-mounted. Test, clean, and maintain equipment to ensure proper working condition. Adjust positions and controls of cameras, printers, and related equipment in order to change focus, exposure, and lighting. Gather and edit raw footage on location to send to television affiliates for broadcast, using electronic news-gathering or film-production equipment. Confer with directors, sound and lighting technicians, electricians, and other crew members to discuss assignments and determine filming sequences, desired effects, camera movements, and lighting requirements. Observe sets or locations for potential problems and to determine filming and lighting requirements. Instruct camera operators regarding camera setups, angles, distances, movement, and variables and cues for starting and stopping filming. Select and assemble cameras, accessories, equipment, and film stock to be used during filming, using knowledge of filming techniques, requirements, and computations. Label and record contents of exposed film and note details on report forms. Read charts and compute ratios to determine variables such as lighting, shutter angles, filter factors, and camera distances. Set up cameras, optical printers, and related equipment to produce photographs and special effects. View films to resolve problems of exposure control, subject and camera movement, changes in subject distance, and related variables. Reload camera magazines with fresh raw film stock. Read and analyze work orders and specifications to determine locations of subject material, work procedures, sequences of operations, and machine setups. Receive raw film stock and maintain film inventories. **SKILLS—Operation Monitoring:** Watching gauges, dials, or other indicators to make sure a machine is working properly. **Equipment Maintenance:** Performing routine maintenance on equipment and determining when and what kind of maintenance is needed. **Troubleshooting:** Determining causes of operating errors and deciding what to do about them. **Operation and Control:** Controlling operations of equipment or systems. **Active Listening:** Giving full attention to what other people are saying, taking time to understand the points being made, asking questions as appropriate, and not interrupting at inappropriate times. **Coordination:** Adjusting actions in relation to others' actions. **Time Management:** Managing one's own time and the time of others. **Social Perceptiveness:** Being aware of others' reactions and understanding why they react as they do. **Persuasion:** Persuading others to change their minds or behavior. **GOE—Interest Area:** 03. Arts and Communication. **Work Group:** 03.09. Media Technology. **Other Jobs in This Work Group:** Audio and Video Equipment Technicians; Broadcast Technicians; Film and Video Editors; Multi-Media Artists and Animators; Photographic Hand Developers; Photographic Reproduction Technicians; Photographic Retouchers and Restorers; Professional Photographers; Radio Operators; Sound Engineering Technicians. **PERSONALITY TYPE:** Artistic. Artistic occupations frequently involve working with forms, designs, and patterns. These occupations often require self-expression, and the work can be done without following a clear set of rules.

EDUCATION/TRAINING PROGRAM(S)— Audiovisual Communications Technologies/Technicians, Other; Cinematography and Film/Video Production; Radio and Television Broadcasting Technology/Technician. **RELATED KNOWLEDGE/ COURSES—Communications and Media:** Knowledge of media production, communication, and dissemination techniques and methods. This includes alternative ways to inform and entertain via written, oral, and visual media. **Computers and Electronics:** Knowledge of circuit boards, processors, chips, electronic equipment, and computer hardware and software, including applications and programming. **Telecommunications:** Knowledge of transmission, broadcasting, switching, control, and operation of telecommunications systems. **Customer and Personal Service:** Knowledge of principles and processes for providing customer and personal services. This includes customer needs assessment, meeting quality standards for services, and evaluation of customer satisfaction. **Engineering and Technology:** Knowledge of the practical application of engineering science and technology. This includes applying principles, techniques, procedures, and equipment to the design and production of various goods and services. **Sales and Marketing:** Knowledge of principles and methods for showing, promoting, and selling products or services. This includes marketing strategy and tactics, product demonstrations, sales techniques, and sales control systems. **Fine Arts:** Knowledge of the theory and techniques required to compose, produce, and perform works of music, dance, the visual arts, drama, and sculpture.

Caption Writers

- ◎ Education/Training Required: Moderate-term on-the-job training
- ◎ Annual Earnings: $44,350
- ◎ Growth: 16.1%
- ◎ Annual Job Openings: 23,000
- ◎ Self-Employed: 67.9%
- ◎ Part-Time: 24.2%

Write caption phrases of dialogue for hearing-impaired and foreign language–speaking viewers of movie or television productions. Writes captions to describe music and background noises. Watches production and reviews captions simultaneously to determine which caption phrases require editing. Enters commands to synchronize captions with dialogue and place on the screen. Translates foreign-language dialogue into English-language captions or English dialogue into foreign-language captions. Operates computerized captioning system for movies or television productions for hearing-impaired and foreign language–speaking viewers. Oversees encoding of captions to master tape of television production. Discusses captions with directors or producers of movie and television productions. Edits translations for correctness of grammar, punctuation, and clarity of expression. **SKILLS—Writing:** Communicating effectively in writing as appropriate for the needs of the audience. **Reading Comprehension:** Understanding written sentences and paragraphs in work-related documents. **Operation and Control:** Controlling operations of equipment or systems. **GOE—Interest Area:** 03. Arts and Communication. **Work Group:** 03.03. News, Broadcasting, and Public Relations. **Other Jobs in This Work Group:** Broadcast News Analysts; Interpreters and Translators; Public Relations Specialists; Reporters and Correspondents. **PERSONALITY TYPE:** Artistic. Artistic occupations frequently involve working with forms, designs, and patterns. These occupations often require self-expression, and the work can be done without following a clear set of rules.

EDUCATION/TRAINING PROGRAM(S)— Broadcast Journalism; Business/Corporate Communications; Communication Studies/Speech Communication and Rhetoric; Communication, Journalism, and Related Programs, Other; Creative Writing; English Composition; Family and Consumer Sciences/Human Sciences Communication; Journalism; Mass Communication/Media Studies; Playwriting and Screenwriting; Technical and Business Writing. **RELATED KNOWLEDGE/COURSES—Foreign Language:** Knowledge of the structure and content of a foreign (non-English) language, including the meaning and spelling of words, rules of composition and grammar, and pronunciation. **Communications and Media:** Knowledge of media production, communication, and dissemination techniques and methods. This includes alternative ways to inform and entertain via written, oral, and visual media. **English Language:** Knowledge of the structure and content of the English language, including the meaning and spelling of words, rules of composition, and grammar. **Computers and Electronics:** Knowledge of circuit boards, processors, chips, electronic equipment, and computer hardware and software, including applications and programming. **Telecommunications:** Knowledge of transmission, broadcasting, switching, control, and operation of telecommunications systems.

Cardiovascular Technologists and Technicians

- ◉ Education/Training Required: Associate degree
- ◉ Annual Earnings: $38,690
- ◉ Growth: 33.5%
- ◉ Annual Job Openings: 6,000
- ◉ Self-Employed: 0.2%
- ◉ Part-Time: 17.5%

Conduct tests on pulmonary or cardiovascular systems of patients for diagnostic purposes. May conduct or assist in electrocardiograms, cardiac catheterizations, pulmonary function tests, lung capacity tests, and similar tests. Monitor patients' blood pressure and heart rate, using electrocardiogram (EKG) equipment, during diagnostic and therapeutic procedures in order to notify the physician if something appears wrong. Monitor patients' comfort and safety during tests, alerting physicians to abnormalities or changes in patient responses. Explain testing procedures to patient to obtain cooperation and reduce anxiety. Prepare reports of diagnostic procedures for interpretation by physician. Observe gauges, recorder, and video screens of data analysis system during imaging of cardiovascular system. Conduct electrocardiogram, phonocardiogram, echocardiogram, stress testing, and other cardiovascular tests to record patients' cardiac activity, using specialized electronic test equipment, recording devices, and laboratory instruments. Prepare and position patients for testing. Obtain and record patient identification, medical history, and test results. Attach electrodes to the patients' chests, arms, and legs, connect electrodes to leads from the electrocardiogram (EKG) machine, and operate the EKG machine to obtain a reading. Adjust equipment and controls according to physicians' orders or established protocol. Check, test, and maintain cardiology equipment, making minor repairs when necessary, to ensure proper operation. Supervise and train other cardiology technologists and students. Assist physicians in diagnosis and treatment of cardiac and peripheral vascular treatments, for example, assisting with balloon angioplasties to treat blood vessel blockages. Operate diagnostic imaging equipment to produce contrast-enhanced radiographs of heart and cardiovascular system. Inject contrast medium into patients' blood vessels. Observe ultrasound display screen and listen to signals to record vascular information such as blood pressure, limb volume changes, oxygen saturation, and cerebral circulation. Assess cardiac physiology and calculate valve areas from blood flow velocity measurements. Compare measurements of heart wall thickness and chamber sizes to standard norms to identify abnormalities. Activate fluoroscope and camera to produce images used to guide catheter through cardiovascular system. **SKILLS—Instructing:** Teaching others how to do something. **Service Orientation:** Actively looking for ways to help people. **Operation Monitoring:** Watching gauges, dials, or other indicators to make sure a machine is working properly. **Active Learning:** Understanding the implications of new information for both current and future problem-solving and decision-making. **Equipment Maintenance:** Performing routine maintenance on equipment and determining when and what kind of maintenance is needed. **Learning Strategies:** Selecting and using training/instructional methods and procedures appropriate for the situation when learning or teaching new things. **Social Perceptiveness:** Being aware of others' reactions and understanding why they react as they do. **Time Management:** Managing one's own time and the time of others. **GOE—Interest Area:** 08. Health Science. **Work Group:** 08.06. Medical Technology. **Other Jobs in This Work Group:** Biological Technicians; Diagnostic Medical Sonographers; Medical and Clinical Laboratory Technicians; Medical and Clinical Lab-

oratory Technologists; Medical Equipment Preparers; Medical Records and Health Information Technicians; Nuclear Medicine Technologists; Opticians, Dispensing; Orthotists and Prosthetists; Radiologic Technicians; Radiologic Technologists. **PERSONALITY TYPE:** Investigative. Investigative occupations frequently involve working with ideas and require an extensive amount of thinking. These occupations can involve searching for facts and figuring out problems mentally.

EDUCATION/TRAINING PROGRAM(S)—Cardiopulmonary Technology/Technologist; Cardiovascular Technology/Technologist; Electrocardiograph Technology/Technician; Perfusion Technology/Perfusionist. **RELATED KNOWLEDGE/COURSES—Medicine and Dentistry:** Knowledge of the information and techniques needed to diagnose and treat human injuries, diseases, and deformities. This includes symptoms, treatment alternatives, drug properties and interactions, and preventive health-care measures. **Customer and Personal Service:** Knowledge of principles and processes for providing customer and personal services. This includes customer needs assessment, meeting quality standards for services, and evaluation of customer satisfaction. **Psychology:** Knowledge of human behavior and performance; individual differences in ability, personality, and interests; learning and motivation; psychological research methods; and the assessment and treatment of behavioral and affective disorders. **Physics:** Knowledge and prediction of physical principles and laws and their interrelationships and applications to understanding fluid, material, and atmospheric dynamics and mechanical, electrical, atomic, and subatomic structures and processes. **Education and Training:** Knowledge of principles and methods for curriculum and training design, teaching and instruction for individuals and groups, and the measurement of training effects. **Computers and Electronics:** Knowledge of circuit boards, processors, chips, electronic equipment, and computer hardware and software, including applications and programming. **Biology:** Knowledge of plant and animal organisms and their tissues, cells, functions, interdependencies, and interactions with each other and the environment.

Cargo and Freight Agents

- ☻ Education/Training Required: Moderate-term on-the-job training
- ☻ Annual Earnings: $34,250
- ☻ Growth: 15.5%
- ☻ Annual Job Openings: 8,000
- ☻ Self-Employed: 0.1%
- ☻ Part-Time: 5.5%

Expedite and route movement of incoming and outgoing cargo and freight shipments in airline, train, and trucking terminals and shipping docks. Take orders from customers and arrange pickup of freight and cargo for delivery to loading platform. Prepare and examine bills of lading to determine shipping charges and tariffs. Advise clients on transportation and payment methods. Arrange insurance coverage for goods. Check import/export documentation to determine cargo contents and classify goods into different fee or tariff groups, using a tariff coding system. Contact vendors and/or claims adjustment departments in order to resolve problems with shipments or contact service depots to arrange for repairs. Determine method of shipment and prepare bills of lading, invoices, and other shipping documents. Direct delivery trucks to shipping doors or designated marshalling areas and help load and unload goods safely. Direct or participate in cargo loading in order to ensure completeness of load and even distribution of weight. Enter shipping information into a computer by hand or by using a hand-held scanner that reads bar codes on goods. Estimate freight or postal rates and record shipment costs and weights. Inspect and count items received and check them against invoices or other documents, recording shortages and rejecting damaged goods. Keep records of all goods shipped, received, and stored. Negotiate and arrange transport of goods with shipping or freight companies. Notify consignees, passengers, or customers of the arrival of freight or baggage and arrange for delivery. Retrieve stored items and trace lost shipments as necessary. Route received goods to first available flight or to appropriate storage areas or departments, using forklifts, handtrucks, or other equipment. Assemble containers and crates used to transport items such as machines or vehicles. Attach address labels, identification codes, and shipping instructions to containers. Coordinate and supervise activities of workers engaged in packing and shipping merchandise. Inspect trucks and vans to ensure cleanliness when shipping such items as grain, flour, and milk. Install straps, braces, and padding to loads in order to prevent shifting or damage during shipment. Maintain a supply of packing materials. Obtain flight numbers, airplane numbers, and names of crew members from dispatchers and record data on airplane flight papers. Open cargo containers and unwrap contents, using steel cutters, crowbars, or other hand tools. **SKILLS—Service Orientation:** Actively looking for ways to help people. **Operation and Control:** Controlling operations of equipment or systems. **Coordination:** Adjusting actions in relation to others' actions. **GOE—Interest Area:** 16. Transportation, Distribution, and Logistics. **Work Group:** 16.07. Transportation Support Work. **Other Jobs in This Work Group:** Bridge and Lock Tenders; Cleaners of Vehicles and Equipment; Freight Inspectors; Public Transportation Inspectors; Railroad Yard Workers; Stevedores, Except Equipment Operators; Traffic Technicians; Train Crew Members. **PERSONALITY TYPE:** Conventional. Conventional occupations frequently involve following set procedures and routines. These occupations can include working with data and details more than with ideas. Usually there is a clear line of authority to follow.

EDUCATION/TRAINING PROGRAM(S)—General Office Occupations and Clerical Services. **RELATED KNOWLEDGE/COURSES—Transportation:** Knowledge of principles and methods for moving people or goods by air, rail, sea, or road, including the relative costs and benefits. **Telecommunications:** Knowledge of transmission, broadcasting, switching, control, and operation of telecommunications systems. **Clerical Practices:** Knowledge of administrative and clerical procedures and systems such as word processing, managing files and records, stenography and transcription, designing forms, and other office procedures and terminology. **Geography:** Knowledge of principles and methods for describing the features of land, sea, and air masses, including their physical characteristics; locations; interrelationships; and distribution of plant, animal, and human life. **Customer and Personal Service:** Knowledge of principles and processes for providing customer and personal services. This includes customer needs assessment, meeting quality standards for services, and evaluation of customer satisfaction.

Carpenter Assemblers and Repairers

- Education/Training Required: Moderate-term on-the-job training
- Annual Earnings: $34,900
- Growth: 10.1%
- Annual Job Openings: 193,000
- Self-Employed: 29.7%
- Part-Time: 5.3%

Perform a variety of tasks requiring a limited knowledge of carpentry, such as applying siding and weatherboard to building exteriors or assembling and erecting prefabricated buildings. Measures and marks location of studs, leaders, and receptacle openings, using tape measure, template, and marker. Cuts sidings and moldings, sections of weatherboard, openings in sheetrock, and lumber, using hand tools and power tools. Lays out and aligns materials on worktable or in assembly jig according to specified instructions. Removes surface defects, using knife, scraper, wet sponge, electric iron, and sanding tools. Trims overlapping edges of wood or weatherboard, using portable router or power saw and hand tools. Installs prefabricated windows and doors; insulation; wall, ceiling, and floor panels; or siding, using adhesives, hoists, hand tools, and power tools. Aligns and fastens materials together, using hand tools and power tools, to form building or bracing. Repairs or replaces defective locks, hinges, cranks, and pieces of wood, using glue, hand tools, and power tools. Applies stain, paint, or crayons to defects and filters to touch up the repaired area. Directs crane operator in positioning floor, wall, ceiling, and roof panel on house foundation. Moves panel or roof section to other workstations or to storage or shipping area, using electric hoist. Studies blueprints, specification sheets, and drawings to determine style and type of window or wall panel required. Fills cracks, seams, depressions, and nail holes with filler. Examines wood surfaces for defects, such as nicks, cracks, or blisters. Measures cut materials to determine conformance

to specifications, using tape measure. Realigns windows and screens to fit casements and oils moving parts. **SKILLS—Repairing:** Repairing machines or systems by using the needed tools. **Installation:** Installing equipment, machines, wiring, or programs to meet specifications. **Management of Material Resources:** Obtaining and seeing to the appropriate use of equipment, facilities, and materials needed to do certain work. **Operation and Control:** Controlling operations of equipment or systems. **Equipment Maintenance:** Performing routine maintenance on equipment and determining when and what kind of maintenance is needed. **GOE—Interest Area:** 02. Architecture and Construction. **Work Group:** 02.06. Construction Support/Labor. **Other Jobs in This Work Group:** Construction Laborers; Grips and Set-Up Workers, Motion Picture Sets, Studios, and Stages; Helpers—Brickmasons, Blockmasons, Stonemasons, and Tile and Marble Setters; Helpers—Carpenters; Helpers—Electricians; Helpers—Installation, Maintenance, and Repair Workers; Helpers—Painters, Paperhangers, Plasterers, and Stucco Masons; Helpers—Pipelayers, Plumbers, Pipefitters, and Steamfitters; Highway Maintenance Workers; Septic Tank Servicers and Sewer Pipe Cleaners. **PERSONALITY TYPE:** Realistic. Realistic occupations frequently involve work activities that include practical, hands-on problems and solutions. These occupations often deal with plants, animals, and real-world materials like wood, tools, and machinery. Many of the occupations require working outside and do not involve a lot of paperwork or working closely with others.

EDUCATION/TRAINING PROGRAM(S)— Carpentry/Carpenter. **RELATED KNOWLEDGE/ COURSES—Building and Construction:** Knowledge of the materials, methods, and tools involved in the construction or repair of houses, buildings, or other structures such as highways and roads. **Design:** Knowledge of design techniques, tools, and principles involved in production of precision technical plans, blueprints, drawings, and models. **Engineering and Technology:** Knowledge of the practical application of engineering science and technology. This includes applying principles, techniques, procedures, and equipment to the design and production of various goods and services.

Carpet Installers

- Education/Training Required: Moderate-term on-the-job training
- Annual Earnings: $34,090
- Growth: 16.8%
- Annual Job Openings: 10,000
- Self-Employed: 53.5%
- Part-Time: 6.9%

Lay and install carpet from rolls or blocks on floors. Install padding and trim flooring materials. Join edges of carpet and seam edges where necessary by sewing or by using tape with glue and heated carpet iron. Cut and trim carpet to fit along wall edges, openings, and projections, finishing the edges with a wall trimmer. Inspect the surface to be covered to determine its condition and correct any imperfections that might show through carpet or cause carpet to wear unevenly. Roll out, measure, mark, and cut carpeting to size with a carpet knife, following floor sketches and allowing extra carpet for final fitting. Plan the layout of the carpet, allowing for expected traffic patterns and placing seams for best appearance and longest wear. Stretch carpet to align with walls and ensure a smooth surface and press carpet in place over tack strips or use staples, tape, tacks, or glue to hold carpet in place. Take measurements and study floor sketches to calculate the area to be carpeted and the amount of material needed. Cut carpet padding to size and install padding, following prescribed method. Install carpet on some floors by using adhesive, following prescribed method. Nail tack strips around area to be carpeted or use old strips to attach edges of new carpet. Fasten metal treads across door openings or where carpet meets flooring to hold carpet in place. Measure, cut, and install tackless strips along the baseboard or wall. Draw building diagrams and record dimensions. Move furniture from area to be carpeted and remove old carpet and padding. Cut and bind material. **SKILLS—Installation:** Installing equipment, machines, wiring, or programs to meet specifications. **Equipment Selection:** Determining the kind of tools and equipment needed to do a job. **Repairing:** Repairing machines or systems by using the needed tools. **Management of Personnel Resources:** Motivating, developing, and directing people as they work, identifying the best people for the job. **Coordination:** Adjusting actions in relation to others' actions. **Mathematics:** Using mathematics to solve problems. **Complex Problem Solving:** Identifying complex problems and reviewing related information to develop and evaluate options and implement solutions. **Learning Strategies:** Selecting and using training/instructional methods and procedures appropriate for the situation when learning or teaching new things. **GOE—Interest Area:** 02. Architecture and Construction. **Work Group:** 02.04. Construction Crafts. **Other Jobs in This Work Group:** Boat Builders and Shipwrights; Boilermakers; Brattice Builders; Brickmasons and Blockmasons; Ceiling Tile Installers; Cement Masons and Concrete Finishers; Commercial Divers; Construction Carpenters; Crane and Tower Operators; Dragline Operators; Drywall Installers; Electricians; Fence Erectors; Floor Layers, Except Carpet, Wood, and Hard Tiles; Floor Sanders and Finishers; Glaziers; Grader, Bulldozer, and Scraper Operators; Hazardous Materials Removal Workers; Insulation Workers, Floor, Ceiling, and Wall; Insulation Workers, Mechanical; Manufactured Building and Mobile Home Installers; Operating Engineers; Painters, Construction and Maintenance; Paperhangers; Paving, Surfacing, and Tamping Equipment Operators; Pile-Driver Operators; Pipe Fitters; Pipelayers; Pipelaying Fitters; Plasterers and Stucco Masons; Plumbers; Rail-Track Laying and Maintenance Equipment Operators; Refractory Materials Repairers, Except Brickmasons; Reinforcing Iron and Rebar Workers; Riggers; Roofers; Rough Carpenters; Security and Fire Alarm Systems Installers; Segmental Pavers; Sheet Metal Workers; Ship Carpenters and Joiners; Stone Cutters and Carvers; Stonemasons; Structural Iron and Steel Workers; Tapers; Terrazzo Workers and Finishers; Tile and Marble Setters. **PERSONALITY TYPE:** Realistic. Realistic occupations frequently involve work activities that include practical, hands-on problems and solutions. These occupations often deal with plants, animals, and real-world materials like wood, tools, and machinery. Many of the occupations require working outside and do not involve a lot of paperwork or working closely with others.

EDUCATION/TRAINING PROGRAM(S)—Construction Trades, Other. **RELATED KNOWLEDGE/COURSES—Public Safety and Security:** Knowledge of relevant equipment, policies, procedures, and strategies to promote effective local, state, or national security operations for the protection of people, data, property, and institutions. **Transportation:** Knowledge of principles and methods for moving people or goods by air, rail, sea, or road, including the relative costs and benefits. **Building and Construction:** Knowledge of the materials, methods, and tools involved in the construction or repair of houses, buildings, or other structures such as highways and roads. **Sales and Marketing:** Knowledge of principles and methods for showing, promoting, and selling products or services. This includes marketing strategy and tactics, product demonstrations, sales techniques, and sales control systems. **Customer and Personal Service:** Knowledge of principles and processes for providing customer and personal services. This includes customer needs assessment, meeting quality standards for services, and evaluation of customer satisfaction. **Personnel and Human Resources:** Knowledge of principles and procedures for personnel recruitment, selection, training, compensation and benefits, labor relations and negotiation, and personnel information systems. **Design:** Knowledge of design techniques, tools, and principles involved in production of precision technical plans, blueprints, drawings, and models.

Cartoonists

- Education/Training Required: Long-term on-the-job training
- Annual Earnings: $38,060
- Growth: 16.5%
- Annual Job Openings: 4,000
- Self-Employed: 55.5%
- Part-Time: 23.1%

Create original artwork by using any of a wide variety of mediums and techniques, such as painting and sculpture. Sketches and submits cartoon or animation for approval. Develops personal ideas for cartoons, comic strips, or animations or reads written material to develop ideas. Makes changes and corrections to cartoon, comic strip, or animation as necessary. Creates and prepares sketches and model drawings of characters, providing details from memory, live models, man-

ufactured products, or reference material. Renders sequential drawings of characters or other subject material which, when photographed and projected at specific speed, become animated. Develops color patterns and moods and paints background layouts to dramatize action for animated cartoon scenes. Discusses ideas for cartoons, comic strips, or animations with editor or publisher's representative. Labels each section with designated colors when colors are used. **SKILLS—Operations Analysis:** Analyzing needs and product requirements to create a design. **GOE—Interest Area:** 03. Arts and Communication. **Work Group:** 03.04. Studio Art. **Other Jobs in This Work Group:** Craft Artists; Painters and Illustrators; Potters; Sculptors; Sketch Artists. **PERSONALITY TYPE:** Artistic. Artistic occupations frequently involve working with forms, designs, and patterns. These occupations often require self-expression, and the work can be done without following a clear set of rules.

EDUCATION/TRAINING PROGRAM(S)— Art/Art Studies, General; Drawing; Fine Arts and Art Studies, Other; Fine/Studio Arts, General; Intermedia/Multimedia; Medical Illustration/Medical Illustrator; Painting; Visual and Performing Arts, General. **RELATED KNOWLEDGE/COURSES—Fine Arts:** Knowledge of the theory and techniques required to compose, produce, and perform works of music, dance, the visual arts, drama, and sculpture. **Communications and Media:** Knowledge of media production, communication, and dissemination techniques and methods. This includes alternative ways to inform and entertain via written, oral, and visual media. **Design:** Knowledge of design techniques, tools, and principles involved in production of precision technical plans, blueprints, drawings, and models. **Sales and Marketing:** Knowledge of principles and methods for showing, promoting, and selling products or services. This includes marketing strategy and tactics, product demonstrations, sales techniques, and sales control systems. **Telecommunications:** Knowledge of transmission, broadcasting, switching, control, and operation of telecommunications systems.

Cashiers

- Education/Training Required: Short-term on-the-job training
- Annual Earnings: $16,240
- Growth: 13.2%
- Annual Job Openings: 1,221,000
- Self-Employed: 1.0%
- Part-Time: 44.8%

Receive and disburse money in establishments other than financial institutions. Usually involves use of electronic scanners, cash registers, or related equipment. Often involved in processing credit or debit card transactions and validating checks. Receive payment by cash, check, credit cards, vouchers, or automatic debits. Issue receipts, refunds, credits, or change due to customers. Count money in cash drawers at the beginning of shifts to ensure that amounts are correct and that there is adequate change. Greet customers entering establishments. Maintain clean and orderly checkout areas. Establish or identify prices of goods, services, or admission and tabulate bills, using calculators, cash registers, or optical price scanners. Issue trading stamps and redeem food stamps and coupons. Resolve customer complaints. Answer customers' questions and provide information on procedures or policies. Cash checks for customers. Weigh items sold by weight in order to determine prices. Calculate total payments received during a time period and reconcile this with total sales. Compute and record totals of transactions. Sell tickets and other items to customers. Keep periodic balance sheets of amounts and numbers of transactions. Bag, box, wrap, or gift-wrap merchandise and prepare packages for shipment. Sort, count, and wrap currency and coins. Process merchandise returns and exchanges. Pay company bills by cash, vouchers, or checks. Request information or assistance by using paging systems. Stock shelves and mark prices on shelves and items. Compile and maintain non-monetary reports and records. Monitor checkout stations to ensure that they have adequate cash available and that they are staffed appropriately. Post charges against guests' or patients' accounts. Offer customers carry-out service at the completion of transactions. **SKILLS—Social Perceptiveness:** Being aware of others' reactions and understanding why they react as they do. **Learning Strategies:** Selecting and using training/instructional methods and procedures appropriate for the situation when learning or teaching new things. **Service Orientation:** Actively looking for ways to help people. **Management of Personnel Resources:** Motivating, developing, and directing people as they work, identifying the best people for the job. **Systems Analysis:** Determining how a system should work and how changes in conditions, operations, and the environment will affect outcomes. **Instructing:** Teaching others how to do something. **Negotiation:** Bringing others together and trying to reconcile differences. **Persuasion:** Persuading others to change their minds or behavior. **GOE—Interest Area:** 14. Retail and Wholesale Sales and Service. **Work Group:** 14.06. Customer Service. **Other Jobs in This Work Group:** Adjustment Clerks; Counter and Rental Clerks; Customer Service Representatives, Utilities; Gaming Change Persons and Booth Cashiers; Order Clerks; Receptionists and Information Clerks. **PERSONALITY TYPE:** Conventional. Conventional occupations frequently involve following set procedures and routines. These occupations can include working with data and details more than with ideas. Usually there is a clear line of authority to follow.

EDUCATION/TRAINING PROGRAM(S)— Retailing and Retail Operations. **RELATED KNOWLEDGE/COURSES—Customer and Personal Service:** Knowledge of principles and processes for providing customer and personal services. This includes customer needs assessment, meeting quality standards for services, and evaluation of customer satisfaction. **Education and Training:** Knowledge of principles and methods for curriculum and training design, teaching and instruction for individuals and groups, and the measurement of training effects. **Foreign Language:** Knowledge of the structure and content of a foreign (non-English) language, including the meaning and spelling of words, rules of composition and grammar, and pronunciation. **English Language:** Knowledge of the structure and content of the English language, including the meaning and spelling of words, rules of composition, and grammar. **Administration and Management:** Knowledge of business and management principles involved in strategic planning, resource allocation, human resources modeling, leadership technique, production methods, and coordination of people and resources. **Mathematics:** Knowledge of arithmetic, algebra, geometry, calculus, and statistics and their applications.

Ceiling Tile Installers

- ◎ Education/Training Required: Moderate-term on-the-job training
- ◎ Annual Earnings: $34,030
- ◎ Growth: 21.4%
- ◎ Annual Job Openings: 17,000
- ◎ Self-Employed: 18.4%
- ◎ Part-Time: 5.9%

Apply or mount acoustical tiles or blocks, strips, or sheets of shock-absorbing materials to ceilings and walls of buildings to reduce or reflect sound. Materials may be of decorative quality. Includes lathers who fasten wooden, metal, or rockboard lath to walls, ceilings, or partitions of buildings to provide support base for plaster, fire-proofing, or acoustical material. Applies acoustical tiles or shock-absorbing materials to ceilings and walls of buildings to reduce or reflect sound and to decorate rooms. Washes concrete surfaces with washing soda and zinc sulfate solution before mounting tile to increase adhesive qualities of surfaces. Inspects furrings, mechanical mountings, and masonry surface for plumbness and level, using spirit or water level. Hangs dry lines (stretched string) to wall molding to guide positioning of main runners. Nails or screws molding to wall to support and seals joint between ceiling tile and wall. Scribes and cuts edges of tile to fit wall where wall molding is not specified. Nails channels or wood furring strips to surfaces to provide mounting for tile. Measures and marks surface to lay out work according to blueprints and drawings. Cuts tiles for fixture and borders, using keyhole saw, and inserts tiles into supporting framework. Applies cement to back of tile and presses tile into place, aligning with layout marks and joints of previously laid tile. **SKILLS**—None met the criteria. **GOE—Interest Area:** 02. Architecture and Construction. **Work Group:** 02.04. Construction Crafts. **Other Jobs in This Work Group:** Boat Builders and Shipwrights; Boilermakers; Brattice Builders; Brickmasons and Blockmasons; Carpet Installers; Cement Masons and Concrete Finishers; Commercial Divers; Construction Carpenters; Crane and Tower Operators; Dragline Operators; Drywall Installers; Electricians; Fence Erectors; Floor Layers, Except Carpet, Wood, and Hard Tiles; Floor Sanders and Finishers; Glaziers; Grader, Bulldozer, and Scraper Operators; Hazardous Materials Removal Workers; Insulation Workers, Floor, Ceiling, and Wall; Insulation Workers, Mechanical; Manufactured Building and Mobile Home Installers; Operating Engineers; Painters, Construction and Maintenance; Paperhangers; Paving, Surfacing, and Tamping Equipment Operators; Pile-Driver Operators; Pipe Fitters; Pipelayers; Pipelaying Fitters; Plasterers and Stucco Masons; Plumbers; Rail-Track Laying and Maintenance Equipment Operators; Refractory Materials Repairers, Except Brickmasons; Reinforcing Iron and Rebar Workers; Riggers; Roofers; Rough Carpenters; Security and Fire Alarm Systems Installers; Segmental Pavers; Sheet Metal Workers; Ship Carpenters and Joiners; Stone Cutters and Carvers; Stonemasons; Structural Iron and Steel Workers; Tapers; Terrazzo Workers and Finishers; Tile and Marble Setters. **PERSONALITY TYPE:** Realistic. Realistic occupations frequently involve work activities that include practical, hands-on problems and solutions. These occupations often deal with plants, animals, and real-world materials like wood, tools, and machinery. Many of the occupations require working outside and do not involve a lot of paperwork or working closely with others.

EDUCATION/TRAINING PROGRAM(S)—Drywall Installation/Drywaller. **RELATED KNOWLEDGE/COURSES**—**Building and Construction:** Knowledge of the materials, methods, and tools involved in the construction or repair of houses, buildings, or other structures such as highways and roads. **Design:** Knowledge of design techniques, tools, and principles involved in production of precision technical plans, blueprints, drawings, and models. **Physics:** Knowledge and prediction of physical principles and laws and their interrelationships and applications to understanding fluid, material, and atmospheric dynamics and mechanical, electrical, atomic, and subatomic structures and processes.

Cement Masons and Concrete Finishers

- Education/Training Required: Long-term on-the-job training
- Annual Earnings: $31,400
- Growth: 26.1%
- Annual Job Openings: 24,000
- Self-Employed: 5.2%
- Part-Time: 5.0%

Smooth and finish surfaces of poured concrete, such as floors, walks, sidewalks, roads, or curbs, using a variety of hand and power tools. Align forms for sidewalks, curbs, or gutters; patch voids; use saws to cut expansion joints. Check the forms that hold the concrete to see that they are properly constructed. Set the forms that hold concrete to the desired pitch and depth and align them. Spread, level, and smooth concrete, using rake, shovel, hand or power trowel, hand or power screed, and float. Mold expansion joints and edges, using edging tools, jointers, and straightedge. Monitor how the wind, heat, or cold affect the curing of the concrete throughout the entire process. Signal truck driver to position truck to facilitate pouring concrete and move chute to direct concrete on forms. Produce rough concrete surface, using broom. Operate power vibrator to compact concrete. Direct the casting of the concrete and supervise laborers who use shovels or special tools to spread it. Mix cement, sand, and water to produce concrete, grout, or slurry, using hoe, trowel, tamper, scraper, or concrete-mixing machine. Cut out damaged areas, drill holes for reinforcing rods, and position reinforcing rods to repair concrete, using power saw and drill. Wet concrete surface and rub with stone to smooth surface and obtain specified finish. Wet surface to prepare for bonding, fill holes and cracks with grout or slurry, and smooth, using trowel. Clean chipped area, using wire brush, and feel and observe surface to determine if it is rough or uneven. Apply hardening and sealing compounds to cure surface of concrete and waterproof or restore surface. Chip, scrape, and grind high spots, ridges, and rough projections to finish concrete, using pneumatic chisels, power grinders, or hand tools. Spread roofing paper on surface of foundation and spread concrete onto roofing paper with trowel to form terrazzo base. Build wooden molds and clamp molds around area to be repaired, using hand tools. Sprinkle colored marble or stone chips, powdered steel, or coloring powder over surface to produce prescribed finish. Cut metal division strips and press them into terrazzo base so that top edges form desired design or pattern. Fabricate concrete beams, columns, and panels. Waterproof or restore concrete surfaces, using appropriate compounds. **SKILLS—Coordination:** Adjusting actions in relation to others' actions. **Mathematics:** Using mathematics to solve problems. **Installation:** Installing equipment, machines, wiring, or programs to meet specifications. **Repairing:** Repairing machines or systems by using the needed tools. **Equipment Maintenance:** Performing routine maintenance on equipment and determining when and what kind of maintenance is needed. **Persuasion:** Persuading others to change their minds or behavior. **Equipment Selection:** Determining the kind of tools and equipment needed to do a job. **Active Learning:** Understanding the implications of new information for both current and future problem-solving and decision-making. **GOE—Interest Area:** 02. Architecture and Construction. **Work Group:** 02.04. Construction Crafts. **Other Jobs in This Work Group:** Boat Builders and Shipwrights; Boilermakers; Brattice Builders; Brickmasons and Blockmasons; Carpet Installers; Ceiling Tile Installers; Commercial Divers; Construction Carpenters; Crane and Tower Operators; Dragline Operators; Drywall Installers; Electricians; Fence Erectors; Floor Layers, Except Carpet, Wood, and Hard Tiles; Floor Sanders and Finishers; Glaziers; Grader, Bulldozer, and Scraper Operators; Hazardous Materials Removal Workers; Insulation Workers, Floor, Ceiling, and Wall; Insulation Workers, Mechanical; Manufactured Building and Mobile Home Installers; Operating Engineers; Painters, Construction and Maintenance; Paperhangers; Paving, Surfacing, and Tamping Equipment Operators; Pile-Driver Operators; Pipe Fitters; Pipelayers; Pipelaying Fitters; Plasterers and Stucco Masons; Plumbers; Rail-Track Laying and Maintenance Equipment Operators; Refractory Materials Repairers, Except Brickmasons; Reinforcing Iron and Rebar Workers; Riggers; Roofers; Rough Carpenters; Security and Fire Alarm Systems Installers; Segmental Pavers; Sheet Metal Workers; Ship Carpenters and Joiners; Stone Cutters and Carvers; Stonemasons; Structural

Iron and Steel Workers; Tapers; Terrazzo Workers and Finishers; Tile and Marble Setters. **PERSONALITY TYPE:** Realistic. Realistic occupations frequently involve work activities that include practical, hands-on problems and solutions. These occupations often deal with plants, animals, and real-world materials like wood, tools, and machinery. Many of the occupations require working outside and do not involve a lot of paperwork or working closely with others.

EDUCATION/TRAINING PROGRAM(S)—Concrete Finishing/Concrete Finisher. **RELATED KNOWLEDGE/COURSES—Building and Construction:** Knowledge of the materials, methods, and tools involved in the construction or repair of houses, buildings, or other structures such as highways and roads. **Public Safety and Security:** Knowledge of relevant equipment, policies, procedures, and strategies to promote effective local, state, or national security operations for the protection of people, data, property, and institutions. **Foreign Language:** Knowledge of the structure and content of a foreign (non-English) language, including the meaning and spelling of words, rules of composition and grammar, and pronunciation. **Economics and Accounting:** Knowledge of economic and accounting principles and practices, the financial markets, banking, and the analysis and reporting of financial data. **Administration and Management:** Knowledge of business and management principles involved in strategic planning, resource allocation, human resources modeling, leadership technique, production methods, and coordination of people and resources. **Mathematics:** Knowledge of arithmetic, algebra, geometry, calculus, and statistics and their applications.

Central Office and PBX Installers and Repairers

- Education/Training Required: Postsecondary vocational training
- Annual Earnings: $49,840
- Growth: –0.6%
- Annual Job Openings: 23,000
- Self-Employed: 4.6%
- Part-Time: 1.7%

Test, analyze, and repair telephone or telegraph circuits and equipment at a central office location, using test meters and hand tools. Analyze and repair defects in communications equipment on customers' premises, using circuit diagrams, polarity probes, meters, and a telephone test set. May install equipment. Tests circuits and components of malfunctioning telecommunication equipment to isolate source of malfunction, using test instruments and circuit diagrams. Analyzes test readings, computer printouts, and trouble reports to determine method of repair. Tests and adjusts installed equipment to ensure circuit continuity and operational performance, using test instruments. Connects wires to equipment, using hand tools, soldering iron, or wire wrap gun. Installs preassembled or partially assembled switching equipment, switchboards, wiring frames, and power apparatus according to floor plans. Retests repaired equipment to ensure that malfunction has been corrected. Repairs or replaces defective components, such as switches, relays, amplifiers, and circuit boards, using hand tools and soldering iron. Removes and remakes connections on wire distributing frame to change circuit layout, following diagrams. Routes cables and trunklines from entry points to specified equipment, following diagrams. Enters codes to correct programming of electronic switching systems. **SKILLS—Repairing:** Repairing machines or systems by using the needed tools. **Installation:** Installing equipment, machines, wiring, or programs to meet specifications. **Troubleshooting:** Determining causes of operating errors and deciding what to do about them. **Technology Design:** Generating or adapting equipment and technology to serve user needs. **Operation Monitoring:** Watching gauges, dials, or other indicators to make sure a machine is working properly. **Science:** Using scientific rules and methods to solve problems. **Equipment Maintenance:** Performing routine maintenance on equipment and determining when and what kind of maintenance is needed. **Quality Control Analysis:** Conducting tests and inspections of products, services, or processes to evaluate quality or performance. **GOE—Interest Area:** 02. Architecture and Construction. **Work Group:** 02.05. Systems and Equipment Installation, Maintenance, and Repair. **Other Jobs in This Work Group:** Communication Equipment Mechanics, Installers, and Repairers; Electric Meter

Installers and Repairers; Electrical and Electronics Repairers, Powerhouse, Substation, and Relay; Electrical Power-Line Installers and Repairers; Elevator Installers and Repairers; Frame Wirers, Central Office; Heating and Air Conditioning Mechanics; Home Appliance Installers; Maintenance and Repair Workers, General; Meter Mechanics; Refrigeration Mechanics; Station Installers and Repairers, Telephone; Telecommunications Facility Examiners; Telecommunications Line Installers and Repairers. **PERSONALITY TYPE:** Realistic. Realistic occupations frequently involve work activities that include practical, hands-on problems and solutions. These occupations often deal with plants, animals, and real-world materials like wood, tools, and machinery. Many of the occupations require working outside and do not involve a lot of paperwork or working closely with others.

EDUCATION/TRAINING PROGRAM(S)— Communications Systems Installation and Repair Technology. **RELATED KNOWLEDGE/COURSES—Telecommunications:** Knowledge of transmission, broadcasting, switching, control, and operation of telecommunications systems. **Computers and Electronics:** Knowledge of circuit boards, processors, chips, electronic equipment, and computer hardware and software, including applications and programming. **Design:** Knowledge of design techniques, tools, and principles involved in production of precision technical plans, blueprints, drawings, and models. **Engineering and Technology:** Knowledge of the practical application of engineering science and technology. This includes applying principles, techniques, procedures, and equipment to the design and production of various goods and services. **Physics:** Knowledge and prediction of physical principles and laws and their interrelationships and applications to understanding fluid, material, and atmospheric dynamics and mechanical, electrical, atomic, and subatomic structures and processes.

Chefs and Head Cooks

- Education/Training Required: Postsecondary vocational training
- Annual Earnings: $30,680
- Growth: 15.8%
- Annual Job Openings: 33,000
- Self-Employed: 7.4%
- Part-Time: 8.6%

Direct the preparation, seasoning, and cooking of salads, soups, fish, meats, vegetables, desserts, or other foods. May plan and price menu items, order supplies, and keep records and accounts. May participate in cooking. Prepare and cook foods of all types, either on a regular basis or for special guests or functions. Supervise and coordinate activities of cooks and workers engaged in food preparation. Collaborate with other personnel to plan and develop recipes and menus, taking into account such factors as seasonal availability of ingredients and the likely number of customers. Check the quality of raw and cooked food products to ensure that standards are met. Check the quantity and quality of received products. Demonstrate new cooking techniques and equipment to staff. Determine how food should be presented and create decorative food displays. Determine production schedules and staff requirements necessary to ensure timely delivery of services. Estimate amounts and costs of required supplies, such as food and ingredients. Inspect supplies, equipment, and work areas to ensure conformance to established standards. Instruct cooks and other workers in the preparation, cooking, garnishing, and presentation of food. Monitor sanitation practices to ensure that employees follow standards and regulations. Order or requisition food and other supplies needed to ensure efficient operation. Recruit and hire staff, including cooks and other kitchen workers. Analyze recipes to assign prices to menu items based on food, labor, and overhead costs. Arrange for equipment purchases and repairs. Meet with customers to discuss menus for special occasions such as weddings, parties, and banquets. Meet with sales representatives in order to negotiate prices and order supplies. Record production and operational data on specified forms. Coordinate planning, budgeting, and purchasing for all the food operations within establishments such as clubs, hotels, or restaurant chains. Plan, direct, and supervise the food preparation and cooking activities of multiple kitchens or restaurants in an establishment such as a restaurant chain, hospital, or hotel. **SKILLS—Management of Financial Resources:** Determining how money will be spent to get the work done and accounting for these expenditures. **Management of Material Resources:** Obtaining and seeing to the appropriate use of equipment, facilities, and materials needed to do certain work. **Management of Personnel Resources:** Motivating, developing, and directing people as they work, identifying the best people for the job. **Coordination:** Adjusting actions in relation to others' actions. **Instructing:** Teaching others how to do something. **Systems Evaluation:** Identifying measures or indicators of system performance and the actions needed to improve or correct performance relative to the goals of the system. **Time Management:** Managing one's own time and the time of others. **Systems Analysis:** Determining how a system should work and how changes in conditions, operations, and the environment will affect outcomes. **GOE—Interest Area:** 09. Hospitality, Tourism, and Recreation. **Work Group:** 09.04. Food and Beverage Preparation. **Other Jobs in This Work Group:** Bakers, Bread and Pastry; Butchers and Meat Cutters; Cooks, Fast Food; Cooks, Institution and Cafeteria; Cooks, Restaurant; Cooks, Short Order; Dishwashers; Food Preparation Workers. **PERSONALITY TYPE:** Enterprising. Enterprising occupations frequently involve starting up and carrying out projects. These occupations can involve leading people and making many decisions. They sometimes require risk taking and often deal with business.

EDUCATION/TRAINING PROGRAM(S)— Cooking and Related Culinary Arts, General; Culinary Arts/Chef Training. **RELATED KNOWLEDGE/ COURSES—Administration and Management:** Knowledge of business and management principles involved in strategic planning, resource allocation, human resources modeling, leadership technique, production methods, and coordination of people and resources. **Personnel and Human Resources:** Knowledge of principles and procedures for personnel recruitment, selection, training, compensation and benefits, labor relations and negotiation, and personnel information systems. **Economics and Accounting:**

Knowledge of economic and accounting principles and practices, the financial markets, banking, and the analysis and reporting of financial data. **Education and Training:** Knowledge of principles and methods for curriculum and training design, teaching and instruction for individuals and groups, and the measurement of training effects. **Food Production:** Knowledge of techniques and equipment for planting, growing, and harvesting food products (both plant and animal) for consumption, including storage/handling techniques. **Biology:** Knowledge of plant and animal organisms and their tissues, cells, functions, interdependencies, and interactions with each other and the environment.

Child Care Workers

- Education/Training Required: Short-term on-the-job training
- Annual Earnings: $16,760
- Growth: 11.7%
- Annual Job Openings: 406,000
- Self-Employed: 43.4%
- Part-Time: 35.2%

Attend to children at schools, businesses, private households, and child care institutions. Perform a variety of tasks, such as dressing, feeding, bathing, and overseeing play. Support children's emotional and social development, encouraging understanding of others and positive self-concepts. Care for children in institutional setting, such as group homes, nursery schools, private businesses, or schools for the handicapped. Sanitize toys and play equipment. Discipline children and recommend or initiate other measures to control behavior, such as caring for own clothing and picking up toys and books. Identify signs of emotional or developmental problems in children and bring them to parents' or guardians' attention. Observe and monitor children's play activities. Keep records on individual children, including daily observations and information about activities, meals served, and medications administered. Instruct children in health and personal habits such as eating, resting, and toilet habits. Read to children and teach them simple painting, drawing, handicrafts, and songs. Organize and participate in recreational activities, such as games.

Assist in preparing food for children, serve meals and refreshments to children, and regulate rest periods. Organize and store toys and materials to ensure order in activity areas. Operate in-house day care centers within businesses. Sterilize bottles and prepare formulas. Provide counseling or therapy to mentally disturbed, delinquent, or handicapped children. Dress children and change diapers. Help children with homework and school work. Perform housekeeping duties such as laundry, cleaning, dishwashing, and changing of linens. Accompany children to and from school, on outings, and to medical appointments. **SKILLS—Learning Strategies:** Selecting and using training/instructional methods and procedures appropriate for the situation when learning or teaching new things. **Social Perceptiveness:** Being aware of others' reactions and understanding why they react as they do. **Negotiation:** Bringing others together and trying to reconcile differences. **Service Orientation:** Actively looking for ways to help people. **Persuasion:** Persuading others to change their minds or behavior. **Time Management:** Managing one's own time and the time of others. **Critical Thinking:** Using logic and reasoning to identify the strengths and weaknesses of alternative solutions, conclusions, or approaches to problems. **Monitoring:** Monitoring or assessing your performance or that of other individuals or organizations to make improvements or take corrective action. **GOE— Interest Area:** 10. Human Service. **Work Group:** 10.03. Child/Personal Care and Services. **Other Jobs in This Work Group:** Funeral Attendants; Nannies; Personal and Home Care Aides. **PERSONALITY TYPE:** Social. Social occupations frequently involve working with, communicating with, and teaching people. These occupations often involve helping or providing service to others.

EDUCATION/TRAINING PROGRAM(S)— Child Care Provider/Assistant. **RELATED KNOWL-EDGE/COURSES—Psychology:** Knowledge of human behavior and performance; individual differences in ability, personality, and interests; learning and motivation; psychological research methods; and the assessment and treatment of behavioral and affective disorders. **Customer and Personal Service:** Knowledge of principles and processes for providing customer and personal services. This includes customer needs assessment, meeting quality standards for services, and eval-uation of customer satisfaction. **Sociology and Anthropology:** Knowledge of group behavior and dynamics, societal trends and influences, human migrations, ethnicity, and cultures and their history and origins. **Public Safety and Security:** Knowledge of relevant equipment, policies, procedures, and strategies to promote effective local, state, or national security operations for the protection of people, data, property, and institutions. **Philosophy and Theology:** Knowl-edge of different philosophical systems and religions. This includes their basic principles, values, ethics, ways of thinking, customs, and practices and their impact on human culture. **Medicine and Dentistry:** Knowl-edge of the information and techniques needed to diagnose and treat human injuries, diseases, and defor-mities. This includes symptoms, treatment alterna-tives, drug properties and interactions, and preventive health-care measures.

Child Support, Missing Persons, and Unemployment Insurance Fraud Investigators

- Education/Training Required: Work experience in a related occupation
- Annual Earnings: $53,990
- Growth: 22.4%
- Annual Job Openings: 11,000
- Self-Employed: 0%
- Part-Time: 0.5%

Conduct investigations to locate, arrest, and return fugitives and persons wanted for non-payment of support payments and unemployment insurance fraud and to locate missing persons. Serves warrants and makes arrests to return persons sought in connec-tion with crimes or for non-payment of child support. Computes amount of child support payments. Testi-fies in court to present evidence regarding cases. Exam-ines medical and dental X rays, fingerprints, and other information to identify bodies held in morgue. Exam-ines case file to determine that divorce decree and court-ordered judgment for payment are in order.

Completes reports to document information acquired during criminal and child support cases and actions taken. Monitors child support payments awarded by court to ensure compliance and enforcement of child support laws. Determines types of court jurisdiction, according to facts and circumstances surrounding case, and files court action. Confers with prosecuting attorney to prepare court case and with court clerk to obtain arrest warrant and schedule court date. Interviews client to obtain information such as relocation of absent parent, amount of child support awarded, and names of witnesses. Interviews and discusses case with parent charged with nonpayment of support to resolve issues in lieu of filing court proceedings. Reviews files and criminal records to develop possible leads, such as previous addresses and aliases. Prepares file indicating data such as wage records of accused, witnesses, and blood test results. Obtains extradition papers to bring about return of fugitive. Contacts employers, neighbors, relatives, and law enforcement agencies to locate person sought and verify information gathered about case. **SKILLS—Active Listening:** Giving full attention to what other people are saying, taking time to understand the points being made, asking questions as appropriate, and not interrupting at inappropriate times. **Speaking:** Talking to others to convey information effectively. **Negotiation:** Bringing others together and trying to reconcile differences. **Critical Thinking:** Using logic and reasoning to identify the strengths and weaknesses of alternative solutions, conclusions, or approaches to problems. **Reading Comprehension:** Understanding written sentences and paragraphs in work-related documents. **Judgment and Decision Making:** Considering the relative costs and benefits of potential actions to choose the most appropriate one. **Writing:** Communicating effectively in writing as appropriate for the needs of the audience. **Persuasion:** Persuading others to change their minds or behavior. **GOE—Interest Area:** 07. Government and Public Administration. **Work Group:** 07.03. Regulations Enforcement. **Other Jobs in This Work Group:** Agricultural Inspectors; Aviation Inspectors; Environmental Compliance Inspectors; Equal Opportunity Representatives and Officers; Financial Examiners; Fire Inspectors; Fish and Game Wardens; Forest Fire Inspectors and Prevention Specialists; Government Property Inspectors and Investigators; Immigration

and Customs Inspectors; Licensing Examiners and Inspectors; Marine Cargo Inspectors; Mechanical Inspectors; Motor Vehicle Inspectors; Nuclear Monitoring Technicians; Occupational Health and Safety Specialists; Pressure Vessel Inspectors; Railroad Inspectors; Tax Examiners, Collectors, and Revenue Agents. **PERSONALITY TYPE:** Enterprising. Enterprising occupations frequently involve starting up and carrying out projects. These occupations can involve leading people and making many decisions. They sometimes require risk taking and often deal with business.

EDUCATION/TRAINING PROGRAM(S)— Criminal Justice/Police Science; Criminalistics and Criminal Science. **RELATED KNOWLEDGE/ COURSES—Law and Government:** Knowledge of laws, legal codes, court procedures, precedents, government regulations, executive orders, agency rules, and the democratic political process. **Public Safety and Security:** Knowledge of relevant equipment, policies, procedures, and strategies to promote effective local, state, or national security operations for the protection of people, data, property, and institutions. **Economics and Accounting:** Knowledge of economic and accounting principles and practices, the financial markets, banking, and the analysis and reporting of financial data. **Geography:** Knowledge of principles and methods for describing the features of land, sea, and air masses, including their physical characteristics; locations; interrelationships; and distribution of plant, animal, and human life. **English Language:** Knowledge of the structure and content of the English language, including the meaning and spelling of words, rules of composition, and grammar. **Sociology and Anthropology:** Knowledge of group behavior and dynamics, societal trends and influences, human migrations, ethnicity, and cultures and their history and origins.

Choreographers

- Education/Training Required: Work experience in a related occupation
- Annual Earnings: $33,670
- Growth: 15.8%
- Annual Job Openings: 3,000
- Self-Employed: 16.7%
- Part-Time: 33.8%

Create and teach dance. May direct and stage presentations. Coordinate production music with music directors. Design dances for individual dancers, dance companies, musical theatre, opera, fashion shows, film, television productions, and special events and for dancers ranging from beginners to professionals. Develop ideas for creating dances, keeping notes and sketches to record influences. Direct rehearsals to instruct dancers in how to use dance steps and in techniques to achieve desired effects. Experiment with different types of dancers, steps, dances, and placements, testing ideas informally to get feedback from dancers. Read and study storylines and musical scores to determine how to translate ideas and moods into dance movements. Record dance movements and their technical aspects, using a technical understanding of the patterns and formations of choreography. Re-stage traditional dances and works in dance companies' repertoires, developing new interpretations. Advise dancers on how to stand and move properly, teaching correct dance techniques to help prevent injuries. Assess students' dancing abilities to determine where improvement or change is needed. Audition performers for one or more dance parts. Choose the music, sound effects, or spoken narrative to accompany a dance. Direct and stage dance presentations for various forms of entertainment. Manage dance schools or assist in their management. Seek influences from other art forms such as theatre, the visual arts, and architecture. Teach students, dancers, and other performers about rhythm and interpretive movement. Train, exercise, and attend dance classes to maintain high levels of technical proficiency, physical ability, and physical fitness. Design sets, lighting, costumes, and other artistic elements of productions in collaboration with cast members. **SKILLS—Instructing:** Teaching others how to do something. **Coordination:** Adjusting actions in relation to others' actions. **GOE—Interest Area:** 03. Arts and Communication. **Work Group:** 03.08. Dance. **Other Jobs in This Work Group:** Dancers. **PERSONALITY TYPE:** Artistic. Artistic occupations frequently involve working with forms, designs, and patterns. They often require self-expression, and the work can be done without following a clear set of rules.

EDUCATION/TRAINING PROGRAM(S)— Dance, General; Dance, Other. **RELATED KNOWLEDGE/COURSES—Fine Arts:** Knowledge of the theory and techniques required to compose, produce, and perform works of music, dance, visual arts, drama, and sculpture. **Communications and Media:** Knowledge of media production, communication, and dissemination techniques and methods. This includes alternative ways to inform and entertain via written, oral, and visual media. **Personnel and Human Resources:** Knowledge of principles and procedures for personnel recruitment, selection, training, compensation and benefits, labor relations and negotiation, and personnel information systems. **Education and Training:** Knowledge of principles and methods for curriculum and training design, teaching and instruction for individuals and groups, and the measurement of training effects.

City and Regional Planning Aides

- Education/Training Required: Associate degree
- Annual Earnings: $34,360
- Growth: 17.5%
- Annual Job Openings: 18,000
- Self-Employed: 1.1%
- Part-Time: 20.2%

Compile data from various sources, such as maps, reports, and field and file investigations, for use by city planner in making planning studies. Prepare, maintain, and update files and records, including land use data and statistics. Respond to public inquiries and complaints. Research, compile, analyze, and organize information from maps, reports, investigations, and books for use in reports and special projects. Prepare, develop, and maintain maps and databases. Serve as a liaison between planning department and other departments and agencies. Prepare reports, using statistics, charts, and graphs, to illustrate planning studies in areas such as population, land use, or zoning. Participate in and support team planning efforts. Provide and process zoning and project permits and applications. Perform clerical duties such as composing, typing, and proofreading documents; scheduling appointments and meetings; handling mail; and posting public notices. Conduct interviews, surveys, and site inspections concerning factors that affect land usage, such as zoning, traffic flow, and housing. Perform code enforcement tasks. Inspect sites and review plans for minor development permit applications. **SKILLS—Service Orientation:** Actively looking for ways to help people. **Coordination:** Adjusting actions in relation to others' actions. **Social Perceptiveness:** Being aware of others' reactions and understanding why they react as they do. **Persuasion:** Persuading others to change their minds or behavior. **Writing:** Communicating effectively in writing as appropriate for the needs of the audience. **Active Learning:** Understanding the implications of new information for both current and future problem-solving and decision-making. **Negotiation:** Bringing others together and trying to reconcile differences. **Learning Strategies:** Selecting and using training/instructional methods and procedures appropriate for the situation when learning or teaching new things. **Complex Problem Solving:** Identifying complex problems and reviewing related information to develop and evaluate options and implement solutions. **GOE—Interest Area:** 07. Government and Public Administration. **Work Group:** 07.02. Public Planning. **Other Jobs in This Work Group:** Urban and Regional Planners. **PERSONALITY TYPE:** Conventional. Conventional occupations frequently involve following set procedures and routines. These occupations can include working with data and details more than with ideas. Usually there is a clear line of authority to follow.

EDUCATION/TRAINING PROGRAM(S)— Social Sciences, General. **RELATED KNOWLEDGE/COURSES—Geography:** Knowledge of principles and methods for describing the features of land, sea, and air masses, including their physical characteristics; locations; interrelationships; and distribu-

tion of plant, animal, and human life. **Design:** Knowledge of design techniques, tools, and principles involved in production of precision technical plans, blueprints, drawings, and models. **Clerical Practices:** Knowledge of administrative and clerical procedures and systems such as word processing, managing files and records, stenography and transcription, designing forms, and other office procedures and terminology. **Law and Government:** Knowledge of laws, legal codes, court procedures, precedents, government regulations, executive orders, agency rules, and the democratic political process. **English Language:** Knowledge of the structure and content of the English language, including the meaning and spelling of words, rules of composition, and grammar. **Customer and Personal Service:** Knowledge of principles and processes for providing customer and personal services. This includes customer needs assessment, meeting quality standards for services, and evaluation of customer satisfaction.

Civil Drafters

- ⊚ Education/Training Required: Postsecondary vocational training
- ⊚ Annual Earnings: $39,190
- ⊚ Growth: 4.2%
- ⊚ Annual Job Openings: 14,000
- ⊚ Self-Employed: 3.7%
- ⊚ Part-Time: 5.1%

Prepare drawings and topographical and relief maps used in civil engineering projects, such as highways, bridges, pipelines, flood control projects, and water and sewerage control systems. Produce drawings by using computer assisted drafting systems (CAD) or drafting machines or by hand, using compasses, dividers, protractors, triangles, and other drafting devices. Draft plans and detailed drawings for structures, installations, and construction projects such as highways, sewage disposal systems, and dikes, working from sketches or notes. Draw maps, diagrams, and profiles, using cross-sections and surveys, to represent elevations, topographical contours, subsurface formations, and structures. Correlate, interpret, and modify data obtained from topographical surveys, well logs, and geophysical prospecting reports. Finish and duplicate drawings and documentation packages according to required mediums and specifications for reproduction, using blueprinting, photography, or other duplicating methods. Review rough sketches, drawings, specifications, and other engineering data received from civil engineers to ensure that they conform to design concepts. Supervise and train other technologists, technicians, and drafters. Supervise or conduct field surveys, inspections, or technical investigations to obtain data required to revise construction drawings. Determine the order of work and method of presentation, such as orthographic or isometric drawing. Calculate excavation tonnage and prepare graphs and fill-hauling diagrams for use in earth-moving operations. Explain drawings to production or construction teams and provide adjustments as necessary. Locate and identify symbols located on topographical surveys to denote geological and geophysical formations or oil field installations. **SKILLS—Mathematics:** Using mathematics to solve problems. **Coordination:** Adjusting actions in relation to others' actions. **Instructing:** Teaching others how to do something. **Operations Analysis:** Analyzing needs and product requirements to create a design. **Active Learning:** Understanding the implications of new information for both current and future problem-solving and decision-making. **Technology Design:** Generating or adapting equipment and technology to serve user needs. **Time Management:** Managing one's own time and the time of others. **Active Listening:** Giving full attention to what other people are saying, taking time to understand the points being made, asking questions as appropriate, and not interrupting at inappropriate times. **GOE—Interest Area:** 02. Architecture and Construction. **Work Group:** 02.03. Architecture/Construction Engineering Technologies. **Other Jobs in This Work Group:** Architectural Drafters; Construction and Building Inspectors; Electrical Drafters; Surveyors. **PERSONALITY TYPE:** Realistic. Realistic occupations frequently involve work activities that include practical, hands-on problems and solutions. These occupations often deal with plants, animals, and real-world materials like wood, tools, and machinery. Many of the occupations require working outside and do not involve a lot of paperwork or working closely with others.

EDUCATION/TRAINING PROGRAM(S)—Architectural Drafting and Architectural CAD/CADD; Architectural Technology/Technician; CAD/CADD Drafting and/or Design Technology/Technician; Civil Drafting and Civil Engineering CAD/CADD; Drafting and Design Technology/Technician, General. **RELATED KNOWLEDGE/COURSES—Design:** Knowledge of design techniques, tools, and principles involved in production of precision technical plans, blueprints, drawings, and models. **Engineering and Technology:** Knowledge of the practical application of engineering science and technology. This includes applying principles, techniques, procedures, and equipment to the design and production of various goods and services. **Computers and Electronics:** Knowledge of circuit boards, processors, chips, electronic equipment, and computer hardware and software, including applications and programming. **Geography:** Knowledge of principles and methods for describing the features of land, sea, and air masses, including their physical characteristics; locations; interrelationships; and distribution of plant, animal, and human life. **Mathematics:** Knowledge of arithmetic, algebra, geometry, calculus, and statistics and their applications. **Law and Government:** Knowledge of laws, legal codes, court procedures, precedents, government regulations, executive orders, agency rules, and the democratic political process.

Civil Engineering Technicians

- Education/Training Required: Associate degree
- Annual Earnings: $38,480
- Growth: 7.6%
- Annual Job Openings: 10,000
- Self-Employed: 0.4%
- Part-Time: 5.0%

Apply theory and principles of civil engineering in planning, designing, and overseeing construction and maintenance of structures and facilities under the direction of engineering staff or physical scientists. Calculate dimensions, square footage, profile and component specifications, and material quantities, using calculator or computer. Draft detailed dimensional drawings and design layouts for projects and to ensure conformance to specifications. Analyze proposed site factors and design maps, graphs, tracings, and diagrams to illustrate findings. Read and review project blueprints and structural specifications to determine dimensions of structure or system and material requirements. Prepare reports and document project activities and data. Confer with supervisor to determine project details, such as plan preparation, acceptance testing, and evaluation of field conditions. Inspect project site and evaluate contractor work to detect design malfunctions and ensure conformance to design specifications and applicable codes. Plan and conduct field surveys to locate new sites and analyze details of project sites. Develop plans and estimate costs for installation of systems, utilization of facilities, or construction of structures. Report maintenance problems occurring at project site to supervisor and negotiate changes to resolve system conflicts. Conduct materials test and analysis, using tools and equipment and applying engineering knowledge. Respond to public suggestions and complaints. Evaluate facility to determine suitability for occupancy and square footage availability. **SKILLS—Mathematics:** Using mathematics to solve problems. **Instructing:** Teaching others how to do something. **Active Learning:** Understanding the implications of new information for both current and future problem-solving and decision-making. **Operations Analysis:** Analyzing needs and product requirements to create a design. **Critical Thinking:** Using logic and reasoning to identify the strengths and weaknesses of alternative solutions, conclusions, or approaches to problems. **Complex Problem Solving:** Identifying complex problems and reviewing related information to develop and evaluate options and implement solutions. **Writing:** Communicating effectively in writing as appropriate for the needs of the audience. **Science:** Using scientific rules and methods to solve problems. **Learning Strategies:** Selecting and using training/instructional methods and procedures appropriate for the situation when learning or teaching new things. **GOE—Interest Area:** 15. Scientific Research, Engineering, and Mathematics. **Work Group:** 15.09. Engineering Technology. **Other Jobs in**

This Work Group: Aerospace Engineering and Operations Technicians; Calibration and Instrumentation Technicians; Cartographers and Photogrammetrists; Electrical Engineering Technicians; Electro-Mechanical Technicians; Electronic Drafters; Electronics Engineering Technicians; Environmental Engineering Technicians; Mapping Technicians; Mechanical Drafters; Mechanical Engineering Technicians; Surveying Technicians. **PERSONALITY TYPE:** Realistic. Realistic occupations frequently involve work activities that include practical, hands-on problems and solutions. These occupations often deal with plants, animals, and real-world materials like wood, tools, and machinery. Many of the occupations require working outside and do not involve a lot of paperwork or working closely with others.

EDUCATION/TRAINING PROGRAM(S)—Civil Engineering Technology/Technician; Construction Engineering Technology/Technician. **RELATED KNOWLEDGE/COURSES—Design:** Knowledge of design techniques, tools, and principles involved in production of precision technical plans, blueprints, drawings, and models. **Building and Construction:** Knowledge of the materials, methods, and tools involved in the construction or repair of houses, buildings, or other structures such as highways and roads. **Engineering and Technology:** Knowledge of the practical application of engineering science and technology. This includes applying principles, techniques, procedures, and equipment to the design and production of various goods and services. **Mathematics:** Knowledge of arithmetic, algebra, geometry, calculus, and statistics and their applications. **Computers and Electronics:** Knowledge of circuit boards, processors, chips, electronic equipment, and computer hardware and software, including applications and programming. **Transportation:** Knowledge of principles and methods for moving people or goods by air, rail, sea, or road, including the relative costs and benefits.

Claims Examiners, Property and Casualty Insurance

- ◉ Education/Training Required: Long-term on-the-job training
- ◉ Annual Earnings: $44,220
- ◉ Growth: 14.2%
- ◉ Annual Job Openings: 31,000
- ◉ Self-Employed: 1.9%
- ◉ Part-Time: 4.9%

Review settled insurance claims to determine that payments and settlements have been made in accordance with company practices and procedures. Report overpayments, underpayments, and other irregularities. Confer with legal counsel on claims requiring litigation. Investigate, evaluate, and settle claims, applying technical knowledge and human relations skills to effect fair and prompt disposal of cases and to contribute to a reduced loss ratio. Pay and process claims within designated authority level. Adjust reserves and provide reserve recommendations to ensure reserving activities consistent with corporate policies. Enter claim payments, reserves, and new claims on computer system, inputting concise yet sufficient file documentation. Resolve complex, severe exposure claims, using high-service-oriented file handling. Maintain claim files, such as records of settled claims and an inventory of claims requiring detailed analysis. Verify and analyze data used in settling claims to ensure that claims are valid and that settlements are made according to company practices and procedures. Examine claims investigated by insurance adjusters, further investigating questionable claims to determine whether to authorize payments. Present cases and participate in their discussion at claim committee meetings. Contact and/or interview claimants, doctors, medical specialists, or employers to get additional information. Confer with legal counsel on claims requiring litigation. Report overpayments, underpayments, and other irregularities. Communicate with reinsurance brokers to obtain information necessary for processing claims. Supervise claims adjusters to ensure that adjusters have followed proper methods.

Conduct detailed bill reviews to implement sound litigation management and expense control. Prepare reports to be submitted to company's data processing department. **SKILLS—Judgment and Decision Making:** Considering the relative costs and benefits of potential actions to choose the most appropriate one. **Persuasion:** Persuading others to change their minds or behavior. **Instructing:** Teaching others how to do something. **Negotiation:** Bringing others together and trying to reconcile differences. **Writing:** Communicating effectively in writing as appropriate for the needs of the audience. **Critical Thinking:** Using logic and reasoning to identify the strengths and weaknesses of alternative solutions, conclusions, or approaches to problems. **Time Management:** Managing one's own time and the time of others. **Reading Comprehension:** Understanding written sentences and paragraphs in work-related documents. **Active Listening:** Giving full attention to what other people are saying, taking time to understand the points being made, asking questions as appropriate, and not interrupting at inappropriate times. **Social Perceptiveness:** Being aware of others' reactions and understanding why they react as they do. **GOE—Interest Area:** 06. Finance and Insurance. **Work Group:** 06.02. Finance/Insurance Investigation and Analysis. **Other Jobs in This Work Group:** Appraisers, Real Estate; Assessors; Cost Estimators; Credit Analysts; Financial Analysts; Insurance Adjusters, Examiners, and Investigators; Insurance Appraisers, Auto Damage; Insurance Underwriters; Loan Counselors; Loan Officers; Market Research Analysts; Survey Researchers. **PERSONALITY TYPE:** Conventional. Conventional occupations frequently involve following set procedures and routines. These occupations can include working with data and details more than with ideas. Usually there is a clear line of authority to follow.

EDUCATION/TRAINING PROGRAM(S)— Health/Medical Claims Examiner; Insurance. **RELATED KNOWLEDGE/COURSES—Customer and Personal Service:** Knowledge of principles and processes for providing customer and personal services. This includes customer needs assessment, meeting quality standards for services, and evaluation of customer satisfaction. **Clerical Practices:** Knowledge of administrative and clerical procedures and systems such as word processing, managing files and records, stenography and transcription, designing forms, and other office procedures and terminology. **Medicine and Dentistry:** Knowledge of the information and techniques needed to diagnose and treat human injuries, diseases, and deformities. This includes symptoms, treatment alternatives, drug properties and interactions, and preventive health-care measures. **Law and Government:** Knowledge of laws, legal codes, court procedures, precedents, government regulations, executive orders, agency rules, and the democratic political process. **Computers and Electronics:** Knowledge of circuit boards, processors, chips, electronic equipment, and computer hardware and software, including applications and programming. **English Language:** Knowledge of the structure and content of the English language, including the meaning and spelling of words, rules of composition, and grammar.

Coaches and Scouts

- Education/Training Required: Long-term on-the-job training
- Annual Earnings: $26,350
- Growth: 18.3%
- Annual Job Openings: 26,000
- Self-Employed: 26.6%
- Part-Time: 36.3%

Instruct or coach groups or individuals in the fundamentals of sports. Demonstrate techniques and methods of participation. May evaluate athletes' strengths and weaknesses as possible recruits or to improve the athletes' technique to prepare them for competition. Those required to hold teaching degrees should be reported in the appropriate teaching category. Plan, organize, and conduct practice sessions. Provide training direction, encouragement, and motivation in order to prepare athletes for games, competitive events, and/or tours. Identify and recruit potential athletes, arranging and offering incentives such as athletic scholarships. Plan strategies and choose team members for individual games and/or sports seasons. Plan and direct physical conditioning programs that will enable athletes to achieve maximum performance. Adjust coaching techniques based on the strengths and weaknesses of athletes. File scouting reports that detail

player assessments, provide recommendations on athlete recruitment, and identify locations and individuals to be targeted for future recruitment efforts. Keep records of athlete, team, and opposing team performance. Instruct individuals or groups in sports rules, game strategies, and performance principles such as specific ways of moving the body, hands, and/or feet in order to achieve desired results. Analyze the strengths and weaknesses of opposing teams in order to develop game strategies. Evaluate athletes' skills and review performance records in order to determine their fitness and potential in a particular area of athletics. Keep abreast of changing rules, techniques, technologies, and philosophies relevant to their sport. Monitor athletes' use of equipment in order to ensure safe and proper use. Develop and arrange competition schedules and programs. Explain and enforce safety rules and regulations. Serve as organizer, leader, instructor, or referee for outdoor and indoor games, such as volleyball, football, and soccer. Explain and demonstrate the use of sports and training equipment, such as trampolines or weights. Perform activities that support a team or a specific sport, such as meeting with media representatives and appearing at fundraising events. Arrange and conduct sports-related activities such as training camps, skill-improvement courses, clinics, and/or pre-season tryouts. Select, acquire, store, and issue equipment and other materials as necessary. **SKILLS—Social Perceptiveness:** Being aware of others' reactions and understanding why they react as they do. **Instructing:** Teaching others how to do something. **Management of Personnel Resources:** Motivating, developing, and directing people as they work, identifying the best people for the job. **Persuasion:** Persuading others to change their minds or behavior. **Negotiation:** Bringing others together and trying to reconcile differences. **Learning Strategies:** Selecting and using training/instructional methods and procedures appropriate for the situation when learning or teaching new things. **Time Management:** Managing one's own time and the time of others. **Management of Financial Resources:** Determining how money will be spent to get the work done and accounting for these expenditures. **GOE—Interest Area:** 09. Hospitality, Tourism, and Recreation. **Work Group:** 09.06. Sports. **Other Jobs in This Work Group:** Athletes and Sports Competitors; Umpires, Referees, and Other

Sports Officials. **PERSONALITY TYPE:** Enterprising. Enterprising occupations frequently involve starting up and carrying out projects. These occupations can involve leading people and making many decisions. They sometimes require risk taking and often deal with business.

EDUCATION/TRAINING PROGRAM(S)— Health and Physical Education, General; Physical Education Teaching and Coaching; Sport and Fitness Administration/Management. **RELATED KNOWLEDGE/COURSES—Psychology:** Knowledge of human behavior and performance; individual differences in ability, personality, and interests; learning and motivation; psychological research methods; and the assessment and treatment of behavioral and affective disorders. **Education and Training:** Knowledge of principles and methods for curriculum and training design, teaching and instruction for individuals and groups, and the measurement of training effects. **Sales and Marketing:** Knowledge of principles and methods for showing, promoting, and selling products or services. This includes marketing strategy and tactics, product demonstrations, sales techniques, and sales control systems. **Therapy and Counseling:** Knowledge of principles, methods, and procedures for diagnosis, treatment, and rehabilitation of physical and mental dysfunctions and for career counseling and guidance. **Personnel and Human Resources:** Knowledge of principles and procedures for personnel recruitment, selection, training, compensation and benefits, labor relations and negotiation, and personnel information systems. **Customer and Personal Service:** Knowledge of principles and processes for providing customer and personal services. This includes customer needs assessment, meeting quality standards for services, and evaluation of customer satisfaction.

Combined Food Preparation and Serving Workers, Including Fast Food

- Education/Training Required: Short-term on-the-job training
- Annual Earnings: $14,690
- Growth: 22.8%
- Annual Job Openings: 734,000
- Self-Employed: 0.1%
- Part-Time: 40.4%

Perform duties which combine both food preparation and food service. Accept payment from customers and make change as necessary. Request and record customer orders and compute bills, using cash registers, multicounting machines, or pencil and paper. Clean and organize eating and service areas. Serve customers in eating places that specialize in fast service and inexpensive carry-out food. Prepare and serve cold drinks or frozen milk drinks or desserts, using drink-dispensing, milkshake, or frozen custard machines. Select food items from serving or storage areas and place them in dishes, on serving trays, or in takeout bags. Prepare simple foods and beverages such as sandwiches, salads, and coffee. Notify kitchen personnel of shortages or special orders. Cook or re-heat food items such as french fries. Wash dishes, glassware, and silverware after meals. Collect and return dirty dishes to the kitchen for washing. Relay food orders to cooks. Distribute food to servers. Serve food and beverages to guests at banquets or other social functions. Provide caterers with assistance in food preparation or service. Pack food, dishes, utensils, tablecloths, and accessories for transportation from catering or food preparation establishments to locations designated by customers. Arrange tables and decorations according to instructions. **SKILLS—Instructing:** Teaching others how to do something. **Service Orientation:** Actively looking for ways to help people. **Social Perceptiveness:** Being aware of others' reactions and understanding why they react as they do. **GOE—Interest Area:** 09. Hospitality, Tourism, and Recreation. **Work Group:** 09.05.

Food and Beverage Service. **Other Jobs in This Work Group:** Bartenders; Counter Attendants, Cafeteria, Food Concession, and Coffee Shop; Dining Room and Cafeteria Attendants and Bartender Helpers; Food Servers, Nonrestaurant; Hosts and Hostesses, Restaurant, Lounge, and Coffee Shop; Waiters and Waitresses. **PERSONALITY TYPE:** Realistic. Realistic occupations frequently involve work activities that include practical, hands-on problems and solutions. These occupations often deal with plants, animals, and real-world materials like wood, tools, and machinery. Many of the occupations require working outside and do not involve a lot of paperwork or working closely with others.

EDUCATION/TRAINING PROGRAM(S)—Food Preparation/Professional Cooking/Kitchen Assistant; Institutional Food Workers. **RELATED KNOWLEDGE/COURSES—Food Production:** Knowledge of techniques and equipment for planting, growing, and harvesting food products (both plant and animal) for consumption, including storage/handling techniques. **Sales and Marketing:** Knowledge of principles and methods for showing, promoting, and selling products or services. This includes marketing strategy and tactics, product demonstrations, sales techniques, and sales control systems. **Customer and Personal Service:** Knowledge of principles and processes for providing customer and personal services. This includes customer needs assessment, meeting quality standards for services, and evaluation of customer satisfaction. **Production and Processing:** Knowledge of raw materials, production processes, quality control, costs, and other techniques for maximizing the effective manufacture and distribution of goods. **Economics and Accounting:** Knowledge of economic and accounting principles and practices, the financial markets, banking, and the analysis and reporting of financial data. **Personnel and Human Resources:** Knowledge of principles and procedures for personnel recruitment, selection, training, compensation and benefits, labor relations and negotiation, and personnel information systems.

Commercial Pilots

- Education/Training Required: Postsecondary vocational training
- Annual Earnings: $53,870
- Growth: 14.9%
- Annual Job Openings: 2,000
- Self-Employed: 11.2%
- Part-Time: 12.9%

Pilot and navigate the flight of small fixed or rotary winged aircraft, primarily for the transport of cargo and passengers. Requires commercial rating. Check aircraft prior to flights to ensure that the engines, controls, instruments, and other systems are functioning properly. Check baggage or cargo to ensure that it has been loaded correctly. Choose routes, altitudes, and speeds that will provide the fastest, safest, and smoothest flights. Consider airport altitudes, outside temperatures, plane weights, and wind speeds and directions in order to calculate the speed needed to become airborne. Contact control towers for takeoff clearances, arrival instructions, and other information, using radio equipment. Coordinate flight activities with ground crews and air traffic control and inform crew members of flight and test procedures. File instrument flight plans with air traffic control so that flights can be coordinated with other air traffic. Monitor engine operation, fuel consumption, and functioning of aircraft systems during flights. Obtain and review data such as load weights, fuel supplies, weather conditions, and flight schedules in order to determine flight plans and to see if changes might be necessary. Order changes in fuel supplies, loads, routes, or schedules to ensure safety of flights. Plan and formulate flight activities and test schedules and prepare flight evaluation reports. Plan flights, following government and company regulations, using aeronautical charts and navigation instruments. Request changes in altitudes or routes as circumstances dictate. Start engines, operate controls, and pilot airplanes to transport passengers, mail, or freight while adhering to flight plans, regulations, and procedures. Use instrumentation to pilot aircraft when visibility is poor. Check the flight performance of new and experimental planes. Conduct in-flight tests and evaluations at specified altitudes and in all types of weather in order to determine the receptivity and other characteristics of equipment and systems. Co-pilot aircraft or perform captain's duties if required. Fly with other pilots or pilot-license applicants to evaluate their proficiency. Instruct other pilots and student pilots in aircraft operations. Perform minor aircraft maintenance and repair work or arrange for major maintenance. **SKILLS— Operation and Control:** Controlling operations of equipment or systems. **Operation Monitoring:** Watching gauges, dials, or other indicators to make sure a machine is working properly. **Instructing:** Teaching others how to do something. **Science:** Using scientific rules and methods to solve problems. **Coordination:** Adjusting actions in relation to others' actions. **Systems Analysis:** Determining how a system should work and how changes in conditions, operations, and the environment will affect outcomes. **Systems Evaluation:** Identifying measures or indicators of system performance and the actions needed to improve or correct performance relative to the goals of the system. **Judgment and Decision Making:** Considering the relative costs and benefits of potential actions to choose the most appropriate one. **GOE—Interest Area:** 16. Transportation, Distribution, and Logistics. **Work Group:** 16.02. Air Vehicle Operation. **Other Jobs in This Work Group:** Airline Pilots, Copilots, and Flight Engineers. **PERSONALITY TYPE:** Realistic. Realistic occupations frequently involve work activities that include practical, hands-on problems and solutions. These occupations often deal with plants, animals, and real-world materials like wood, tools, and machinery. Many of the occupations require working outside and do not involve a lot of paperwork or working closely with others.

EDUCATION/TRAINING PROGRAM(S)—Airline/Commercial/Professional Pilot and Flight Crew; Flight Instructor. **RELATED KNOWLEDGE/ COURSES—Transportation:** Knowledge of principles and methods for moving people or goods by air, rail, sea, or road, including the relative costs and benefits. **Geography:** Knowledge of principles and methods for describing the features of land, sea, and air masses, including their physical characteristics; locations; interrelationships; and distribution of plant, animal, and human life. **Public Safety and Security:** Knowledge of relevant equipment, policies, procedures, and strategies to promote effective local, state, or national

security operations for the protection of people, data, property, and institutions. **Mechanical Devices:** Knowledge of machines and tools, including their designs, uses, repair, and maintenance. **Education and Training:** Knowledge of principles and methods for curriculum and training design, teaching and instruction for individuals and groups, and the measurement of training effects. **Physics:** Knowledge and prediction of physical principles and laws and their interrelationships and applications to understanding fluid, material, and atmospheric dynamics and mechanical, electrical, atomic, and subatomic structures and processes.

Communication Equipment Mechanics, Installers, and Repairers

- ◎ Education/Training Required: Postsecondary vocational training
- ◎ Annual Earnings: $49,840
- ◎ Growth: –0.6%
- ◎ Annual Job Openings: 23,000
- ◎ Self-Employed: 4.6%
- ◎ Part-Time: 1.7%

Install, maintain, test, and repair communication cables and equipment. Examines and tests malfunctioning equipment to determine defects, using blueprints and electrical measuring instruments. Tests installed equipment for conformance to specifications, using test equipment. Assembles and installs communication equipment, such as data communication lines and equipment, computer systems, and antennas and towers, using hand tools. Repairs, replaces, or adjusts defective components. Disassembles equipment to adjust, repair, or replace parts, using hand tools. Evaluates quality of performance of installed equipment by observance and using test equipment. Digs holes or trenches. Answers customers' inquiries or complaints. Cleans and maintains tools, test equipment, and motor vehicle. Communicates with base, using telephone or two-way radio to receive instructions or technical advice or to report unauthorized use of equipment. Demonstrates equipment and instructs customer in use of equipment. Determines viability of site through observation and discusses site location and construction requirements with customer. Measures distance from landmarks to identify exact installation site. Climbs poles and ladders; constructs pole, roof mounts, or reinforcements; and mixes concrete to enable equipment installation. Plans layout and installation of data communications equipment. Reviews work orders, building permits, manufacturer's instructions, and ordinances to move, change, install, repair, or remove communication equipment. Adjusts or modifies equipment in accordance with customer request or to enhance performance of equipment. Performs routine maintenance on equipment, which includes adjustment, repair, and painting. Measures, cuts, splices, connects, solders, and installs wires and cables. **SKILLS—Repairing:** Repairing machines or systems by using the needed tools. **Installation:** Installing equipment, machines, wiring, or programs to meet specifications. **Troubleshooting:** Determining causes of operating errors and deciding what to do about them. **Equipment Maintenance:** Performing routine maintenance on equipment and determining when and what kind of maintenance is needed. **Quality Control Analysis:** Conducting tests and inspections of products, services, or processes to evaluate quality or performance. **Technology Design:** Generating or adapting equipment and technology to serve user needs. **Operation Monitoring:** Watching gauges, dials, or other indicators to make sure a machine is working properly. **Operation and Control:** Controlling operations of equipment or systems. **GOE— Interest Area:** 02. Architecture and Construction. **Work Group:** 02.05. Systems and Equipment Installation, Maintenance, and Repair. **Other Jobs in This Work Group:** Central Office and PBX Installers and Repairers; Electric Meter Installers and Repairers; Electrical and Electronics Repairers, Powerhouse, Substation, and Relay; Electrical Power-Line Installers and Repairers; Elevator Installers and Repairers; Frame Wirers, Central Office; Heating and Air Conditioning Mechanics; Home Appliance Installers; Maintenance and Repair Workers, General; Meter Mechanics; Refrigeration Mechanics; Station Installers and Repairers, Telephone; Telecommunications Facility Examiners; Telecommunications Line Installers and Repairers. **PERSONALITY TYPE:** Realistic. Realistic occupations frequently involve work activities that include practical, hands-on problems and solutions. These occupations often deal with plants, animals, and real-world materials like wood, tools, and machinery. Many of the occupations require working outside and do not involve a lot of paperwork or working closely with others.

EDUCATION/TRAINING PROGRAM(S)— Communications Systems Installation and Repair Technology. **RELATED KNOWLEDGE/COURSES—Telecommunications:** Knowledge of transmission, broadcasting, switching, control, and operation of telecommunications systems. **Computers and Electronics:** Knowledge of circuit boards, processors, chips, electronic equipment, and computer hardware and software, including applications and programming. **Design:** Knowledge of design techniques, tools, and principles involved in production of precision technical plans, blueprints, drawings, and models. **Mechanical Devices:** Knowledge of machines and tools, including their designs, uses, repair, and maintenance. **Engineering and Technology:** Knowledge of the practical application of engineering science and technology. This includes applying principles, techniques, procedures, and equipment to the design and production of various goods and services.

Computer Support Specialists

- ◎ Education/Training Required: Associate degree
- ◎ Annual Earnings: $40,430
- ◎ Growth: 30.3%
- ◎ Annual Job Openings: 71,000
- ◎ Self-Employed: 0.6%
- ◎ Part-Time: 6.8%

Provide technical assistance to computer system users. Answer questions or resolve computer problems for clients in person, via telephone, or from remote location. May provide assistance concerning the use of computer hardware and software, including printing, installation, word processing, electronic mail, and operating systems. Answer users' inquiries

regarding computer software and hardware operation to resolve problems. Enter commands and observe system functioning to verify correct operations and detect errors. Install and perform minor repairs to hardware, software, and peripheral equipment, following design or installation specifications. Oversee the daily performance of computer systems. Set up equipment for employee use, performing or ensuring proper installation of cable, operating systems, and appropriate software. Maintain record of daily data communication transactions, problems and remedial action taken, and installation activities. Read technical manuals, confer with users, and conduct computer diagnostics to investigate and resolve problems and to provide technical assistance and support. Confer with staff, users, and management to establish requirements for new systems or modifications. Develop training materials and procedures and/or train users in the proper use of hardware and software. Refer major hardware or software problems or defective products to vendors or technicians for service. Prepare evaluations of software or hardware and recommend improvements or upgrades. Read trade magazines and technical manuals and attend conferences and seminars to maintain knowledge of hardware and software. Supervise and coordinate workers engaged in problem-solving, monitoring, and installing data communication equipment and software. Inspect equipment and read order sheets to prepare for delivery to users. Modify and customize commercial programs for internal needs. **SKILLS— Troubleshooting:** Determining causes of operating errors and deciding what to do about them. **Repairing:** Repairing machines or systems by using the needed tools. **Social Perceptiveness:** Being aware of others' reactions and understanding why they react as they do. **Installation:** Installing equipment, machines, wiring, or programs to meet specifications. **Persuasion:** Persuading others to change their minds or behavior. **Equipment Maintenance:** Performing routine maintenance on equipment and determining when and what kind of maintenance is needed. **Writing:** Communicating effectively in writing as appropriate for the needs of the audience. **Instructing:** Teaching others how to do something. **GOE—Interest Area:** 11. Information Technology. **Work Group:** 11.02. Information Technology Specialties. **Other Jobs in This Work Group:** Computer Operators; Computer Program-

mers; Computer Security Specialists; Computer Software Engineers, Applications; Computer Software Engineers, Systems Software; Computer Systems Analysts; Database Administrators; Network Systems and Data Communications Analysts. **PERSONALITY TYPE:** Investigative. Investigative occupations frequently involve working with ideas and require an extensive amount of thinking. These occupations can involve searching for facts and figuring out problems mentally.

EDUCATION/TRAINING PROGRAM(S)— Accounting and Computer Science; Agricultural Business Technology; Computer Hardware Technology/ Technician; Computer Software Technology/Technician; Data Processing and Data Processing Technology/Technician; Medical Office Computer Specialist/Assistant. **RELATED KNOWLEDGE/ COURSES—Computers and Electronics:** Knowledge of circuit boards, processors, chips, electronic equipment, and computer hardware and software, including applications and programming. **Customer and Personal Service:** Knowledge of principles and processes for providing customer and personal services. This includes customer needs assessment, meeting quality standards for services, and evaluation of customer satisfaction. **Telecommunications:** Knowledge of transmission, broadcasting, switching, control, and operation of telecommunications systems. **Production and Processing:** Knowledge of raw materials, production processes, quality control, costs, and other techniques for maximizing the effective manufacture and distribution of goods. **Engineering and Technology:** Knowledge of the practical application of engineering science and technology. This includes applying principles, techniques, procedures, and equipment to the design and production of various goods and services. **Design:** Knowledge of design techniques, tools, and principles involved in production of precision technical plans, blueprints, drawings, and models.

Construction and Building Inspectors

- ⊚ Education/Training Required: Work experience in a related occupation
- ⊚ Annual Earnings: $43,670
- ⊚ Growth: 13.8%
- ⊚ Annual Job Openings: 10,000
- ⊚ Self-Employed: 8.1%
- ⊚ Part-Time: 5.9%

Inspect structures, using engineering skills to determine structural soundness and compliance with specifications, building codes, and other regulations. Inspections may be general in nature or may be limited to a specific area, such as electrical systems or plumbing. Use survey instruments; metering devices; tape measures; and test equipment, such as concrete strength measurers, to perform inspections. Inspect bridges, dams, highways, buildings, wiring, plumbing, electrical circuits, sewers, heating systems, and foundations during and after construction for structural quality, general safety, and conformance to specifications and codes. Maintain daily logs and supplement inspection records with photographs. Review and interpret plans, blueprints, site layouts, specifications, and construction methods to ensure compliance to legal requirements and safety regulations. Inspect and monitor construction sites to ensure adherence to safety standards, building codes, and specifications. Measure dimensions and verify level, alignment, and elevation of structures and fixtures to ensure compliance to building plans and codes. Issue violation notices and stop-work orders, conferring with owners, violators, and authorities to explain regulations and recommend rectifications. Issue permits for construction, relocation, demolition, and occupancy. Approve and sign plans that meet required specifications. Compute estimates of work completed or of needed renovations or upgrades and approve payment for contractors. Monitor installation of plumbing, wiring, equipment, and appliances to ensure that installation is performed properly and is in compliance with applicable regulations. Examine lifting and conveying devices, such as elevators, escalators, moving sidewalks, lifts and hoists, inclined railways, ski lifts, and amusement rides, to ensure safety and proper functioning. Train, direct, and supervise other construction inspectors. Evaluate premises for cleanliness, including proper garbage disposal and lack of vermin infestation. **SKILLS—Persuasion:** Persuading others to change their minds or behavior. **Mathematics:** Using mathematics to solve problems. **Time Management:** Managing one's own time and the time of others. **Reading Comprehension:** Understanding written sentences and paragraphs in work-related documents. **Active Listening:** Giving full attention to what other people are saying, taking time to understand the points being made, asking questions as appropriate, and not interrupting at inappropriate times. **Coordination:** Adjusting actions in relation to others' actions. **Active Learning:** Understanding the implications of new information for both current and future problem-solving and decision-making. **Social Perceptiveness:** Being aware of others' reactions and understanding why they react as they do. **Negotiation:** Bringing others together and trying to reconcile differences. **Instructing:** Teaching others how to do something. **GOE—Interest Area:** 02. Architecture and Construction. **Work Group:** 02.03. Architecture/Construction Engineering Technologies. **Other Jobs in This Work Group:** Architectural Drafters; Civil Drafters; Electrical Drafters; Surveyors. **PERSONALITY TYPE:** Conventional. Conventional occupations frequently involve following set procedures and routines. These occupations can include working with data and details more than with ideas. Usually there is a clear line of authority to follow.

EDUCATION/TRAINING PROGRAM(S)—Building/Home/Construction Inspection/Inspector. **RELATED KNOWLEDGE/COURSES—Building and Construction:** Knowledge of the materials, methods, and tools involved in the construction or repair of houses, buildings, or other structures such as highways and roads. **Design:** Knowledge of design techniques, tools, and principles involved in production of precision technical plans, blueprints, drawings, and models. **Engineering and Technology:** Knowledge of the practical application of engineering science and technology. This includes applying principles, techniques, procedures, and equipment to the design and production of various goods and services. **Public Safety and Security:** Knowledge of relevant equipment, policies, procedures, and strategies to promote effective local, state, or national security operations for the protection of people, data, property, and institutions. **Customer and Personal Service:** Knowledge of principles and processes for providing customer and personal services. This includes customer needs assessment, meeting quality standards for services, and evaluation of customer satisfaction. **Administration and Management:** Knowledge of business and management principles involved in strategic planning, resource allocation, human resources modeling, leadership technique, production methods, and coordination of people and resources. **Mechanical Devices:** Knowledge of machines and tools, including their designs, uses, repair, and maintenance.

Construction Carpenters

- Education/Training Required: Long-term on-the-job training
- Annual Earnings: $34,900
- Growth: 10.1%
- Annual Job Openings: 193,000
- Self-Employed: 29.7%
- Part-Time: 5.3%

Construct, erect, install, and repair structures and fixtures of wood, plywood, and wallboard, using carpenter's hand tools and power tools. Measure and mark cutting lines on materials, using ruler, pencil, chalk, and marking gauge. Follow established safety rules and regulations and maintain a safe and clean environment. Verify trueness of structure, using plumb bob and level. Shape or cut materials to specified measurements, using hand tools, machines, or power saw. Study specifications in blueprints, sketches, or building plans to prepare project layout and determine dimensions and materials required. Assemble and fasten materials to make framework or props, using hand tools and wood screws, nails, dowel pins, or glue. Build or repair cabinets, doors, frameworks, floors, and other wooden fixtures used in buildings, using woodworking machines, carpenter's hand tools, and power tools. Erect scaffolding and ladders for assembling structures above ground level. Remove damaged or defective parts or sections of structures and repair or replace, using hand tools. Install structures and fixtures, such as windows, frames, floorings, and trim, or hardware, using carpenter's hand and power tools. Select and order lumber and other required materials. Maintain records, document actions, and present written progress reports. Finish surfaces of woodwork or wallboard in houses and buildings, using paint, hand tools, and paneling. Prepare cost estimates for clients or employers. Arrange for subcontractors to deal with special areas such as heating and electrical wiring work. **SKILLS—Management of Personnel Resources:** Motivating, developing, and directing people as they work, identifying the best people for the job. **Management of Material Resources:** Obtaining and seeing to the appropriate use of equipment, facilities, and materials needed to do certain work. **Management of Financial Resources:** Determining how money will be spent to get the work done and accounting for these expenditures. **Equipment Maintenance:** Performing routine maintenance on equipment and determining when and what kind of maintenance is needed. **Repairing:** Repairing machines or systems by using the needed tools. **Quality Control Analysis:** Conducting tests and inspections of products, services, or processes to evaluate quality or performance. **Service Orientation:** Actively looking for ways to help people. **Speaking:** Talking to others to convey information effectively. **GOE—Interest Area:** 02. Architecture and Construction. **Work Group:** 02.04. Construction Crafts. **Other Jobs in This Work Group:** Boat Builders and Shipwrights; Boilermakers; Brattice Builders; Brickmasons and Blockmasons; Carpet Installers; Ceiling Tile Installers; Cement Masons and Concrete Finishers; Commercial Divers; Crane and Tower Operators; Dragline Operators; Drywall Installers; Electricians; Fence Erectors; Floor Layers, Except Carpet, Wood, and Hard Tiles; Floor Sanders and Finishers; Glaziers; Grader, Bulldozer, and Scraper Operators; Hazardous Materials Removal Workers; Insulation Workers, Floor, Ceiling, and Wall; Insulation Workers, Mechanical; Manufactured Building and Mobile Home Installers; Operating Engineers; Painters, Construction and Maintenance; Paperhangers; Paving, Surfacing, and Tamping Equipment Operators; Pile-Driver Operators; Pipe Fitters; Pipelayers; Pipelaying Fitters; Plasterers and Stucco Masons; Plumbers; Rail-Track Laying and Maintenance Equip-

C

ment Operators; Refractory Materials Repairers, Except Brickmasons; Reinforcing Iron and Rebar Workers; Riggers; Roofers; Rough Carpenters; Security and Fire Alarm Systems Installers; Segmental Pavers; Sheet Metal Workers; Ship Carpenters and Joiners; Stone Cutters and Carvers; Stonemasons; Structural Iron and Steel Workers; Tapers; Terrazzo Workers and Finishers; Tile and Marble Setters. **PERSONALITY TYPE:** Realistic. Realistic occupations frequently involve work activities that include practical, hands-on problems and solutions. These occupations often deal with plants, animals, and real-world materials like wood, tools, and machinery. Many of the occupations require working outside and do not involve a lot of paperwork or working closely with others.

EDUCATION/TRAINING PROGRAM(S)—Carpentry/Carpenter. **RELATED KNOWLEDGE/ COURSES—Building and Construction:** Knowledge of the materials, methods, and tools involved in the construction or repair of houses, buildings, or other structures such as highways and roads. **Production and Processing:** Knowledge of raw materials, production processes, quality control, costs, and other techniques for maximizing the effective manufacture and distribution of goods. **Engineering and Technology:** Knowledge of the practical application of engineering science and technology. This includes applying principles, techniques, procedures, and equipment to the design and production of various goods and services. **Design:** Knowledge of design techniques, tools, and principles involved in production of precision technical plans, blueprints, drawings, and models. **Public Safety and Security:** Knowledge of relevant equipment, policies, procedures, and strategies to promote effective local, state, or national security operations for the protection of people, data, property, and institutions. **Mechanical Devices:** Knowledge of machines and tools, including their designs, uses, repair, and maintenance.

Construction Laborers

◎ Education/Training Required: Moderate-term on-the-job training
◎ Annual Earnings: $25,160
◎ Growth: 14.2%
◎ Annual Job Openings: 166,000
◎ Self-Employed: 13.3%
◎ Part-Time: 7.9%

Perform tasks involving physical labor at building, highway, and heavy construction projects; tunnel and shaft excavations; and demolition sites. May operate hand and power tools of all types: air hammers, earth tampers, cement mixers, small mechanical hoists, surveying and measuring equipment, and a variety of other equipment and instruments. May clean and prepare sites; dig trenches; set braces to support the sides of excavations; erect scaffolding; clean up rubble and debris; and remove asbestos, lead, and other hazardous waste materials. May assist other craft workers. Apply caulking compounds by hand or using caulking guns. Build and position forms for pouring concrete and dismantle forms after use, using saws, hammers, nails, or bolts. Clean and prepare construction sites to eliminate possible hazards. Control traffic passing near, in, and around work zones. Dig ditches or trenches, backfill excavations, and compact and level earth to grade specifications, using picks, shovels, pneumatic tampers, and rakes. Erect and disassemble scaffolding, shoring, braces, traffic barricades, ramps, and other temporary structures. Grind, scrape, sand, or polish surfaces such as concrete, marble, terrazzo, or wood flooring, using abrasive tools or machines. Install sewer, water, and storm drain pipes, using pipe-laying machinery and laser guidance equipment. Load, unload, and identify building materials, machinery, and tools and distribute them to the appropriate locations according to project plans and specifications. Measure, mark, and record openings and distances to lay out areas where construction work will be performed. Mix ingredients to create compounds for covering or cleaning surfaces. Mop, brush, or spread paints, cleaning solutions, or other compounds over surfaces to clean them or to provide protection. Operate jackhammers and drills to break up concrete or pavement. Place, consolidate, and protect case-in-place concrete or masonry structures. Position, join, align, and seal structural components, such as concrete wall sections and pipes. Shovel cement and other materials into portable cement mixers and mix, pour, and spread concrete. Signal equipment operators to facilitate alignment, movement, and adjustment of machinery, equipment, and materials. Smooth and finish freshly poured cement or concrete, using floats, trowels, screeds, or powered cement-finishing tools. Spray materials such as water, sand, steam, vinyl, paint, or stucco through hoses to clean, coat, or seal surfaces. Tend machines that pump concrete, grout, cement, sand, plaster, or stucco through spray guns for application to ceilings and walls. Tend pumps, compressors, and generators to provide power for tools, machinery, and equipment or to heat and move materials such as asphalt. **SKILLS—Equipment Maintenance:** Performing routine maintenance on equipment and determining when and what kind of maintenance is needed. **GOE—Interest Area:** 02. Architecture and Construction. **Work Group:** 02.06. Construction Support/Labor. **Other Jobs in This Work Group:** Carpenter Assemblers and Repairers; Grips and Set-Up Workers, Motion Picture Sets, Studios, and Stages; Helpers—Brickmasons, Blockmasons, Stonemasons, and Tile and Marble Setters; Helpers—Carpenters; Helpers—Electricians; Helpers—Installation, Maintenance, and Repair Workers; Helpers—Painters, Paperhangers, Plasterers, and Stucco Masons; Helpers—Pipelayers, Plumbers, Pipefitters, and Steamfitters; Highway Maintenance Workers; Septic Tank Servicers and Sewer Pipe Cleaners. **PERSONALITY TYPE:** Realistic. Realistic occupations frequently involve work activities that include practical, hands-on problems and solutions. These occupations often deal with plants, animals, and real-world materials like wood, tools, and machinery. Many of the occupations require working outside and do not involve a lot of paperwork or working closely with others.

EDUCATION/TRAINING PROGRAM(S)—Construction Trades, Other. **RELATED KNOWLEDGE/COURSES—Building and Construction:** Knowledge of the materials, methods, and tools involved in the construction or repair of houses, buildings, or other structures such as highways and roads.

Mechanical Devices: Knowledge of machines and tools, including their designs, uses, repair, and maintenance. **Production and Processing:** Knowledge of raw materials, production processes, quality control, costs, and other techniques for maximizing the effective manufacture and distribution of goods. **Engineering and Technology:** Knowledge of the practical application of engineering science and technology. This includes applying principles, techniques, procedures, and equipment to the design and production of various goods and services. **Physics:** Knowledge and prediction of physical principles and laws and their interrelationships and applications to understanding fluid, material, and atmospheric dynamics and mechanical, electrical, atomic, and subatomic structures and processes. **Design:** Knowledge of design techniques, tools, and principles involved in production of precision technical plans, blueprints, drawings, and models.

Cooks, Restaurant

- Education/Training Required: Long-term on-the-job training
- Annual Earnings: $19,520
- Growth: 15.9%
- Annual Job Openings: 211,000
- Self-Employed: 1.3%
- Part-Time: 31.6%

Prepare, season, and cook soups, meats, vegetables, desserts, or other foodstuffs in restaurants. May order supplies, keep records and accounts, price items on menu, or plan menu. Inspect food preparation and serving areas to ensure observance of safe, sanitary food-handling practices. Turn or stir foods to ensure even cooking. Season and cook food according to recipes or personal judgment and experience. Observe and test foods to determine if they have been cooked sufficiently, using methods such as tasting, smelling, or piercing them with utensils. Weigh, measure, and mix ingredients according to recipes or personal judgment, using various kitchen utensils and equipment. Portion, arrange, and garnish food and serve food to waiters or patrons. Regulate temperature of ovens, broilers, grills, and roasters. Substitute for or assist other cooks during emergencies or rush periods. Bake, roast, broil, and steam meats, fish, vegetables, and other foods. Wash, peel, cut, and seed fruits and vegetables to prepare them for consumption. Estimate expected food consumption; then requisition or purchase supplies or procure food from storage. Carve and trim meats such as beef, veal, ham, pork, and lamb for hot or cold service or for sandwiches. Coordinate and supervise work of kitchen staff. Consult with supervisory staff to plan menus, taking into consideration factors such as costs and special event needs. Butcher and dress animals, fowl, or shellfish or cut and bone meat prior to cooking. Bake breads, rolls, cakes, and pastries. Prepare relishes and hors d'oeuvres. Keep records and accounts. Plan and price menu items. **SKILLS—Equipment Maintenance:** Performing routine maintenance on equipment and determining when and what kind of maintenance is needed. **Instructing:** Teaching others how to do something. **Active Learning:** Understanding the implications of new information for both current and future problem-solving and decision-making. **Learning Strategies:** Selecting and using training/instructional methods and procedures appropriate for the situation when learning or teaching new things. **Time Management:** Managing one's own time and the time of others. **Management of Personnel Resources:** Motivating, developing, and directing people as they work, identifying the best people for the job. **Social Perceptiveness:** Being aware of others' reactions and understanding why they react as they do. **Repairing:** Repairing machines or systems by using the needed tools. **GOE—Interest Area:** 09. Hospitality, Tourism, and Recreation. **Work Group:** 09.04. Food and Beverage Preparation. **Other Jobs in This Work Group:** Bakers, Bread and Pastry; Butchers and Meat Cutters; Chefs and Head Cooks; Cooks, Fast Food; Cooks, Institution and Cafeteria; Cooks, Short Order; Dishwashers; Food Preparation Workers. **PERSONALITY TYPE:** Realistic. Realistic occupations frequently involve work activities that include practical, hands-on problems and solutions. These occupations often deal with plants, animals, and real-world materials like wood, tools, and machinery. Many of the occupations require working outside and do not involve a lot of paperwork or working closely with others.

EDUCATION/TRAINING PROGRAM(S)— Cooking and Related Culinary Arts, General; Culinary Arts/Chef Training. **RELATED KNOWLEDGE/ COURSES—Food Production:** Knowledge of techniques and equipment for planting, growing, and harvesting food products (both plant and animal) for consumption, including storage/handling techniques. **Production and Processing:** Knowledge of raw materials, production processes, quality control, costs, and other techniques for maximizing the effective manufacture and distribution of goods. **Customer and Personal Service:** Knowledge of principles and processes for providing customer and personal services. This includes customer needs assessment, meeting quality standards for services, and evaluation of customer satisfaction. **Foreign Language:** Knowledge of the structure and content of a foreign (non-English) language, including the meaning and spelling of words, rules of composition and grammar, and pronunciation. **Chemistry:** Knowledge of the chemical composition, structure, and properties of substances and of the chemical processes and transformations that they undergo. This includes uses of chemicals and their danger signs, production techniques, and disposal methods. **Administration and Management:** Knowledge of business and management principles involved in strategic planning, resource allocation, human resources modeling, leadership technique, production methods, and coordination of people and resources. **Education and Training:** Knowledge of principles and methods for curriculum and training design, teaching and instruction for individuals and groups, and the measurement of training effects.

Coroners

◎ Education/Training Required: Work experience in a related occupation
◎ Annual Earnings: $47,390
◎ Growth: 9.8%
◎ Annual Job Openings: 20,000
◎ Self-Employed: 0.9%
◎ Part-Time: 5.3%

Direct activities such as autopsies, pathological and toxicological analyses, and inquests relating to the investigation of deaths occurring within a legal jurisdiction to determine cause of death or to fix respon-

sibility for accidental, violent, or unexplained deaths. Collect and document any pertinent medical history information. Complete death certificates, including the assignment of a cause and manner of death. Complete reports and forms required to finalize cases. Direct activities of workers who conduct autopsies, perform pathological and toxicological analyses, and prepare documents for permanent records. Inquire into the cause, manner, and circumstances of human deaths and establish the identities of deceased persons. Interview persons present at death scenes to obtain information useful in determining the manner of death. Observe and record the positions and conditions of bodies and of related evidence. Observe, record, and preserve any objects or personal property related to deaths, including objects such as medication containers and suicide notes. Perform medico-legal examinations and autopsies, conducting preliminary examinations of the body in order to identify victims, to locate signs of trauma, and to identify factors that would indicate time of death. Testify at inquests, hearings, and court trials. Arrange for the next of kin to be notified of deaths. Collect wills, burial instructions, and other documentation needed for investigations and for handling of the remains. Confer with officials of public health and law enforcement agencies in order to coordinate interdepartmental activities. Coordinate the release of personal effects to authorized persons and facilitate the disposition of unclaimed corpses and personal effects. Inventory personal effects, such as jewelry or wallets, that are recovered from bodies. Locate and document information regarding the next of kin, including their relationship to the deceased and the status of notification attempts. Provide information concerning the circumstances of death to relatives of the deceased. Remove or supervise removal of bodies from death scenes, using the proper equipment and supplies, and arrange for transportation to morgues. Witness and certify deaths that are the result of a judicial order. Record the disposition of minor children, as well as details of arrangements made for their care. **SKILLS—Science:** Using scientific rules and methods to solve problems. **Reading Comprehension:** Understanding written sentences and paragraphs in work-related documents. **Speaking:** Talking to others to convey information effectively. **Writing:** Communicating effectively in writing as appropriate for the needs of the audience. **Critical Thinking:** Using logic and reasoning to identify the strengths and weaknesses of alternative solutions, conclusions, or approaches to problems. **Mathematics:** Using mathematics to solve problems. **Management of Personnel Resources:** Motivating, developing, and directing people as they work, identifying the best people for the job. **Active Listening:** Giving full attention to what other people are saying, taking time to understand the points being made, asking questions as appropriate, and not interrupting at inappropriate times. **Complex Problem Solving:** Identifying complex problems and reviewing related information to develop and evaluate options and implement solutions. **GOE—Interest Area:** 08. Health Science. **Work Group:** 08.01. Managerial Work in Medical and Health Services. **Other Jobs in This Work Group:** First-Line Supervisors and Manager/Supervisors—Animal Care Workers, Except Livestock; Medical and Health Services Managers. **PERSONALITY TYPE:** Investigative. Investigative occupations frequently involve working with ideas and require an extensive amount of thinking. These occupations can involve searching for facts and figuring out problems mentally.

EDUCATION/TRAINING PROGRAM(S)—No data available. **RELATED KNOWLEDGE/COURSES—Medicine and Dentistry:** Knowledge of the information and techniques needed to diagnose and treat human injuries, diseases, and deformities. This includes symptoms, treatment alternatives, drug properties and interactions, and preventive health-care measures. **Biology:** Knowledge of plant and animal organisms and their tissues, cells, functions, interdependencies, and interactions with each other and the environment. **Chemistry:** Knowledge of the chemical composition, structure, and properties of substances and of the chemical processes and transformations that they undergo. This includes uses of chemicals and their danger signs, production techniques, and disposal methods. **Administration and Management:** Knowledge of business and management principles involved in strategic planning, resource allocation, human resources modeling, leadership technique, production methods, and coordination of people and resources. **Law and Government:** Knowledge of laws, legal codes, court procedures, precedents, government regulations, executive orders, agency rules, and the democratic political process. **Public Safety and Security:** Knowledge of relevant equipment, policies, procedures, and strategies to promote effective local, state, or national security operations for the protection of people, data, property, and institutions.

Correctional Officers and Jailers

- ◎ Education/Training Required: Moderate-term on-the-job training
- ◎ Annual Earnings: $33,600
- ◎ Growth: 24.2%
- ◎ Annual Job Openings: 49,000
- ◎ Self-Employed: 0%
- ◎ Part-Time: 1.3%

Guard inmates in penal or rehabilitative institution in accordance with established regulations and procedures. May guard prisoners in transit between jail, courtroom, prison, or other point. Includes deputy sheriffs and police who spend the majority of their time guarding prisoners in correctional institutions. Monitor conduct of prisoners according to established policies, regulations, and procedures in order to prevent escape or violence. Inspect conditions of locks, window bars, grills, doors, and gates at correctional facilities in order to ensure that they will prevent escapes. Search prisoners, cells, and vehicles for weapons, valuables, or drugs. Guard facility entrances in order to screen visitors. Search for and recapture escapees. Inspect mail for the presence of contraband. Take prisoners into custody and escort to locations within and outside of facility, such as visiting room, courtroom, or airport. Record information such as prisoner identification, charges, and incidences of inmate disturbance. Use weapons, handcuffs, and physical force to maintain discipline and order among prisoners. Conduct fire, safety, and sanitation inspections. Provide to supervisors oral and written reports of the quality and quantity of work performed by inmates, inmate disturbances and rule violations, and unusual occurrences. Settle disputes between inmates. Drive passenger vehicles and trucks used to transport inmates to other institutions, courtrooms, hospitals, and work sites. Arrange daily schedules for prisoners, including library visits, work assignments, family visits, and counseling appointments. Assign duties to inmates, providing instructions as needed. Issue clothing, tools, and other authorized items to inmates. Serve meals and distribute commissary items to prisoners. Investigate crimes that have occurred within an institution or assist police in their investigations of crimes and inmates. Maintain records of prisoners' identification and charges. Supervise and coordinate work of other correctional service officers. Sponsor inmate recreational activities such as newspapers and self-help groups. **SKILLS—Social Perceptiveness:** Being aware of others' reactions and understanding why they react as they do. **Persuasion:** Persuading others to change their minds or behavior. **Negotiation:** Bringing others together and trying to reconcile differences. **Speaking:** Talking to others to convey information effectively. **Instructing:** Teaching others how to do something. **Writing:** Communicating effectively in writing as appropriate for the needs of the audience. **Monitoring:** Monitoring or assessing your performance or that of other individuals or organizations to make improvements or take corrective action. **Active Listening:** Giving full attention to what other people are saying, taking time to understand the points being made, asking questions as appropriate, and not interrupting at inappropriate times. **GOE—Interest Area:** 12. Law and Public Safety. **Work Group:** 12.04. Law Enforcement and Public Safety. **Other Jobs in This Work Group:** Bailiffs; Criminal Investigators and Special Agents; Fire Investigators; Forensic Science Technicians; Highway Patrol Pilots; Parking Enforcement Workers; Police Detectives; Police Identification and Records Officers; Police Patrol Officers; Sheriffs and Deputy Sheriffs; Transit and Railroad Police. **PERSONALITY TYPE:** Realistic. Realistic occupations frequently involve work activities that include practical, hands-on problems and solutions. These occupations often deal with plants, animals, and real-world materials like wood, tools, and machinery. Many of the occupations require working outside and do not involve a lot of paperwork or working closely with others.

EDUCATION/TRAINING PROGRAM(S)—Corrections; Corrections and Criminal Justice, Other; Juvenile Corrections. **RELATED KNOWLEDGE/**

COURSES—**Psychology:** Knowledge of human behavior and performance; individual differences in ability, personality, and interests; learning and motivation; psychological research methods; and the assessment and treatment of behavioral and affective disorders. **Public Safety and Security:** Knowledge of relevant equipment, policies, procedures, and strategies to promote effective local, state, or national security operations for the protection of people, data, property, and institutions. **Law and Government:** Knowledge of laws, legal codes, court procedures, precedents, government regulations, executive orders, agency rules, and the democratic political process. **Philosophy and Theology:** Knowledge of different philosophical systems and religions. This includes their basic principles, values, ethics, ways of thinking, customs, and practices and their impact on human culture. **Sociology and Anthropology:** Knowledge of group behavior and dynamics, societal trends and influences, human migrations, ethnicity, and cultures and their history and origins. **Transportation:** Knowledge of principles and methods for moving people or goods by air, rail, sea, or road, including the relative costs and benefits.

Costume Attendants

- Education/Training Required: Moderate-term on-the-job training
- Annual Earnings: $25,050
- Growth: 27.8%
- Annual Job Openings: 66,000
- Self-Employed: 0.4%
- Part-Time: 51.9%

Select, fit, and take care of costumes for cast members and aid entertainers. Arrange costumes in order of use to facilitate quick-change procedures for performances. Assign lockers to employees and maintain locker rooms, dressing rooms, wig rooms, and costume storage and laundry areas. Care for non-clothing items such as flags, table skirts, and draperies. Check the appearance of costumes on stage and under lights in order to determine whether desired effects are being achieved. Clean and press costumes before and after performances and perform any minor repairs. Collaborate with production designers, costume designers, and other production staff in order to discuss and execute costume design details. Create worksheets for dressing lists, show notes, and costume checks. Distribute costumes and related equipment and keep records of item status. Examine costume fit on cast members and sketch or write notes for alterations. Inventory stock in order to determine types and conditions of available costuming. Monitor, maintain, and secure inventories of costumes, wigs, and makeup, providing keys or access to assigned directors, costume designers, and wardrobe mistresses/masters. Provide assistance to cast members in wearing costumes or assign cast dressers to assist specific cast members with costume changes. Return borrowed or rented items when productions are complete and return other items to storage. Design and construct costumes or send them to tailors for construction, major repairs, or alterations. Direct the work of wardrobe crews during dress rehearsals and performances. Participate in the hiring, training, scheduling, and supervision of alteration workers. Provide managers with budget recommendations and take responsibility for budgetary line items related to costumes, storage, and makeup needs. Purchase, rent, or requisition costumes and other wardrobe necessities. Recommend vendors and monitor their work. Review scripts or other production information in order to determine a story's locale and period as well as the number of characters and required costumes. Study books, pictures, and examples of period clothing in order to determine styles worn during specific periods in history. **SKILLS—Management of Material Resources:** Obtaining and seeing to the appropriate use of equipment, facilities, and materials needed to do certain work. **Management of Financial Resources:** Determining how money will be spent to get the work done and accounting for these expenditures. **Repairing:** Repairing machines or systems by using the needed tools. **GOE—Interest Area:** 03. Arts and Communication. **Work Group:** 03.06. Drama. **Other Jobs in This Work Group:** Actors; Directors—Stage, Motion Pictures, Television, and Radio; Makeup Artists, Theatrical and Performance; Public Address System and Other Announcers; Radio and Television Announcers. **PERSONALITY TYPE:** Artistic. Artistic occupations frequently involve working with forms, designs, and patterns. These occupations often require self-expression, and the work can be done without following a clear set of rules.

EDUCATION/TRAINING PROGRAM(S)—No data available. RELATED KNOWLEDGE/COURS-ES—Fine Arts: Knowledge of the theory and techniques required to compose, produce, and perform works of music, dance, the visual arts, drama, and sculpture. Design: Knowledge of design techniques, tools, and principles involved in production of precision technical plans, blueprints, drawings, and models. Sociology and Anthropology: Knowledge of group behavior and dynamics, societal trends and influences, human migrations, ethnicity, and cultures and their history and origins. Geography: Knowledge of principles and methods for describing the features of land, sea, and air masses, including their physical characteristics; locations; interrelationships; and distribution of plant, animal, and human life. History and Archeology: Knowledge of historical events and their causes, indicators, and effects on civilizations and cultures.

Counter and Rental Clerks

- Education/Training Required: Short-term on-the-job training
- Annual Earnings: $18,280
- Growth: 26.3%
- Annual Job Openings: 144,000
- Self-Employed: 1.3%
- Part-Time: 35.9%

Receive orders for repairs, rentals, and services. May describe available options, compute cost, and accept payment. Compute charges for merchandise or services and receive payments. Prepare merchandise for display or for purchase or rental. Recommend and provide advice on a wide variety of products and services. Answer telephones to provide information and receive orders. Greet customers and discuss the type, quality, and quantity of merchandise sought for rental. Keep records of transactions and of the number of customers entering an establishment. Prepare rental forms, obtaining customer signature and other information, such as required licenses. Receive, examine, and tag articles to be altered, cleaned, stored, or repaired. Inspect and adjust rental items to meet needs of customer. Explain rental fees, policies, and procedures. Reserve items for requested times and keep records of items rented. Receive orders for services such as rentals, repairs, dry cleaning, and storage. Rent items, arrange for provision of services to customers, and accept returns. Provide information about rental items, such as availability, operation, or description. Advise customers on use and care of merchandise. **SKILLS—Instructing:** Teaching others how to do something. **Service Orientation:** Actively looking for ways to help people. **GOE—Interest Area:** 14. Retail and Wholesale Sales and Service. **Work Group:** 14.06. Customer Service. **Other Jobs in This Work Group:** Adjustment Clerks; Cashiers; Customer Service Representatives, Utilities; Gaming Change Persons and Booth Cashiers; Order Clerks; Receptionists and Information Clerks. **PERSONALITY TYPE:** Conventional. Conventional occupations frequently involve following set procedures and routines. These occupations can include working with data and details more than with ideas. Usually there is a clear line of authority to follow.

EDUCATION/TRAINING PROGRAM(S)—Selling Skills and Sales Operations. RELATED KNOWLEDGE/COURSES—Food Production: Knowledge of techniques and equipment for planting, growing, and harvesting food products (both plant and animal) for consumption, including storage/handling techniques. Administration and Management: Knowledge of business and management principles involved in strategic planning, resource allocation, human resources modeling, leadership technique, production methods, and coordination of people and resources. Sales and Marketing: Knowledge of principles and methods for showing, promoting, and selling products or services. This includes marketing strategy and tactics, product demonstrations, sales techniques, and sales control systems. Personnel and Human Resources: Knowledge of principles and procedures for personnel recruitment, selection, training, compensation and benefits, labor relations and negotiation, and personnel information systems. Clerical Practices: Knowledge of administrative and clerical procedures and systems such as word processing, managing files and records, stenography and transcription, designing forms, and other office procedures and terminology. Mathematics: Knowledge of arithmetic, algebra, geometry, calculus, and statistics and their applications. English Language: Knowledge of the structure and content of the English language, including the meaning and spelling of words, rules of composition, and grammar.

Counter Attendants, Cafeteria, Food Concession, and Coffee Shop

◎ Education/Training Required: Short-term on-the-job training
◎ Annual Earnings: $15,660
◎ Growth: 16.7%
◎ Annual Job Openings: 190,000
◎ Self-Employed: 0.9%
◎ Part-Time: 65.8%

Serve food to diners at counter or from a steam table. Scrub and polish counters, steam tables, and other equipment and clean glasses, dishes, and fountain equipment. Serve food, beverages, or desserts to customers in such settings as take-out counters of restaurants or lunchrooms, business or industrial establishments, hotel rooms, and cars. Replenish foods at serving stations. Take customers' orders and write ordered items on tickets, giving ticket stubs to customers when needed to identify filled orders. Prepare food such as sandwiches, salads, and ice cream dishes, using standard formulas or following directions. Wrap menu items such as sandwiches, hot entrees, and desserts for serving or for takeout. Prepare bills for food, using cash registers, calculators, or adding machines, and accept payment and make change. Deliver orders to kitchens and pick up and serve food when it is ready. Serve salads, vegetables, meat, breads, and cocktails; ladle soups and sauces; portion desserts; and fill beverage cups and glasses. Add relishes and garnishes to food orders according to instructions. Carve meat. Order items needed to replenish supplies. Set up dining areas for meals and clear them following meals. Brew coffee and tea and fill containers with requested beverages. Balance receipts and payments in cash registers. Arrange reservations for patrons of dining establishments. **SKILLS—Social Perceptiveness:** Being aware of others' reactions and understanding why they react as they do. **Management of Personnel Resources:** Motivating, developing, and directing people as they work, identifying the best people for the job. **Negotiation:** Bringing others together and trying to reconcile differences. **Equipment Maintenance:** Performing routine maintenance on equipment and determining when and what kind of maintenance is needed. **Service Orientation:** Actively looking for ways to help people. **Troubleshooting:** Determining causes of operating errors and deciding what to do about them. **Repairing:** Repairing machines or systems by using the needed tools. **Learning Strategies:** Selecting and using training/instructional methods and procedures appropriate for the situation when learning or teaching new things. **GOE—Interest Area:** 09. Hospitality, Tourism, and Recreation. **Work Group:** 09.05. Food and Beverage Service. **Other Jobs in This Work Group:** Bartenders; Combined Food Preparation and Serving Workers, Including Fast Food; Dining Room and Cafeteria Attendants and Bartender Helpers; Food Servers, Nonrestaurant; Hosts and Hostesses, Restaurant, Lounge, and Coffee Shop; Waiters and Waitresses. **PERSONALITY TYPE:** Social. Social occupations frequently involve working with, communicating with, and teaching people. These occupations often involve helping or providing service to others.

EDUCATION/TRAINING PROGRAM(S)—Food Service, Waiter/Waitress, and Dining Room Management/Manager. **RELATED KNOWLEDGE/COURSES—Food Production:** Knowledge of techniques and equipment for planting, growing, and harvesting food products (both plant and animal) for consumption, including storage/handling techniques. **Sales and Marketing:** Knowledge of principles and methods for showing, promoting, and selling products or services. This includes marketing strategy and tactics, product demonstrations, sales techniques, and sales control systems. **Customer and Personal Service:** Knowledge of principles and processes for providing customer and personal services. This includes customer needs assessment, meeting quality standards for services, and evaluation of customer satisfaction. **Psychology:** Knowledge of human behavior and performance; individual differences in ability, personality, and interests; learning and motivation; psychological research methods; and the assessment and treatment of behavioral and affective disorders. **Public Safety and Security:** Knowledge of relevant equipment, policies, procedures, and strategies to promote effective local, state, or national security operations for the protection of people, data, property, and institutions. **Administration and Management:** Knowledge of business and management principles involved in strategic planning, resource allocation, human resources modeling, leadership technique, production methods, and coordination of people and resources. **Chemistry:** Knowledge of the chemical composition, structure, and properties of substances and of the chemical processes and transformations that they undergo. This includes uses of chemicals and their danger signs, production techniques, and disposal methods.

Court Clerks

- ◉ Education/Training Required: Short-term on-the-job training
- ◉ Annual Earnings: $28,430
- ◉ Growth: 12.3%
- ◉ Annual Job Openings: 14,000
- ◉ Self-Employed: 2.6%
- ◉ Part-Time: 8.3%

Perform clerical duties in court of law; prepare docket of cases to be called; secure information for judges; and contact witnesses, attorneys, and litigants to obtain information for court. Prepare dockets or calendars of cases to be called, using typewriters or computers. Record case dispositions, court orders, and arrangements made for payment of court fees. Answer inquiries from the general public regarding judicial procedures, court appearances, trial dates, adjournments, outstanding warrants, summonses, subpoenas, witness fees, and payment of fines. Prepare and issue orders of the court, including probation orders, release documentation, sentencing information, and summonses. Prepare documents recording the outcomes of court proceedings. Instruct parties about timing of court appearances. Explain procedures or forms to parties in cases or to the general public. Search files and contact witnesses, attorneys, and litigants in order to obtain information for the court. Follow procedures to secure courtrooms and exhibits such as money, drugs,

and weapons. Amend indictments when necessary and endorse indictments with pertinent information. Read charges and related information to the court and, if necessary, record defendants' pleas. Swear in jury members, interpreters, witnesses, and defendants. Collect court fees or fines and record amounts collected. Direct support staff in handling of paperwork processed by clerks' offices. Prepare and mark all applicable court exhibits and evidence. Examine legal documents submitted to courts for adherence to laws or court procedures. Record court proceedings, using recording equipment, or record minutes of court proceedings, using stenotype machines or shorthand. Prepare courtrooms with paper, pens, water, easels, and electronic equipment and ensure that recording equipment is working. Conduct roll calls and poll jurors. Open courts, calling them to order and announcing judges. Meet with judges, lawyers, parole officers, police, and social agency officials in order to coordinate the functions of the court. **SKILLS—Instructing:** Teaching others how to do something. **Active Listening:** Giving full attention to what other people are saying, taking time to understand the points being made, asking questions as appropriate, and not interrupting at inappropriate times. **Service Orientation:** Actively looking for ways to help people. **Coordination:** Adjusting actions in relation to others' actions. **Learning Strategies:** Selecting and using training/instructional methods and procedures appropriate for the situation when learning or teaching new things. **Critical Thinking:** Using logic and reasoning to identify the strengths and weaknesses of alternative solutions, conclusions, or approaches to problems. **Writing:** Communicating effectively in writing as appropriate for the needs of the audience. **Time Management:** Managing one's own time and the time of others. **GOE—Interest Area:** 07. Government and Public Administration. **Work Group:** 07.04. Public Administration Clerical Support. **Other Jobs in This Work Group:** Court Reporters; License Clerks; Municipal Clerks. **PERSONALITY TYPE:** Conventional. Conventional occupations frequently involve following set procedures and routines. These occupations can include working with data and details more than with ideas. Usually there is a clear line of authority to follow.

EDUCATION/TRAINING PROGRAM(S)—General Office Occupations and Clerical Services.

RELATED KNOWLEDGE/COURSES—Clerical Practices: Knowledge of administrative and clerical procedures and systems such as word processing, managing files and records, stenography and transcription, designing forms, and other office procedures and terminology. **Customer and Personal Service:** Knowledge of principles and processes for providing customer and personal services. This includes customer needs assessment, meeting quality standards for services, and evaluation of customer satisfaction. **Law and Government:** Knowledge of laws, legal codes, court procedures, precedents, government regulations, executive orders, agency rules, and the democratic political process. **Computers and Electronics:** Knowledge of circuit boards, processors, chips, electronic equipment, and computer hardware and software, including applications and programming. **English Language:** Knowledge of the structure and content of the English language, including the meaning and spelling of words, rules of composition, and grammar.

Court Reporters

- ◉ Education/Training Required: Postsecondary vocational training
- ◉ Annual Earnings: $42,920
- ◉ Growth: 12.7%
- ◉ Annual Job Openings: 2,000
- ◉ Self-Employed: 11.0%
- ◉ Part-Time: 12.6%

Use verbatim methods and equipment to capture, store, retrieve, and transcribe pretrial and trial proceedings or other information. Includes stenocaptioners who operate computerized stenographic captioning equipment to provide captions of live or prerecorded broadcasts for hearing-impaired viewers. Ask speakers to clarify inaudible statements. File a legible transcript of records of a court case with the court clerk's office. Provide transcripts of proceedings upon request of judges, lawyers, or the public. Record verbatim proceedings of courts, legislative assemblies, committee meetings, and other proceedings, using computerized recording equipment, electronic stenograph machines, or stenomasks. Respond to requests during court sessions to read portions of the proceed-

ings already recorded. Transcribe recorded proceedings in accordance with established formats. Verify accuracy of transcripts by checking copies against original records of proceedings and accuracy of rulings by checking with judges. Caption news, emergency broadcasts, sporting events, and other programming for television networks or cable stations. File and store shorthand notes of court session. Record depositions and other proceedings for attorneys. Record symbols on computer disks or CD-ROM and then translate and display them as text in computer-aided transcription process. Take notes in shorthand or use a stenotype or shorthand machine that prints letters on a paper tape. **SKILLS**—No data available. **GOE— Interest Area:** 07. Government and Public Administration. **Work Group:** 07.04. Public Administration Clerical Support. **Other Jobs in This Work Group:** Court Clerks; License Clerks; Municipal Clerks. **PERSONALITY TYPE:** No data available.

EDUCATION/TRAINING PROGRAM(S)— Court Reporting/Court Reporter. **RELATED KNOWLEDGE/COURSES**—No data available.

Crane and Tower Operators

- ◉ Education/Training Required: Moderate-term on-the-job training
- ◉ Annual Earnings: $37,410
- ◉ Growth: 10.8%
- ◉ Annual Job Openings: 5,000
- ◉ Self-Employed: 1.9%
- ◉ Part-Time: 1.2%

Operate mechanical boom and cable or tower and cable equipment to lift and move materials, machines, or products in many directions. Determine load weights and check them against lifting capacities in order to prevent overload. Direct helpers engaged in placing blocking and outrigging under cranes. Load and unload bundles from trucks and move containers to storage bins, using moving equipment. Move levers, depress foot pedals, and turn dials to operate cranes, cherry pickers, electromagnets, or other moving equipment for lifting, moving, and placing loads. Review daily work and delivery schedules to determine orders, sequences of deliveries, and special loading instructions. Weigh bundles, using floor scales, and record weights for company records. Clean, lubricate, and maintain mechanisms such as cables, pulleys, and grappling devices, making repairs as necessary. Direct truck drivers backing vehicles into loading bays and cover, uncover, and secure loads for delivery. Inspect and adjust crane mechanisms and lifting accessories in order to prevent malfunctions and damage. Inspect bundle packaging for conformance to regulations and customer requirements and remove and batch packaging tickets. Inspect cables and grappling devices for wear and install or replace cables as needed. **SKILLS— Operation and Control:** Controlling operations of equipment or systems. **Repairing:** Repairing machines or systems by using the needed tools. **Installation:** Installing equipment, machines, wiring, or programs to meet specifications. **Operation Monitoring:** Watching gauges, dials, or other indicators to make sure a machine is working properly. **Equipment Maintenance:** Performing routine maintenance on equipment and determining when and what kind of maintenance is needed. **GOE—Interest Area:** 02. Architecture and Construction. **Work Group:** 02.04. Construction Crafts. **Other Jobs in This Work Group:** Boat Builders and Shipwrights; Boilermakers; Brattice Builders; Brickmasons and Blockmasons; Carpet Installers; Ceiling Tile Installers; Cement Masons and Concrete Finishers; Commercial Divers; Construction Carpenters; Dragline Operators; Drywall Installers; Electricians; Fence Erectors; Floor Layers, Except Carpet, Wood, and Hard Tiles; Floor Sanders and Finishers; Glaziers; Grader, Bulldozer, and Scraper Operators; Hazardous Materials Removal Workers; Insulation Workers, Floor, Ceiling, and Wall; Insulation Workers, Mechanical; Manufactured Building and Mobile Home Installers; Operating Engineers; Painters, Construction and Maintenance; Paperhangers; Paving, Surfacing, and Tamping Equipment Operators; Pile-Driver Operators; Pipe Fitters; Pipelayers; Pipelaying Fitters; Plasterers and Stucco Masons; Plumbers; Rail-Track Laying and Maintenance Equipment Operators; Refractory Materials Repairers, Except Brickmasons; Reinforcing Iron and Rebar Workers; Riggers; Roofers; Rough Carpenters; Security and Fire Alarm Systems Installers; Segmental Pavers;

Sheet Metal Workers; Ship Carpenters and Joiners; Stone Cutters and Carvers; Stonemasons; Structural Iron and Steel Workers; Tapers; Terrazzo Workers and Finishers; Tile and Marble Setters. **PERSONALITY TYPE:** Realistic. Realistic occupations frequently involve work activities that include practical, hands-on problems and solutions. These occupations often deal with plants, animals, and real-world materials like wood, tools, and machinery. Many of the occupations require working outside and do not involve a lot of paperwork or working closely with others.

EDUCATION/TRAINING PROGRAM(S)—Construction/Heavy Equipment/Earthmoving Equipment Operation; Mobil Crane Operation/Operator. **RELATED KNOWLEDGE/COURSES—Mechanical Devices:** Knowledge of machines and tools, including their designs, uses, repair, and maintenance. **Transportation:** Knowledge of principles and methods for moving people or goods by air, rail, sea, or road, including the relative costs and benefits. **Building and Construction:** Knowledge of the materials, methods, and tools involved in the construction or repair of houses, buildings, or other structures such as highways and roads.

Criminal Investigators and Special Agents

- Education/Training Required: Work experience in a related occupation
- Annual Earnings: $53,990
- Growth: 22.4%
- Annual Job Openings: 11,000
- Self-Employed: 0%
- Part-Time: 0.5%

Investigate alleged or suspected criminal violations of federal, state, or local laws to determine if evidence is sufficient to recommend prosecution. Determine scope, timing, and direction of investigations. Develop relationships with informants in order to obtain information related to cases. Examine records in order to locate links in chains of evidence or information. Identify case issues and evidence needed based on analysis of charges, complaints, or allegations of law violations.

Obtain and use search and arrest warrants. Obtain and verify evidence by interviewing and observing suspects and witnesses or by analyzing records. Perform undercover assignments and maintain surveillance, including monitoring authorized wiretaps. Prepare reports that detail investigation findings. Analyze evidence in laboratories or in the field. Collaborate with other authorities on activities such as surveillance, transcription, and research. Collaborate with other offices and agencies in order to exchange information and coordinate activities. Collect and record physical information about arrested suspects, including fingerprints, height and weight measurements, and photographs. Compare crime scene fingerprints with those from suspects or fingerprint files to identify perpetrators, using computers. Investigate organized crime, public corruption, financial crime, copyright infringement, civil rights violations, bank robbery, extortion, kidnapping, and other violations of federal or state statutes. Manage security programs designed to protect personnel, facilities, and information. Record evidence and documents, using equipment such as cameras and photocopy machines. Search for and collect evidence such as fingerprints, using investigative equipment. Serve subpoenas or other official papers. Testify before grand juries concerning criminal activity investigations. Administer counter-terrorism and counter-narcotics reward programs. Issue security clearances. Provide protection for individuals such as government leaders, political candidates and visiting foreign dignitaries. Train foreign civilian police. **SKILLS—Social Perceptiveness:** Being aware of others' reactions and understanding why they react as they do. **Speaking:** Talking to others to convey information effectively. **Active Listening:** Giving full attention to what other people are saying, taking time to understand the points being made, asking questions as appropriate, and not interrupting at inappropriate times. **Persuasion:** Persuading others to change their minds or behavior. **Writing:** Communicating effectively in writing as appropriate for the needs of the audience. **Complex Problem Solving:** Identifying complex problems and reviewing related information to develop and evaluate options and implement solutions. **Judgment and Decision Making:** Considering the relative costs and benefits of potential actions to choose the most appropriate one. **Critical Thinking:** Using logic and reasoning to identify the strengths and weaknesses of alternative solutions, conclusions, or approaches to problems. **Coordination:** Adjusting actions in relation to others' actions. **GOE—Interest Area:** 12. Law and Public Safety. **Work Group:** 12.04. Law Enforcement and Public Safety. **Other Jobs in This Work Group:** Bailiffs; Correctional Officers and Jailers; Fire Investigators; Forensic Science Technicians; Highway Patrol Pilots; Parking Enforcement Workers; Police Detectives; Police Identification and Records Officers; Police Patrol Officers; Sheriffs and Deputy Sheriffs; Transit and Railroad Police. **PERSONALITY TYPE:** Enterprising. Enterprising occupations frequently involve starting up and carrying out projects. These occupations can involve leading people and making many decisions. They sometimes require risk taking and often deal with business.

EDUCATION/TRAINING PROGRAM(S)— Criminal Justice/Police Science; Criminalistics and Criminal Science. **RELATED KNOWLEDGE/ COURSES—Public Safety and Security:** Knowledge of relevant equipment, policies, procedures, and strategies to promote effective local, state, or national security operations for the protection of people, data, property, and institutions. **Law and Government:** Knowledge of laws, legal codes, court procedures, precedents, government regulations, executive orders, agency rules, and the democratic political process. **Psychology:** Knowledge of human behavior and performance; individual differences in ability, personality, and interests; learning and motivation; psychological research methods; and the assessment and treatment of behavioral and affective disorders. **Telecommunications:** Knowledge of transmission, broadcasting, switching, control, and operation of telecommunications systems. **Sociology and Anthropology:** Knowledge of group behavior and dynamics, societal trends and influences, human migrations, ethnicity, and cultures and their history and origins. **Geography:** Knowledge of principles and methods for describing the features of land, sea, and air masses, including their physical characteristics; locations; interrelationships; and distribution of plant, animal, and human life.

Customer Service Representatives, Utilities

- ◉ Education/Training Required: Moderate-term on-the-job training
- ◉ Annual Earnings: $27,020
- ◉ Growth: 24.3%
- ◉ Annual Job Openings: 419,000
- ◉ Self-Employed: 0.5%
- ◉ Part-Time: 14.8%

Interview applicants for water, gas, electric, or telephone service. Talk with customer by phone or in person and receive orders for installation, turn-on, discontinuance, or change in services. Confers with customer by phone or in person to receive orders for installation, turn-on, discontinuance, or change in service. Completes contract forms, prepares change of address records, and issues discontinuance orders, using computer. Determines charges for service requested and collects deposits. Solicits sale of new or additional utility services. Resolves billing or service complaints and refers grievances to designated departments for investigation. **SKILLS—Service Orientation:** Actively looking for ways to help people. **Active Listening:** Giving full attention to what other people are saying, taking time to understand the points being made, asking questions as appropriate, and not interrupting at inappropriate times. **Speaking:** Talking to others to convey information effectively. **GOE—Interest Area:** 14. Retail and Wholesale Sales and Service. **Work Group:** 14.06. Customer Service. **Other Jobs in This Work Group:** Adjustment Clerks; Cashiers; Counter and Rental Clerks; Gaming Change Persons and Booth Cashiers; Order Clerks; Receptionists and Information Clerks. **PERSONALITY TYPE:** Conventional. Conventional occupations frequently involve following set procedures and routines. These occupations can include working with data and details more than with ideas. Usually there is a clear line of authority to follow.

EDUCATION/TRAINING PROGRAM(S)—Customer Service Support/Call Center/Teleservice Operation; Receptionist. **RELATED KNOWLEDGE/ COURSES—Sales and Marketing:** Knowledge of principles and methods for showing, promoting, and selling products or services. This includes marketing strategy and tactics, product demonstrations, sales techniques, and sales control systems. **Customer and Personal Service:** Knowledge of principles and processes for providing customer and personal services. This includes customer needs assessment, meeting quality standards for services, and evaluation of customer satisfaction. **Economics and Accounting:** Knowledge of economic and accounting principles and practices, the financial markets, banking, and the analysis and reporting of financial data. **Telecommunications:** Knowledge of transmission, broadcasting, switching, control, and operation of telecommunications systems. **Clerical Practices:** Knowledge of administrative and clerical procedures and systems such as word processing, managing files and records, stenography and transcription, designing forms, and other office procedures and terminology.

Data Processing Equipment Repairers

- ◉ Education/Training Required: Postsecondary vocational training
- ◉ Annual Earnings: $35,150
- ◉ Growth: 15.1%
- ◉ Annual Job Openings: 19,000
- ◉ Self-Employed: 12.2%
- ◉ Part-Time: 8.2%

Repair, maintain, and install computer hardware such as peripheral equipment and word-processing systems. Replaces defective components and wiring. Tests faulty equipment and applies knowledge of functional operation of electronic units and systems to diagnose cause of malfunction. Aligns, adjusts, and calibrates equipment according to specifications. Calibrates testing instruments. Adjusts mechanical parts, using hand tools and soldering iron. Converses with equipment operators to ascertain problems with equipment before breakdown or cause of breakdown. Tests electronic components and circuits to locate defects, using oscilloscopes, signal generators, ammeters, and voltmeters. Maintains records of repairs, calibrations, and tests. Enters information into computer to copy program from one electronic component to another or to draw, modify, or store schematics. **SKILLS—Installation:** Installing equipment, machines, wiring, or programs to meet specifications. **Repairing:** Repairing machines or systems by using the needed tools. **Troubleshooting:** Determining causes of operating errors and deciding what to do about them. **Science:** Using scientific rules and methods to solve problems. **Equipment Maintenance:** Performing routine maintenance on equipment and determining when and what kind of maintenance is needed. **Operation Monitoring:** Watching gauges, dials, or other indicators to make sure a machine is working properly. **Quality Control Analysis:** Conducting tests and inspections of products, services, or processes to evaluate quality or performance. **Operation and Control:** Controlling operations of equipment or systems. **GOE—Interest Area:** 11. Information Technology. **Work Group:** 11.03. Digital Equipment Repair. **Other Jobs in This Work Group:** Automatic Teller Machine Servicers; Coin, Vending, and Amusement Machine Servicers and Repairers; Office Machine and Cash Register Servicers. **PERSONALITY TYPE:** Realistic. Realistic occupations frequently involve work activities that include practical, hands-on problems and solutions. These occupations often deal with plants, animals, and real-world materials like wood, tools, and machinery. Many of the occupations require working outside and do not involve a lot of paperwork or working closely with others.

EDUCATION/TRAINING PROGRAM(S)—Business Machine Repair; Computer Installation and Repair Technology/Technician. **RELATED KNOWLEDGE/COURSES—Computers and Electronics:** Knowledge of circuit boards, processors, chips, electronic equipment, and computer hardware and software, including applications and programming. **Telecommunications:** Knowledge of transmission, broadcasting, switching, control, and operation of telecommunications systems. **Design:** Knowledge of design techniques, tools, and principles involved in production of precision technical plans, blueprints, drawings, and models. **Mechanical Devices:** Knowledge of machines and tools, including their designs, uses, repair, and maintenance. **Physics:** Knowledge and prediction of physical principles and laws and

their interrelationships and applications to understanding fluid, material, and atmospheric dynamics and mechanical, electrical, atomic, and subatomic structures and processes. **Engineering and Technology:** Knowledge of the practical application of engineering science and technology. This includes applying principles, techniques, procedures, and equipment to the design and production of various goods and services.

Demonstrators and Product Promoters

- ◎ Education/Training Required: Moderate-term on-the-job training
- ◎ Annual Earnings: $20,700
- ◎ Growth: 17.0%
- ◎ Annual Job Openings: 38,000
- ◎ Self-Employed: 42.1%
- ◎ Part-Time: 52.5%

Demonstrate merchandise and answer questions for the purpose of creating public interest in buying the product. May sell demonstrated merchandise. Demonstrate and explain products, methods, or services in order to persuade customers to purchase products or utilize services. Identify interested and qualified customers in order to provide them with additional information. Keep areas neat while working and return items to correct locations following demonstrations. Practice demonstrations to ensure that they will run smoothly. Prepare and alter presentation contents to target specific audiences. Provide product information, using lectures, films, charts, and/or slide shows. Provide product samples, coupons, informational brochures, and other incentives to persuade people to buy products. Record and report demonstration-related information such as the number of questions asked by the audience and the number of coupons distributed. Research and investigate products to be presented to prepare for demonstrations. Sell products being promoted and keep records of sales. Set up and arrange displays and demonstration areas to attract the attention of prospective customers. Stock shelves with products. Suggest specific product purchases to meet customers' needs. Transport, assemble, and disassemble materials used in presentations. Visit trade shows, stores, community organizations, and other venues to demonstrate products or services and to answer questions from potential customers. Collect fees or accept donations. Contact businesses and civic establishments to arrange to exhibit and sell merchandise. Develop lists of prospective clients from sources such as newspaper items, company records, local merchants, and customers. Give tours of plants where specific products are made. Instruct customers in alteration of products. Learn about competitors' products and consumers' interests and concerns in order to answer questions and provide more-complete information. Recommend product or service improvements to employers. Train demonstrators to present a company's products or services. Wear costumes or signboards and walk in public to promote merchandise, services, or events. Work as part of a team of demonstrators to accommodate large crowds. **SKILLS—Persuasion:** Persuading others to change their minds or behavior. **Speaking:** Talking to others to convey information effectively. **Social Perceptiveness:** Being aware of others' reactions and understanding why they react as they do. **Learning Strategies:** Selecting and using training/instructional methods and procedures appropriate for the situation when learning or teaching new things. **Instructing:** Teaching others how to do something. **Writing:** Communicating effectively in writing as appropriate for the needs of the audience. **Active Learning:** Understanding the implications of new information for both current and future problem-solving and decision-making. **Systems Evaluation:** Identifying measures or indicators of system performance and the actions needed to improve or correct performance relative to the goals of the system. **GOE—Interest Area:** 14. Retail and Wholesale Sales and Service. **Work Group:** 14.04. Personal Soliciting. **Other Jobs in This Work Group:** Door-To-Door Sales Workers, News and Street Vendors, and Related Workers; Models; Telemarketers. **PERSONALITY TYPE:** Enterprising. Enterprising occupations frequently involve starting up and carrying out projects. These occupations can involve leading people and making many decisions. They sometimes require risk taking and often deal with business.

EDUCATION/TRAINING PROGRAM(S)— Retailing and Retail Operations. **RELATED KNOWLEDGE/COURSES—Sales and Marketing:** Knowledge of principles and methods for showing, promoting, and selling products or services. This includes marketing strategy and tactics, product demonstrations, sales techniques, and sales control systems. **Communications and Media:** Knowledge of media production, communication, and dissemination techniques and methods. This includes alternative ways to inform and entertain via written, oral, and visual media. **Education and Training:** Knowledge of principles and methods for curriculum and training design, teaching and instruction for individuals and groups, and the measurement of training effects. **English Language:** Knowledge of the structure and content of the English language, including the meaning and spelling of words, rules of composition, and grammar. **Economics and Accounting:** Knowledge of economic and accounting principles and practices, the financial markets, banking, and the analysis and reporting of financial data. **Clerical Practices:** Knowledge of administrative and clerical procedures and systems such as word processing, managing files and records, stenography and transcription, designing forms, and other office procedures and terminology.

Dental Assistants

- Education/Training Required: Moderate-term on-the-job training
- Annual Earnings: $28,330
- Growth: 42.5%
- Annual Job Openings: 35,000
- Self-Employed: 0%
- Part-Time: 35.6%

Assist dentist, set up patient and equipment, and keep records. Prepare patient, sterilize and disinfect instruments, set up instrument trays, prepare materials, and assist dentist during dental procedures. Expose dental diagnostic X rays. Record treatment information in patient records. Take and record medical and dental histories and vital signs of patients. Provide postoperative instructions prescribed by dentist. Assist dentist in management of medical and dental emergencies. Pour, trim, and polish study casts. Instruct patients in oral hygiene and plaque control programs. Make preliminary impressions for study casts and occlusal registrations for mounting study casts. Clean and polish removable appliances. Clean teeth, using dental instruments. Apply protective coating of fluoride to teeth. Fabricate temporary restorations and custom impressions from preliminary impressions. Schedule appointments, prepare bills and receive payment for dental services, complete insurance forms, and maintain records, manually or using computer. **SKILLS—Social Perceptiveness:** Being aware of others' reactions and understanding why they react as they do. **Equipment Maintenance:** Performing routine maintenance on equipment and determining when and what kind of maintenance is needed. **Management of Material Resources:** Obtaining and seeing to the appropriate use of equipment, facilities, and materials needed to do certain work. **Instructing:** Teaching others how to do something. **Service Orientation:** Actively looking for ways to help people. **Operation and Control:** Controlling operations of equipment or systems. **Persuasion:** Persuading others to change their minds or behavior. **Time Management:** Managing one's own time and the time of others. **GOE—Interest Area:** 08. Health Science. **Work Group:** 08.03. Dentistry. **Other Jobs in This Work Group:** Dental Hygienists; Dentists, General; Oral and Maxillofacial Surgeons; Orthodontists; Prosthodontists. **PERSONALITY TYPE:** Social. Social occupations frequently involve working with, communicating with, and teaching people. These occupations often involve helping or providing service to others.

EDUCATION/TRAINING PROGRAM(S)— Dental Assisting/Assistant. **RELATED KNOWLEDGE/COURSES—Medicine and Dentistry:** Knowledge of the information and techniques needed to diagnose and treat human injuries, diseases, and deformities. This includes symptoms, treatment alternatives, drug properties and interactions, and preventive health-care measures. **Customer and Personal Service:** Knowledge of principles and processes for providing customer and personal services. This includes customer needs assessment, meeting quality standards for services, and evaluation of customer satisfaction. **Chemistry:** Knowledge of the chemical composition, structure, and properties of substances and of the chemical processes and transformations that they undergo. This includes uses of chemicals and their danger signs, production techniques, and disposal methods. **Clerical Practices:** Knowledge of administrative and clerical procedures and systems such as word processing, managing files and records, stenography and transcription, designing forms, and other office procedures and terminology. **Psychology:** Knowledge of human behavior and performance; individual differences in ability, personality, and interests; learning and motivation; psychological research methods; and the assessment and treatment of behavioral and affective disorders. **Computers and Electronics:** Knowledge of circuit boards, processors, chips, electronic equipment, and computer hardware and software, including applications and programming.

Dental Hygienists

- ◎ Education/Training Required: Associate degree
- ◎ Annual Earnings: $58,350
- ◎ Growth: 43.1%
- ◎ Annual Job Openings: 9,000
- ◎ Self-Employed: 0.7%
- ◎ Part-Time: 57.8%

Clean teeth and examine oral areas, head, and neck for signs of oral disease. May educate patients on oral hygiene, take and develop X rays, or apply fluoride or sealants. Clean calcareous deposits, accretions, and stains from teeth and beneath margins of gums, using dental instruments. Feel and visually examine gums for sores and signs of disease. Chart conditions of decay and disease for diagnosis and treatment by dentist. Feel lymph nodes under patient's chin to detect swelling or tenderness that could indicate presence of oral cancer. Apply fluorides and other cavity-preventing agents to arrest dental decay. Examine gums, using probes, to locate periodontal recessed gums and signs of gum disease. Expose and develop X-ray film. Provide clinical services and health education to improve and maintain oral health of schoolchildren. Remove excess cement from coronal surfaces of teeth. Make impressions for study casts. Place, carve, and finish amalgam restorations. Administer local anesthetic agents. Conduct dental health clinics for community groups to augment services of dentist. **SKILLS—Time Management:** Managing one's own time and the time of others. **Active Learning:** Understanding the implications of new information for both current and future problem-solving and decision-making. **Social Perceptiveness:** Being aware of others' reactions and understanding why they react as they do. **Instructing:** Teaching others how to do something. **Persuasion:** Persuading others to change their minds or behavior. **Learning Strategies:** Selecting and using training/instructional methods and procedures appropriate for the situation when learning or teaching new things. **Reading Comprehension:** Understanding written sentences and paragraphs in work-related documents. **Active Listening:** Giving full attention to what other people are saying, taking time to understand the points being made, asking questions as appropriate, and not interrupting at inappropriate times. **Service Orientation:** Actively looking for ways to help people. **GOE—Interest Area:** 08. Health Science. **Work Group:** 08.03. Dentistry. **Other Jobs in This Work Group:** Dental Assistants; Dentists, General; Oral and Maxillofacial Surgeons; Orthodontists; Prosthodontists. **PERSONALITY TYPE:** Social. Social occupations frequently involve working with, communicating with, and teaching people. These occupations often involve helping or providing service to others.

EDUCATION/TRAINING PROGRAM(S)— Dental Hygiene/Hygienist. **RELATED KNOWLEDGE/COURSES—Medicine and Dentistry:** Knowledge of the information and techniques needed to diagnose and treat human injuries, diseases, and deformities. This includes symptoms, treatment alternatives, drug properties and interactions, and preventive health-care measures. **Biology:** Knowledge of plant and animal organisms and their tissues, cells, functions, interdependencies, and interactions with each other and the environment. **Customer and Personal Service:** Knowledge of principles and processes for providing customer and personal services. This includes customer needs assessment, meeting quality standards for services, and evaluation of customer satisfaction. **Chemistry:** Knowledge of the chemical composition, structure, and properties of substances and of

the chemical processes and transformations that they undergo. This includes uses of chemicals and their danger signs, production techniques, and disposal methods. **Psychology:** Knowledge of human behavior and performance; individual differences in ability, personality, and interests; learning and motivation; psychological research methods; and the assessment and treatment of behavioral and affective disorders. **Sales and Marketing:** Knowledge of principles and methods for showing, promoting, and selling products or services. This includes marketing strategy and tactics, product demonstrations, sales techniques, and sales control systems.

Desktop Publishers

- ◎ Education/Training Required: Postsecondary vocational training
- ◎ Annual Earnings: $32,340
- ◎ Growth: 29.2%
- ◎ Annual Job Openings: 4,000
- ◎ Self-Employed: 0%
- ◎ Part-Time: 17.5%

Format typescript and graphic elements, using computer software to produce publication-ready material. Check preliminary and final proofs for errors and make necessary corrections. Operate desktop publishing software and equipment to design, lay out, and produce camera-ready copy. View monitors for visual representation of work in progress and for instructions and feedback throughout process, making modifications as necessary. Enter text into computer keyboard and select the size and style of type, column width, and appropriate spacing for printed materials. Store copies of publications on paper, magnetic tape, film, or diskette. Position text and art elements from a variety of databases in a visually appealing way in order to design print or Web pages, using knowledge of type styles and size and layout patterns. Enter digitized data into electronic prepress system computer memory, using scanner, camera, keyboard, or mouse. Edit graphics and photos, using pixel or bitmap editing, airbrushing, masking, or image retouching. Import text and art elements such as electronic clip art or electronic files from photographs that have been scanned or produced with a digital camera, using computer software. Prepare sample layouts for approval, using computer software. Study layout or other design instructions to determine work to be done and sequence of operations. Load floppy disks or tapes containing information into system. Convert various types of files for printing or for the Internet, using computer software. Enter data, such as coordinates of images and color specifications, into system to retouch and make color corrections. Select number of colors and determine color separations. Transmit, deliver, or mail publication master to printer for production into film and plates. Collaborate with graphic artists, editors, and writers to produce master copies according to design specifications. Create special effects such as vignettes, mosaics, and image combining and add elements such as sound and animation to electronic publications. **SKILLS—Time Management:** Managing one's own time and the time of others. **Service Orientation:** Actively looking for ways to help people. **Operation and Control:** Controlling operations of equipment or systems. **Instructing:** Teaching others how to do something. **Active Listening:** Giving full attention to what other people are saying, taking time to understand the points being made, asking questions as appropriate, and not interrupting at inappropriate times. **Operations Analysis:** Analyzing needs and product requirements to create a design. **Technology Design:** Generating or adapting equipment and technology to serve user needs. **Reading Comprehension:** Understanding written sentences and paragraphs in work-related documents. **GOE—Interest Area:** 13. Manufacturing. **Work Group:** 13.08. Graphic Arts Production. **Other Jobs in This Work Group:** Bindery Machine Operators and Tenders; Camera Operators; Design Printing Machine Setters and Set-Up Operators; Dot Etchers; Electronic Masking System Operators; Electrotypers and Stereotypers; Embossing Machine Set-Up Operators; Engraver Set-Up Operators; Engravers, Hand; Engravers/Carvers; Etchers; Etchers, Hand; Film Laboratory Technicians; Hand Compositors and Typesetters; Job Printers; Letterpress Setters and Set-Up Operators; Marking and Identification Printing Machine Setters and Set-Up Operators; Offset Lithographic Press Setters and Set-Up Operators; Pantograph Engravers; Paste-Up Workers; Photo-

engravers; Photoengraving and Lithographing Machine Operators and Tenders; Photographic Processing Machine Operators; Plate Finishers; Platemakers; Precision Etchers and Engravers, Hand or Machine; Precision Printing Workers; Printing Press Machine Operators and Tenders; Scanner Operators; Strippers; Typesetting and Composing Machine Operators and Tenders. **PERSONALITY TYPE:** Realistic. Realistic occupations frequently involve work activities that include practical, hands-on problems and solutions. These occupations often deal with plants, animals, and real-world materials like wood, tools, and machinery. Many of the occupations require working outside and do not involve a lot of paperwork or working closely with others.

EDUCATION/TRAINING PROGRAM(S)—Prepress/Desktop Publishing and Digital Imaging Design. **RELATED KNOWLEDGE/COURSES—Computers and Electronics:** Knowledge of circuit boards, processors, chips, electronic equipment, and computer hardware and software, including applications and programming. **Production and Processing:** Knowledge of raw materials, production processes, quality control, costs, and other techniques for maximizing the effective manufacture and distribution of goods. **English Language:** Knowledge of the structure and content of the English language, including the meaning and spelling of words, rules of composition, and grammar. **Clerical Practices:** Knowledge of administrative and clerical procedures and systems such as word processing, managing files and records, stenography and transcription, designing forms, and other office procedures and terminology. **Customer and Personal Service:** Knowledge of principles and processes for providing customer and personal services. This includes customer needs assessment, meeting quality standards for services, and evaluation of customer satisfaction. **Telecommunications:** Knowledge of transmission, broadcasting, switching, control, and operation of telecommunications systems.

Diagnostic Medical Sonographers

- Education/Training Required: Associate degree
- Annual Earnings: $52,490
- Growth: 24.0%
- Annual Job Openings: 4,000
- Self-Employed: 0.2%
- Part-Time: 17.5%

Produce ultrasonic recordings of internal organs for use by physicians. Decide which images to include, looking for differences between healthy and pathological areas. Observe screen during scan to ensure that image produced is satisfactory for diagnostic purposes, making adjustments to equipment as required. Observe and care for patients throughout examinations to ensure their safety and comfort. Provide sonogram and oral or written summary of technical findings to physician for use in medical diagnosis. Operate ultrasound equipment to produce and record images of the motion, shape, and composition of blood, organs, tissues, and bodily masses such as fluid accumulations. Select appropriate equipment settings and adjust patient positions to obtain the best sites and angles. Determine whether scope of exam should be extended, based on findings. Process and code film from procedures and complete appropriate documentation. Obtain and record accurate patient history, including prior test results and information from physical examinations. Prepare patient for exam by explaining procedure, transferring them to ultrasound table, scrubbing skin and applying gel, and positioning them properly. Record and store suitable images, using camera unit connected to the ultrasound equipment. Coordinate work with physicians and other healthcare team members, including providing assistance during invasive procedures. Maintain records that include patient information, sonographs and interpretations, files of correspondence, publications and regulations, and quality assurance records (e.g., pathology, biopsy, post-operative reports). Perform legal and ethical duties, including preparing safety and accident reports, obtaining written consent from patient to perform invasive procedures, and reporting symptoms of abuse and neglect. Supervise and train students and other medical sonographers. Maintain stock and supplies, preparing supplies for special examinations and ordering supplies when necessary. Clean, check, and maintain sonographic equipment, submitting maintenance requests or performing minor repairs as necessary. Perform clerical duties such as scheduling exams and special procedures, keeping records, and archiving computerized images. **SKILLS—Social Perceptiveness:** Being aware of others' reactions and understanding why they react as they do. **Reading Comprehension:** Understanding written sentences and paragraphs in work-related documents. **Learning Strategies:** Selecting and using training/instructional methods and procedures appropriate for the situation when learning or teaching new things. **Instructing:** Teaching others how to do something. **Operation and Control:** Controlling operations of equipment or systems. **Active Listening:** Giving full attention to what other people are saying, taking time to understand the points being made, asking questions as appropriate, and not interrupting at inappropriate times. **Service Orientation:** Actively looking for ways to help people. **Active Learning:** Understanding the implications of new information for both current and future problem-solving and decision-making. **GOE—Interest Area:** 08. Health Science. **Work Group:** 08.06. Medical Technology. **Other Jobs in This Work Group:** Biological Technicians; Cardiovascular Technologists and Technicians; Medical and Clinical Laboratory Technicians; Medical and Clinical Laboratory Technologists; Medical Equipment Preparers; Medical Records and Health Information Technicians; Nuclear Medicine Technologists; Opticians, Dispensing; Orthotists and Prosthetists; Radiologic Technicians; Radiologic Technologists. **PERSONALITY TYPE:** No data available.

EDUCATION/TRAINING PROGRAM(S)— Allied Health Diagnostic, Intervention, and Treatment Professions, Other; Diagnostic Medical Sonography/Sonographer and Ultrasound Technician. **RELATED KNOWLEDGE/COURSES—Medicine and Dentistry:** Knowledge of the information and techniques needed to diagnose and treat human injuries, diseases, and deformities. This includes symptoms, treatment alternatives, drug properties and interactions, and preventive health-care measures. **Physics:** Knowledge and prediction of physical principles and laws and their interrelationships and applications to understanding fluid, material, and atmospheric dynamics and mechanical, electrical, atomic, and sub-atomic structures and processes. **Biology:** Knowledge of plant and animal organisms and their tissues, cells, functions, interdependencies, and interactions with each other and the environment. **Customer and Personal Service:** Knowledge of principles and processes for providing customer and personal services. This includes customer needs assessment, meeting quality standards for services, and evaluation of customer satisfaction. **Education and Training:** Knowledge of principles and methods for curriculum and training design, teaching and instruction for individuals and groups, and the measurement of training effects. **Psychology:** Knowledge of human behavior and performance; individual differences in ability, personality, and interests; learning and motivation; psychological research methods; and the assessment and treatment of behavioral and affective disorders.

Dining Room and Cafeteria Attendants and Bartender Helpers

- ◎ Education/Training Required: Short-term on-the-job training
- ◎ Annual Earnings: $14,770
- ◎ Growth: 14.9%
- ◎ Annual Job Openings: 143,000
- ◎ Self-Employed: 0.1%
- ◎ Part-Time: 54.0%

Facilitate food service. Clean tables, carry dirty dishes, replace soiled table linens; set tables; replenish supply of clean linens, silverware, glassware, and dishes; supply service bar with food; and serve water, butter, and coffee to patrons. Perform serving, cleaning, and stocking duties in establishments such as cafeterias or dining rooms in order to facilitate customer service. Clean up spilled food, drink, and broken dishes and remove empty bottles and trash. Carry food, dishes, trays, and silverware from kitchens and supply departments to serving counters. Carry trays from food counters to tables for cafeteria patrons. Fill bever-

age and ice dispensers. Garnish foods and position them on tables to make them visible and accessible. Maintain adequate supplies of items such as clean linens, silverware, glassware, dishes, and trays. Mix and prepare flavors for mixed drinks. Replenish supplies of food and equipment at steam tables and service bars. Scrape and stack dirty dishes and carry dishes and other tableware to kitchens for cleaning. Serve food to customers when waiters and waitresses need assistance. Serve ice water, coffee, rolls, and butter to patrons. Set tables with clean linens, condiments, and other supplies. Slice and pit fruit used to garnish drinks. Stock cabinets and serving areas with condiments and refill condiment containers as necessary. Stock refrigerating units with wines and bottled beer and replace empty beer kegs. Wash glasses and other serving equipment at bars. Wipe tables and seats with dampened cloths and replace dirty tablecloths. Carry linens to and from laundry areas. Clean and polish counters, shelves, walls, furniture, and equipment in food service areas and other areas of restaurants and mop and vacuum floors. Locate items requested by customers. Run cash registers. Stock vending machines with food. **SKILLS**—None met the criteria. **GOE—Interest Area:** 09. Hospitality, Tourism, and Recreation. **Work Group:** 09.05. Food and Beverage Service. **Other Jobs in This Work Group:** Bartenders; Combined Food Preparation and Serving Workers, Including Fast Food; Counter Attendants, Cafeteria, Food Concession, and Coffee Shop; Food Servers, Nonrestaurant; Hosts and Hostesses, Restaurant, Lounge, and Coffee Shop; Waiters and Waitresses. **PERSONALITY TYPE:** Realistic. Realistic occupations frequently involve work activities that include practical, hands-on problems and solutions. These occupations often deal with plants, animals, and real-world materials like wood, tools, and machinery. Many of the occupations require working outside and do not involve a lot of paperwork or working closely with others.

EDUCATION/TRAINING PROGRAM(S)—Food Service, Waiter/Waitress, and Dining Room Management/Manager. **RELATED KNOWLEDGE/ COURSES—Administration and Management:** Knowledge of business and management principles involved in strategic planning, resource allocation, human resources modeling, leadership technique, production methods, and coordination of people and resources. **Clerical Practices:** Knowledge of administrative and clerical procedures and systems such as word processing, managing files and records, stenography and transcription, designing forms, and other office procedures and terminology.

Dispatchers, Except Police, Fire, and Ambulance

◉ Education/Training Required: Moderate-term on-the-job training
◉ Annual Earnings: $30,920
◉ Growth: 14.4%
◉ Annual Job Openings: 28,000
◉ Self-Employed: 0.6%
◉ Part-Time: 8.5%

Schedule and dispatch workers, work crews, equipment, or service vehicles for conveyance of materials, freight, or passengers or for normal installation, service, or emergency repairs rendered outside the place of business. Duties may include using radio, telephone, or computer to transmit assignments and compiling statistics and reports on work progress. Schedule and dispatch workers, work crews, equipment, or service vehicles to appropriate locations according to customer requests, specifications, or needs, using radios or telephones. Arrange for necessary repairs in order to restore service and schedules. Relay work orders, messages, and information to or from work crews, supervisors, and field inspectors, using telephones or two-way radios. Confer with customers or supervising personnel in order to address questions, problems, and requests for service or equipment. Prepare daily work and run schedules. Receive or prepare work orders. Oversee all communications within specifically assigned territories. Monitor personnel and/or equipment locations and utilization in order to coordinate service and schedules. Record and maintain files and records of customer requests, work or services performed, charges, expenses, inventory, and other dispatch information. Determine types or amounts of equipment, vehicles, materials, or personnel required according to work orders or specifications. Advise personnel about traffic problems such as construction areas, accidents, congestion, weather conditions, and other hazards. Ensure timely and efficient movement of trains according to train orders and schedules. Order supplies and equipment and issue them to personnel. **SKILLS—Service Orientation:** Actively looking for ways to help people. **Operations Analysis:** Analyzing needs and product requirements to create a design. **Management of Personnel Resources:** Motivating, developing, and directing people as they work, identifying the best people for the job. **Learning Strategies:** Selecting and using training/instructional methods and procedures appropriate for the situation when learning or teaching new things. **Critical Thinking:** Using logic and reasoning to identify the strengths and weaknesses of alternative solutions, conclusions, or approaches to problems. **Social Perceptiveness:** Being aware of others' reactions and understanding why they react as they do. **Instructing:** Teaching others how to do something. **Troubleshooting:** Determining causes of operating errors and deciding what to do about them. **GOE—Interest Area:** 03. Arts and Communication. **Work Group:** 03.10. Communications Technology. **Other Jobs in This Work Group:** Air Traffic Controllers; Airfield Operations Specialists; Central Office Operators; Directory Assistance Operators; Police, Fire, and Ambulance Dispatchers. **PERSONALITY TYPE:** Conventional. Conventional occupations frequently involve following set procedures and routines. These occupations can include working with data and details more than with ideas. Usually there is a clear line of authority to follow.

EDUCATION/TRAINING PROGRAM(S)— No data available. **RELATED KNOWLEDGE/ COURSES—Transportation:** Knowledge of principles and methods for moving people or goods by air, rail, sea, or road, including the relative costs and benefits. **Clerical Practices:** Knowledge of administrative and clerical procedures and systems such as word processing, managing files and records, stenography and transcription, designing forms, and other office procedures and terminology. **Public Safety and Security:** Knowledge of relevant equipment, policies, procedures, and strategies to promote effective local, state, or national security operations for the protection of people, data, property, and institutions. **Customer and Personal Service:** Knowledge of principles and processes for providing customer and personal services. This includes customer needs assessment, meeting quality standards for services, and evaluation of customer satisfaction. **Computers and Electronics:** Knowledge of circuit boards, processors, chips, electronic equipment, and computer hardware and software, including applications and programming. **Telecommunications:** Knowledge of transmission, broadcasting, switching, control, and operation of telecommunications systems.

Dragline Operators

- ◎ Education/Training Required: Moderate-term on-the-job training
- ◎ Annual Earnings: $31,970
- ◎ Growth: 8.9%
- ◎ Annual Job Openings: 14,000
- ◎ Self-Employed: 16.9%
- ◎ Part-Time: 2.7%

Operate power-driven crane equipment with dragline bucket to excavate or move sand, gravel, mud, or other materials. Moves controls to position boom, lower and drag bucket through material, and release material at unloading point. Directs workers engaged in placing blocks and outriggers to prevent capsizing of machine when lifting heavy loads. Drives machine to work site. **SKILLS—Operation and Control:** Controlling operations of equipment or systems. **Operation Monitoring:** Watching gauges, dials, or other indicators to make sure a machine is working properly. **GOE—Interest Area:** 02. Architecture and Construction. **Work Group:** 02.04. Construction Crafts. **Other Jobs in This Work Group:** Boat Builders and Shipwrights; Boilermakers; Brattice Builders; Brickmasons and Blockmasons; Carpet Installers; Ceiling Tile Installers; Cement Masons and Concrete Finishers; Commercial Divers; Construction Carpenters; Crane and Tower Operators; Drywall Installers; Electricians; Fence Erectors; Floor Layers, Except Carpet, Wood, and Hard Tiles; Floor Sanders and Finishers; Glaziers; Grader, Bulldozer, and Scraper Operators; Hazardous Materials Removal Workers; Insulation Workers, Floor, Ceiling, and Wall; Insulation Workers, Mechanical; Manufactured Building and Mobile Home Installers; Operating Engineers; Painters, Construction and Maintenance; Paperhangers; Paving, Surfacing, and Tamping Equipment Operators; Pile-Driver Operators; Pipe Fitters; Pipelayers; Pipelaying Fitters; Plasterers and Stucco Masons; Plumbers; Rail-Track Laying and Maintenance Equipment Operators; Refractory Materials Repairers, Except Brickmasons; Reinforcing Iron and Rebar Workers; Riggers; Roofers; Rough Carpenters; Security and Fire Alarm Systems Installers; Segmental Pavers; Sheet Metal Workers; Ship Carpenters and Joiners; Stone Cutters and Carvers; Stonemasons; Structural Iron and Steel Workers; Tapers; Terrazzo Workers and Finishers; Tile and Marble Setters. **PERSONALITY TYPE:** Realistic. Realistic occupations frequently involve work activities that include practical, hands-on problems and solutions. These occupations often deal with plants, animals, and real-world materials like wood, tools, and machinery. Many of the occupations require working outside and do not involve a lot of paperwork or working closely with others.

EDUCATION/TRAINING PROGRAM(S)—Construction/Heavy Equipment/Earthmoving Equipment Operation. **RELATED KNOWLEDGE/COURSES—Building and Construction:** Knowledge of the materials, methods, and tools involved in the construction or repair of houses, buildings, or other structures such as highways and roads. **Transportation:** Knowledge of principles and methods for moving people or goods by air, rail, sea, or road, including the relative costs and benefits. **Physics:** Knowledge and prediction of physical principles and laws and their interrelationships and applications to understanding fluid, material, and atmospheric dynamics and mechanical, electrical, atomic, and subatomic structures and processes. **Engineering and Technology:** Knowledge of the practical application of engineering science and technology. This includes applying principles, techniques, procedures, and equipment to the design and production of various goods and services. **Mechanical Devices:** Knowledge of machines and tools, including their designs, uses, repair, and maintenance. **Public Safety and Security:** Knowledge of relevant equipment, policies, procedures, and strategies to promote effective local, state, or national security operations for the protection of people, data, property, and institutions.

Drywall Installers

- ◉ Education/Training Required: Moderate-term on-the-job training
- ◉ Annual Earnings: $34,030
- ◉ Growth: 21.4%
- ◉ Annual Job Openings: 17,000
- ◉ Self-Employed: 18.4%
- ◉ Part-Time: 5.9%

Apply plasterboard or other wallboard to ceilings and interior walls of buildings. Trims rough edges from wallboard to maintain even joints, using knife. Fits and fastens wallboard or sheetrock into specified position, using hand tools, portable power tools, or adhesive. Measures and marks cutting lines on framing, drywall, and trim, using tape measure, straightedge or square, and marking devices. Installs blanket insulation between studs and tacks plastic moisture barrier over insulation. Removes plaster, drywall, or paneling, using crowbar and hammer. Assembles and installs metal framing and decorative trim for windows, doorways, and bents. Reads blueprints and other specifications to determine method of installation, work procedures, and material and tool requirements. Lays out reference lines and points, computes position of framing and furring channels, and marks position, using chalkline. Suspends angle iron grid and channel iron from ceiling, using wire. Installs horizontal and vertical metal or wooden studs for attachment of wallboard on interior walls, using hand tools. Cuts metal or wood framing, angle and channel iron, and trim to size, using cutting tools. Cuts openings into board for electrical outlets, windows, vents, or fixtures, using keyhole saw or other cutting tools. **SKILLS—Installation:** Installing equipment, machines, wiring, or programs to meet specifications. **GOE—Interest Area:** 02. Architecture and Construction. **Work Group:** 02.04. Construction Crafts. **Other Jobs in This Work Group:** Boat Builders and Shipwrights; Boilermakers; Brattice Builders; Brickmasons and Blockmasons; Car-

pet Installers; Ceiling Tile Installers; Cement Masons and Concrete Finishers; Commercial Divers; Construction Carpenters; Crane and Tower Operators; Dragline Operators; Electricians; Fence Erectors; Floor Layers, Except Carpet, Wood, and Hard Tiles; Floor Sanders and Finishers; Glaziers; Grader, Bulldozer, and Scraper Operators; Hazardous Materials Removal Workers; Insulation Workers, Floor, Ceiling, and Wall; Insulation Workers, Mechanical; Manufactured Building and Mobile Home Installers; Operating Engineers; Painters, Construction and Maintenance; Paperhangers; Paving, Surfacing, and Tamping Equipment Operators; Pile-Driver Operators; Pipe Fitters; Pipelayers; Pipelaying Fitters; Plasterers and Stucco Masons; Plumbers; Rail-Track Laying and Maintenance Equipment Operators; Refractory Materials Repairers, Except Brickmasons; Reinforcing Iron and Rebar Workers; Riggers; Roofers; Rough Carpenters; Security and Fire Alarm Systems Installers; Segmental Pavers; Sheet Metal Workers; Ship Carpenters and Joiners; Stone Cutters and Carvers; Stonemasons; Structural Iron and Steel Workers; Tapers; Terrazzo Workers and Finishers; Tile and Marble Setters. **PERSONALITY TYPE:** Realistic. Realistic occupations frequently involve work activities that include practical, hands-on problems and solutions. These occupations often deal with plants, animals, and real-world materials like wood, tools, and machinery. Many of the occupations require working outside and do not involve a lot of paperwork or working closely with others.

EDUCATION/TRAINING PROGRAM(S)—Drywall Installation/Drywaller. **RELATED KNOWLEDGE/COURSES—Building and Construction:** Knowledge of the materials, methods, and tools involved in the construction or repair of houses, buildings, or other structures such as highways and roads. **Design:** Knowledge of design techniques, tools, and principles involved in production of precision technical plans, blueprints, drawings, and models. **Engineering and Technology:** Knowledge of the practical application of engineering science and technology. This includes applying principles, techniques, procedures, and equipment to the design and production of various goods and services. **Mechanical Devices:** Knowledge of machines and tools, including their designs, uses, repair, and maintenance.

Electric Meter Installers and Repairers

◎ Education/Training Required: Moderate-term on-the-job training
◎ Annual Earnings: $43,710
◎ Growth: 12.0%
◎ Annual Job Openings: 5,000
◎ Self-Employed: 0.7%
◎ Part-Time: 2.0%

Install electric meters on customers' premises or on pole. Test meters and perform necessary repairs. Turn current on/off by connecting/disconnecting service drop. Mounts and installs meter and other electric equipment, such as time clocks, transformers, and circuit breakers, using electrician's hand tools. Inspects and tests electric meters, relays, and power to detect cause of malfunction and inaccuracy, using hand tools and testing equipment. Splices and connects cable from meter or current transformer to pull box or switchboard, using hand tools, to provide power. Disconnects and removes electric power meters when defective or when customer accounts are in default, using hand tools. Records meter reading and installation data on meter cards, work orders, or field service orders. Cleans meter parts, using chemical solutions, brushes, sandpaper, and soap and water. Makes adjustments to meter components, such as setscrews or timing mechanism, to conform to specifications. Repairs electric meters and components, such as transformers and relays, and changes faulty or incorrect wiring, using hand tools. **SKILLS—Installation:** Installing equipment, machines, wiring, or programs to meet specifications. **Troubleshooting:** Determining causes of operating errors and deciding what to do about them. **Repairing:** Repairing machines or systems by using the needed tools. **Technology Design:** Generating or adapting equipment and technology to serve user needs. **Equipment Maintenance:** Performing routine maintenance on equipment and determining when and what kind of maintenance is needed. **Quality Control Analysis:** Conducting tests and inspections of products, services, or processes to evaluate quality or performance. **Science:** Using scientific rules and methods to solve problems. **Operation Monitor-

ing:** Watching gauges, dials, or other indicators to make sure a machine is working properly. **GOE— Interest Area:** 02. Architecture and Construction. **Work Group:** 02.05. Systems and Equipment Installation, Maintenance, and Repair. **Other Jobs in This Work Group:** Central Office and PBX Installers and Repairers; Communication Equipment Mechanics, Installers, and Repairers; Electrical and Electronics Repairers, Powerhouse, Substation, and Relay; Electrical Power-Line Installers and Repairers; Elevator Installers and Repairers; Frame Wirers, Central Office; Heating and Air Conditioning Mechanics; Home Appliance Installers; Maintenance and Repair Workers, General; Meter Mechanics; Refrigeration Mechanics; Station Installers and Repairers, Telephone; Telecommunications Facility Examiners; Telecommunications Line Installers and Repairers. **PERSONALITY TYPE:** Realistic. Realistic occupations frequently involve work activities that include practical, hands-on problems and solutions. These occupations often deal with plants, animals, and real-world materials like wood, tools, and machinery. Many of the occupations require working outside and do not involve a lot of paperwork or working closely with others.

EDUCATION/TRAINING PROGRAM(S)— Electromechanical and Instrumentation and Maintenance Technologies/Technicians, Other. **RELATED KNOWLEDGE/COURSES—Mechanical Devices:** Knowledge of machines and tools, including their designs, uses, repair, and maintenance. **Computers and Electronics:** Knowledge of circuit boards, processors, chips, electronic equipment, and computer hardware and software, including applications and programming. **Engineering and Technology:** Knowledge of the practical application of engineering science and technology. This includes applying principles, techniques, procedures, and equipment to the design and production of various goods and services. **Design:** Knowledge of design techniques, tools, and principles involved in production of precision technical plans, blueprints, drawings, and models. **Telecommunications:** Knowledge of transmission, broadcasting, switching, control, and operation of telecommunications systems. **Building and Construction:** Knowledge of the materials, methods, and tools involved in the construction or repair of houses, buildings, or other structures such as highways and roads. **Geography:**

E

Knowledge of principles and methods for describing the features of land, sea, and air masses, including their physical characteristics; locations; interrelationships; and distribution of plant, animal, and human life.

Electrical and Electronic Inspectors and Testers

- Education/Training Required: Moderate-term on-the-job training
- Annual Earnings: $28,410
- Growth: 4.7%
- Annual Job Openings: 87,000
- Self-Employed: 1.2%
- Part-Time: 5.0%

Inspect and test electrical and electronic systems, such as radar navigational equipment, computer memory units, and television and radio transmitters, using precision measuring instruments. Tests and measures finished products, components, or assemblies for functioning, operation, accuracy, or assembly to verify adherence to functional specifications. Reads dials and meters to verify functioning of equipment according to specifications. Analyzes and interprets blueprints, sample data, and other materials to determine, change, or measure specifications or inspection and testing procedures. Marks items for acceptance or rejection, records test results and inspection data, and compares findings with specifications to ensure conformance to standards. Inspects materials, products, and work in progress for conformance to specifications and adjusts process or assembly equipment to meet standards. Computes and/or calculates sample data and test results. Confers with vendors and others regarding inspection results; recommends corrective procedures; and compiles reports of results, recommendations, and needed repairs. Writes and installs computer programs to control test equipment. Installs, positions, or connects new or replacement parts, components, and instruments. Reviews maintenance records to ensure that plant equipment functions properly. Disassembles defective parts and components. Cleans and maintains test equipment and instruments to ensure proper functioning. Positions or

directs other workers to position products, components, or parts for testing. Operates or tends machinery and equipment and uses hand tools. Examines and adjusts or repairs finished products and components or parts. **SKILLS—Programming:** Writing computer programs for various purposes. **Quality Control Analysis:** Conducting tests and inspections of products, services, or processes to evaluate quality or performance. **Installation:** Installing equipment, machines, wiring, or programs to meet specifications. **Troubleshooting:** Determining causes of operating errors and deciding what to do about them. **Repairing:** Repairing machines or systems by using the needed tools. **Operation Monitoring:** Watching gauges, dials, or other indicators to make sure a machine is working properly. **Science:** Using scientific rules and methods to solve problems. **Equipment Maintenance:** Performing routine maintenance on equipment and determining when and what kind of maintenance is needed. **GOE—Interest Area:** 13. Manufacturing. **Work Group:** 13.07. Production Quality Control. **Other Jobs in This Work Group:** Graders and Sorters, Agricultural Products; Materials Inspectors; Precision Devices Inspectors and Testers; Production Inspectors, Testers, Graders, Sorters, Samplers, Weighers. **PERSONALITY TYPE:** Realistic. Realistic occupations frequently involve work activities that include practical, hands-on problems and solutions. These occupations often deal with plants, animals, and real-world materials like wood, tools, and machinery. Many of the occupations require working outside and do not involve a lot of paperwork or working closely with others.

EDUCATION/TRAINING PROGRAM(S)— Quality Control Technology/Technician. **RELATED KNOWLEDGE/COURSES—Computers and Electronics:** Knowledge of circuit boards, processors, chips, electronic equipment, and computer hardware and software, including applications and programming. **Telecommunications:** Knowledge of transmission, broadcasting, switching, control, and operation of telecommunications systems. **Design:** Knowledge of design techniques, tools, and principles involved in production of precision technical plans, blueprints, drawings, and models. **Mechanical Devices:** Knowledge of machines and tools, including their designs, uses, repair, and maintenance. **Engineering and Technology:** Knowledge of the practical application of engineering science and technology. This includes applying principles, techniques, procedures, and equipment to the design and production of various goods and services. **Production and Processing:** Knowledge of raw materials, production processes, quality control, costs, and other techniques for maximizing the effective manufacture and distribution of goods.

Electrical and Electronics Repairers, Commercial and Industrial Equipment

◎ Education/Training Required: Postsecondary vocational training

◎ Annual Earnings: $42,600

◎ Growth: 10.3%

◎ Annual Job Openings: 10,000

◎ Self-Employed: 0.7%

◎ Part-Time: 1.2%

Repair, test, adjust, or install electronic equipment, such as industrial controls, transmitters, and antennas. Perform scheduled preventive maintenance tasks, such as checking, cleaning, and repairing equipment, to detect and prevent problems. Examine work orders and converse with equipment operators to detect equipment problems and to ascertain whether mechanical or human errors contributed to the problems. Set up and test industrial equipment to ensure that it functions properly. Operate equipment to demonstrate proper use and to analyze malfunctions. Test faulty equipment to diagnose malfunctions, using test equipment and software and applying knowledge of the functional operation of electronic units and systems. Repair and adjust equipment, machines, and defective components, replacing worn parts such as gaskets and seals in watertight electrical equipment. Calibrate testing instruments and installed or repaired equipment to prescribed specifications. Advise management regarding customer satisfaction, product performance, and suggestions for product improvements. Inspect components of industrial equipment for accu-

rate assembly and installation and for defects such as loose connections and frayed wires. Study blueprints, schematics, manuals, and other specifications to determine installation procedures. Maintain equipment logs that record performance problems, repairs, calibrations, and tests. Coordinate efforts with other workers involved in installing and maintaining equipment or components. Maintain inventory of spare parts. Consult with customers, supervisors, and engineers to plan layout of equipment and to resolve problems in system operation and maintenance. Send defective units to the manufacturer or to a specialized repair shop for repair. Install repaired equipment in various settings, such as industrial or military establishments. Determine feasibility of using standardized equipment and develop specifications for equipment required to perform additional functions. Enter information into computer to copy program or to draw, modify, or store schematics, applying knowledge of software package used. Sign overhaul documents for equipment replaced or repaired. Develop or modify industrial electronic devices, circuits, and equipment according to available specifications. **SKILLS—Installation:** Installing equipment, machines, wiring, or programs to meet specifications. **Troubleshooting:** Determining causes of operating errors and deciding what to do about them. **Repairing:** Repairing machines or systems by using the needed tools. **Operation Monitoring:** Watching gauges, dials, or other indicators to make sure a machine is working properly. **Equipment Maintenance:** Performing routine maintenance on equipment and determining when and what kind of maintenance is needed. **Systems Analysis:** Determining how a system should work and how changes in conditions, operations, and the environment will affect outcomes. **Operation and Control:** Controlling operations of equipment or systems. **Coordination:** Adjusting actions in relation to others' actions. **GOE—Interest Area:** 13. Manufacturing. **Work Group:** 13.12. Electrical and Electronic Repair. **Other Jobs in This Work Group:** Avionics Technicians; Battery Repairers; Electric Home Appliance and Power Tool Repairers; Electric Motor and Switch Assemblers and Repairers; Electrical and Electronics Installers and Repairers, Transportation Equipment; Electrical Parts Reconditioners; Electronic Equipment Installers and Repairers, Motor Vehicles; Electronic Home Entertainment Equipment Installers and

Repairers; Radio Mechanics; Transformer Repairers. **PERSONALITY TYPE:** Realistic. Realistic occupations frequently involve work activities that include practical, hands-on problems and solutions. These occupations often deal with plants, animals, and real-world materials like wood, tools, and machinery. Many of the occupations require working outside and do not involve a lot of paperwork or working closely with others.

EDUCATION/TRAINING PROGRAM(S)— Computer Installation and Repair Technology/Technician; Industrial Electronics Technology/Technician. **RELATED KNOWLEDGE/COURSES—Mechanical Devices:** Knowledge of machines and tools, including their designs, uses, repair, and maintenance. **Computers and Electronics:** Knowledge of circuit boards, processors, chips, electronic equipment, and computer hardware and software, including applications and programming. **Telecommunications:** Knowledge of transmission, broadcasting, switching, control, and operation of telecommunications systems. **Design:** Knowledge of design techniques, tools, and principles involved in production of precision technical plans, blueprints, drawings, and models. **Engineering and Technology:** Knowledge of the practical application of engineering science and technology. This includes applying principles, techniques, procedures, and equipment to the design and production of various goods and services. **Transportation:** Knowledge of principles and methods for moving people or goods by air, rail, sea, or road, including the relative costs and benefits.

Electrical Engineering Technicians

- Education/Training Required: Associate degree
- Annual Earnings: $46,310
- Growth: 10.0%
- Annual Job Openings: 24,000
- Self-Employed: 0.4%
- Part-Time: 5.0%

Apply electrical theory and related knowledge to test and modify developmental or operational electrical machinery and electrical control equipment and circuitry in industrial or commercial plants and laboratories. Usually work under direction of engineering staff. Provide technical assistance and resolution when electrical or engineering problems are encountered before, during, and after construction. Assemble electrical and electronic systems and prototypes according to engineering data and knowledge of electrical principles, using hand tools and measuring instruments. Install and maintain electrical control systems and solid state equipment. Modify electrical prototypes, parts, assemblies, and systems to correct functional deviations. Set up and operate test equipment to evaluate performance of developmental parts, assemblies, or systems under simulated operating conditions and record results. Collaborate with electrical engineers and other personnel to identify, define, and solve developmental problems. Build, calibrate, maintain, troubleshoot, and repair electrical instruments or testing equipment. Analyze and interpret test information to resolve design-related problems. Write commissioning procedures for electrical installations. Prepare project cost and work-time estimates. Evaluate engineering proposals, shop drawings, and design comments for sound electrical engineering practice and conformance with established safety and design criteria and recommend approval or disapproval. Draw or modify diagrams and write engineering specifications to clarify design details and functional criteria of experimental electronics units. Conduct inspections for quality control and assurance programs, reporting findings and recommendations. Prepare contracts and initiate, review, and coordinate modifications to contract specifications and plans throughout the construction process. Plan, schedule, and monitor work of support personnel to assist supervisor. Review existing electrical engineering criteria to identify necessary revisions, deletions, or amendments to outdated material. Perform supervisory duties such as recommending work assignments, approving leaves, and completing performance evaluations. Plan method and sequence of operations for developing and testing experimental electronic and electrical equipment. **SKILLS— Troubleshooting:** Determining causes of operating errors and deciding what to do about them. **Repairing:**

Repairing machines or systems by using the needed tools. **Installation:** Installing equipment, machines, wiring, or programs to meet specifications. **Technology Design:** Generating or adapting equipment and technology to serve user needs. **Operations Analysis:** Analyzing needs and product requirements to create a design. **Equipment Maintenance:** Performing routine maintenance on equipment and determining when and what kind of maintenance is needed. **Mathematics:** Using mathematics to solve problems. **Science:** Using scientific rules and methods to solve problems. **GOE—Interest Area:** 15. Scientific Research, Engineering, and Mathematics. **Work Group:** 15.09. Engineering Technology. **Other Jobs in This Work Group:** Aerospace Engineering and Operations Technicians; Calibration and Instrumentation Technicians; Cartographers and Photogrammetrists; Civil Engineering Technicians; Electro-Mechanical Technicians; Electronic Drafters; Electronics Engineering Technicians; Environmental Engineering Technicians; Mapping Technicians; Mechanical Drafters; Mechanical Engineering Technicians; Surveying Technicians. **PERSONALITY TYPE:** Realistic. Realistic occupations frequently involve work activities that include practical, hands-on problems and solutions. These occupations often deal with plants, animals, and real-world materials like wood, tools, and machinery. Many of the occupations require working outside and do not involve a lot of paperwork or working closely with others.

EDUCATION/TRAINING PROGRAM(S)— Computer Engineering Technology/Technician; Computer Technology/Computer Systems Technology; Electrical and Electronic Engineering Technologies/Technicians, Other; Electrical, Electronic, and Communications Engineering Technology/Technician; Telecommunications Technology/Technician. **RELATED KNOWLEDGE/COURSES—Engineering and Technology:** Knowledge of the practical application of engineering science and technology. This includes applying principles, techniques, procedures, and equipment to the design and production of various goods and services. **Design:** Knowledge of design techniques, tools, and principles involved in production of precision technical plans, blueprints, drawings, and models. **Computers and Electronics:** Knowledge of circuit boards, processors, chips, electronic equip-

ment, and computer hardware and software, including applications and programming. **Physics:** Knowledge and prediction of physical principles and laws and their interrelationships and applications to understanding fluid, material, and atmospheric dynamics and mechanical, electrical, atomic, and subatomic structures and processes. **Mechanical Devices:** Knowledge of machines and tools, including their designs, uses, repair, and maintenance. **Telecommunications:** Knowledge of transmission, broadcasting, switching, control, and operation of telecommunications systems.

Electrical Power-Line Installers and Repairers

- Education/Training Required: Long-term on-the-job training
- Annual Earnings: $49,100
- Growth: 1.6%
- Annual Job Openings: 9,000
- Self-Employed: 3.1%
- Part-Time: 1.3%

Install or repair cables or wires used in electrical power or distribution systems. May erect poles and light- or heavy-duty transmission towers. Adhere to safety practices and procedures, such as checking equipment regularly and erecting barriers around work areas. Attach crossarms, insulators, and auxiliary equipment to poles prior to installing them. Clean, tin, and splice corresponding conductors by twisting ends together or by joining ends with metal clamps and soldering connections. Climb poles or use truck-mounted buckets to access equipment. Cut and peel lead sheathing and insulation from defective or newly installed cables and conduits prior to splicing. Identify defective sectionalizing devices, circuit breakers, fuses, voltage regulators, transformers, switches, relays, or wiring, using wiring diagrams and electrical-testing instruments. Inspect and test power lines and auxiliary equipment to locate and identify problems, using reading and testing instruments. Install, maintain, and repair electrical distribution and transmission systems, including conduits, cables, wires, and related equipment such as transformers, circuit breakers, and switches. Lay underground cable directly in trenches or string it through conduit running through the trenches. Open switches or attach grounding devices in order to remove electrical hazards from disturbed or fallen lines or to facilitate repairs. Place insulating or fireproofing materials over conductors and joints. Pull up cable by hand from large reels mounted on trucks. Replace damaged poles with new poles and straighten the poles. Splice or solder cables together or to overhead transmission lines, customer service lines, or street light lines, using hand tools, epoxies, or specialized equipment. String wire conductors and cables between poles, towers, trenches, pylons, and buildings, setting lines in place and using winches to adjust tension. Test conductors according to electrical diagrams and specifications to identify corresponding conductors and to prevent incorrect connections. Coordinate work assignment preparation and completion with other workers. Cut trenches for laying underground cables, using trenchers and cable plows. Dig holes, using augers, and set poles, using cranes and power equipment. **SKILLS—Installation:** Installing equipment, machines, wiring, or programs to meet specifications. **Repairing:** Repairing machines or systems by using the needed tools. **Troubleshooting:** Determining causes of operating errors and deciding what to do about them. **Equipment Maintenance:** Performing routine maintenance on equipment and determining when and what kind of maintenance is needed. **Science:** Using scientific rules and methods to solve problems. **Quality Control Analysis:** Conducting tests and inspections of products, services, or processes to evaluate quality or performance. **Technology Design:** Generating or adapting equipment and technology to serve user needs. **Operation and Control:** Controlling operations of equipment or systems. **GOE—Interest Area:** 02. Architecture and Construction. **Work Group:** 02.05. Systems and Equipment Installation, Maintenance, and Repair. **Other Jobs in This Work Group:** Central Office and PBX Installers and Repairers; Communication Equipment Mechanics, Installers, and Repairers; Electric Meter Installers and Repairers; Electrical and Electronics Repairers, Powerhouse, Substation, and Relay; Elevator Installers and Repairers; Frame Wirers, Central Office; Heating and Air Conditioning Mechanics; Home Appliance Installers;

Maintenance and Repair Workers, General; Meter Mechanics; Refrigeration Mechanics; Station Installers and Repairers, Telephone; Telecommunications Facility Examiners; Telecommunications Line Installers and Repairers. **PERSONALITY TYPE:** Realistic. Realistic occupations frequently involve work activities that include practical, hands-on problems and solutions. These occupations often deal with plants, animals, and real-world materials like wood, tools, and machinery. Many of the occupations require working outside and do not involve a lot of paperwork or working closely with others.

EDUCATION/TRAINING PROGRAM(S)—Electrical and Power Transmission Installation/Installer, General; Electrical and Power Transmission Installers, Other; Lineworker. **RELATED KNOWLEDGE/ COURSES—Mechanical Devices:** Knowledge of machines and tools, including their designs, uses, repair, and maintenance. **Public Safety and Security:** Knowledge of relevant equipment, policies, procedures, and strategies to promote effective local, state, or national security operations for the protection of people, data, property, and institutions. **Design:** Knowledge of design techniques, tools, and principles involved in production of precision technical plans, blueprints, drawings, and models. **Engineering and Technology:** Knowledge of the practical application of engineering science and technology. This includes applying principles, techniques, procedures, and equipment to the design and production of various goods and services. **Building and Construction:** Knowledge of the materials, methods, and tools involved in the construction or repair of houses, buildings, or other structures such as highways and roads. **Computers and Electronics:** Knowledge of circuit boards, processors, chips, electronic equipment, and computer hardware and software, including applications and programming.

Electricians

- ◎ Education/Training Required: Long-term on-the-job training
- ◎ Annual Earnings: $42,300
- ◎ Growth: 23.4%
- ◎ Annual Job Openings: 65,000
- ◎ Self-Employed: 9.1%
- ◎ Part-Time: 2.2%

Install, maintain, and repair electrical wiring, equipment, and fixtures. Ensure that work is in accordance with relevant codes. May install or service street lights, intercom systems, or electrical control systems. Assemble, install, test, and maintain electrical or electronic wiring, equipment, appliances, apparatus, and fixtures, using hand tools and power tools. Diagnose malfunctioning systems, apparatus, and components, using test equipment and hand tools, to locate the cause of a breakdown and correct the problem. Connect wires to circuit breakers, transformers, or other components. Inspect electrical systems, equipment, and components to identify hazards, defects, and the need for adjustment or repair and to ensure compliance with codes. Advise management on whether continued operation of equipment could be hazardous. Test electrical systems and continuity of circuits in electrical wiring, equipment, and fixtures, using testing devices such as ohmmeters, voltmeters, and oscilloscopes, to ensure compatibility and safety of system. Maintain current electrician's license or identification card to meet governmental regulations. Plan layout and installation of electrical wiring, equipment, and fixtures based on job specifications and local codes. Direct and train workers to install, maintain, or repair electrical wiring, equipment, and fixtures. Prepare sketches or follow blueprints to determine the location of wiring and equipment and to ensure conformance to building and safety codes. Use a variety of tools and equipment, such as power construction equipment; measuring devices; power tools; and testing equipment, including oscilloscopes, ammeters, and test lamps. Install ground leads and connect power cables to equipment such as motors. Perform business management duties such as maintaining records and files, preparing reports, and ordering supplies and equipment. Repair or replace wiring, equipment, and fixtures, using hand tools and power tools. Work from ladders, scaffolds, and roofs to install, maintain, or repair electrical wiring, equipment, and fixtures. Place conduit (pipes or tubing) inside designated partitions, walls, or other concealed areas and pull insulated wires or cables through the conduit to complete circuits between boxes. Construct and fabricate parts, using hand tools and specifications. **SKILLS—Installation:** Installing equipment, machines, wiring, or programs to meet specifications. **Repairing:** Repairing machines or systems by using the needed tools. **Troubleshooting:** Determining causes of operating errors and deciding what to do about them. **Equipment Maintenance:** Performing routine maintenance on equipment and determining when and what kind of maintenance is needed. **Technology Design:** Generating or adapting equipment and technology to serve user needs. **Equipment Selection:** Determining the kind of tools and equipment needed to do a job. **Operations Analysis:** Analyzing needs and product requirements to create a design. **Operation Monitoring:** Watching gauges, dials, or other indicators to make sure a machine is working properly. **Management of Financial Resources:** Determining how money will be spent to get the work done and accounting for these expenditures. **GOE—Interest Area:** 02. Architecture and Construction. **Work Group:** 02.04. Construction Crafts. **Other Jobs in This Work Group:** Boat Builders and Shipwrights; Boilermakers; Brattice Builders; Brickmasons and Blockmasons; Carpet Installers; Ceiling Tile Installers; Cement Masons and Concrete Finishers; Commercial Divers; Construction Carpenters; Crane and Tower Operators; Dragline Operators; Drywall Installers; Fence Erectors; Floor Layers, Except Carpet, Wood, and Hard Tiles; Floor Sanders and Finishers; Glaziers; Grader, Bulldozer, and Scraper Operators; Hazardous Materials Removal Workers; Insulation Workers, Floor, Ceiling, and Wall; Insulation Workers, Mechanical; Manufactured Building and Mobile Home Installers; Operating Engineers; Painters, Construction and Maintenance; Paperhangers; Paving, Surfacing, and Tamping Equipment Operators; Pile-Driver Operators; Pipe Fitters; Pipelayers; Pipelaying Fitters; Plasterers and Stucco Masons; Plumbers; Rail-Track Laying and Maintenance Equipment Operators; Refractory Materials Repairers,

Except Brickmasons; Reinforcing Iron and Rebar Workers; Riggers; Roofers; Rough Carpenters; Security and Fire Alarm Systems Installers; Segmental Pavers; Sheet Metal Workers; Ship Carpenters and Joiners; Stone Cutters and Carvers; Stonemasons; Structural Iron and Steel Workers; Tapers; Terrazzo Workers and Finishers; Tile and Marble Setters. **PERSONALITY TYPE:** Realistic. Realistic occupations frequently involve work activities that include practical, hands-on problems and solutions. These occupations often deal with plants, animals, and real-world materials like wood, tools, and machinery. Many of the occupations require working outside and do not involve a lot of paperwork or working closely with others.

EDUCATION/TRAINING PROGRAM(S)—Electrician. **RELATED KNOWLEDGE/COURSES— Building and Construction:** Knowledge of the materials, methods, and tools involved in the construction or repair of houses, buildings, or other structures such as highways and roads. **Mechanical Devices:** Knowledge of machines and tools, including their designs, uses, repair, and maintenance. **Design:** Knowledge of design techniques, tools, and principles involved in production of precision technical plans, blueprints, drawings, and models. **Production and Processing:** Knowledge of raw materials, production processes, quality control, costs, and other techniques for maximizing the effective manufacture and distribution of goods. **Physics:** Knowledge and prediction of physical principles and laws and their interrelationships and applications to understanding fluid, material, and atmospheric dynamics and mechanical, electrical, atomic, and subatomic structures and processes. **Customer and Personal Service:** Knowledge of principles and processes for providing customer and personal services. This includes customer needs assessment, meeting quality standards for services, and evaluation of customer satisfaction.

Electro-Mechanical Technicians

◉ Education/Training Required: Associate degree
◉ Annual Earnings: $41,440
◉ Growth: 11.5%
◉ Annual Job Openings: 4,000
◉ Self-Employed: 0.6%
◉ Part-Time: 5.0%

Operate, test, and maintain unmanned, automated, servo-mechanical, or electromechanical equipment. May operate unmanned submarines, aircraft, or other equipment at work sites, such as oil rigs, deep ocean exploration, or hazardous waste removal. May assist engineers in testing and designing robotics equipment. Analyze and record test results and prepare written testing documentation. Inspect parts for surface defects. Install electrical and electronic parts and hardware in housings or assemblies, using soldering equipment and hand tools. Read blueprints, schematics, diagrams, and technical orders to determine methods and sequences of assembly. Repair, rework, and calibrate hydraulic and pneumatic assemblies and systems to meet operational specifications and tolerances. Test performance of electromechanical assemblies, using test instruments such as oscilloscopes, electronic voltmeters, and bridges. Verify dimensions and clearances of parts to ensure conformance to specifications, using precision measuring instruments. Develop, test, and program new robots. Operate metalworking machines to fabricate housings, jigs, fittings, and fixtures. Train others to install, use, and maintain robots. Align, fit, and assemble component parts, using hand tools, power tools, fixtures, templates, and microscopes. **SKILLS—Repairing:** Repairing machines or systems by using the needed tools. **Troubleshooting:** Determining causes of operating errors and deciding what to do about them. **Equipment Maintenance:** Performing routine maintenance on equipment and determining when and what kind of maintenance is needed. **Quality Control Analysis:** Conducting tests and inspections of products, services, or processes to evaluate quality or performance. **Installation:** Installing equipment, machines, wiring, or programs to meet specifications. **Operation Monitoring:** Watching gauges, dials, or other indicators to make sure a machine is working properly. **Science:** Using scientific rules and methods to solve problems. **Operation and Control:** Controlling operations of equipment or systems. **GOE—Interest Area:** 15. Scientific Research, Engineering, and Mathematics. **Work Group:** 15.09. Engineering Technology. **Other Jobs in This Work Group:** Aerospace Engineering and Operations Technicians; Calibration and Instrumentation Technicians; Cartographers and Photogrammetrists; Civil Engineering Technicians; Electrical Engineering Technicians; Electronic Drafters; Electronics Engineering Technicians; Environmental Engineering Technicians; Mapping Technicians; Mechanical Drafters; Mechanical Engineering Technicians; Surveying Technicians. **PERSONALITY TYPE:** Realistic. Realistic occupations frequently involve work activities that include practical, hands-on problems and solutions. These occupations often deal with plants, animals, and real-world materials like wood, tools, and machinery. Many of the occupations require working outside and do not involve a lot of paperwork or working closely with others.

EDUCATION/TRAINING PROGRAM(S)—Engineering Technologies/Technicians, Other. **RELATED KNOWLEDGE/COURSES—Mechanical Devices:** Knowledge of machines and tools, including their designs, uses, repair, and maintenance. **Production and Processing:** Knowledge of raw materials, production processes, quality control, costs, and other techniques for maximizing the effective manufacture and distribution of goods. **Engineering and Technology:** Knowledge of the practical application of engineering science and technology. This includes applying principles, techniques, procedures, and equipment to the design and production of various goods and services. **Computers and Electronics:** Knowledge of circuit boards, processors, chips, electronic equipment, and computer hardware and software, including applications and programming. **Design:** Knowledge of design techniques, tools, and principles involved in production of precision technical plans, blueprints, drawings, and models. **Physics:** Knowledge and prediction of physical principles and laws and their interrelationships and applications to understanding fluid, material, and atmospheric dynamics and mechanical,

electrical, atomic, and subatomic structures and processes.

Electronics Engineering Technicians

- Education/Training Required: Associate degree
- Annual Earnings: $46,310
- Growth: 10.0%
- Annual Job Openings: 24,000
- Self-Employed: 0.4%
- Part-Time: 5.0%

Lay out, build, test, troubleshoot, repair, and modify developmental and production electronic components, parts, equipment, and systems, such as computer equipment, missile control instrumentation, electron tubes, test equipment, and machine tool numerical controls, applying principles and theories of electronics, electrical circuitry, engineering mathematics, electronic and electrical testing, and physics. Usually work under direction of engineering staff. Test electronics units, using standard test equipment, and analyze results to evaluate performance and determine need for adjustment. Perform preventative maintenance and calibration of equipment and systems. Read blueprints, wiring diagrams, schematic drawings, and engineering instructions for assembling electronics units, applying knowledge of electronic theory and components. Identify and resolve equipment malfunctions, working with manufacturers and field representatives as necessary to procure replacement parts. Maintain system logs and manuals to document testing and operation of equipment. Assemble, test, and maintain circuitry or electronic components according to engineering instructions, technical manuals, and knowledge of electronics, using hand and power tools. Adjust and replace defective or improperly functioning circuitry and electronics components, using hand tools and soldering iron. Procure parts and maintain inventory and related documentation. Maintain working knowledge of state-of-the-art tools, software, etc., through reading and/or attending conferences, workshops, or other training. Provide user applications and engineering support and recommendations for new and existing equipment with regard to installation, upgrades, and enhancement. Write reports and record data on testing techniques, laboratory equipment, and specifications to assist engineers. Provide customer support and education, working with users to identify needs, determine sources of problems, and provide information on product use. Design basic circuitry and draft sketches for clarification of details and design documentation under engineers' direction, using drafting instruments and computer-aided design equipment. Build prototypes from rough sketches or plans. Develop and upgrade preventative maintenance procedures for components, equipment, parts, and systems. Fabricate parts, such as coils, terminal boards, and chassis, using bench lathes, drills, or other machine tools. Research equipment and component needs, sources, competitive prices, delivery times, and ongoing operational costs. **SKILLS—Repairing:** Repairing machines or systems by using the needed tools. **Troubleshooting:** Determining causes of operating errors and deciding what to do about them. **Equipment Maintenance:** Performing routine maintenance on equipment and determining when and what kind of maintenance is needed. **Installation:** Installing equipment, machines, wiring, or programs to meet specifications. **Technology Design:** Generating or adapting equipment and technology to serve user needs. **Operation Monitoring:** Watching gauges, dials, or other indicators to make sure a machine is working properly. **Systems Evaluation:** Identifying measures or indicators of system performance and the actions needed to improve or correct performance relative to the goals of the system. **Systems Analysis:** Determining how a system should work and how changes in conditions, operations, and the environment will affect outcomes. **GOE—Interest Area:** 15. Scientific Research, Engineering, and Mathematics. **Work Group:** 15.09. Engineering Technology. **Other Jobs in This Work Group:** Aerospace Engineering and Operations Technicians; Calibration and Instrumentation Technicians; Cartographers and Photogrammetrists; Civil Engineering Technicians; Electrical Engineering Technicians; Electro-Mechanical Technicians; Electronic Drafters; Environmental Engineering Technicians; Mapping Technicians; Mechanical Drafters; Mechanical Engineering Technicians; Surveying Technicians. **PER-**

SONALITY TYPE: Realistic. Realistic occupations frequently involve work activities that include practical, hands-on problems and solutions. These occupations often deal with plants, animals, and real-world materials like wood, tools, and machinery. Many of the occupations require working outside and do not involve a lot of paperwork or working closely with others. **EDUCATION/TRAINING PROGRAM(S)—** Computer Engineering Technology/Technician; Computer Technology/Computer Systems Technology; Electrical and Electronic Engineering Technologies/Technicians, Other; Electrical, Electronic, and Communications Engineering Technology/Technician; Telecommunications Technology/Technician. **RELATED KNOWLEDGE/COURSES—Engineering and Technology:** Knowledge of the practical application of engineering science and technology. This includes applying principles, techniques, procedures, and equipment to the design and production of various goods and services. **Computers and Electronics:** Knowledge of circuit boards, processors, chips, electronic equipment, and computer hardware and software, including applications and programming. **Mechanical Devices:** Knowledge of machines and tools, including their designs, uses, repair, and maintenance. **Design:** Knowledge of design techniques, tools, and principles involved in production of precision technical plans, blueprints, drawings, and models. **Mathematics:** Knowledge of arithmetic, algebra, geometry, calculus, and statistics and their applications. **Telecommunications:** Knowledge of transmission, broadcasting, switching, control, and operation of telecommunications systems.

Elevator Installers and Repairers

- Education/Training Required: Long-term on-the-job training
- Annual Earnings: $58,710
- Growth: 17.1%
- Annual Job Openings: 3,000
- Self-Employed: 0%
- Part-Time: 0.2%

Assemble, install, repair, or maintain electric or hydraulic freight or passenger elevators, escalators, or dumbwaiters. Adjust safety controls; counterweights; door mechanisms; and components such as valves, ratchets, seals, and brake linings. Assemble electrically powered stairs, steel frameworks, and tracks and install associated motors and electrical wiring. Assemble elevator cars, installing each car's platform, walls, and doors. Assemble, install, repair, and maintain elevators, escalators, moving sidewalks, and dumbwaiters, using hand and power tools and testing devices such as test lamps, ammeters, and voltmeters. Attach guide shoes and rollers to minimize the lateral motion of cars as they travel through shafts. Bolt or weld steel rails to the walls of shafts to guide elevators, working from scaffolding or platforms. Check that safety regulations and building codes are met and complete service reports verifying conformance to standards. Connect car frames to counterweights, using steel cables. Connect electrical wiring to control panels and electric motors. Cut prefabricated sections of framework, rails, and other components to specified dimensions. Disassemble defective units and repair or replace parts such as locks, gears, cables, and electric wiring. Inspect wiring connections, control panel hookups, door installations, and alignments and clearances of cars and hoistways to ensure that equipment will operate properly. Install electrical wires and controls by attaching conduit along shaft walls from floor to floor and then pulling plastic-covered wires through the conduit. Install outer doors and door frames at elevator entrances on each floor of a structure. Locate malfunctions in brakes, motors, switches, and signal and control systems, using test equipment. Maintain logbooks that detail all repairs and checks performed. Operate elevators to determine power demands and test power consumption to detect overload factors. Read and interpret blueprints to determine the layout of system components, frameworks, and foundations and to select installation equipment. Test newly installed equipment to ensure that it meets specifications, such as stopping at floors for set amounts of time. **SKILLS—Installation:** Installing equipment, machines, wiring, or programs to meet specifications. **Repairing:** Repairing machines or systems by using the needed tools. **Equipment Maintenance:** Performing routine maintenance on equipment and determining when and what kind of maintenance is needed. **Troubleshooting:** Determining causes of operating errors and deciding what to do about them. **Quality Control Analysis:** Conducting tests and inspections of products, services, or processes to evaluate quality or performance. **Operation Monitoring:** Watching gauges, dials, or other indicators to make sure a machine is working properly. **Systems Analysis:** Determining how a system should work and how changes in conditions, operations, and the environment will affect outcomes. **Operation and Control:** Controlling operations of equipment or systems. **GOE—Interest Area:** 02. Architecture and Construction. **Work Group:** 02.05. Systems and Equipment Installation, Maintenance, and Repair. **Other Jobs in This Work Group:** Central Office and PBX Installers and Repairers; Communication Equipment Mechanics, Installers, and Repairers; Electric Meter Installers and Repairers; Electrical and Electronics Repairers, Powerhouse, Substation, and Relay; Electrical Power-Line Installers and Repairers; Frame Wirers, Central Office; Heating and Air Conditioning Mechanics; Home Appliance Installers; Maintenance and Repair Workers, General; Meter Mechanics; Refrigeration Mechanics; Station Installers and Repairers, Telephone; Telecommunications Facility Examiners; Telecommunications Line Installers and Repairers. **PERSONALITY TYPE:** Realistic. Realistic occupations frequently involve work activities that include practical, hands-on problems and solutions. These occupations often deal with plants, animals, and real-world materials like wood, tools, and machinery. Many of the occupations require working outside and do not involve a lot of paperwork or working closely with others.

EDUCATION/TRAINING PROGRAM(S)— Industrial Mechanics and Maintenance Technology. **RELATED KNOWLEDGE/COURSES—Building and Construction:** Knowledge of the materials, methods, and tools involved in the construction or repair of houses, buildings, or other structures such as highways and roads. **Mechanical Devices:** Knowledge of machines and tools, including their designs, uses, repair, and maintenance. **Engineering and Technology:** Knowledge of the practical application of engineering science and technology. This includes applying principles, techniques, procedures, and equipment to the design and production of various goods and services. **Physics:** Knowledge and prediction of physical principles and laws and their interrelationships and applications to understanding fluid, material, and atmospheric dynamics and mechanical, electrical, atomic, and subatomic structures and processes. **Telecommunications:** Knowledge of transmission, broadcasting, switching, control, and operation of telecommunications systems. **Public Safety and Security:** Knowledge of relevant equipment, policies, procedures, and strategies to promote effective local, state, or national security operations for the protection of people, data, property, and institutions.

Emergency Management Specialists

- Education/Training Required: Work experience in a related occupation
- Annual Earnings: $45,390
- Growth: 28.2%
- Annual Job Openings: 2,000
- Self-Employed: 0%
- Part-Time: 7.4%

Coordinate disaster response or crisis management activities; provide disaster-preparedness training; and prepare emergency plans and procedures for natural (e.g., hurricanes, floods, earthquakes), wartime, or technological (e.g., nuclear power plant emergencies, hazardous materials spills) disasters or hostage situations. Collaborate with other officials in order to prepare and analyze damage assessments following disasters or emergencies. Conduct surveys to determine the types of emergency-related needs that will need to be addressed in disaster planning or provide technical support to others conducting such surveys. Consult with officials of local and area governments, schools, hospitals, and other institutions in order to determine their needs and capabilities in the event of a natural disaster or other emergency. Coordinate disaster response or crisis management activities such as ordering evacuations, opening public shelters, and implementing special needs plans and programs. Design and administer emergency/disaster-preparedness training courses that teach people how to effec-

tively respond to major emergencies and disasters. Develop and maintain liaisons with municipalities, county departments, and similar entities in order to facilitate plan development, response effort coordination, and exchanges of personnel and equipment. Develop and perform tests and evaluations of emergency management plans in accordance with state and federal regulations. Inspect facilities and equipment such as emergency management centers and communications equipment in order to determine their operational and functional capabilities in emergency situations. Keep informed of activities or changes that could affect the likelihood of an emergency, as well as those that could affect response efforts and details of plan implementation. Keep informed of federal, state, and local regulations affecting emergency plans and ensure that plans adhere to these regulations. Maintain and update all resource materials associated with emergency-preparedness plans. Prepare emergency situation status reports that describe response and recovery efforts, needs, and preliminary damage assessments. Prepare plans that outline operating procedures to be used in response to disasters/emergencies such as hurricanes, nuclear accidents, and terrorist attacks and in recovery from these events. Propose alteration of emergency response procedures based on regulatory changes, technological changes, or knowledge gained from outcomes of previous emergency situations. **SKILLS**—No data available. **GOE**—Interest Area: 12. Law and Public Safety. **Work Group:** 12.01. Managerial Work in Law and Public Safety. **Other Jobs in This Work Group:** First-Line Supervisors/Managers of Correctional Officers; First-Line Supervisors/Managers of Police and Detectives; Forest Fire Fighting and Prevention Supervisors; Municipal Fire Fighting and Prevention Supervisors. **PERSONALITY TYPE:** No data available.

EDUCATION/TRAINING PROGRAM(S)—Community Organization and Advocacy; Public Administration. **RELATED KNOWLEDGE/COURSES**—No data available.

Emergency Medical Technicians and Paramedics

- ◎ Education/Training Required: Postsecondary vocational training
- ◎ Annual Earnings: $25,310
- ◎ Growth: 33.1%
- ◎ Annual Job Openings: 32,000
- ◎ Self-Employed: 0.8%
- ◎ Part-Time: 8.4%

Assess injuries, administer emergency medical care, and extricate trapped individuals. Transport injured or sick persons to medical facilities. Administer first-aid treatment and life-support care to sick or injured persons in prehospital setting. Operate equipment such as EKGs, external defibrillators, and bag-valve mask resuscitators in advanced life-support environments. Assess nature and extent of illness or injury to establish and prioritize medical procedures. Maintain vehicles and medical and communication equipment and replenish first-aid equipment and supplies. Observe, record, and report to physician the patient's condition or injury, the treatment provided, and reactions to drugs and treatment. Perform emergency diagnostic and treatment procedures, such as stomach suction, airway management, and heart monitoring, during ambulance ride. Administer drugs, orally or by injection, and perform intravenous procedures under a physician's direction. Comfort and reassure patients. Coordinate work with other emergency medical team members and police and fire department personnel. Communicate with dispatchers and treatment center personnel to provide information about situation, to arrange reception of victims, and to receive instructions for further treatment. Immobilize patient for placement on stretcher and ambulance transport, using backboard or other spinal immobilization device. Decontaminate ambulance interior following treatment of patient with infectious disease and report case to proper authorities. Drive mobile intensive care unit to specified location, following instructions from emergency medical dispatcher. Coordinate with treatment center personnel to obtain patients' vital statistics and medical history, to determine the circumstances of the emergency, and to administer emergency treatment. **SKILLS—Equipment Maintenance:** Performing routine maintenance on equipment and determining when and what kind of maintenance is needed. **Social Perceptiveness:** Being aware of others' reactions and understanding why they react as they do. **Service Orientation:** Actively looking for ways to help people. **Coordination:** Adjusting actions in relation to others' actions. **Instructing:** Teaching others how to do something. **Negotiation:** Bringing others together and trying to reconcile differences. **Speaking:** Talking to others to convey information effectively. **Operation Monitoring:** Watching gauges, dials, or other indicators to make sure a machine is working properly. **GOE—Interest Area:** 12. Law and Public Safety. **Work Group:** 12.06. Emergency Responding. **Other Jobs in This Work Group:** Forest Fire Fighters; Municipal Fire Fighters. **PERSONALITY TYPE:** Social. Social occupations frequently involve working with, communicating with, and teaching people. These occupations often involve helping or providing service to others.

EDUCATION/TRAINING PROGRAM(S)— Emergency Care Attendant (EMT Ambulance); Emergency Medical Technology/Technician (EMT Paramedic). **RELATED KNOWLEDGE/COURSES—Customer and Personal Service:** Knowledge of principles and processes for providing customer and personal services. This includes customer needs assessment, meeting quality standards for services, and evaluation of customer satisfaction. **Medicine and Dentistry:** Knowledge of the information and techniques needed to diagnose and treat human injuries, diseases, and deformities. This includes symptoms, treatment alternatives, drug properties and interactions, and preventive health-care measures. **Psychology:** Knowledge of human behavior and performance; individual differences in ability, personality, and interests; learning and motivation; psychological research methods; and the assessment and treatment of behavioral and affective disorders. **Chemistry:** Knowledge of the chemical composition, structure, and properties of substances and of the chemical processes and transformations that they undergo. This includes uses of chemicals and their danger signs, production techniques, and disposal methods. **Public Safety and Secu-**

rity: Knowledge of relevant equipment, policies, procedures, and strategies to promote effective local, state, or national security operations for the protection of people, data, property, and institutions. **Therapy and Counseling:** Knowledge of principles, methods, and procedures for diagnosis, treatment, and rehabilitation of physical and mental dysfunctions and for career counseling and guidance.

Environmental Compliance Inspectors

- Education/Training Required: Long-term on-the-job training
- Annual Earnings: $47,390
- Growth: 9.8%
- Annual Job Openings: 20,000
- Self-Employed: 0.9%
- Part-Time: 5.3%

Inspect and investigate sources of pollution to protect the public and environment and ensure conformance with federal, state, and local regulations and ordinances. Inform health professionals, property owners, and the public about harmful properties and related problems of water pollution and contaminated wastewater. Participate in the development of spill prevention programs and hazardous waste rules and regulations and recommend corrective actions for hazardous waste problems. Prepare data to calculate sewer service charges and capacity fees. Prepare written, oral, tabular, and graphic reports summarizing requirements and regulations, including enforcement and chain of custody documentation. Research and keep informed of pertinent information and developments in areas such as EPA laws and regulations. Respond to questions and inquiries, such as those concerning service charges and capacity fees, or refer them to supervisors. Maintain and repair materials, work sites, and equipment. Analyze and implement state, federal, or local requirements as necessary to maintain approved pretreatment, pollution prevention, and storm water runoff programs. Conduct research on hazardous waste management projects in order to determine the magnitude of problems and treatment or disposal

alternatives and costs. Determine the nature of code violations and actions to be taken and issue written notices of violation; participate in enforcement hearings as necessary. Determine sampling locations and methods and collect water or wastewater samples for analysis, preserving samples with appropriate containers and preservation methods. Determine which sites and violation reports to investigate and coordinate compliance and enforcement activities with other government agencies. Examine permits, licenses, applications, and records to ensure compliance with licensing requirements. Inform individuals and groups of pollution control regulations and inspection findings and explain how problems can be corrected. Inspect waste pretreatment, treatment, and disposal facilities and systems for conformance to federal, state, or local regulations. Interview individuals to determine the nature of suspected violations and to obtain evidence of violations. Investigate complaints and suspected violations regarding illegal dumping, pollution, pesticides, product quality, or labeling laws. **SKILLS—Science:** Using scientific rules and methods to solve problems. **Systems Evaluation:** Identifying measures or indicators of system performance and the actions needed to improve or correct performance relative to the goals of the system. **Reading Comprehension:** Understanding written sentences and paragraphs in work-related documents. **Systems Analysis:** Determining how a system should work and how changes in conditions, operations, and the environment will affect outcomes. **Speaking:** Talking to others to convey information effectively. **Negotiation:** Bringing others together and trying to reconcile differences. **Critical Thinking:** Using logic and reasoning to identify the strengths and weaknesses of alternative solutions, conclusions, or approaches to problems. **Writing:** Communicating effectively in writing as appropriate for the needs of the audience. **Judgment and Decision Making:** Considering the relative costs and benefits of potential actions to choose the most appropriate one. **GOE—Interest Area:** 07. Government and Public Administration. **Work Group:** 07.03. Regulations Enforcement. **Other Jobs in This Work Group:** Agricultural Inspectors; Aviation Inspectors; Child Support, Missing Persons, and Unemployment Insurance Fraud Investigators; Equal Opportunity Representatives and Officers; Financial Examiners; Fire Inspectors; Fish and Game

Wardens; Forest Fire Inspectors and Prevention Specialists; Government Property Inspectors and Investigators; Immigration and Customs Inspectors; Licensing Examiners and Inspectors; Marine Cargo Inspectors; Mechanical Inspectors; Motor Vehicle Inspectors; Nuclear Monitoring Technicians; Occupational Health and Safety Specialists; Pressure Vessel Inspectors; Railroad Inspectors; Tax Examiners, Collectors, and Revenue Agents. **PERSONALITY TYPE:** Investigative. Investigative occupations frequently involve working with ideas and require an extensive amount of thinking. These occupations can involve searching for facts and figuring out problems mentally.

EDUCATION/TRAINING PROGRAM(S)—No data available. **RELATED KNOWLEDGE/COURSES—Chemistry:** Knowledge of the chemical composition, structure, and properties of substances and of the chemical processes and transformations that they undergo. This includes uses of chemicals and their danger signs, production techniques, and disposal methods. **Public Safety and Security:** Knowledge of relevant equipment, policies, procedures, and strategies to promote effective local, state, or national security operations for the protection of people, data, property, and institutions. **Law and Government:** Knowledge of laws, legal codes, court procedures, precedents, government regulations, executive orders, agency rules, and the democratic political process. **Physics:** Knowledge and prediction of physical principles and laws and their interrelationships and applications to understanding fluid, material, and atmospheric dynamics and mechanical, electrical, atomic, and subatomic structures and processes. **Production and Processing:** Knowledge of raw materials, production processes, quality control, costs, and other techniques for maximizing the effective manufacture and distribution of goods. **Biology:** Knowledge of plant and animal organisms and their tissues, cells, functions, interdependencies, and interactions with each other and the environment.

Environmental Engineering Technicians

- Education/Training Required: Associate degree
- Annual Earnings: $38,550
- Growth: 28.4%
- Annual Job Openings: 3,000
- Self-Employed: 0.4%
- Part-Time: 5.0%

Apply theory and principles of environmental engineering to modify, test, and operate equipment and devices used in the prevention, control, and remediation of environmental pollution, including waste treatment and site remediation. May assist in the development of environmental pollution remediation devices under direction of engineer. Receive, set up, test, and decontaminate equipment. Maintain project logbook records and computer program files. Conduct pollution surveys, collecting and analyzing samples such as air and groundwater. Perform environmental quality work in field and office settings. Review technical documents to ensure completeness and conformance to requirements. Perform laboratory work such as logging numerical and visual observations, preparing and packaging samples, recording test results, and performing photo documentation. Review work plans to schedule activities. Obtain product information, identify vendors and suppliers, and order materials and equipment to maintain inventory. Arrange for the disposal of lead, asbestos, and other hazardous materials. Inspect facilities to monitor compliance with regulations governing substances such as asbestos, lead, and wastewater. Provide technical engineering support in the planning of projects, such as wastewater treatment plants, to ensure compliance with environmental regulations and policies. Improve chemical processes to reduce toxic emissions. Oversee support staff. Assist in the cleanup of hazardous material spills. Produce environmental assessment reports, tabulating data and preparing charts, graphs, and sketches. Maintain process parameters and evaluate process anomalies. Work with customers to assess the environmental impact of proposed construction and to develop pollution prevention programs. Perform statistical analy-

E

sis and correction of air and/or water pollution data submitted by industry and other agencies. Develop work plans, including writing specifications and establishing material, manpower, and facilities needs. **SKILLS—Troubleshooting:** Determining causes of operating errors and deciding what to do about them. **Science:** Using scientific rules and methods to solve problems. **Repairing:** Repairing machines or systems by using the needed tools. **Coordination:** Adjusting actions in relation to others' actions. **Equipment Maintenance:** Performing routine maintenance on equipment and determining when and what kind of maintenance is needed. **Operation Monitoring:** Watching gauges, dials, or other indicators to make sure a machine is working properly. **Time Management:** Managing one's own time and the time of others. **Service Orientation:** Actively looking for ways to help people. **Management of Financial Resources:** Determining how money will be spent to get the work done and accounting for these expenditures. **GOE—Interest Area:** 15. Scientific Research, Engineering, and Mathematics. **Work Group:** 15.09. Engineering Technology. **Other Jobs in This Work Group:** Aerospace Engineering and Operations Technicians; Calibration and Instrumentation Technicians; Cartographers and Photogrammetrists; Civil Engineering Technicians; Electrical Engineering Technicians; Electro-Mechanical Technicians; Electronic Drafters; Electronics Engineering Technicians; Mapping Technicians; Mechanical Drafters; Mechanical Engineering Technicians; Surveying Technicians. **PERSONALITY TYPE:** No data available.

EDUCATION/TRAINING PROGRAM(S)—Environmental Engineering Technology/Environmental Technology; Hazardous Materials Information Systems Technology/Technician. **RELATED KNOWLEDGE/COURSES—Engineering and Technology:** Knowledge of the practical application of engineering science and technology. This includes applying principles, techniques, procedures, and equipment to the design and production of various goods and services. **Design:** Knowledge of design techniques, tools, and principles involved in production of precision technical plans, blueprints, drawings, and models. **Building and Construction:** Knowledge of the materials, methods, and tools involved in the construction or repair of houses, buildings, or other structures such as highways

and roads. **Physics:** Knowledge and prediction of physical principles and laws and their interrelationships and applications to understanding fluid, material, and atmospheric dynamics and mechanical, electrical, atomic, and subatomic structures and processes. **Law and Government:** Knowledge of laws, legal codes, court procedures, precedents, government regulations, executive orders, agency rules, and the democratic political process. **Administration and Management:** Knowledge of business and management principles involved in strategic planning, resource allocation, human resources modeling, leadership technique, production methods, and coordination of people and resources. **Customer and Personal Service:** Knowledge of principles and processes for providing customer and personal services. This includes customer needs assessment, meeting quality standards for services, and evaluation of customer satisfaction. **Chemistry:** Knowledge of the chemical composition, structure, and properties of substances and of the chemical processes and transformations that they undergo. This includes uses of chemicals and their danger signs, production techniques, and disposal methods.

Environmental Science and Protection Technicians, Including Health

- Education/Training Required: Associate degree
- Annual Earnings: $35,340
- Growth: 36.8%
- Annual Job Openings: 4,000
- Self-Employed: 1.1%
- Part-Time: 20.2%

Performs laboratory and field tests to monitor the environment and investigate sources of pollution, including those that affect health. Under direction of an environmental scientist or specialist, may collect samples of gases, soil, water, and other materials for testing and take corrective actions as assigned. Record

for curriculum and training design, teaching
uction for individuals and groups, and the
ment of training effects.

l Opportunity
esentatives and
cers

cation/Training Required: Long-term
he-job training
ual Earnings: $47,390
wth: 9.8%
ual Job Openings: 20,000
f-Employed: 0.9%
t-Time: 5.3%

or and evaluate compliance with equal oppor-
laws, guidelines, and policies to ensure that
yment practices and contracting arrangements
qual opportunity without regard to race, reli-
color, national origin, sex, age, or disability.
uct surveys and evaluate findings in order to
mine if systematic discrimination exists. Counsel
hired members of minority and disadvantaged
s, informing them about details of civil rights
Interpret civil rights laws and equal opportunity
ations for individuals and employers. Investigate
oyment practices and alleged violations of laws in
to document and correct discriminatory factors.
with persons involved in equal opportunity com-
ts in order to verify case information and to arbi-
and settle disputes. Prepare reports of selection,
ey, and other statistics and recommendations for
ective action. Provide information, technical assis-
e, and training to supervisors, managers, and
loyees on topics such as employee supervision, hir-
grievance procedures, and staff development.
iew company contracts to determine actions
uired to meet governmental equal opportunity pro-
ons. Study equal opportunity complaints in order
larify issues. Act as liaisons between minority place-
nt agencies and employers or between job search
mmittees and other equal opportunity administra-
s. Consult with community representatives to

develop technical assistance agreements in accordance
with governmental regulations. Coordinate, monitor,
and revise complaint procedures to ensure timely processing and review of complaints. Develop guidelines
for non-discriminatory employment practices and
monitor their implementation and impact. Meet with
job search committees or coordinators to explain the
role of the equal opportunity coordinator, to provide
resources for advertising, and to explain expectations
for future contacts. Participate in the recruitment of
employees through job fairs, career days, and advertising plans. Verify that all job descriptions are submitted
for review and approval and that descriptions meet regulatory standards. **SKILLS—Negotiation:** Bringing
others together and trying to reconcile differences.
Writing: Communicating effectively in writing as
appropriate for the needs of the audience. **Speaking:**
Talking to others to convey information effectively.
Persuasion: Persuading others to change their minds
or behavior. **Systems Analysis:** Determining how a system should work and how changes in conditions,
operations, and the environment will affect outcomes.
Reading Comprehension: Understanding written sentences and paragraphs in work-related documents.
Active Listening: Giving full attention to what other
people are saying, taking time to understand the points
being made, asking questions as appropriate, and not
interrupting at inappropriate times. **Systems Evaluation:** Identifying measures or indicators of system performance and the actions needed to improve or correct
performance relative to the goals of the system.
GOE—Interest Area: 07. Government and Public
Administration. **Work Group:** 07.03. Regulations
Enforcement. **Other Jobs in This Work Group:** Agricultural Inspectors; Aviation Inspectors; Child Support, Missing Persons, and Unemployment Insurance
Fraud Investigators; Environmental Compliance
Inspectors; Financial Examiners; Fire Inspectors; Fish
and Game Wardens; Forest Fire Inspectors and Pre-
vention Specialists; Government Property Inspectors
and Investigators; Immigration and Customs Inspec-
tors; Licensing Examiners and Inspectors; Marine
Cargo Inspectors; Mechanical Inspectors; Motor Vehicle Inspectors; Nuclear Monitoring Technicians;
Occupational Health and Safety Specialists; Pressure
Vessel Inspectors; Railroad Inspectors; Tax Examiners,
Collectors, and Revenue Agents. **PERSONALITY**

test data and prepare reports, summaries, and charts that interpret test results. Collect samples of gases, soils, water, industrial wastewater, and asbestos products to conduct tests on pollutant levels and identify sources of pollution. Respond to and investigate hazardous conditions or spills or outbreaks of disease or food poisoning, collecting samples for analysis. Provide information and technical and program assistance to government representatives, employers, and the general public on the issues of public health, environmental protection, or workplace safety. Calibrate microscopes and test instruments. Make recommendations to control or eliminate unsafe conditions at workplaces or public facilities. Inspect sanitary conditions at public facilities. Prepare samples or photomicrographs for testing and analysis. Calculate amount of pollutant in samples or compute air pollution or gas flow in industrial processes, using chemical and mathematical formulas. Initiate procedures to close down or fine establishments violating environmental and/or health regulations. Determine amounts and kinds of chemicals to use in destroying harmful organisms and removing impurities from purification systems. Discuss test results and analyses with customers. Maintain files such as hazardous waste databases, chemical usage data, personnel exposure information, and diagrams showing equipment locations. Perform statistical analysis of environmental data. Set up equipment or stations to monitor and collect pollutants from sites such as smoke stacks, manufacturing plants, or mechanical equipment. Distribute permits, closure plans, and cleanup plans. Inspect workplaces to ensure the absence of health and safety hazards such as high noise levels, radiation, or potential lighting hazards. Weigh, analyze, and measure collected sample particles, such as lead, coal dust, or rock, to determine concentration of pollutants. Examine and analyze material for presence and concentration of contaminants such as asbestos, using variety of microscopes. Develop testing procedures and direct activities of workers in laboratory. **SKILLS—Science:** Using scientific rules and methods to solve problems. **Persuasion:** Persuading others to change their minds or behavior. **Active Learning:** Understanding the implications of new information for both current and future problem-solving and decision-making. **Instructing:** Teaching others how to do something. **Reading Comprehension:**

Understanding writt
work-related docum
logic and reasoning tc
nesses of alternativ
approaches to probler
aware of others' reactic
react as they do. **Troul**
es of operating errors a
them. **GOE—Interest**
ural Resources. **Work (**
nologies for Plants, An
Other Jobs in This Wor
cians; Food Science Tec
Technologists; Geologica
cal Sample Test Technicia
Investigative. Investigati
involve working with ide
amount of thinking. The
searching for facts and figu

EDUCATION/TRAININ
ronmental Science; Envirc
Science Technologies/Tecl
Technologies/Technicians,
KNOWLEDGE/COURSE
of plant and animal organisi
functions, interdependencie:
each other and the environ
Technology: Knowledge of th
engineering science and tec
applying principles, technic
equipment to the design and
goods and services. **Chemist.**
chemical composition, structu
substances and of the chemical
mations that they undergo. 1
chemicals and their danger sig
niques, and disposal methods.
and prediction of physical prir
their interrelationships and ap;
standing fluid, material, and at
and mechanical, electrical, aton
structures and processes. **Custome**
vice: Knowledge of principles anc
viding customer and personal ser\
customer needs assessment, meetin
for services, and evaluation of cus
Education and Training: Knowledg

methods
and instr
measurer

Equa
Rep|
Offi

◉ Edu
   on-
◉ An|
◉ Gr\
◉ An
◉ Se
◉ Pa

Monit
tunity
emplc
give e
gion,
  Cond
determ
newly
group
laws.
regul
emp
orde
  Mee
plair
trate
surv
corr
tanc
em|
ing
  Re
req
vis
to
m
co
to

TYPE: Social. Social occupations frequently involve working with, communicating with, and teaching people. These occupations often involve helping or providing service to others.

EDUCATION/TRAINING PROGRAM(S)—No data available. RELATED KNOWLEDGE/COURSES—Personnel and Human Resources: Knowledge of principles and procedures for personnel recruitment, selection, training, compensation and benefits, labor relations and negotiation, and personnel information systems. Law and Government: Knowledge of laws, legal codes, court procedures, precedents, government regulations, executive orders, agency rules, and the democratic political process. Sociology and Anthropology: Knowledge of group behavior and dynamics, societal trends and influences, human migrations, ethnicity, and cultures and their history and origins. English Language: Knowledge of the structure and content of the English language, including the meaning and spelling of words, rules of composition, and grammar. Mathematics: Knowledge of arithmetic, algebra, geometry, calculus, and statistics and their applications. Communications and Media: Knowledge of media production, communication, and dissemination techniques and methods. This includes alternative ways to inform and entertain via written, oral, and visual media.

Excavating and Loading Machine Operators

- Education/Training Required: Moderate-term on-the-job training
- Annual Earnings: $31,970
- Growth: 8.9%
- Annual Job Openings: 14,000
- Self-Employed: 16.9%
- Part-Time: 2.7%

Operate machinery equipped with scoops, shovels, or buckets to excavate and load loose materials. Operates power machinery, such as powered shovel, stripping shovel, scraper loader (mucking machine), or backhoe (trench-excavating machine) to excavate and load material. Observes hand signals, grade stakes, and other markings when operating machines. Receives written or oral instructions to move or excavate material. Measures and verifies levels of rock or gravel, base, and other excavated material. Lubricates and repairs machinery and replaces parts such as gears, bearings, and bucket teeth. Directs ground workers engaged in activities such as moving stakes or markers. SKILLS—Operation and Control: Controlling operations of equipment or systems. Operation Monitoring: Watching gauges, dials, or other indicators to make sure a machine is working properly. Repairing: Repairing machines or systems by using the needed tools. Equipment Maintenance: Performing routine maintenance on equipment and determining when and what kind of maintenance is needed. Management of Personnel Resources: Motivating, developing, and directing people as they work, identifying the best people for the job. Troubleshooting: Determining causes of operating errors and deciding what to do about them. Equipment Selection: Determining the kind of tools and equipment needed to do a job. Installation: Installing equipment, machines, wiring, or programs to meet specifications. GOE—Interest Area: 01. Agriculture and Natural Resources. Work Group: 01.08. Mining and Drilling. Other Jobs in This Work Group: Construction Drillers; Continuous Mining Machine Operators; Derrick Operators, Oil and Gas; Explosives Workers, Ordnance Handling Experts, and Blasters; Helpers—Extraction Workers; Loading Machine Operators, Underground Mining; Mine Cutting and Channeling Machine Operators; Rock Splitters, Quarry; Roof Bolters, Mining; Rotary Drill Operators, Oil and Gas; Roustabouts, Oil and Gas; Service Unit Operators, Oil, Gas, and Mining; Shuttle Car Operators; Well and Core Drill Operators; Wellhead Pumpers. PERSONALITY TYPE: Realistic. Realistic occupations frequently involve work activities that include practical, hands-on problems and solutions. These occupations often deal with plants, animals, and real-world materials like wood, tools, and machinery. Many of the occupations require working outside and do not involve a lot of paperwork or working closely with others.

EDUCATION/TRAINING PROGRAM(S)—Construction/Heavy Equipment/Earthmoving Equipment Operation. RELATED KNOWLEDGE/COURSES—Mechanical Devices: Knowledge of machines and tools, including their designs, uses, repair, and maintenance. **Engineering and Technology:** Knowledge of the practical application of engineering science and technology. This includes applying principles, techniques, procedures, and equipment to the design and production of various goods and services. **Physics:** Knowledge and prediction of physical principles and laws and their interrelationships and applications to understanding fluid, material, and atmospheric dynamics and mechanical, electrical, atomic, and subatomic structures and processes.

Executive Secretaries and Administrative Assistants

- Education/Training Required: Moderate-term on-the-job training
- Annual Earnings: $34,970
- Growth: 8.7%
- Annual Job Openings: 210,000
- Self-Employed: 1.6%
- Part-Time: 17.5%

Provide high-level administrative support by conducting research; preparing statistical reports; handling information requests; and performing clerical functions such as preparing correspondence, receiving visitors, arranging conference calls, and scheduling meetings. May also train and supervise lower-level clerical staff. Manage and maintain executives' schedules. Prepare invoices, reports, memos, letters, financial statements, and other documents, using word-processing, spreadsheet, database, and/or presentation software. Read and analyze incoming memos, submissions, and reports in order to determine their significance and plan their distribution. Open, sort, and distribute incoming correspondence, including faxes and e-mail. File and retrieve corporate documents, records, and reports. Greet visitors and determine whether they should be given access to specific individuals. Prepare responses to correspondence containing routine inquiries. Perform general office duties such as ordering supplies, maintaining records management systems, and performing basic bookkeeping work. Prepare agendas and make arrangements for committee, board, and other meetings. Make travel arrangements for executives. Conduct research, compile data, and prepare papers for consideration and presentation by executives, committees, and boards of directors. Compile, transcribe, and distribute minutes of meetings. Attend meetings in order to record minutes. Coordinate and direct office services, such as records and budget preparation, personnel, and housekeeping, in order to aid executives. Meet with individuals, special interest groups, and others on behalf of executives, committees, and boards of directors. Set up and oversee administrative policies and procedures for offices and/or organizations. Supervise and train other clerical staff. Review operating practices and procedures in order to determine whether improvements can be made in areas such as workflow, reporting procedures, or expenditures. Interpret administrative and operating policies and procedures for employees. **SKILLS—Active Listening:** Giving full attention to what other people are saying, taking time to understand the points being made, asking questions as appropriate, and not interrupting at inappropriate times. **Time Management:** Managing one's own time and the time of others. **Writing:** Communicating effectively in writing as appropriate for the needs of the audience. **Speaking:** Talking to others to convey information effectively. **Service Orientation:** Actively looking for ways to help people. **Management of Material Resources:** Obtaining and seeing to the appropriate use of equipment, facilities, and materials needed to do certain work. **Instructing:** Teaching others how to do something. **Management of Financial Resources:** Determining how money will be spent to get the work done and accounting for these expenditures. **GOE—Interest Area:** 04. Business and Administration. **Work Group:** 04.04. Secretarial Support. **Other Jobs in This Work Group:** Legal Secretaries; Medical Secretaries; Secretaries, Except Legal, Medical, and Executive. **PERSONALITY TYPE:** Conventional. Conventional occupations frequently involve following set procedures and routines. These occupations can include working with data and details more than with ideas. Usually there is a clear line of authority to follow.

EDUCATION/TRAINING PROGRAM(S)— Administrative Assistant and Secretarial Science, General; Executive Assistant/Executive Secretary; Medical Administrative/Executive Assistant and Medical

Secretary. **RELATED KNOWLEDGE/COURSES— Clerical Practices:** Knowledge of administrative and clerical procedures and systems such as word processing, managing files and records, stenography and transcription, designing forms, and other office procedures and terminology. **Customer and Personal Service:** Knowledge of principles and processes for providing customer and personal services. This includes customer needs assessment, meeting quality standards for services, and evaluation of customer satisfaction. **English Language:** Knowledge of the structure and content of the English language, including the meaning and spelling of words, rules of composition, and grammar. **Computers and Electronics:** Knowledge of circuit boards, processors, chips, electronic equipment, and computer hardware and software, including applications and programming. **Communications and Media:** Knowledge of media production, communication, and dissemination techniques and methods. This includes alternative ways to inform and entertain via written, oral, and visual media. **Administration and Management:** Knowledge of business and management principles involved in strategic planning, resource allocation, human resources modeling, leadership technique, production methods, and coordination of people and resources.

Farmers and Ranchers

- ◎ Education/Training Required: Long-term on-the-job training
- ◎ Annual Earnings: $40,440
- ◎ Growth: –20.6%
- ◎ Annual Job Openings: 118,000
- ◎ Self-Employed: 99.3%
- ◎ Part-Time: 17.7%

On an ownership or rental basis, operate farms, ranches, greenhouses, nurseries, timber tracts, or other agricultural production establishments that produce crops, horticultural specialties, livestock, poultry, finfish, shellfish, or animal specialties. May plant, cultivate, harvest, perform post-harvest activities for, and market crops and livestock; may hire, train, and supervise farm workers or supervise a farm labor contractor; may prepare cost, production, and other records. **May maintain and operate machinery and perform physical work.** Assist in animal births and care for newborn livestock. Breed and raise stock such as cattle, poultry, and honeybees, using recognized breeding practices to ensure continued improvement in stock. Clean and disinfect buildings and yards and remove manure. Clean and sanitize milking equipment, storage tanks, collection cups, and cows' udders or ensure that procedures are followed to maintain sanitary conditions for handling of milk. Clean, grade, and package crops for marketing. Control the spread of disease and parasites in herds by using vaccination and medication and by separating sick animals. Destroy diseased or superfluous crops. Determine types and quantities of crops or livestock to be raised according to factors such as market conditions, federal program availability, and soil conditions. Evaluate product marketing alternatives and then promote and market farm products, acting as the sales agent for livestock and crops. Harvest crops and collect specialty products such as royal jelly, wax, pollen, and honey from bee colonies. Install and shift irrigation systems to irrigate fields evenly or according to crop need. Maintain pastures or grazing lands to ensure that animals have enough feed, employing pasture-conservation measures such as arranging rotational grazing. Milk cows, using milking machinery. Monitor crops as they grow in order to ensure that they are growing properly and are free from diseases and contaminants. Negotiate and arrange with buyers for the sale, storage, and shipment of crops. Perform crop production duties such as planning, tilling, planting, fertilizing, cultivating, spraying, and harvesting. Plan crop activities based on factors such as crop maturity and weather conditions. Purchase and store livestock feed. Remove lower-quality or older animals from herds and purchase other livestock to replace culled animals. Select and purchase supplies and equipment such as seed, fertilizers, and farm machinery. Select animals for market and provide transportation of livestock to market. Set up and operate farm machinery to cultivate, harvest, and haul crops. **SKILLS—Management of Financial Resources:** Determining how money will be spent to get the work done and accounting for these expenditures. **Management of Personnel Resources:** Motivating, developing, and directing people as they work, identifying the best people for the job. **Installa-**

tion: Installing equipment, machines, wiring, or programs to meet specifications. **Management of Material Resources:** Obtaining and seeing to the appropriate use of equipment, facilities, and materials needed to do certain work. **Equipment Selection:** Determining the kind of tools and equipment needed to do a job. **Operation and Control:** Controlling operations of equipment or systems. **Equipment Maintenance:** Performing routine maintenance on equipment and determining when and what kind of maintenance is needed. **Repairing:** Repairing machines or systems by using the needed tools. **GOE—Interest Area:** 01. Agriculture and Natural Resources. **Work Group:** 01.01. Managerial Work in Agriculture and Natural Resources. **Other Jobs in This Work Group:** Agricultural Crop Farm Managers; First-Line Supervisors and Manager/Supervisors—Agricultural Crop Workers; First-Line Supervisors and Manager/Supervisors—Animal Husbandry Workers; First-Line Supervisors and Manager/Supervisors—Extractive Workers; First-Line Supervisors and Manager/Supervisors—Fishery Workers; First-Line Supervisors and Manager/Supervisors—Horticultural Workers; First-Line Supervisors and Manager/Supervisors—Landscaping Workers; First-Line Supervisors and Manager/Supervisors—Logging Workers; Fish Hatchery Managers; Lawn Service Managers; Nursery and Greenhouse Managers; Park Naturalists; Purchasing Agents and Buyers, Farm Products. **PERSONALITY TYPE:** Realistic. Realistic occupations frequently involve work activities that include practical, hands-on problems and solutions. These occupations often deal with plants, animals, and real-world materials like wood, tools, and machinery. Many of the occupations require working outside and do not involve a lot of paperwork or working closely with others.

EDUCATION/TRAINING PROGRAM(S)—Agribusiness/Agricultural Business Operations; Agricultural Animal Breeding; Agricultural Business and Management, General; Agricultural Production Operations, General; Agricultural Production Operations, Other; Agronomy and Crop Science; Animal Nutrition; Animal Sciences, General; Animal/Livestock Husbandry and Production; Aquaculture; Crop Production; Dairy Husbandry and Production; Dairy Science; Farm/Farm and Ranch Management; Greenhouse Operations and Management; Horticul-

tural Science; Livestock Management; Ornamental Horticulture; Plant Nursery Operations and Management; Plant Protection and Integrated Pest Management; Plant Sciences, General; Poultry Science; Range Science and Management. **RELATED KNOWLEDGE/COURSES—Food Production:** Knowledge of techniques and equipment for planting, growing, and harvesting food products (both plant and animal) for consumption, including storage/handling techniques. **Economics and Accounting:** Knowledge of economic and accounting principles and practices, the financial markets, banking, and the analysis and reporting of financial data. **Personnel and Human Resources:** Knowledge of principles and procedures for personnel recruitment, selection, training, compensation and benefits, labor relations and negotiation, and personnel information systems. **Production and Processing:** Knowledge of raw materials, production processes, quality control, costs, and other techniques for maximizing the effective manufacture and distribution of goods. **Sales and Marketing:** Knowledge of principles and methods for showing, promoting, and selling products or services. This includes marketing strategy and tactics, product demonstrations, sales techniques, and sales control systems. **Transportation:** Knowledge of principles and methods for moving people or goods by air, rail, sea, or road, including the relative costs and benefits.

First-Line Supervisors and Manager/Supervisors— Agricultural Crop Workers

- Education/Training Required: Associate degree
- Annual Earnings: $35,490
- Growth: 11.4%
- Annual Job Openings: 6,000
- Self-Employed: 0.9%
- Part-Time: 6.1%

Directly supervise and coordinate activities of agricultural crop workers. Manager/supervisors are generally found in smaller establishments, where they perform both supervisory and management func-

tions, such as accounting, marketing, and personnel work, and may also engage in the same agricultural work as the workers they supervise. Assigns duties, such as tilling soil, planting, irrigating, storing crops, and maintaining machines, and assigns fields or rows to workers. Determines number and kind of workers needed to perform required work and schedules activities. Observes workers to detect inefficient and unsafe work procedures or identify problems and initiates actions to correct improper procedure or solve problem. Issues farm implements and machinery, ladders, or containers to workers and collects them at end of workday. Investigates grievances and settles disputes to maintain harmony among workers. Opens gate to permit entry of water into ditches or pipes and signals worker to start flow of water to irrigate fields. Drives and operates farm machinery, such as trucks, tractors, or self-propelled harvesters, to transport workers or cultivate and harvest fields. Requisitions and purchases farm supplies, such as insecticides, machine parts or lubricants, and tools. Confers with manager to evaluate weather and soil conditions and to develop and revise plans and procedures. Prepares time, payroll, and production reports, such as farm conditions, amount of yield, machinery breakdowns, and labor problems. Directs or assists in adjustment, repair, and maintenance of farm machinery and equipment. Trains workers in methods of field work and safety regulations and briefs them on identifying characteristic of insects and diseases. Contracts with seasonal workers and farmers to provide employment and arranges for transportation, equipment, and living quarters. Recruits, hires, and discharges workers. Inspects crops and fields to determine maturity, yield, infestation, or work requirements, such as cultivating, spraying, weeding, or harvesting. **SKILLS—Management of Personnel Resources:** Motivating, developing, and directing people as they work, identifying the best people for the job. **Management of Material Resources:** Obtaining and seeing to the appropriate use of equipment, facilities, and materials needed to do certain work. **Coordination:** Adjusting actions in relation to others' actions. **Equipment Maintenance:** Performing routine maintenance on equipment and determining when and what kind of maintenance is needed. **Repairing:** Repairing machines or systems by using the needed tools. **Time Management:** Managing one's

own time and the time of others. **Instructing:** Teaching others how to do something. **Management of Financial Resources:** Determining how money will be spent to get the work done and accounting for these expenditures. **GOE—Interest Area:** 01. Agriculture and Natural Resources. **Work Group:** 01.01. Managerial Work in Agriculture and Natural Resources. **Other Jobs in This Work Group:** Agricultural Crop Farm Managers; Farmers and Ranchers; First-Line Supervisors and Manager/Supervisors—Animal Husbandry Workers; First-Line Supervisors and Manager/Supervisors—Extractive Workers; First-Line Supervisors and Manager/Supervisors—Fishery Workers; First-Line Supervisors and Manager/Supervisors—Horticultural Workers; First-Line Supervisors and Manager/Supervisors—Landscaping Workers; First-Line Supervisors and Manager/Supervisors—Logging Workers; Fish Hatchery Managers; Lawn Service Managers; Nursery and Greenhouse Managers; Park Naturalists; Purchasing Agents and Buyers, Farm Products. **PERSONALITY TYPE:** Enterprising. Enterprising occupations frequently involve starting up and carrying out projects. These occupations can involve leading people and making many decisions. They sometimes require risk taking and often deal with business.

EDUCATION/TRAINING PROGRAM(S)—Agricultural Business and Management, Other; Agricultural Production Operations, General; Agricultural Production Operations, Other; Agriculture, Agriculture Operations, and Related Sciences, Other; Agronomy and Crop Science; Aquaculture; Crop Production; Farm/Farm and Ranch Management; Fishing and Fisheries Sciences and Management; Plant Sciences, General; Range Science and Management. **RELATED KNOWLEDGE/COURSES—Food Production:** Knowledge of techniques and equipment for planting, growing, and harvesting food products (both plant and animal) for consumption, including storage/handling techniques. **Personnel and Human Resources:** Knowledge of principles and procedures for personnel recruitment, selection, training, compensation and benefits, labor relations and negotiation, and personnel information systems. **Administration and Management:** Knowledge of business and management principles involved in strategic planning, resource allocation, human resources modeling, leadership technique, production methods, and coordination of people and resources. **Biology:** Knowledge of plant and animal organisms and their tissues, cells, functions, interdependencies, and interactions with each other and the environment. **Mechanical Devices:** Knowledge of machines and tools, including their designs, uses, repair, and maintenance. **Chemistry:** Knowledge of the chemical composition, structure, and properties of substances and of the chemical processes and transformations that they undergo. This includes uses of chemicals and their danger signs, production techniques, and disposal methods.

First-Line Supervisors and Manager/Supervisors— Animal Care Workers, Except Livestock

- Education/Training Required: Associate degree
- Annual Earnings: $35,490
- Growth: 11.4%
- Annual Job Openings: 6,000
- Self-Employed: 0.9%
- Part-Time: 6.1%

Directly supervise and coordinate activities of animal care workers. Manager/supervisors are generally found in smaller establishments, where they perform both supervisory and management functions, such as accounting, marketing, and personnel work, and may also engage in the same animal care work as the workers they supervise. Assigns workers to tasks such as feeding and treatment of animals and cleaning and maintenance of animal quarters. Establishes work schedule and procedures of animal care. Monitors animal care, inspects facilities to identify problems, and discusses solutions with workers. Trains workers in animal care procedures, maintenance duties, and safety precautions. Plans budget and arranges for purchase of animals, feed, or supplies. Prepares reports concerning activity of facility, employees' time records, and animal treatment. Delivers lectures to public to stimulate interest in animals and communicate humane philos-

ophy to public. Operates euthanasia equipment to destroy animals. Investigates complaints of animal neglect or cruelty and follows up on complaints appearing to justify prosecution. Observes and examines animals to detect signs of illness and determine need of services from veterinarian. Directs and assists workers in maintenance and repair of facilities. **SKILLS—Management of Financial Resources:** Determining how money will be spent to get the work done and accounting for these expenditures. **Management of Personnel Resources:** Motivating, developing, and directing people as they work, identifying the best people for the job. **Instructing:** Teaching others how to do something. **Management of Material Resources:** Obtaining and seeing to the appropriate use of equipment, facilities, and materials needed to do certain work. **Systems Evaluation:** Identifying measures or indicators of system performance and the actions needed to improve or correct performance relative to the goals of the system. **Writing:** Communicating effectively in writing as appropriate for the needs of the audience. **Speaking:** Talking to others to convey information effectively. **Systems Analysis:** Determining how a system should work and how changes in conditions, operations, and the environment will affect outcomes. **GOE—Interest Area:** 08. Health Science. **Work Group:** 08.01. Managerial Work in Medical and Health Services. **Other Jobs in This Work Group:** Coroners; Medical and Health Services Managers. **PERSONALITY TYPE:** Realistic. Realistic occupations frequently involve work activities that include practical, hands-on problems and solutions. These occupations often deal with plants, animals, and real-world materials like wood, tools, and machinery. Many of the occupations require working outside and do not involve a lot of paperwork or working closely with others.

EDUCATION/TRAINING PROGRAM(S)—Agricultural Business and Management, Other; Agricultural Production Operations, General; Agricultural Production Operations, Other; Agriculture, Agriculture Operations, and Related Sciences, Other; Animal Nutrition; Animal Sciences, General; Aquaculture; Farm/Farm and Ranch Management; Fishing and Fisheries Sciences and Management; Range Science and Management. **RELATED KNOWLEDGE/ COURSES—Administration and Management:**

Knowledge of business and management principles involved in strategic planning, resource allocation, human resources modeling, leadership technique, production methods, and coordination of people and resources. **Biology:** Knowledge of plant and animal organisms and their tissues, cells, functions, interdependencies, and interactions with each other and the environment. **Medicine and Dentistry:** Knowledge of the information and techniques needed to diagnose and treat human injuries, diseases, and deformities. This includes symptoms, treatment alternatives, drug properties and interactions, and preventive health-care measures. **Economics and Accounting:** Knowledge of economic and accounting principles and practices, the financial markets, banking, and the analysis and reporting of financial data. **Personnel and Human Resources:** Knowledge of principles and procedures for personnel recruitment, selection, training, compensation and benefits, labor relations and negotiation, and personnel information systems. **Education and Training:** Knowledge of principles and methods for curriculum and training design, teaching and instruction for individuals and groups, and the measurement of training effects.

First-Line Supervisors and Manager/Supervisors— Animal Husbandry Workers

- ◎ Education/Training Required: Associate degree
- ◎ Annual Earnings: $35,490
- ◎ Growth: 11.4%
- ◎ Annual Job Openings: 6,000
- ◎ Self-Employed: 16.9%
- ◎ Part-Time: 6.1%

Directly supervise and coordinate activities of animal husbandry workers. Manager/supervisors are generally found in smaller establishments, where they perform both supervisory and management functions, such as accounting, marketing, and personnel work, and may also engage in the same animal husbandry work as the workers they supervise. Assigns workers to tasks such as feeding and treating animals, cleaning quarters, transferring animals, and maintaining facilities. Notifies veterinarian and manager of serious illnesses or injuries to animals. Monitors eggs and adjusts incubator thermometer and gauges to ascertain hatching progress and maintain specified conditions. Treats animal illness or injury, following experience or instructions of veterinarian. Inseminates livestock artificially to produce desired offspring and to demonstrate techniques to farmers. Transports or arranges for transport of animals, equipment, food, animal feed, and other supplies to and from work site. Requisitions equipment, materials, and supplies. Prepares animal condition, production, feed consumption, and worker attendance reports. Trains workers in animal care, artificial insemination techniques, egg candling and sorting, and transfer of animals. Observes animals, such as cattle, sheep, poultry, or game animals, for signs of illness, injury, nervousness, or unnatural behavior. Plans and prepares work schedules. Recruits, hires, and pays workers. Confers with manager to discuss and ascertain production requirements, condition of equipment and supplies, and work schedules. Inspects buildings, fences, fields or range, supplies, and equipment to determine work to be done. Studies feed, weight, health, genetic, or milk production records to determine feed formula and rations or breeding schedule. Oversees animal care, maintenance, breeding, or packing and transfer activities to ensure work is done correctly and to identify and solve problems. **SKILLS—Management of Personnel Resources:** Motivating, developing, and directing people as they work, identifying the best people for the job. **Management of Material Resources:** Obtaining and seeing to the appropriate use of equipment, facilities, and materials needed to do certain work. **Systems Evaluation:** Identifying measures or indicators of system performance and the actions needed to improve or correct performance relative to the goals of the system. **Instructing:** Teaching others how to do something. **Systems Analysis:** Determining how a system should work and how changes in conditions, operations, and the environment will affect outcomes. **Time Management:** Managing one's own time and the time of others. **Coordination:** Adjusting actions in relation to others' actions. **Equipment Selection:** Determining the kind of tools and equipment needed to do a job. **Management of Financial Resources:** Determining how money will be spent to get the work done and accounting for these expenditures. **GOE—Interest Area:** 01. Agriculture and Natural Resources. **Work Group:** 01.01. Managerial Work in Agriculture and Natural Resources. **Other Jobs in This Work Group:** Agricultural Crop Farm Managers; Farmers and Ranchers; First-Line Supervisors and Manager/Supervisors—Agricultural Crop Workers; First-Line Supervisors and Manager/Supervisors—Extractive Workers; First-Line Supervisors and Manager/Supervisors—Fishery Workers; First-Line Supervisors and Manager/Supervisors—Horticultural Workers; First-Line Supervisors and Manager/Supervisors—Landscaping Workers; First-Line Supervisors and Manager/Supervisors—Logging Workers; Fish Hatchery Managers; Lawn Service Managers; Nursery and Greenhouse Managers; Park Naturalists; Purchasing Agents and Buyers, Farm Products. **PERSONALITY TYPE:** Enterprising. Enterprising occupations frequently involve starting up and carrying out projects. These occupations can involve leading people and making many decisions. They sometimes require risk taking and often deal with business.

EDUCATION/TRAINING PROGRAM(S)—Agricultural Animal Breeding; Agricultural Business and Management, Other; Agricultural Production Operations, General; Agricultural Production Operations, Other; Agriculture, Agriculture Operations, and Related Sciences, Other; Animal Nutrition; Animal Sciences, General; Animal/Livestock Husbandry and Production; Aquaculture; Dairy Husbandry and Production; Dairy Science; Farm/Farm and Ranch Management; Fishing and Fisheries Sciences and Management; Horse Husbandry/Equine Science and Management; Livestock Management; Poultry Science; Range Science and Management. **RELATED KNOWLEDGE/COURSES—Food Production:** Knowledge of techniques and equipment for planting, growing, and harvesting food products (both plant and animal) for consumption, including storage/handling techniques. **Biology:** Knowledge of plant and animal organisms and their tissues, cells, functions, interdependencies, and interactions with each other and the environment. **Personnel and Human Resources:** Knowledge of principles and procedures for personnel recruitment, selection, training, compensation and benefits, labor relations and negotiation, and personnel information systems. **Administration and Management:** Knowledge of business and management principles involved in strategic planning, resource allocation, human resources modeling, leadership technique, production methods, and coordination of people and resources. **Medicine and Dentistry:** Knowledge of the information and techniques needed to diagnose and treat human injuries, diseases, and deformities. This includes symptoms, treatment alternatives, drug properties and interactions, and preventive health-care measures. **Transportation:** Knowledge of principles and methods for moving people or goods by air, rail, sea, or road, including the relative costs and benefits.

First-Line Supervisors and Manager/Supervisors— Construction Trades Workers

- Education/Training Required: Work experience in a related occupation
- Annual Earnings: $50,450
- Growth: 14.1%
- Annual Job Openings: 67,000
- Self-Employed: 20.1%
- Part-Time: 2.1%

Directly supervise and coordinate activities of construction trades workers and their helpers. Manager/supervisors are generally found in smaller establishments, where they perform both supervisory and management functions, such as accounting, marketing, and personnel work, and may also engage in the same construction trades work as the workers they supervise. Suggests and initiates personnel actions, such as promotions, transfers, and hires. Analyzes and resolves worker problems and recommends motivational plans. Examines and inspects work progress, equipment, and construction sites to verify safety and ensure that specifications are met. Estimates material and worker requirements to complete job. Reads specifications, such as blueprints and data, to determine construction requirements. Analyzes and plans installation and construction of equipment and structures. Locates, measures, and marks location and placement of structures and equipment. Records information, such as personnel, production, and operational data, on specified forms and reports. Trains workers in construction methods and operation of equipment. Recommends measures to improve production methods and equipment performance to increase efficiency and safety. Assists workers engaged in construction activities, using hand tools and equipment. Supervises and coordinates activities of construction trades workers. Directs and leads workers engaged in construction activities. Assigns work to employees, using material and worker requirements data. Confers with staff and worker to ensure production and personnel problems are resolved. **SKILLS— Management of Personnel Resources:** Motivating, developing, and directing people as they work, identifying the best people for the job. **Management of Material Resources:** Obtaining and seeing to the appropriate use of equipment, facilities, and materials needed to do certain work. **Installation:** Installing equipment, machines, wiring, or programs to meet specifications. **Systems Analysis:** Determining how a system should work and how changes in conditions, operations, and the environment will affect outcomes. **Systems Evaluation:** Identifying measures or indicators of system performance and the actions needed to improve or correct performance relative to the goals of the system. **Time Management:** Managing one's own time and the time of others. **Coordination:** Adjusting actions in relation to others' actions. **Quality Control Analysis:** Conducting tests and inspections of products, services, or processes to evaluate quality or performance. **GOE—Interest Area:** 02. Architecture and Construction. **Work Group:** 02.01. Managerial Work in Architecture and Construction. **Other Jobs in This Work Group:** Construction Managers. **PERSONALITY TYPE:** Enterprising. Enterprising occupations frequently involve starting up and carrying out projects. These occupations can involve leading people and making many decisions. They sometimes require risk taking and often deal with business.

EDUCATION/TRAINING PROGRAM(S)— Building/Construction Finishing, Management, and Inspection, Other; Building/Construction Site Management/Manager; Building/Home/Construction Inspection/Inspector; Building/Property Maintenance and Management; Carpentry/Carpenter; Concrete Finishing/Concrete Finisher; Construction Trades, Other; Drywall Installation/Drywaller; Electrical and Power Transmission Installation/Installer, General; Electrical and Power Transmission Installers, Other; Electrician; Glazier; Lineworker; Mason/Masonry; Painting/Painter and Wall Coverer; Plumbing Technology/Plumber; Roofer; Well Drilling/Driller. **RELATED KNOWLEDGE/COURSES—Building and Construction:** Knowledge of the materials, methods, and tools involved in the construction or repair of houses, buildings, or other structures such as highways and roads. **Personnel and Human Resources:** Knowledge of principles and procedures for personnel recruitment, selection, training, compensation and benefits, labor relations and negotiation, and personnel information systems. **Administration and Management:** Knowledge of business and management principles involved in strategic planning, resource allocation, human resources modeling, leadership technique, production methods, and coordination of people and resources. **Design:** Knowledge of design techniques, tools, and principles involved in production of precision technical plans, blueprints, drawings, and models. **Engineering and Technology:** Knowledge of the practical application of engineering science and technology. This includes applying principles, techniques, procedures, and equipment to the design and production of various goods and services. **Mechanical Devices:** Knowledge of machines and tools, including their designs, uses, repair, and maintenance.

First-Line Supervisors and Manager/Supervisors— Extractive Workers

- ◎ Education/Training Required: Work experience in a related occupation
- ◎ Annual Earnings: $50,450
- ◎ Growth: 14.1%
- ◎ Annual Job Openings: 67,000
- ◎ Self-Employed: 20.1%
- ◎ Part-Time: 2.1%

Directly supervise and coordinate activities of extractive workers and their helpers. **Manager/supervisors are generally found in smaller establishments, where they perform both supervisory and management functions, such as accounting, marketing, and personnel work, and may also engage in the same extractive work as the workers they supervise.** Supervises and coordinates activities of workers engaged in the extraction of geological materials. Directs and leads workers engaged in extraction of geological materials. Assigns work to employees, using material and worker requirements data. Confers with staff and workers to ensure production personnel problems are resolved. Analyzes and resolves worker problems and recommends motivational plans. Analyzes and plans extraction process of geological materials. Trains workers in construction methods and operation of equipment. Examines and inspects equipment, site, and materials to verify specifications are met. Recommends measures to improve production methods and equipment performance to increase efficiency and safety. Suggests and initiates personnel actions, such as promotions, transfers, and hires. Records information such as personnel, production, and operational data on specified forms. Assists workers engaged in extraction activities, using hand tools and equipment. Locates, measures, and marks materials and site location, using measuring and marking equipment. Orders materials, supplies, and repair of equipment and machinery. **SKILLS—Management of Personnel Resources:** Motivating, developing, and directing people as they work, identifying the best people for the job. **Management of Material Resources:** Obtaining and seeing to the appropriate use of equipment, facilities, and materials needed to do certain work. **Instructing:** Teaching others how to do something. **Systems Evaluation:** Identifying measures or indicators of system performance and the actions needed to improve or correct performance relative to the goals of the system. **Systems Analysis:** Determining how a system should work and how changes in conditions, operations, and the environment will affect outcomes. **Coordination:** Adjusting actions in relation to others' actions. **Operation Monitoring:** Watching gauges, dials, or other indicators to make sure a machine is working properly. **Social Perceptiveness:** Being aware of others' reactions and understanding why they react as they do. **Negotiation:** Bringing others together and trying to reconcile differences. **Time Management:** Managing one's own time and the time of others. **GOE—Interest Area:** 01. Agriculture and Natural Resources. **Work Group:** 01.01. Managerial Work in Agriculture and Natural Resources. **Other Jobs in This Work Group:** Agricultural Crop Farm Managers; Farmers and Ranchers; First-Line Supervisors and Manager/Supervisors—Agricultural Crop Workers; First-Line Supervisors and Manager/Supervisors—Animal Husbandry Workers; First-Line Supervisors and Manager/Supervisors—Fishery Workers; First-Line Supervisors and Manager/Supervisors—Horticultural Workers; First-Line Supervisors and Manager/Supervisors—Landscaping Workers; First-Line Supervisors and Manager/Supervisors—Logging Workers; Fish Hatchery Managers; Lawn Service Managers; Nursery and Greenhouse Managers; Park Naturalists; Purchasing Agents and Buyers, Farm Products. **PERSONALITY TYPE:** Enterprising. Enterprising occupations frequently involve starting up and carrying out projects. These occupations can involve leading people and making many decisions. They sometimes require risk taking and often deal with business.

EDUCATION/TRAINING PROGRAM(S)—Blasting/Blaster; Well Drilling/Driller. **RELATED KNOWLEDGE/COURSES—Personnel and Human Resources:** Knowledge of principles and procedures for personnel recruitment, selection, training, compensation and benefits, labor relations and negotiation, and personnel information systems. **Administration and Management:** Knowledge of business and management principles involved in strategic planning, resource allocation, human resources modeling, leadership technique, production methods, and coordination of people and resources. **Engineering and Technology:** Knowledge of the practical application of engineering science and technology. This includes applying principles, techniques, procedures, and equipment to the design and production of various goods and services. **Physics:** Knowledge and prediction of physical principles and laws and their interrelationships and applications to understanding fluid, material, and atmospheric dynamics and mechanical, electrical, atomic, and subatomic structures and processes. **Production and Processing:** Knowledge of raw materials, production processes, quality control, costs, and other techniques for maximizing the effective manufacture and distribution of goods. **Mechanical Devices:** Knowledge of machines and tools, including their designs, uses, repair, and maintenance.

First-Line Supervisors and Manager/Supervisors— Fishery Workers

- Education/Training Required: Associate degree
- Annual Earnings: $35,490
- Growth: 11.4%
- Annual Job Openings: 6,000
- Self-Employed: 16.9%
- Part-Time: 6.1%

Directly supervise and coordinate activities of fishery workers. Manager/supervisors are generally found in smaller establishments, where they perform both supervisory and management functions, such as accounting, marketing, and personnel work, and may also engage in the same fishery work as the workers they supervise. Assigns workers to duties such as fertilizing and incubating spawn; feeding and transferring fish; and planting, cultivating, and harvesting shellfish beds. Oversees worker activities, such as treatment and rearing of fingerlings, maintenance of equipment, and harvesting of fish or shellfish. Directs workers to correct deviations or problems, such as disease, quality of seed distribution, or adequacy of cultivation. Plans work schedules according to availability of personnel and equipment, tidal levels, feeding schedules, or need for transfer or harvest. Observes fish and beds or ponds to detect diseases, determine quality of fish, or determine completeness of harvesting. Records number and type of fish or shellfish reared and harvested and keeps workers' time records. Confers with manager to determine time and place of seed planting and cultivating, feeding, or harvesting of fish or shellfish. Trains workers in spawning, rearing, cultivating, and harvesting methods and use of equipment. **SKILLS—Management of Personnel Resources:** Motivating, developing, and directing people as they work, identifying the best people for the job. **Instructing:** Teaching others how to

do something. **Management of Material Resources:** Obtaining and seeing to the appropriate use of equipment, facilities, and materials needed to do certain work. **Systems Analysis:** Determining how a system should work and how changes in conditions, operations, and the environment will affect outcomes. **Time Management:** Managing one's own time and the time of others. **Coordination:** Adjusting actions in relation to others' actions. **Systems Evaluation:** Identifying measures or indicators of system performance and the actions needed to improve or correct performance relative to the goals of the system. **Learning Strategies:** Selecting and using training/instructional methods and procedures appropriate for the situation when learning or teaching new things. **GOE—Interest Area:** 01. Agriculture and Natural Resources. **Work Group:** 01.01. Managerial Work in Agriculture and Natural Resources. **Other Jobs in This Work Group:** Agricultural Crop Farm Managers; Farmers and Ranchers; First-Line Supervisors and Manager/Supervisors— Agricultural Crop Workers; First-Line Supervisors and Manager/Supervisors—Animal Husbandry Workers; First-Line Supervisors and Manager/Supervisors— Extractive Workers; First-Line Supervisors and Manager/Supervisors—Horticultural Workers; First-Line Supervisors and Manager/Supervisors—Landscaping Workers; First-Line Supervisors and Manager/Supervisors—Logging Workers; Fish Hatchery Managers; Lawn Service Managers; Nursery and Greenhouse Managers; Park Naturalists; Purchasing Agents and Buyers, Farm Products. **PERSONALITY TYPE:** Realistic. Realistic occupations frequently involve work activities that include practical, hands-on problems and solutions. These occupations often deal with plants, animals, and real-world materials like wood, tools, and machinery. Many of the occupations require working outside and do not involve a lot of paperwork or working closely with others.

EDUCATION/TRAINING PROGRAM(S)—Agricultural Animal Breeding; Agricultural Business and Management, Other; Agricultural Production Operations, General; Agricultural Production Operations, Other; Agriculture, Agriculture Operations, and Related Sciences, Other; Animal Nutrition; Animal Sciences, General; Animal/Livestock Husbandry and Production; Farm/Farm and Ranch Management; Fishing and Fisheries Sciences and Management.

RELATED KNOWLEDGE/COURSES—Food Production: Knowledge of techniques and equipment for planting, growing, and harvesting food products (both plant and animal) for consumption, including storage/handling techniques. Biology: Knowledge of plant and animal organisms and their tissues, cells, functions, interdependencies, and interactions with each other and the environment. Personnel and Human Resources: Knowledge of principles and procedures for personnel recruitment, selection, training, compensation and benefits, labor relations and negotiation, and personnel information systems. Production and Processing: Knowledge of raw materials, production processes, quality control, costs, and other techniques for maximizing the effective manufacture and distribution of goods. Administration and Management: Knowledge of business and management principles involved in strategic planning, resource allocation, human resources modeling, leadership technique, production methods, and coordination of people and resources. Chemistry: Knowledge of the chemical composition, structure, and properties of substances and of the chemical processes and transformations that they undergo. This includes uses of chemicals and their danger signs, production techniques, and disposal methods.

First-Line Supervisors and Manager/Supervisors— Horticultural Workers

- Education/Training Required: Associate degree
- Annual Earnings: $35,490
- Growth: 11.4%
- Annual Job Openings: 6,000
- Self-Employed: 16.9%
- Part-Time: 6.1%

Directly supervise and coordinate activities of horticultural workers. Manager/supervisors are generally found in smaller establishments, where they perform both supervisory and management functions, such as accounting, marketing, and personnel work, and may also engage in the same horticultural work as the workers they supervise. Assigns workers to duties such as cultivation, harvesting, maintenance, grading and packing products, or altering greenhouse environmental conditions. Estimates work-hour requirements to plant, cultivate, or harvest and prepares work schedule. Confers with management to report conditions; plan planting and harvesting schedules; and discuss changes in fertilizer, herbicides, or cultivating techniques. Drives and operates heavy machinery, such as dump truck, tractor, or growth-media tiller, to transport materials and supplies. Maintains records of employees' hours worked and work completed. Prepares and submits written or oral reports of personnel actions, such as performance evaluations, hires, promotions, and discipline. Trains employees in horticultural techniques, such as transplanting and weeding, shearing and harvesting trees, and grading and packing flowers. Inspects facilities to determine maintenance needs, such as malfunctioning environmental-control system, clogged sprinklers, or missing glass panes in greenhouse. Observes plants, flowers, shrubs, and trees in greenhouses, cold frames, or fields to ascertain condition. Reads inventory records, customer orders, and shipping schedules to ascertain day's activities. Reviews employees' work to ascertain quality and quantity of work performed. SKILLS—Management of Personnel Resources: Motivating, developing, and directing people as they work, identifying the best people for the job. Management of Material Resources: Obtaining and seeing to the appropriate use of equipment, facilities, and materials needed to do certain work. Instructing: Teaching others how to do something. Coordination: Adjusting actions in relation to others' actions. Operation Monitoring: Watching gauges, dials, or other indicators to make sure a machine is working properly. Systems Analysis: Determining how a system should work and how changes in conditions, operations, and the environment will affect outcomes. Repairing: Repairing machines or systems by using the needed tools. Troubleshooting: Determining causes of operating errors and deciding what to do about them. Time Management: Managing one's own time and the time of others. GOE—Interest Area: 01. Agriculture and Natural Resources. Work Group: 01.01. Managerial Work in Agriculture and Natural Resources. Other Jobs in This Work Group: Agricultural Crop Farm Managers; Farmers and Ranchers;

First-Line Supervisors and Manager/Supervisors—Agricultural Crop Workers; First-Line Supervisors and Manager/Supervisors—Animal Husbandry Workers; First-Line Supervisors and Manager/Supervisors—Extractive Workers; First-Line Supervisors and Manager/Supervisors—Fishery Workers; First-Line Supervisors and Manager/Supervisors—Landscaping Workers; First-Line Supervisors and Manager/Supervisors—Logging Workers; Fish Hatchery Managers; Lawn Service Managers; Nursery and Greenhouse Managers; Park Naturalists; Purchasing Agents and Buyers, Farm Products. **PERSONALITY TYPE:** Realistic. Realistic occupations frequently involve work activities that include practical, hands-on problems and solutions. These occupations often deal with plants, animals, and real-world materials like wood, tools, and machinery. Many of the occupations require working outside and do not involve a lot of paperwork or working closely with others.

EDUCATION/TRAINING PROGRAM(S)—Agricultural Business and Management, Other; Agricultural Production Operations, General; Agricultural Production Operations, Other; Agriculture, Agriculture Operations, and Related Sciences, Other; Agronomy and Crop Science; Crop Production; Farm/Farm and Ranch Management; Plant Sciences, General. **RELATED KNOWLEDGE/COURSES—Biology:** Knowledge of plant and animal organisms and their tissues, cells, functions, interdependencies, and interactions with each other and the environment. **Personnel and Human Resources:** Knowledge of principles and procedures for personnel recruitment, selection, training, compensation and benefits, labor relations and negotiation, and personnel information systems. **Food Production:** Knowledge of techniques and equipment for planting, growing, and harvesting food products (both plant and animal) for consumption, including storage/handling techniques. **Administration and Management:** Knowledge of business and management principles involved in strategic planning, resource allocation, human resources modeling, leadership technique, production methods, and coordination of people and resources. **Chemistry:** Knowledge of the chemical composition, structure, and properties of substances and of the chemical processes and transformations that they undergo. This includes uses of chemicals and their danger signs, production tech-niques, and disposal methods. **Production and Processing:** Knowledge of raw materials, production processes, quality control, costs, and other techniques for maximizing the effective manufacture and distribution of goods.

First-Line Supervisors and Manager/Supervisors—Landscaping Workers

- Education/Training Required: Work experience in a related occupation
- Annual Earnings: $35,340
- Growth: 21.6%
- Annual Job Openings: 18,000
- Self-Employed: 34.7%
- Part-Time: 5.9%

Directly supervise and coordinate activities of landscaping workers. Manager/supervisors are generally found in smaller establishment, where they perform both supervisory and management functions, such as accounting, marketing, and personnel work, and may also engage in the same landscaping work as the workers they supervise. Directs workers in maintenance and repair of driveways, walkways, benches, graves, and mausoleums. Observes ongoing work to ascertain if work is being performed according to instructions and will be completed on time. Determines work priority and crew and equipment requirements and assigns workers tasks, such as planting, fertilizing, irrigating, and mowing. Directs and assists workers engaged in maintenance and repair of equipment such as power mower and backhoe, using hand tools and power tools. Confers with manager to develop plans and schedules for maintenance and improvement of grounds. Keeps employee time records and records daily work performed. Interviews, hires, and discharges workers. Assists workers in performing work when completion is critical. Tours grounds, such as park, botanical garden, cemetery, or golf course, to inspect conditions. Trains workers in tasks such as transplanting and pruning trees and shrubs, finishing cement, using equipment, and caring for turf. Mixes and prepares spray and dust solutions and directs application of fertilizer, insecticide, and fungicide. **SKILLS—Management of Personnel Resources:** Motivating, developing, and directing people as they work, identifying the best people for the job. **Management of Material Resources:** Obtaining and seeing to the appropriate use of equipment, facilities, and materials needed to do certain work. **Coordination:** Adjusting actions in relation to others' actions. **Systems Analysis:** Determining how a system should work and how changes in conditions, operations, and the environment will affect outcomes. **Systems Evaluation:** Identifying measures or indicators of system performance and the actions needed to improve or correct performance relative to the goals of the system. **Instructing:** Teaching others how to do something. **Time Management:** Managing one's own time and the time of others. **Speaking:** Talking to others to convey information effectively. **GOE—Interest Area:** 01. Agriculture and Natural Resources. **Work Group:** 01.01. Managerial Work in Agriculture and Natural Resources. **Other Jobs in This Work Group:** Agricultural Crop Farm Managers; Farmers and Ranchers; First-Line Supervisors and Manager/Supervisors—Agricultural Crop Workers; First-Line Supervisors and Manager/Supervisors—Animal Husbandry Workers; First-Line Supervisors and Manager/Supervisors—Extractive Workers; First-Line Supervisors and Manager/Supervisors—Fishery Workers; First-Line Supervisors and Manager/Supervisors—Horticultural Workers; First-Line Supervisors and Manager/Supervisors—Logging Workers; Fish Hatchery Managers; Lawn Service Managers; Nursery and Greenhouse Managers; Park Naturalists; Purchasing Agents and Buyers, Farm Products. **PERSONALITY TYPE:** Realistic. Realistic occupations frequently involve work activities that include practical, hands-on problems and solutions. These occupations often deal with plants, animals, and real-world materials like wood, tools, and machinery. Many of the occupations require working outside and do not involve a lot of paperwork or working closely with others.

EDUCATION/TRAINING PROGRAM(S)— Landscaping and Groundskeeping; Ornamental Horticulture; Turf and Turfgrass Management. **RELATED KNOWLEDGE/COURSES—Personnel and Human Resources:** Knowledge of principles and procedures for personnel recruitment, selection, training,

compensation and benefits, labor relations and negotiation, and personnel information systems. **Administration and Management:** Knowledge of business and management principles involved in strategic planning, resource allocation, human resources modeling, leadership technique, production methods, and coordination of people and resources. **Chemistry:** Knowledge of the chemical composition, structure, and properties of substances and of the chemical processes and transformations that they undergo. This includes uses of chemicals and their danger signs, production techniques, and disposal methods. **Mechanical Devices:** Knowledge of machines and tools, including their designs, uses, repair, and maintenance. **Biology:** Knowledge of plant and animal organisms and their tissues, cells, functions, interdependencies, and interactions with each other and the environment. **Building and Construction:** Knowledge of the materials, methods, and tools involved in the construction or repair of houses, buildings, or other structures such as highways and roads.

First-Line Supervisors, Administrative Support

- Education/Training Required: Work experience in a related occupation
- Annual Earnings: $41,030
- Growth: 6.6%
- Annual Job Openings: 140,000
- Self-Employed: 0.9%
- Part-Time: 6.7%

Supervise and coordinate activities of workers involved in providing administrative support. Supervises and coordinates activities of workers engaged in clerical or administrative support activities. Plans, prepares, and revises work schedules and duty assignments according to budget allotments, customer needs, problems, workloads, and statistical forecasts. Verifies completeness and accuracy of subordinates' work, computations, and records. Interviews, selects, and discharges employees. Oversees, coordinates, or performs activities associated with shipping, receiving, distribution, and transportation. Evaluates subordinate job performance and conformance to regulations and recommends appropriate personnel action. Consults with supervisor and other personnel to resolve problems such as equipment performance, output quality, and work schedules. Trains employees in work and safety procedures and company policies. Computes figures such as balances, totals, and commissions. Analyzes financial activities of establishment or department and assists in planning budget. Inspects equipment for defects and notifies maintenance personnel or outside service contractors for repairs. Plans layout of stockroom, warehouse, or other storage areas, considering turnover, size, weight, and related factors pertaining to items stored. Compiles reports and information required by management or governmental agencies. Identifies and resolves discrepancies or errors. Maintains records of such matters as inventory, personnel, orders, supplies, and machine maintenance. Examines procedures and recommends changes to save time, labor, and other costs and to improve quality control and operating efficiency. Participates in work of subordinates to facilitate productivity or overcome difficult aspects of work. Requisitions supplies. Reviews records and reports pertaining to such activities as production, operation, payroll, customer accounts, and shipping. **SKILLS—Management of Personnel Resources:** Motivating, developing, and directing people as they work, identifying the best people for the job. **Management of Financial Resources:** Determining how money will be spent to get the work done and accounting for these expenditures. **Management of Material Resources:** Obtaining and seeing to the appropriate use of equipment, facilities, and materials needed to do certain work. **Social Perceptiveness:** Being aware of others' reactions and understanding why they react as they do. **Systems Evaluation:** Identifying measures or indicators of system performance and the actions needed to improve or correct performance relative to the goals of the system. **Time Management:** Managing one's own time and the time of others. **Systems Analysis:** Determining how a system should work and how changes in conditions, operations, and the environment will affect outcomes. **Learning Strategies:** Selecting and using training/instructional methods and procedures appropriate for the situation when learning or teaching new things. **GOE—Interest Area:** 04. Business and Administration. **Work Group:** 04.02.

Managerial Work in Business Detail. **Other Jobs in This Work Group:** Administrative Services Managers; First-Line Supervisors, Customer Service; Housekeeping Supervisors; Janitorial Supervisors; Meeting and Convention Planners. **PERSONALITY TYPE:** Enterprising. Enterprising occupations frequently involve starting up and carrying out projects. These occupations can involve leading people and making many decisions. They sometimes require risk taking and often deal with business.

EDUCATION/TRAINING PROGRAM(S)—Agricultural Business Technology; Customer Service Management; Medical/Health Management and Clinical Assistant/Specialist; Office Management and Supervision. **RELATED KNOWLEDGE/COURSES—Clerical Practices:** Knowledge of administrative and clerical procedures and systems such as word processing, managing files and records, stenography and transcription, designing forms, and other office procedures and terminology. **Personnel and Human Resources:** Knowledge of principles and procedures for personnel recruitment, selection, training, compensation and benefits, labor relations and negotiation, and personnel information systems. **Transportation:** Knowledge of principles and methods for moving people or goods by air, rail, sea, or road, including the relative costs and benefits. **Economics and Accounting:** Knowledge of economic and accounting principles and practices, the financial markets, banking, and the analysis and reporting of financial data. **Administration and Management:** Knowledge of business and management principles involved in strategic planning, resource allocation, human resources modeling, leadership technique, production methods, and coordination of people and resources. **Law and Government:** Knowledge of laws, legal codes, court procedures, precedents, government regulations, executive orders, agency rules, and the democratic political process.

First-Line Supervisors, Customer Service

- Education/Training Required: Work experience in a related occupation
- Annual Earnings: $41,030
- Growth: 6.6%
- Annual Job Openings: 140,000
- Self-Employed: 0.9%
- Part-Time: 6.7%

Supervise and coordinate activities of workers involved in providing customer service. Supervises and coordinates activities of workers engaged in customer service activities. Plans, prepares, and devises work schedules according to budgets and workloads. Observes and evaluates workers' performance. Issues instructions and assigns duties to workers. Trains and instructs employees. Hires and discharges workers. Communicates with other departments and management to resolve problems and expedite work. Interprets and communicates work procedures and company policies to staff. Helps workers in resolving problems and completing work. Resolves complaints and answers questions of customers regarding services and procedures. Reviews and checks work of subordinates, such as reports, records, and applications, for accuracy and content and corrects errors. Prepares, maintains, and submits reports and records, such as budgets and operational and personnel reports. Makes recommendations to management concerning staff and improvement of procedures. Plans and develops improved procedures. Requisitions or purchases supplies. **SKILLS—Management of Personnel Resources:** Motivating, developing, and directing people as they work, identifying the best people for the job. **Management of Financial Resources:** Determining how money will be spent to get the work done and accounting for these expenditures. **Service Orientation:** Actively looking for ways to help people. **Social Perceptiveness:** Being aware of others' reactions and understanding why they react as they do. **Systems Evaluation:** Identifying measures or indicators of system performance and the actions needed to improve or correct performance relative to the goals of the system. **Coordination:** Adjusting actions in relation to others'

actions. **Time Management:** Managing one's own time and the time of others. **Learning Strategies:** Selecting and using training/instructional methods and procedures appropriate for the situation when learning or teaching new things. **Systems Analysis:** Determining how a system should work and how changes in conditions, operations, and the environment will affect outcomes. **GOE—Interest Area:** 04. Business and Administration. **Work Group:** 04.02. Managerial Work in Business Detail. **Other Jobs in This Work Group:** Administrative Services Managers; First-Line Supervisors, Administrative Support; Housekeeping Supervisors; Janitorial Supervisors; Meeting and Convention Planners. **PERSONALITY TYPE:** Enterprising. Enterprising occupations frequently involve starting up and carrying out projects. These occupations can involve leading people and making many decisions. They sometimes require risk taking and often deal with business.

EDUCATION/TRAINING PROGRAM(S)—Agricultural Business Technology; Customer Service Management; Medical/Health Management and Clinical Assistant/Specialist; Office Management and Supervision. **RELATED KNOWLEDGE/COURSES—Customer and Personal Service:** Knowledge of principles and processes for providing customer and personal services. This includes customer needs assessment, meeting quality standards for services, and evaluation of customer satisfaction. **Personnel and Human Resources:** Knowledge of principles and procedures for personnel recruitment, selection, training, compensation and benefits, labor relations and negotiation, and personnel information systems. **Economics and Accounting:** Knowledge of economic and accounting principles and practices, the financial markets, banking, and the analysis and reporting of financial data. **Administration and Management:** Knowledge of business and management principles involved in strategic planning, resource allocation, human resources modeling, leadership technique, production methods, and coordination of people and resources. **Clerical Practices:** Knowledge of administrative and clerical procedures and systems such as word processing, managing files and records, stenography and transcription, designing forms, and other office procedures and terminology. **Education and Training:** Knowledge of principles and methods for curriculum and training design, teaching and instruction for individuals and groups, and the measurement of training effects.

First-Line Supervisors/ Managers of Correctional Officers

- Education/Training Required: Work experience in a related occupation
- Annual Earnings: $44,720
- Growth: 19.0%
- Annual Job Openings: 4,000
- Self-Employed: 0%
- Part-Time: 1.4%

Supervise and coordinate activities of correctional officers and jailers. Complete administrative paperwork and supervise the preparation and maintenance of records, forms, and reports. Conduct roll calls of correctional officers. Develop work and security procedures. Instruct employees and provide on-the-job training. Maintain knowledge of, comply with, and enforce all institutional policies, rules, procedures, and regulations. Maintain order, discipline, and security within assigned areas in accordance with relevant rules, regulations, policies, and laws. Monitor behavior of subordinates to ensure alert, courteous, and professional behavior toward inmates, parolees, fellow employees, visitors, and the public. Read and review offender information to identify issues that require special attention. Respond to emergencies such as escapes. Restrain, secure, and control offenders, using chemical agents, firearms, and other weapons of force as necessary. Set up employee work schedules. Supervise and direct the work of correctional officers to ensure the safe custody, discipline, and welfare of inmates. Supervise and perform searches of inmates and their quarters to locate contraband items. Supervise activities such as searches, shakedowns, riot control, and institutional tours. Take, receive, and check periodic inmate counts. Carry injured offenders or employees to safety and provide emergency first aid when necessary. Convey correctional officers' and

inmates' complaints to superiors. Examine incoming and outgoing mail to ensure conformance with regulations. Rate behavior of inmates, promoting acceptable attitudes and behaviors to those with low ratings. Resolve problems between inmates. Supervise and provide security for offenders performing tasks such as construction, maintenance, laundry, food service, and other industrial or agricultural operations. Transfer and transport offenders on foot or by driving vehicles such as trailers, vans, and buses. **SKILLS**—No data available. **GOE—Interest Area:** 12. Law and Public Safety. **Work Group:** 12.01. Managerial Work in Law and Public Safety. **Other Jobs in This Work Group:** Emergency Management Specialists; First-Line Supervisors/Managers of Police and Detectives; Forest Fire Fighting and Prevention Supervisors; Municipal Fire Fighting and Prevention Supervisors. **PERSONALITY TYPE:** No data available.

EDUCATION/TRAINING PROGRAM(S)—Corrections; Corrections Administration. **RELATED KNOWLEDGE/COURSES**—No data available.

First-Line Supervisors/ Managers of Food Preparation and Serving Workers

- Education/Training Required: Work experience in a related occupation
- Annual Earnings: $25,410
- Growth: 15.5%
- Annual Job Openings: 154,000
- Self-Employed: 4.5%
- Part-Time: 14.7%

Supervise workers engaged in preparing and serving food. Compile and balance cash receipts at the end of the day or shift. Resolve customer complaints regarding food service. Train workers in food preparation and in service, sanitation, and safety procedures. Inspect supplies, equipment, and work areas in order to ensure efficient service and conformance to standards. Control inventories of food, equipment, smallware, and liquor and report shortages to designated personnel. Observe and evaluate workers and work procedures in order to ensure quality standards and service. Assign duties, responsibilities, and work stations to employees in accordance with work requirements. Estimate ingredients and supplies required to prepare a recipe. Perform personnel actions such as hiring and firing staff, consulting with other managers as necessary. Analyze operational problems, such as theft and wastage, and establish procedures to alleviate these problems. Specify food portions and courses, production and time sequences, and workstation and equipment arrangements. Recommend measures for improving work procedures and worker performance in order to increase service quality and enhance job safety. Greet and seat guests and present menus and wine lists. Present bills and accept payments. Forecast staff, equipment, and supply requirements based on a master menu. Perform serving duties such as carving meat, preparing flambe dishes, or serving wine and liquor. Record production and operational data on specified forms. Purchase or requisition supplies and equipment needed to ensure quality and timely delivery of services. Collaborate with other personnel in order to plan menus, serving arrangements, and related details. Supervise and check the assembly of regular and special diet trays and the delivery of food trolleys to hospital patients. Schedule parties and take reservations. Develop departmental objectives, budgets, policies, procedures, and strategies. Develop equipment maintenance schedules and arrange for repairs. Evaluate new products for usefulness and suitability. **SKILLS— Management of Personnel Resources:** Motivating, developing, and directing people as they work, identifying the best people for the job. **Management of Financial Resources:** Determining how money will be spent to get the work done and accounting for these expenditures. **Equipment Maintenance:** Performing routine maintenance on equipment and determining when and what kind of maintenance is needed. **Instructing:** Teaching others how to do something. **Learning Strategies:** Selecting and using training/instructional methods and procedures appropriate for the situation when learning or teaching new things. **Service Orientation:** Actively looking for ways to help people. **Monitoring:** Monitoring or assessing your performance or that of other individuals or

organizations to make improvements or take corrective action. **Speaking:** Talking to others to convey information effectively. **GOE—Interest Area:** 09. Hospitality, Tourism, and Recreation. **Work Group:** 09.01. Managerial Work in Hospitality and Tourism. **Other Jobs in This Work Group:** First-Line Supervisors/Managers of Personal Service Workers; Food Service Managers; Gaming Managers; Gaming Supervisors; Lodging Managers. **PERSONALITY TYPE:** Enterprising. Enterprising occupations frequently involve starting up and carrying out projects. These occupations can involve leading people and making many decisions. They sometimes require risk taking and often deal with business.

EDUCATION/TRAINING PROGRAM(S)— Cooking and Related Culinary Arts, General; Foodservice Systems Administration/Management; Restaurant, Culinary, and Catering Management/ Manager. **RELATED KNOWLEDGE/COURSES— Customer and Personal Service:** Knowledge of principles and processes for providing customer and personal services. This includes customer needs assessment, meeting quality standards for services, and evaluation of customer satisfaction. **Food Production:** Knowledge of techniques and equipment for planting, growing, and harvesting food products (both plant and animal) for consumption, including storage/handling techniques. **Administration and Management:** Knowledge of business and management principles involved in strategic planning, resource allocation, human resources modeling, leadership technique, production methods, and coordination of people and resources. **Sales and Marketing:** Knowledge of principles and methods for showing, promoting, and selling products or services. This includes marketing strategy and tactics, product demonstrations, sales techniques, and sales control systems. **Production and Processing:** Knowledge of raw materials, production processes, quality control, costs, and other techniques for maximizing the effective manufacture and distribution of goods. **Personnel and Human Resources:** Knowledge of principles and procedures for personnel recruitment, selection, training, compensation and benefits, labor relations and negotiation, and personnel information systems. **Education and Training:** Knowledge of principles and methods for curriculum and training design, teaching and instruction for individuals and groups, and the measurement of training effects.

First-Line Supervisors/ Managers of Helpers, Laborers, and Material Movers, Hand

- ◉ Education/Training Required: Work experience in a related occupation
- ◉ Annual Earnings: $38,280
- ◉ Growth: 14.0%
- ◉ Annual Job Openings: 16,000
- ◉ Self-Employed: 0.2%
- ◉ Part-Time: 6.6%

Supervise and coordinate the activities of helpers, laborers, or material movers. Assess training needs of staff; then arrange for or provide appropriate instruction. Collaborate with workers and managers to solve work-related problems. Conduct staff meetings to relay general information or to address specific topics such as safety. Estimate material, time, and staffing requirements for a given project, based on work orders, job specifications, and experience. Evaluate employee performance and prepare performance appraisals. Examine freight to determine loading sequences. Perform the same work duties as those whom they supervise and/or perform more difficult or skilled tasks or assist in their performance. Plan work schedules and assign duties to maintain adequate staffing levels, to ensure that activities are performed effectively, and to respond to fluctuating workloads. Prepare and maintain work records and reports that include information such as employee time and wages, daily receipts, and inspection results. Provide assistance in balancing books, tracking, monitoring, and projecting a unit's budget needs and in developing unit policies and procedures. Recommend or initiate personnel actions such as promotions, transfers, and disciplinary measures. Resolve personnel problems, complaints, and formal grievances when possible, or refer them to higher-level supervisors for resolution. Review work throughout the work process and at completion in order to ensure that it has been performed properly. Transmit and explain work orders to laborers. Check specifications of materials loaded or unloaded against information contained in work orders. Counsel employees in work-related activities, personal growth, and career development. Inform designated employees or departments of items loaded and problems encountered. Inspect equipment for wear and for conformance to specifications. Inspect job sites to determine the extent of maintenance or repairs needed. Inventory supplies and requisition or purchase additional items as necessary. Participate in the hiring process by reviewing credentials, conducting interviews, and/or making hiring decisions or recommendations. **SKILLS—Management of Personnel Resources:** Motivating, developing, and directing people as they work, identifying the best people for the job. **Social Perceptiveness:** Being aware of others' reactions and understanding why they react as they do. **Systems Analysis:** Determining how a system should work and how changes in conditions, operations, and the environment will affect outcomes. **Instructing:** Teaching others how to do something. **Systems Evaluation:** Identifying measures or indicators of system performance and the actions needed to improve or correct performance relative to the goals of the system. **Learning Strategies:** Selecting and using training/instructional methods and procedures appropriate for the situation when learning or teaching new things. **Management of Material Resources:** Obtaining and seeing to the appropriate use of equipment, facilities, and materials needed to do certain work. **Time Management:** Managing one's own time and the time of others. **GOE— Interest Area:** 13. Manufacturing. **Work Group:** 13.01. Managerial Work in Manufacturing. **Other Jobs in This Work Group:** First-Line Supervisors/Managers of Mechanics, Installers, and Repairers; First-Line Supervisors/Managers of Production and Operating Workers; Industrial Production Managers. **PERSONALITY TYPE:** Enterprising. Enterprising occupations frequently involve starting up and carrying out projects. These occupations can involve leading people and making many decisions. They sometimes require risk taking and often deal with business.

EDUCATION/TRAINING PROGRAM(S)—No data available. RELATED KNOWLEDGE/COURSES—Production and Processing: Knowledge of raw materials, production processes, quality control, costs, and other techniques for maximizing the effective manufacture and distribution of goods. Economics and Accounting: Knowledge of economic and accounting principles and practices, the financial markets, banking, and the analysis and reporting of financial data. Administration and Management: Knowledge of business and management principles involved in strategic planning, resource allocation, human resources modeling, leadership technique, production methods, and coordination of people and resources. Personnel and Human Resources: Knowledge of principles and procedures for personnel recruitment, selection, training, compensation and benefits, labor relations and negotiation, and personnel information systems. Education and Training: Knowledge of principles and methods for curriculum and training design, teaching and instruction for individuals and groups, and the measurement of training effects. Mathematics: Knowledge of arithmetic, algebra, geometry, calculus, and statistics and their applications.

First-Line Supervisors/ Managers of Mechanics, Installers, and Repairers

- Education/Training Required: Work experience in a related occupation
- Annual Earnings: $50,340
- Growth: 15.4%
- Annual Job Openings: 42,000
- Self-Employed: 0.1%
- Part-Time: 1.3%

Supervise and coordinate the activities of mechanics, installers, and repairers. Determine schedules, sequences, and assignments for work activities based on work priority, quantity of equipment and skill of personnel. Patrol and monitor work areas and examine tools and equipment in order to detect unsafe conditions or violations of procedures or safety rules. Monitor employees' work levels and review work performance. Examine objects, systems, or facilities and analyze information to determine needed installations, services, or repairs. Participate in budget preparation and administration, coordinating purchasing and documentation and monitoring departmental expenditures. Counsel employees about work-related issues and assist employees in correcting job-skill deficiencies. Requisition materials and supplies, such as tools, equipment, and replacement parts. Compute estimates and actual costs of factors such as materials, labor, and outside contractors. Interpret specifications, blueprints, and job orders in order to construct templates and lay out reference points for workers. Conduct or arrange for worker training in safety, repair, and maintenance techniques; operational procedures; and equipment use. Investigate accidents and injuries and prepare reports of findings. Confer with personnel, such as management, engineering, quality control, customer, and union workers' representatives, in order to coordinate work activities, resolve employee grievances, and identify and review resource needs. Recommend or initiate personnel actions, such as hires, promotions, transfers, discharges, and disciplinary measures. Perform skilled repair and maintenance operations, using equipment such as hand and power tools, hydraulic presses and shears, and welding equipment. Compile operational and personnel records, such as time and production records, inventory data, repair and maintenance statistics, and test results. Develop, implement, and evaluate maintenance policies and procedures. Monitor tool inventories and the condition and maintenance of shops in order to ensure adequate working conditions. Inspect, test, and measure completed work, using devices such as hand tools and gauges to verify conformance to standards and repair requirements. SKILLS—Management of Personnel Resources: Motivating, developing, and directing people as they work, identifying the best people for the job. Installation: Installing equipment, machines, wiring, or programs to meet specifications. Repairing: Repairing machines or systems by using the needed tools. Management of Material Resources: Obtaining and seeing to the appropriate use of equipment, facilities, and materials needed to do certain work. Management of Financial Resources: Determining how money will be spent to get the work done and accounting for these expenditures. **Equipment Maintenance:** Performing routine maintenance on equipment and determining when and what kind of maintenance is needed. **Negotiation:** Bringing others together and trying to reconcile differences. **Troubleshooting:** Determining causes of operating errors and deciding what to do about them. **GOE—Interest Area:** 13. Manufacturing. **Work Group:** 13.01. Managerial Work in Manufacturing. **Other Jobs in This Work Group:** First-Line Supervisors/Managers of Helpers, Laborers, and Material Movers, Hand; First-Line Supervisors/Managers of Production and Operating Workers; Industrial Production Managers. **PERSONALITY TYPE:** Enterprising. Enterprising occupations frequently involve starting up and carrying out projects. These occupations can involve leading people and making many decisions. They sometimes require risk taking and often deal with business.

EDUCATION/TRAINING PROGRAM(S)— Operations Management and Supervision. **RELATED KNOWLEDGE/COURSES—Mechanical Devices:** Knowledge of machines and tools, including their designs, uses, repair, and maintenance. **Building and Construction:** Knowledge of the materials, methods, and tools involved in the construction or repair of houses, buildings, or other structures such as highways and roads. **Design:** Knowledge of design techniques, tools, and principles involved in production of precision technical plans, blueprints, drawings, and models. **Personnel and Human Resources:** Knowledge of principles and procedures for personnel recruitment, selection, training, compensation and benefits, labor relations and negotiation, and personnel information systems. **Administration and Management:** Knowledge of business and management principles involved in strategic planning, resource allocation, human resources modeling, leadership technique, production methods, and coordination of people and resources. **Customer and Personal Service:** Knowledge of principles and processes for providing customer and personal services. This includes customer needs assessment, meeting quality standards for services, and evaluation of customer satisfaction.

First-Line Supervisors/ Managers of Non-Retail Sales Workers

- Education/Training Required: Work experience in a related occupation
- Annual Earnings: $59,300
- Growth: 6.8%
- Annual Job Openings: 72,000
- Self-Employed: 44.7%
- Part-Time: 5.7%

Directly supervise and coordinate activities of sales workers other than retail sales workers. May perform duties such as budgeting, accounting, and personnel work in addition to supervisory duties. Analyze details of sales territories to assess their growth potential and to set quotas. Direct and supervise employees engaged in sales, inventory-taking, reconciling cash receipts, or performing specific services such as pumping gasoline for customers. Hire, train, and evaluate personnel. Inventory stock and reorder when inventories drop to specified levels. Keep records pertaining to purchases, sales, and requisitions. Listen to and resolve customer complaints regarding services, products, or personnel. Monitor sales staff performance to ensure that goals are met. Plan and prepare work schedules and assign employees to specific duties. Prepare sales and inventory reports for management and budget departments. Provide staff with assistance in performing difficult or complicated duties. Attend company meetings to exchange product information and coordinate work activities with other departments. Confer with company officials to develop methods and procedures to increase sales, expand markets, and promote business. Coordinate sales promotion activities and prepare merchandise displays and advertising copy. Examine merchandise to ensure correct pricing and display and that it functions as advertised. Examine products purchased for resale or received for storage to determine product condition. Formulate pricing policies on merchandise according to profitability requirements. Prepare rental or lease agreements, specifying charges and payment procedures for use of machinery, tools, or other items. Visit retailers and sales representatives to promote products and gather information. **SKILLS—Management of Personnel Resources:** Motivating, developing, and directing people as they work, identifying the best people for the job. **Management of Material Resources:** Obtaining and seeing to the appropriate use of equipment, facilities, and materials needed to do certain work. **Management of Financial Resources:** Determining how money will be spent to get the work done and accounting for these expenditures. **Systems Evaluation:** Identifying measures or indicators of system performance and the actions needed to improve or correct performance relative to the goals of the system. **Systems Analysis:** Determining how a system should work and how changes in conditions, operations, and the environment will affect outcomes. **Negotiation:** Bringing others together and trying to reconcile differences. **Social Perceptiveness:** Being aware of others' reactions and understanding why they react as they do. **Coordination:** Adjusting actions in relation to others' actions. **GOE—Interest Area:** 14. Retail and Wholesale Sales and Service. **Work Group:** 14.01. Managerial Work in Retail/Wholesale Sales and Service. **Other Jobs in This Work Group:** Advertising and Promotions Managers; First-Line Supervisors/Managers of Retail Sales Workers; Funeral Directors; Marketing Managers; Property, Real Estate, and Community Association Managers; Purchasing Managers; Sales Managers. **PERSONALITY TYPE:** Enterprising. Enterprising occupations frequently involve starting up and carrying out projects. These occupations can involve leading people and making many decisions. They sometimes require risk taking and often deal with business.

EDUCATION/TRAINING PROGRAM(S)—Business, Management, Marketing, and Related Support Services, Other; General Merchandising, Sales, and Related Marketing Operations, Other; Special Products Marketing Operations; Specialized Merchandising, Sales, and Related Marketing Operations, Other. **RELATED KNOWLEDGE/COURSES—Sales and Marketing:** Knowledge of principles and methods for showing, promoting, and selling products or services. This includes marketing strategy and tactics, product demonstrations, sales techniques, and sales control systems. **Economics and Accounting:** Knowledge of economic and accounting principles and practices, the

financial markets, banking, and the analysis and reporting of financial data. **Personnel and Human Resources:** Knowledge of principles and procedures for personnel recruitment, selection, training, compensation and benefits, labor relations and negotiation, and personnel information systems. **Administration and Management:** Knowledge of business and management principles involved in strategic planning, resource allocation, human resources modeling, leadership technique, production methods, and coordination of people and resources. **Mathematics:** Knowledge of arithmetic, algebra, geometry, calculus, and statistics and their applications. **Customer and Personal Service:** Knowledge of principles and processes for providing customer and personal services. This includes customer needs assessment, meeting quality standards for services, and evaluation of customer satisfaction.

First-Line Supervisors/ Managers of Personal Service Workers

- ◎ Education/Training Required: Work experience in a related occupation
- ◎ Annual Earnings: $30,350
- ◎ Growth: 9.4%
- ◎ Annual Job Openings: 26,000
- ◎ Self-Employed: 49.4%
- ◎ Part-Time: 16.1%

Supervise and coordinate activities of personal service workers, such as flight attendants, hairdressers, or caddies. Analyze and record personnel and operational data and write related activity reports. Apply customer/guest feedback to service improvement efforts. Assign work schedules, following work requirements, to ensure quality and timely delivery of service. Direct and coordinate the activities of workers such as flight attendants, hotel staff, or hairstylists. Inspect work areas and operating equipment to ensure conformance to established standards in areas such as cleanliness and maintenance. Meet with managers and other supervisors to stay informed of changes affecting operations. Observe and evaluate workers' appearance and performance to ensure quality service and compliance with specifications. Recruit and hire staff members. Requisition necessary supplies, equipment, and services. Resolve customer complaints regarding worker performance and services rendered. Take disciplinary action to address performance problems. Train workers in proper operational procedures and functions and explain company policies. Collaborate with staff members to plan and develop programs of events, schedules of activities, or menus. Direct marketing, advertising, and other customer recruitment efforts. Furnish customers with information on events and activities. Inform workers about interests and special needs of specific groups. Participate in continuing education to stay abreast of industry trends and developments. **SKILLS—Service Orientation:** Actively looking for ways to help people. **Management of Personnel Resources:** Motivating, developing, and directing people as they work, identifying the best people for the job. **Coordination:** Adjusting actions in relation to others' actions. **Time Management:** Managing one's own time and the time of others. **Management of Financial Resources:** Determining how money will be spent to get the work done and accounting for these expenditures. **Management of Material Resources:** Obtaining and seeing to the appropriate use of equipment, facilities, and materials needed to do certain work. **Learning Strategies:** Selecting and using training/instructional methods and procedures appropriate for the situation when learning or teaching new things. **Systems Evaluation:** Identifying measures or indicators of system performance and the actions needed to improve or correct performance relative to the goals of the system. **GOE—Interest Area:** 09. Hospitality, Tourism, and Recreation. **Work Group:** 09.01. Managerial Work in Hospitality and Tourism. **Other Jobs in This Work Group:** First-Line Supervisors/Managers of Food Preparation and Serving Workers; Food Service Managers; Gaming Managers; Gaming Supervisors; Lodging Managers. **PERSONALITY TYPE:** Enterprising. Enterprising occupations frequently involve starting up and carrying out projects. These occupations can involve leading people and making many decisions. They sometimes require risk taking and often deal with business.

EDUCATION/TRAINING PROGRAM(S)—No data available. **RELATED KNOWLEDGE/COURSES—Administration and Management:** Knowledge of business and management principles involved in strategic planning, resource allocation, human resources modeling, leadership technique, production methods, and coordination of people and resources. **Customer and Personal Service:** Knowledge of principles and processes for providing customer and personal services. This includes customer needs assessment, meeting quality standards for services, and evaluation of customer satisfaction. **Personnel and Human Resources:** Knowledge of principles and procedures for personnel recruitment, selection, training, compensation and benefits, labor relations and negotiation, and personnel information systems. **Psychology:** Knowledge of human behavior and performance; individual differences in ability, personality, and interests; learning and motivation; psychological research methods; and the assessment and treatment of behavioral and affective disorders. **Economics and Accounting:** Knowledge of economic and accounting principles and practices, the financial markets, banking, and the analysis and reporting of financial data. **Education and Training:** Knowledge of principles and methods for curriculum and training design, teaching and instruction for individuals and groups, and the measurement of training effects.

First-Line Supervisors/ Managers of Police and Detectives

- Education/Training Required: Work experience in a related occupation
- Annual Earnings: $64,430
- Growth: 15.3%
- Annual Job Openings: 14,000
- Self-Employed: 0%
- Part-Time: 1.4%

Supervise and coordinate activities of members of police force. Explain police operations to subordinates to assist them in performing their job duties. Inform personnel of changes in regulations and policies, implications of new or amended laws, and new techniques of police work. Supervise and coordinate the investigation of criminal cases, offering guidance and expertise to investigators and ensuring that procedures are conducted in accordance with laws and regulations. Investigate and resolve personnel problems within organization and charges of misconduct against staff. Train staff in proper police work procedures. Maintain logs; prepare reports; and direct the preparation, handling, and maintenance of departmental records. Monitor and evaluate the job performance of subordinates and authorize promotions and transfers. Direct collection, preparation, and handling of evidence and personal property of prisoners. Develop, implement, and revise departmental policies and procedures. Conduct raids and order detention of witnesses and suspects for questioning. Prepare work schedules and assign duties to subordinates. Discipline staff for violation of department rules and regulations. Cooperate with court personnel and officials from other law enforcement agencies and testify in court as necessary. Review contents of written orders to ensure adherence to legal requirements. Inspect facilities, supplies, vehicles, and equipment to ensure conformance to standards. Prepare news releases and respond to police correspondence. Requisition and issue equipment and supplies. Meet with civic, educational, and community groups to develop community programs and events and to discuss law enforcement subjects. Direct release or transfer of prisoners. Prepare budgets and manage expenditures of department funds. **SKILLS—Management of Personnel Resources:** Motivating, developing, and directing people as they work, identifying the best people for the job. **Persuasion:** Persuading others to change their minds or behavior. **Negotiation:** Bringing others together and trying to reconcile differences. **Social Perceptiveness:** Being aware of others' reactions and understanding why they react as they do. **Service Orientation:** Actively looking for ways to help people. **Monitoring:** Monitoring or assessing your performance or that of other individuals or organizations to make improvements or take corrective action. **Instructing:** Teaching others how to do something. **Learning Strategies:** Selecting and using training/instructional methods and procedures appropriate for the situation when learning or teaching new

things. **Coordination:** Adjusting actions in relation to others' actions. **GOE—Interest Area:** 12. Law and Public Safety. **Work Group:** 12.01. Managerial Work in Law and Public Safety. **Other Jobs in This Work Group:** Emergency Management Specialists; First-Line Supervisors/Managers of Correctional Officers; Forest Fire Fighting and Prevention Supervisors; Municipal Fire Fighting and Prevention Supervisors. **PERSONALITY TYPE:** Enterprising. Enterprising occupations frequently involve starting up and carrying out projects. These occupations can involve leading people and making many decisions. They sometimes require risk taking and often deal with business.

EDUCATION/TRAINING PROGRAM(S)—Corrections; Criminal Justice/Law Enforcement Administration; Criminal Justice/Safety Studies. **RELATED KNOWLEDGE/COURSES—Public Safety and Security:** Knowledge of relevant equipment, policies, procedures, and strategies to promote effective local, state, or national security operations for the protection of people, data, property, and institutions. **Psychology:** Knowledge of human behavior and performance; individual differences in ability, personality, and interests; learning and motivation; psychological research methods; and the assessment and treatment of behavioral and affective disorders. **Law and Government:** Knowledge of laws, legal codes, court procedures, precedents, government regulations, executive orders, agency rules, and the democratic political process. **Customer and Personal Service:** Knowledge of principles and processes for providing customer and personal services. This includes customer needs assessment, meeting quality standards for services, and evaluation of customer satisfaction. **Personnel and Human Resources:** Knowledge of principles and procedures for personnel recruitment, selection, training, compensation and benefits, labor relations and negotiation, and personnel information systems. **Education and Training:** Knowledge of principles and methods for curriculum and training design, teaching and instruction for individuals and groups, and the measurement of training effects.

First-Line Supervisors/ Managers of Production and Operating Workers

- Education/Training Required: Work experience in a related occupation
- Annual Earnings: $44,740
- Growth: 9.5%
- Annual Job Openings: 66,000
- Self-Employed: 2.2%
- Part-Time: 1.9%

Supervise and coordinate the activities of production and operating workers, such as inspectors, precision workers, machine setters and operators, assemblers, fabricators, and plant and system operators. Calculate labor and equipment requirements and production specifications, using standard formulas. Confer with management or subordinates to resolve worker problems, complaints, or grievances. Confer with other supervisors to coordinate operations and activities within or between departments. Demonstrate equipment operations and work and safety procedures to new employees or assign employees to experienced workers for training. Direct and coordinate the activities of employees engaged in the production or processing of goods, such as inspectors, machine setters, and fabricators. Inspect materials, products, or equipment to detect defects or malfunctions. Interpret specifications, blueprints, job orders, and company policies and procedures for workers. Maintain operations data such as time, production, and cost records and prepare management reports of production results. Observe work and monitor gauges, dials, and other indicators to ensure that operators conform to production or processing standards. Plan and establish work schedules, assignments, and production sequences to meet production goals. Recommend or implement measures to motivate employees and to improve production methods, equipment performance, product quality, or efficiency. Requisition materials, supplies, equipment parts, or repair services. Determine standards, budgets, production goals, and rates based on company policies, equipment and labor availability, and workloads. Enforce safety and sanitation regulations. Plan and

develop new products and production processes. Read and analyze charts, work orders, production schedules, and other records and reports in order to determine production requirements and to evaluate current production estimates and outputs. Recommend personnel actions such as hirings and promotions. Set up and adjust machines and equipment. **SKILLS—Management of Personnel Resources:** Motivating, developing, and directing people as they work, identifying the best people for the job. **Management of Material Resources:** Obtaining and seeing to the appropriate use of equipment, facilities, and materials needed to do certain work. **Systems Analysis:** Determining how a system should work and how changes in conditions, operations, and the environment will affect outcomes. **Negotiation:** Bringing others together and trying to reconcile differences. **Operation Monitoring:** Watching gauges, dials, or other indicators to make sure a machine is working properly. **Coordination:** Adjusting actions in relation to others' actions. **Social Perceptiveness:** Being aware of others' reactions and understanding why they react as they do. **Systems Evaluation:** Identifying measures or indicators of system performance and the actions needed to improve or correct performance relative to the goals of the system. **Management of Financial Resources:** Determining how money will be spent to get the work done and accounting for these expenditures. **GOE—Interest Area:** 13. Manufacturing. **Work Group:** 13.01. Managerial Work in Manufacturing. **Other Jobs in This Work Group:** First-Line Supervisors/Managers of Helpers, Laborers, and Material Movers, Hand; First-Line Supervisors/Managers of Mechanics, Installers, and Repairers; Industrial Production Managers. **PERSONALITY TYPE:** Enterprising. Enterprising occupations frequently involve starting up and carrying out projects. These occupations can involve leading people and making many decisions. They sometimes require risk taking and often deal with business.

EDUCATION/TRAINING PROGRAM(S)— Operations Management and Supervision. **RELATED KNOWLEDGE/COURSES—Production and Processing:** Knowledge of raw materials, production processes, quality control, costs, and other techniques for maximizing the effective manufacture and distribution of goods. **Personnel and Human Resources:** Knowledge of principles and procedures for personnel recruitment, selection, training, compensation and benefits, labor relations and negotiation, and personnel information systems. **Administration and Management:** Knowledge of business and management principles involved in strategic planning, resource allocation, human resources modeling, leadership technique, production methods, and coordination of people and resources. **Economics and Accounting:** Knowledge of economic and accounting principles and practices, the financial markets, banking, and the analysis and reporting of financial data. **Psychology:** Knowledge of human behavior and performance; individual differences in ability, personality, and interests; learning and motivation; psychological research methods; and the assessment and treatment of behavioral and affective disorders. **Mathematics:** Knowledge of arithmetic, algebra, geometry, calculus, and statistics and their applications.

First-Line Supervisors/ Managers of Retail Sales Workers

- ◎ Education/Training Required: Work experience in a related occupation
- ◎ Annual Earnings: $32,720
- ◎ Growth: 9.1%
- ◎ Annual Job Openings: 251,000
- ◎ Self-Employed: 33.0%
- ◎ Part-Time: 7.3%

Directly supervise sales workers in a retail establishment or department. Duties may include management functions, such as purchasing, budgeting, accounting, and personnel work, in addition to supervisory duties. Provide customer service by greeting and assisting customers and responding to customer inquiries and complaints. Monitor sales activities to ensure that customers receive satisfactory service and quality goods. Assign employees to specific duties. Direct and supervise employees engaged in sales, inventory-taking, reconciling cash receipts, or performing services for customers. Inventory stock and reorder when inventory drops to a specified level. Keep

records of purchases, sales, and requisitions. Enforce safety, health, and security rules. Examine products purchased for resale or received for storage to assess the condition of each product or item. Hire, train, and evaluate personnel in sales or marketing establishments, promoting or firing workers when appropriate. Perform work activities of subordinates, such as cleaning and organizing shelves and displays and selling merchandise. Establish and implement policies, goals, objectives, and procedures for their department. Instruct staff on how to handle difficult and complicated sales. Formulate pricing policies for merchandise according to profitability requirements. Estimate consumer demand and determine the types and amounts of goods to be sold. Examine merchandise to ensure that it is correctly priced and displayed and that it functions as advertised. Plan and prepare work schedules and keep records of employees' work schedules and time cards. Review inventory and sales records to prepare reports for management and budget departments. Plan and coordinate advertising campaigns and sales promotions and prepare merchandise displays and advertising copy. Confer with company officials to develop methods and procedures to increase sales, expand markets, and promote business. Establish credit policies and operating procedures. Plan budgets and authorize payments and merchandise returns. **SKILLS—Management of Personnel Resources:** Motivating, developing, and directing people as they work, identifying the best people for the job. **Persuasion:** Persuading others to change their minds or behavior. **Instructing:** Teaching others how to do something. **Management of Financial Resources:** Determining how money will be spent to get the work done and accounting for these expenditures. **Social Perceptiveness:** Being aware of others' reactions and understanding why they react as they do. **Service Orientation:** Actively looking for ways to help people. **Time Management:** Managing one's own time and the time of others. **Monitoring:** Monitoring or assessing your performance or that of other individuals or organizations to make improvements or take corrective action. **Negotiation:** Bringing others together and trying to reconcile differences. **GOE—Interest Area:** 14. Retail and Wholesale Sales and Service. **Work Group:** 14.01. Managerial Work in Retail/Wholesale Sales and Service. **Other Jobs in This Work Group:** Advertising and Promotions Managers; First-Line Supervisors/ Managers of Non-Retail Sales Workers; Funeral Directors; Marketing Managers; Property, Real Estate, and Community Association Managers; Purchasing Managers; Sales Managers. **PERSONALITY TYPE:** Enterprising. Enterprising occupations frequently involve starting up and carrying out projects. These occupations can involve leading people and making many decisions. They sometimes require risk taking and often deal with business.

EDUCATION/TRAINING PROGRAM(S)—Business, Management, Marketing, and Related Support Services, Other; Consumer Merchandising/Retailing Management; E-Commerce/Electronic Commerce; Floriculture/Floristry Operations and Management; Retailing and Retail Operations; Selling Skills and Sales Operations; Special Products Marketing Operations; Specialized Merchandising, Sales, and Related Marketing Operations, Other. **RELATED KNOWLEDGE/COURSES—Sales and Marketing:** Knowledge of principles and methods for showing, promoting, and selling products or services. This includes marketing strategy and tactics, product demonstrations, sales techniques, and sales control systems. **Customer and Personal Service:** Knowledge of principles and processes for providing customer and personal services. This includes customer needs assessment, meeting quality standards for services, and evaluation of customer satisfaction. **Administration and Management:** Knowledge of business and management principles involved in strategic planning, resource allocation, human resources modeling, leadership technique, production methods, and coordination of people and resources. **Personnel and Human Resources:** Knowledge of principles and procedures for personnel recruitment, selection, training, compensation and benefits, labor relations and negotiation, and personnel information systems. **Food Production:** Knowledge of techniques and equipment for planting, growing, and harvesting food products (both plant and animal) for consumption, including storage/handling techniques. **Economics and Accounting:** Knowledge of economic and accounting principles and practices, the financial markets, banking, and the analysis and reporting of financial data. **Public Safety and Security:** Knowledge of relevant

equipment, policies, procedures, and strategies to promote effective local, state, or national security operations for the protection of people, data, property, and institutions.

First-Line Supervisors/ Managers of Transportation and Material-Moving Machine and Vehicle Operators

- ◎ Education/Training Required: Work experience in a related occupation
- ◎ Annual Earnings: $44,810
- ◎ Growth: 12.1%
- ◎ Annual Job Openings: 23,000
- ◎ Self-Employed: 0.2%
- ◎ Part-Time: 6.6%

Directly supervise and coordinate activities of transportation and material-moving machine and vehicle operators and helpers. Confer with customers, supervisors, contractors, and other personnel to exchange information and to resolve problems. Direct workers in transportation or related services, such as pumping, moving, storing, and loading/unloading of materials or people. Enforce safety rules and regulations. Explain and demonstrate work tasks to new workers or assign workers to more experienced workers for further training. Interpret transportation and tariff regulations, shipping orders, safety regulations, and company policies and procedures for workers. Maintain or verify records of time, materials, expenditures, and crew activities. Monitor fieldwork to ensure that it is being performed properly and that materials are being used as they should be. Plan work assignments and equipment allocations in order to meet transportation, operations, or production goals. Prepare, compile, and submit reports on work activities, operations, production, and work-related accidents. Recommend or implement personnel actions such as employee selection, evaluation, and rewards or disciplinary actions. Requisition needed personnel, supplies, equipment, parts, or repair services. Resolve worker problems or collaborate with employees to assist in problem resolution. Review orders, production schedules, blueprints, and shipping/receiving notices to determine work sequences and material shipping dates, types, volumes, and destinations. Compute and estimate cash, payroll, transportation, personnel, and storage requirements. Dispatch personnel and vehicles in response to telephone or radio reports of emergencies. Drive vehicles or operate machines or equipment to complete work assignments or to assist workers. Examine, measure, and weigh cargo or materials to determine specific handling requirements. Inspect or test materials, stock, vehicles, equipment, and facilities to ensure that they are safe, are free of defects, and meet specifications. Perform or schedule repairs and preventive maintenance of vehicles and other equipment. Plan and establish transportation routes. Provide workers with assistance in performing tasks such as coupling railroad cars or loading vehicles. **SKILLS—Management of Financial Resources:** Determining how money will be spent to get the work done and accounting for these expenditures. **Management of Personnel Resources:** Motivating, developing, and directing people as they work, identifying the best people for the job. **Management of Material Resources:** Obtaining and seeing to the appropriate use of equipment, facilities, and materials needed to do certain work. **Systems Analysis:** Determining how a system should work and how changes in conditions, operations, and the environment will affect outcomes. **Operations Analysis:** Analyzing needs and product requirements to create a design. **Equipment Maintenance:** Performing routine maintenance on equipment and determining when and what kind of maintenance is needed. **Negotiation:** Bringing others together and trying to reconcile differences. **Coordination:** Adjusting actions in relation to others' actions. **Systems Evaluation:** Identifying measures or indicators of system performance and the actions needed to improve or correct performance relative to the goals of the system. **GOE—Interest Area:** 16. Transportation, Distribution, and Logistics. **Work Group:** 16.01. Managerial Work in Transportation. **Other Jobs in This Work Group:** Aircraft Cargo Handling Supervisors; Postmasters and Mail Superintendents; Railroad Conductors and Yardmasters; Storage and Distribution Managers; Transportation Managers.

PERSONALITY TYPE: Enterprising. Enterprising occupations frequently involve starting up and carrying out projects. These occupations can involve leading people and making many decisions. They sometimes require risk taking and often deal with business.

EDUCATION/TRAINING PROGRAM(S)—No data available. **RELATED KNOWLEDGE/COURSES—Economics and Accounting:** Knowledge of economic and accounting principles and practices, the financial markets, banking, and the analysis and reporting of financial data. **Transportation:** Knowledge of principles and methods for moving people or goods by air, rail, sea, or road, including the relative costs and benefits. **Personnel and Human Resources:** Knowledge of principles and procedures for personnel recruitment, selection, training, compensation and benefits, labor relations and negotiation, and personnel information systems. **Administration and Management:** Knowledge of business and management principles involved in strategic planning, resource allocation, human resources modeling, leadership technique, production methods, and coordination of people and resources. **Production and Processing:** Knowledge of raw materials, production processes, quality control, costs, and other techniques for maximizing the effective manufacture and distribution of goods. **Sales and Marketing:** Knowledge of principles and methods for showing, promoting, and selling products or services. This includes marketing strategy and tactics, product demonstrations, sales techniques, and sales control systems.

Fish Hatchery Managers

- ◎ Education/Training Required: Work experience in a related occupation
- ◎ Annual Earnings: $50,700
- ◎ Growth: 5.1%
- ◎ Annual Job Openings: 25,000
- ◎ Self-Employed: 0.9%
- ◎ Part-Time: 9.2%

Direct and coordinate, through subordinate supervisory personnel, activities of workers engaged in fish

hatchery production for corporations, cooperatives, or other owners. Determines, administers, and executes policies relating to administration, standards of hatchery operations, and facility maintenance. Oversees trapping and spawning of fish, egg incubation, and fry rearing, applying knowledge of management and fish culturing techniques. Oversees movement of mature fish to lakes, ponds, streams, or commercial tanks. Collects information regarding techniques for collecting, fertilizing, incubating spawn, and treatment of spawn and fry. Accounts for and dispenses funds. Prepares reports required by state and federal laws. Prepares budget reports. Confers with biologists and other fishery personnel to obtain data concerning fish habits, food, and environmental requirements. Approves employment and discharge of employees, signs payrolls, and performs personnel duties. **SKILLS—Management of Financial Resources:** Determining how money will be spent to get the work done and accounting for these expenditures. **Management of Personnel Resources:** Motivating, developing, and directing people as they work, identifying the best people for the job. **Management of Material Resources:** Obtaining and seeing to the appropriate use of equipment, facilities, and materials needed to do certain work. **Science:** Using scientific rules and methods to solve problems. **Reading Comprehension:** Understanding written sentences and paragraphs in work-related documents. **Systems Analysis:** Determining how a system should work and how changes in conditions, operations, and the environment will affect outcomes. **Writing:** Communicating effectively in writing as appropriate for the needs of the audience. **Time Management:** Managing one's own time and the time of others. **GOE—Interest Area:** 01. Agriculture and Natural Resources. **Work Group:** 01.01. Managerial Work in Agriculture and Natural Resources. **Other Jobs in This Work Group:** Agricultural Crop Farm Managers; Farmers and Ranchers; First-Line Supervisors and Manager/Supervisors—Agricultural Crop Workers; First-Line Supervisors and Manager/Supervisors—Animal Husbandry Workers; First-Line Supervisors and Manager/Supervisors—Extractive Workers; First-Line Supervisors and Manager/Supervisors—Fishery Workers; First-Line Supervisors and Manager/Supervisors—Horticultural Workers; First-Line Supervisors and Manager/Supervisors—Landscaping Workers; First-Line Supervisors

and Manager/Supervisors—Logging Workers; Lawn Service Managers; Nursery and Greenhouse Managers; Park Naturalists; Purchasing Agents and Buyers, Farm Products. **PERSONALITY TYPE:** Enterprising. Enterprising occupations frequently involve starting up and carrying out projects. These occupations can involve leading people and making many decisions. They sometimes require risk taking and often deal with business.

EDUCATION/TRAINING PROGRAM(S)— Agribusiness/Agricultural Business Operations; Agricultural Animal Breeding; Agricultural Business and Management, General; Agricultural Business and Management, Other; Agricultural Production Operations, General; Agricultural Production Operations, Other; Animal Nutrition; Animal Sciences, General; Animal/Livestock Husbandry and Production; Farm/Farm and Ranch Management; Livestock Management. **RELATED KNOWLEDGE/COURSES— Food Production:** Knowledge of techniques and equipment for planting, growing, and harvesting food products (both plant and animal) for consumption, including storage/handling techniques. **Administration and Management:** Knowledge of business and management principles involved in strategic planning, resource allocation, human resources modeling, leadership technique, production methods, and coordination of people and resources. **Personnel and Human Resources:** Knowledge of principles and procedures for personnel recruitment, selection, training, compensation and benefits, labor relations and negotiation, and personnel information systems. **Economics and Accounting:** Knowledge of economic and accounting principles and practices, the financial markets, banking, and the analysis and reporting of financial data. **Biology:** Knowledge of plant and animal organisms and their tissues, cells, functions, interdependencies, and interactions with each other and the environment. **Law and Government:** Knowledge of laws, legal codes, court procedures, precedents, government regulations, executive orders, agency rules, and the democratic political process.

Fitness Trainers and Aerobics Instructors

◎ Education/Training Required: Postsecondary vocational training

◎ Annual Earnings: $25,470

◎ Growth: 44.5%

◎ Annual Job Openings: 38,000

◎ Self-Employed: 5.4%

◎ Part-Time: 35.6%

Instruct or coach groups or individuals in exercise activities and the fundamentals of sports. Demonstrate techniques and methods of participation. Observe participants and inform them of corrective measures necessary to improve their skills. Those required to hold teaching degrees should be reported in the appropriate teaching category. Explain and enforce safety rules and regulations governing sports, recreational activities, and the use of exercise equipment. Offer alternatives during classes to accommodate different levels of fitness. Plan routines, choose appropriate music, and choose different movements for each set of muscles, depending on participants' capabilities and limitations. Observe participants and inform them of corrective measures necessary for skill improvement. Teach proper breathing techniques used during physical exertion. Instruct participants in maintaining exertion levels in order to maximize benefits from exercise routines. Teach and demonstrate use of gymnastic and training equipment such as trampolines and weights. Maintain fitness equipment. Conduct therapeutic, recreational, or athletic activities. Monitor participants' progress and adapt programs as needed. Evaluate individuals' abilities, needs, and physical conditions and develop suitable training programs to meet any special requirements. Plan physical education programs to promote development of participants' physical attributes and social skills. Provide students with information and resources regarding nutrition, weight control, and lifestyle issues. Administer emergency first aid, wrap injuries, treat minor chronic disabilities, or refer injured persons to physicians. Advise clients about proper clothing and shoes. Wrap ankles, fingers, wrists, or other body parts with synthetic skin, gauze, or adhesive tape in order to support muscles and liga-

ments. Teach individual and team sports to participants through instruction and demonstration, utilizing knowledge of sports techniques and of participants' physical capabilities. Promote health clubs through membership sales and record member information. Organize, lead, and referee indoor and outdoor games such as volleyball, baseball, and basketball. Maintain equipment inventories and select, store, and issue equipment as needed. Organize and conduct competitions and tournaments. Advise participants in use of heat or ultraviolet treatments and hot baths. Massage body parts to relieve soreness, strains, and bruises. **SKILLS—Instructing:** Teaching others how to do something. **Service Orientation:** Actively looking for ways to help people. **Coordination:** Adjusting actions in relation to others' actions. **Monitoring:** Monitoring or assessing your performance or that of other individuals or organizations to make improvements or take corrective action. **Equipment Selection:** Determining the kind of tools and equipment needed to do a job. **Social Perceptiveness:** Being aware of others' reactions and understanding why they react as they do. **Learning Strategies:** Selecting and using training/instructional methods and procedures appropriate for the situation when learning or teaching new things. **Time Management:** Managing one's own time and the time of others. **GOE—Interest Area:** 05. Education and Training. **Work Group:** 05.06. Counseling, Health, and Fitness Education. **Other Jobs in This Work Group:** Educational, Vocational, and School Counselors; Health Educators. **PERSONALITY TYPE:** Social. Social occupations frequently involve working with, communicating with, and teaching people. These occupations often involve helping or providing service to others.

EDUCATION/TRAINING PROGRAM(S)— Health and Physical Education, General; Physical Education Teaching and Coaching; Sport and Fitness Administration/Management. **RELATED KNOWLEDGE/COURSES—Customer and Personal Service:** Knowledge of principles and processes for providing customer and personal services. This includes customer needs assessment, meeting quality standards for services, and evaluation of customer satisfaction. **Psychology:** Knowledge of human behavior and performance; individual differences in ability, personality, and interests; learning and motivation; psychological research methods; and the assessment and treatment of behavioral and affective disorders. **Medicine and Dentistry:** Knowledge of the information and techniques needed to diagnose and treat human injuries, diseases, and deformities. This includes symptoms, treatment alternatives, drug properties and interactions, and preventive health-care measures. **Education and Training:** Knowledge of principles and methods for curriculum and training design, teaching and instruction for individuals and groups, and the measurement of training effects. **Sociology and Anthropology:** Knowledge of group behavior and dynamics, societal trends and influences, human migrations, ethnicity, and cultures and their history and origins. **Fine Arts:** Knowledge of the theory and techniques required to compose, produce, and perform works of music, dance, the visual arts, drama, and sculpture.

Flight Attendants

- ◎ Education/Training Required: Long-term on-the-job training
- ◎ Annual Earnings: $43,440
- ◎ Growth: 15.9%
- ◎ Annual Job Openings: 23,000
- ◎ Self-Employed: 0%
- ◎ Part-Time: 29.9%

Provide personal services to ensure the safety and comfort of airline passengers during flight. Greet passengers, verify tickets, explain use of safety equipment, and serve food or beverages. Administer first aid to passengers in distress. Inspect and clean cabins, checking for any problems and making sure that cabins are in order. Inspect passenger tickets to verify information and to obtain destination information. Operate audio and video systems. Prepare reports showing places of departure and destination, passenger ticket numbers, meal and beverage inventories, the conditions of cabin equipment, and any problems encountered by passengers. Reassure passengers when situations such as turbulence are encountered. Verify that first aid kits and other emergency equipment, including fire extinguishers and oxygen bottles, are in working order. Announce and demonstrate safety and emergency procedures such as the use of oxygen masks, seat belts, and life jackets. Answer passengers' questions about flights, aircraft, weather, travel routes and services, arrival times, and/or schedules. Assist passengers in placing carry-on luggage in overhead, garment, or under-seat storage. Assist passengers while entering or disembarking the aircraft. Attend preflight briefings concerning weather, altitudes, routes, emergency procedures, crew coordination, lengths of flights, food and beverage services offered, and numbers of passengers. Check to ensure that food, beverages, blankets, reading material, emergency equipment, and other supplies are aboard and are in adequate supply. Collect money for meals and beverages. Conduct periodic trips through the cabin to ensure passenger comfort and to distribute reading material, headphones, pillows, playing cards, and blankets. Determine special assistance needs of passengers such as small children, the elderly, or disabled persons. Direct and assist passengers in the event of an emergency, such as directing passengers to evacuate a plane following an emergency landing. Prepare passengers and aircraft for landing, following procedures. Greet passengers boarding aircraft and direct them to assigned seats. Heat and serve prepared foods. Announce flight delays and descent preparations. Sell alcoholic beverages to passengers. Take inventory of headsets, alcoholic beverages, and money collected. **SKILLS—Service Orientation:** Actively looking for ways to help people. **Social Perceptiveness:** Being aware of others' reactions and understanding why they react as they do. **GOE—Interest Area:** 09. Hospitality, Tourism, and Recreation. **Work Group:** 09.03. Hospitality and Travel Services. **Other Jobs in This Work Group:** Baggage Porters and Bellhops; Concierges; Hotel, Motel, and Resort Desk Clerks; Janitors and Cleaners, Except Maids and Housekeeping Cleaners; Maids and Housekeeping Cleaners; Reservation and Transportation Ticket Agents; Tour Guides and Escorts; Transportation Attendants, Except Flight Attendants and Baggage Porters; Travel Agents; Travel Clerks; Travel Guides. **PERSONALITY TYPE:** Enterprising. Enterprising occupations frequently involve starting up and carrying out projects. These occupations can involve leading people and making many decisions. They sometimes require risk taking and often deal with business.

EDUCATION/TRAINING PROGRAM(S)—Airline Flight Attendant. **RELATED KNOWLEDGE/ COURSES—Customer and Personal Service:** Knowledge of principles and processes for providing customer and personal services. This includes customer needs assessment, meeting quality standards for services, and evaluation of customer satisfaction. **Medicine and Dentistry:** Knowledge of the information and techniques needed to diagnose and treat human injuries, diseases, and deformities. This includes symptoms, treatment alternatives, drug properties and interactions, and preventive health-care measures. **Transportation:** Knowledge of principles and methods for moving people or goods by air, rail, sea, or road, including the relative costs and benefits. **Geography:** Knowledge of principles and methods for describing the features of land, sea, and air masses, including their physical characteristics; locations; interrelationships; and distribution of plant, animal, and human life. **Public Safety and Security:** Knowledge of relevant equipment, policies, procedures, and strategies to promote effective local, state, or national security operations for the protection of people, data, property, and institutions. **Psychology:** Knowledge of human behavior and performance; individual differences in ability, personality, and interests; learning and motivation; psychological research methods; and the assessment and treatment of behavioral and affective disorders.

Food Preparation Workers

- ◎ Education/Training Required: Short-term on-the-job training
- ◎ Annual Earnings: $16,710
- ◎ Growth: 20.2%
- ◎ Annual Job Openings: 267,000
- ◎ Self-Employed: 0.6%
- ◎ Part-Time: 41.9%

Perform a variety of food preparation duties other than cooking, such as preparing cold foods and shellfish, slicing meat, and brewing coffee or tea. Clean work areas, equipment, utensils, dishes, and silverware. Store food in designated containers and storage areas to prevent spoilage. Prepare a variety of foods according to customers' orders or supervisors' instructions, following approved procedures. Package take-out foods and/or serve food to customers. Portion and wrap the food or place it directly on plates for service to patrons. Place food trays over food warmers for immediate service or store them in refrigerated storage cabinets. Inform supervisors when supplies are getting low or equipment is not working properly. Weigh or measure ingredients. Assist cooks and kitchen staff with various tasks as needed and provide cooks with needed items. Wash, peel, and/or cut various foods to prepare for cooking or serving. Receive and store food supplies, equipment, and utensils in refrigerators, cupboards, and other storage areas. Stock cupboards and refrigerators and tend salad bars and buffet meals. Remove trash and clean kitchen garbage containers. Prepare and serve a variety of beverages such as coffee, tea, and soft drinks. Carry food supplies, equipment, and utensils to and from storage and work areas. Make special dressings and sauces as condiments for sandwiches. Scrape leftovers from dishes into garbage containers. Use manual and/or electric appliances to clean, peel, slice, and trim foods. Stir and strain soups and sauces. Distribute food to waiters and waitresses to serve to customers. Keep records of the quantities of food used. Load dishes, glasses, and tableware into dishwashing machines. Butcher and clean fowl, fish, poultry, and shellfish to prepare for cooking or serving. Cut, slice, and/or grind meat, poultry, and seafood to prepare for cooking. Work on assembly lines, adding cutlery, napkins, food, and other items to trays in hospitals, cafeterias, airline kitchens, and similar establishments. Mix ingredients for green salads, molded fruit salads, vegetable salads, and pasta salads. Distribute menus to hospital patients, collect diet sheets, and deliver food trays and snacks to nursing units or directly to patients. **SKILLS—Management of Personnel Resources:** Motivating, developing, and directing people as they work, identifying the best people for the job. **Service Orientation:** Actively looking for ways to help people. **Instructing:** Teaching others how to do something. **Social Perceptiveness:** Being aware of others' reactions and understanding why they react as they do. **Learning Strategies:** Selecting and using training/instructional methods and procedures appropriate for the situation when learning or teaching new things. **Negotiation:** Bringing others together and trying to reconcile differences. **Persuasion:** Persuading others to change their minds or behavior. **Operation Monitoring:** Watching gauges, dials, or other indicators to make sure a machine is working properly. **Equipment Maintenance:** Performing routine maintenance on equipment and determining when and what kind of maintenance is needed. **GOE—Interest Area:** 09. Hospitality, Tourism, and Recreation. **Work Group:** 09.04. Food and Beverage Preparation. **Other Jobs in This Work Group:** Bakers, Bread and Pastry; Butchers and Meat Cutters; Chefs and Head Cooks; Cooks, Fast Food; Cooks, Institution and Cafeteria; Cooks, Restaurant; Cooks, Short Order; Dishwashers. **PERSONALITY TYPE:** Realistic. Realistic occupations frequently involve work activities that include practical, hands-on problems and solutions. These occupations often deal with plants, animals, and real-world materials like wood, tools, and machinery. Many of the occupations require working outside and do not involve a lot of paperwork or working closely with others.

EDUCATION/TRAINING PROGRAM(S)— Cooking and Related Culinary Arts, General; Food Preparation/Professional Cooking/Kitchen Assistant; Institutional Food Workers. **RELATED KNOWLEDGE/COURSES—Food Production:** Knowledge of techniques and equipment for planting, growing, and harvesting food products (both plant and animal) for consumption, including storage/handling techniques. **Customer and Personal Service:** Knowledge of principles and processes for providing customer and personal services. This includes customer needs assessment, meeting quality standards for services, and evaluation of customer satisfaction. **Production and Processing:** Knowledge of raw materials, production processes, quality control, costs, and other techniques for maximizing the effective manufacture and distribution of goods. **Administration and Management:** Knowledge of business and management principles involved in strategic planning, resource allocation, human resources modeling, leadership technique, production methods, and coordination of people and resources. **Sales and Marketing:** Knowledge of principles and methods for showing, promoting, and selling products or services. This includes marketing strategy and tactics, product demonstrations, sales techniques, and sales control systems. **Economics and Accounting:** Knowledge of economic and accounting principles

and practices, the financial markets, banking, and the analysis and reporting of financial data. **Public Safety and Security:** Knowledge of relevant equipment, policies, procedures, and strategies to promote effective local, state, or national security operations for the protection of people, data, property, and institutions.

Food Service Managers

- ◎ Education/Training Required: Work experience in a related occupation
- ◎ Annual Earnings: $39,610
- ◎ Growth: 11.5%
- ◎ Annual Job Openings: 58,000
- ◎ Self-Employed: 34.7%
- ◎ Part-Time: 8.6%

Plan, direct, or coordinate activities of an organization or department that serves food and beverages. Test cooked food by tasting and smelling it in order to ensure palatability and flavor conformity. Investigate and resolve complaints regarding food quality, service, or accommodations. Schedule and receive food and beverage deliveries, checking delivery contents in order to verify product quality and quantity. Monitor food preparation methods, portion sizes, and garnishing and presentation of food in order to ensure that food is prepared and presented in an acceptable manner. Monitor budgets and payroll records and review financial transactions in order to ensure that expenditures are authorized and budgeted. Schedule staff hours and assign duties. Monitor compliance with health and fire regulations regarding food preparation and serving and building maintenance in lodging and dining facilities. Coordinate assignments of cooking personnel in order to ensure economical use of food and timely preparation. Keep records required by government agencies regarding sanitation and food subsidies when appropriate. Establish standards for personnel performance and customer service. Estimate food, liquor, wine, and other beverage consumption in order to anticipate amounts to be purchased or requisitioned. Review work procedures and operational problems in order to determine ways to improve service, performance, and/or safety. Perform some food preparation or service tasks such as cooking, clearing tables, and serving food and drinks when necessary. Maintain food and equipment inventories and keep inventory records. Organize and direct worker training programs, resolve personnel problems, hire new staff, and evaluate employee performance in dining and lodging facilities. Order and purchase equipment and supplies. Review menus and analyze recipes in order to determine labor and overhead costs and assign prices to menu items. Record the number, type, and cost of items sold in order to determine which items may be unpopular or less profitable. Assess staffing needs and recruit staff, using methods such as newspaper advertisements or attendance at job fairs. Arrange for equipment maintenance and repairs and coordinate a variety of services such as waste removal and pest control. **SKILLS— Management of Personnel Resources:** Motivating, developing, and directing people as they work, identifying the best people for the job. **Management of Financial Resources:** Determining how money will be spent to get the work done and accounting for these expenditures. **Time Management:** Managing one's own time and the time of others. **Learning Strategies:** Selecting and using training/instructional methods and procedures appropriate for the situation when learning or teaching new things. **Monitoring:** Monitoring or assessing your performance or that of other individuals or organizations to make improvements or take corrective action. **Instructing:** Teaching others how to do something. **Service Orientation:** Actively looking for ways to help people. **Management of Material Resources:** Obtaining and seeing to the appropriate use of equipment, facilities, and materials needed to do certain work. **GOE—Interest Area:** 09. Hospitality, Tourism, and Recreation. **Work Group:** 09.01. Managerial Work in Hospitality and Tourism. **Other Jobs in This Work Group:** First-Line Supervisors/Managers of Food Preparation and Serving Workers; First-Line Supervisors/Managers of Personal Service Workers; Gaming Managers; Gaming Supervisors; Lodging Managers. **PERSONALITY TYPE:** Enterprising. Enterprising occupations frequently involve starting up and carrying out projects. These occupations can involve leading people and making many decisions. They sometimes require risk taking and often deal with business.

EDUCATION/TRAINING PROGRAM(S)—Hospitality Administration/Management, General;

Hotel/Motel Administration/Management; Restaurant, Culinary, and Catering Management/Manager; Restaurant/Food Services Management. **RELATED KNOWLEDGE/COURSES—Customer and Personal Service:** Knowledge of principles and processes for providing customer and personal services. This includes customer needs assessment, meeting quality standards for services, and evaluation of customer satisfaction. **Food Production:** Knowledge of techniques and equipment for planting, growing, and harvesting food products (both plant and animal) for consumption, including storage/handling techniques. **Sales and Marketing:** Knowledge of principles and methods for showing, promoting, and selling products or services. This includes marketing strategy and tactics, product demonstrations, sales techniques, and sales control systems. **Production and Processing:** Knowledge of raw materials, production processes, quality control, costs, and other techniques for maximizing the effective manufacture and distribution of goods. **Administration and Management:** Knowledge of business and management principles involved in strategic planning, resource allocation, human resources modeling, leadership technique, production methods, and coordination of people and resources. **Personnel and Human Resources:** Knowledge of principles and procedures for personnel recruitment, selection, training, compensation and benefits, labor relations and negotiation, and personnel information systems.

Forensic Science Technicians

- Education/Training Required: Associate degree
- Annual Earnings: $44,010
- Growth: 18.9%
- Annual Job Openings: 1,000
- Self-Employed: 1.0%
- Part-Time: 20.2%

Collect, identify, classify, and analyze physical evidence related to criminal investigations. Perform tests on weapons or substances such as fiber, hair, and tissue to determine significance to investigation. May

testify as expert witnesses on evidence or crime laboratory techniques. **May serve as specialists in area of expertise, such as ballistics, fingerprinting, handwriting, or biochemistry.** Testify in court about investigative and analytical methods and findings. Keep records and prepare reports detailing findings, investigative methods, and laboratory techniques. Interpret laboratory findings and test results in order to identify and classify substances, materials, and other evidence collected at crime scenes. Operate and maintain laboratory equipment and apparatus. Prepare solutions, reagents, and sample formulations needed for laboratory work. Analyze and classify biological fluids, using DNA typing or serological techniques. Collect evidence from crime scenes, storing it in conditions that preserve its integrity. Identify and quantify drugs and poisons found in biological fluids and tissues, in foods, and at crime scenes. Analyze handwritten and machine-produced textual evidence to decipher altered or obliterated text or to determine authorship, age, and/or source. Reconstruct crime scenes in order to determine relationships among pieces of evidence. Examine DNA samples to determine if they match other samples. Collect impressions of dust from surfaces in order to obtain and identify fingerprints. Analyze gunshot residue and bullet paths in order to determine how shootings occurred. Visit morgues, examine scenes of crimes, or contact other sources in order to obtain evidence or information to be used in investigations. Examine physical evidence such as hair, fiber, wood, or soil residues in order to obtain information about its source and composition. Determine types of bullets used in shooting and if they were fired from a specific weapon. Examine firearms in order to determine mechanical condition and legal status, performing restoration work on damaged firearms in order to obtain information such as serial numbers. Interpret the pharmacological effects of a drug or a combination of drugs on an individual. Confer with ballistics, fingerprinting, handwriting, documents, electronics, medical, chemical, or metallurgical experts concerning evidence and its interpretation. Compare objects such as tools with impression marks in order to determine whether a specific object is responsible for a specific mark. **SKILLS—Science:** Using scientific rules and methods to solve problems. **Quality Control Analysis:** Conducting tests and inspections of products, services, or processes to evaluate quality or performance. **Troubleshooting:** Determining causes of operating errors and deciding what to do about them. **Active Learning:** Understanding the implications of new information for both current and future problem-solving and decision-making. **Instructing:** Teaching others how to do something. **Speaking:** Talking to others to convey information effectively. **Reading Comprehension:** Understanding written sentences and paragraphs in work-related documents. **Critical Thinking:** Using logic and reasoning to identify the strengths and weaknesses of alternative solutions, conclusions, or approaches to problems. **GOE—Interest Area:** 12. Law and Public Safety. **Work Group:** 12.04. Law Enforcement and Public Safety. **Other Jobs in This Work Group:** Bailiffs; Correctional Officers and Jailers; Criminal Investigators and Special Agents; Fire Investigators; Highway Patrol Pilots; Parking Enforcement Workers; Police Detectives; Police Identification and Records Officers; Police Patrol Officers; Sheriffs and Deputy Sheriffs; Transit and Railroad Police. **PERSONALITY TYPE:** Investigative. Investigative occupations frequently involve working with ideas and require an extensive amount of thinking. These occupations can involve searching for facts and figuring out problems mentally.

EDUCATION/TRAINING PROGRAM(S)— Forensic Science and Technology. **RELATED KNOWLEDGE/COURSES—Chemistry:** Knowledge of the chemical composition, structure, and properties of substances and of the chemical processes and transformations that they undergo. This includes uses of chemicals and their danger signs, production techniques, and disposal methods. **Law and Government:** Knowledge of laws, legal codes, court procedures, precedents, government regulations, executive orders, agency rules, and the democratic political process. **Customer and Personal Service:** Knowledge of principles and processes for providing customer and personal services. This includes customer needs assessment, meeting quality standards for services, and evaluation of customer satisfaction. **Public Safety and Security:** Knowledge of relevant equipment, policies, procedures, and strategies to promote effective local, state, or national security operations for the protection of people, data, property, and institutions. **English Language:** Knowledge of the structure and content of the

English language, including the meaning and spelling of words, rules of composition, and grammar. **Biology:** Knowledge of plant and animal organisms and their tissues, cells, functions, interdependencies, and interactions with each other and the environment.

Forest Fire Fighters

- Education/Training Required: Long-term on-the-job training
- Annual Earnings: $38,330
- Growth: 20.7%
- Annual Job Openings: 29,000
- Self-Employed: 0%
- Part-Time: 1.1%

Control and suppress fires in forests or vacant public land. Maintain contact with fire dispatchers at all times in order to notify them of the need for additional fire fighters and supplies or to detail any difficulties encountered. Rescue fire victims and administer emergency medical aid. Collaborate with other fire fighters as a member of a firefighting crew. Patrol burned areas after fires to locate and eliminate hot spots that may restart fires. Extinguish flames and embers to suppress fires, using shovels or engine- or hand-driven water or chemical pumps. Fell trees, cut and clear brush, and dig trenches in order to create firelines, using axes, chain saws, or shovels. Maintain knowledge of current firefighting practices by participating in drills and by attending seminars, conventions, and conferences. Operate pumps connected to high-pressure hoses. Participate in physical training in order to maintain high levels of physical fitness. Establish water supplies, connect hoses, and direct water onto fires. Maintain fire equipment and firehouse living quarters. Inform and educate the public about fire prevention. Take action to contain any hazardous chemicals that could catch fire, leak, or spill. Organize fire caches, positioning equipment for the most effective response. Transport personnel and cargo to and from fire areas. Participate in fire prevention and inspection programs. Perform forest maintenance and improvement tasks such as cutting brush, planting trees, building trails, and marking timber. Test and maintain tools, equipment, jump gear, and parachutes in order to ensure readiness for fire-suppression activities. Observe forest areas from fire lookout towers in order to spot potential problems. Orient self in relation to fire, using compass and map, and collect supplies and equipment dropped by parachute. Serve as fully trained lead helicopter crew member and as helispot manager. Drop weighted paper streamers from aircraft to determine the speed and direction of the wind at fire sites. **SKILLS—Management of Personnel Resources:** Motivating, developing, and directing people as they work, identifying the best people for the job. **Service Orientation:** Actively looking for ways to help people. **Equipment Maintenance:** Performing routine maintenance on equipment and determining when and what kind of maintenance is needed. **Repairing:** Repairing machines or systems by using the needed tools. **Coordination:** Adjusting actions in relation to others' actions. **Operation Monitoring:** Watching gauges, dials, or other indicators to make sure a machine is working properly. **Equipment Selection:** Determining the kind of tools and equipment needed to do a job. **Systems Analysis:** Determining how a system should work and how changes in conditions, operations, and the environment will affect outcomes. **GOE—Interest Area:** 12. Law and Public Safety. **Work Group:** 12.06. Emergency Responding. **Other Jobs in This Work Group:** Emergency Medical Technicians and Paramedics; Municipal Fire Fighters. **PERSONALITY TYPE:** Realistic. Realistic occupations frequently involve work activities that include practical, hands-on problems and solutions. These occupations often deal with plants, animals, and real-world materials like wood, tools, and machinery. Many of the occupations require working outside and do not involve a lot of paperwork or working closely with others.

EDUCATION/TRAINING PROGRAM(S)—Fire Protection, Other; Fire Science/Firefighting. **RELATED KNOWLEDGE/COURSES—Customer and Personal Service:** Knowledge of principles and processes for providing customer and personal services. This includes customer needs assessment, meeting quality standards for services, and evaluation of customer satisfaction. **Geography:** Knowledge of principles and methods for describing the features of land, sea, and air masses, including their physical characteristics; locations; interrelationships; and distribution of plant, animal, and human life. **Education and Train-**

ing: Knowledge of principles and methods for curriculum and training design, teaching and instruction for individuals and groups, and the measurement of training effects. **Mechanical Devices:** Knowledge of machines and tools, including their designs, uses, repair, and maintenance. **Public Safety and Security:** Knowledge of relevant equipment, policies, procedures, and strategies to promote effective local, state, or national security operations for the protection of people, data, property, and institutions. **Psychology:** Knowledge of human behavior and performance; individual differences in ability, personality, and interests; learning and motivation; psychological research methods; and the assessment and treatment of behavioral and affective disorders.

Forest Fire Fighting and Prevention Supervisors

- ◎ Education/Training Required: Work experience in a related occupation
- ◎ Annual Earnings: $58,920
- ◎ Growth: 18.7%
- ◎ Annual Job Openings: 8,000
- ◎ Self-Employed: 0%
- ◎ Part-Time: 0.1%

Supervise fire fighters who control and suppress fires in forests or vacant public land. Communicate fire details to superiors, subordinates, and interagency dispatch centers, using two-way radios. Direct investigations of suspected arsons in wildfires, working closely with other investigating agencies. Direct the loading of fire suppression equipment into aircraft and the parachuting of equipment to crews on the ground. Evaluate size, location, and condition of forest fires in order to request and dispatch crews and position equipment so fires can be contained safely and effectively. Identify staff training and development needs in order to ensure that appropriate training can be arranged. Maintain fire suppression equipment in good condition, checking equipment periodically in order to ensure that it is ready for use. Maintain knowledge of forest fire laws and fire prevention techniques and tactics. Monitor prescribed burns to ensure that they are conducted safely and effectively. Observe fires and crews from air to determine firefighting force requirements and to note changing conditions that will affect firefighting efforts. Operate wildland fire engines and hoselays. Perform administrative duties such as compiling and maintaining records, completing forms, preparing reports, and composing correspondence. Recruit and hire forest fire—fighting personnel. Review and evaluate employee performance. Schedule employee work assignments and set work priorities. Serve as working leader of an engine, hand, helicopter, or prescribed fire crew of three or more fire fighters. Train workers in such skills as parachute jumping, fire suppression, aerial observation, and radio communication both in the classroom and on the job. Appraise damage caused by fires in order to prepare damage reports. Direct and supervise prescribed burn projects and prepare post-burn reports analyzing burn conditions and results. Drive crew carriers in order to transport fire fighters to fire sites. Educate the public about forest fire prevention by participating in activities such as exhibits and presentations and by distributing promotional materials. Inspect all stations, uniforms, equipment, and recreation areas in order to ensure compliance with safety standards, taking corrective action as necessary. **SKILLS—Management of Personnel Resources:** Motivating, developing, and directing people as they work, identifying the best people for the job. **Management of Material Resources:** Obtaining and seeing to the appropriate use of equipment, facilities, and materials needed to do certain work. **Systems Analysis:** Determining how a system should work and how changes in conditions, operations, and the environment will affect outcomes. **Systems Evaluation:** Identifying measures or indicators of system performance and the actions needed to improve or correct performance relative to the goals of the system. **Service Orientation:** Actively looking for ways to help people. **Coordination:** Adjusting actions in relation to others' actions. **Instructing:** Teaching others how to do something. **Judgment and Decision Making:** Considering the relative costs and benefits of potential actions to choose the most appropriate one. **GOE—Interest Area:** 12. Law and Public Safety. **Work Group:** 12.01. Managerial Work in Law and Public Safety. **Other Jobs in This Work Group:** Emergency Management Specialists; First-Line Supervisors/Managers of Correctional Officers; First-Line Supervisors/Managers of Police and Detectives; Municipal Fire Fighting and Prevention Supervisors. **PERSONALITY TYPE:** Realistic. Realistic occupations frequently involve work activities that include practical, hands-on problems and solutions. These occupations often deal with plants, animals, and real-world materials like wood, tools, and machinery. Many of the occupations require working outside and do not involve a lot of paperwork or working closely with others.

EDUCATION/TRAINING PROGRAM(S)—Fire Protection and Safety Technology/Technician; Fire Services Administration. **RELATED KNOWLEDGE/COURSES**—**Public Safety and Security:** Knowledge of relevant equipment, policies, procedures, and strategies to promote effective local, state, or national security operations for the protection of people, data, property, and institutions. **Transportation:** Knowledge of principles and methods for moving people or goods by air, rail, sea, or road, including the relative costs and benefits. **Education and Training:** Knowledge of principles and methods for curriculum and training design, teaching and instruction for individuals and groups, and the measurement of training effects. **Administration and Management:** Knowledge of business and management principles involved in strategic planning, resource allocation, human resources modeling, leadership technique, production methods, and coordination of people and resources. **Geography:** Knowledge of principles and methods for describing the features of land, sea, and air masses, including their physical characteristics; locations; interrelationships; and distribution of plant, animal, and human life. **Chemistry:** Knowledge of the chemical composition, structure, and properties of substances and of the chemical processes and transformations that they undergo. This includes uses of chemicals and their danger signs, production techniques, and disposal methods.

Frame Wirers, Central Office

- Education/Training Required: Postsecondary vocational training
- Annual Earnings: $49,840
- Growth: –0.6%
- Annual Job Openings: 23,000
- Self-Employed: 4.6%
- Part-Time: 1.7%

Connect wires from telephone lines and cables to distributing frames in telephone company central office, using soldering iron and other hand tools. Solders connections, following diagram or oral instructions. Strings distributing frames with connecting wires. Tests circuit connections, using voltmeter or ammeter. Assists in locating and correcting malfunction in wiring on distributing frame. Lubricates moving switch parts. Cleans switches and replaces contact points, using vacuum hose, solvents, and hand tools. Removes and remakes connections to change circuit layouts. **SKILLS**—**Installation:** Installing equipment, machines, wiring, or programs to meet specifications. **Repairing:** Repairing machines or systems by using the needed tools. **Quality Control Analysis:** Conducting tests and inspections of products, services, or processes to evaluate quality or performance. **Troubleshooting:** Determining causes of operating errors and deciding what to do about them. **Operation Monitoring:** Watching gauges, dials, or other indicators to make sure a machine is working properly. **Equipment Maintenance:** Performing routine maintenance on equipment and determining when and what kind of maintenance is needed. **GOE**—**Interest Area:** 02. Architecture and Construction. **Work Group:** 02.05. Systems and Equipment Installation, Maintenance, and Repair. **Other Jobs in This Work Group:** Central Office and PBX Installers and Repairers; Communication Equipment Mechanics, Installers, and Repairers; Electric Meter Installers and Repairers; Electrical and Electronics Repairers, Powerhouse, Substation, and Relay; Electrical Power-Line Installers and Repairers; Elevator Installers and Repairers; Heating and Air Conditioning Mechanics; Home Appliance Installers; Maintenance and Repair Workers, General; Meter

Mechanics; Refrigeration Mechanics; Station Installers and Repairers, Telephone; Telecommunications Facility Examiners; Telecommunications Line Installers and Repairers. **PERSONALITY TYPE:** Realistic. Realistic occupations frequently involve work activities that include practical, hands-on problems and solutions. These occupations often deal with plants, animals, and real-world materials like wood, tools, and machinery. Many of the occupations require working outside and do not involve a lot of paperwork or working closely with others.

EDUCATION/TRAINING PROGRAM(S)— Communications Systems Installation and Repair Technology. **RELATED KNOWLEDGE/COURSES**—**Telecommunications:** Knowledge of transmission, broadcasting, switching, control, and operation of telecommunications systems. **Engineering and Technology:** Knowledge of the practical application of engineering science and technology. This includes applying principles, techniques, procedures, and equipment to the design and production of various goods and services. **Mechanical Devices:** Knowledge of machines and tools, including their designs, uses, repair, and maintenance. **Physics:** Knowledge and prediction of physical principles and laws and their interrelationships and applications to understanding fluid, material, and atmospheric dynamics and mechanical, electrical, atomic, and subatomic structures and processes. **Design:** Knowledge of design techniques, tools, and principles involved in production of precision technical plans, blueprints, drawings, and models.

Freight Inspectors

- ◎ Education/Training Required: Work experience in a related occupation
- ◎ Annual Earnings: $50,380
- ◎ Growth: 7.7%
- ◎ Annual Job Openings: 5,000
- ◎ Self-Employed: 0.4%
- ◎ Part-Time: 3.2%

Inspect freight for proper storage according to specifications. Inspects shipment to ascertain that freight is securely braced and blocked. Observes loading of freight to ensure that crews comply with procedures. Monitors temperature and humidity of freight storage area. Records freight condition and handling and notifies crews to reload freight or insert additional bracing or packing. Measures height and width of loads that will pass over bridges or through tunnels. Notifies workers of special treatment required for shipments. Prepares and submits report after trip. Posts warning signs on vehicles containing explosives or inflammatory or radioactive materials. **SKILLS**—**Systems Analysis:** Determining how a system should work and how changes in conditions, operations, and the environment will affect outcomes. **GOE**—**Interest Area:** 16. Transportation, Distribution, and Logistics. **Work Group:** 16.07. Transportation Support Work. **Other Jobs in This Work Group:** Bridge and Lock Tenders; Cargo and Freight Agents; Cleaners of Vehicles and Equipment; Public Transportation Inspectors; Railroad Yard Workers; Stevedores, Except Equipment Operators; Traffic Technicians; Train Crew Members. **PERSONALITY TYPE:** Conventional. Conventional occupations frequently involve following set procedures and routines. These occupations can include working with data and details more than with ideas. Usually there is a clear line of authority to follow.

EDUCATION/TRAINING PROGRAM(S)—No data available. **RELATED KNOWLEDGE/COURSES**—**Transportation:** Knowledge of principles and methods for moving people or goods by air, rail, sea, or road, including the relative costs and benefits. **Public Safety and Security:** Knowledge of relevant equipment, policies, procedures, and strategies to promote effective local, state, or national security operations for the protection of people, data, property, and institutions. **Production and Processing:** Knowledge of raw materials, production processes, quality control, costs, and other techniques for maximizing the effective manufacture and distribution of goods. **Geography:** Knowledge of principles and methods for describing the features of land, sea, and air masses, including their physical characteristics; locations; interrelationships; and distribution of plant, animal, and human life.

Gaming Change Persons and Booth Cashiers

- Education/Training Required: Short-term on-the-job training
- Annual Earnings: $20,530
- Growth: 24.1%
- Annual Job Openings: 12,000
- Self-Employed: 1.0%
- Part-Time: 44.8%

Exchange coins and tokens for patrons' money. May issue payoffs and obtain customer's signature on receipt when winnings exceed the amount held in the slot machine. May operate a booth in the slot machine area and furnish change persons with money bank at the start of the shift or count and audit money in drawers. Count money and audit money drawers. Keep accurate records of monetary exchanges, authorization forms, and transaction reconciliations. Exchange money, credit, and casino chips and make change for customers. Work in and monitor an assigned area on the casino floor where slot machines are located. Listen for jackpot alarm bells and issue payoffs to winners. Maintain cage security according to rules. Obtain customers' signatures on receipts when winnings exceed the amount held in a slot machine. Reconcile daily summaries of transactions to balance books. Sell gambling chips, tokens, or tickets to patrons or to other workers for resale to patrons. Calculate the value of chips won or lost by players. Furnish change persons with a money bank at the start of each shift. Accept credit applications and verify credit references in order to provide check-cashing authorization or to establish house credit accounts. **SKILLS—Service Orientation:** Actively looking for ways to help people. **Time Management:** Managing one's own time and the time of others. **GOE—Interest Area:** 14. Retail and Wholesale Sales and Service. **Work Group:** 14.06. Customer Service. **Other Jobs in This Work Group:** Adjustment Clerks; Cashiers; Counter and Rental Clerks; Customer Service Representatives, Utilities; Order Clerks; Receptionists and Information Clerks. **PERSONALITY TYPE:** No data available.

EDUCATION/TRAINING PROGRAM(S)— Retailing and Retail Operations. **RELATED**

KNOWLEDGE/COURSES—Customer and Personal Service: Knowledge of principles and processes for providing customer and personal services. This includes customer needs assessment, meeting quality standards for services, and evaluation of customer satisfaction. **Public Safety and Security:** Knowledge of relevant equipment, policies, procedures, and strategies to promote effective local, state, or national security operations for the protection of people, data, property, and institutions. **Sales and Marketing:** Knowledge of principles and methods for showing, promoting, and selling products or services. This includes marketing strategy and tactics, product demonstrations, sales techniques, and sales control systems. **Engineering and Technology:** Knowledge of the practical application of engineering science and technology. This includes applying principles, techniques, procedures, and equipment to the design and production of various goods and services. **Administration and Management:** Knowledge of business and management principles involved in strategic planning, resource allocation, human resources modeling, leadership technique, production methods, and coordination of people and resources. **Economics and Accounting:** Knowledge of economic and accounting principles and practices, the financial markets, banking, and the analysis and reporting of financial data.

Gaming Dealers

- Education/Training Required: Postsecondary vocational training
- Annual Earnings: $14,340
- Growth: 24.7%
- Annual Job Openings: 26,000
- Self-Employed: 2.5%
- Part-Time: 16.3%

Operate table games. Stand or sit behind table and operate games of chance by dispensing the appropriate number of cards or blocks to players or operating other gaming equipment. Compare the house's hand against players' hands and pay off or collect players' money or chips. Exchange paper currency for playing chips or coin money. Pay winnings or collect losing bets as established by the rules and procedures of a specific game. Deal cards to house hands and compare these with players' hands to determine winners, as in blackjack. Conduct gambling games such as dice, roulette, cards, or keno, following all applicable rules and regulations. Check to ensure that all players have placed bets before play begins. Stand behind a gaming table and deal the appropriate number of cards to each player. Inspect cards and equipment to be used in games to ensure that they are in good condition. Start and control games and gaming equipment and announce winning numbers or colors. Open and close cash floats and game tables. Compute amounts of players' wins or losses or scan winning tickets presented by patrons to calculate the amount of money won. Apply rule variations to card games such as poker, in which players bet on the value of their hands. Receive, verify, and record patrons' cash wagers. Answer questions about game rules and casino policies. Refer patrons to gaming cashiers to collect winnings. Work as part of a team of dealers in games such as baccarat or craps. Participate in games for gambling establishments in order to provide the minimum complement of players at a table. Seat patrons at gaming tables. Prepare collection reports for submission to supervisors. Monitor gambling tables and supervise staff. Train new dealers. **SKILLS—Service Orientation:** Actively looking for ways to help people. **Speaking:** Talking to others to convey information effectively. **Social Perceptiveness:** Being aware of others' reactions and understanding why they react as they do. **Mathematics:** Using mathematics to solve problems. **Coordination:** Adjusting actions in relation to others' actions. **Critical Thinking:** Using logic and reasoning to identify the strengths and weaknesses of alternative solutions, conclusions, or approaches to problems. **Active Listening:** Giving full attention to what other people are saying, taking time to understand the points being made, asking questions as appropriate, and not interrupting at inappropriate times. **Learning Strategies:** Selecting and using training/instructional methods and procedures appropriate for the situation when learning or teaching new things. **Instructing:** Teaching others how to do something. **GOE—Interest Area:** 09. Hospitality, Tourism, and Recreation. **Work Group:** 09.02. Recreational Services. **Other Jobs in This Work Group:** Amusement and Recreation Attendants; Gaming and Sports Book Writers and Runners;

Locker Room, Coatroom, and Dressing Room Attendants; Motion Picture Projectionists; Recreation Workers; Slot Key Persons; Ushers, Lobby Attendants, and Ticket Takers. **PERSONALITY TYPE:** Enterprising. Enterprising occupations frequently involve starting up and carrying out projects. These occupations can involve leading people and making many decisions. They sometimes require risk taking and often deal with business.

EDUCATION/TRAINING PROGRAM(S)— No data available. **RELATED KNOWLEDGE/ COURSES—Customer and Personal Service:** Knowledge of principles and processes for providing customer and personal services. This includes customer needs assessment, meeting quality standards for services, and evaluation of customer satisfaction. **Psychology:** Knowledge of human behavior and performance; individual differences in ability, personality, and interests; learning and motivation; psychological research methods; and the assessment and treatment of behavioral and affective disorders. **Mathematics:** Knowledge of arithmetic, algebra, geometry, calculus, and statistics and their applications. **Sales and Marketing:** Knowledge of principles and methods for showing, promoting, and selling products or services. This includes marketing strategy and tactics, product demonstrations, sales techniques, and sales control systems. **Economics and Accounting:** Knowledge of economic and accounting principles and practices, the financial markets, banking, and the analysis and reporting of financial data. **Law and Government:** Knowledge of laws, legal codes, court procedures, precedents, government regulations, executive orders, agency rules, and the democratic political process.

Gaming Supervisors

- ◎ Education/Training Required: Postsecondary vocational training
- ◎ Annual Earnings: $40,840
- ◎ Growth: 15.7%
- ◎ Annual Job Openings: 6,000
- ◎ Self-Employed: 33.8%
- ◎ Part-Time: 15.2%

Supervise gaming operations and personnel in an assigned area. Circulate among tables and observe operations. Ensure that stations and games are covered for each shift. May explain and interpret operating rules of house to patrons. May plan and organize activities and create friendly atmosphere for guests in hotels/casinos. May adjust service complaints. Monitor game operations to ensure that house rules are followed; that tribal, state, and federal regulations are adhered to; and that employees provide prompt and courteous service. Observe gamblers' behavior for signs of cheating such as marking, switching, or counting cards; notify security staff of suspected cheating. Maintain familiarity with the games at a facility and with strategies and tricks used by cheaters at such games. Perform paperwork required for monetary transactions. Resolve customer and employee complaints. Greet customers and ask about the quality of service they are receiving. Establish and maintain banks and table limits for each game. Monitor stations and games and move dealers from game to game to ensure adequate staffing. Report customer-related incidents occurring in gaming areas to supervisors. Explain and interpret house rules, such as game rules and betting limits, for patrons. Supervise the distribution of complimentary meals, hotel rooms, discounts, and other items given to players based on length of play and amount bet. Evaluate workers' performance and prepare written performance evaluations. Monitor patrons for signs of compulsive gambling, offering assistance if necessary. Record, issue receipts for, and pay off bets. Monitor and verify the counting, wrapping, weighing, and distribution of currency and coins. Direct workers compiling summary sheets for each race or event to record amounts wagered and amounts to be paid to winners. Determine how many gaming tables to open each day and schedule staff accordingly. Establish policies on types of gambling offered, odds, and extension of credit. Interview, hire, and train workers. Provide fire protection and first-aid assistance when necessary. Review operational expenses, budget estimates, betting accounts, and collection reports for accuracy. **SKILLS—Instructing:** Teaching others how to do something. **Management of Personnel Resources:** Motivating, developing, and directing people as they work, identifying the best people for the job. **Social Perceptiveness:** Being aware of others' reactions and understanding why they react as they do. **Service Orientation:** Actively looking for ways to help people. **Monitoring:** Monitoring or assessing your performance or that of other individuals or organizations to make improvements or take corrective action. **Critical Thinking:** Using logic and reasoning to identify the strengths and weaknesses of alternative solutions, conclusions, or approaches to problems. **Learning Strategies:** Selecting and using training/instructional methods and procedures appropriate for the situation when learning or teaching new things. **Persuasion:** Persuading others to change their minds or behavior. **GOE—Interest Area:** 09. Hospitality, Tourism, and Recreation. **Work Group:** 09.01. Managerial Work in Hospitality and Tourism. **Other Jobs in This Work Group:** First-Line Supervisors/Managers of Food Preparation and Serving Workers; First-Line Supervisors/Managers of Personal Service Workers; Food Service Managers; Gaming Managers; Lodging Managers. **PERSONALITY TYPE:** Enterprising. Enterprising occupations frequently involve starting up and carrying out projects. These occupations can involve leading people and making many decisions. They sometimes require risk taking and often deal with business.

EDUCATION/TRAINING PROGRAM(S)— No data available. **RELATED KNOWLEDGE/ COURSES—Customer and Personal Service:** Knowledge of principles and processes for providing customer and personal services. This includes customer needs assessment, meeting quality standards for services, and evaluation of customer satisfaction. **Psychology:** Knowledge of human behavior and performance; individual differences in ability, personality, and interests; learning and motivation; psychological research methods; and the assessment and treatment of behavioral and affective disorders. **Education and Training:** Knowledge of principles and methods for curriculum and training design, teaching and instruction for individuals and groups, and the measurement of training effects. **Mathematics:** Knowledge of arithmetic, algebra, geometry, calculus, and statistics and their applications. **Law and Government:** Knowledge of laws, legal codes, court procedures, precedents, government regulations, executive orders, agency rules, and the democratic political process. **Administration and Management:** Knowledge of business and management principles involved in strategic planning, resource allocation, human resources modeling, leadership technique, production methods, and coordination of people and resources. **Personnel and Human Resources:** Knowledge of principles and procedures for personnel recruitment, selection, training, compensation and benefits, labor relations and negotiation, and personnel information systems.

Glaziers

- Education/Training Required: Long-term on-the-job training
- Annual Earnings: $32,650
- Growth: 17.2%
- Annual Job Openings: 7,000
- Self-Employed: 5.6%
- Part-Time: 3.1%

Install glass in windows, skylights, store fronts, and display cases or on surfaces such as building fronts, interior walls, ceilings, and tabletops. Cut and attach mounting strips, metal or wood moldings, rubber gaskets, or metal clips to surfaces in preparation for mirror installation. Secure mirrors in position, using mastic cement, putty, bolts, or screws. Cut and remove broken glass prior to installing replacement glass. Cut, fit, install, repair, and replace glass and glass substitutes, such as plastic and aluminum, in building interiors or exteriors and in furniture or other products. Determine plumb of walls or ceilings, using plumb lines and levels. Fasten glass panes into wood sashes or frames with clips, points, or moldings, adding weather seals or putty around pane edges to seal joints. Grind and polish glass and smooth edges when necessary. Measure and mark outlines or patterns on glass to indicate cutting lines. Score glass with cutters' wheels, breaking off excess glass by hand or with notched tools. Measure mirrors and dimensions of areas to be covered in order to determine work procedures. Measure, cut, fit, and press anti-glare adhesive film to glass or spray glass with tinting solution to prevent light glare. Pack spaces between moldings and glass with glazing compounds and trim excess material with glazing knives. Prepare glass for cutting by resting it on rack edges or against cutting tables and brushing thin layer of oil along cutting lines or dipping cutting tools in oil. Read and interpret blueprints and specifications to determine size, shape, color, type, and thickness of glass; location of framing; installation procedures; and staging and scaffolding materials required. Select the type and color of glass or mirror according to specifications. Assemble and cement sections of stained glass together. Assemble, erect, and dismantle scaffolds, rigging, and hoisting equipment. Confer with customers to determine project requirements and to provide cost estimates. Create patterns on glass by etching, sandblasting, or painting designs. Cut, assemble, fit, and attach metal-framed glass enclosures for showers, bathtubs, display cases, skylights, solariums, and other structures. Drive trucks to installation sites and unload mirrors, glass equipment, and tools. **SKILLS—Installation:** Installing equipment, machines, wiring, or programs to meet specifications. **Technology Design:** Generating or adapting equipment and technology to serve user needs. **Repairing:** Repairing machines or systems by using the needed tools. **Mathematics:** Using mathematics to solve problems. **GOE—Interest Area:** 02. Architecture and Construction. **Work Group:** 02.04. Construction Crafts. **Other Jobs in This Work Group:** Boat Builders and Shipwrights; Boilermakers; Brattice Builders; Brickmasons and Blockmasons; Carpet Installers; Ceiling Tile Installers; Cement Masons and Concrete Finishers; Commercial Divers; Construction Carpenters; Crane and Tower Operators; Dragline Operators; Drywall Installers; Electricians; Fence Erectors; Floor Layers, Except Carpet, Wood, and Hard Tiles; Floor Sanders and Finishers; Grader, Bulldozer, and Scraper Operators; Hazardous Materials Removal Workers; Insulation Workers, Floor, Ceiling, and Wall; Insulation Workers, Mechanical; Manufactured Building and Mobile Home Installers; Operating Engineers; Painters, Construction and Maintenance; Paperhangers; Paving, Surfacing, and Tamping Equipment Operators; Pile-Driver Operators; Pipe Fitters; Pipelayers; Pipelaying Fitters; Plasterers and Stucco Masons; Plumbers; Rail-Track Laying and Maintenance Equipment Operators; Refractory Materials Repairers, Except Brickmasons; Reinforcing Iron and Rebar Workers; Riggers; Roofers; Rough Carpenters; Security and Fire Alarm Systems Installers; Segmental Pavers; Sheet Metal Workers; Ship Carpenters and Joiners; Stone Cutters and

Carvers; Stonemasons; Structural Iron and Steel Workers; Tapers; Terrazzo Workers and Finishers; Tile and Marble Setters. **PERSONALITY TYPE:** Realistic. Realistic occupations frequently involve work activities that include practical, hands-on problems and solutions. These occupations often deal with plants, animals, and real-world materials like wood, tools, and machinery. Many of the occupations require working outside and do not involve a lot of paperwork or working closely with others.

EDUCATION/TRAINING PROGRAM(S)— Glazier. **RELATED KNOWLEDGE/COURSES— Building and Construction:** Knowledge of the materials, methods, and tools involved in the construction or repair of houses, buildings, or other structures such as highways and roads. **Production and Processing:** Knowledge of raw materials, production processes, quality control, costs, and other techniques for maximizing the effective manufacture and distribution of goods. **Design:** Knowledge of design techniques, tools, and principles involved in production of precision technical plans, blueprints, drawings, and models. **Engineering and Technology:** Knowledge of the practical application of engineering science and technology. This includes applying principles, techniques, procedures, and equipment to the design and production of various goods and services. **Geography:** Knowledge of principles and methods for describing the features of land, sea, and air masses, including their physical characteristics; locations; interrelationships; and distribution of plant, animal, and human life.

Government Property Inspectors and Investigators

- ◎ Education/Training Required: Long-term on-the-job training
- ◎ Annual Earnings: $47,390
- ◎ Growth: 9.8%
- ◎ Annual Job Openings: 20,000
- ◎ Self-Employed: 0.9%
- ◎ Part-Time: 5.3%

Investigate or inspect government property to ensure compliance with contract agreements and government regulations. Collect, identify, evaluate, and preserve case evidence. Examine records, reports, and documents in order to establish facts and detect discrepancies. Inspect government-owned equipment and materials in the possession of private contractors in order to ensure compliance with contracts and regulations and to prevent misuse. Inspect manufactured or processed products to ensure compliance with contract specifications and legal requirements. Locate and interview plaintiffs, witnesses, or representatives of business or government in order to gather facts relevant to inspections or alleged violations. Prepare correspondence, reports of inspections or investigations, and recommendations for action. Recommend legal or administrative action to protect government property. Submit samples of products to government laboratories for testing as required. Coordinate with and assist law enforcement agencies in matters of mutual concern. Investigate applications for special licenses or permits, as well as alleged license or permit violations. Testify in court or at administrative proceedings concerning investigation findings. Monitor investigations of suspected offenders to ensure that they are conducted in accordance with constitutional requirements. **SKILLS—Systems Analysis:** Determining how a system should work and how changes in conditions, operations, and the environment will affect outcomes. **Negotiation:** Bringing others together and trying to reconcile differences. **Speaking:** Talking to others to convey information effectively. **Judgment and Decision Making:** Considering the relative costs and benefits of potential actions to choose the most appropriate one. **Writing:** Communicating effectively in writing as appropriate for the needs of the audience. **Reading Comprehension:** Understanding written sentences and paragraphs in work-related documents. **Critical Thinking:** Using logic and reasoning to identify the strengths and weaknesses of alternative solutions, conclusions, or approaches to problems. **Systems Evaluation:** Identifying measures or indicators of system performance and the actions needed to improve or correct performance relative to the goals of the system. **GOE—Interest Area:** 07. Government and Public Administration. **Work Group:** 07.03. Regulations Enforcement. **Other Jobs in This Work Group:** Agricultural Inspectors; Aviation Inspectors; Child Support, Missing Persons, and Unemployment Insurance Fraud Investigators; Environmental Compliance Inspectors; Equal Opportunity Representatives and Officers; Financial Examiners; Fire Inspectors; Fish and Game Wardens; Forest Fire Inspectors and Prevention Specialists; Immigration and Customs Inspectors; Licensing Examiners and Inspectors; Marine Cargo Inspectors; Mechanical Inspectors; Motor Vehicle Inspectors; Nuclear Monitoring Technicians; Occupational Health and Safety Specialists; Pressure Vessel Inspectors; Railroad Inspectors; Tax Examiners, Collectors, and Revenue Agents. **PERSONALITY TYPE:** Enterprising. Enterprising occupations frequently involve starting up and carrying out projects. These occupations can involve leading people and making many decisions. They sometimes require risk taking and often deal with business.

EDUCATION/TRAINING PROGRAM(S)— No data available. **RELATED KNOWLEDGE/ COURSES—Law and Government:** Knowledge of laws, legal codes, court procedures, precedents, government regulations, executive orders, agency rules, and the democratic political process. **Personnel and Human Resources:** Knowledge of principles and procedures for personnel recruitment, selection, training, compensation and benefits, labor relations and negotiation, and personnel information systems. **Public Safety and Security:** Knowledge of relevant equipment, policies, procedures, and strategies to promote effective local, state, or national security operations for the protection of people, data, property, and institutions. **English Language:** Knowledge of the structure and content of the English language, including the meaning and spelling of words, rules of composition, and grammar. **Communications and Media:** Knowledge of media production, communication, and dissemination techniques and methods. This includes alternative ways to inform and entertain via written, oral, and visual media. **Production and Processing:** Knowledge of raw materials, production processes, quality control, costs, and other techniques for maximizing the effective manufacture and distribution of goods.

Grader, Bulldozer, and Scraper Operators

- Education/Training Required: Moderate-term on-the-job training
- Annual Earnings: $35,360
- Growth: 10.4%
- Annual Job Openings: 45,000
- Self-Employed: 3.7%
- Part-Time: 2.6%

Operate machines or vehicles equipped with blades to remove, distribute, level, or grade earth. Connects hydraulic hoses, belts, mechanical linkage, or power takeoff shaft to tractor. Starts engine; moves throttle, switches, and levers; and depresses pedals to operate machines, equipment, and attachments. Drives equipment in successive passes over working area to achieve specified result, such as grading terrain or removing, dumping, or spreading earth and rock. Aligns machine, cutterhead, or depth gauge marker with reference stakes and guidelines on ground or positions equipment, following hand signals of assistant. Fastens bulldozer blade or other attachment to tractor, using hitches. Greases, oils, and performs minor repairs on tractor, using grease gun, oilcans, and hand tools. Signals operator to guide movement of tractor-drawn machine. **SKILLS—Operation and Control:** Controlling operations of equipment or systems. **Repairing:** Repairing machines or systems by using the needed tools. **Operation Monitoring:** Watching gauges, dials, or other indicators to make sure a machine is working properly. **Equipment Selection:** Determining the kind of tools and equipment needed to do a job. **Equipment Maintenance:** Performing routine maintenance on equipment and determining when and what kind of maintenance is needed. **GOE—Interest Area:** 02. Architecture and Construction. **Work Group:** 02.04. Construction Crafts. **Other Jobs in This Work Group:** Boat Builders and Shipwrights; Boilermakers; Brattice Builders; Brickmasons and Blockmasons; Carpet Installers; Ceiling Tile Installers; Cement Masons and Concrete Finishers; Commercial Divers; Construction Carpenters; Crane and Tower Operators; Dragline Operators; Drywall Installers; Electricians; Fence Erectors; Floor Layers, Except Carpet, Wood, and Hard Tiles; Floor Sanders and Finishers; Glaziers; Hazardous Materials Removal Workers; Insulation Workers, Floor, Ceiling, and Wall; Insulation Workers, Mechanical; Manufactured Building and Mobile Home Installers; Operating Engineers; Painters, Construction and Maintenance; Paperhangers; Paving, Surfacing, and Tamping Equipment Operators; Pile-Driver Operators; Pipe Fitters; Pipelayers; Pipelaying Fitters; Plasterers and Stucco Masons; Plumbers; Rail-Track Laying and Maintenance Equipment Operators; Refractory Materials Repairers, Except Brickmasons; Reinforcing Iron and Rebar Workers; Riggers; Roofers; Rough Carpenters; Security and Fire Alarm Systems Installers; Segmental Pavers; Sheet Metal Workers; Ship Carpenters and Joiners; Stone Cutters and Carvers; Stonemasons; Structural Iron and Steel Workers; Tapers; Terrazzo Workers and Finishers; Tile and Marble Setters. **PERSONALITY TYPE:** Realistic. Realistic occupations frequently involve work activities that include practical, hands-on problems and solutions. These occupations often deal with plants, animals, and real-world materials like wood, tools, and machinery. Many of the occupations require working outside and do not involve a lot of paperwork or working closely with others.

EDUCATION/TRAINING PROGRAM(S)—Construction/Heavy Equipment/Earthmoving Equipment Operation; Mobil Crane Operation/Operator. **RELATED KNOWLEDGE/COURSES— Mechanical Devices:** Knowledge of machines and tools, including their designs, uses, repair, and maintenance. **Transportation:** Knowledge of principles and methods for moving people or goods by air, rail, sea, or road, including the relative costs and benefits. **Physics:** Knowledge and prediction of physical principles and laws and their interrelationships and applications to understanding fluid, material, and atmospheric dynamics and mechanical, electrical, atomic, and subatomic structures and processes.

Hairdressers, Hairstylists, and Cosmetologists

- ◎ Education/Training Required: Postsecondary vocational training
- ◎ Annual Earnings: $19,800
- ◎ Growth: 14.7%
- ◎ Annual Job Openings: 68,000
- ◎ Self-Employed: 44.3%
- ◎ Part-Time: 31.1%

Provide beauty services, such as shampooing, cutting, coloring, and styling hair and massaging and treating scalp. May also apply makeup, dress wigs, perform hair removal, and provide nail and skin care services. Keep work stations clean and sanitize tools such as scissors and combs. Cut, trim, and shape hair or hairpieces, based on customers' instructions, hair type, and facial features, using clippers, scissors, trimmers, and razors. Analyze patrons' hair and other physical features to determine and recommend beauty treatment or suggest hairstyles. Schedule client appointments. Bleach, dye, or tint hair, using applicator or brush. Update and maintain customer information records, such as beauty services provided. Shampoo, rinse, condition, and dry hair and scalp or hairpieces with water, liquid soap, or other solutions. Operate cash registers to receive payments from patrons. Demonstrate and sell hair care products and cosmetics. Develop new styles and techniques. Apply water or setting, straightening, or waving solutions to hair and use curlers, rollers, hot combs, and curling irons to press and curl hair. Comb, brush, and spray hair or wigs to set style. Shape eyebrows and remove facial hair, using depilatory cream, tweezers, electrolysis, or wax. Administer therapeutic medication and advise patron to seek medical treatment for chronic or contagious scalp conditions. Massage and treat scalp for hygienic and remedial purposes, using hands, fingers, or vibrating equipment. Shave, trim, and shape beards and moustaches. Train or supervise other hairstylists, hairdressers, and assistants. Recommend and explain the use of cosmetics, lotions, and creams to soften and lubricate skin and enhance and restore natural appearance. Give facials to patrons, using special compounds such as lotions and creams. Clean, shape, and polish fingernails and toenails, using files and nail polish. Apply artificial fingernails. **SKILLS—Learning Strategies:** Selecting and using training/instructional methods and procedures appropriate for the situation when learning or teaching new things. **Social Perceptiveness:** Being aware of others' reactions and understanding why they react as they do. **Time Management:** Managing one's own time and the time of others. **Management of Financial Resources:** Determining how money will be spent to get the work done and accounting for these expenditures. **Science:** Using scientific rules and methods to solve problems. **Service Orientation:** Actively looking for ways to help people. **Operations Analysis:** Analyzing needs and product requirements to create a design. **Persuasion:** Persuading others to change their minds or behavior. **Equipment Selection:** Determining the kind of tools and equipment needed to do a job. **GOE—Interest Area:** 09. Hospitality, Tourism, and Recreation. **Work Group:** 09.07. Barber and Beauty Services. **Other Jobs in This Work Group:** Barbers; Manicurists and Pedicurists; Shampooers; Skin Care Specialists. **PERSONALITY TYPE:** Enterprising. Enterprising occupations frequently involve starting up and carrying out projects. These occupations can involve leading people and making many decisions. They sometimes require risk taking and often deal with business.

EDUCATION/TRAINING PROGRAM(S)— Cosmetology and Related Personal Grooming Arts, Other; Cosmetology, Barber/Styling, and Nail Instructor; Cosmetology/Cosmetologist, General; Electrolysis/Electrology and Electrolysis Technician; Hair Styling/Stylist and Hair Design; Make-Up Artist/Specialist; Permanent Cosmetics/Makeup and Tattooing; Salon/Beauty Salon Management/Manager. **RELATED KNOWLEDGE/COURSES—Chemistry:** Knowledge of the chemical composition, structure, and properties of substances and of the chemical processes and transformations that they undergo. This includes uses of chemicals and their danger signs, production techniques, and disposal methods. **Customer and Personal Service:** Knowledge of principles and processes for providing customer and personal services. This includes customer needs assessment, meeting quality standards for services, and evaluation of customer satisfaction. **Sales and Marketing:** Knowledge

of principles and methods for showing, promoting, and selling products or services. This includes marketing strategy and tactics, product demonstrations, sales techniques, and sales control systems. **Education and Training:** Knowledge of principles and methods for curriculum and training design, teaching and instruction for individuals and groups, and the measurement of training effects. **Administration and Management:** Knowledge of business and management principles involved in strategic planning, resource allocation, human resources modeling, leadership technique, production methods, and coordination of people and resources. **Psychology:** Knowledge of human behavior and performance; individual differences in ability, personality, and interests; learning and motivation; psychological research methods; and the assessment and treatment of behavioral and affective disorders.

Hazardous Materials Removal Workers

- Education/Training Required: Moderate-term on-the-job training
- Annual Earnings: $33,320
- Growth: 43.1%
- Annual Job Openings: 8,000
- Self-Employed: 0%
- Part-Time: 5.7%

Identify, remove, pack, transport, or dispose of hazardous materials, including asbestos, lead-based paint, waste oil, fuel, transmission fluid, radioactive materials, contaminated soil, etc. Specialized training and certification in hazardous materials handling or a confined entry permit are generally required. May operate earth-moving equipment or trucks. Clean contaminated equipment or areas for re-use, using detergents and solvents, sandblasters, filter pumps, and steam cleaners. Drive trucks or other heavy equipment to convey contaminated waste to designated sea or ground locations. Follow prescribed safety procedures and comply with federal laws regulating waste disposal methods. Identify asbestos, lead, or other hazardous materials that need to be removed, using monitoring devices. Load and unload materials into containers and onto trucks, using hoists or forklifts. Mix and pour concrete into forms to encase waste material for disposal. Operate cranes to move and load baskets, casks, and canisters. Operate machines and equipment to remove, package, store, or transport loads of waste materials. Record numbers of containers stored at disposal sites and specify amounts and types of equipment and waste disposed. Apply chemical compounds to lead-based paint, allow compounds to dry, and then scrape the hazardous material into containers for removal and/or storage. Construct scaffolding or build containment areas prior to beginning abatement or decontamination work. Manipulate handgrips of mechanical arms to place irradiated fuel elements into baskets. Organize and track the locations of hazardous items in landfills. Package, store, and move irradiated fuel elements in the underwater storage basin of a nuclear reactor plant, using machines and equipment. Pull tram cars along underwater tracks and position cars to receive irradiated fuel elements; then pull loaded cars to mechanisms that automatically unload elements onto underwater tables. Remove asbestos and/or lead from surfaces, using hand and power tools such as scrapers, vacuums, and high-pressure sprayers. Unload baskets of irradiated elements onto packaging machines that automatically insert fuel elements into canisters and secure lids. **SKILLS**—No data available. **GOE**—**Interest Area:** 02. Architecture and Construction. **Work Group:** 02.04. Construction Crafts. **Other Jobs in This Work Group:** Boat Builders and Shipwrights; Boilermakers; Brattice Builders; Brickmasons and Blockmasons; Carpet Installers; Ceiling Tile Installers; Cement Masons and Concrete Finishers; Commercial Divers; Construction Carpenters; Crane and Tower Operators; Dragline Operators; Drywall Installers; Electricians; Fence Erectors; Floor Layers, Except Carpet, Wood, and Hard Tiles; Floor Sanders and Finishers; Glaziers; Grader, Bulldozer, and Scraper Operators; Insulation Workers, Floor, Ceiling, and Wall; Insulation Workers, Mechanical; Manufactured Building and Mobile Home Installers; Operating Engineers; Painters, Construction and Maintenance; Paperhangers; Paving, Surfacing, and Tamping Equipment Operators; Pile-Driver Operators; Pipe Fitters; Pipelayers; Pipelaying Fitters; Plasterers and Stucco Masons; Plumbers; Rail-Track Laying and Maintenance Equipment Operators; Refractory Materials Repairers, Except Brickmasons; Reinforcing Iron and Rebar Workers; Riggers; Roofers; Rough Carpenters; Security and Fire Alarm Systems Installers; Segmental Pavers; Sheet Metal Workers; Ship Carpenters and Joiners; Stone Cutters and Carvers; Stonemasons; Structural Iron and Steel Workers; Tapers; Terrazzo Workers and Finishers; Tile and Marble Setters. **PERSONALITY TYPE:** No data available.

EDUCATION/TRAINING PROGRAM(S)—Construction Trades, Other; Hazardous Materials Management and Waste Technology/Technician; Mechanic and Repair Technologies/Technicians, Other. **RELATED KNOWLEDGE/COURSES**—No data available.

Heating and Air Conditioning Mechanics

- Education/Training Required: Long-term on-the-job training
- Annual Earnings: $36,260
- Growth: 31.8%
- Annual Job Openings: 35,000
- Self-Employed: 15.4%
- Part-Time: 3.1%

Install, service, and repair heating and air conditioning systems in residences and commercial establishments. Obtain and maintain required certification(s). Comply with all applicable standards, policies, and procedures, including safety procedures and the maintenance of a clean work area. Repair or replace defective equipment, components, or wiring. Test electrical circuits and components for continuity, using electrical test equipment. Reassemble and test equipment following repairs. Inspect and test system to verify system compliance with plans and specifications and to detect and locate malfunctions. Discuss heating-cooling system malfunctions with users to isolate problems or to verify that malfunctions have been corrected. Record and report all faults, deficiencies, and other unusual occurrences, as well as the time and materials expended on work orders. Test pipe or tubing joints and connections for leaks, using pressure gauge or soap-and-water solution. Adjust system controls to setting recommended by manufacturer to balance system, using hand tools. Recommend, develop, and perform preventive and general maintenance procedures such as cleaning, power-washing, and vacuuming equipment; oiling parts; and changing filters. Lay out and connect electrical wiring between controls and equipment according to wiring diagram, using electrician's hand tools. Install auxiliary components to heating-cooling equipment, such as expansion and discharge valves, air ducts, pipes, blowers, dampers, flues, and stokers, following blueprints. Assist with other work in coordination with repair and maintenance teams. Install, connect, and adjust thermostats, humidistats and timers, using hand tools. Generate work orders that address deficiencies in need of correction. Join pipes or tubing to equipment and to fuel, water, or refrigerant source to form complete circuit. Assemble, position, and mount heating or cooling equipment, following blueprints. Study blueprints, design specifications, and manufacturers' recommendations to ascertain the configuration of heating or cooling equipment components and to ensure the proper installation of components. Cut and drill holes in floors, walls, and roof to install equipment, using power saws and drills. **SKILLS—Repairing:** Repairing machines or systems by using the needed tools. **Installation:** Installing equipment, machines, wiring, or programs to meet specifications. **Equipment Maintenance:** Performing routine maintenance on equipment and determining when and what kind of maintenance is needed. **Troubleshooting:** Determining causes of operating errors and deciding what to do about them. **Systems Evaluation:** Identifying measures or indicators of system performance and the actions needed to improve or correct performance relative to the goals of the system. **Coordination:** Adjusting actions in relation to others' actions. **Negotiation:** Bringing others together and trying to reconcile differences. **Persuasion:** Persuading others to change their minds or behavior. **GOE—Interest Area:** 02. Architecture and Construction. **Work Group:** 02.05. Systems and Equipment Installation, Maintenance, and Repair. **Other Jobs in This Work Group:** Central Office and PBX Installers and Repairers; Communication Equipment Mechanics, Installers, and Repairers; Electric Meter Installers and Repairers; Electrical and Electronics Repairers, Powerhouse, Substation, and

Relay; Electrical Power-Line Installers and Repairers; Elevator Installers and Repairers; Frame Wirers, Central Office; Home Appliance Installers; Maintenance and Repair Workers, General; Meter Mechanics; Refrigeration Mechanics; Station Installers and Repairers, Telephone; Telecommunications Facility Examiners; Telecommunications Line Installers and Repairers. **PERSONALITY TYPE:** Realistic. Realistic occupations frequently involve work activities that include practical, hands-on problems and solutions. These occupations often deal with plants, animals, and real-world materials like wood, tools, and machinery. Many of the occupations require working outside and do not involve a lot of paperwork or working closely with others.

EDUCATION/TRAINING PROGRAM(S)— Heating, Air Conditioning, and Refrigeration Technology/Technician (ACH/ACR/ACHR/HRAC/HVAC/AC Technology); Heating, Air Conditioning, Ventilation, and Refrigeration Maintenance Technology/Technician (HAC, HACR, HVAC, HVACR); Solar Energy Technology/Technician. **RELATED KNOWLEDGE/COURSES—Mechanical Devices:** Knowledge of machines and tools, including their designs, uses, repair, and maintenance. **Building and Construction:** Knowledge of the materials, methods, and tools involved in the construction or repair of houses, buildings, or other structures such as highways and roads. **Design:** Knowledge of design techniques, tools, and principles involved in production of precision technical plans, blueprints, drawings, and models. **Engineering and Technology:** Knowledge of the practical application of engineering science and technology. This includes applying principles, techniques, procedures, and equipment to the design and production of various goods and services. **Physics:** Knowledge and prediction of physical principles and laws and their interrelationships and applications to understanding fluid, material, and atmospheric dynamics and mechanical, electrical, atomic, and subatomic structures and processes. **Customer and Personal Service:** Knowledge of principles and processes for providing customer and personal services. This includes customer needs assessment, meeting quality standards for services, and evaluation of customer satisfaction.

Helpers—Electricians

- Education/Training Required: Short-term on-the-job training
- Annual Earnings: $23,420
- Growth: 17.9%
- Annual Job Openings: 17,000
- Self-Employed: 0.4%
- Part-Time: 13.2%

Help electricians by performing duties of lesser skill. Duties include using, supplying or holding materials or tools and cleaning work area and equipment. Trace out short circuits in wiring, using test meter. Measure, cut, and bend wire and conduit, using measuring instruments and hand tools. Maintain tools, vehicles, and equipment and keep parts and supplies in order. Drill holes and pull or push wiring through openings, using hand and power tools. Perform semi-skilled and unskilled laboring duties related to the installation, maintenance, and repair of a wide variety of electrical systems and equipment. Disassemble defective electrical equipment, replace defective or worn parts, and reassemble equipment, using hand tools. Transport tools, materials, equipment, and supplies to work site by hand; handtruck; or heavy, motorized truck. Examine electrical units for loose connections and broken insulation and tighten connections, using hand tools. Strip insulation from wire ends, using wire-stripping pliers, and attach wires to terminals for subsequent soldering. Thread conduit ends, connect couplings, and fabricate and secure conduit support brackets, using hand tools. Construct controllers and panels, using power drills, drill presses, taps, saws, and punches. String transmission lines or cables through ducts or conduits, under the ground, through equipment, or to towers. Clean work area and wash parts. Erect electrical system components and barricades and rig scaffolds, hoists, and shoring. Install copper-clad ground rods, using a manual post driver. Raise, lower, or position equipment, tools, and materials, using hoist, hand line, or block and tackle. Dig trenches or holes for installation of conduit or supports. Requisition materials, using warehouse requisition or release forms. Bolt component parts together to form tower assemblies, using hand tools. Paint a variety of objects related to electrical functions. Operate cutting torches and welding equipment while working with conduit and metal components to construct devices associated with electrical functions. **SKILLS—Installation:** Installing equipment, machines, wiring, or programs to meet specifications. **Troubleshooting:** Determining causes of operating errors and deciding what to do about them. **Repairing:** Repairing machines or systems by using the needed tools. **Complex Problem Solving:** Identifying complex problems and reviewing related information to develop and evaluate options and implement solutions. **Mathematics:** Using mathematics to solve problems. **Equipment Selection:** Determining the kind of tools and equipment needed to do a job. **Instructing:** Teaching others how to do something. **Critical Thinking:** Using logic and reasoning to identify the strengths and weaknesses of alternative solutions, conclusions, or approaches to problems. **Learning Strategies:** Selecting and using training/instructional methods and procedures appropriate for the situation when learning or teaching new things. **Time Management:** Managing one's own time and the time of others. **GOE—Interest Area:** 02. Architecture and Construction. **Work Group:** 02.06. Construction Support/Labor. **Other Jobs in This Work Group:** Carpenter Assemblers and Repairers; Construction Laborers; Grips and Set-Up Workers, Motion Picture Sets, Studios, and Stages; Helpers—Brickmasons, Blockmasons, Stonemasons, and Tile and Marble Setters; Helpers—Carpenters; Helpers—Installation, Maintenance, and Repair Workers; Helpers—Painters, Paperhangers, Plasterers, and Stucco Masons; Helpers—Pipelayers, Plumbers, Pipefitters, and Steamfitters; Highway Maintenance Workers; Septic Tank Servicers and Sewer Pipe Cleaners. **PERSONALITY TYPE:** Realistic. Realistic occupations frequently involve work activities that include practical, hands-on problems and solutions. These occupations often deal with plants, animals, and real-world materials like wood, tools, and machinery. Many of the occupations require working outside and do not involve a lot of paperwork or working closely with others.

EDUCATION/TRAINING PROGRAM(S)—Electrician. **RELATED KNOWLEDGE/COURSES—Building and Construction:** Knowledge of the materials, methods, and tools involved in the construction or repair of houses, buildings, or other structures such as highways and roads. **Mechanical Devices:** Knowledge of machines and tools, including their designs, uses, repair, and maintenance. **Design:** Knowledge of design techniques, tools, and principles involved in production of precision technical plans, blueprints, drawings, and models. **Public Safety and Security:** Knowledge of relevant equipment, policies, procedures, and strategies to promote effective local, state, or national security operations for the protection of people, data, property, and institutions. **Mathematics:** Knowledge of arithmetic, algebra, geometry, calculus, and statistics and their applications. **Engineering and Technology:** Knowledge of the practical application of engineering science and technology. This includes applying principles, techniques, procedures, and equipment to the design and production of various goods and services.

Helpers—Installation, Maintenance, and Repair Workers

- Education/Training Required: Short-term on-the-job training
- Annual Earnings: $21,310
- Growth: 20.3%
- Annual Job Openings: 33,000
- Self-Employed: 0%
- Part-Time: 19.2%

Help installation, maintenance, and repair workers in maintenance, parts replacement, and repair of vehicles, industrial machinery, and electrical and electronic equipment. Perform duties such as furnishing tools, materials, and supplies to other workers; cleaning work area, machines, and tools; and holding materials or tools for other workers. Tend and observe equipment and machinery in order to verify efficient and safe operation. Examine and test machinery, equipment, components, and parts for defects and to ensure proper functioning. Adjust, connect, or disconnect wiring, piping, tubing, and other parts, using hand tools or power tools. Install or replace machinery, equipment, and new or replacement parts and instru-

ments, using hand tools or power tools. Clean or lubricate vehicles, machinery, equipment, instruments, tools, work areas, and other objects, using hand tools, power tools, and cleaning equipment. Apply protective materials to equipment, components, and parts in order to prevent defects and corrosion. Transfer tools, parts, equipment, and supplies to and from work stations and other areas. Disassemble broken or defective equipment in order to facilitate repair; reassemble equipment when repairs are complete. Assemble and maintain physical structures, using hand tools or power tools. Provide assistance to more-skilled workers involved in the adjustment, maintenance, part replacement, and repair of tools, equipment, and machines. Position vehicles, machinery, equipment, physical structures, and other objects for assembly or installation, using hand tools, power tools, and moving equipment. Hold or supply tools, parts, equipment, and supplies for other workers. Prepare work stations so mechanics and repairers can conduct work. **SKILLS— Installation:** Installing equipment, machines, wiring, or programs to meet specifications. **Operation Monitoring:** Watching gauges, dials, or other indicators to make sure a machine is working properly. **Repairing:** Repairing machines or systems by using the needed tools. **Equipment Maintenance:** Performing routine maintenance on equipment and determining when and what kind of maintenance is needed. **Troubleshooting:** Determining causes of operating errors and deciding what to do about them. **Operations Analysis:** Analyzing needs and product requirements to create a design. **Persuasion:** Persuading others to change their minds or behavior. **Operation and Control:** Controlling operations of equipment or systems. **GOE—Interest Area:** 02. Architecture and Construction. **Work Group:** 02.06. Construction Support/Labor. **Other Jobs in This Work Group:** Carpenter Assemblers and Repairers; Construction Laborers; Grips and Set-Up Workers, Motion Picture Sets, Studios, and Stages; Helpers—Brickmasons, Blockmasons, Stonemasons, and Tile and Marble Setters; Helpers—Carpenters; Helpers—Electricians; Helpers—Painters, Paperhangers, Plasterers, and Stucco Masons; Helpers—Pipelayers, Plumbers, Pipefitters, and Steamfitters; Highway Maintenance Workers; Septic Tank Servicers and Sewer Pipe Cleaners. **PERSONALITY TYPE:** Realistic. Realistic occupations frequently involve work activities that include practical, hands-on problems and solutions. These occupations often deal with plants, animals, and real-world materials like wood, tools, and machinery. Many of the occupations require working outside and do not involve a lot of paperwork or working closely with others.

EDUCATION/TRAINING PROGRAM(S)— Industrial Mechanics and Maintenance Technology. **RELATED KNOWLEDGE/COURSES—Mechanical Devices:** Knowledge of machines and tools, including their designs, uses, repair, and maintenance. **Engineering and Technology:** Knowledge of the practical application of engineering science and technology. This includes applying principles, techniques, procedures, and equipment to the design and production of various goods and services. **Design:** Knowledge of design techniques, tools, and principles involved in production of precision technical plans, blueprints, drawings, and models. **Chemistry:** Knowledge of the chemical composition, structure, and properties of substances and of the chemical processes and transformations that they undergo. This includes uses of chemicals and their danger signs, production techniques, and disposal methods. **Building and Construction:** Knowledge of the materials, methods, and tools involved in the construction or repair of houses, buildings, or other structures such as highways and roads. **Public Safety and Security:** Knowledge of relevant equipment, policies, procedures, and strategies to promote effective local, state, or national security operations for the protection of people, data, property, and institutions.

Highway Maintenance Workers

- Education/Training Required: Moderate-term on-the-job training
- Annual Earnings: $29,550
- Growth: 10.4%
- Annual Job Openings: 25,000
- Self-Employed: 1.6%
- Part-Time: 1.8%

Maintain highways, municipal and rural roads, airport runways, and rights-of-way. Duties include patching broken or eroded pavement, repairing guard rails, highway markers, and snow fences. May also mow or clear brush from along road or plow snow from roadway. Flag motorists to warn them of obstacles or repair work ahead. Set out signs and cones around work areas to divert traffic. Drive trucks or tractors with adjustable attachments to sweep debris from paved surfaces, mow grass and weeds, and remove snow and ice. Dump, spread, and tamp asphalt, using pneumatic tampers, to repair joints and patch broken pavement. Drive trucks to transport crews and equipment to work sites. Inspect, clean, and repair drainage systems, bridges, tunnels, and other structures. Haul and spread sand, gravel, and clay to fill washouts and repair road shoulders. Erect, install, or repair guardrails, road shoulders, berms, highway markers, warning signals, and highway lighting, using hand tools and power tools. Remove litter and debris from roadways, including debris from rock and mud slides. Clean and clear debris from culverts, catch basins, drop inlets, ditches, and other drain structures. Perform roadside landscaping work, such as clearing weeds and brush and planting and trimming trees. Paint traffic control lines and place pavement traffic messages by hand or using machines. Inspect markers to verify accurate installation. Apply poisons along roadsides and in animal burrows to eliminate unwanted roadside vegetation and rodents. Measure and mark locations for installation of markers, using tape, string, or chalk. Apply oil to road surfaces, using sprayers. Blend compounds to form adhesive mixtures used for marker installation. Place and remove snow fences used to prevent the accumulation of drifting snow on highways. **SKILLS—Equipment Maintenance:** Performing routine maintenance on equipment and determining when and what kind of maintenance is needed. **Repairing:** Repairing machines or systems by using the needed tools. **Installation:** Installing equipment, machines, wiring, or programs to meet specifications. **Management of Material Resources:** Obtaining and seeing to the appropriate use of equipment, facilities, and materials needed to do certain work. **Troubleshooting:** Determining causes of operating errors and deciding what to do about them. **Management of Personnel Resources:** Motivating, developing, and directing people as they work, identifying the best people for the job. **Coordination:** Adjusting actions in relation to others' actions. **Instructing:** Teaching others how to do something. **GOE—Interest Area:** 02. Architecture and Construction. **Work Group:** 02.06. Construction Support/Labor. **Other Jobs in This Work Group:** Carpenter Assemblers and Repairers; Construction Laborers; Grips and Set-Up Workers, Motion Picture Sets, Studios, and Stages; Helpers—Brickmasons, Blockmasons, Stonemasons, and Tile and Marble Setters; Helpers—Carpenters; Helpers—Electricians; Helpers—Installation, Maintenance, and Repair Workers; Helpers—Painters, Paperhangers, Plasterers, and Stucco Masons; Helpers—Pipelayers, Plumbers, Pipefitters, and Steamfitters; Septic Tank Servicers and Sewer Pipe Cleaners. **PERSONALITY TYPE:** Realistic. Realistic occupations frequently involve work activities that include practical, hands-on problems and solutions. These occupations often deal with plants, animals, and real-world materials like wood, tools, and machinery. Many of the occupations require working outside and do not involve a lot of paperwork or working closely with others.

EDUCATION/TRAINING PROGRAM(S)—Construction/Heavy Equipment/Earthmoving Equipment Operation. **RELATED KNOWLEDGE/COURSES—Transportation:** Knowledge of principles and methods for moving people or goods by air, rail, sea, or road, including the relative costs and benefits. **Building and Construction:** Knowledge of the materials, methods, and tools involved in the construction or repair of houses, buildings, or other structures such as highways and roads. **Customer and Personal Service:** Knowledge of principles and processes for providing customer and personal services. This includes customer needs assessment, meeting quality standards for services, and evaluation of customer satisfaction. **Public Safety and Security:** Knowledge of relevant equipment, policies, procedures, and strategies to promote effective local, state, or national security operations for the protection of people, data, property, and institutions. **Mechanical Devices:** Knowledge of machines and tools, including their designs, uses, repair, and maintenance. **Geography:** Knowledge of principles and methods for describing the features of land, sea, and air masses, including their physical characteristics; locations; interrelationships; and distribution of plant, animal, and human life.

Highway Patrol Pilots

- Education/Training Required: Long-term on-the-job training
- Annual Earnings: $45,210
- Growth: 24.7%
- Annual Job Openings: 67,000
- Self-Employed: 0%
- Part-Time: 1.4%

Pilot aircraft to patrol highway and enforce traffic laws. Pilots airplane to maintain order, respond to emergencies, enforce traffic and criminal laws, and apprehend criminals. Investigates traffic accidents and other accidents to determine causes and to determine if crime was committed. Arrests perpetrator of criminal act or submits citation or warning to violator of motor vehicle ordinance. Informs ground personnel where to re-route traffic in case of emergencies. Informs ground personnel of traffic congestion or unsafe driving conditions to ensure traffic flow and reduce incidence of accidents. Reviews facts to determine if criminal act or statute violation was involved. Expedites processing of prisoners, prepares and maintains records of prisoner bookings, and maintains record of prisoner status during booking and pre-trial process. Prepares reports to document activities. Relays complaint and emergency request information to appropriate agency dispatcher. Evaluates complaint and emergency request information to determine response requirements. Renders aid to accident victims and other persons requiring first aid for physical injuries. Testifies in court to present evidence or act as witness in traffic and criminal cases. Records facts, photographs and diagrams crime or accident scene, and interviews witnesses to gather information for possible use in legal action or safety programs. **SKILLS—Operation and Control:** Controlling operations of equipment or systems. **Social Perceptiveness:** Being aware of others' reactions and understanding why they react as they do. **Service Orientation:** Actively looking for ways to help people. **Operation Monitoring:**

Watching gauges, dials, or other indicators to make sure a machine is working properly. **Judgment and Decision Making:** Considering the relative costs and benefits of potential actions to choose the most appropriate one. **Active Listening:** Giving full attention to what other people are saying, taking time to understand the points being made, asking questions as appropriate, and not interrupting at inappropriate times. **Critical Thinking:** Using logic and reasoning to identify the strengths and weaknesses of alternative solutions, conclusions, or approaches to problems. **Reading Comprehension:** Understanding written sentences and paragraphs in work-related documents. **GOE—Interest Area:** 12. Law and Public Safety. **Work Group:** 12.04. Law Enforcement and Public Safety. **Other Jobs in This Work Group:** Bailiffs; Correctional Officers and Jailers; Criminal Investigators and Special Agents; Fire Investigators; Forensic Science Technicians; Parking Enforcement Workers; Police Detectives; Police Identification and Records Officers; Police Patrol Officers; Sheriffs and Deputy Sheriffs; Transit and Railroad Police. **PERSONALITY TYPE:** Realistic. Realistic occupations frequently involve work activities that include practical, hands-on problems and solutions. These occupations often deal with plants, animals, and real-world materials like wood, tools, and machinery. Many of the occupations require working outside and do not involve a lot of paperwork or working closely with others.

EDUCATION/TRAINING PROGRAM(S)— Criminal Justice/Police Science; Criminalistics and Criminal Science. **RELATED KNOWLEDGE/ COURSES—Public Safety and Security:** Knowledge of relevant equipment, policies, procedures, and strategies to promote effective local, state, or national security operations for the protection of people, data, property, and institutions. **Transportation:** Knowledge of principles and methods for moving people or goods by air, rail, sea, or road, including the relative costs and benefits. **Law and Government:** Knowledge of laws, legal codes, court procedures, precedents, government regulations, executive orders, agency rules, and the democratic political process. **Customer and Personal Service:** Knowledge of principles and processes for providing customer and personal services. This includes customer needs assessment, meeting quality standards for services, and evaluation of customer satisfaction. **Medicine and Dentistry:** Knowledge of the information and techniques needed to diagnose and treat human injuries, diseases, and deformities. This includes symptoms, treatment alternatives, drug properties and interactions, and preventive health-care measures. **Psychology:** Knowledge of human behavior and performance; individual differences in ability, personality, and interests; learning and motivation; psychological research methods; and the assessment and treatment of behavioral and affective disorders.

Home Health Aides

- Education/Training Required: Short-term on-the-job training
- Annual Earnings: $18,330
- Growth: 48.1%
- Annual Job Openings: 141,000
- Self-Employed: 1.6%
- Part-Time: 21.9%

Provide routine, personal health care, such as bathing, dressing, or grooming, to elderly, convalescent, or disabled persons in the home of patients or in a residential care facility. Maintain records of patient care, condition, progress, and problems in order to report and discuss observations with a supervisor or case manager. Provide patients with help moving in and out of beds, baths, wheelchairs, or automobiles and with dressing and grooming. Provide patients and families with emotional support and instruction in areas such as infant care, preparing healthy meals, independent living, and adaptation to disability or illness. Change bed linens, wash and iron patients' laundry, and clean patients' quarters. Entertain, converse with, or read aloud to patients to keep them mentally healthy and alert. Plan, purchase, prepare, and serve meals to patients and other family members according to prescribed diets. Direct patients in simple prescribed exercises and in the use of braces or artificial limbs. Check patients' pulse, temperature, and respiration. Change dressings. Perform a variety of duties as requested by client, such as obtaining household supplies and running errands. Accompany clients to doctors' offices and on other trips outside the home, providing transportation, assistance, and companionship. Administer prescribed oral medications under written direction of physician or as directed by home care nurse and aide. Care for children who are disabled or who have sick or disabled parents. Massage patients and apply preparations and treatments such as liniment, alcohol rubs, and heat-lamp stimulation. **SKILLS—Social Perceptiveness:** Being aware of others' reactions and understanding why they react as they do. **Service Orientation:** Actively looking for ways to help people. **Reading Comprehension:** Understanding written sentences and paragraphs in work-related documents. **Writing:** Communicating effectively in writing as appropriate for the needs of the audience. **Instructing:** Teaching others how to do something. **Active Listening:** Giving full attention to what other people are saying, taking time to understand the points being made, asking questions as appropriate, and not interrupting at inappropriate times. **Learning Strategies:** Selecting and using training/instructional methods and procedures appropriate for the situation when learning or teaching new things. **Persuasion:** Persuading others to change their minds or behavior. **GOE—Interest Area:** 08. Health Science. **Work Group:** 08.08. Patient Care and Assistance. **Other Jobs in This Work Group:** Licensed Practical and Licensed Vocational Nurses; Nursing Aides, Orderlies, and Attendants; Psychiatric Aides; Psychiatric Technicians. **PERSONALITY TYPE:** Social. Social occupations frequently involve working with, communicating with, and teaching people. These occupations often involve helping or providing service to others.

EDUCATION/TRAINING PROGRAM(S)— Home Health Aide/Home Attendant. **RELATED KNOWLEDGE/COURSES—Medicine and Dentistry:** Knowledge of the information and techniques needed to diagnose and treat human injuries, diseases, and deformities. This includes symptoms, treatment alternatives, drug properties and interactions, and preventive health-care measures. **Psychology:** Knowledge of human behavior and performance; individual differences in ability, personality, and interests; learning and motivation; psychological research methods; and the assessment and treatment of behavioral and affective disorders. **Therapy and Counseling:** Knowledge of principles, methods, and procedures for diagnosis, treatment, and rehabilitation of physical and mental

dysfunctions and for career counseling and guidance. **Philosophy and Theology:** Knowledge of different philosophical systems and religions. This includes their basic principles, values, ethics, ways of thinking, customs, and practices and their impact on human culture. **Food Production:** Knowledge of techniques and equipment for planting, growing, and harvesting food products (both plant and animal) for consumption, including storage/handling techniques. **Public Safety and Security:** Knowledge of relevant equipment, policies, procedures, and strategies to promote effective local, state, or national security operations for the protection of people, data, property, and institutions.

Hosts and Hostesses, Restaurant, Lounge, and Coffee Shop

- ◎ Education/Training Required: Short-term on-the-job training
- ◎ Annual Earnings: $15,630
- ◎ Growth: 16.4%
- ◎ Annual Job Openings: 95,000
- ◎ Self-Employed: 0.6%
- ◎ Part-Time: 66.9%

Welcome patrons, seat them at tables or in lounge, and help ensure quality of facilities and service. Provide guests with menus. Greet guests and seat them at tables or in waiting areas. Assign patrons to tables suitable for their needs. Inspect dining and serving areas to ensure cleanliness and proper setup. Speak with patrons to ensure satisfaction with food and service and to respond to complaints. Receive and record patrons' dining reservations. Maintain contact with kitchen staff, management, serving staff, and customers to ensure that dining details are handled properly and customers' concerns are addressed. Inform patrons of establishment specialties and features. Direct patrons to coatrooms and waiting areas such as lounges. Operate cash registers to accept payments for food and beverages. Prepare cash receipts after establishments close and make bank deposits. Supervise and coordinate activities of dining room staff to ensure that patrons receive prompt and courteous service. Prepare staff work schedules. Order or requisition supplies and equipment for tables and serving stations. Hire, train, and supervise food and beverage service staff. Plan parties or other special events and services. Confer with other staff to help plan establishments' menus. Perform marketing and advertising services. **SKILLS— Service Orientation:** Actively looking for ways to help people. **Persuasion:** Persuading others to change their minds or behavior. **Instructing:** Teaching others how to do something. **Social Perceptiveness:** Being aware of others' reactions and understanding why they react as they do. **Learning Strategies:** Selecting and using training/instructional methods and procedures appropriate for the situation when learning or teaching new things. **Negotiation:** Bringing others together and trying to reconcile differences. **GOE—Interest Area:** 09. Hospitality, Tourism, and Recreation. **Work Group:** 09.05. Food and Beverage Service. **Other Jobs in This Work Group:** Bartenders; Combined Food Preparation and Serving Workers, Including Fast Food; Counter Attendants, Cafeteria, Food Concession, and Coffee Shop; Dining Room and Cafeteria Attendants and Bartender Helpers; Food Servers, Nonrestaurant; Waiters and Waitresses. **PERSONALITY TYPE:** Enterprising. Enterprising occupations frequently involve starting up and carrying out projects. These occupations can involve leading people and making many decisions. They sometimes require risk taking and often deal with business.

EDUCATION/TRAINING PROGRAM(S)— Food Service, Waiter/Waitress, and Dining Room Management/Manager. **RELATED KNOWLEDGE/ COURSES—Customer and Personal Service:** Knowledge of principles and processes for providing customer and personal services. This includes customer needs assessment, meeting quality standards for services, and evaluation of customer satisfaction. **Food Production:** Knowledge of techniques and equipment for planting, growing, and harvesting food products (both plant and animal) for consumption, including storage/handling techniques. **Sales and Marketing:** Knowledge of principles and methods for showing, promoting, and selling products or services. This includes marketing strategy and tactics, product demonstrations, sales techniques, and sales control systems. **Public Safety and Security:** Knowledge of relevant equipment, policies, procedures, and strategies to promote effective local, state, or national security operations for the protection of people, data, property, and institutions. **Administration and Management:** Knowledge of business and management principles involved in strategic planning, resource allocation, human resources modeling, leadership technique, production methods, and coordination of people and resources.

Hotel, Motel, and Resort Desk Clerks

- Education/Training Required: Short-term on-the-job training
- Annual Earnings: $17,700
- Growth: 23.9%
- Annual Job Openings: 46,000
- Self-Employed: 0%
- Part-Time: 27.2%

Accommodate hotel, motel, and resort patrons by registering and assigning rooms to guests, issuing room keys, transmitting and receiving messages, keeping records of occupied rooms and guests' accounts, making and confirming reservations, and presenting statements to and collecting payments from departing guests. Greet, register, and assign rooms to guests of hotels or motels. Verify customers' credit and establish how the customer will pay for the accommodation. Keep records of room availability and guests' accounts manually or by using computers. Compute bills, collect payments, and make change for guests. Perform simple bookkeeping activities such as balancing cash accounts. Issue room keys and escort instructions to bellhops. Review accounts and charges with guests during the checkout process. Post charges, such as those for rooms, food, liquor, or telephone calls, to ledgers manually or by using computers. Transmit and receive messages, using telephones or telephone switchboards. Contact housekeeping or maintenance staff when guests report problems. Make and confirm reservations. Answer inquiries pertaining to hotel services; registration of guests; and shopping, dining, entertainment, and travel directions. Record guest comments or complaints, referring customers to managers as necessary. Advise housekeeping staff when rooms have been vacated and are ready for cleaning. Arrange tours, taxis, and restaurants for customers. Deposit guests' valuables in hotel safes or safe-deposit boxes. Date-stamp, sort, and rack incoming mail and messages. **SKILLS—Service Orientation:** Actively looking for ways to help people. **Instructing:** Teaching others how to do something. **Learning Strategies:** Selecting and using training/instructional methods and procedures appropriate for the situation when learning or teaching new things. **Critical Thinking:** Using logic and reasoning to identify the strengths and weaknesses of alternative solutions, conclusions, or approaches to problems. **Social Perceptiveness:** Being aware of others' reactions and understanding why they react as they do. **Active Listening:** Giving full attention to what other people are saying, taking time to understand the points being made, asking questions as appropriate, and not interrupting at inappropriate times. **Persuasion:** Persuading others to change their minds or behavior. **Negotiation:** Bringing others together and trying to reconcile differences. **GOE—Interest Area:** 09. Hospitality, Tourism, and Recreation. **Work Group:** 09.03. Hospitality and Travel Services. **Other Jobs in This Work Group:** Baggage Porters and Bellhops; Concierges; Flight Attendants; Janitors and Cleaners, Except Maids and Housekeeping Cleaners; Maids and Housekeeping Cleaners; Reservation and Transportation Ticket Agents; Tour Guides and Escorts; Transportation Attendants, Except Flight Attendants and Baggage Porters; Travel Agents; Travel Clerks; Travel Guides. **PERSONALITY TYPE:** Conventional. Conventional occupations frequently involve following set procedures and routines. These occupations can include working with data and details more than with ideas. Usually there is a clear line of authority to follow.

EDUCATION/TRAINING PROGRAM(S)— Selling Skills and Sales Operations. **RELATED KNOWLEDGE/COURSES—Customer and Personal Service:** Knowledge of principles and processes for providing customer and personal services. This includes customer needs assessment, meeting quality standards for services, and evaluation of customer satisfaction. **Clerical Practices:** Knowledge of administrative and clerical procedures and systems such as word processing, managing files and records, stenography

and transcription, designing forms, and other office procedures and terminology. **Sales and Marketing:** Knowledge of principles and methods for showing, promoting, and selling products or services. This includes marketing strategy and tactics, product demonstrations, sales techniques, and sales control systems. **Computers and Electronics:** Knowledge of circuit boards, processors, chips, electronic equipment, and computer hardware and software, including applications and programming. **Administration and Management:** Knowledge of business and management principles involved in strategic planning, resource allocation, human resources modeling, leadership technique, production methods, and coordination of people and resources. **Economics and Accounting:** Knowledge of economic and accounting principles and practices, the financial markets, banking, and the analysis and reporting of financial data.

Housekeeping Supervisors

- ◎ Education/Training Required: Work experience in a related occupation
- ◎ Annual Earnings: $29,510
- ◎ Growth: 16.2%
- ◎ Annual Job Openings: 28,000
- ◎ Self-Employed: 5.6%
- ◎ Part-Time: 6.6%

Supervise work activities of cleaning personnel to ensure clean, orderly, and attractive rooms in hotels, hospitals, educational institutions, and similar establishments. Assign duties, inspect work, and investigate complaints regarding housekeeping service and equipment and take corrective action. May purchase housekeeping supplies and equipment, take periodic inventories, screen applicants, train new employees, and recommend dismissals. Assigns workers their duties and inspects work for conformance to prescribed standards of cleanliness. Investigates complaints regarding housekeeping service and equipment and takes corrective action. Obtains list of rooms to be cleaned immediately and list of prospective check-outs or discharges to prepare work assignments. Coordinates work activities among departments. Conducts orientation training and in-service training to explain policies and work procedures and to demonstrate use and maintenance of equipment. Inventories stock to ensure adequate supplies. Evaluates records to forecast department personnel requirements. Makes recommendations to improve service and ensure more efficient operation. Prepares reports concerning room occupancy, payroll, and department expenses. Selects and purchases new furnishings. Performs cleaning duties in cases of emergency or staff shortage. Examines building to determine need for repairs or replacement of furniture or equipment and makes recommendations to management. Attends staff meetings to discuss company policies and patrons' complaints. Issues supplies and equipment to workers. Establishes standards and procedures for work of housekeeping staff. Advises manager, desk clerk, or admitting personnel of rooms ready for occupancy. Records data regarding work assignments, personnel actions, and time cards and prepares periodic reports. Screens job applicants; hires new employees; and recommends promotions, transfers, and dismissals. **SKILLS—Management of Personnel Resources:** Motivating, developing, and directing people as they work, identifying the best people for the job. **Time Management:** Managing one's own time and the time of others. **Management of Material Resources:** Obtaining and seeing to the appropriate use of equipment, facilities, and materials needed to do certain work. **Management of Financial Resources:** Determining how money will be spent to get the work done and accounting for these expenditures. **Systems Analysis:** Determining how a system should work and how changes in conditions, operations, and the environment will affect outcomes. **Coordination:** Adjusting actions in relation to others' actions. **Systems Evaluation:** Identifying measures or indicators of system performance and the actions needed to improve or correct performance relative to the goals of the system. **Speaking:** Talking to others to convey information effectively. **GOE—Interest Area:** 04. Business and Administration. **Work Group:** 04.02. Managerial Work in Business Detail. **Other Jobs in This Work Group:** Administrative Services Managers; First-Line Supervisors, Administrative Support; First-Line Supervisors, Customer Service; Janitorial Supervisors; Meeting and Convention Planners. **PERSONALITY TYPE:** Enterprising. Enterprising occupations frequently involve starting up and carrying out projects.

These occupations can involve leading people and making many decisions. They sometimes require risk taking and often deal with business.

EDUCATION/TRAINING PROGRAM(S)—No data available. **RELATED KNOWLEDGE/COURSES—Personnel and Human Resources:** Knowledge of principles and procedures for personnel recruitment, selection, training, compensation and benefits, labor relations and negotiation, and personnel information systems. **Administration and Management:** Knowledge of business and management principles involved in strategic planning, resource allocation, human resources modeling, leadership technique, production methods, and coordination of people and resources. **Customer and Personal Service:** Knowledge of principles and processes for providing customer and personal services. This includes customer needs assessment, meeting quality standards for services, and evaluation of customer satisfaction. **Clerical Practices:** Knowledge of administrative and clerical procedures and systems such as word processing, managing files and records, stenography and transcription, designing forms, and other office procedures and terminology. **Education and Training:** Knowledge of principles and methods for curriculum and training design, teaching and instruction for individuals and groups, and the measurement of training effects. **Foreign Language:** Knowledge of the structure and content of a foreign (non-English) language, including the meaning and spelling of words, rules of composition and grammar, and pronunciation.

Human Resources Assistants, Except Payroll and Timekeeping

- ◎ Education/Training Required: Short-term on-the-job training
- ◎ Annual Earnings: $31,750
- ◎ Growth: 19.3%
- ◎ Annual Job Openings: 36,000
- ◎ Self-Employed: 0%
- ◎ Part-Time: 15.1%

Compile and keep personnel records. **Record data for each employee, such as address, weekly earnings, absences, amount of sales or production, supervisory reports on ability, and date of and reason for termination. Compile and type reports from employment records. File employment records. Search employee files and furnish information to authorized persons.** Explain company personnel policies, benefits, and procedures to employees or job applicants. Process, verify, and maintain documentation relating to personnel activities such as staffing, recruitment, training, grievances, performance evaluations, and classifications. Record data for each employee, including such information as addresses, weekly earnings, absences, amount of sales or production, supervisory reports on performance, and dates of and reasons for terminations. Process and review employment applications in order to evaluate qualifications or eligibility of applicants. Answer questions regarding examinations, eligibility, salaries, benefits, and other pertinent information. Examine employee files to answer inquiries and provide information for personnel actions. Gather personnel records from other departments and/or employees. Search employee files in order to obtain information for authorized persons and organizations, such as credit bureaus and finance companies. Interview job applicants to obtain and verify information used to screen and evaluate them. Request information from law enforcement officials, previous employers, and other references in order to determine applicants' employment acceptability. Compile and prepare reports and documents pertaining to personnel activities. Inform job applicants of their acceptance or rejection of employment. Select applicants meeting specified job requirements and refer them to hiring personnel. Arrange for in-house and external training activities. Arrange for advertising or posting of job vacancies and notify eligible workers of position availability. Provide assistance in administering employee benefit programs and worker's compensation plans. Prepare badges, passes, and identification cards and perform other security-related duties. Administer and score applicant and employee aptitude, personality, and interest assessment instruments. **SKILLS—Active Listening:** Giving full attention to what other people are saying, taking time to understand the points being made, asking questions as

appropriate, and not interrupting at inappropriate times. **Social Perceptiveness:** Being aware of others' reactions and understanding why they react as they do. **Management of Personnel Resources:** Motivating, developing, and directing people as they work, identifying the best people for the job. **Service Orientation:** Actively looking for ways to help people. **Time Management:** Managing one's own time and the time of others. **Writing:** Communicating effectively in writing as appropriate for the needs of the audience. **Speaking:** Talking to others to convey information effectively. **Instructing:** Teaching others how to do something. **GOE—Interest Area:** 04. Business and Administration. **Work Group:** 04.07. Records and Materials Processing. **Other Jobs in This Work Group:** Correspondence Clerks; File Clerks; Mail Clerks, Except Mail Machine Operators and Postal Service; Marking Clerks; Meter Readers, Utilities; Office Clerks, General; Order Fillers, Wholesale and Retail Sales; Postal Service Clerks; Postal Service Mail Sorters, Processors, and Processing Machine Operators; Procurement Clerks; Production, Planning, and Expediting Clerks; Shipping, Receiving, and Traffic Clerks; Stock Clerks, Sales Floor; Stock Clerks—Stockroom, Warehouse, or Storage Yard; Weighers, Measurers, Checkers, and Samplers, Recordkeeping. **PERSONALITY TYPE:** Conventional. Conventional occupations frequently involve following set procedures and routines. These occupations can include working with data and details more than with ideas. Usually there is a clear line of authority to follow.

EDUCATION/TRAINING PROGRAM(S)—General Office Occupations and Clerical Services. **RELATED KNOWLEDGE/COURSES—Clerical Practices:** Knowledge of administrative and clerical procedures and systems such as word processing, managing files and records, stenography and transcription, designing forms, and other office procedures and terminology. **Personnel and Human Resources:** Knowledge of principles and procedures for personnel recruitment, selection, training, compensation and benefits, labor relations and negotiation, and personnel information systems. **Customer and Personal Service:** Knowledge of principles and processes for providing customer and personal services. This includes customer needs assessment, meeting quality standards for services, and evaluation of customer satisfaction. **Computers and Electronics:** Knowledge of circuit boards, processors, chips, electronic equipment, and computer hardware and software, including applications and programming. **Education and Training:** Knowledge of principles and methods for curriculum and training design, teaching and instruction for individuals and groups, and the measurement of training effects. **English Language:** Knowledge of the structure and content of the English language, including the meaning and spelling of words, rules of composition, and grammar.

Immigration and Customs Inspectors

- ◉ Education/Training Required: Work experience in a related occupation
- ◉ Annual Earnings: $53,990
- ◉ Growth: 22.4%
- ◉ Annual Job Openings: 11,000
- ◉ Self-Employed: 0%
- ◉ Part-Time: 0.5%

Investigate and inspect persons, common carriers, goods, and merchandise arriving in or departing from the United States or moving between states to detect violations of immigration and customs laws and regulations. Detain persons found to be in violation of customs or immigration laws and arrange for legal action such as deportation. Determine duty and taxes to be paid on goods. Examine immigration applications, visas, and passports and interview persons in order to determine eligibility for admission, residence, and travel in the United States. Inspect cargo, baggage, and personal articles entering or leaving the United States for compliance with revenue laws and U.S. Customs Service regulations. Interpret and explain laws and regulations to travelers, prospective immigrants, shippers, and manufacturers. Investigate applications for duty refunds and petition for remission or mitigation of penalties when warranted. Locate and seize contraband; undeclared merchandise; and vehicles, aircraft, or boats that contain such merchandise. Record and report job-related activities, findings, transactions,

violations, discrepancies, and decisions. Collect samples of merchandise for examination, appraisal, or testing. Institute civil and criminal prosecutions and cooperate with other law enforcement agencies in the investigation and prosecution of those in violation of immigration or customs laws. Testify regarding decisions at immigration appeals or in federal court. **SKILLS—Writing:** Communicating effectively in writing as appropriate for the needs of the audience. **Speaking:** Talking to others to convey information effectively. **Negotiation:** Bringing others together and trying to reconcile differences. **Judgment and Decision Making:** Considering the relative costs and benefits of potential actions to choose the most appropriate one. **Systems Analysis:** Determining how a system should work and how changes in conditions, operations, and the environment will affect outcomes. **GOE—Interest Area:** 07. Government and Public Administration. **Work Group:** 07.03. Regulations Enforcement. **Other Jobs in This Work Group:** Agricultural Inspectors; Aviation Inspectors; Child Support, Missing Persons, and Unemployment Insurance Fraud Investigators; Environmental Compliance Inspectors; Equal Opportunity Representatives and Officers; Financial Examiners; Fire Inspectors; Fish and Game Wardens; Forest Fire Inspectors and Prevention Specialists; Government Property Inspectors and Investigators; Licensing Examiners and Inspectors; Marine Cargo Inspectors; Mechanical Inspectors; Motor Vehicle Inspectors; Nuclear Monitoring Technicians; Occupational Health and Safety Specialists; Pressure Vessel Inspectors; Railroad Inspectors; Tax Examiners, Collectors, and Revenue Agents. **PERSONALITY TYPE:** Conventional. Conventional occupations frequently involve following set procedures and routines. These occupations can include working with data and details more than with ideas. Usually there is a clear line of authority to follow.

EDUCATION/TRAINING PROGRAM(S)— Criminal Justice/Police Science; Criminalistics and Criminal Science. **RELATED KNOWLEDGE/ COURSES—Law and Government:** Knowledge of laws, legal codes, court procedures, precedents, government regulations, executive orders, agency rules, and the democratic political process. **Geography:** Knowledge of principles and methods for describing the features of land, sea, and air masses, including their physical characteristics; locations; interrelationships; and distribution of plant, animal, and human life. **Public Safety and Security:** Knowledge of relevant equipment, policies, procedures, and strategies to promote effective local, state, or national security operations for the protection of people, data, property, and institutions. **Transportation:** Knowledge of principles and methods for moving people or goods by air, rail, sea, or road, including the relative costs and benefits. **Foreign Language:** Knowledge of the structure and content of a foreign (non-English) language, including the meaning and spelling of words, rules of composition and grammar, and pronunciation. **Communications and Media:** Knowledge of media production, communication, and dissemination techniques and methods. This includes alternative ways to inform and entertain via written, oral, and visual media.

Industrial Engineering Technicians

- ◎ Education/Training Required: Associate degree
- ◎ Annual Earnings: $43,590
- ◎ Growth: 8.7%
- ◎ Annual Job Openings: 7,000
- ◎ Self-Employed: 0.4%
- ◎ Part-Time: 5.0%

Apply engineering theory and principles to problems of industrial layout or manufacturing production, usually under the direction of engineering staff. May study and record time, motion, method, and speed involved in performance of production, maintenance, clerical, and other worker operations for such purposes as establishing standard production rates or improving efficiency. Recommend revision to methods of operation, material handling, equipment layout, or other changes to increase production or improve standards. Study time, motion, methods, and speed involved in maintenance, production, and other operations to establish standard production rate and improve efficiency. Interpret engineering drawings, schematic diagrams, or formulas and confer with man-

agement or engineering staff to determine quality and reliability standards. Recommend modifications to existing quality or production standards to achieve optimum quality within limits of equipment capability. Aid in planning work assignments in accordance with worker performance, machine capacity, production schedules, and anticipated delays. Observe worker using equipment to verify that equipment is being operated and maintained according to quality assurance standards. Observe workers operating equipment or performing tasks to determine time involved and fatigue rate, using timing devices. Prepare charts, graphs, and diagrams to illustrate workflow, routing, floor layouts, material handling, and machine utilization. Evaluate data and write reports to validate or indicate deviations from existing standards. Read worker logs, product processing sheets, and specification sheets to verify that records adhere to quality assurance specifications. Prepare graphs or charts of data or enter data into computer for analysis. Record test data, applying statistical quality control procedures. Select products for tests at specified stages in production process and test products for performance characteristics and adherence to specifications. Compile and evaluate statistical data to determine and maintain quality and reliability of products. **SKILLS—Troubleshooting:** Determining causes of operating errors and deciding what to do about them. **Coordination:** Adjusting actions in relation to others' actions. **Persuasion:** Persuading others to change their minds or behavior. **Technology Design:** Generating or adapting equipment and technology to serve user needs. **Instructing:** Teaching others how to do something. **Operations Analysis:** Analyzing needs and product requirements to create a design. **Active Learning:** Understanding the implications of new information for both current and future problem-solving and decision-making. **Negotiation:** Bringing others together and trying to reconcile differences. **GOE—Interest Area:** 04. Business and Administration. **Work Group:** 04.05. Accounting, Auditing, and Analytical Support. **Other Jobs in This Work Group:** Accountants; Auditors; Budget Analysts; Logisticians; Management Analysts; Operations Research Analysts. **PERSONALITY TYPE:** Investigative. Investigative occupations frequently involve working with ideas and require an extensive amount of thinking. These occupations can involve searching for facts and figuring out problems mentally.

EDUCATION/TRAINING PROGRAM(S)— Engineering/Industrial Management; Industrial Production Technologies/Technicians, Other; Industrial Technology/Technician; Manufacturing Technology/Technician. **RELATED KNOWLEDGE/COURSES—Production and Processing:** Knowledge of raw materials, production processes, quality control, costs, and other techniques for maximizing the effective manufacture and distribution of goods. **Engineering and Technology:** Knowledge of the practical application of engineering science and technology. This includes applying principles, techniques, procedures, and equipment to the design and production of various goods and services. **Clerical Practices:** Knowledge of administrative and clerical procedures and systems such as word processing, managing files and records, stenography and transcription, designing forms, and other office procedures and terminology. **Design:** Knowledge of design techniques, tools, and principles involved in production of precision technical plans, blueprints, drawings, and models. **Mathematics:** Knowledge of arithmetic, algebra, geometry, calculus, and statistics and their applications. **Education and Training:** Knowledge of principles and methods for curriculum and training design, teaching and instruction for individuals and groups, and the measurement of training effects.

Industrial Machinery Mechanics

- ◎ Education/Training Required: Long-term on-the-job training
- ◎ Annual Earnings: $39,060
- ◎ Growth: 5.5%
- ◎ Annual Job Openings: 19,000
- ◎ Self-Employed: 6.3%
- ◎ Part-Time: 2.1%

Repair, install, adjust, or maintain industrial production and processing machinery or refinery and pipeline distribution systems. Analyze test results, machine error messages, and information obtained from operators in order to diagnose equipment problems. Clean, lubricate, and adjust parts, equipment, and machinery. Disassemble machinery and equipment to remove parts and make repairs. Examine parts for defects such as breakage and excessive wear. Observe and test the operation of machinery and equipment in order to diagnose malfunctions, using voltmeters and other testing devices. Operate newly repaired machinery and equipment to verify the adequacy of repairs. Reassemble equipment after completion of inspections, testing, or repairs. Repair and maintain the operating condition of industrial production and processing machinery and equipment. Repair and replace broken or malfunctioning components of machinery and equipment. Study blueprints and manufacturers' manuals to determine correct installation and operation of machinery. Cut and weld metal to repair broken metal parts, fabricate new parts, and assemble new equipment. Demonstrate equipment functions and features to machine operators. Enter codes and instructions to program computer-controlled machinery. Record parts and materials used and order or requisition new parts and materials as necessary. Record repairs and maintenance performed. **SKILLS—Repairing:** Repairing machines or systems by using the needed tools. **Equipment Maintenance:** Performing routine maintenance on equipment and determining when and what kind of maintenance is needed. **Troubleshooting:** Determining causes of operating errors and deciding what to do about them. **Operation Monitoring:** Watching gauges, dials, or other indicators to make sure a machine is working properly. **Quality Control Analysis:** Conducting tests and inspections of products, services, or processes to evaluate quality or performance. **Installation:** Installing equipment, machines, wiring, or programs to meet specifications. **Operation and Control:** Controlling operations of equipment or systems. **Technology Design:** Generating or adapting equipment and technology to serve user needs. **GOE—Interest Area:** 13. Manufacturing. **Work Group:** 13.13. Machinery Repair. **Other Jobs in This Work Group:** Bicycle Repairers; Gas Appliance Repairers; Hand and Portable Power Tool Repairers; Locksmiths and Safe Repairers; Maintenance Workers, Machinery; Mechanical Door Repairers; Millwrights; Signal and Track Switch Repairers; Valve and Regulator Repairers. **PERSON-**

ALITY TYPE: Realistic. Realistic occupations frequently involve work activities that include practical, hands-on problems and solutions. These occupations often deal with plants, animals, and real-world materials like wood, tools, and machinery. Many of the occupations require working outside and do not involve a lot of paperwork or working closely with others.

EDUCATION/TRAINING PROGRAM(S)—Heavy/Industrial Equipment Maintenance Technologies, Other; Industrial Mechanics and Maintenance Technology. RELATED KNOWLEDGE/COURSES—Mechanical Devices: Knowledge of machines and tools, including their designs, uses, repair, and maintenance. Engineering and Technology: Knowledge of the practical application of engineering science and technology. This includes applying principles, techniques, procedures, and equipment to the design and production of various goods and services. Computers and Electronics: Knowledge of circuit boards, processors, chips, electronic equipment, and computer hardware and software, including applications and programming. Physics: Knowledge and prediction of physical principles and laws and their interrelationships and applications to understanding fluid, material, and atmospheric dynamics and mechanical, electrical, atomic, and subatomic structures and processes. Public Safety and Security: Knowledge of relevant equipment, policies, procedures, and strategies to promote effective local, state, or national security operations for the protection of people, data, property, and institutions. Design: Knowledge of design techniques, tools, and principles involved in production of precision technical plans, blueprints, drawings, and models.

Industrial Truck and Tractor Operators

- Education/Training Required: Short-term on-the-job training
- Annual Earnings: $26,580
- Growth: 11.1%
- Annual Job Openings: 94,000
- Self-Employed: 0.1%
- Part-Time: 2.1%

Operate industrial trucks or tractors equipped to move materials around a warehouse, storage yard, factory, construction site, or similar location. Move controls to drive gasoline- or electric-powered trucks, cars, or tractors and transport materials between loading, processing, and storage areas. Move levers and controls that operate lifting devices, such as forklifts, lift beams and swivel-hooks, hoists, and elevating platforms, in order to load, unload, transport, and stack material. Position lifting devices under, over, or around loaded pallets, skids, and boxes and secure material or products for transport to designated areas. Manually load or unload materials onto or off pallets, skids, platforms, cars, or lifting devices. Perform routine maintenance on vehicles and auxiliary equipment, such as cleaning, lubricating, recharging batteries, fueling, or replacing liquefied-gas tank. Weigh materials or products and record weight and other production data on tags or labels. Operate or tend automatic stacking, loading, packaging, or cutting machines. Signal workers to discharge, dump, or level materials. Hook tow trucks to trailer hitches and fasten attachments such as graders, plows, rollers, and winch cables to tractors, using hitchpins. SKILLS—Operation Monitoring: Watching gauges, dials, or other indicators to make sure a machine is working properly. Equipment Maintenance: Performing routine maintenance on equipment and determining when and what kind of maintenance is needed. Instructing: Teaching others how to do something. Repairing: Repairing machines or systems by using the needed tools. Operation and Control: Controlling operations of equipment or systems. Troubleshooting: Determining causes of operating errors and deciding what to do about them. Systems Analysis: Determining how a system should work and how changes in conditions, operations, and the environment will affect outcomes. Learning Strategies: Selecting and using training/instructional methods and procedures appropriate for the situation when learning or teaching new things. Equipment Selection: Determining the kind of tools and equipment needed to do a job. GOE—Interest Area: 13. Manufacturing. Work Group: 13.17. Loading, Moving, Hoisting, and Conveying. Other Jobs in This Work Group: Conveyor Operators and Tenders; Freight, Stock, and Material Movers, Hand; Hoist and Winch Operators; Irradiated-Fuel Handlers; Machine

Feeders and Offbearers; Packers and Packagers, Hand; Pump Operators, Except Wellhead Pumpers; Refuse and Recyclable Material Collectors; Tank Car, Truck, and Ship Loaders. **PERSONALITY TYPE:** Realistic. Realistic occupations frequently involve work activities that include practical, hands-on problems and solutions. These occupations often deal with plants, animals, and real-world materials like wood, tools, and machinery. Many of the occupations require working outside and do not involve a lot of paperwork or working closely with others.

EDUCATION/TRAINING PROGRAM(S)— Ground Transportation, Other. **RELATED KNOWL-EDGE/COURSES—Transportation:** Knowledge of principles and methods for moving people or goods by air, rail, sea, or road, including the relative costs and benefits. **Mechanical Devices:** Knowledge of machines and tools, including their designs, uses, repair, and maintenance. **Chemistry:** Knowledge of the chemical composition, structure, and properties of substances and of the chemical processes and transformations that they undergo. This includes uses of chemicals and their danger signs, production techniques, and disposal methods. **Geography:** Knowledge of principles and methods for describing the features of land, sea, and air masses, including their physical characteristics; locations; interrelationships; and distribution of plant, animal, and human life. **Production and Processing:** Knowledge of raw materials, production processes, quality control, costs, and other techniques for maximizing the effective manufacture and distribution of goods. **Mathematics:** Knowledge of arithmetic, algebra, geometry, calculus, and statistics and their applications. **Telecommunications:** Knowledge of transmission, broadcasting, switching, control, and operation of telecommunications systems.

Insulation Workers, Floor, Ceiling, and Wall

- Education/Training Required: Moderate-term on-the-job training
- Annual Earnings: $30,310
- Growth: 15.8%
- Annual Job Openings: 9,000
- Self-Employed: 3.9%
- Part-Time: 2.0%

Line and cover structures with insulating materials. May work with batt, roll, or blown insulation materials. Cover and line structures with blown or rolled forms of materials to insulate against cold, heat, or moisture, using saws, knives, rasps, trowels, blowers, and other tools and implements. Cover, seal, or finish insulated surfaces or access holes with plastic covers, canvas ships, sealants, tape, cement, or asphalt mastic. Distribute insulating materials evenly into small spaces within floors, ceilings, or walls, using blowers and hose attachments or cement mortars. Fill blower hoppers with insulating materials. Fit, wrap, staple, or glue insulating materials to structures or surfaces, using hand tools or wires. Measure and cut insulation for covering surfaces, using tape measures, handsaws, power saws, knives, or scissors. Move controls, buttons, or levers to start blowers and regulate flow of materials through nozzles. Prepare surfaces for insulation application by brushing or spreading on adhesives, cement, or asphalt or by attaching metal pins to surfaces. Read blueprints and select appropriate insulation, based on space characteristics and the heat-retaining or -excluding characteristics of the material. Remove old insulation such as asbestos, following safety procedures. **SKILLS—Installation:** Installing equipment, machines, wiring, or programs to meet specifications. **GOE—Interest Area:** 02. Architecture and Construction. **Work Group:** 02.04. Construction Crafts. **Other Jobs in This Work Group:** Boat Builders and Shipwrights; Boilermakers; Brattice Builders; Brickmasons and Blockmasons; Carpet Installers; Ceiling Tile Installers; Cement Masons and Concrete Finishers; Commercial Divers; Construction Carpenters; Crane and Tower Operators; Dragline Operators, Drywall Installers; Electricians; Fence

Erectors; Floor Layers, Except Carpet, Wood, and Hard Tiles; Floor Sanders and Finishers; Glaziers; Grader, Bulldozer, and Scraper Operators; Hazardous Materials Removal Workers; Insulation Workers, Mechanical; Manufactured Building and Mobile Home Installers; Operating Engineers; Painters, Construction and Maintenance; Paperhangers; Paving, Surfacing, and Tamping Equipment Operators; Pile-Driver Operators; Pipe Fitters; Pipelayers; Pipelaying Fitters; Plasterers and Stucco Masons; Plumbers; Rail-Track Laying and Maintenance Equipment Operators; Refractory Materials Repairers, Except Brickmasons; Reinforcing Iron and Rebar Workers; Riggers; Roofers; Rough Carpenters; Security and Fire Alarm Systems Installers; Segmental Pavers; Sheet Metal Workers; Ship Carpenters and Joiners; Stone Cutters and Carvers; Stonemasons; Structural Iron and Steel Workers; Tapers; Terrazzo Workers and Finishers; Tile and Marble Setters. **PERSONALITY TYPE:** Realistic. Realistic occupations frequently involve work activities that include practical, hands-on problems and solutions. These occupations often deal with plants, animals, and real-world materials like wood, tools, and machinery. Many of the occupations require working outside and do not involve a lot of paperwork or working closely with others.

EDUCATION/TRAINING PROGRAM(S)—Construction Trades, Other. **RELATED KNOWLEDGE/COURSES—Building and Construction:** Knowledge of the materials, methods, and tools involved in the construction or repair of houses, buildings, or other structures such as highways and roads. **Mechanical Devices:** Knowledge of machines and tools, including their designs, uses, repair, and maintenance.

Insulation Workers, Mechanical

- Education/Training Required: Moderate-term on-the-job training
- Annual Earnings: $33,330
- Growth: 15.8%
- Annual Job Openings: 9,000
- Self-Employed: 3.9%
- Part-Time: 2.0%

Apply insulating materials to pipes or ductwork or other mechanical systems in order to help control and maintain temperature. Apply, remove, and repair insulation on industrial equipment, pipes, ductwork, or other mechanical systems such as heat exchangers, tanks, and vessels to help control noise and maintain temperatures. Cover, seal, and finish insulated surfaces or access holes with plastic covers, canvas ships, sealant, tape, cement, or asphalt mastic. Determine the amounts and types of insulation needed and methods of installation, based on factors such as location, surface shape, and equipment use. Fit insulation around obstructions and shape insulating materials and protective coverings as required. Install sheet metal around insulated pipes with screws in order to protect the insulation from weather conditions or physical damage. Measure and cut insulation for covering surfaces, using tape measures, handsaws, knives, and scissors. Prepare surfaces for insulation application by brushing or spreading on adhesives, cement, or asphalt or by attaching metal pins to surfaces. Read blueprints and specifications to determine job requirements. Select appropriate insulation such as fiberglass, Styrofoam, or cork, based on the heat-retaining or -excluding characteristics of the material. Distribute insulating materials evenly into small spaces within floors, ceilings, or walls, using blowers and hose attachments or cement mortar. Fill blower hoppers with insulating materials. Move controls, buttons, or levers to start blowers and to regulate flow of materials through nozzles. Remove or seal off old asbestos insulation, following safety procedures. **SKILLS—Installation:** Installing equipment, machines, wiring, or programs to meet specifications. **GOE—Interest Area:** 02. Architecture and Construction. **Work Group:** 02.04. Construction Crafts. **Other**

Jobs in This Work Group: Boat Builders and Ship-wrights; Boilermakers; Brattice Builders; Brickmasons and Blockmasons; Carpet Installers; Ceiling Tile Installers; Cement Masons and Concrete Finishers; Commercial Divers; Construction Carpenters; Crane and Tower Operators; Dragline Operators; Drywall Installers; Electricians; Fence Erectors; Floor Layers, Except Carpet, Wood, and Hard Tiles; Floor Sanders and Finishers; Glaziers; Grader, Bulldozer, and Scraper Operators; Hazardous Materials Removal Workers; Insulation Workers, Floor, Ceiling, and Wall; Manufactured Building and Mobile Home Installers; Operating Engineers; Painters, Construction and Maintenance; Paperhangers; Paving, Surfacing, and Tamping Equipment Operators; Pile-Driver Operators; Pipe Fitters; Pipelayers; Pipelaying Fitters; Plasterers and Stucco Masons; Plumbers; Rail-Track Laying and Maintenance Equipment Operators; Refractory Materials Repairers, Except Brickmasons; Reinforcing Iron and Rebar Workers; Riggers; Roofers; Rough Carpenters; Security and Fire Alarm Systems Installers; Segmental Pavers; Sheet Metal Workers; Ship Carpenters and Joiners; Stone Cutters and Carvers; Stonemasons; Structural Iron and Steel Workers; Tapers; Terrazzo Workers and Finishers; Tile and Marble Setters. **PERSONALITY TYPE:** Realistic. Realistic occupations frequently involve work activities that include practical, hands-on problems and solutions. These occupations often deal with plants, animals, and real-world materials like wood, tools, and machinery. Many of the occupations require working outside and do not involve a lot of paperwork or working closely with others.

EDUCATION/TRAINING PROGRAM(S)—Construction Trades, Other. **RELATED KNOWL-EDGE/COURSES—Building and Construction:** Knowledge of the materials, methods, and tools involved in the construction or repair of houses, buildings, or other structures such as highways and roads. **Mechanical Devices:** Knowledge of machines and tools, including their designs, uses, repair, and maintenance.

Insurance Adjusters, Examiners, and Investigators

- Education/Training Required: Long-term on-the-job training
- Annual Earnings: $44,220
- Growth: 14.2%
- Annual Job Openings: 31,000
- Self-Employed: 1.9%
- Part-Time: 4.9%

Investigate, analyze, and determine the extent of insurance company's liability concerning personal, casualty, or property loss or damages and attempt to effect settlement with claimants. Correspond with or interview medical specialists, agents, witnesses, or claimants to compile information. Calculate benefit payments and approve payment of claims within a certain monetary limit. Interview or correspond with claimant and witnesses, consult police and hospital records, and inspect property damage to determine extent of liability. Investigate and assess damage to property. Examine claims form and other records to determine insurance coverage. Analyze information gathered by investigation and report findings and recommendations. Negotiate claim settlements and recommend litigation when settlement cannot be negotiated. Prepare report of findings of investigation. Collect evidence to support contested claims in court. Interview or correspond with agents and claimants to correct errors or omissions and to investigate questionable claims. Refer questionable claims to investigator or claims adjuster for investigation or settlement. Examine titles to property to determine validity and act as company agent in transactions with property owners. Obtain credit information from banks and other credit services. Communicate with former associates to verify employment record and to obtain background information regarding persons or businesses applying for credit. **SKILLS—Negotiation:** Bringing others together and trying to reconcile differences. **Persuasion:** Persuading others to change their minds or behavior. **Time Management:** Managing one's own time and the time of others. **Judgment and Decision**

Making: Considering the relative costs and benefits of potential actions to choose the most appropriate one. **Social Perceptiveness:** Being aware of others' reactions and understanding why they react as they do. **Reading Comprehension:** Understanding written sentences and paragraphs in work-related documents. **Learning Strategies:** Selecting and using training/instructional methods and procedures appropriate for the situation when learning or teaching new things. **Service Orientation:** Actively looking for ways to help people. **GOE—Interest Area:** 06. Finance and Insurance. **Work Group:** 06.02. Finance/Insurance Investigation and Analysis. **Other Jobs in This Work Group:** Appraisers, Real Estate; Assessors; Claims Examiners, Property and Casualty Insurance; Cost Estimators; Credit Analysts; Financial Analysts; Insurance Appraisers, Auto Damage; Insurance Underwriters; Loan Counselors; Loan Officers; Market Research Analysts; Survey Researchers. **PERSONALITY TYPE:** Enterprising. Enterprising occupations frequently involve starting up and carrying out projects. These occupations can involve leading people and making many decisions. They sometimes require risk taking and often deal with business.

EDUCATION/TRAINING PROGRAM(S)—Health/Medical Claims Examiner; Insurance. **RELATED KNOWLEDGE/COURSES—Customer and Personal Service:** Knowledge of principles and processes for providing customer and personal services. This includes customer needs assessment, meeting quality standards for services, and evaluation of customer satisfaction. **Clerical Practices:** Knowledge of administrative and clerical procedures and systems such as word processing, managing files and records, stenography and transcription, designing forms, and other office procedures and terminology. **Computers and Electronics:** Knowledge of circuit boards, processors, chips, electronic equipment, and computer hardware and software, including applications and programming. **Law and Government:** Knowledge of laws, legal codes, court procedures, precedents, government regulations, executive orders, agency rules, and the democratic political process. **English Language:** Knowledge of the structure and content of the English language, including the meaning and spelling of words, rules of composition, and grammar. **Mathe-**

matics: Knowledge of arithmetic, algebra, geometry, calculus, and statistics and their applications. **Medicine and Dentistry:** Knowledge of the information and techniques needed to diagnose and treat human injuries, diseases, and deformities. This includes symptoms, treatment alternatives, drug properties and interactions, and preventive health-care measures.

Insurance Appraisers, Auto Damage

- ⊚ Education/Training Required: Long-term on-the-job training
- ⊚ Annual Earnings: $45,330
- ⊚ Growth: 11.7%
- ⊚ Annual Job Openings: 2,000
- ⊚ Self-Employed: 1.8%
- ⊚ Part-Time: 4.9%

Appraise automobile or other vehicle damage to determine cost of repair for insurance claim settlement and seek agreement with automotive repair shop on cost of repair. Prepare insurance forms to indicate repair cost or cost estimates and recommendations. Estimate parts and labor to repair damage, using standard automotive labor and parts-cost manuals and knowledge of automotive repair. Review repair-cost estimates with automobile-repair shop to secure agreement on cost of repairs. Prepare insurance forms to indicate repair-cost estimates and recommendations. Examine damaged vehicle to determine extent of structural, body, mechanical, electrical, or interior damage. Arrange to have damage appraised by another appraiser to resolve disagreement with shop on repair cost. Determine salvage value on total-loss vehicle. Evaluate practicality of repair as opposed to payment of market value of vehicle before accident. **SKILLS—Negotiation:** Bringing others together and trying to reconcile differences. **Mathematics:** Using mathematics to solve problems. **Judgment and Decision Making:** Considering the relative costs and benefits of potential actions to choose the most appropriate one. **Management of Financial Resources:** Determining how money will be spent to get the work done and accounting for these expenditures. **Systems Evalua-**

tion: Identifying measures or indicators of system performance and the actions needed to improve or correct performance relative to the goals of the system. **Writing:** Communicating effectively in writing as appropriate for the needs of the audience. **Speaking:** Talking to others to convey information effectively. **GOE—Interest Area:** 06. Finance and Insurance. **Work Group:** 06.02. Finance/Insurance Investigation and Analysis. **Other Jobs in This Work Group:** Appraisers, Real Estate; Assessors; Claims Examiners, Property and Casualty Insurance; Cost Estimators; Credit Analysts; Financial Analysts; Insurance Adjusters, Examiners, and Investigators; Insurance Underwriters; Loan Counselors; Loan Officers; Market Research Analysts; Survey Researchers. **PERSONALITY TYPE:** Conventional. Conventional occupations frequently involve following set procedures and routines. These occupations can include working with data and details more than with ideas. Usually there is a clear line of authority to follow.

EDUCATION/TRAINING PROGRAM(S)— Insurance. **RELATED KNOWLEDGE/COURSES—Economics and Accounting:** Knowledge of economic and accounting principles and practices, the financial markets, banking, and the analysis and reporting of financial data. **Mechanical Devices:** Knowledge of machines and tools, including their designs, uses, repair, and maintenance. **Clerical Practices:** Knowledge of administrative and clerical procedures and systems such as word processing, managing files and records, stenography and transcription, designing forms, and other office procedures and terminology. **Mathematics:** Knowledge of arithmetic, algebra, geometry, calculus, and statistics and their applications. **Telecommunications:** Knowledge of transmission, broadcasting, switching, control, and operation of telecommunications systems.

Interpreters and Translators

- Education/Training Required: Long-term on-the-job training
- Annual Earnings: $33,860
- Growth: 22.1%
- Annual Job Openings: 4,000
- Self-Employed: 19.6%
- Part-Time: 26.3%

Translate or interpret written, oral, or sign language text into another language for others. Check original texts or confer with authors to ensure that translations retain the content, meaning, and feeling of the original material. Check translations of technical terms and terminology to ensure that they are accurate and remain consistent throughout translation revisions. Compile terminology and information to be used in translations, including technical terms such as those for legal or medical material. Discuss translation requirements with clients and determine any fees to be charged for services provided. Listen to speakers' statements in order to determine meanings and to prepare translations, using electronic listening systems as necessary. Proofread, edit, and revise translated materials. Read written materials such as legal documents, scientific works, or news reports and rewrite material into specified languages. Refer to reference materials such as dictionaries, lexicons, encyclopedias, and computerized terminology banks as needed to ensure translation accuracy. Translate messages simultaneously or consecutively into specified languages orally or by using hand signs, maintaining message content, context, and style as much as possible. Adapt translations to students' cognitive and grade levels, collaborating with educational team members as necessary. Follow ethical codes that protect the confidentiality of information. Identify and resolve conflicts related to the meanings of words, concepts, practices, or behaviors. Compile information about the content and context of information to be translated, as well as details of the groups for whom translation or interpretation is being performed. Adapt software and accompanying technical documents to another language and culture. Educate students, parents, staff, and teachers about the roles and functions of educational interpreters. Train and supervise other translators/interpreters. Travel with or guide tourists who speak another language. **SKILLS— Active Listening:** Giving full attention to what other people are saying, taking time to understand the points being made, asking questions as appropriate, and not interrupting at inappropriate times. **Writing:** Communicating effectively in writing as appropriate for the needs of the audience. **Reading Comprehension:** Understanding written sentences and paragraphs in work-related documents. **Speaking:** Talking to others to convey information effectively. **Service Orientation:** Actively looking for ways to help people. **GOE— Interest Area:** 03. Arts and Communication. **Work Group:** 03.03. News, Broadcasting, and Public Relations. **Other Jobs in This Work Group:** Broadcast News Analysts; Caption Writers; Public Relations Specialists; Reporters and Correspondents. **PERSONALITY TYPE:** Artistic. Artistic occupations frequently involve working with forms, designs, and patterns. These occupations often require self-expression, and the work can be done without following a clear set of rules.

EDUCATION/TRAINING PROGRAM(S)— African Languages, Literatures, and Linguistics; Albanian Language and Literature; American Indian/Native American Languages, Literatures, and Linguistics; Ancient Near Eastern and Biblical Languages, Literatures, and Linguistics; Ancient/Classical Greek Language and Literature; Arabic Language and Literature; Australian/Oceanic/Pacific Languages, Literatures, and Linguistics; Bahasa Indonesian/Bahasa Malay Languages and Literatures; Baltic Languages, Literatures, and Linguistics; Bengali Language and Literature; Bulgarian Language and Literature; Burmese Language and Literature; Catalan Language and Literature; Celtic Languages, Literatures, and Linguistics; Chinese Language and Literature; Classics and Classical Languages, Literatures, and Linguistics, General; Classics and Classical Languages, Literatures, and Linguistics, Other; Czech Language and Literature; Danish Language and Literature; Dutch/Flemish Language and Literature; East Asian Languages, Literatures, and Linguistics, General; East Asian Languages, Literatures, and Linguistics, Other; Filipino/Tagalog Language and Literature; Finnish and Related Languages, Literatures, and Linguistics; Foreign Languages and Literatures, General; Foreign Languages, Literatures, and Linguistics, Other; French Language and Literature; German Language and Literature; Germanic Languages, Literatures, and Linguistics, General; Germanic Languages, Literatures, and Linguistics, Other; Hebrew Language and Literature; Hindi Language and Literature; Hungarian/Magyar Language and Literature; Iranian/Persian Languages, Literatures, and Linguistics; Italian Language and Literature; Japanese Language and Literature; Khmer/Cambodian Language and Literature; Korean Language and Literature; Language Interpretation and Translation; Lao/Laotian Language and Literature; Latin Language and Literature; Latin Teacher Education; Linguistics; Middle/Near Eastern and Semitic Languages, Literatures, and Linguistics, Other; others. **RELATED KNOWLEDGE/COURSES—Foreign Language:** Knowledge of the structure and content of a foreign (non-English) language, including the meaning and spelling of words, rules of composition and grammar, and pronunciation. **Communications and Media:** Knowledge of media production, communication, and dissemination techniques and methods. This includes alternative ways to inform and entertain via written, oral, and visual media. **English Language:** Knowledge of the structure and content of the English language, including the meaning and spelling of words, rules of composition, and grammar. **Sociology and Anthropology:** Knowledge of group behavior and dynamics, societal trends and influences, human migrations, ethnicity, and cultures and their history and origins. **History and Archeology:** Knowledge of historical events and their causes, indicators, and effects on civilizations and cultures.

Interviewers, Except Eligibility and Loan

- ◎ Education/Training Required: Short-term on-the-job training
- ◎ Annual Earnings: $23,670
- ◎ Growth: 28.0%
- ◎ Annual Job Openings: 46,000
- ◎ Self-Employed: 0.7%
- ◎ Part-Time: 30.4%

Interview persons by telephone, by mail, in person, or by other means for the purpose of completing forms, applications, or questionnaires. Ask specific questions, record answers, and assist persons with completing form. May sort, classify, and file forms. Ask questions in accordance with instructions to obtain various specified information, such as person's name, address, age, religious preference, and state of residency. Identify and resolve inconsistencies in interviewees' responses by means of appropriate questioning and/or explanation. Compile, record, and code results and data from interview or survey, using computer or specified form. Review data obtained from interview for completeness and accuracy. Contact individuals to be interviewed at home, place of business, or field location by telephone, by mail, or in person. Assist individuals in filling out applications or questionnaires. Ensure payment for services by verifying benefits with the person's insurance provider or working out financing options. Identify and report problems in obtaining valid data. Explain survey objectives and procedures to interviewees and interpret survey questions to help interviewees' comprehension. Perform patient services, such as answering the telephone and assisting patients with financial and medical questions. Prepare reports to provide answers in response to specific problems. Locate and list addresses and households. Perform other office duties as needed, such as telemarketing and customer service inquiries, billing patients, and receiving payments. Meet with supervisor daily to submit completed assignments and discuss progress. Collect and analyze data, such as studying old records; tallying the number of outpatients entering each day or week; or participating in federal, state, or local population surveys as a Census Enumerator. **SKILLS—Service Orientation:** Actively looking for ways to help people. **Social Perceptiveness:** Being aware of others' reactions and understanding why they react as they do. **Speaking:** Talking to others to convey information effectively. **Active Listening:** Giving full attention to what other people are saying, taking time to understand the points being made, asking questions as appropriate, and not interrupting at inappropriate times. **Persuasion:** Persuading others to change their minds or behavior. **Learning Strategies:** Selecting and using training/instructional methods and procedures appropriate for the situation when learning or teaching

new things. **Negotiation:** Bringing others together and trying to reconcile differences. **Writing:** Communicating effectively in writing as appropriate for the needs of the audience. **GOE—Interest Area:** 10. Human Service. **Work Group:** 10.04. Client Interviewing. **Other Jobs in This Work Group:** Claims Takers, Unemployment Benefits; Welfare Eligibility Workers and Interviewers. **PERSONALITY TYPE:** Conventional. Conventional occupations frequently involve following set procedures and routines. These occupations can include working with data and details more than with ideas. Usually there is a clear line of authority to follow.

EDUCATION/TRAINING PROGRAM(S)— Receptionist. **RELATED KNOWLEDGE/COURSES—Customer and Personal Service:** Knowledge of principles and processes for providing customer and personal services. This includes customer needs assessment, meeting quality standards for services, and evaluation of customer satisfaction. **Therapy and Counseling:** Knowledge of principles, methods, and procedures for diagnosis, treatment, and rehabilitation of physical and mental dysfunctions and for career counseling and guidance. **Sales and Marketing:** Knowledge of principles and methods for showing, promoting, and selling products or services. This includes marketing strategy and tactics, product demonstrations, sales techniques, and sales control systems. **Education and Training:** Knowledge of principles and methods for curriculum and training design, teaching and instruction for individuals and groups, and the measurement of training effects. **Psychology:** Knowledge of human behavior and performance; individual differences in ability, personality, and interests; learning and motivation; psychological research methods; and the assessment and treatment of behavioral and affective disorders. **Philosophy and Theology:** Knowledge of different philosophical systems and religions. This includes their basic principles, values, ethics, ways of thinking, customs, and practices and their impact on human culture.

Irradiated-Fuel Handlers

- Education/Training Required: Moderate-term on-the-job training
- Annual Earnings: $33,320
- Growth: 43.1%
- Annual Job Openings: 8,000
- Self-Employed: 0%
- Part-Time: 5.7%

Package, store, and convey irradiated fuels and wastes, using hoists, mechanical arms, shovels, and industrial truck. Operates machines and equipment to package, store, or transport loads of waste materials. Follows prescribed safety procedures and complies with federal laws regulating waste disposal methods. Cleans contaminated equipment for reuse, using detergents and solvents, sandblasters, filter pumps, and steam cleaners. Records number of containers stored at disposal site and specifies amount and type of equipment and waste disposed. Mixes and pours concrete into forms to encase waste material for disposal. Drives truck to convey contaminated waste to designated sea or ground location. Loads and unloads materials into containers and onto trucks, using hoists or forklift. **SKILLS—Operation and Control:** Controlling operations of equipment or systems. **GOE—Interest Area:** 13. Manufacturing. **Work Group:** 13.17. Loading, Moving, Hoisting, and Conveying. **Other Jobs in This Work Group:** Conveyor Operators and Tenders; Freight, Stock, and Material Movers, Hand; Hoist and Winch Operators; Industrial Truck and Tractor Operators; Machine Feeders and Offbearers; Packers and Packagers, Hand; Pump Operators, Except Wellhead Pumpers; Refuse and Recyclable Material Collectors; Tank Car, Truck, and Ship Loaders. **PERSONALITY TYPE:** Realistic. Realistic occupations frequently involve work activities that include practical, hands-on problems and solutions. These occupations often deal with plants, animals, and real-world materials like wood, tools, and machinery. Many of the occupations require working outside and do not involve a lot of paperwork or working closely with others. **EDUCATION/TRAINING PROGRAM(S)—** Hazardous Materials Management and Waste Technology/Technician. **RELATED KNOWLEDGE/**

COURSES—Transportation: Knowledge of principles and methods for moving people or goods by air, rail, sea, or road, including the relative costs and benefits. **Production and Processing:** Knowledge of raw materials, production processes, quality control, costs, and other techniques for maximizing the effective manufacture and distribution of goods. **Chemistry:** Knowledge of the chemical composition, structure, and properties of substances and of the chemical processes and transformations that they undergo. This includes uses of chemicals and their danger signs, production techniques, and disposal methods. **Public Safety and Security:** Knowledge of relevant equipment, policies, procedures, and strategies to promote effective local, state, or national security operations for the protection of people, data, property, and institutions. **Law and Government:** Knowledge of laws, legal codes, court procedures, precedents, government regulations, executive orders, agency rules, and the democratic political process. **Building and Construction:** Knowledge of the materials, methods, and tools involved in the construction or repair of houses, buildings, or other structures such as highways and roads.

Janitorial Supervisors

- Education/Training Required: Work experience in a related occupation
- Annual Earnings: $29,510
- Growth: 16.2%
- Annual Job Openings: 28,000
- Self-Employed: 5.6%
- Part-Time: 6.6%

Supervise work activities of janitorial personnel in commercial and industrial establishments. Assign duties, inspect work, and investigate complaints regarding janitorial services and take corrective action. May purchase janitorial supplies and equipment, take periodic inventories, screen applicants, train new employees, and recommend dismissals. Supervises and coordinates activities of workers engaged in janitorial services. Assigns janitorial work to employees, following material and work requirements. Inspects work performed to ensure conformance to specifications and established standards.

Records personnel data on specified forms. Recommends personnel actions, such as hires and discharges, to ensure proper staffing. Confers with staff to resolve production and personnel problems. Trains workers in janitorial methods and procedures and proper operation of equipment. Issues janitorial supplies and equipment to workers to ensure quality and timely delivery of services. **SKILLS—Management of Personnel Resources:** Motivating, developing, and directing people as they work, identifying the best people for the job. **Coordination:** Adjusting actions in relation to others' actions. **Time Management:** Managing one's own time and the time of others. **Social Perceptiveness:** Being aware of others' reactions and understanding why they react as they do. **Persuasion:** Persuading others to change their minds or behavior. **Negotiation:** Bringing others together and trying to reconcile differences. **Management of Material Resources:** Obtaining and seeing to the appropriate use of equipment, facilities, and materials needed to do certain work. **Speaking:** Talking to others to convey information effectively. **GOE—Interest Area:** 04. Business and Administration. **Work Group:** 04.02. Managerial Work in Business Detail. **Other Jobs in This Work Group:** Administrative Services Managers; First-Line Supervisors, Administrative Support; First-Line Supervisors, Customer Service; Housekeeping Supervisors; Meeting and Convention Planners. **PERSONALITY TYPE:** Enterprising. Enterprising occupations frequently involve starting up and carrying out projects. These occupations can involve leading people and making many decisions. They sometimes require risk taking and often deal with business.

EDUCATION/TRAINING PROGRAM(S)—No data available. **RELATED KNOWLEDGE/COURSES—Personnel and Human Resources:** Knowledge of principles and procedures for personnel recruitment, selection, training, compensation and benefits, labor relations and negotiation, and personnel information systems. **Administration and Management:** Knowledge of business and management principles involved in strategic planning, resource allocation, human resources modeling, leadership technique, production methods, and coordination of people and resources. **Customer and Personal Service:** Knowledge of principles and processes for providing customer and personal services. This includes customer needs assessment, meeting quality standards for services, and evaluation of customer satisfaction.

Janitors and Cleaners, Except Maids and Housekeeping Cleaners

- Education/Training Required: Short-term on-the-job training
- Annual Earnings: $18,790
- Growth: 18.3%
- Annual Job Openings: 454,000
- Self-Employed: 4.7%
- Part-Time: 21.7%

Keep buildings in clean and orderly condition. Perform heavy cleaning duties, such as cleaning floors, shampooing rugs, washing walls and glass, and removing rubbish. Duties may include tending furnace and boiler, performing routine maintenance activities, notifying management of need for repairs, and cleaning snow or debris from sidewalk. Clean building floors by sweeping, mopping, scrubbing, or vacuuming them. Gather and empty trash. Service, clean, and supply restrooms. Clean and polish furniture and fixtures. Clean windows, glass partitions, and mirrors, using soapy water or other cleaners, sponges, and squeegees. Dust furniture, walls, machines, and equipment. Make adjustments and minor repairs to heating, cooling, ventilating, plumbing, and electrical systems. Mix water and detergents or acids in containers to prepare cleaning solutions according to specifications. Steam-clean or shampoo carpets. Strip, seal, finish, and polish floors. Clean and restore building interiors damaged by fire, smoke, or water, using commercial cleaning equipment. Clean chimneys, flues, and connecting pipes, using power and hand tools. Clean laboratory equipment, such as glassware and metal instruments, using solvents, brushes, rags, and power-cleaning equipment. Drive vehicles required to perform or travel to cleaning work, including vans, industrial trucks, or industrial vacuum cleaners. Follow procedures for the use of chemical cleaners and power equipment in order to prevent damage to floors and fixtures. Monitor building security and safety by performing such tasks as locking doors after operating hours and checking electrical appliance use to ensure that hazards are not created. Move heavy furniture, equipment, and supplies either manually or by using hand trucks. Mow and trim lawns and shrubbery, using mowers and hand and power trimmers, and clear debris from grounds. Notify managers concerning the need for major repairs or additions to building operating systems. Remove snow from sidewalks, driveways, and parking areas, using snowplows, snow blowers, and snow shovels, and spread snow-melting chemicals. Requisition supplies and equipment needed for cleaning and maintenance duties. Set up, arrange, and remove decorations, tables, chairs, ladders, and scaffolding to prepare facilities for events such as banquets and meetings. Spray insecticides and fumigants to prevent insect and rodent infestation. **SKILLS—Repairing:** Repairing machines or systems by using the needed tools. **Equipment Maintenance:** Performing routine maintenance on equipment and determining when and what kind of maintenance is needed. **Installation:** Installing equipment, machines, wiring, or programs to meet specifications. **Troubleshooting:** Determining causes of operating errors and deciding what to do about them. **GOE—Interest Area:** 09. Hospitality, Tourism, and Recreation. **Work Group:** 09.03. Hospitality and Travel Services. **Other Jobs in This Work Group:** Baggage Porters and Bellhops; Concierges; Flight Attendants; Hotel, Motel, and Resort Desk Clerks; Maids and Housekeeping Cleaners; Reservation and Transportation Ticket Agents; Tour Guides and Escorts; Transportation Attendants, Except Flight Attendants and Baggage Porters; Travel Agents; Travel Clerks; Travel Guides. **PERSONALITY TYPE:** Realistic. Realistic occupations frequently involve work activities that include practical, hands-on problems and solutions. These occupations often deal with plants, animals, and real-world materials like wood, tools, and machinery. Many of the occupations require working outside and do not involve a lot of paperwork or working closely with others.

EDUCATION/TRAINING PROGRAM(S)—No data available. **RELATED KNOWLEDGE/COURSES—Mechanical Devices:** Knowledge of machines and tools, including their designs, uses, repair, and maintenance. **Chemistry:** Knowledge of the chemical composition, structure, and properties of substances and of the chemical processes and transformations that they undergo. This includes uses of chemicals and their danger signs, production techniques, and disposal methods. **Building and Construction:** Knowledge of the materials, methods, and tools involved in the construction or repair of houses, buildings, or other structures such as highways and roads. **Transportation:** Knowledge of principles and methods for moving people or goods by air, rail, sea, or road, including the relative costs and benefits. **Physics:** Knowledge and prediction of physical principles and laws and their interrelationships and applications to understanding fluid, material, and atmospheric dynamics and mechanical, electrical, atomic, and subatomic structures and processes. **Public Safety and Security:** Knowledge of relevant equipment, policies, procedures, and strategies to promote effective local, state, or national security operations for the protection of people, data, property, and institutions.

Landscaping and Groundskeeping Workers

- Education/Training Required: Short-term on-the-job training
- Annual Earnings: $20,420
- Growth: 22.0%
- Annual Job Openings: 203,000
- Self-Employed: 23.3%
- Part-Time: 15.3%

Landscape or maintain grounds of property, using hand or power tools or equipment. Workers typically perform a variety of tasks, which may include any combination of the following: sod laying, mowing, trimming, planting, watering, fertilizing, digging, raking, sprinkler installation, and installation of mortarless segmental concrete masonry wall units. Care for established lawns by mulching; aerating; weeding; grubbing and removing thatch; and trimming and edging around flowerbeds, walks, and walls. Mix and spray or spread fertilizers, herbicides, or insecticides onto grass, shrubs, and trees, using hand or automatic sprayers or spreaders. Mow and edge lawns, using power mowers and edgers. Plant seeds, bulbs, foliage, flowering plants, grass, ground cover, trees, and shrubs and apply mulch for protection, using gardening tools. Attach wires from planted trees to support stakes. Decorate gardens with stones and plants. Follow planned landscaping designs to determine where to lay sod, sow grass, or plant flowers and foliage. Gather and remove litter. Haul or spread topsoil and spread straw over seeded soil to hold soil in place. Maintain irrigation systems, including winterizing the systems and starting them up in spring. Plan and cultivate lawns and gardens. Prune and trim trees, shrubs, and hedges, using shears, pruners, or chain saws. Rake, mulch, and compost leaves. Trim and pick flowers and clean flowerbeds. Water lawns, trees, and plants, using portable sprinkler systems, hoses, or watering cans. Advise customers on plant selection and care. Build forms and mix and pour cement to form garden borders. Install rock gardens, ponds, decks, drainage systems, irrigation systems, retaining walls, fences, planters, and/or playground equipment. Maintain and repair tools; equipment; and structures such as buildings, greenhouses, fences, and benches, using hand and power tools. Provide proper upkeep of sidewalks, driveways, parking lots, fountains, planters, burial sites, and other grounds features. Shovel snow from walks, driveways, and parking lots and spread salt in those areas. Use irrigation methods to adjust the amount of water consumption and to prevent waste. Care for artificial turf fields, periodically removing the turf and replacing cushioning pads and vacuuming and disinfecting the turf after use to prevent the growth of harmful bacteria. Care for natural turf fields, making sure the underlying soil has the required composition to allow proper drainage and to support the grasses used on the fields. **SKILLS—Repairing:** Repairing machines or systems by using the needed tools. **Operation and Control:** Controlling operations of equipment or systems. **Equipment Maintenance:** Performing routine maintenance on equipment and determining when and what kind of maintenance is needed. **Installation:** Installing equipment, machines, wiring, or programs to meet specifications. **GOE— Interest Area:** 01. Agriculture and Natural Resources. **Work Group:** 01.05. Nursery, Groundskeeping, and Pest Control. **Other Jobs in This Work Group:** Nursery Workers; Pest Control Workers; Pesticide Handlers, Sprayers, and Applicators, Vegetation; Tree Trimmers and Pruners. **PERSONALITY TYPE:** Realistic. Realistic occupations frequently involve work activities that include practical, hands-on problems and solutions. These occupations often deal with plants, animals, and real-world materials like wood, tools, and machinery. Many of the occupations require working outside and do not involve a lot of paperwork or working closely with others.

EDUCATION/TRAINING PROGRAM(S)— Landscaping and Groundskeeping; Turf and Turfgrass Management. **RELATED KNOWLEDGE/COURSES—Chemistry:** Knowledge of the chemical composition, structure, and properties of substances and of the chemical processes and transformations that they undergo. This includes uses of chemicals and their danger signs, production techniques, and disposal methods. **Building and Construction:** Knowledge of the materials, methods, and tools involved in the construction or repair of houses, buildings, or other structures such as highways and roads. **Mechanical Devices:** Knowledge of machines and tools, including their designs, uses, repair, and maintenance.

Lawn Service Managers

- Education/Training Required: Work experience in a related occupation
- Annual Earnings: $35,340
- Growth: 21.6%
- Annual Job Openings: 18,000
- Self-Employed: 34.7%
- Part-Time: 5.9%

Plan, direct, and coordinate activities of workers engaged in pruning trees and shrubs, cultivating lawns, and applying pesticides and other chemicals according to service contract specifications. Supervises workers who provide groundskeeping services on a contract basis. Investigates customer complaints. Prepares work activity and personnel reports. Suggests changes in work procedures and orders corrective work done. Spot-checks completed work to improve quality of service and to ensure contract compliance. Schedules work for crew according to weather conditions, availability of equipment, and seasonal limitations.

Reviews contracts to ascertain service, machine, and workforce requirements for job. Prepares service cost estimates for customers. Answers customers' questions about groundskeeping care requirements. **SKILLS— Management of Personnel Resources:** Motivating, developing, and directing people as they work, identifying the best people for the job. **Time Management:** Managing one's own time and the time of others. **Management of Financial Resources:** Determining how money will be spent to get the work done and accounting for these expenditures. **Systems Analysis:** Determining how a system should work and how changes in conditions, operations, and the environment will affect outcomes. **Systems Evaluation:** Identifying measures or indicators of system performance and the actions needed to improve or correct performance relative to the goals of the system. **Management of Material Resources:** Obtaining and seeing to the appropriate use of equipment, facilities, and materials needed to do certain work. **Coordination:** Adjusting actions in relation to others' actions. **Mathematics:** Using mathematics to solve problems. **Negotiation:** Bringing others together and trying to reconcile differences. **GOE—Interest Area:** 01. Agriculture and Natural Resources. **Work Group:** 01.01. Managerial Work in Agriculture and Natural Resources. **Other Jobs in This Work Group:** Agricultural Crop Farm Managers; Farmers and Ranchers; First-Line Supervisors and Manager/Supervisors—Agricultural Crop Workers; First-Line Supervisors and Manager/Supervisors— Animal Husbandry Workers; First-Line Supervisors and Manager/Supervisors—Extractive Workers; First-Line Supervisors and Manager/Supervisors—Fishery Workers; First-Line Supervisors and Manager/Supervisors—Horticultural Workers; First-Line Supervisors and Manager/Supervisors—Landscaping Workers; First-Line Supervisors and Manager/Supervisors— Logging Workers; Fish Hatchery Managers; Nursery and Greenhouse Managers; Park Naturalists; Purchasing Agents and Buyers, Farm Products. **PERSONALITY TYPE:** Enterprising. Enterprising occupations frequently involve starting up and carrying out projects. These occupations can involve leading people and making many decisions. They sometimes require risk taking and often deal with business.

EDUCATION/TRAINING PROGRAM(S)— Landscaping and Groundskeeping; Ornamental Hor-

ticulture; Turf and Turfgrass Management. **RELATED KNOWLEDGE/COURSES—Administration and Management:** Knowledge of business and management principles involved in strategic planning, resource allocation, human resources modeling, leadership technique, production methods, and coordination of people and resources. **Economics and Accounting:** Knowledge of economic and accounting principles and practices, the financial markets, banking, and the analysis and reporting of financial data. **Customer and Personal Service:** Knowledge of principles and processes for providing customer and personal services. This includes customer needs assessment, meeting quality standards for services, and evaluation of customer satisfaction. **Personnel and Human Resources:** Knowledge of principles and procedures for personnel recruitment, selection, training, compensation and benefits, labor relations and negotiation, and personnel information systems. **Sales and Marketing:** Knowledge of principles and methods for showing, promoting, and selling products or services. This includes marketing strategy and tactics, product demonstrations, sales techniques, and sales control systems. **Chemistry:** Knowledge of the chemical composition, structure, and properties of substances and of the chemical processes and transformations that they undergo. This includes uses of chemicals and their danger signs, production techniques, and disposal methods.

Legal Secretaries

- Education/Training Required: Postsecondary vocational training
- Annual Earnings: $36,720
- Growth: 18.8%
- Annual Job Openings: 39,000
- Self-Employed: 1.7%
- Part-Time: 17.5%

Perform secretarial duties, utilizing legal terminology, procedures, and documents. Prepare legal papers and correspondence, such as summonses, complaints, motions, and subpoenas. May also assist with legal research. Prepare and process legal documents and papers, such as summonses, subpoenas, complaints, appeals, motions, and pretrial agreements. Mail, fax, or arrange for delivery of legal correspondence to clients, witnesses, and court officials. Receive and place telephone calls. Schedule and make appointments. Make photocopies of correspondence, document, and other printed matter. Organize and maintain law libraries and document and case files. Assist attorneys in collecting information such as employment, medical, and other records. Attend legal meetings, such as client interviews, hearings, or depositions, and take notes. Draft and type office memos. Review legal publications and perform database searches to identify laws and court decisions relevant to pending cases. Submit articles and information from searches to attorneys for review and approval for use. Complete various forms, such as accident reports, trial and courtroom requests, and applications for clients. **SKILLS—Writing:** Communicating effectively in writing as appropriate for the needs of the audience. **Time Management:** Managing one's own time and the time of others. **Social Perceptiveness:** Being aware of others' reactions and understanding why they react as they do. **Reading Comprehension:** Understanding written sentences and paragraphs in work-related documents. **Learning Strategies:** Selecting and using training/instructional methods and procedures appropriate for the situation when learning or teaching new things. **Negotiation:** Bringing others together and trying to reconcile differences. **Active Listening:** Giving full attention to what other people are saying, taking time to understand the points being made, asking questions as appropriate, and not interrupting at inappropriate times. **Persuasion:** Persuading others to change their minds or behavior. **GOE—Interest Area:** 04. Business and Administration. **Work Group:** 04.04. Secretarial Support. **Other Jobs in This Work Group:** Executive Secretaries and Administrative Assistants; Medical Secretaries; Secretaries, Except Legal, Medical, and Executive. **PERSONALITY TYPE:** Conventional. Conventional occupations frequently involve following set procedures and routines. These occupations can include working with data and details more than with ideas. Usually there is a clear line of authority to follow.

EDUCATION/TRAINING PROGRAM(S)—Legal Administrative Assistant/Secretary. **RELATED KNOWLEDGE/COURSES—Clerical Practices:** Knowledge of administrative and clerical procedures

and systems such as word processing, managing files and records, stenography and transcription, designing forms, and other office procedures and terminology. **Law and Government:** Knowledge of laws, legal codes, court procedures, precedents, government regulations, executive orders, agency rules, and the democratic political process. **Customer and Personal Service:** Knowledge of principles and processes for providing customer and personal services. This includes customer needs assessment, meeting quality standards for services, and evaluation of customer satisfaction. **Economics and Accounting:** Knowledge of economic and accounting principles and practices, the financial markets, banking, and the analysis and reporting of financial data. **Computers and Electronics:** Knowledge of circuit boards, processors, chips, electronic equipment, and computer hardware and software, including applications and programming. **English Language:** Knowledge of the structure and content of the English language, including the meaning and spelling of words, rules of composition, and grammar.

Library Assistants, Clerical

- Education/Training Required: Short-term on-the-job training
- Annual Earnings: $20,720
- Growth: 21.5%
- Annual Job Openings: 27,000
- Self-Employed: 0.1%
- Part-Time: 50.4%

Compile records, sort and shelve books, and issue and receive library materials such as pictures, cards, slides and microfilm. Locate library materials for loan and replace material in shelving area, stacks, or files according to identification number and title. Register patrons to permit them to borrow books, periodicals, and other library materials. Lend and collect books, periodicals, videotapes, and other materials at circulation desks. Enter and update patrons' records on computers. Process new materials, including books, audiovisual materials, and computer software. Sort books, publications, and other items according to established procedure and return them to shelves, files, or other designated storage areas. Locate library materials for patrons, including books, periodicals, tape cassettes, Braille volumes, and pictures. Instruct patrons on how to use reference sources, card catalogs, and automated information systems. Inspect returned books for condition and due-date status and compute any applicable fines. Answer routine inquiries and refer patrons in need of professional assistance to librarians. Maintain records of items received, stored, issued, and returned and file catalog cards according to system used. Perform clerical activities such as filing, typing, word processing, photocopying and mailing out material, and mail sorting. Provide assistance to librarians in the maintenance of collections of books, periodicals, magazines, newspapers, and audiovisual and other materials. Take action to deal with disruptive or problem patrons. Classify and catalog items according to content and purpose. Register new patrons and issue borrower identification cards that permit patrons to borrow books and other materials. Send out notices and accept fine payments for lost or overdue books. Operate small branch libraries under the direction of off-site librarian supervisors. Prepare, store, and retrieve classification and catalog information, lecture notes, or other information related to stored documents, using computers. Schedule and supervise clerical workers, volunteers, and student assistants. Operate and maintain audiovisual equipment. Review records, such as microfilm and issue cards, in order to identify titles of overdue materials and delinquent borrowers. Select substitute titles when requested materials are unavailable, following criteria such as age, education, and interests. Repair books, using mending tape, paste, and brushes. **SKILLS—Service Orientation:** Actively looking for ways to help people. **Reading Comprehension:** Understanding written sentences and paragraphs in work-related documents. **Instructing:** Teaching others how to do something. **Learning Strategies:** Selecting and using training/instructional methods and procedures appropriate for the situation when learning or teaching new things. **Active Listening:** Giving full attention to what other people are saying, taking time to understand the points being made, asking questions as appropriate, and not interrupting at inappropriate times. **Social Perceptiveness:** Being aware of others' reactions and understanding why they react as they do. **Time Management:** Managing one's own time and the time of others. **Writing:** Communi-cating effectively in writing as appropriate for the needs of the audience. **GOE—Interest Area:** 05. Education and Training. **Work Group:** 05.04. Library Services. **Other Jobs in This Work Group:** Librarians; Library Technicians. **PERSONALITY TYPE:** Conventional. Conventional occupations frequently involve following set procedures and routines. These occupations can include working with data and details more than with ideas. Usually there is a clear line of authority to follow.

EDUCATION/TRAINING PROGRAM(S)— Library Assistant/Technician. **RELATED KNOWL-EDGE/COURSES—Clerical Practices:** Knowledge of administrative and clerical procedures and systems such as word processing, managing files and records, stenography and transcription, designing forms, and other office procedures and terminology. **Computers and Electronics:** Knowledge of circuit boards, processors, chips, electronic equipment, and computer hardware and software, including applications and programming. **Customer and Personal Service:** Knowledge of principles and processes for providing customer and personal services. This includes customer needs assessment, meeting quality standards for services, and evaluation of customer satisfaction. **English Language:** Knowledge of the structure and content of the English language, including the meaning and spelling of words, rules of composition, and grammar. **History and Archeology:** Knowledge of historical events and their causes, indicators, and effects on civilizations and cultures. **Communications and Media:** Knowledge of media production, communication, and dissemination techniques and methods. This includes alternative ways to inform and entertain via written, oral, and visual media.

Library Technicians

- Education/Training Required: Short-term on-the-job training
- Annual Earnings: $24,940
- Growth: 16.8%
- Annual Job Openings: 22,000
- Self-Employed: 0%
- Part-Time: 53.4%

Assist librarians by helping readers in the use of library catalogs, databases, and indexes to locate books and other materials and by answering questions that require only brief consultation of standard reference. Compile records; sort and shelve books; remove or repair damaged books; register patrons; check materials in and out of the circulation process. Replace materials in shelving area (stacks) or files. Includes bookmobile drivers who operate bookmobiles or light trucks that pull trailers to specific locations on a predetermined schedule and assist with providing services in mobile libraries. Reserve, circulate, renew, and discharge books and other materials. Enter and update patrons' records on computers. Provide assistance to teachers and students by locating materials and helping to complete special projects. Answer routine reference inquiries and refer patrons needing further assistance to librarians. Guide patrons in finding and using library resources, including reference materials, audiovisual equipment, computers, and electronic resources. Train other staff, volunteers, and/or student assistants and schedule and supervise their work. Sort books, publications, and other items according to procedure and return them to shelves, files, or other designated storage areas. Conduct reference searches, using printed materials and in-house and online databases. Deliver and retrieve items throughout the library by hand or using pushcart. Take actions to halt disruption of library activities by problem patrons. Process interlibrary loans for patrons. Process print and non-print library materials to prepare them for inclusion in library collections. Retrieve information from central databases for storage in a library's computer. Organize and maintain periodicals and reference materials. Compile and maintain records relating to circulation, materials, and equipment. Collect fines and respond to complaints about fines. Issue identification cards to borrowers. Verify bibliographical data for materials, including author, title, publisher, publication date, and edition. Review subject matter of materials to be classified and select classification numbers and headings according to classification systems. Send out notices about lost or overdue books. Prepare order slips for materials to be acquired, checking prices and figuring costs. Design, customize, and maintain databases, Web pages, and local area networks. Operate and maintain audiovisual equipment such as projectors, tape recorders, and videocassette recorders. File catalog cards according to system used. Prepare volumes for binding. Conduct children's programs and other specialized programs such as library tours. Compose explanatory summaries of contents of books and other reference materials. **SKILLS—Service Orientation:** Actively looking for ways to help people. **Instructing:** Teaching others how to do something. **Learning Strategies:** Selecting and using training/instructional methods and procedures appropriate for the situation when learning or teaching new things. **Social Perceptiveness:** Being aware of others' reactions and understanding why they react as they do. **Reading Comprehension:** Understanding written sentences and paragraphs in work-related documents. **Active Listening:** Giving full attention to what other people are saying, taking time to understand the points being made, asking questions as appropriate, and not interrupting at inappropriate times. **Management of Personnel Resources:** Motivating, developing, and directing people as they work, identifying the best people for the job. **Writing:** Communicating effectively in writing as appropriate for the needs of the audience. **Critical Thinking:** Using logic and reasoning to identify the strengths and weaknesses of alternative solutions, conclusions, or approaches to problems. **Time Management:** Managing one's own time and the time of others. **GOE—Interest Area:** 05. Education and Training. **Work Group:** 05.04. Library Services. **Other Jobs in This Work Group:** Librarians; Library Assistants, Clerical. **PERSONALITY TYPE:** Conventional. Conventional occupations frequently involve following set procedures and routines. These occupations can include working with data and details more than with ideas. Usually there is a clear line of authority to follow.

EDUCATION/TRAINING PROGRAM(S)— Library Assistant/Technician. **RELATED KNOWLEDGE/COURSES—Clerical Practices:** Knowledge of administrative and clerical procedures and systems such as word processing, managing files and records, stenography and transcription, designing forms, and other office procedures and terminology. **Customer and Personal Service:** Knowledge of principles and processes for providing customer and personal services. This includes customer needs assessment, meeting quality standards for services, and evaluation of customer satisfaction. **Computers and Electronics:** Knowledge of circuit boards, processors, chips, electronic equipment, and computer hardware and software, including applications and programming. **Geography:** Knowledge of principles and methods for describing the features of land, sea, and air masses, including their physical characteristics; locations; interrelationships; and distribution of plant, animal, and human life. **Education and Training:** Knowledge of principles and methods for curriculum and training design, teaching and instruction for individuals and groups, and the measurement of training effects. **English Language:** Knowledge of the structure and content of the English language, including the meaning and spelling of words, rules of composition, and grammar.

License Clerks

- Education/Training Required: Short-term on-the-job training
- Annual Earnings: $28,430
- Growth: 12.3%
- Annual Job Openings: 14,000
- Self-Employed: 2.6%
- Part-Time: 8.3%

Issue licenses or permits to qualified applicants. Obtain necessary information, record data, advise applicants on requirements, collect fees, and issue licenses. May conduct oral, written, visual, or performance testing. Answer questions and provide advice to the public regarding licensing policies, procedures, and regulations. Assemble photographs with printed license information in order to produce completed documents. Collect prescribed fees for licenses. Conduct and score oral, visual, written, or performance tests to determine applicant qualifications and notify applicants of their scores. Evaluate information on applications to verify completeness and accuracy and to determine whether applicants are qualified to obtain desired licenses. Instruct customers in the completion of drivers' license application forms and other forms such as voter registration cards and organ donor forms. Maintain records of applications made and licensing fees collected. Operate specialized photographic equipment in order to obtain photographs for drivers' licenses and photo identification cards. Perform routine data entry and other office support activities, including creating, sorting, photocopying, distributing, and filing documents. Question applicants to obtain required information, such as name, address, and age, and record data on prescribed forms. Stock counters with adequate supplies of forms, film, licenses, and other required materials. Update operational records and licensing information, using computer terminals. Code information on license applications for entry into computers. Inform customers by mail or telephone of additional steps they need to take to obtain licenses. Perform record checks on past and current licensees as required by investigations. Prepare bank deposits and take them to banks. Prepare lists of overdue accounts and license suspensions and issuances. Train other workers and coordinate their work as necessary. Send drivers' licenses by mail to out-of-county or out-of-state applicants. Enforce canine licensing regulations, contacting noncompliant owners in person or by mail to inform them of the required regulations and potential enforcement actions. Perform driver education program enrollments for participating schools. Provide assistance in the preparation of insurance examinations covering a variety of types of insurance. **SKILLS—Speaking:** Talking to others to convey information effectively. **GOE—Interest Area:** 07. Government and Public Administration. **Work Group:** 07.04. Public Administration Clerical Support. **Other Jobs in This Work Group:** Court Clerks; Court Reporters; Municipal Clerks. **PERSONALITY TYPE:** Conventional. Conventional occupations frequently involve following set procedures and routines. These occupations can include working with data and details more than with ideas. Usually there is a clear line of authority to follow.

EDUCATION/TRAINING PROGRAM(S)—General Office Occupations and Clerical Services. **RELATED KNOWLEDGE/COURSES—Clerical Practices:** Knowledge of administrative and clerical procedures and systems such as word processing, managing files and records, stenography and transcription, designing forms, and other office procedures and terminology. **Law and Government:** Knowledge of laws, legal codes, court procedures, precedents, government regulations, executive orders, agency rules, and the democratic political process. **Economics and Account-**

ing: Knowledge of economic and accounting principles and practices, the financial markets, banking, and the analysis and reporting of financial data. **Transportation:** Knowledge of principles and methods for moving people or goods by air, rail, sea, or road, including the relative costs and benefits. **Telecommunications:** Knowledge of transmission, broadcasting, switching, control, and operation of telecommunications systems.

Licensed Practical and Licensed Vocational Nurses

- Education/Training Required: Postsecondary vocational training
- Annual Earnings: $33,970
- Growth: 20.2%
- Annual Job Openings: 105,000
- Self-Employed: 0.6%
- Part-Time: 19.1%

Care for ill, injured, convalescent, or disabled persons in hospitals, nursing homes, clinics, private homes, group homes, and similar institutions. May work under the supervision of a registered nurse. Licensing required. Observe patients, charting and reporting changes in patients' conditions such as adverse reactions to medication or treatment and taking any necessary action. Administer prescribed medications or start intravenous fluids and note times and amounts on patients' charts. Answer patients' calls and determine how to assist them. Measure and record patients' vital signs, such as height, weight, temperature, blood pressure, pulse, and respiration. Provide basic patient care and treatments, such as taking temperatures and blood pressure; dressing wounds; treating bedsores; giving enemas, douches, alcohol rubs, and massages; or performing catheterizations. Help patients with bathing, dressing, personal hygiene, moving in bed, and standing and walking. Supervise nurses' aides and assistants. Work as part of a health-care team to assess patient needs, plan and modify care, and implement interventions. Record food and fluid intake and out-

put. Evaluate nursing intervention outcomes, conferring with other health-care team members as necessary. Assemble and use equipment such as catheters, tracheotomy tubes, and oxygen suppliers. Collect samples such as blood, urine, and sputum from patients and perform routine laboratory tests on samples. Prepare patients for examinations, tests, and treatments and explain procedures. Prepare food trays and examine them for conformance to prescribed diet. Apply compresses, ice bags, and hot water bottles. Clean rooms and make beds. Inventory and requisition supplies and instruments. Provide medical treatment and personal care to patients in private home settings, such as cooking, keeping rooms orderly, seeing that patients are comfortable and in good spirits, and instructing family members in simple nursing tasks. Sterilize equipment and supplies, using germicides, sterilizer, or autoclave. Assist in delivery, care, and feeding of infants. Wash and dress bodies of deceased persons. Make appointments, keep records, and perform other clerical duties in doctors' offices and clinics. Set up equipment and prepare medical treatment rooms. **SKILLS—Service Orientation:** Actively looking for ways to help people. **Science:** Using scientific rules and methods to solve problems. **Active Listening:** Giving full attention to what other people are saying, taking time to understand the points being made, asking questions as appropriate, and not interrupting at inappropriate times. **Judgment and Decision Making:** Considering the relative costs and benefits of potential actions to choose the most appropriate one. **Time Management:** Managing one's own time and the time of others. **Operation Monitoring:** Watching gauges, dials, or other indicators to make sure a machine is working properly. **Management of Personnel Resources:** Motivating, developing, and directing people as they work, identifying the best people for the job. **Instructing:** Teaching others how to do something. **GOE—Interest Area:** 08. Health Science. **Work Group:** 08.08. Patient Care and Assistance. **Other Jobs in This Work Group:** Home Health Aides; Nursing Aides, Orderlies, and Attendants; Psychiatric Aides; Psychiatric Technicians. **PERSONALITY TYPE:** Social. Social occupations frequently involve working with, communicating with, and teaching people. These occupations often involve helping or providing service to others.

EDUCATION/TRAINING PROGRAM(S)—Licensed Practical/Vocational Nurse Training (LPN, LVN, Cert, Dipl, AAS). **RELATED KNOWLEDGE/COURSES—Psychology:** Knowledge of human behavior and performance; individual differences in ability, personality, and interests; learning and motivation; psychological research methods; and the assessment and treatment of behavioral and affective disorders. **Customer and Personal Service:** Knowledge of principles and processes for providing customer and personal services. This includes customer needs assessment, meeting quality standards for services, and evaluation of customer satisfaction. **Therapy and Counseling:** Knowledge of principles, methods, and procedures for diagnosis, treatment, and rehabilitation of physical and mental dysfunctions and for career counseling and guidance. **Medicine and Dentistry:** Knowledge of the information and techniques needed to diagnose and treat human injuries, diseases, and deformities. This includes symptoms, treatment alternatives, drug properties and interactions, and preventive health-care measures. **Philosophy and Theology:** Knowledge of different philosophical systems and religions. This includes their basic principles, values, ethics, ways of thinking, customs, and practices and their impact on human culture. **Education and Training:** Knowledge of principles and methods for curriculum and training design, teaching and instruction for individuals and groups, and the measurement of training effects.

Licensing Examiners and Inspectors

- Education/Training Required: Long-term on-the-job training
- Annual Earnings: $47,390
- Growth: 9.8%
- Annual Job Openings: 20,000
- Self-Employed: 0.9%
- Part-Time: 5.3%

Examine, evaluate, and investigate eligibility for, conformity with, or liability under licenses or permits. Administer oral, written, road, or flight tests to license applicants. Advise licensees and other individuals or groups concerning licensing, permit, or passport regulations. Evaluate applications, records, and documents in order to gather information about eligibility or liability issues. Issue licenses to individuals meeting standards. Prepare correspondence to inform concerned parties of licensing decisions and of appeals processes. Prepare reports of activities, evaluations, recommendations, and decisions. Report law or regulation violations to appropriate boards and agencies. Score tests and observe equipment operation and control in order to rate ability of applicants. Confer with and interview officials, technical or professional specialists, and applicants in order to obtain information or to clarify facts relevant to licensing decisions. Visit establishments to verify that valid licenses and permits are displayed and that licensing standards are being upheld. Warn violators of infractions or penalties. **SKILLS—Speaking:** Talking to others to convey information effectively. **Reading Comprehension:** Understanding written sentences and paragraphs in work-related documents. **Active Listening:** Giving full attention to what other people are saying, taking time to understand the points being made, asking questions as appropriate, and not interrupting at inappropriate times. **Writing:** Communicating effectively in writing as appropriate for the needs of the audience. **Monitoring:** Monitoring or assessing your performance or that of other individuals or organizations to make improvements or take corrective action. **Judgment and Decision Making:** Considering the relative costs and benefits of potential actions to choose the most appropriate one. **Mathematics:** Using mathematics to solve problems. **Quality Control Analysis:** Conducting tests and inspections of products, services, or processes to evaluate quality or performance. **Systems Analysis:** Determining how a system should work and how changes in conditions, operations, and the environment will affect outcomes. **GOE—Interest Area:** 07. Government and Public Administration. **Work Group:** 07.03. Regulations Enforcement. **Other Jobs in This Work Group:** Agricultural Inspectors; Aviation Inspectors; Child Support, Missing Persons, and Unemployment Insurance Fraud Investigators; Environmental Compliance Inspectors; Equal Opportunity Representatives and Officers; Financial Examiners; Fire Inspectors; Fish and Game Wardens; Forest Fire Inspectors and Prevention Specialists; Government Property Inspectors and Investigators; Immigration and Customs Inspectors; Marine Cargo Inspectors; Mechanical Inspectors; Motor Vehicle Inspectors; Nuclear Monitoring Technicians; Occupational Health and Safety Specialists; Pressure Vessel Inspectors; Railroad Inspectors; Tax Examiners, Collectors, and Revenue Agents. **PERSONALITY TYPE:** Conventional. Conventional occupations frequently involve following set procedures and routines. These occupations can include working with data and details more than with ideas. Usually there is a clear line of authority to follow.

EDUCATION/TRAINING PROGRAM(S)—No data available. **RELATED KNOWLEDGE/COURSES—Law and Government:** Knowledge of laws, legal codes, court procedures, precedents, government regulations, executive orders, agency rules, and the democratic political process. **Transportation:** Knowledge of principles and methods for moving people or goods by air, rail, sea, or road, including the relative costs and benefits. **Clerical Practices:** Knowledge of administrative and clerical procedures and systems such as word processing, managing files and records, stenography and transcription, designing forms, and other office procedures and terminology. **Communications and Media:** Knowledge of media production, communication, and dissemination techniques and methods. This includes alternative ways to inform and entertain via written, oral, and visual media. **English Language:** Knowledge of the structure and content of the English language, including the meaning and spelling of words, rules of composition, and grammar.

Loading Machine Operators, Underground Mining

- ◎ Education/Training Required: Moderate-term on-the-job training
- ◎ Annual Earnings: $33,250
- ◎ Growth: 8.9%
- ◎ Annual Job Openings: 14,000
- ◎ Self-Employed: 16.5%
- ◎ Part-Time: 2.7%

Operate underground loading machine to load coal, ore, or rock into shuttle or mine car or onto conveyors. Loading equipment may include power shovels, hoisting engines equipped with cable-drawn scraper or scoop, or machines equipped with gathering arms and conveyor. Advance machines in order to gather material and convey it into cars. Drive machines into piles of material blasted from working faces. Operate levers to move conveyor booms or shovels so that mine contents such as coal, rock, and ore can be placed into cars or onto conveyors. Signal workers to move loaded cars. Start conveyor booms and gathering-arm motors and operate winches to position cars under boom-conveyors for loading. Stop gathering arms when cars are full. Clean hoppers and clean spillage from tracks, walks, driveways, and conveyor decking. Estimate and record amounts of material in bins. Inspect boarding and locking of open-top box cars and wedging of side-drop and hopper cars in order to prevent loss of material in transit. Move trailing electrical cables clear of obstructions, using rubber safety gloves. Notify switching departments to deliver specific types of cars. Observe and record car numbers, carriers, customers, tonnages, and grades and conditions of material. Oil, lubricate, and adjust conveyors, crushers, and other equipment, using hand tools and lubricating equipment. Pry off loose material from roofs and move it into the paths of machines, using crowbars. Replace hydraulic hoses, headlight bulbs, and gathering-arm teeth. **SKILLS—Repairing:** Repairing machines or systems by using the needed tools. **Equipment Maintenance:** Performing routine maintenance on equipment and determining when and what kind of maintenance is needed. **Operation and Control:** Controlling operations of equipment or systems. **Operation Monitoring:** Watching gauges, dials, or other indicators to make sure a machine is working properly. **GOE—Interest Area:** 01. Agriculture and Natural Resources. **Work Group:** 01.08. Mining and Drilling. **Other Jobs in This Work Group:** Construction Drillers; Continuous Mining Machine Operators; Derrick Operators, Oil and Gas; Excavating and Loading Machine Operators; Explosives Workers, Ordnance Handling Experts, and Blasters; Helpers—Extraction Workers; Mine Cutting and Channeling Machine Operators; Rock Splitters, Quarry; Roof Bolters, Mining; Rotary Drill Operators, Oil and Gas; Roustabouts, Oil and Gas; Service Unit Operators, Oil, Gas, and Mining; Shuttle Car Operators; Well and Core Drill Operators; Wellhead Pumpers. **PERSONALITY TYPE:** Realistic. Realistic occupations frequently involve work activities that include practical, hands-on problems and solutions. These occupations often deal with plants, animals, and real-world materials like wood, tools, and machinery. Many of the occupations require working outside and do not involve a lot of paperwork or working closely with others.

EDUCATION/TRAINING PROGRAM(S)— Ground Transportation, Other. **RELATED KNOWLEDGE/COURSES—Mechanical Devices:** Knowledge of machines and tools, including their designs, uses, repair, and maintenance. **Engineering and Technology:** Knowledge of the practical application of engineering science and technology. This includes applying principles, techniques, procedures, and equipment to the design and production of various goods and services. **Physics:** Knowledge and prediction of physical principles and laws and their interrelationships and applications to understanding fluid, material, and atmospheric dynamics and mechanical, electrical, atomic, and subatomic structures and processes. **Public Safety and Security:** Knowledge of relevant equipment, policies, procedures, and strategies to promote effective local, state, or national security operations for the protection of people, data, property, and institutions. **Transportation:** Knowledge of principles and methods for moving people or goods by air, rail, sea, or road, including the relative costs and benefits. **Production and Processing:** Knowledge of raw materials, production processes, quality control, costs, and other techniques for maximizing the effective manufacture and distribution of goods.

Locker Room, Coatroom, and Dressing Room Attendants

- Education/Training Required: Short-term on-the-job training
- Annual Earnings: $17,550
- Growth: 27.8%
- Annual Job Openings: 66,000
- Self-Employed: 0.3%
- Part-Time: 51.9%

Provide personal items to patrons or customers in locker rooms, dressing rooms, or coatrooms. Assign dressing room facilities, locker space, or clothing containers to patrons of athletic or bathing establishments. Answer customer inquiries and explain cost, availability, policies, and procedures of facilities. Check supplies to ensure adequate availability and order new supplies when necessary. Refer guest problems or complaints to supervisors. Clean and polish footwear, using brushes, sponges, cleaning fluid, polishes, waxes, liquid or sole dressing, and daubers. Report and document safety hazards, potentially hazardous conditions, and unsafe practices and procedures. Operate washing machines and dryers in order to clean soiled apparel and towels. Monitor patrons' facility use in order to ensure that rules and regulations are followed and safety and order are maintained. Procure beverages, food, and other items as requested. Activate emergency action plans and administer first aid as necessary. Store personal possessions for patrons, issue claim checks for articles stored, and return articles on receipt of checks. Provide towels and sheets to clients in public baths, steam rooms, and restrooms. Collect soiled linen or clothing for laundering. Operate controls that regulate temperatures or room environments. Attend to needs of athletic teams in clubhouses. Provide assistance to patrons by performing duties such as opening doors and carrying bags. Stencil identifying information on equipment. Maintain inventories of clothing or uniforms, accessories, equipment, and/or linens. **SKILLS—Service Orientation:** Actively looking for ways to help people. **Negotiation:** Bringing others together and trying to reconcile differences. **Social Perceptiveness:**

Being aware of others' reactions and understanding why they react as they do. **Instructing:** Teaching others how to do something. **Critical Thinking:** Using logic and reasoning to identify the strengths and weaknesses of alternative solutions, conclusions, or approaches to problems. **Persuasion:** Persuading others to change their minds or behavior. **Reading Comprehension:** Understanding written sentences and paragraphs in work-related documents. **Speaking:** Talking to others to convey information effectively. **GOE—Interest Area:** 09. Hospitality, Tourism, and Recreation. **Work Group:** 09.02. Recreational Services. **Other Jobs in This Work Group:** Amusement and Recreation Attendants; Gaming and Sports Book Writers and Runners; Gaming Dealers; Motion Picture Projectionists; Recreation Workers; Slot Key Persons; Ushers, Lobby Attendants, and Ticket Takers. **PERSONALITY TYPE:** Social. Social occupations frequently involve working with, communicating with, and teaching people. These occupations often involve helping or providing service to others.

EDUCATION/TRAINING PROGRAM(S)—No data available. **RELATED KNOWLEDGE/COURSES—Customer and Personal Service:** Knowledge of principles and processes for providing customer and personal services. This includes customer needs assessment, meeting quality standards for services, and evaluation of customer satisfaction. **Sales and Marketing:** Knowledge of principles and methods for showing, promoting, and selling products or services. This includes marketing strategy and tactics, product demonstrations, sales techniques, and sales control systems.

Locksmiths and Safe Repairers

◎ Education/Training Required: Moderate-term on-the-job training
◎ Annual Earnings: $30,360
◎ Growth: 21.0%
◎ Annual Job Openings: 3,000
◎ Self-Employed: 16.8%
◎ Part-Time: 6.9%

Repair and open locks, make keys, change locks and safe combinations, and install and repair safes. Cut new or duplicate keys, using key-cutting machines. Keep records of company locks and keys. Insert new or repaired tumblers into locks in order to change combinations. Move picklocks in cylinders in order to open door locks without keys. Disassemble mechanical or electrical locking devices and repair or replace worn tumblers, springs, and other parts, using hand tools. Repair and adjust safes, vault doors, and vault components, using hand tools, lathes, drill presses, and welding and acetylene cutting apparatus. Install safes, vault doors, and deposit boxes according to blueprints, using equipment such as powered drills, taps, dies, truck cranes, and dollies. Open safe locks by drilling. **SKILLS—Installation:** Installing equipment, machines, wiring, or programs to meet specifications. **Repairing:** Repairing machines or systems by using the needed tools. **Equipment Maintenance:** Performing routine maintenance on equipment and determining when and what kind of maintenance is needed. **Troubleshooting:** Determining causes of operating errors and deciding what to do about them. **Service Orientation:** Actively looking for ways to help people. **Equipment Selection:** Determining the kind of tools and equipment needed to do a job. **Technology Design:** Generating or adapting equipment and technology to serve user needs. **Management of Material Resources:** Obtaining and seeing to the appropriate use of equipment, facilities, and materials needed to do certain work. **GOE—Interest Area:** 13. Manufacturing. **Work Group:** 13.13. Machinery Repair. **Other Jobs in This Work Group:** Bicycle Repairers; Gas Appliance Repairers; Hand and Portable Power Tool Repairers; Industrial Machinery Mechanics; Maintenance Workers, Machinery; Mechanical Door Repairers; Millwrights; Signal and Track Switch Repairers; Valve and Regulator Repairers. **PERSONALITY TYPE:** Realistic. Realistic occupations frequently involve work activities that include practical, hands-on problems and solutions. These occupations often deal with plants, animals, and real-world materials like wood, tools, and machinery. Many of the occupations require working outside and do not involve a lot of paperwork or working closely with others.

EDUCATION/TRAINING PROGRAM(S)— Locksmithing and Safe Repair. **RELATED KNOWL-**

EDGE/COURSES—**Customer and Personal Service:** Knowledge of principles and processes for providing customer and personal services. This includes customer needs assessment, meeting quality standards for services, and evaluation of customer satisfaction. **Administration and Management:** Knowledge of business and management principles involved in strategic planning, resource allocation, human resources modeling, leadership technique, production methods, and coordination of people and resources. **Clerical Practices:** Knowledge of administrative and clerical procedures and systems such as word processing, managing files and records, stenography and transcription, designing forms, and other office procedures and terminology. **Sales and Marketing:** Knowledge of principles and methods for showing, promoting, and selling products or services. This includes marketing strategy and tactics, product demonstrations, sales techniques, and sales control systems. **Public Safety and Security:** Knowledge of relevant equipment, policies, procedures, and strategies to promote effective local, state, or national security operations for the protection of people, data, property, and institutions. **Mechanical Devices:** Knowledge of machines and tools, including their designs, uses, repair, and maintenance. **Law and Government:** Knowledge of laws, legal codes, court procedures, precedents, government regulations, executive orders, agency rules, and the democratic political process.

Lodging Managers

- ◎ Education/Training Required: Work experience in a related occupation
- ◎ Annual Earnings: $37,660
- ◎ Growth: 6.6%
- ◎ Annual Job Openings: 10,000
- ◎ Self-Employed: 50.3%
- ◎ Part-Time: 7.2%

Plan, direct, or coordinate activities of an organization or department that provides lodging and other accommodations. Greet and register guests. Answer inquiries pertaining to hotel policies and services and resolve occupants' complaints. Assign duties to workers and schedule shifts. Coordinate front-office activities of hotels or motels and resolve problems. Participate in financial activities such as the setting of room rates, the establishment of budgets, and the allocation of funds to departments. Confer and cooperate with other managers in order to ensure coordination of hotel activities. Collect payments and record data pertaining to funds and expenditures. Manage and maintain temporary or permanent lodging facilities. Observe and monitor staff performance in order to ensure efficient operations and adherence to facility's policies and procedures. Train staff members in their duties. Show, rent, or assign accommodations. Develop and implement policies and procedures for the operation of a department or establishment. Inspect guest rooms, public areas, and grounds for cleanliness and appearance. Prepare required paperwork pertaining to departmental functions. Interview and hire applicants. Purchase supplies and arrange for outside services, such as deliveries, laundry, maintenance and repair, and trash collection. Arrange telephone answering services, deliver mail and packages, and answer questions regarding locations for eating and entertainment. Perform marketing and public relations activities. Organize and coordinate the work of staff and convention personnel for meetings to be held at a particular facility. Receive and process advance registration payments, send out letters of confirmation, and return checks when registrations cannot be accepted. Meet with clients in order to schedule and plan details of conventions, banquets, receptions, and other functions. Provide assistance to staff members by performing activities such as inspecting rooms, setting tables, and doing laundry. SKILLS—**Management of Financial Resources:** Determining how money will be spent to get the work done and accounting for these expenditures. **Social Perceptiveness:** Being aware of others' reactions and understanding why they react as they do. **Negotiation:** Bringing others together and trying to reconcile differences. **Management of Material Resources:** Obtaining and seeing to the appropriate use of equipment, facilities, and materials needed to do certain work. **Monitoring:** Monitoring or assessing your performance or that of other individuals or organizations to make improvements or take corrective action. **Management of Personnel Resources:** Motivating, developing, and directing people as they work, identifying the best people for the job. **Persuasion:** Persuading others to change their minds or behavior. **Time Management:** Managing one's own time and the time of others. **GOE—Interest Area:** 09. Hospitality, Tourism, and Recreation. **Work Group:** 09.01. Managerial Work in Hospitality and Tourism. **Other Jobs in This Work Group:** First-Line Supervisors/Managers of Food Preparation and Serving Workers; First-Line Supervisors/Managers of Personal Service Workers; Food Service Managers; Gaming Managers; Gaming Supervisors. **PERSONALITY TYPE:** Enterprising. Enterprising occupations frequently involve starting up and carrying out projects. These occupations can involve leading people and making many decisions. They sometimes require risk taking and often deal with business.

EDUCATION/TRAINING PROGRAM(S)—Hospitality Administration/Management, General; Hospitality and Recreation Marketing Operations; Hotel/Motel Administration/Management; Resort Management; Selling Skills and Sales Operations. **RELATED KNOWLEDGE/COURSES—Clerical Practices:** Knowledge of administrative and clerical procedures and systems such as word processing, managing files and records, stenography and transcription, designing forms, and other office procedures and terminology. **Sales and Marketing:** Knowledge of principles and methods for showing, promoting, and selling products or services. This includes marketing strategy and tactics, product demonstrations, sales techniques, and sales control systems. **Customer and Personal Service:** Knowledge of principles and processes for providing customer and personal services. This includes customer needs assessment, meeting quality standards for services, and evaluation of customer satisfaction. **Personnel and Human Resources:** Knowledge of principles and procedures for personnel recruitment, selection, training, compensation and benefits, labor relations and negotiation, and personnel information systems. **Psychology:** Knowledge of human behavior and performance; individual differences in ability, personality, and interests; learning and motivation; psychological research methods; and the assessment and treatment of behavioral and affective disorders. **Economics and Accounting:** Knowledge of economic and accounting principles and practices, the financial markets, banking, and the analysis and reporting of financial data.

Machinists

◉ Education/Training Required: Long-term on-the-job training
◉ Annual Earnings: $33,960
◉ Growth: 8.2%
◉ Annual Job Openings: 30,000
◉ Self-Employed: 2.7%
◉ Part-Time: 2.1%

Set up and operate a variety of machine tools to produce precision parts and instruments. Includes precision instrument makers who fabricate, modify, or repair mechanical instruments. May also fabricate and modify parts to make or repair machine tools or maintain industrial machines, applying knowledge of mechanics, shop mathematics, metal properties, layout, and machining procedures. Calculate dimensions and tolerances, using knowledge of mathematics and instruments such as micrometers and vernier calipers. Machine parts to specifications, using machine tools such as lathes, milling machines, shapers, or grinders. Measure, examine, and test completed units in order to detect defects and ensure conformance to specifications, using precision instruments such as micrometers. Set up, adjust, and operate all of the basic machine tools and many specialized or advanced variation tools in order to perform precision machining operations. Align and secure holding fixtures, cutting tools, attachments, accessories, and materials onto machines. Monitor the feed and speed of machines during the machining process. Study sample parts, blueprints, drawings, and engineering information in order to determine methods and sequences of operations needed to fabricate products and determine product dimensions and tolerances. Select the appropriate tools, machines, and materials to be used in preparation of machinery work. Lay out, measure, and mark metal stock in order to display placement of cuts. Observe and listen to operating machines or equipment in order to diagnose machine malfunctions and to determine need for adjustments or repairs. Check workpieces to ensure that they are properly lubricated and cooled. Maintain industrial machines, applying knowledge of mechanics, shop mathematics, metal properties, layout, and machining procedures. Position and fasten workpieces. Operate equipment to verify operational efficiency. Install repaired parts into equipment or install new equipment. Clean and lubricate machines, tools, and equipment in order to remove grease, rust, stains, and foreign matter. Advise clients about the materials being used for finished products. Program computers and electronic instruments such as numerically controlled machine tools. Set controls to regulate machining or enter commands to retrieve, input, or edit computerized machine control media. Confer with engineering, supervisory, and manufacturing personnel in order to exchange technical information. **SKILLS—Operation Monitoring:** Watching gauges, dials, or other indicators to make sure a machine is working properly. **Operation and Control:** Controlling operations of equipment or systems. **Equipment Maintenance:** Performing routine maintenance on equipment and determining when and what kind of maintenance is needed. **Quality Control Analysis:** Conducting tests and inspections of products, services, or processes to evaluate quality or performance. **Installation:** Installing equipment, machines, wiring, or programs to meet specifications. **Troubleshooting:** Determining causes of operating errors and deciding what to do about them. **Equipment Selection:** Determining the kind of tools and equipment needed to do a job. **Repairing:** Repairing machines or systems by using the needed tools. **GOE—Interest Area:** 13. Manufacturing. **Work Group:** 13.05. Production Machining Technology. **Other Jobs in This Work Group:** Foundry Mold and Coremakers; Lay-Out Workers, Metal and Plastic; Model Makers, Metal and Plastic; Numerical Control Machine Tool Operators and Tenders, Metal and Plastic; Numerical Tool and Process Control Programmers; Patternmakers, Metal and Plastic; Tool and Die Makers; Tool Grinders, Filers, and Sharpeners. **PERSONALITY TYPE:** Realistic. Realistic occupations frequently involve work activities that include practical, hands-on problems and solutions. These occupations often deal with plants, animals, and real-world materials like wood, tools, and machinery. Many of the occupations require working outside and do not involve a lot of paperwork or working closely with others.

EDUCATION/TRAINING PROGRAM(S)— Machine Shop Technology/Assistant; Machine Tool Technology/Machinist. **RELATED KNOWL-**EDGE/COURSES—Mechanical Devices: Knowledge of machines and tools, including their designs, uses, repair, and maintenance. **Mathematics:** Knowledge of arithmetic, algebra, geometry, calculus, and statistics and their applications. **Engineering and Technology:** Knowledge of the practical application of engineering science and technology. This includes applying principles, techniques, procedures, and equipment to the design and production of various goods and services. **Design:** Knowledge of design techniques, tools, and principles involved in production of precision technical plans, blueprints, drawings, and models. **Production and Processing:** Knowledge of raw materials, production processes, quality control, costs, and other techniques for maximizing the effective manufacture and distribution of goods. **Computers and Electronics:** Knowledge of circuit boards, processors, chips, electronic equipment, and computer hardware and software, including applications and programming.

Maintenance and Repair Workers, General

- Education/Training Required: Long-term on-the-job training
- Annual Earnings: $30,710
- Growth: 16.3%
- Annual Job Openings: 155,000
- Self-Employed: 0.9%
- Part-Time: 4.5%

Perform work involving the skills of two or more maintenance or craft occupations to keep machines, mechanical equipment, or the structure of an establishment in repair. Duties may involve pipe fitting; boilermaking; insulating; welding; machining; carpentry; repairing electrical or mechanical equipment; installing, aligning, and balancing new equipment; and repairing buildings, floors, or stairs. Repair or replace defective equipment parts, using hand tools and power tools, and reassemble equipment. Perform routine preventive maintenance to ensure that machines continue to run smoothly, building systems operate efficiently, and the physical condition of buildings does not deteriorate. Inspect drives, motors, and belts; check fluid levels; replace filters; and perform other maintenance actions, following checklists. Use tools ranging from common hand and power tools, such as hammers, hoists, saws, drills, and wrenches, to precision measuring instruments and electrical and electronic testing devices. Assemble, install, and/or repair wiring, electrical and electronic components, pipe systems and plumbing, machinery, and equipment. Diagnose mechanical problems and determine how to correct them, checking blueprints, repair manuals, and parts catalogs as necessary. Inspect, operate, and test machinery and equipment in order to diagnose machine malfunctions. Record maintenance and repair work performed and the costs of the work. Clean and lubricate shafts, bearings, gears, and other parts of machinery. Dismantle devices to gain access to and remove defective parts, using hoists, cranes, hand tools, and power tools. Plan and lay out repair work, using diagrams, drawings, blueprints, maintenance manuals, and schematic diagrams. Order parts, supplies, and equipment from catalogs and suppliers or obtain them from storerooms. Adjust functional parts of devices and control instruments, using hand tools, levels, plumb bobs, and straightedges. Paint and repair roofs, windows, doors, floors, woodwork, plaster, drywall, and other parts of building structures. Operate cutting torches or welding equipment to cut or join metal parts. Align and balance new equipment after installation. Inspect used parts to determine changes in dimensional requirements, using rules, calipers, micrometers, and other measuring instruments. Set up and operate machine tools to repair or fabricate machine parts, jigs and fixtures, and tools. Maintain and repair specialized equipment and machinery found in cafeterias, laundries, hospitals, stores, offices, and factories. **SKILLS—Equipment Maintenance:** Performing routine maintenance on equipment and determining when and what kind of maintenance is needed. **Installation:** Installing equipment, machines, wiring, or programs to meet specifications. **Repairing:** Repairing machines or systems by using the needed tools. **Troubleshooting:** Determining causes of operating errors and deciding what to do about them. **Operation Monitoring:** Watching gauges, dials, or other indicators to make sure a machine is working properly. **Equipment Selection:** Determining the kind of

tools and equipment needed to do a job. **Operation and Control:** Controlling operations of equipment or systems. **Technology Design:** Generating or adapting equipment and technology to serve user needs. **GOE—Interest Area:** 02. Architecture and Construction. **Work Group:** 02.05. Systems and Equipment Installation, Maintenance, and Repair. **Other Jobs in This Work Group:** Central Office and PBX Installers and Repairers; Communication Equipment Mechanics, Installers, and Repairers; Electric Meter Installers and Repairers; Electrical and Electronics Repairers, Powerhouse, Substation, and Relay; Electrical Power-Line Installers and Repairers; Elevator Installers and Repairers; Frame Wirers, Central Office; Heating and Air Conditioning Mechanics; Home Appliance Installers; Meter Mechanics; Refrigeration Mechanics; Station Installers and Repairers, Telephone; Telecommunications Facility Examiners; Telecommunications Line Installers and Repairers. **PERSONALITY TYPE:** Realistic. Realistic occupations frequently involve work activities that include practical, hands-on problems and solutions. These occupations often deal with plants, animals, and real-world materials like wood, tools, and machinery. Many of the occupations require working outside and do not involve a lot of paperwork or working closely with others.

EDUCATION/TRAINING PROGRAM(S)— Building/Construction Site Management/Manager. **RELATED KNOWLEDGE/COURSES—Mechanical Devices:** Knowledge of machines and tools, including their designs, uses, repair, and maintenance. **Building and Construction:** Knowledge of the materials, methods, and tools involved in the construction or repair of houses, buildings, or other structures such as highways and roads. **Design:** Knowledge of design techniques, tools, and principles involved in production of precision technical plans, blueprints, drawings, and models. **Public Safety and Security:** Knowledge of relevant equipment, policies, procedures, and strategies to promote effective local, state, or national security operations for the protection of people, data, property, and institutions. **Engineering and Technology:** Knowledge of the practical application of engineering science and technology. This includes applying principles, techniques, procedures, and equipment to the design and production of various goods and services. **Physics:** Knowledge and prediction of physical principles and laws and their interrelationships and applications to understanding fluid, material, and atmospheric dynamics and mechanical, electrical, atomic, and subatomic structures and processes.

Mapping Technicians

- ◎ Education/Training Required: Moderate-term on-the-job training
- ◎ Annual Earnings: $30,380
- ◎ Growth: 23.1%
- ◎ Annual Job Openings: 10,000
- ◎ Self-Employed: 5.5%
- ◎ Part-Time: 7.0%

Calculate mapmaking information from field notes and draw and verify accuracy of topographical maps. Analyze aerial photographs in order to detect and interpret significant military, industrial, resource, or topographical data. Calculate latitudes, longitudes, angles, areas, and other information for mapmaking, using survey field notes and reference tables. Check all layers of maps in order to ensure accuracy, identifying and marking errors and making corrections. Compare topographical features and contour lines with images from aerial photographs, old maps, and other reference materials in order to verify the accuracy of their identification. Compute and measure scaled distances between reference points in order to establish relative positions of adjoining prints and enable the creation of photographic mosaics. Form three-dimensional images of aerial photographs taken from different locations, using mathematical techniques and plotting instruments. Lay out and match aerial photographs in sequences in which they were taken and identify any areas missing from photographs. Monitor mapping work and the updating of maps in order to ensure accuracy, the inclusion of new and/or changed information, and compliance with rules and regulations. Produce and update overlay maps in order to show information boundaries, water locations, and topographic features on various base maps and at different scales. Redraw and correct maps, such as revising parcel maps to reflect tax code area changes, using information from official records and surveys. Trace contours and topographic details in order to generate maps that denote specific land and property locations and geographic attributes. Trim, align, and join prints in order to form photographic mosaics, maintaining scaled distances between reference points. Complete detailed source and method notes detailing the location of routine and complex land parcels. Create survey description pages and historical records related to the mapping activities and specifications of section plats. Determine scales, line sizes, and colors to be used for hard copies of computerized maps, using plotters. Enter GPS data, legal deeds, field notes, and land survey reports into GIS workstations so that information can be transformed into graphic land descriptions, such as maps and drawings. **SKILLS—Mathematics:** Using mathematics to solve problems. **Technology Design:** Generating or adapting equipment and technology to serve user needs. **Management of Personnel Resources:** Motivating, developing, and directing people as they work, identifying the best people for the job. **Operations Analysis:** Analyzing needs and product requirements to create a design. **GOE—Interest Area:** 15. Scientific Research, Engineering, and Mathematics. **Work Group:** 15.09. Engineering Technology. **Other Jobs in This Work Group:** Aerospace Engineering and Operations Technicians; Calibration and Instrumentation Technicians; Cartographers and Photogrammetrists; Civil Engineering Technicians; Electrical Engineering Technicians; Electro-Mechanical Technicians; Electronic Drafters; Electronics Engineering Technicians; Environmental Engineering Technicians; Mechanical Drafters; Mechanical Engineering Technicians; Surveying Technicians. **PERSONALITY TYPE:** Conventional. Conventional occupations frequently involve following set procedures and routines. These occupations can include working with data and details more than with ideas. Usually there is a clear line of authority to follow.

EDUCATION/TRAINING PROGRAM(S)—Cartography; Surveying Technology/Surveying. **RELATED KNOWLEDGE/COURSES—Geography:** Knowledge of principles and methods for describing the features of land, sea, and air masses, including their physical characteristics; locations; interrelationships; and distribution of plant, animal, and human life. **Design:** Knowledge of design techniques, tools, and principles involved in production of precision technical plans, blueprints, drawings, and models. **Mathe-**

matics: Knowledge of arithmetic, algebra, geometry, calculus, and statistics and their applications. **Computers and Electronics:** Knowledge of circuit boards, processors, chips, electronic equipment, and computer hardware and software, including applications and programming. **Administration and Management:** Knowledge of business and management principles involved in strategic planning, resource allocation, human resources modeling, leadership technique, production methods, and coordination of people and resources. **Engineering and Technology:** Knowledge of the practical application of engineering science and technology. This includes applying principles, techniques, procedures, and equipment to the design and production of various goods and services.

Marine Cargo Inspectors

- ◎ Education/Training Required: Work experience in a related occupation
- ◎ Annual Earnings: $50,380
- ◎ Growth: 7.7%
- ◎ Annual Job Openings: 5,000
- ◎ Self-Employed: 0.4%
- ◎ Part-Time: 3.2%

Inspect cargoes of seagoing vessels to certify compliance with health and safety regulations in cargo handling and stowage. Inspects loaded cargo in holds and cargo-handling devices to determine compliance with regulations and need for maintenance. Reads vessel documents to ascertain cargo capabilities according to design and cargo regulations. Calculates gross and net tonnage, hold capacities, volume of stored fuel and water, cargo weight, and ship stability factors, using mathematical formulas. Determines type of license and safety equipment required and computes applicable tolls and wharfage fees. Examines blueprints of ship and takes physical measurements to determine capacity and depth of vessel in water, using measuring instruments. Writes certificates of admeasurement, listing details such as design, length, depth, and breadth of vessel and method of propulsion. Issues certificate of compliance when violations are not detected or recommends remedial procedures to correct deficiencies. Times roll of ship, using stopwatch. Analyzes data, for-

mulates recommendations, and writes reports of findings. Advises crew in techniques of stowing dangerous and heavy cargo according to knowledge of hazardous cargo. **SKILLS—Mathematics:** Using mathematics to solve problems. **Writing:** Communicating effectively in writing as appropriate for the needs of the audience. **Systems Evaluation:** Identifying measures or indicators of system performance and the actions needed to improve or correct performance relative to the goals of the system. **Systems Analysis:** Determining how a system should work and how changes in conditions, operations, and the environment will affect outcomes. **Reading Comprehension:** Understanding written sentences and paragraphs in work-related documents. **Active Listening:** Giving full attention to what other people are saying, taking time to understand the points being made, asking questions as appropriate, and not interrupting at inappropriate times. **Speaking:** Talking to others to convey information effectively. **Judgment and Decision Making:** Considering the relative costs and benefits of potential actions to choose the most appropriate one. **GOE—Interest Area:** 07. Government and Public Administration. **Work Group:** 07.03. Regulations Enforcement. **Other Jobs in This Work Group:** Agricultural Inspectors; Aviation Inspectors; Child Support, Missing Persons, and Unemployment Insurance Fraud Investigators; Environmental Compliance Inspectors; Equal Opportunity Representatives and Officers; Financial Examiners; Fire Inspectors; Fish and Game Wardens; Forest Fire Inspectors and Prevention Specialists; Government Property Inspectors and Investigators; Immigration and Customs Inspectors; Licensing Examiners and Inspectors; Mechanical Inspectors; Motor Vehicle Inspectors; Nuclear Monitoring Technicians; Occupational Health and Safety Specialists; Pressure Vessel Inspectors; Railroad Inspectors; Tax Examiners, Collectors, and Revenue Agents. **PERSONALITY TYPE:** Conventional. Conventional occupations frequently involve following set procedures and routines. These occupations can include working with data and details more than with ideas. Usually there is a clear line of authority to follow.

EDUCATION/TRAINING PROGRAM(S)—No data available. **RELATED KNOWLEDGE/COURSES—Public Safety and Security:** Knowledge of relevant equipment, policies, procedures, and strategies to promote effective local, state, or national security operations for the protection of people, data, property, and institutions. **Mathematics:** Knowledge of arithmetic, algebra, geometry, calculus, and statistics and their applications. **Transportation:** Knowledge of principles and methods for moving people or goods by air, rail, sea, or road, including the relative costs and benefits. **Design:** Knowledge of design techniques, tools, and principles involved in production of precision technical plans, blueprints, drawings, and models. **Physics:** Knowledge and prediction of physical principles and laws and their interrelationships and applications to understanding fluid, material, and atmospheric dynamics and mechanical, electrical, atomic, and subatomic structures and processes. **Law and Government:** Knowledge of laws, legal codes, court procedures, precedents, government regulations, executive orders, agency rules, and the democratic political process.

Massage Therapists

- Education/Training Required: Postsecondary vocational training
- Annual Earnings: $31,960
- Growth: 27.1%
- Annual Job Openings: 24,000
- Self-Employed: 70.1%
- Part-Time: 41.2%

Massage customers for hygienic or remedial purposes. Apply finger and hand pressure to specific points of the body. Assess clients' soft tissue condition, joint quality and function, muscle strength, and range of motion. Confer with clients about their medical histories and any problems with stress and/or pain in order to determine whether massage would be helpful. Develop and propose client treatment plans that specify which types of massage are to be used. Massage and knead the muscles and soft tissues of the human body in order to provide courses of treatment for medical conditions and injuries or wellness maintenance. Prepare and blend oils and apply the blends to clients' skin. Consult with other health care professionals such as physiotherapists, chiropractors, physicians, and psychologists in order to develop treatment plans for

clients. Maintain treatment records. Provide clients with guidance and information about techniques for postural improvement and stretching, strengthening, relaxation, and rehabilitative exercises. Refer clients to other types of therapists when necessary. Use complementary aids such as infrared lamps, wet compresses, ice, and whirlpool baths in order to promote clients' recovery, relaxation, and well-being. Treat clients in own offices or travel to clients' offices and homes. **SKILLS**—No data available. **GOE—Interest Area:** 08. Health Science. **Work Group:** 08.07. Medical Therapy. **Other Jobs in This Work Group:** Audiologists; Occupational Therapist Aides; Occupational Therapist Assistants; Occupational Therapists; Physical Therapist Aides; Physical Therapist Assistants; Physical Therapists; Radiation Therapists; Recreational Therapists; Respiratory Therapists; Respiratory Therapy Technicians; Speech-Language Pathologists. **PERSONALITY TYPE:** No data available.

EDUCATION/TRAINING PROGRAM(S)—Asian Bodywork Therapy; Massage Therapy/Therapeutic Massage; Somatic Bodywork; Somatic Bodywork and Related Therapeutic Services, Other. **RELATED KNOWLEDGE/COURSES**—No data available.

Materials Inspectors

- Education/Training Required: Moderate-term on-the-job training
- Annual Earnings: $28,410
- Growth: 4.7%
- Annual Job Openings: 87,000
- Self-Employed: 1.2%
- Part-Time: 5.0%

Examine and inspect materials and finished parts and products for defects and wear and to ensure conformance with work orders, diagrams, blueprints, and template specifications. Usually specialize in a single phase of inspection. Inspects materials, products, and work in progress for conformance to specifications and adjusts process or assembly equipment to meet standards. Collects samples for testing and computes findings. Reads dials and meters to verify functioning of equipment according to specifications. Analyzes and

M

interprets blueprints, sample data, and other materials to determine, change, or measure specifications or inspection and testing procedures. Tests and measures finished products, components, or assemblies for functioning, operation, accuracy, or assembly to verify adherence to functional specifications. Observes and monitors production operations and equipment to ensure proper assembly of parts or assists in testing and monitoring activities. Marks items for acceptance or rejection, records test results and inspection data, and compares findings with specifications to ensure conformance to standards. Confers with vendors and others regarding inspection results; recommends corrective procedures; and compiles reports of results, recommendations, and needed repairs. Supervises testing or drilling activities and adjusts equipment to obtain sample fluids or to direct drilling. Operates or tends machinery and equipment and uses hand tools. Fabricates, installs, positions, or connects components, parts, finished products, or instruments for testing or operational purposes. **SKILLS—Quality Control Analysis:** Conducting tests and inspections of products, services, or processes to evaluate quality or performance. **Operation Monitoring:** Watching gauges, dials, or other indicators to make sure a machine is working properly. **Troubleshooting:** Determining causes of operating errors and deciding what to do about them. **Operation and Control:** Controlling operations of equipment or systems. **Technology Design:** Generating or adapting equipment and technology to serve user needs. **Installation:** Installing equipment, machines, wiring, or programs to meet specifications. **Science:** Using scientific rules and methods to solve problems. **Mathematics:** Using mathematics to solve problems. **GOE—Interest Area:** 13. Manufacturing. **Work Group:** 13.07. Production Quality Control. **Other Jobs in This Work Group:** Electrical and Electronic Inspectors and Testers; Graders and Sorters, Agricultural Products; Precision Devices Inspectors and Testers; Production Inspectors, Testers, Graders, Sorters, Samplers, Weighers. **PERSONALITY TYPE:** Realistic. Realistic occupations frequently involve work activities that include practical, hands-on problems and solutions. These occupations often deal with plants, animals, and real-world materials like wood, tools, and machinery. Many of the occupations require working outside and do not

involve a lot of paperwork or working closely with others.

EDUCATION/TRAINING PROGRAM(S)—Quality Control Technology/Technician. **RELATED KNOWLEDGE/COURSES—Design:** Knowledge of design techniques, tools, and principles involved in production of precision technical plans, blueprints, drawings, and models. **Mechanical Devices:** Knowledge of machines and tools, including their designs, uses, repair, and maintenance. **Production and Processing:** Knowledge of raw materials, production processes, quality control, costs, and other techniques for maximizing the effective manufacture and distribution of goods. **Engineering and Technology:** Knowledge of the practical application of engineering science and technology. This includes applying principles, techniques, procedures, and equipment to the design and production of various goods and services. **Physics:** Knowledge and prediction of physical principles and laws and their interrelationships and applications to understanding fluid, material, and atmospheric dynamics and mechanical, electrical, atomic, and subatomic structures and processes. **Public Safety and Security:** Knowledge of relevant equipment, policies, procedures, and strategies to promote effective local, state, or national security operations for the protection of people, data, property, and institutions.

Mechanical Engineering Technicians

- Education/Training Required: Associate degree
- Annual Earnings: $43,400
- Growth: 11.0%
- Annual Job Openings: 6,000
- Self-Employed: 0.4%
- Part-Time: 5.0%

Apply theory and principles of mechanical engineering to modify, develop, and test machinery and equipment under direction of engineering staff or physical scientists. Prepare parts sketches and write work orders and purchase requests to be furnished by outside contractors. Draft detail drawing or sketch for drafting room completion or to request parts fabrication by machine, sheet, or wood shops. Review project instructions and blueprints to ascertain test specifications, procedures, and objectives and test nature of technical problems, such as redesign. Review project instructions and specifications to identify, modify, and plan requirements fabrication, assembly, and testing. Devise, fabricate, and assemble new or modified mechanical components for products such as industrial machinery or equipment and measuring instruments. Discuss changes in design, method of manufacture and assembly, and drafting techniques and procedures with staff and coordinate corrections. Set up and conduct tests of complete units and components under operational conditions to investigate proposals for improving equipment performance. Inspect lines and figures for clarity and return erroneous drawings to designer for correction. Analyze test results in relation to design or rated specifications and test objectives and modify or adjust equipment to meet specifications. Evaluate tool drawing designs by measuring drawing dimensions and comparing with original specifications for form and function, using engineering skills. Confer with technicians, submit reports of test results to engineering department, and recommend design or material changes. Calculate required capacities for equipment of proposed system to obtain specified performance and submit data to engineering personnel for approval. Record test procedures and results, numerical and graphical data, and recommendations for changes in product or test methods. Read dials and meters to determine amperage, voltage, and electrical output and input at specific operating temperature to analyze parts performance. Estimate cost factors, including labor and material for purchased and fabricated parts and costs for assembly, testing, and installing. Set up prototype and test apparatus and operate test, controlling equipment to observe and record prototype test results. **SKILLS— Troubleshooting:** Determining causes of operating errors and deciding what to do about them. **Installation:** Installing equipment, machines, wiring, or programs to meet specifications. **Coordination:** Adjusting actions in relation to others' actions. **Technology Design:** Generating or adapting equipment and technology to serve user needs. **Equipment Selection:** Determining the kind of tools and equipment needed

to do a job. **Service Orientation:** Actively looking for ways to help people. **Operations Analysis:** Analyzing needs and product requirements to create a design. **Time Management:** Managing one's own time and the time of others. **GOE—Interest Area:** 15. Scientific Research, Engineering, and Mathematics. **Work Group:** 15.09. Engineering Technology. **Other Jobs in This Work Group:** Aerospace Engineering and Operations Technicians; Calibration and Instrumentation Technicians; Cartographers and Photogrammetrists; Civil Engineering Technicians; Electrical Engineering Technicians; Electro-Mechanical Technicians; Electronic Drafters; Electronics Engineering Technicians; Environmental Engineering Technicians; Mapping Technicians; Mechanical Drafters; Surveying Technicians. **PERSONALITY TYPE:** Realistic. Realistic occupations frequently involve work activities that include practical, hands-on problems and solutions. These occupations often deal with plants, animals, and real-world materials like wood, tools, and machinery. Many of the occupations require working outside and do not involve a lot of paperwork or working closely with others.

EDUCATION/TRAINING PROGRAM(S)— Mechanical Engineering–Related Technologies/Technicians, Other; Mechanical Engineering/Mechanical Technology/Technician. **RELATED KNOWLEDGE/COURSES—Engineering and Technology:** Knowledge of the practical application of engineering science and technology. This includes applying principles, techniques, procedures, and equipment to the design and production of various goods and services. **Design:** Knowledge of design techniques, tools, and principles involved in production of precision technical plans, blueprints, drawings, and models. **Mechanical Devices:** Knowledge of machines and tools, including their designs, uses, repair, and maintenance. **Physics:** Knowledge and prediction of physical principles and laws and their interrelationships and applications to understanding fluid, material, and atmospheric dynamics and mechanical, electrical, atomic, and subatomic structures and processes. **Computers and Electronics:** Knowledge of circuit boards, processors, chips, electronic equipment, and computer hardware and software, including applications and programming. **Production and Processing:** Knowledge of raw materials, production processes, quality control, costs, and other techniques for maximizing the effective manufacture and distribution of goods.

Mechanical Inspectors

- Education/Training Required: Long-term on-the-job training
- Annual Earnings: $28,410
- Growth: 4.7%
- Annual Job Openings: 87,000
- Self-Employed: 1.2%
- Part-Time: 5.0%

Inspect and test mechanical assemblies and systems, such as motors, vehicles, and transportation equipment, for defects and wear to ensure compliance with specifications. Tests and measures finished products, components, or assemblies for functioning, operation, accuracy, or assembly to verify adherence to functional specifications. Inspects materials, products, and work in progress for conformance to specifications and adjusts process or assembly equipment to meet standards. Starts and operates finished products for testing or inspection. Reads dials and meters to ensure that equipment is operating according to specifications. Collects samples for testing and computes findings. Marks items for acceptance or rejection, records test results and inspection data, and compares findings with specifications to ensure conformance to standards. Discards or rejects products, materials, and equipment not meeting specifications. Reads and interprets materials such as work orders, inspection manuals, and blueprints to determine inspection and test procedures. Analyzes and interprets sample data. Installs and positions new or replacement parts, components, and instruments. Estimates and records operational data. Completes necessary procedures to satisfy licensing requirements and indicates concurrence with acceptance or rejection decisions. Confers with vendors and others regarding inspection results; recommends corrective procedures; and compiles reports of results, recommendations, and needed repairs. Cleans and maintains test equipment and instruments to ensure proper functioning. **SKILLS—Quality Control Analysis:** Conducting tests and inspections of products, services, or processes to evaluate quality or

performance. **Science:** Using scientific rules and methods to solve problems. **Installation:** Installing equipment, machines, wiring, or programs to meet specifications. **Operation Monitoring:** Watching gauges, dials, or other indicators to make sure a machine is working properly. **Troubleshooting:** Determining causes of operating errors and deciding what to do about them. **Operation and Control:** Controlling operations of equipment or systems. **Equipment Maintenance:** Performing routine maintenance on equipment and determining when and what kind of maintenance is needed. **Repairing:** Repairing machines or systems by using the needed tools. **GOE—Interest Area:** 07. Government and Public Administration. **Work Group:** 07.03. Regulations Enforcement. **Other Jobs in This Work Group:** Agricultural Inspectors; Aviation Inspectors; Child Support, Missing Persons, and Unemployment Insurance Fraud Investigators; Environmental Compliance Inspectors; Equal Opportunity Representatives and Officers; Financial Examiners; Fire Inspectors; Fish and Game Wardens; Forest Fire Inspectors and Prevention Specialists; Government Property Inspectors and Investigators; Immigration and Customs Inspectors; Licensing Examiners and Inspectors; Marine Cargo Inspectors; Motor Vehicle Inspectors; Nuclear Monitoring Technicians; Occupational Health and Safety Specialists; Pressure Vessel Inspectors; Railroad Inspectors; Tax Examiners, Collectors, and Revenue Agents. **PERSONALITY TYPE:** Realistic. Realistic occupations frequently involve work activities that include practical, hands-on problems and solutions. These occupations often deal with plants, animals, and real-world materials like wood, tools, and machinery. Many of the occupations require working outside and do not involve a lot of paperwork or working closely with others.

EDUCATION/TRAINING PROGRAM(S)— Quality Control Technology/Technician. **RELATED KNOWLEDGE/COURSES—Mechanical Devices:** Knowledge of machines and tools, including their designs, uses, repair, and maintenance. **Design:** Knowledge of design techniques, tools, and principles involved in production of precision technical plans, blueprints, drawings, and models. **Engineering and Technology:** Knowledge of the practical application of engineering science and technology. This includes applying principles, techniques, procedures, and equipment to the design and production of various goods and services. **Production and Processing:** Knowledge of raw materials, production processes, quality control, costs, and other techniques for maximizing the effective manufacture and distribution of goods. **Public Safety and Security:** Knowledge of relevant equipment, policies, procedures, and strategies to promote effective local, state, or national security operations for the protection of people, data, property, and institutions. **Physics:** Knowledge and prediction of physical principles and laws and their interrelationships and applications to understanding fluid, material, and atmospheric dynamics and mechanical, electrical, atomic, and subatomic structures and processes.

Medical and Clinical Laboratory Technicians

- Education/Training Required: Associate degree
- Annual Earnings: $30,840
- Growth: 19.4%
- Annual Job Openings: 21,000
- Self-Employed: 1.6%
- Part-Time: 16.0%

Perform routine medical laboratory tests for the diagnosis, treatment, and prevention of disease. May work under the supervision of a medical technologist. Conduct chemical analyses of body fluids, such as blood and urine, using microscope or automatic analyzer to detect abnormalities or diseases, and enter findings into computer. Set up, adjust, maintain, and clean medical laboratory equipment. Analyze the results of tests and experiments to ensure conformity to specifications, using special mechanical and electrical devices. Analyze and record test data to issue reports that use charts, graphs, and narratives. Perform medical research to further control and cure disease. Conduct blood tests for transfusion purposes and perform blood counts. Obtain specimens, cultivating, isolating, and identifying microorganisms for analysis. Examine cells stained with dye to locate abnormalities.

Collect blood or tissue samples from patients, observing principles of asepsis to obtain blood sample. Consult with a pathologist to determine a final diagnosis when abnormal cells are found. Inoculate fertilized eggs, broths, or other bacteriological media with organisms. Cut, stain, and mount tissue samples for examination by pathologists. Supervise and instruct other technicians and laboratory assistants. Prepare standard volumetric solutions and reagents to be combined with samples, following standardized formulas or experimental procedures. Prepare vaccines and serums by standard laboratory methods, testing for virus inactivity and sterility. Test raw materials, processes, and finished products to determine quality and quantity of materials or characteristics of a substance. **SKILLS—Equipment Maintenance:** Performing routine maintenance on equipment and determining when and what kind of maintenance is needed. **Science:** Using scientific rules and methods to solve problems. **Troubleshooting:** Determining causes of operating errors and deciding what to do about them. **Instructing:** Teaching others how to do something. **Monitoring:** Monitoring or assessing your performance or that of other individuals or organizations to make improvements or take corrective action. **Service Orientation:** Actively looking for ways to help people. **Operation Monitoring:** Watching gauges, dials, or other indicators to make sure a machine is working properly. **Quality Control Analysis:** Conducting tests and inspections of products, services, or processes to evaluate quality or performance. **Time Management:** Managing one's own time and the time of others. **GOE—Interest Area:** 08. Health Science. **Work Group:** 08.06. Medical Technology. **Other Jobs in This Work Group:** Biological Technicians; Cardiovascular Technologists and Technicians; Diagnostic Medical Sonographers; Medical and Clinical Laboratory Technologists; Medical Equipment Preparers; Medical Records and Health Information Technicians; Nuclear Medicine Technologists; Opticians, Dispensing; Orthotists and Prosthetists; Radiologic Technicians; Radiologic Technologists. **PERSONALITY TYPE:** Realistic. Realistic occupations frequently involve work activities that include practical, hands-on problems and solutions. These occupations often deal with plants, animals, and real-world materials like wood, tools, and machinery. Many of the occupations require working outside and do not involve a lot of paperwork or working closely with others.

EDUCATION/TRAINING PROGRAM(S)— Blood Bank Technology Specialist; Clinical/Medical Laboratory Assistant; Clinical/Medical Laboratory Technician; Hematology Technology/Technician; Histologic Technician. **RELATED KNOWLEDGE/ COURSES—Medicine and Dentistry:** Knowledge of the information and techniques needed to diagnose and treat human injuries, diseases, and deformities. This includes symptoms, treatment alternatives, drug properties and interactions, and preventive health-care measures. **Therapy and Counseling:** Knowledge of principles, methods, and procedures for diagnosis, treatment, and rehabilitation of physical and mental dysfunctions and for career counseling and guidance. **Clerical Practices:** Knowledge of administrative and clerical procedures and systems such as word processing, managing files and records, stenography and transcription, designing forms, and other office procedures and terminology. **Biology:** Knowledge of plant and animal organisms and their tissues, cells, functions, interdependencies, and interactions with each other and the environment. **Chemistry:** Knowledge of the chemical composition, structure, and properties of substances and of the chemical processes and transformations that they undergo. This includes uses of chemicals and their danger signs, production techniques, and disposal methods. **Customer and Personal Service:** Knowledge of principles and processes for providing customer and personal services. This includes customer needs assessment, meeting quality standards for services, and evaluation of customer satisfaction.

Medical Assistants

- Education/Training Required: Moderate-term on-the-job training
- Annual Earnings: $24,610
- Growth: 58.9%
- Annual Job Openings: 78,000
- Self-Employed: 2.3%
- Part-Time: 25.3%

Perform administrative and certain clinical duties under the direction of physician. Administrative duties may include scheduling appointments, maintaining medical records, billing, and coding for insurance purposes. Clinical duties may include taking and recording vital signs and medical histories, preparing patients for examination, drawing blood, and administering medications as directed by physician. Interview patients to obtain medical information and measure their vital signs, weight, and height. Show patients to examination rooms and prepare them for the physician. Record patients' medical history, vital statistics, and information such as test results in medical records. Prepare and administer medications as directed by a physician. Collect blood, tissue, or other laboratory specimens; log the specimens; and prepare them for testing. Explain treatment procedures, medications, diets, and physicians' instructions to patients. Help physicians examine and treat patients, handing them instruments and materials or performing such tasks as giving injections and removing sutures. Authorize drug refills and provide prescription information to pharmacies. Prepare treatment rooms for patient examinations, keeping the rooms neat and clean. Clean and sterilize instruments and dispose of contaminated supplies. Schedule appointments for patients. Change dressings on wounds. Greet and log in patients arriving at office or clinic. Contact medical facilities or departments to schedule patients for tests and/or admission. Perform general office duties such as answering telephones, taking dictation, and completing insurance forms. Inventory and order medical, lab, and office supplies and equipment. Perform routine laboratory tests and sample analyses. Set up medical laboratory equipment. Keep financial records and perform other bookkeeping duties, such as handling credit and collections and mailing monthly statements to patients. Operate X-ray, electrocardiogram (EKG), and other equipment to administer routine diagnostic tests. **SKILLS—Social Perceptiveness:** Being aware of others' reactions and understanding why they react as they do. **Service Orientation:** Actively looking for ways to help people. **Instructing:** Teaching others how to do something. **Active Listening:** Giving full attention to what other people are saying, taking time to understand the points being made, asking questions as appropriate, and not interrupting at inappropriate times. **Learning Strategies:** Selecting and using training/instructional methods and procedures appropriate for the situation when learning or teaching new things. **Negotiation:** Bringing others together and trying to reconcile differences. **Troubleshooting:** Determining causes of operating errors and deciding what to do about them. **Reading Comprehension:** Understanding written sentences and paragraphs in work-related documents. **Operation Monitoring:** Watching gauges, dials, or other indicators to make sure a machine is working properly. **GOE—Interest Area:** 08. Health Science. **Work Group:** 08.02. Medicine and Surgery. **Other Jobs in This Work Group:** Anesthesiologists; Family and General Practitioners; Internists, General; Medical Transcriptionists; Obstetricians and Gynecologists; Pediatricians, General; Pharmacists; Pharmacy Aides; Pharmacy Technicians; Physician Assistants; Psychiatrists; Registered Nurses; Surgeons; Surgical Technologists. **PERSONALITY TYPE:** Social. Social occupations frequently involve working with, communicating with, and teaching people. These occupations often involve helping or providing service to others.

EDUCATION/TRAINING PROGRAM(S)— Allied Health and Medical Assisting Services, Other; Anesthesiologist Assistant; Chiropractic Assistant/ Technician; Medical Administrative/Executive Assistant and Medical Secretary; Medical Insurance Coding Specialist/Coder; Medical Office Assistant/Specialist; Medical Office Management/Administration; Medical Reception/Receptionist; Medical/Clinical Assistant; Opthalmic Technician/Technologist; Optomeric Technician/Assistant; Orthoptics/Orthoptist. **RELATED KNOWLEDGE/COURSES—Medicine and Dentistry:** Knowledge of the information and techniques needed to diagnose and treat human injuries, diseases, and deformities. This includes symptoms, treatment alternatives, drug properties and interactions, and preventive health-care measures. **Customer and Personal Service:** Knowledge of principles and processes for providing customer and personal services. This includes customer needs assessment, meeting quality standards for services, and evaluation of customer satisfaction. **Clerical Practices:** Knowledge of administrative and clerical procedures and systems such as word processing, managing files and records, stenography and transcription, designing forms, and other office procedures and terminology. **Psychology:** Knowledge

of human behavior and performance; individual differences in ability, personality, and interests; learning and motivation; psychological research methods; and the assessment and treatment of behavioral and affective disorders. **Therapy and Counseling:** Knowledge of principles, methods, and procedures for diagnosis, treatment, and rehabilitation of physical and mental dysfunctions and for career counseling and guidance. **English Language:** Knowledge of the structure and content of the English language, including the meaning and spelling of words, rules of composition, and grammar.

Medical Equipment Repairers

- Education/Training Required: Moderate-term on-the-job training
- Annual Earnings: $37,220
- Growth: 14.8%
- Annual Job Openings: 4,000
- Self-Employed: 23.2%
- Part-Time: 10.1%

Test, adjust, or repair biomedical or electromedical equipment. Inspect and test malfunctioning medical and related equipment, following manufacturers' specifications and using test and analysis instruments. Examine medical equipment and facility's structural environment and check for proper use of equipment to protect patients and staff from electrical or mechanical hazards and to ensure compliance with safety regulations. Disassemble malfunctioning equipment and remove, repair, and replace defective parts such as motors, clutches, or transformers. Keep records of maintenance, repair, and required updates of equipment. Perform preventive maintenance or service such as cleaning, lubricating, and adjusting equipment. Test and calibrate components and equipment, following manufacturers' manuals and troubleshooting techniques and using hand tools, power tools, and measuring devices. Explain and demonstrate correct operation and preventive maintenance of medical equipment to personnel. Study technical manuals and attend training sessions provided by equipment manufacturers to maintain current knowledge. Plan and carry out work assignments, using blueprints, schematic drawings, technical manuals, wiring diagrams, and liquid and air flow sheets, while following prescribed regulations, directives, and other instructions as required. Solder loose connections, using soldering iron. Test, evaluate, and classify excess or in-use medial equipment and determine serviceability, condition, and disposition in accordance with regulations. Research catalogs and repair part lists to locate sources for repair parts, requisitioning parts and recording their receipt. Evaluate technical specifications to identify equipment and systems best suited for intended use and possible purchase based on specifications, user needs, and technical requirements. Contribute expertise to develop medical maintenance standard operating procedures. Compute power and space requirements for installing medical, dental, or related equipment and install units to manufacturers' specifications. Supervise and advise subordinate personnel. **SKILLS—Repairing:** Repairing machines or systems by using the needed tools. **Installation:** Installing equipment, machines, wiring, or programs to meet specifications. **Equipment Maintenance:** Performing routine maintenance on equipment and determining when and what kind of maintenance is needed. **Troubleshooting:** Determining causes of operating errors and deciding what to do about them. **Systems Analysis:** Determining how a system should work and how changes in conditions, operations, and the environment will affect outcomes. **Service Orientation:** Actively looking for ways to help people. **Operation Monitoring:** Watching gauges, dials, or other indicators to make sure a machine is working properly. **Instructing:** Teaching others how to do something. **GOE—Interest Area:** 13. Manufacturing. **Work Group:** 13.15. Medical and Technical Equipment Repair. **Other Jobs in This Work Group:** Camera and Photographic Equipment Repairers; Watch Repairers. **PERSONALITY TYPE:** Realistic. Realistic occupations frequently involve work activities that include practical, hands-on problems and solutions. These occupations often deal with plants, animals, and real-world materials like wood, tools, and machinery. Many of the occupations require working outside and do not involve a lot of paperwork or working closely with others.

EDUCATION/TRAINING PROGRAM(S)—Biomedical Technology/Technician. **RELATED KNOWLEDGE/COURSES—Computers and Electronics:** Knowledge of circuit boards, processors, chips, electronic equipment, and computer hardware and software, including applications and programming. **Mechanical Devices:** Knowledge of machines and tools, including their designs, uses, repair, and maintenance. **Engineering and Technology:** Knowledge of the practical application of engineering science and technology. This includes applying principles, techniques, procedures, and equipment to the design and production of various goods and services. **Customer and Personal Service:** Knowledge of principles and processes for providing customer and personal services. This includes customer needs assessment, meeting quality standards for services, and evaluation of customer satisfaction. **Physics:** Knowledge and prediction of physical principles and laws and their interrelationships and applications to understanding fluid, material, and atmospheric dynamics and mechanical, electrical, atomic, and subatomic structures and processes. **Chemistry:** Knowledge of the chemical composition, structure, and properties of substances and of the chemical processes and transformations that they undergo. This includes uses of chemicals and their danger signs, production techniques, and disposal methods. **Telecommunications:** Knowledge of transmission, broadcasting, switching, control, and operation of telecommunications systems.

Medical Records and Health Information Technicians

- Education/Training Required: Associate degree
- Annual Earnings: $25,590
- Growth: 46.8%
- Annual Job Openings: 24,000
- Self-Employed: 1.1%
- Part-Time: 17.6%

Compile, process, and maintain medical records of hospital and clinic patients in a manner consistent with medical, administrative, ethical, legal, and regulatory requirements of the health-care system. Process, maintain, compile, and report patient information for health requirements and standards. Protect the security of medical records to ensure that confidentiality is maintained. Process patient admission and discharge documents. Review records for completeness, accuracy, and compliance with regulations. Compile and maintain patients' medical records to document condition and treatment and to provide data for research or cost control and care improvement efforts. Enter data such as demographic characteristics, history and extent of disease, diagnostic procedures, and treatment into computer. Release information to persons and agencies according to regulations. Plan, develop, maintain, and operate a variety of health record indexes and storage and retrieval systems to collect, classify, store, and analyze information. Manage the department and supervise clerical workers, directing and controlling activities of personnel in the medical records department. Transcribe medical reports. Identify, compile, abstract, and code patient data, using standard classification systems. Resolve/clarify codes and diagnoses with conflicting, missing, or unclear information by consulting with doctors or others to get additional information and by participating in the coding team's regular meetings. Train medical records staff. Assign the patient to one of several hundred "diagnosis-related groups," or DRGs, using appropriate computer software. Post medical insurance billings. Process and prepare business and government forms. Contact discharged patients, their families, and physicians to maintain registry with follow-up information, such as quality of life and length of survival of cancer patients. Prepare statistical reports, narrative reports, and graphic presentations of information such as tumor registry data for use by hospital staff, researchers, and other users. Consult classification manuals to locate information about disease processes. Compile medical care and census data for statistical reports on diseases treated, surgery performed, and use of hospital beds. Develop in-service educational materials. **SKILLS—Instructing:** Teaching others how to do something. **Systems Evaluation:** Identifying measures or indicators of system performance and the

actions needed to improve or correct performance relative to the goals of the system. **Active Listening:** Giving full attention to what other people are saying, taking time to understand the points being made, asking questions as appropriate, and not interrupting at inappropriate times. **Learning Strategies:** Selecting and using training/instructional methods and procedures appropriate for the situation when learning or teaching new things. **Time Management:** Managing one's own time and the time of others. **Service Orientation:** Actively looking for ways to help people. **Critical Thinking:** Using logic and reasoning to identify the strengths and weaknesses of alternative solutions, conclusions, or approaches to problems. **Reading Comprehension:** Understanding written sentences and paragraphs in work-related documents. **Social Perceptiveness:** Being aware of others' reactions and understanding why they react as they do. **GOE—Interest Area:** 08. Health Science. **Work Group:** 08.06. Medical Technology. **Other Jobs in This Work Group:** Biological Technicians; Cardiovascular Technologists and Technicians; Diagnostic Medical Sonographers; Medical and Clinical Laboratory Technicians; Medical and Clinical Laboratory Technologists; Medical Equipment Preparers; Nuclear Medicine Technologists; Opticians, Dispensing; Orthotists and Prosthetists; Radiologic Technicians; Radiologic Technologists. **PERSONALITY TYPE:** Conventional. Conventional occupations frequently involve following set procedures and routines. These occupations can include working with data and details more than with ideas. Usually there is a clear line of authority to follow.

EDUCATION/TRAINING PROGRAM(S)— Health Information/Medical Records Technology/ Technician; Medical Insurance Coding Specialist/Coder. **RELATED KNOWLEDGE/ COURSES—Clerical Practices:** Knowledge of administrative and clerical procedures and systems such as word processing, managing files and records, stenography and transcription, designing forms, and other office procedures and terminology. **Customer and Personal Service:** Knowledge of principles and processes for providing customer and personal services. This includes customer needs assessment, meeting quality standards for services, and evaluation of customer satisfaction. **Medicine and Dentistry:** Knowledge of the information and techniques needed to

M

diagnose and treat human injuries, diseases, and deformities. This includes symptoms, treatment alternatives, drug properties and interactions, and preventive health-care measures. **Administration and Management:** Knowledge of business and management principles involved in strategic planning, resource allocation, human resources modeling, leadership technique, production methods, and coordination of people and resources. **Personnel and Human Resources:** Knowledge of principles and procedures for personnel recruitment, selection, training, compensation and benefits, labor relations and negotiation, and personnel information systems. **Computers and Electronics:** Knowledge of circuit boards, processors, chips, electronic equipment, and computer hardware and software, including applications and programming.

Medical Secretaries

◎ Education/Training Required: Postsecondary vocational training
◎ Annual Earnings: $26,540
◎ Growth: 17.2%
◎ Annual Job Openings: 50,000
◎ Self-Employed: 1.6%
◎ Part-Time: 17.5%

Perform secretarial duties, utilizing specific knowledge of medical terminology and hospital, clinic, or laboratory procedures. Duties include scheduling appointments; billing patients; and compiling and recording medical charts, reports, and correspondence. Schedule and confirm patient diagnostic appointments, surgeries, and medical consultations. Compile and record medical charts, reports, and correspondence, using typewriter or personal computer. Answer telephones and direct calls to appropriate staff. Receive and route messages and documents such as laboratory results to appropriate staff. Greet visitors, ascertain purpose of visit, and direct them to appropriate staff. Interview patients in order to complete documents, case histories, and forms such as intake and insurance forms. Maintain medical records, technical library, and correspondence files. Operate office equipment such as voice mail messaging systems and use word-processing, spreadsheet, and other software

applications to prepare reports, invoices, financial statements, letters, case histories, and medical records. Transmit correspondence and medical records by mail, e-mail, or fax. Perform various clerical and administrative functions, such as ordering and maintaining an inventory of supplies. Arrange hospital admissions for patients. Transcribe recorded messages and practitioners' diagnoses and recommendations into patients' medical records. Perform bookkeeping duties, such as credits and collections, preparing and sending financial statements and bills, and keeping financial records. Complete insurance and other claim forms. Prepare correspondence and assist physicians or medical scientists with preparation of reports, speeches, articles, and conference proceedings. **SKILLS—Social Perceptiveness:** Being aware of others' reactions and understanding why they react as they do. **Active Listening:** Giving full attention to what other people are saying, taking time to understand the points being made, asking questions as appropriate, and not interrupting at inappropriate times. **Instructing:** Teaching others how to do something. **Writing:** Communicating effectively in writing as appropriate for the needs of the audience. **Management of Personnel Resources:** Motivating, developing, and directing people as they work, identifying the best people for the job. **Time Management:** Managing one's own time and the time of others. **Reading Comprehension:** Understanding written sentences and paragraphs in work-related documents. **Management of Material Resources:** Obtaining and seeing to the appropriate use of equipment, facilities, and materials needed to do certain work. **GOE— Interest Area:** 04. Business and Administration. **Work Group:** 04.04. Secretarial Support. **Other Jobs in This Work Group:** Executive Secretaries and Administrative Assistants; Legal Secretaries; Secretaries, Except Legal, Medical, and Executive. **PERSONALITY TYPE:** Conventional. Conventional occupations frequently involve following set procedures and routines. These occupations can include working with data and details more than with ideas. Usually there is a clear line of authority to follow.

EDUCATION/TRAINING PROGRAM(S)—Medical Administrative/Executive Assistant and Medical Secretary; Medical Insurance Specialist/Medical Biller; Medical Office Assistant/Specialist. **RELATED KNOWLEDGE/COURSES—Customer and Per-**

sonal Service: Knowledge of principles and processes for providing customer and personal services. This includes customer needs assessment, meeting quality standards for services, and evaluation of customer satisfaction. **Clerical Practices:** Knowledge of administrative and clerical procedures and systems such as word processing, managing files and records, stenography and transcription, designing forms, and other office procedures and terminology. **Telecommunications:** Knowledge of transmission, broadcasting, switching, control, and operation of telecommunications systems. **Computers and Electronics:** Knowledge of circuit boards, processors, chips, electronic equipment, and computer hardware and software, including applications and programming. **English Language:** Knowledge of the structure and content of the English language, including the meaning and spelling of words, rules of composition, and grammar. **Communications and Media:** Knowledge of media production, communication, and dissemination techniques and methods. This includes alternative ways to inform and entertain via written, oral, and visual media.

Medical Transcriptionists

- Education/Training Required: Associate degree
- Annual Earnings: $28,380
- Growth: 22.6%
- Annual Job Openings: 18,000
- Self-Employed: 2.3%
- Part-Time: 25.3%

Use transcribing machines with headset and foot pedal to listen to recordings of physicians and other health-care professionals dictating a variety of medical reports, such as emergency room visits, diagnostic imaging studies, operations, chart reviews, and final summaries. Transcribe dictated reports and translate medical jargon and abbreviations into their expanded forms. Edit as necessary and return reports in either printed or electronic form to the dictator for review and signature or correction. Decide which information should be included or excluded in reports. Distinguish between homonyms and recognize inconsistencies and mistakes in medical terms, referring to dictionaries; drug references; and other sources on anatomy, physiology, and medicine. Identify mistakes in reports and check with doctors to obtain the correct information. Perform data entry and data retrieval services, providing data for inclusion in medical records and for transmission to physicians. Produce medical reports, correspondence, records, patient-care information, statistics, medical research, and administrative material. Return dictated reports in printed or electronic form for physicians' review, signature, and corrections and for inclusion in patients' medical records. Review and edit transcribed reports or dictated material for spelling, grammar, clarity, consistency, and proper medical terminology. Take dictation, using either shorthand or a stenotype machine or using headsets and transcribing machines; then convert dictated materials or rough notes to written form. Transcribe dictation for a variety of medical reports, such as patient histories, physical examinations, emergency room visits, operations, chart reviews, consultation, and/or discharge summaries. Translate medical jargon and abbreviations into their expanded forms to ensure the accuracy of patient and health-care facility records. Answer inquiries concerning the progress of medical cases within the limits of confidentiality laws. Perform a variety of clerical and office tasks, such as handling incoming and outgoing mail, completing and submitting insurance claims, typing, filing, and operating office machines. Receive patients, schedule appointments, and maintain patient records. Set up and maintain medical files and databases, including records such as X-ray, lab, and procedure reports; medical histories; diagnostic workups; admission and discharge summaries; and clinical resumes. Receive and screen telephone calls and visitors. **SKILLS**—No data available. **GOE—Interest Area:** 08. Health Science. **Work Group:** 08.02. Medicine and Surgery. **Other Jobs in This Work Group:** Anesthesiologists; Family and General Practitioners; Internists, General; Medical Assistants; Obstetricians and Gynecologists; Pediatricians, General; Pharmacists; Pharmacy Aides; Pharmacy Technicians; Physician Assistants; Psychiatrists; Registered Nurses; Surgeons; Surgical Technologists. **PERSONALITY TYPE:** No data available.

EDUCATION/TRAINING PROGRAM(S)—Medical Transcription/Transcriptionist. **RELATED KNOWLEDGE/COURSES**—No data available.

Meter Mechanics

- Education/Training Required: Moderate-term on-the-job training
- Annual Earnings: $43,710
- Growth: 12.0%
- Annual Job Openings: 5,000
- Self-Employed: 0.7%
- Part-Time: 2.0%

Test, adjust, and repair gas, water, and oil meters. Adjusts meter and repeats test until meter registration is within specified limits. Inspects, repairs, and maintains gas meters at wells or processing plants. Dismantles meter and replaces defective parts, such as case, shafts, gears, disks, and recording mechanisms, using soldering iron and hand tools. Connects gas, oil, water, or air meter to test apparatus to detect leaks. Reassembles meter and meter parts, using soldering gun, power tools, and hand tools. Lubricates moving meter parts, using oil gun. Records test results, materials used, and meters needing repair on log or card and segregates meters requiring repair. Caps meter housing and activates controls on paint booth to spray-paint meter case. Cleans plant growth, scale, and rust from meter housing, using wire brush, buffer, sandblaster, or cleaning compounds. Analyzes test results to determine cause of persistent meter registration errors. **SKILLS—Repairing:** Repairing machines or systems by using the needed tools. **Installation:** Installing equipment, machines, wiring, or programs to meet specifications. **Equipment Maintenance:** Performing routine maintenance on equipment and determining when and what kind of maintenance is needed. **Quality Control Analysis:** Conducting tests and inspections of products, services, or processes to evaluate quality or performance. **Troubleshooting:** Determining causes of operating errors and deciding what to do about them. **Operation Monitoring:** Watching gauges, dials, or other indicators to make sure a machine is working properly. **Operation and Control:** Controlling operations of equipment or systems. **GOE—Interest Area:** 02. Architecture and Construction. **Work Group:** 02.05. Systems and Equipment Installation, Maintenance, and Repair. **Other Jobs in This Work Group:** Central Office and PBX Installers

and Repairers; Communication Equipment Mechanics, Installers, and Repairers; Electric Meter Installers and Repairers; Electrical and Electronics Repairers, Powerhouse, Substation, and Relay; Electrical Power-Line Installers and Repairers; Elevator Installers and Repairers; Frame Wirers, Central Office; Heating and Air Conditioning Mechanics; Home Appliance Installers; Maintenance and Repair Workers, General; Refrigeration Mechanics; Station Installers and Repairers, Telephone; Telecommunications Facility Examiners; Telecommunications Line Installers and Repairers. **PERSONALITY TYPE:** Realistic. Realistic occupations frequently involve work activities that include practical, hands-on problems and solutions. These occupations often deal with plants, animals, and real-world materials like wood, tools, and machinery. Many of the occupations require working outside and do not involve a lot of paperwork or working closely with others.

EDUCATION/TRAINING PROGRAM(S)— Electromechanical and Instrumentation and Maintenance Technologies/Technicians, Other. **RELATED KNOWLEDGE/COURSES—Mechanical Devices:** Knowledge of machines and tools, including their designs, uses, repair, and maintenance. **Engineering and Technology:** Knowledge of the practical application of engineering science and technology. This includes applying principles, techniques, procedures, and equipment to the design and production of various goods and services.

Millwrights

- Education/Training Required: Long-term on-the-job training
- Annual Earnings: $43,720
- Growth: 5.3%
- Annual Job Openings: 7,000
- Self-Employed: 1.5%
- Part-Time: 1.6%

Install, dismantle, or move machinery and heavy equipment according to layout plans, blueprints, or other drawings. Replace defective parts of machine or adjust clearances and alignment of moving parts. Align machines and equipment, using hoists, jacks, hand tools, squares, rules, micrometers, and plumb bobs. Connect power unit to machines or steam piping to equipment and test unit to evaluate its mechanical operation. Repair and lubricate machines and equipment. Assemble and install equipment, using hand tools and power tools. Position steel beams to support bedplates of machines and equipment, using blueprints and schematic drawings to determine work procedures. Signal crane operator to lower basic assembly units to bedplate and align unit to centerline. Insert shims, adjust tension on nuts and bolts, or position parts, using hand tools and measuring instruments, to set specified clearances between moving and stationary parts. Move machinery and equipment, using hoists, dollies, rollers, and trucks. Attach moving parts and subassemblies to basic assembly unit, using hand tools and power tools. Assemble machines and bolt, weld, rivet, or otherwise fasten them to foundation or other structures, using hand tools and power tools. Lay out mounting holes, using measuring instruments, and drill holes with power drill. Bolt parts, such as side and deck plates, jaw plates, and journals, to basic assembly unit. Level bedplate and establish centerline, using straightedge, levels, and transit. Dismantle machines, using hammers, wrenches, crowbars, and other hand tools. Shrink-fit bushings, sleeves, rings, liners, gears, and wheels to specified items, using portable gas heating equipment. Dismantle machinery and equipment for shipment to installation site, usually performing installation and maintenance work as part of team. Construct foundation for machines, using hand tools and building materials such as wood, cement, and steel. **SKILLS—Installation:** Installing equipment, machines, wiring, or programs to meet specifications. **Repairing:** Repairing machines or systems by using the needed tools. **Troubleshooting:** Determining causes of operating errors and deciding what to do about them. **Equipment Maintenance:** Performing routine maintenance on equipment and determining when and what kind of maintenance is needed. **Mathematics:** Using mathematics to solve problems. **Equipment Selection:** Determining the kind of tools and equipment needed to do a job. **Technology Design:** Generating or adapting equipment and technology to serve user needs. **Coordination:** Adjusting actions in relation to others' actions. **GOE—Interest Area:** 13. Manufacturing.

Work Group: 13.13. Machinery Repair. **Other Jobs in This Work Group:** Bicycle Repairers; Gas Appliance Repairers; Hand and Portable Power Tool Repairers; Industrial Machinery Mechanics; Locksmiths and Safe Repairers; Maintenance Workers, Machinery; Mechanical Door Repairers; Signal and Track Switch Repairers; Valve and Regulator Repairers. **PERSONALITY TYPE:** Realistic. Realistic occupations frequently involve work activities that include practical, hands-on problems and solutions. These occupations often deal with plants, animals, and real-world materials like wood, tools, and machinery. Many of the occupations require working outside and do not involve a lot of paperwork or working closely with others.

EDUCATION/TRAINING PROGRAM(S)— Heavy/Industrial Equipment Maintenance Technologies, Other; Industrial Mechanics and Maintenance Technology. **RELATED KNOWLEDGE/COURSES—Mechanical Devices:** Knowledge of machines and tools, including their designs, uses, repair, and maintenance. **Building and Construction:** Knowledge of the materials, methods, and tools involved in the construction or repair of houses, buildings, or other structures such as highways and roads. **Engineering and Technology:** Knowledge of the practical application of engineering science and technology. This includes applying principles, techniques, procedures, and equipment to the design and production of various goods and services. **Design:** Knowledge of design techniques, tools, and principles involved in production of precision technical plans, blueprints, drawings, and models. **Physics:** Knowledge and prediction of physical principles and laws and their interrelationships and applications to understanding fluid, material, and atmospheric dynamics and mechanical, electrical, atomic, and subatomic structures and processes. **Public Safety and Security:** Knowledge of relevant equipment, policies, procedures, and strategies to promote effective local, state, or national security operations for the protection of people, data, property, and institutions.

M

Mobile Heavy Equipment Mechanics, Except Engines

- Education/Training Required: Postsecondary vocational training
- Annual Earnings: $38,150
- Growth: 9.6%
- Annual Job Openings: 12,000
- Self-Employed: 4.4%
- Part-Time: 2.8%

Diagnose, adjust, repair, or overhaul mobile mechanical, hydraulic, and pneumatic equipment, such as cranes, bulldozers, graders, and conveyors, used in construction, logging, and surface mining. Test mechanical products and equipment after repair or assembly to ensure proper performance and compliance with manufacturers' specifications. Repair and replace damaged or worn parts. Operate and inspect machines or heavy equipment in order to diagnose defects. Diagnose faults or malfunctions to determine required repairs, using engine diagnostic equipment such as computerized test equipment and calibration devices. Dismantle and reassemble heavy equipment, using hoists and hand tools. Clean, lubricate, and perform other routine maintenance work on equipment and vehicles. Examine parts for damage or excessive wear, using micrometers and gauges. Schedule maintenance for industrial machines and equipment and keep equipment service records. Read and understand operating manuals, blueprints, and technical drawings. Overhaul and test machines or equipment to ensure operating efficiency. Assemble gear systems and align frames and gears. Fit bearings to adjust, repair, or overhaul mobile mechanical, hydraulic, and pneumatic equipment. Weld or solder broken parts and structural members, using electric or gas welders and soldering tools. Clean parts by spraying them with grease solvent or immersing them in tanks of solvent. Adjust, maintain, and repair or replace subassemblies, such as transmissions and crawler heads, using hand tools, jacks, and cranes. Adjust and maintain industrial machinery, using control and regulating devices. Fabricate needed parts or items from sheet metal. Direct workers who are assembling or disassembling equipment or cleaning parts. **SKILLS—Installation:** Installing equipment, machines, wiring, or programs to meet specifications. **Equipment Maintenance:** Performing routine maintenance on equipment and determining when and what kind of maintenance is needed. **Repairing:** Repairing machines or systems by using the needed tools. **Troubleshooting:** Determining causes of operating errors and deciding what to do about them. **Operation Monitoring:** Watching gauges, dials, or other indicators to make sure a machine is working properly. **Equipment Selection:** Determining the kind of tools and equipment needed to do a job. **Operation and Control:** Controlling operations of equipment or systems. **Technology Design:** Generating or adapting equipment and technology to serve user needs. **GOE—Interest Area:** 13. Manufacturing. **Work Group:** 13.14. Vehicle and Facility Mechanical Work. **Other Jobs in This Work Group:** Aircraft Body and Bonded Structure Repairers; Aircraft Engine Specialists; Aircraft Rigging Assemblers; Aircraft Structure Assemblers, Precision; Aircraft Systems Assemblers, Precision; Airframe-and-Power-Plant Mechanics; Automotive Body and Related Repairers; Automotive Glass Installers and Repairers; Automotive Master Mechanics; Automotive Specialty Technicians; Bus and Truck Mechanics and Diesel Engine Specialists; Farm Equipment Mechanics; Fiberglass Laminators and Fabricators; Motorboat Mechanics; Motorcycle Mechanics; Outdoor Power Equipment and Other Small Engine Mechanics; Rail Car Repairers; Recreational Vehicle Service Technicians; Tire Repairers and Changers. **PERSONALITY TYPE:** Realistic. Realistic occupations frequently involve work activities that include practical, hands-on problems and solutions. These occupations often deal with plants, animals, and real-world materials like wood, tools, and machinery. Many of the occupations require working outside and do not involve a lot of paperwork or working closely with others.

EDUCATION/TRAINING PROGRAM(S)— Agricultural Mechanics and Equipment/Machine Technology; Heavy Equipment Maintenance Technology/Technician. **RELATED KNOWLEDGE/ COURSES—Mechanical Devices:** Knowledge of machines and tools, including their designs, uses, repair, and maintenance. **Engineering and Technolo-**

gy: Knowledge of the practical application of engineering science and technology. This includes applying principles, techniques, procedures, and equipment to the design and production of various goods and services. **Physics:** Knowledge and prediction of physical principles and laws and their interrelationships and applications to understanding fluid, material, and atmospheric dynamics and mechanical, electrical, atomic, and subatomic structures and processes. **Customer and Personal Service:** Knowledge of principles and processes for providing customer and personal services. This includes customer needs assessment, meeting quality standards for services, and evaluation of customer satisfaction. **Chemistry:** Knowledge of the chemical composition, structure, and properties of substances and of the chemical processes and transformations that they undergo. This includes uses of chemicals and their danger signs, production techniques, and disposal methods. **Transportation:** Knowledge of principles and methods for moving people or goods by air, rail, sea, or road, including the relative costs and benefits.

Model Makers, Metal and Plastic

- Education/Training Required: Moderate-term on-the-job training
- Annual Earnings: $44,250
- Growth: 14.6%
- Annual Job Openings: 1,000
- Self-Employed: 0%
- Part-Time: 6.0%

Set up and operate machines such as lathes, milling and engraving machines, and jig borers to make working models of metal or plastic objects. Align, fit, and join parts by using bolts and screws or by welding or gluing. Cut, shape, and form metal parts, using lathes, power saws, snips, power brakes and shears, files, and mallets. Drill, countersink, and ream holes in parts and assemblies for bolts, screws, and other fasteners, using power tools. Grind, file, and sand parts to finished dimensions. Inspect and test products to verify conformance to specifications, using precision measuring instruments or circuit testers. Lay out and mark reference points and dimensions on materials, using measuring instruments and drawing or scribing tools. Set up and operate machines such as lathes, drill presses, punch presses, or bandsaws to fabricate prototypes or models. Study blueprints, drawings, and sketches to determine material dimensions, required equipment, and operations sequences. Assemble mechanical, electrical, and electronic components into models or prototypes, using hand tools, power tools, and fabricating machines. Consult and confer with engineering personnel to discuss developmental problems and to recommend product modifications. Devise and construct tools, dies, molds, jigs, and fixtures or modify existing tools and equipment. Record specifications, production operations, and final dimensions of models for use in establishing operating standards and procedures. Rework or alter component model or parts as required to ensure that products meet standards. Wire and solder electrical and electronic connections and components. **SKILLS—Technology Design:** Generating or adapting equipment and technology to serve user needs. **Quality Control Analysis:** Conducting tests and inspections of products, services, or processes to evaluate quality or performance. **Operations Analysis:** Analyzing needs and product requirements to create a design. **Equipment Selection:** Determining the kind of tools and equipment needed to do a job. **Troubleshooting:** Determining causes of operating errors and deciding what to do about them. **Operation Monitoring:** Watching gauges, dials, or other indicators to make sure a machine is working properly. **Systems Analysis:** Determining how a system should work and how changes in conditions, operations, and the environment will affect outcomes. **Operation and Control:** Controlling operations of equipment or systems. **GOE—Interest Area:** 13. Manufacturing. **Work Group:** 13.05. Production Machining Technology. **Other Jobs in This Work Group:** Foundry Mold and Coremakers; Lay-Out Workers, Metal and Plastic; Machinists; Numerical Control Machine Tool Operators and Tenders, Metal and Plastic; Numerical Tool and Process Control Programmers; Patternmakers, Metal and Plastic; Tool and Die Makers; Tool Grinders, Filers, and Sharpeners. **PERSONALITY TYPE:** Realistic. Realistic occupations frequently involve work activities that include practical, hands-on problems and solutions. These occupations often deal with plants, animals, and real-world materials like wood, tools, and machinery. Many of the occupations require working outside and do not involve a lot of paperwork or working closely with others.

EDUCATION/TRAINING PROGRAM(S)—Sheet Metal Technology/Sheetworking. **RELATED KNOWLEDGE/COURSES—Mechanical Devices:** Knowledge of machines and tools, including their designs, uses, repair, and maintenance. **Design:** Knowledge of design techniques, tools, and principles involved in production of precision technical plans, blueprints, drawings, and models. **Building and Construction:** Knowledge of the materials, methods, and tools involved in the construction or repair of houses, buildings, or other structures such as highways and roads. **Engineering and Technology:** Knowledge of the practical application of engineering science and technology. This includes applying principles, techniques, procedures, and equipment to the design and production of various goods and services. **Computers and Electronics:** Knowledge of circuit boards, processors, chips, electronic equipment, and computer hardware and software, including applications and programming. **Telecommunications:** Knowledge of transmission, broadcasting, switching, control, and operation of telecommunications systems.

Motor Vehicle Inspectors

◎ Education/Training Required: Work experience in a related occupation
◎ Annual Earnings: $50,380
◎ Growth: 7.7%
◎ Annual Job Openings: 5,000
◎ Self-Employed: 0.4%
◎ Part-Time: 3.2%

Inspect automotive vehicles to ensure compliance with governmental regulations and safety standards. Inspects truck accessories, air lines, and electric circuits and reports needed repairs. Examines vehicles for damage and drives vehicle to detect malfunctions. Tests vehicle components for wear, damage, or improper adjustment, using mechanical or electrical devices. Applies inspection sticker to vehicles that pass inspec-

tion and rejection sticker to vehicles that fail. Prepares report on each vehicle for follow-up action by owner or police. Prepares and keeps record of vehicles delivered. Positions trailer and drives car onto truck trailer. Notifies authorities of owners having illegal equipment installed on vehicle. Services vehicles with fuel and water. **SKILLS—Science:** Using scientific rules and methods to solve problems. **Troubleshooting:** Determining causes of operating errors and deciding what to do about them. **Quality Control Analysis:** Conducting tests and inspections of products, services, or processes to evaluate quality or performance. **Operation Monitoring:** Watching gauges, dials, or other indicators to make sure a machine is working properly. **Technology Design:** Generating or adapting equipment and technology to serve user needs. **Systems Evaluation:** Identifying measures or indicators of system performance and the actions needed to improve or correct performance relative to the goals of the system. **Equipment Maintenance:** Performing routine maintenance on equipment and determining when and what kind of maintenance is needed. **GOE—Interest Area:** 07. Government and Public Administration. **Work Group:** 07.03. Regulations Enforcement. **Other Jobs in This Work Group:** Agricultural Inspectors; Aviation Inspectors; Child Support, Missing Persons, and Unemployment Insurance Fraud Investigators; Environmental Compliance Inspectors; Equal Opportunity Representatives and Officers; Financial Examiners; Fire Inspectors; Fish and Game Wardens; Forest Fire Inspectors and Prevention Specialists; Government Property Inspectors and Investigators; Immigration and Customs Inspectors; Licensing Examiners and Inspectors; Marine Cargo Inspectors; Mechanical Inspectors; Nuclear Monitoring Technicians; Occupational Health and Safety Specialists; Pressure Vessel Inspectors; Railroad Inspectors; Tax Examiners, Collectors, and Revenue Agents. **PERSONALITY TYPE:** Realistic. Realistic occupations frequently involve work activities that include practical, hands-on problems and solutions. These occupations often deal with plants, animals, and real-world materials like wood, tools, and machinery. Many of the occupations require working outside and do not involve a lot of paperwork or working closely with others.

EDUCATION/TRAINING PROGRAM(S)— No data available. **RELATED KNOWLEDGE/**

COURSES—**Public Safety and Security:** Knowledge of relevant equipment, policies, procedures, and strategies to promote effective local, state, or national security operations for the protection of people, data, property, and institutions. **Mechanical Devices:** Knowledge of machines and tools, including their designs, uses, repair, and maintenance. **Computers and Electronics:** Knowledge of circuit boards, processors, chips, electronic equipment, and computer hardware and software, including applications and programming. **Engineering and Technology:** Knowledge of the practical application of engineering science and technology. This includes applying principles, techniques, procedures, and equipment to the design and production of various goods and services.

Municipal Clerks

◎ Education/Training Required: Short-term on-the-job training
◎ Annual Earnings: $28,430
◎ Growth: 12.3%
◎ Annual Job Openings: 14,000
◎ Self-Employed: 2.6%
◎ Part-Time: 8.3%

Draft agendas and bylaws for town or city council, record minutes of council meetings, answer official correspondence, keep fiscal records and accounts, and prepare reports on civic needs. Participate in the administration of municipal elections, including preparation and distribution of ballots, appointment and training of election officers, and tabulation and certification of results. Record and edit the minutes of meetings and then distribute them to appropriate officials and staff members. Plan and direct the maintenance, filing, safekeeping, and computerization of all municipal documents. Issue public notification of all official activities and meetings. Maintain and update documents such as municipal codes and city charters. Prepare meeting agendas and packets of related information. Prepare ordinances, resolutions, and proclamations so that they can be executed, recorded, archived, and distributed. Respond to requests for information from the public, other municipalities, state officials, and state and federal legislative offices.

Maintain fiscal records and accounts. Perform budgeting duties, including assisting in budget preparation, expenditure review, and budget administration. Perform general office duties such as taking and transcribing dictation, typing and proofreading correspondence, distributing and filing official forms, and scheduling appointments. Coordinate and maintain office-tracking systems for correspondence and follow-up actions. Research information in the municipal archives upon request of public officials and private citizens. Perform contract administration duties, assisting with bid openings and the awarding of contracts. Collaborate with other staff to assist in the development and implementation of goals, objectives, policies, and priorities. Represent municipalities at community events and serve as liaisons on community committees. Serve as a notary of the public. Issue various permits and licenses, including marriage, fishing, hunting, and dog licenses, and collect appropriate fees. Provide assistance to persons with disabilities in reaching less-accessible areas of municipal facilities. Process claims against the municipality, maintaining files and log of claims, and coordinate claim response and handling with municipal claims administrators. **SKILLS—Service Orientation:** Actively looking for ways to help people. **Social Perceptiveness:** Being aware of others' reactions and understanding why they react as they do. **Management of Financial Resources:** Determining how money will be spent to get the work done and accounting for these expenditures. **Active Listening:** Giving full attention to what other people are saying, taking time to understand the points being made, asking questions as appropriate, and not interrupting at inappropriate times. **Writing:** Communicating effectively in writing as appropriate for the needs of the audience. **Persuasion:** Persuading others to change their minds or behavior. **Time Management:** Managing one's own time and the time of others. **Management of Personnel Resources:** Motivating, developing, and directing people as they work, identifying the best people for the job. **GOE—Interest Area:** 07. Government and Public Administration. **Work Group:** 07.04. Public Administration Clerical Support. **Other Jobs in This Work Group:** Court Clerks; Court Reporters; License Clerks. **PERSONALITY TYPE:** Conventional. Conventional occupations frequently involve following set proce-

M

dures and routines. These occupations can include working with data and details more than with ideas. Usually there is a clear line of authority to follow.

EDUCATION/TRAINING PROGRAM(S)—General Office Occupations and Clerical Services. **RELATED KNOWLEDGE/COURSES**—**Clerical Practices:** Knowledge of administrative and clerical procedures and systems such as word processing, managing files and records, stenography and transcription, designing forms, and other office procedures and terminology. **Law and Government:** Knowledge of laws, legal codes, court procedures, precedents, government regulations, executive orders, agency rules, and the democratic political process. **English Language:** Knowledge of the structure and content of the English language, including the meaning and spelling of words, rules of composition, and grammar. **Customer and Personal Service:** Knowledge of principles and processes for providing customer and personal services. This includes customer needs assessment, meeting quality standards for services, and evaluation of customer satisfaction. **Personnel and Human Resources:** Knowledge of principles and procedures for personnel recruitment, selection, training, compensation and benefits, labor relations and negotiation, and personnel information systems. **Administration and Management:** Knowledge of business and management principles involved in strategic planning, resource allocation, human resources modeling, leadership technique, production methods, and coordination of people and resources.

Municipal Fire Fighters

- ⊚ Education/Training Required: Long-term on-the-job training
- ⊚ Annual Earnings: $38,330
- ⊚ Growth: 20.7%
- ⊚ Annual Job Openings: 29,000
- ⊚ Self-Employed: 0%
- ⊚ Part-Time: 1.1%

Control and extinguish municipal fires, protect life and property, and conduct rescue efforts. Administer first aid and cardiopulmonary resuscitation to injured persons. Rescue victims from burning buildings and accident sites. Search burning buildings to locate fire victims. Drive and operate firefighting vehicles and equipment. Dress with equipment such as fire-resistant clothing and breathing apparatus. Move toward the source of a fire, using knowledge of types of fires, construction design, building materials, and physical layout of properties. Position and climb ladders in order to gain access to upper levels of buildings or to rescue individuals from burning structures. Take action to contain hazardous chemicals that might catch fire, leak, or spill. Assess fires and situations and report conditions to superiors in order to receive instructions, using two-way radios. Respond to fire alarms and other calls for assistance, such as automobile and industrial accidents. Operate pumps connected to high-pressure hoses. Select and attach hose nozzles, depending on fire type, and direct streams of water or chemicals onto fires. Create openings in buildings for ventilation or entrance, using axes, chisels, crowbars, electric saws, or core cutters. Inspect fire sites after flames have been extinguished in order to ensure that there is no further danger. Lay hose lines and connect them to water supplies. Protect property from water and smoke, using waterproof salvage covers, smoke ejectors, and deodorants. Participate in physical training activities in order to maintain a high level of physical fitness. Salvage property by removing broken glass, pumping out water, and ventilating buildings to remove smoke. Participate in fire drills and demonstrations of firefighting techniques. Clean and maintain fire stations and firefighting equipment and apparatus. Collaborate with police to respond to accidents, disasters, and arson investigation calls. Establish firelines to prevent unauthorized persons from entering areas near fires. Inform and educate the public on fire prevention. Inspect buildings for fire hazards and compliance with fire prevention ordinances, testing and checking smoke alarms and fire suppression equipment as necessary. **SKILLS**—**Service Orientation:** Actively looking for ways to help people. **Equipment Maintenance:** Performing routine maintenance on equipment and determining when and what kind of maintenance is needed. **Social Perceptiveness:** Being aware of others' reactions and understanding why they react as they do. **Equipment Selection:** Determining the kind of tools and equipment needed to do a job. **Coordination:** Adjusting actions in relation to others' actions. **Learning Strategies:** Selecting and using training/instructional methods and procedures appropriate for the situation when learning or teaching new things. **Operation Monitoring:** Watching gauges, dials, or other indicators to make sure a machine is working properly. **Complex Problem Solving:** Identifying complex problems and reviewing related information to develop and evaluate options and implement solutions. **GOE—Interest Area:** 12. Law and Public Safety. **Work Group:** 12.06. Emergency Responding. **Other Jobs in This Work Group:** Emergency Medical Technicians and Paramedics; Forest Fire Fighters. **PERSONALITY TYPE:** Realistic. Realistic occupations frequently involve work activities that include practical, hands-on problems and solutions. These occupations often deal with plants, animals, and real-world materials like wood, tools, and machinery. Many of the occupations require working outside and do not involve a lot of paperwork or working closely with others.

EDUCATION/TRAINING PROGRAM(S)—Fire Protection, Other; Fire Science/Firefighting. **RELATED KNOWLEDGE/COURSES—Customer and Personal Service:** Knowledge of principles and processes for providing customer and personal services. This includes customer needs assessment, meeting quality standards for services, and evaluation of customer satisfaction. **Medicine and Dentistry:** Knowledge of the information and techniques needed to diagnose and treat human injuries, diseases, and deformities. This includes symptoms, treatment alternatives, drug properties and interactions, and preventive health-care measures. **Physics:** Knowledge and prediction of physical principles and laws and their interrelationships and applications to understanding fluid, material, and atmospheric dynamics and mechanical, electrical, atomic, and subatomic structures and processes. **Public Safety and Security:** Knowledge of relevant equipment, policies, procedures, and strategies to promote effective local, state, or national security operations for the protection of people, data, property, and institutions. **Building and Construction:** Knowledge of the materials, methods, and tools involved in the construction or repair of houses, buildings, or other structures such as highways and roads. **Psychology:** Knowledge of human behavior and performance;

individual differences in ability, personality, and interests; learning and motivation; psychological research methods; and the assessment and treatment of behavioral and affective disorders.

Municipal Fire Fighting and Prevention Supervisors

◎ Education/Training Required: Work experience in a related occupation

◎ Annual Earnings: $58,920

◎ Growth: 18.7%

◎ Annual Job Openings: 8,000

◎ Self-Employed: 0%

◎ Part-Time: 0.1%

Supervise fire fighters who control and extinguish municipal fires, protect life and property, and conduct rescue efforts. Assign firefighters to jobs at strategic locations in order to facilitate rescue of persons and maximize application of extinguishing agents. Provide emergency medical services as required and perform light to heavy rescue functions at emergencies. Assess nature and extent of fire, condition of building, danger to adjacent buildings, and water supply status in order to determine crew or company requirements. Instruct and drill fire department personnel in assigned duties, including firefighting, medical care, hazardous materials response, fire prevention, and related subjects. Evaluate the performance of assigned firefighting personnel. Direct the training of firefighters, assigning of instructors to training classes, and providing of supervisors with reports on training progress and status. Prepare activity reports listing fire call locations, actions taken, fire types and probable causes, damage estimates, and situation dispositions. Maintain required maps and records. Attend in-service training classes to remain current in knowledge of codes, laws, ordinances, and regulations. Evaluate fire station procedures in order to ensure efficiency and enforcement of departmental regulations. Direct firefighters in station maintenance duties and participate in these duties. Compile and maintain equipment and personnel records, including accident reports. Direct investigation of cases of suspected arson, hazards, and false alarms and submit reports outlining findings. Recommend personnel actions related to disciplinary procedures, performance, leaves of absence, and grievances. Supervise and participate in the inspection of properties in order to ensure that they are in compliance with applicable fire codes, ordinances, laws, regulations, and standards. Write and submit proposals for repair, modification, or replacement of firefighting equipment. Coordinate the distribution of fire-prevention promotional materials. Identify corrective actions needed to bring properties into compliance with applicable fire codes and ordinances and conduct follow-up inspections to see if corrective actions have been taken. **SKILLS—Service Orientation:** Actively looking for ways to help people. **Management of Personnel Resources:** Motivating, developing, and directing people as they work, identifying the best people for the job. **Equipment Maintenance:** Performing routine maintenance on equipment and determining when and what kind of maintenance is needed. **Coordination:** Adjusting actions in relation to others' actions. **Instructing:** Teaching others how to do something. **Judgment and Decision Making:** Considering the relative costs and benefits of potential actions to choose the most appropriate one. **Operation Monitoring:** Watching gauges, dials, or other indicators to make sure a machine is working properly. **Management of Material Resources:** Obtaining and seeing to the appropriate use of equipment, facilities, and materials needed to do certain work. **GOE—Interest Area:** 12. Law and Public Safety. **Work Group:** 12.01. Managerial Work in Law and Public Safety. **Other Jobs in This Work Group:** Emergency Management Specialists; First-Line Supervisors/Managers of Correctional Officers; First-Line Supervisors/Managers of Police and Detectives; Forest Fire Fighting and Prevention Supervisors. **PERSONALITY TYPE:** Realistic. Realistic occupations frequently involve work activities that include practical, hands-on problems and solutions. These occupations often deal with plants, animals, and real-world materials like wood, tools, and machinery. Many of the occupations require working outside and do not involve a lot of paperwork or working closely with others.

EDUCATION/TRAINING PROGRAM(S)—Fire Protection and Safety Technology/Technician; Fire Services Administration. **RELATED KNOWLEDGE/COURSES—Public Safety and Security:** Knowledge of relevant equipment, policies, procedures, and strategies to promote effective local, state, or national security operations for the protection of people, data, property, and institutions. **Customer and Personal Service:** Knowledge of principles and processes for providing customer and personal services. This includes customer needs assessment, meeting quality standards for services, and evaluation of customer satisfaction. **Education and Training:** Knowledge of principles and methods for curriculum and training design, teaching and instruction for individuals and groups, and the measurement of training effects. **Building and Construction:** Knowledge of the materials, methods, and tools involved in the construction or repair of houses, buildings, or other structures such as highways and roads. **Medicine and Dentistry:** Knowledge of the information and techniques needed to diagnose and treat human injuries, diseases, and deformities. This includes symptoms, treatment alternatives, drug properties and interactions, and preventive health-care measures. **Psychology:** Knowledge of human behavior and performance; individual differences in ability, personality, and interests; learning and motivation; psychological research methods; and the assessment and treatment of behavioral and affective disorders.

Nannies

- Education/Training Required: Short-term on-the-job training
- Annual Earnings: $16,760
- Growth: 11.7%
- Annual Job Openings: 406,000
- Self-Employed: 43.4%
- Part-Time: 35.2%

Care for children in private households and provide support and expertise to parents in satisfying children's physical, emotional, intellectual, and social needs. Duties may include meal planning and preparation, laundry and clothing care, organization of play activities and outings, discipline, intellectual stimulation, language activities, and transportation. Perform first aid or CPR when required. Regulate children's rest periods and nap schedules. Meet regularly with parents to discuss children's activities and development. Help prepare and serve nutritionally balanced meals and snacks for children. Instruct children in safe behavior, such as seeking adult assistance when crossing the street and avoiding contact or play with unsafe objects. Organize and conduct age-appropriate recreational activities, such as games, arts and crafts, sports, walks, and play dates. Observe children's behavior for irregularities, take temperature, transport children to doctor, or administer medications as directed to maintain children's health. Model appropriate social behaviors and encourage concern for others to cultivate development of interpersonal relationships and communication skills. Work with parents to develop and implement discipline programs to promote desirable child behavior. Help develop and/or monitor family schedule. Supervise and assist with homework. Assign appropriate chores and praise targeted behaviors to encourage development of self-control, self-confidence, and responsibility. Transport children to schools, social outings, and medical appointments. Perform housekeeping and cleaning duties related to children's care. Instruct and assist children in the development of health and personal habits, such as eating, resting, and toilet behavior. Keep records of play, meal schedules, and bill payment. Teach and perform age-appropriate activities such as lap play, reading, and arts and crafts to encourage intellectual development of children. Remove hazards and develop appropriate boundaries and rules to create a safe environment for children. **SKILLS—Negotiation:** Bringing others together and trying to reconcile differences. **Social Perceptiveness:** Being aware of others' reactions and understanding why they react as they do. **Time Management:** Managing one's own time and the time of others. **Persuasion:** Persuading others to change their minds or behavior. **Instructing:** Teaching others how to do something. **Management of Financial Resources:** Determining how money will be spent to get the work done and accounting for these expenditures. **Speaking:** Talking to others to convey information effectively. **Active Listening:** Giving full attention to what other people are saying, taking time to understand the points being made, asking questions as appropriate, and not interrupting at inappropriate times. **Learning Strategies:** Selecting and using training/instructional methods and procedures appropriate for the situation when learning or teaching new things. **Service Orientation:** Actively looking for ways to help people. **GOE—Interest Area:** 10. Human Service. **Work Group:** 10.03. Child/Personal Care and Services. **Other Jobs in This Work Group:** Child Care Workers; Funeral Attendants; Personal and Home Care Aides. **PERSONALITY TYPE:** No data available.

EDUCATION/TRAINING PROGRAM(S)— Child Care Provider/Assistant. **RELATED KNOWLEDGE/COURSES—Philosophy and Theology:** Knowledge of different philosophical systems and religions. This includes their basic principles, values, ethics, ways of thinking, customs, and practices and their impact on human culture. **Medicine and Dentistry:** Knowledge of the information and techniques needed to diagnose and treat human injuries, diseases, and deformities. This includes symptoms, treatment alternatives, drug properties and interactions, and preventive health-care measures. **Psychology:** Knowledge of human behavior and performance; individual differences in ability, personality, and interests; learning and motivation; psychological research methods; and the assessment and treatment of behavioral and affective disorders. **Geography:** Knowledge of principles and methods for describing the features of land, sea, and air masses, including their physical characteristics; locations; interrelationships; and distribution of plant, animal, and human life. **Sociology and Anthropology:** Knowledge of group behavior and dynamics, societal trends and influences, human migrations, ethnicity, and cultures and their history and origins. **Therapy and Counseling:** Knowledge of principles, methods, and procedures for diagnosis, treatment, and rehabilitation of physical and mental dysfunctions and for career counseling and guidance.

N

New Accounts Clerks

- Education/Training Required: Work experience in a related occupation
- Annual Earnings: $26,860
- Growth: 11.2%
- Annual Job Openings: 24,000
- Self-Employed: 0%
- Part-Time: 14.8%

Interview persons desiring to open bank accounts. Explain banking services available to prospective customers and assist them in preparing application form. Answer customers' questions and explain available services such as deposit accounts, bonds, and securities. Compile information about new accounts, enter account information into computers, and file related forms or other documents. Refer customers to appropriate bank personnel in order to meet their financial needs. Interview customers in order to obtain information needed for opening accounts or renting safe-deposit boxes. Inform customers of procedures for applying for services such as ATM cards, direct deposit of checks, and certificates of deposit. Obtain credit records from reporting agencies. Collect and record customer deposits and fees and issue receipts, using computers. Investigate and correct errors upon customers' request, according to customer and bank records. Perform teller duties as required. Execute wire transfers of funds. Duplicate records for distribution to branch offices. Issue initial and replacement safe-deposit keys to customers and admit customers to vaults. Perform foreign-currency transactions and sell traveler's checks. Schedule repairs for locks on safe-deposit boxes. **SKILLS—Service Orientation:** Actively looking for ways to help people. **Active Listening:** Giving full attention to what other people are saying, taking time to understand the points being made, asking questions as appropriate, and not interrupting at inappropriate times. **Social Perceptiveness:** Being aware of others' reactions and understanding why they react as they do. **Critical Thinking:** Using logic and reasoning to identify the strengths and weaknesses of alternative solutions, conclusions, or approaches to problems. **Writing:** Communicating effectively in writing as appropriate for the needs of the audience.

Speaking: Talking to others to convey information effectively. **Judgment and Decision Making:** Considering the relative costs and benefits of potential actions to choose the most appropriate one. **Reading Comprehension:** Understanding written sentences and paragraphs in work-related documents. **GOE—Interest Area:** 06. Finance and Insurance. **Work Group:** 06.04. Finance/Insurance Customer Service. **Other Jobs in This Work Group:** Bill and Account Collectors; Loan Interviewers and Clerks; Tellers. **PERSONALITY TYPE:** Conventional. Conventional occupations frequently involve following set procedures and routines. These occupations can include working with data and details more than with ideas. Usually there is a clear line of authority to follow.

EDUCATION/TRAINING PROGRAM(S)— Banking and Financial Support Services. **RELATED KNOWLEDGE/COURSES—Customer and Personal Service:** Knowledge of principles and processes for providing customer and personal services. This includes customer needs assessment, meeting quality standards for services, and evaluation of customer satisfaction. **Sales and Marketing:** Knowledge of principles and methods for showing, promoting, and selling products or services. This includes marketing strategy and tactics, product demonstrations, sales techniques, and sales control systems. **Economics and Accounting:** Knowledge of economic and accounting principles and practices, the financial markets, banking, and the analysis and reporting of financial data. **Mathematics:** Knowledge of arithmetic, algebra, geometry, calculus, and statistics and their applications. **Clerical Practices:** Knowledge of administrative and clerical procedures and systems such as word processing, managing files and records, stenography and transcription, designing forms, and other office procedures and terminology. **Personnel and Human Resources:** Knowledge of principles and procedures for personnel recruitment, selection, training, compensation and benefits, labor relations and negotiation, and personnel information systems. **Law and Government:** Knowledge of laws, legal codes, court procedures, precedents, government regulations, executive orders, agency rules, and the democratic political process.

Nonfarm Animal Caretakers

- ◎ Education/Training Required: Short-term on-the-job training
- ◎ Annual Earnings: $17,460
- ◎ Growth: 22.2%
- ◎ Annual Job Openings: 32,000
- ◎ Self-Employed: 27.3%
- ◎ Part-Time: 31.7%

Feed, water, groom, bathe, exercise, or otherwise care for pets and other nonfarm animals, such as dogs, cats, ornamental fish or birds, zoo animals, and mice. Work in settings such as kennels, animal shelters, zoos, circuses, and aquariums. May keep records of feedings, treatments, and animals received or discharged. May clean, disinfect, and repair cages, pens, or fish tanks. Feed and water animals according to schedules and feeding instructions. Clean, organize, and disinfect animal quarters such as pens, stables, cages, and yards and animal equipment such as saddles and bridles. Answer telephones and schedule appointments. Examine and observe animals in order to detect signs of illness, disease, or injury. Respond to questions from patrons and provide information about animals, such as behavior, habitat, breeding habits, or facility activities. Provide treatment to sick or injured animals or contact veterinarians in order to secure treatment. Collect and record animal information such as weight, size, physical condition, treatments received, medications given, and food intake. Perform animal grooming duties such as washing, brushing, clipping, and trimming coats; cutting nails; and cleaning ears. Exercise animals in order to maintain their physical and mental health. Order, unload, and store feed and supplies. Mix food, liquid formulas, medications, or food supplements according to instructions, prescriptions, and knowledge of animal species. Clean and disinfect surgical equipment. Discuss with clients their pets' grooming needs. Observe and caution children petting and feeding animals in designated areas in order to ensure the safety of humans and animals. Find homes for stray or unwanted animals. Adjust controls to regulate specified temperature and humidity of animal quarters, nurseries, or exhibit areas. Anesthetize and

inoculate animals according to instructions. Transfer animals between enclosures in order to facilitate breeding, birthing, shipping, or rearrangement of exhibits. Install, maintain, and repair animal care facility equipment such as infrared lights, feeding devices, and cages. Train animals to perform certain tasks. Teach obedience classes. **SKILLS—Time Management:** Managing one's own time and the time of others. **Social Perceptiveness:** Being aware of others' reactions and understanding why they react as they do. **Persuasion:** Persuading others to change their minds or behavior. **Management of Financial Resources:** Determining how money will be spent to get the work done and accounting for these expenditures. **Instructing:** Teaching others how to do something. **Active Listening:** Giving full attention to what other people are saying, taking time to understand the points being made, asking questions as appropriate, and not interrupting at inappropriate times. **Coordination:** Adjusting actions in relation to others' actions. **Management of Material Resources:** Obtaining and seeing to the appropriate use of equipment, facilities, and materials needed to do certain work. **GOE—Interest Area:** 08. Health Science. **Work Group:** 08.05. Animal Care. **Other Jobs in This Work Group:** Animal Breeders; Animal Trainers; Veterinarians; Veterinary Assistants and Laboratory Animal Caretakers; Veterinary Technologists and Technicians. **PERSONALITY TYPE:** Realistic. Realistic occupations frequently involve work activities that include practical, hands-on problems and solutions. These occupations often deal with plants, animals, and real-world materials like wood, tools, and machinery. Many of the occupations require working outside and do not involve a lot of paperwork or working closely with others.

EDUCATION/TRAINING PROGRAM(S)—Agricultural/Farm Supplies Retailing and Wholesaling; Dog/Pet/Animal Grooming. **RELATED KNOWLEDGE/COURSES—Customer and Personal Service:** Knowledge of principles and processes for providing customer and personal services. This includes customer needs assessment, meeting quality standards for services, and evaluation of customer satisfaction. **Public Safety and Security:** Knowledge of relevant equipment, policies, procedures, and strategies to promote effective local, state, or national security operations for the protection of people, data, property, and institutions. **Sales and Marketing:** Knowledge of principles and methods for showing, promoting, and selling products or services. This includes marketing strategy and tactics, product demonstrations, sales techniques, and sales control systems. **Biology:** Knowledge of plant and animal organisms and their tissues, cells, functions, interdependencies, and interactions with each other and the environment. **Psychology:** Knowledge of human behavior and performance; individual differences in ability, personality, and interests; learning and motivation; psychological research methods; and the assessment and treatment of behavioral and affective disorders. **Medicine and Dentistry:** Knowledge of the information and techniques needed to diagnose and treat human injuries, diseases, and deformities. This includes symptoms, treatment alternatives, drug properties and interactions, and preventive health-care measures.

Nuclear Medicine Technologists

- Education/Training Required: Associate degree
- Annual Earnings: $56,450
- Growth: 23.6%
- Annual Job Openings: 2,000
- Self-Employed: 0.2%
- Part-Time: 17.5%

Prepare, administer, and measure radioactive isotopes in therapeutic, diagnostic, and tracer studies, utilizing a variety of radioisotope equipment. Prepare stock solutions of radioactive materials and calculate doses to be administered by radiologists. Subject patients to radiation. Execute blood volume, red cell survival, and fat absorption studies, following standard laboratory techniques. Calculate, measure and record radiation dosage or radiopharmaceuticals received, used, and disposed, using computer and following physician's prescription. Detect and map radiopharmaceuticals in patients' bodies, using a camera to produce photographic or computer images. Explain test procedures and safety precautions to patients and provide them with assistance during test procedures.

Administer radiopharmaceuticals or radiation to patients to detect or treat diseases, using radioisotope equipment, under direction of physician. Produce a computer-generated or film image for interpretation by a physician. Process cardiac function studies, using computer. Dispose of radioactive materials and store radiopharmaceuticals, following radiation safety procedures. Record and process results of procedures. Prepare stock radiopharmaceuticals, adhering to safety standards that minimize radiation exposure to workers and patients. Maintain and calibrate radioisotope and laboratory equipment. Gather information on patients' illnesses and medical history to guide the choice of diagnostic procedures for therapy. Measure glandular activity, blood volume, red-cell survival, and radioactivity of patient, using scanners, Geiger counters, scintillometers, and other laboratory equipment. Train and supervise student or subordinate nuclear medicine technologists. Position radiation fields, radiation beams, and patient to allow for most effective treatment of patient's disease, using computer. Add radioactive substances to biological specimens, such as blood, urine, and feces, to determine therapeutic drug or hormone levels. Develop treatment procedures for nuclear medicine treatment programs. **SKILLS—Science:** Using scientific rules and methods to solve problems. **Operation Monitoring:** Watching gauges, dials, or other indicators to make sure a machine is working properly. **Social Perceptiveness:** Being aware of others' reactions and understanding why they react as they do. **Service Orientation:** Actively looking for ways to help people. **Instructing:** Teaching others how to do something. **Operation and Control:** Controlling operations of equipment or systems. **Learning Strategies:** Selecting and using training/instructional methods and procedures appropriate for the situation when learning or teaching new things. **Active Learning:** Understanding the implications of new information for both current and future problem-solving and decision-making. **GOE—Interest Area:** 08. Health Science. **Work Group:** 08.06. Medical Technology. **Other Jobs in This Work Group:** Biological Technicians; Cardiovascular Technologists and Technicians; Diagnostic Medical Sonographers; Medical and Clinical Laboratory Technicians; Medical and Clinical Laboratory Technologists; Medical Equipment Preparers; Medical Records and Health Information Technicians; Opticians, Dispensing; Orthotists and Prosthetists; Radiologic Technicians; Radiologic Technologists. **PERSONALITY TYPE:** Investigative. Investigative occupations frequently involve working with ideas and require an extensive amount of thinking. These occupations can involve searching for facts and figuring out problems mentally.

EDUCATION/TRAINING PROGRAM(S)— Nuclear Medical Technology/Technologist; Radiation Protection/Health Physics Technician. **RELATED KNOWLEDGE/COURSES—Medicine and Dentistry:** Knowledge of the information and techniques needed to diagnose and treat human injuries, diseases, and deformities. This includes symptoms, treatment alternatives, drug properties and interactions, and preventive health-care measures. **Customer and Personal Service:** Knowledge of principles and processes for providing customer and personal services. This includes customer needs assessment, meeting quality standards for services, and evaluation of customer satisfaction. **Biology:** Knowledge of plant and animal organisms and their tissues, cells, functions, interdependencies, and interactions with each other and the environment. **Physics:** Knowledge and prediction of physical principles and laws and their interrelationships and applications to understanding fluid, material, and atmospheric dynamics and mechanical, electrical, atomic, and subatomic structures and processes. **Chemistry:** Knowledge of the chemical composition, structure, and properties of substances and of the chemical processes and transformations that they undergo. This includes uses of chemicals and their danger signs, production techniques, and disposal methods. **Computers and Electronics:** Knowledge of circuit boards, processors, chips, electronic equipment, and computer hardware and software, including applications and programming.

Nursery and Greenhouse Managers

- Education/Training Required: Work experience in a related occupation
- Annual Earnings: $50,700
- Growth: 5.1%
- Annual Job Openings: 25,000
- Self-Employed: 0.9%
- Part-Time: 9.2%

Plan, organize, direct, control, and coordinate activities of workers engaged in propagating, cultivating, and harvesting horticultural specialties, such as trees, shrubs, flowers, mushrooms, and other plants. Confer with horticultural personnel in order to plan facility renovations or additions. Construct structures and accessories such as greenhouses and benches. Coordinate clerical, record-keeping, inventory, requisitioning, and marketing activities. Cut and prune trees, shrubs, flowers, and plants. Graft plants. Inspect facilities and equipment for signs of disrepair and perform necessary maintenance work. Negotiate contracts such as those for land leases or tree purchases. Assign work schedules and duties to nursery or greenhouse staff and supervise their work. Determine plant growing conditions, such as greenhouses, hydroponics, or natural settings, and set planting and care schedules. Determine types and quantities of horticultural plants to be grown, based on budgets, projected sales volumes, and/or executive directives. Explain and enforce safety regulations and policies. Hire employees and train them in gardening techniques. Identify plants as well as problems such as diseases, weeds, and insect pests. Manage nurseries that grow horticultural plants for sale to trade or retail customers, for display or exhibition, or for research. Select and purchase seeds, plant nutrients, disease control chemicals, and garden and lawn care equipment. Tour work areas to observe work being done, to inspect crops, and to evaluate plant and soil conditions. Apply pesticides and fertilizers to plants. Position and regulate plant irrigation systems and program environmental and irrigation control computers. Prepare soil for planting and plant or transplant seeds, bulbs, and cuttings. Provide information to customers on the care of trees, shrubs, flowers, plants, and lawns. **SKILLS—**

N

Management of Personnel Resources: Motivating, developing, and directing people as they work, identifying the best people for the job. **Management of Financial Resources:** Determining how money will be spent to get the work done and accounting for these expenditures. **Management of Material Resources:** Obtaining and seeing to the appropriate use of equipment, facilities, and materials needed to do certain work. **Negotiation:** Bringing others together and trying to reconcile differences. **Systems Analysis:** Determining how a system should work and how changes in conditions, operations, and the environment will affect outcomes. **Systems Evaluation:** Identifying measures or indicators of system performance and the actions needed to improve or correct performance relative to the goals of the system. **Coordination:** Adjusting actions in relation to others' actions. **Operations Analysis:** Analyzing needs and product requirements to create a design. **Time Management:** Managing one's own time and the time of others. **GOE—Interest Area:** 01. Agriculture and Natural Resources. **Work Group:** 01.01. Managerial Work in Agriculture and Natural Resources. **Other Jobs in This Work Group:** Agricultural Crop Farm Managers; Farmers and Ranchers; First-Line Supervisors and Manager/Supervisors—Agricultural Crop Workers; First-Line Supervisors and Manager/Supervisors—Animal Husbandry Workers; First-Line Supervisors and Manager/Supervisors—Extractive Workers; First-Line Supervisors and Manager/Supervisors—Fishery Workers; First-Line Supervisors and Manager/Supervisors—Horticultural Workers; First-Line Supervisors and Manager/Supervisors—Landscaping Workers; First-Line Supervisors and Manager/Supervisors—Logging Workers; Fish Hatchery Managers; Lawn Service Managers; Park Naturalists; Purchasing Agents and Buyers, Farm Products. **PERSONALITY TYPE:** Enterprising. Enterprising occupations frequently involve starting up and carrying out projects. These occupations can involve leading people and making many decisions. They sometimes require risk taking and often deal with business.

EDUCATION/TRAINING PROGRAM(S)— Agribusiness/Agricultural Business Operations; Agricultural Business and Management, General; Agricultural Business and Management, Other; Agricultural Production Operations, General; Agricultural Production Operations, Other; Agronomy and Crop Science; Crop Production; Farm/Farm and Ranch Management; Greenhouse Operations and Management; Horticultural Science; Ornamental Horticulture; Plant Nursery Operations and Management; Plant Protection and Integrated Pest Management; Plant Sciences, General; Range Science and Management. **RELATED KNOWLEDGE/COURSES— Biology:** Knowledge of plant and animal organisms and their tissues, cells, functions, interdependencies, and interactions with each other and the environment. **Administration and Management:** Knowledge of business and management principles involved in strategic planning, resource allocation, human resources modeling, leadership technique, production methods, and coordination of people and resources. **Personnel and Human Resources:** Knowledge of principles and procedures for personnel recruitment, selection, training, compensation and benefits, labor relations and negotiation, and personnel information systems. **Chemistry:** Knowledge of the chemical composition, structure, and properties of substances and of the chemical processes and transformations that they undergo. This includes uses of chemicals and their danger signs, production techniques, and disposal methods. **Food Production:** Knowledge of techniques and equipment for planting, growing, and harvesting food products (both plant and animal) for consumption, including storage/handling techniques. **Production and Processing:** Knowledge of raw materials, production processes, quality control, costs, and other techniques for maximizing the effective manufacture and distribution of goods.

Nursing Aides, Orderlies, and Attendants

◎ Education/Training Required: Short-term on-the-job training
◎ Annual Earnings: $20,980
◎ Growth: 24.9%
◎ Annual Job Openings: 302,000
◎ Self-Employed: 1.6%
◎ Part-Time: 21.9%

Provide basic patient care under direction of nursing staff. Perform duties such as feeding, bathing, dressing, grooming, or moving patients or changing linens. Turn and re-position bedridden patients, alone or with assistance, to prevent bedsores. Answer patients' call signals. Feed patients who are unable to feed themselves. Observe patients' conditions, measuring and recording food and liquid intake and output and vital signs, and report changes to professional staff. Provide patient care by supplying and emptying bedpans, applying dressings, and supervising exercise routines. Provide patients with help walking, exercising, and moving in and out of bed. Bathe, groom, shave, dress, and/or drape patients to prepare them for surgery, treatment, or examination. Collect specimens such as urine, feces, or sputum. Prepare, serve, and collect food trays. Clean rooms and change linens. Transport patients to treatment units, using a wheelchair or stretcher. Deliver messages, documents, and specimens. Answer phones and direct visitors. Administer medications and treatments, such as catheterizations, suppositories, irrigations, enemas, massages, and douches, as directed by a physician or nurse. Restrain patients if necessary. Maintain inventory by storing, preparing, sterilizing, and issuing supplies such as dressing packs and treatment trays. Explain medical instructions to patients and family members. Perform clerical duties such as processing documents and scheduling appointments. Work as part of a medical team that examines and treats clinic outpatients. Set up equipment such as oxygen tents, portable X-ray machines, and overhead irrigation bottles. **SKILLS— Social Perceptiveness:** Being aware of others' reactions and understanding why they react as they do. **Time Management:** Managing one's own time and the time of others. **Instructing:** Teaching others how to do something. **Service Orientation:** Actively looking for ways to help people. **Monitoring:** Monitoring or assessing your performance or that of other individuals or organizations to make improvements or take corrective action. **Operation Monitoring:** Watching gauges, dials, or other indicators to make sure a machine is working properly. **Coordination:** Adjusting actions in relation to others' actions. **Persuasion:** Persuading others to change their minds or behavior. **GOE—Interest Area:** 08. Health Science. **Work Group:** 08.08. Patient Care and Assistance. **Other**

Jobs in This Work Group: Home Health Aides; Licensed Practical and Licensed Vocational Nurses; Psychiatric Aides; Psychiatric Technicians. **PERSONALITY TYPE:** Social. Social occupations frequently involve working with, communicating with, and teaching people. These occupations often involve helping or providing service to others.

EDUCATION/TRAINING PROGRAM(S)— Health Aide; Nurse/Nursing Assistant/Aide and Patient Care Assistant. **RELATED KNOWLEDGE/COURSES—Psychology:** Knowledge of human behavior and performance; individual differences in ability, personality, and interests; learning and motivation; psychological research methods; and the assessment and treatment of behavioral and affective disorders. **Customer and Personal Service:** Knowledge of principles and processes for providing customer and personal services. This includes customer needs assessment, meeting quality standards for services, and evaluation of customer satisfaction. **Medicine and Dentistry:** Knowledge of the information and techniques needed to diagnose and treat human injuries, diseases, and deformities. This includes symptoms, treatment alternatives, drug properties and interactions, and preventive health-care measures. **Education and Training:** Knowledge of principles and methods for curriculum and training design, teaching and instruction for individuals and groups, and the measurement of training effects. **Foreign Language:** Knowledge of the structure and content of a foreign (non-English) language, including the meaning and spelling of words, rules of composition and grammar, and pronunciation. **English Language:** Knowledge of the structure and content of the English language, including the meaning and spelling of words, rules of composition, and grammar.

Occupational Therapist Assistants

- Education/Training Required: Associate degree
- Annual Earnings: $38,430
- Growth: 39.2%
- Annual Job Openings: 3,000
- Self-Employed: 2.9%
- Part-Time: 25.5%

Assist occupational therapists in providing occupational therapy treatments and procedures. May, in accordance with state laws, assist in development of treatment plans, carry out routine functions, direct activity programs, and document the progress of treatments. Generally requires formal training. Observe and record patients' progress, attitudes, and behavior and maintain this information in client records. Maintain and promote a positive attitude toward clients and their treatment programs. Monitor patients' performance in therapy activities, providing encouragement. Select therapy activities to fit patients' needs and capabilities. Instruct, or assist in instructing, patients and families in home programs, basic living skills, and the care and use of adaptive equipment. Evaluate the daily living skills and capacities of physically, developmentally, or emotionally disabled clients. Aid patients in dressing and grooming themselves. Implement, or assist occupational therapists with implementing, treatment plans designed to help clients function independently. Report to supervisors, verbally or in writing, on patients' progress, attitudes, and behavior. Alter treatment programs to obtain better results if treatment is not having the intended effect. Work under the direction of occupational therapists to plan, implement, and administer educational, vocational, and recreational programs that restore and enhance performance in individuals with functional impairments. Design, fabricate, and repair assistive devices and make adaptive changes to equipment and environments. Assemble, clean, and maintain equipment and materials for patient use. Teach patients how to deal constructively with their emotions. Perform clerical duties such as scheduling appointments, collecting data, and documenting health insurance billings. Transport patients to and from the occupational therapy work area. Demonstrate therapy techniques, such as manual and creative arts and games. Order any needed educational or treatment supplies. Assist educational specialists or clinical psychologists in administering situational or diagnostic tests to measure client's abilities or progress. **SKILLS—Social Perceptiveness:** Being aware of others' reactions and understanding why they react as they do. **Service Orientation:** Actively looking for ways to help people. **Instructing:** Teaching others how to do something. **Learning Strategies:** Selecting and using training/instructional methods and procedures appropriate for the situation when learning or teaching new things. **Persuasion:** Persuading others to change their minds or behavior. **Time Management:** Managing one's own time and the time of others. **Monitoring:** Monitoring or assessing your performance or that of other individuals or organizations to make improvements or take corrective action. **Active Listening:** Giving full attention to what other people are saying, taking time to understand the points being made, asking questions as appropriate, and not interrupting at inappropriate times. **GOE—Interest Area:** 08. Health Science. **Work Group:** 08.07. Medical Therapy. **Other Jobs in This Work Group:** Audiologists; Massage Therapists; Occupational Therapist Aides; Occupational Therapists; Physical Therapist Aides; Physical Therapist Assistants; Physical Therapists; Radiation Therapists; Recreational Therapists; Respiratory Therapists; Respiratory Therapy Technicians; Speech-Language Pathologists. **PERSONALITY TYPE:** Social. Social occupations frequently involve working with, communicating with, and teaching people. These occupations often involve helping or providing service to others.

EDUCATION/TRAINING PROGRAM(S)— Occupational Therapist Assistant. **RELATED KNOWLEDGE/COURSES—Psychology:** Knowledge of human behavior and performance; individual differences in ability, personality, and interests; learning and motivation; psychological research methods; and the assessment and treatment of behavioral and affective disorders. **Therapy and Counseling:** Knowledge of principles, methods, and procedures for diagnosis, treatment, and rehabilitation of physical and mental dysfunctions and for career counseling and guidance. **Sociology and Anthropology:** Knowledge of group behavior and dynamics, societal trends and influences, human migrations, ethnicity, and cultures and their history and origins. **Philosophy and Theology:** Knowledge of different philosophical systems and religions. This includes their basic principles, values, ethics, ways of thinking, customs, and practices and their impact on human culture. **Customer and Personal Service:** Knowledge of principles and processes for providing customer and personal services. This includes customer needs assessment, meeting quality standards for services, and evaluation of customer satisfaction. **Medicine and Dentistry:** Knowledge of the information and techniques needed to diagnose and treat human injuries, diseases, and deformities. This includes symptoms, treatment alternatives, drug properties and interactions, and preventive health-care measures.

Office Clerks, General

- Education/Training Required: Short-term on-the-job training
- Annual Earnings: $22,770
- Growth: 10.4%
- Annual Job Openings: 550,000
- Self-Employed: 0.5%
- Part-Time: 25.7%

Perform duties too varied and diverse to be classified in any specific office clerical occupation and requiring limited knowledge of office management systems and procedures. Clerical duties may be assigned in accordance with the office procedures of individual establishments and may include a combination of answering telephones, bookkeeping, typing or word processing, stenography, office machine operation, and filing. Collect, count, and disburse money; do basic bookkeeping; and complete banking transactions. Communicate with customers, employees, and other individuals to answer questions, disseminate or explain information, take orders, and address complaints. Answer telephones, direct calls, and take messages. Compile, copy, sort, and file records of office activities, business transactions, and other activities. Complete and mail bills, contracts, policies, invoices,

or checks. Operate office machines, such as photocopiers and scanners, facsimile machines, voice mail systems, and personal computers. Compute, record, and proofread data and other information, such as records or reports. Maintain and update filing, inventory, mailing, and database systems either manually or using a computer. Open, sort, and route incoming mail; answer correspondence; and prepare outgoing mail. Review files, records, and other documents to obtain information to respond to requests. Deliver messages and run errands. Inventory and order materials, supplies, and services. Complete work schedules, manage calendars, and arrange appointments. Process and prepare documents such as business or government forms and expense reports. Monitor and direct the work of lower-level clerks. Type, format, proofread, and edit correspondence and other documents from notes or dictating machines, using computers or typewriters. Count, weigh, measure, and/or organize materials. Train other staff members to perform work activities such as using computer applications. Prepare meeting agendas, attend meetings, and record and transcribe minutes. Troubleshoot problems involving office equipment, such as computer hardware and software. **SKILLS—Active Listening:** Giving full attention to what other people are saying, taking time to understand the points being made, asking questions as appropriate, and not interrupting at inappropriate times. **Reading Comprehension:** Understanding written sentences and paragraphs in work-related documents. **Social Perceptiveness:** Being aware of others' reactions and understanding why they react as they do. **Service Orientation:** Actively looking for ways to help people. **Writing:** Communicating effectively in writing as appropriate for the needs of the audience. **Speaking:** Talking to others to convey information effectively. **Learning Strategies:** Selecting and using training/instructional methods and procedures appropriate for the situation when learning or teaching new things. **GOE—Interest Area:** 04. Business and Administration. **Work Group:** 04.07. Records and Materials Processing. **Other Jobs in This Work Group:** Correspondence Clerks; File Clerks; Human Resources Assistants, Except Payroll and Timekeeping; Mail Clerks, Except Mail Machine Operators and Postal Service; Marking Clerks; Meter Readers, Utilities; Order Fillers, Wholesale and Retail Sales; Postal

Service Clerks; Postal Service Mail Sorters, Processors, and Processing Machine Operators; Procurement Clerks; Production, Planning, and Expediting Clerks; Shipping, Receiving, and Traffic Clerks; Stock Clerks, Sales Floor; Stock Clerks—Stockroom, Warehouse, or Storage Yard; Weighers, Measurers, Checkers, and Samplers, Recordkeeping. **PERSONALITY TYPE:** Conventional. Conventional occupations frequently involve following set procedures and routines. These occupations can include working with data and details more than with ideas. Usually there is a clear line of authority to follow.

EDUCATION/TRAINING PROGRAM(S)—General Office Occupations and Clerical Services. **RELATED KNOWLEDGE/COURSES—Clerical Practices:** Knowledge of administrative and clerical procedures and systems such as word processing, managing files and records, stenography and transcription, designing forms, and other office procedures and terminology. **Customer and Personal Service:** Knowledge of principles and processes for providing customer and personal services. This includes customer needs assessment, meeting quality standards for services, and evaluation of customer satisfaction. **Economics and Accounting:** Knowledge of economic and accounting principles and practices, the financial markets, banking, and the analysis and reporting of financial data. **Personnel and Human Resources:** Knowledge of principles and procedures for personnel recruitment, selection, training, compensation and benefits, labor relations and negotiation, and personnel information systems. **Computers and Electronics:** Knowledge of circuit boards, processors, chips, electronic equipment, and computer hardware and software, including applications and programming. **Mathematics:** Knowledge of arithmetic, algebra, geometry, calculus, and statistics and their applications. **English Language:** Knowledge of the structure and content of the English language, including the meaning and spelling of words, rules of composition, and grammar.

Office Machine and Cash Register Servicers

◎ Education/Training Required: Long-term on-the-job training
◎ Annual Earnings: $35,150
◎ Growth: 15.1%
◎ Annual Job Openings: 19,000
◎ Self-Employed: 12.2%
◎ Part-Time: 8.2%

Repair and service office machines, such as adding, accounting, calculating, duplicating, and typewriting machines. Includes the repair of manual, electrical, and electronic office machines. Tests machine to locate cause of electrical problems, using testing devices such as voltmeter, ohmmeter, and circuit test equipment. Disassembles machine and examines parts such as wires, gears, and bearings for wear and defects, using hand tools, power tools, and measuring devices. Operates machine such as typewriter, cash register, or adding machine to test functioning of parts and mechanisms. Assembles and installs machine according to specifications, using hand tools, power tools, and measuring devices. Cleans and oils mechanical parts to maintain machine. Reads specifications such as blueprints, charts, and schematics to determine machine settings and adjustments. Repairs, adjusts, or replaces electrical and mechanical components and parts, using hand tools, power tools, and soldering or welding equipment. Instructs operators and servicers in operation, maintenance, and repair of machine. **SKILLS— Installation:** Installing equipment, machines, wiring, or programs to meet specifications. **Repairing:** Repairing machines or systems by using the needed tools. **Equipment Maintenance:** Performing routine maintenance on equipment and determining when and what kind of maintenance is needed. **Instructing:** Teaching others how to do something. **Technology Design:** Generating or adapting equipment and technology to serve user needs. **Troubleshooting:** Determining causes of operating errors and deciding what to do about them. **Quality Control Analysis:** Conducting tests and inspections of products, services, or processes to evaluate quality or performance. **Science:** Using scientific rules and methods to solve problems. **Operation Mon-**

itoring: Watching gauges, dials, or other indicators to make sure a machine is working properly. **GOE— Interest Area:** 11. Information Technology. **Work Group:** 11.03. Digital Equipment Repair. **Other Jobs in This Work Group:** Automatic Teller Machine Servicers; Coin, Vending, and Amusement Machine Servicers and Repairers; Data Processing Equipment Repairers. **PERSONALITY TYPE:** Realistic. Realistic occupations frequently involve work activities that include practical, hands-on problems and solutions. These occupations often deal with plants, animals, and real-world materials like wood, tools, and machinery. Many of the occupations require working outside and do not involve a lot of paperwork or working closely with others.

EDUCATION/TRAINING PROGRAM(S)—Business Machine Repair; Computer Installation and Repair Technology/Technician. **RELATED KNOWLEDGE/COURSES—Computers and Electronics:** Knowledge of circuit boards, processors, chips, electronic equipment, and computer hardware and software, including applications and programming. **Mechanical Devices:** Knowledge of machines and tools, including their designs, uses, repair, and maintenance. **Engineering and Technology:** Knowledge of the practical application of engineering science and technology. This includes applying principles, techniques, procedures, and equipment to the design and production of various goods and services. **Design:** Knowledge of design techniques, tools, and principles involved in production of precision technical plans, blueprints, drawings, and models. **Telecommunications:** Knowledge of transmission, broadcasting, switching, control, and operation of telecommunications systems. **Education and Training:** Knowledge of principles and methods for curriculum and training design, teaching and instruction for individuals and groups, and the measurement of training effects.

Operating Engineers

- Education/Training Required: Moderate-term on-the-job training
- Annual Earnings: $35,360
- Growth: 10.4%
- Annual Job Openings: 45,000
- Self-Employed: 3.7%
- Part-Time: 2.6%

Operate several types of power construction equipment, such as compressors, pumps, hoists, derricks, cranes, shovels, tractors, scrapers, or motor graders, to excavate, move, and grade earth; erect structures; or pour concrete or other hard-surface pavement. May repair and maintain equipment in addition to other duties. Adjusts handwheels and depresses pedals to drive machines and control attachments, such as blades, buckets, scrapers, and swing booms. Turns valves to control air and water output of compressors and pumps. Repairs and maintains equipment. **SKILLS—Repairing:** Repairing machines or systems by using the needed tools. **Operation and Control:** Controlling operations of equipment or systems. **Equipment Maintenance:** Performing routine maintenance on equipment and determining when and what kind of maintenance is needed. **Operation Monitoring:** Watching gauges, dials, or other indicators to make sure a machine is working properly. **Troubleshooting:** Determining causes of operating errors and deciding what to do about them. **GOE—Interest Area:** 02. Architecture and Construction. **Work Group:** 02.04. Construction Crafts. **Other Jobs in This Work Group:** Boat Builders and Shipwrights; Boilermakers; Brattice Builders; Brickmasons and Blockmasons; Carpet Installers; Ceiling Tile Installers; Cement Masons and Concrete Finishers; Commercial Divers; Construction Carpenters; Crane and Tower Operators; Dragline Operators; Drywall Installers; Electricians; Fence Erectors; Floor Layers, Except Carpet, Wood, and Hard Tiles; Floor Sanders and Finishers; Glaziers; Grader, Bulldozer, and Scraper Operators; Hazardous Materials Removal Workers; Insulation Workers, Floor, Ceiling, and Wall; Insulation Workers, Mechanical; Manufactured Building and Mobile Home Installers; Painters, Construction and Maintenance; Paperhangers; Paving, Surfacing, and Tamping Equipment Operators; Pile-Driver Operators; Pipe Fitters; Pipelayers; Pipelaying Fitters; Plasterers and Stucco Masons; Plumbers; Rail-Track Laying and Maintenance Equipment Operators; Refractory Materials Repairers, Except Brickmasons; Reinforcing Iron and Rebar Workers; Riggers; Roofers; Rough Carpenters; Security and Fire Alarm Systems Installers; Segmental Pavers; Sheet Metal Workers; Ship Carpenters and Joiners; Stone Cutters and Carvers; Stonemasons; Structural Iron and Steel Workers; Tapers; Terrazzo Workers and Finishers; Tile and Marble Setters. **PERSONALITY TYPE:** Realistic. Realistic occupations frequently involve work activities that include practical, hands-on problems and solutions. These occupations often deal with plants, animals, and real-world materials like wood, tools, and machinery. Many of the occupations require working outside and do not involve a lot of paperwork or working closely with others.

EDUCATION/TRAINING PROGRAM(S)—Construction/Heavy Equipment/Earthmoving Equipment Operation; Mobil Crane Operation/Operator. **RELATED KNOWLEDGE/COURSES—Mechanical Devices:** Knowledge of machines and tools, including their designs, uses, repair, and maintenance. **Building and Construction:** Knowledge of the materials, methods, and tools involved in the construction or repair of houses, buildings, or other structures such as highways and roads. **Sales and Marketing:** Knowledge of principles and methods for showing, promoting, and selling products or services. This includes marketing strategy and tactics, product demonstrations, sales techniques, and sales control systems. **Physics:** Knowledge and prediction of physical principles and laws and their interrelationships and applications to understanding fluid, material, and atmospheric dynamics and mechanical, electrical, atomic, and subatomic structures and processes. **Engineering and Technology:** Knowledge of the practical application of engineering science and technology. This includes applying principles, techniques, procedures, and equipment to the design and production of various goods and services. **Public Safety and Security:** Knowledge of relevant equipment, policies, procedures, and strategies to promote effective local, state, or national security oper-

ations for the protection of people, data, property, and institutions.

Opticians, Dispensing

- Education/Training Required: Long-term on-the-job training
- Annual Earnings: $27,950
- Growth: 18.2%
- Annual Job Openings: 10,000
- Self-Employed: 2.8%
- Part-Time: 19.9%

Design, measure, fit, and adapt lenses and frames for client according to written optical prescription or specification. Assist client with selecting frames. Measure customer for size of eyeglasses and coordinate frames with facial and eye measurements and optical prescription. Prepare work order for optical laboratory containing instructions for grinding and mounting lenses in frames. Verify exactness of finished lens spectacles. Adjust frame and lens position to fit client. May shape or reshape frames. Measure clients' bridge and eye size, temple length, vertex distance, pupillary distance, and optical centers of eyes, using measuring devices. Verify that finished lenses are ground to specifications. Prepare work orders and instructions for grinding lenses and fabricating eyeglasses. Assist clients in selecting frames according to style and color and ensure that frames are coordinated with facial and eye measurements and optical prescriptions. Maintain records of customer prescriptions, work orders, and payments. Perform administrative duties such as tracking inventory and sales, submitting patient insurance information, and performing simple bookkeeping. Recommend specific lenses, lens coatings, and frames to suit client needs. Sell goods such as contact lenses, spectacles, sunglasses, and other goods related to eyes in general. Heat, shape, or bend plastic or metal frames in order to adjust eyeglasses to fit clients, using pliers and hands. Evaluate prescriptions in conjunction with clients' vocational and avocational visual requirements. Instruct clients in how to wear and care for eyeglasses. Determine clients' current lens prescriptions, when necessary, using lensometers or lens analyzers and clients' eyeglasses. Show customers how to insert, remove, and care for their contact lenses. Repair damaged frames. Obtain a customer's previous record or verify a prescription with the examining optometrist or ophthalmologist. Arrange and maintain displays of optical merchandise. Fabricate lenses to meet prescription specifications. Grind lens edges or apply coatings to lenses. Assemble eyeglasses by cutting and edging lenses and then fitting the lenses into frames. Supervise the training of student opticians. **SKILLS—Persuasion:** Persuading others to change their minds or behavior. **Service Orientation:** Actively looking for ways to help people. **Technology Design:** Generating or adapting equipment and technology to serve user needs. **Speaking:** Talking to others to convey information effectively. **Social Perceptiveness:** Being aware of others' reactions and understanding why they react as they do. **Equipment Selection:** Determining the kind of tools and equipment needed to do a job. **Active Learning:** Understanding the implications of new information for both current and future problem-solving and decision-making. **Instructing:** Teaching others how to do something. **Management of Financial Resources:** Determining how money will be spent to get the work done and accounting for these expenditures. **GOE—Interest Area:** 08. Health Science. **Work Group:** 08.06. Medical Technology. **Other Jobs in This Work Group:** Biological Technicians; Cardiovascular Technologists and Technicians; Diagnostic Medical Sonographers; Medical and Clinical Laboratory Technicians; Medical and Clinical Laboratory Technologists; Medical Equipment Preparers; Medical Records and Health Information Technicians; Nuclear Medicine Technologists; Orthotists and Prosthetists; Radiologic Technicians; Radiologic Technologists. **PERSONALITY TYPE:** Enterprising. Enterprising occupations frequently involve starting up and carrying out projects. These occupations can involve leading people and making many decisions. They sometimes require risk taking and often deal with business.

EDUCATION/TRAINING PROGRAM(S)—Opticianry/Ophthalmic Dispensing Optician. **RELATED KNOWLEDGE/COURSES—Sales and Marketing:** Knowledge of principles and methods for showing, promoting, and selling products or services. This includes marketing strategy and tactics, product

demonstrations, sales techniques, and sales control systems. **Customer and Personal Service:** Knowledge of principles and processes for providing customer and personal services. This includes customer needs assessment, meeting quality standards for services, and evaluation of customer satisfaction. **Production and Processing:** Knowledge of raw materials, production processes, quality control, costs, and other techniques for maximizing the effective manufacture and distribution of goods. **Clerical Practices:** Knowledge of administrative and clerical procedures and systems such as word processing, managing files and records, stenography and transcription, designing forms, and other office procedures and terminology. **Psychology:** Knowledge of human behavior and performance; individual differences in ability, personality, and interests; learning and motivation; psychological research methods; and the assessment and treatment of behavioral and affective disorders. **Administration and Management:** Knowledge of business and management principles involved in strategic planning, resource allocation, human resources modeling, leadership technique, production methods, and coordination of people and resources.

Packaging and Filling Machine Operators and Tenders

- Education/Training Required: Short-term on-the-job training
- Annual Earnings: $22,200
- Growth: 21.1%
- Annual Job Openings: 69,000
- Self-Employed: 0%
- Part-Time: 5.7%

Operate or tend machines to prepare industrial or consumer products for storage or shipment. Includes cannery workers who pack food products. Observe machine operations to ensure quality and conformity of filled or packaged products to standards. Adjust machine components and machine tension and pressure according to size or processing angle of product.

Tend or operate machine that packages product. Remove finished packaged items from machine and separate rejected items. Regulate machine flow, speed, or temperature. Stop or reset machines when malfunctions occur, clear machine jams, and report malfunctions to a supervisor. Secure finished packaged items by hand-tying, sewing, gluing, stapling, or attaching fastener. Stock and sort product for packaging or filling machine operation and replenish packaging supplies such as wrapping paper, plastic sheet, boxes, cartons, glue, ink, or labels. Inspect and remove defective products and packaging material. Clean and remove damaged or otherwise inferior materials to prepare raw products for processing. Sort, grade, weigh, and inspect products, verifying and adjusting product weight or measurement to meet specifications. Clean, oil, and make minor adjustments or repairs to machinery and equipment, such as opening valves or setting guides. Monitor the production line, watching for problems such as pile-ups, jams, or glue that isn't sticking properly. Stack finished packaged items or wrap protective material around each item and pack the items in cartons or containers. Start machine by engaging controls. Count and record finished and rejected packaged items. Package the product in the form in which it will be sent out, for example, filling bags with flour from a chute or spout. Supply materials to spindles, conveyors, hoppers, or other feeding devices and unload packaged product. Attach identification labels to finished packaged items or cut stencils and stencil information on containers, such as lot numbers or shipping destinations. Clean packaging containers, line and pad crates, and/or assemble cartons to prepare for product packing. **SKILLS—Equipment Maintenance:** Performing routine maintenance on equipment and determining when and what kind of maintenance is needed. **Instructing:** Teaching others how to do something. **Quality Control Analysis:** Conducting tests and inspections of products, services, or processes to evaluate quality or performance. **Operation Monitoring:** Watching gauges, dials, or other indicators to make sure a machine is working properly. **Troubleshooting:** Determining causes of operating errors and deciding what to do about them. **Operation and Control:** Controlling operations of equipment or systems. **Coordination:** Adjusting actions in relation to others' actions. **Repairing:** Repairing machines or systems by using the needed tools. **GOE—Interest Area:** 13. Manufacturing. **Work Group:** 13.03. Production Work, Assorted Materials Processing. **Other Jobs in This Work Group:** Bakers, Manufacturing; Cementing and Gluing Machine Operators and Tenders; Chemical Equipment Controllers and Operators; Chemical Equipment Tenders; Cleaning, Washing, and Metal Pickling Equipment Operators and Tenders; Coating, Painting, and Spraying Machine Operators and Tenders; Combination Machine Tool Operators and Tenders, Metal and Plastic; Cooling and Freezing Equipment Operators and Tenders; Cutting and Slicing Machine Operators and Tenders; Electrolytic Plating and Coating Machine Operators and Tenders, Metal and Plastic; Extruding and Forming Machine Operators and Tenders, Synthetic or Glass Fibers; Extruding, Forming, Pressing, and Compacting Machine Operators and Tenders; Food and Tobacco Roasting, Baking, and Drying Machine Operators and Tenders; Food Batchmakers; Food Cooking Machine Operators and Tenders; Furnace, Kiln, Oven, Drier, and Kettle Operators and Tenders; Heat Treating, Annealing, and Tempering Machine Operators and Tenders, Metal and Plastic; Heaters, Metal and Plastic; Meat, Poultry, and Fish Cutters and Trimmers; Metal-Refining Furnace Operators and Tenders; Mixing and Blending Machine Setters, Operators, and Tenders; Nonelectrolytic Plating and Coating Machine Operators and Tenders, Metal and Plastic; Plastic Molding and Casting Machine Operators and Tenders; Pourers and Casters, Metal; Pressing Machine Operators and Tenders—Textile, Garment, and Related Materials; Production Helpers; Production Laborers; Sawing Machine Operators and Tenders; Separating, Filtering, Clarifying, Precipitating, and Still Machine Setters, Operators, and Tenders; Sewing Machine Operators, Garment; Sewing Machine Operators, Non-Garment; Shoe Machine Operators and Tenders; Slaughterers and Meat Packers; Stone Sawyers; Team Assemblers; Textile Bleaching and Dyeing Machine Operators and Tenders; Tire Builders; Woodworking Machine Operators and Tenders, Except Sawing. **PERSONALITY TYPE:** Realistic. Realistic occupations frequently involve work activities that include practical, hands-on problems and solutions. These occupations often deal with plants, animals, and real-world materials like wood, tools, and machinery. Many of the occupations require working outside and do not involve a lot of paperwork or working closely with others.

EDUCATION/TRAINING PROGRAM(S)—No data available. **RELATED KNOWLEDGE/COURS-ES—Production and Processing:** Knowledge of raw materials, production processes, quality control, costs, and other techniques for maximizing the effective manufacture and distribution of goods. **Mechanical Devices:** Knowledge of machines and tools, including their designs, uses, repair, and maintenance. **Psychology:** Knowledge of human behavior and performance; individual differences in ability, personality, and interests; learning and motivation; psychological research methods; and the assessment and treatment of behavioral and affective disorders. **Sociology and Anthropology:** Knowledge of group behavior and dynamics, societal trends and influences, human migrations, ethnicity, and cultures and their history and origins. **Public Safety and Security:** Knowledge of relevant equipment, policies, procedures, and strategies to promote effective local, state, or national security operations for the protection of people, data, property, and institutions. **Education and Training:** Knowledge of principles and methods for curriculum and training design, teaching and instruction for individuals and groups, and the measurement of training effects.

Packers and Packagers, Hand

- ◉ Education/Training Required: Short-term on-the-job training
- ◉ Annual Earnings: $17,150
- ◉ Growth: 14.4%
- ◉ Annual Job Openings: 198,000
- ◉ Self-Employed: 0.1%
- ◉ Part-Time: 15.3%

Pack or package by hand a wide variety of products and materials. Mark and label containers, container tags, or products, using marking tools. Measure, weigh, and count products and materials. Examine and inspect containers, materials, and products in order to ensure that packing specifications are met.

Record product, packaging, and order information on specified forms and records. Remove completed or defective products or materials, placing them on moving equipment such as conveyors or in specified areas such as loading docks. Seal containers or materials, using glues, fasteners, nails, and hand tools. Load materials and products into package-processing equipment. Assemble, line, and pad cartons, crates, and containers, using hand tools. Clean containers, materials, supplies, or work areas, using cleaning solutions and hand tools. Transport packages to customers' vehicles. Place or pour products or materials into containers, using hand tools and equipment, or fill containers from spouts or chutes. Obtain, move, and sort products, materials, containers, and orders, using hand tools. **SKILLS—Persuasion:** Persuading others to change their minds or behavior. **Active Listening:** Giving full attention to what other people are saying, taking time to understand the points being made, asking questions as appropriate, and not interrupting at inappropriate times. **Management of Personnel Resources:** Motivating, developing, and directing people as they work, identifying the best people for the job. **Social Perceptiveness:** Being aware of others' reactions and understanding why they react as they do. **Learning Strategies:** Selecting and using training/instructional methods and procedures appropriate for the situation when learning or teaching new things. **Instructing:** Teaching others how to do something. **Coordination:** Adjusting actions in relation to others' actions. **Service Orientation:** Actively looking for ways to help people. **Quality Control Analysis:** Conducting tests and inspections of products, services, or processes to evaluate quality or performance. **GOE—Interest Area:** 13. Manufacturing. **Work Group:** 13.17. Loading, Moving, Hoisting, and Conveying. **Other Jobs in This Work Group:** Conveyor Operators and Tenders; Freight, Stock, and Material Movers, Hand; Hoist and Winch Operators; Industrial Truck and Tractor Operators; Irradiated-Fuel Handlers; Machine Feeders and Offbearers; Pump Operators, Except Wellhead Pumpers; Refuse and Recyclable Material Collectors; Tank Car, Truck, and Ship Loaders. **PERSONALITY TYPE:** Realistic. Realistic occupations frequently involve work activities that include practical, hands-on problems and solutions. These occupations often deal with plants, animals, and real-world materials like wood, tools, and machinery. Many of the occupations require working outside and do not involve a lot of paperwork or working closely with others.

EDUCATION/TRAINING PROGRAM(S)—No data available. RELATED KNOWLEDGE/COURS- ES—Production and Processing: Knowledge of raw materials, production processes, quality control, costs, and other techniques for maximizing the effective manufacture and distribution of goods. Public Safety and Security: Knowledge of relevant equipment, poli- cies, procedures, and strategies to promote effective local, state, or national security operations for the pro- tection of people, data, property, and institutions. Food Production: Knowledge of techniques and equipment for planting, growing, and harvesting food products (both plant and animal) for consumption, including storage/handling techniques. Transporta- tion: Knowledge of principles and methods for mov- ing people or goods by air, rail, sea, or road, including the relative costs and benefits. Administration and Management: Knowledge of business and manage- ment principles involved in strategic planning, resource allocation, human resources modeling, leader- ship technique, production methods, and coordina- tion of people and resources. Clerical Practices: Knowledge of administrative and clerical procedures and systems such as word processing, managing files and records, stenography and transcription, designing forms, and other office procedures and terminology.

Painters and Illustrators

◎ Education/Training Required: Long-term on-the-job training
◎ Annual Earnings: $38,060
◎ Growth: 16.5%
◎ Annual Job Openings: 4,000
◎ Self-Employed: 55.5%
◎ Part-Time: 23.1%

Paint or draw subject material to produce original artwork or illustrations, using watercolors, oils, acrylics, tempera, or other paint mediums. Renders drawings, illustrations, and sketches of buildings, man- ufactured products, or models, working from sketches, blueprints, memory, or reference materials. Paints sce- nic backgrounds, murals, and portraiture for motion picture and television production sets, glass artworks, and exhibits. Etches, carves, paints, or draws artwork on material such as stone, glass, canvas, wood, and linoleum. Develops drawings, paintings, diagrams, and models of medical or biological subjects for use in publications, exhibits, consultations, research, and teaching. Studies style, techniques, colors, textures, and materials used by artist to maintain consistency in reconstruction or retouching procedures. Removes painting from frame or paint layer from canvas to restore artwork, following specified technique and equipment. Examines surfaces of paintings and proofs of artwork, using magnifying device, to determine method of restoration or needed corrections. Installs finished stained glass in window or door frame. Assem- bles, leads, and solders finished glass to fabricate stained glass article. Applies select solvents and clean- ing agents to clean surface of painting and remove accretions, discolorations, and deteriorated varnish. Performs tests to determine factors such as age, struc- ture, pigment stability, and probable reaction to vari- ous cleaning agents and solvents. Confers with professional personnel or client to discuss objectives of artwork and develop illustration ideas and theme to be portrayed. Brushes or sprays protective or decorative finish on completed background panels, information- al legends, exhibit accessories, or finished painting. Integrates and develops visual elements, such as line, space, mass, color, and perspective to produce desired effect. SKILLS—Operations Analysis: Analyzing needs and product requirements to create a design. Management of Material Resources: Obtaining and seeing to the appropriate use of equipment, facilities, and materials needed to do certain work. Installation: Installing equipment, machines, wiring, or programs to meet specifications. Quality Control Analysis: Conducting tests and inspections of products, services, or processes to evaluate quality or performance. Repairing: Repairing machines or systems by using the needed tools. GOE—Interest Area: 03. Arts and Communication. Work Group: 03.04. Studio Art. Other Jobs in This Work Group: Cartoonists; Craft Artists; Potters; Sculptors; Sketch Artists. PERSON- ALITY TYPE: Artistic. Artistic occupations frequent- ly involve working with forms, designs, and patterns.

These occupations often require self-expression, and the work can be done without following a clear set of rules.

EDUCATION/TRAINING PROGRAM(S)— Art/Art Studies, General; Drawing; Fine Arts and Art Studies, Other; Fine/Studio Arts, General; Medical Illustration/Medical Illustrator; Painting; Visual and Performing Arts, General. **RELATED KNOWL-EDGE/COURSES—Fine Arts:** Knowledge of the theory and techniques required to compose, produce, and perform works of music, dance, the visual arts, drama, and sculpture. **Design:** Knowledge of design techniques, tools, and principles involved in production of precision technical plans, blueprints, drawings, and models. **Chemistry:** Knowledge of the chemical composition, structure, and properties of substances and of the chemical processes and transformations that they undergo. This includes uses of chemicals and their danger signs, production techniques, and disposal methods. **History and Archeology:** Knowledge of historical events and their causes, indicators, and effects on civilizations and cultures. **Communications and Media:** Knowledge of media production, communication, and dissemination techniques and methods. This includes alternative ways to inform and entertain via written, oral, and visual media. **Engineering and Technology:** Knowledge of the practical application of engineering science and technology. This includes applying principles, techniques, procedures, and equipment to the design and production of various goods and services.

Painters, Construction and Maintenance

- ◎ Education/Training Required: Moderate-term on-the-job training
- ◎ Annual Earnings: $30,260
- ◎ Growth: 11.6%
- ◎ Annual Job Openings: 69,000
- ◎ Self-Employed: 41.7%
- ◎ Part-Time: 9.0%

Paint walls, equipment, buildings, bridges, and other structural surfaces, using brushes, rollers, and spray guns. May remove old paint to prepare surface prior to painting. May mix colors or oils to obtain desired color or consistency. Apply paint, stain, varnish, enamel, and other finishes to equipment, buildings, bridges, and/or other structures, using brushes, spray guns, or rollers. Apply primers or sealers to prepare new surfaces, such as bare wood or metal, for finish coats. Calculate amounts of required materials and estimate costs, based on surface measurements and/or work orders. Cover surfaces with dropcloths or masking tape and paper to protect surfaces during painting. Fill cracks, holes, and joints with caulk, putty, plaster, or other fillers, using caulking guns or putty knives. Mix and match colors of paint, stain, or varnish with oil and thinning and drying additives in order to obtain desired colors and consistencies. Polish final coats to specified finishes. Read work orders or receive instructions from supervisors or homeowners in order to determine work requirements. Remove fixtures such as pictures, doorknobs, lamps, and electric switch covers prior to painting. Remove old finishes by stripping, sanding, wire brushing, burning, or using water and/or abrasive blasting. Smooth surfaces, using sandpaper, scrapers, brushes, steel wool, and/or sanding machines. Wash and treat surfaces with oil, turpentine, mildew remover, or other preparations and sand rough spots to ensure that finishes will adhere properly. Bake finishes on painted and enameled articles, using baking ovens. Cut stencils and brush and spray lettering and decorations on surfaces. Erect scaffolding and swing gates or set up ladders to work above ground level. Select and purchase tools and finishes for surfaces to be covered, considering durability, ease of handling, methods of application, and customers' wishes. Spray or brush hot plastics or pitch onto surfaces. Use special finishing techniques such as sponging, ragging, layering, or faux finishing. Waterproof buildings, using waterproofers and caulking. **SKILLS**—None met the criteria. **GOE—Interest Area:** 02. Architecture and Construction. **Work Group:** 02.04. Construction Crafts. **Other Jobs in This Work Group:** Boat Builders and Shipwrights; Boilermakers; Brattice Builders; Brickmasons and Blockmasons; Carpet Installers; Ceiling Tile Installers; Cement Masons and Concrete Finishers; Commercial Divers; Construction Carpenters; Crane and Tower Operators; Dragline Operators; Drywall Installers; Electricians; Fence Erectors; Floor Layers, Except Carpet, Wood, and Hard Tiles; Floor Sanders and Finishers; Glaziers; Grader, Bulldozer, and Scraper Operators; Hazardous Materials Removal Workers; Insulation Workers, Floor, Ceiling, and Wall; Insulation Workers, Mechanical; Manufactured Building and Mobile Home Installers; Operating Engineers; Paperhangers; Paving, Surfacing, and Tamping Equipment Operators; Pile-Driver Operators; Pipe Fitters; Pipelayers; Pipelaying Fitters; Plasterers and Stucco Masons; Plumbers; Rail-Track Laying and Maintenance Equipment Operators; Refractory Materials Repairers, Except Brickmasons; Reinforcing Iron and Rebar Workers; Riggers; Roofers; Rough Carpenters; Security and Fire Alarm Systems Installers; Segmental Pavers; Sheet Metal Workers; Ship Carpenters and Joiners; Stone Cutters and Carvers; Stonemasons; Structural Iron and Steel Workers; Tapers; Terrazzo Workers and Finishers; Tile and Marble Setters. **PERSONALITY TYPE:** Realistic. Realistic occupations frequently involve work activities that include practical, hands-on problems and solutions. These occupations often deal with plants, animals, and real-world materials like wood, tools, and machinery. Many of the occupations require working outside and do not involve a lot of paperwork or working closely with others.

EDUCATION/TRAINING PROGRAM(S)— Painting/Painter and Wall Coverer. **RELATED KNOWLEDGE/COURSES—Building and Construction:** Knowledge of the materials, methods, and tools involved in the construction or repair of houses, buildings, or other structures such as highways and roads. **Sales and Marketing:** Knowledge of principles and methods for showing, promoting, and selling products or services. This includes marketing strategy and tactics, product demonstrations, sales techniques, and sales control systems.

Painters, Transportation Equipment

- Education/Training Required: Moderate-term on-the-job training
- Annual Earnings: $35,120
- Growth: 17.5%
- Annual Job Openings: 9,000
- Self-Employed: 7.8%
- Part-Time: 4.5%

Operate or tend painting machines to paint surfaces of transportation equipment, such as automobiles, buses, trucks, trains, boats, and airplanes. Adjust controls on infrared ovens, heat lamps, portable ventilators, and exhaust units in order to speed the drying of vehicles between coats. Allow the sprayed product to dry and then touch up any spots that may have been missed. Apply designs, lettering, or other identifying or decorative items to finished products, using paint brushes or paint sprayers. Apply primer over any repairs made to vehicle surfaces. Apply rust-resistant undercoats and caulk and seal seams. Buff and wax the finished paintwork. Fill small dents and scratches with body fillers and smooth surfaces in order to prepare vehicles for painting. Lay out logos, symbols, or designs on painted surfaces according to blueprint specifications, using measuring instruments, stencils, and patterns. Mix paints to match color specifications or vehicles' original colors and then stir and thin the paints, using spatulas or power-mixing equipment. Monitor painting operations in order to identify flaws such as blisters and streaks so that their causes can be corrected. Operate lifting and moving devices in order to move equipment or materials so that areas to be painted are accessible. Paint by hand areas that cannot be reached with a spray gun or those that need retouching, using brushes. Pour paint into spray guns and adjust nozzles and paint mixes in order to get the proper paint flow and coating thickness. Remove accessories from vehicles, such as chrome or mirrors, and mask other surfaces with tape or paper in order to protect them from paint. Remove grease, dirt, paint, and rust from vehicle surfaces in preparation for paint application, using abrasives, solvents, brushes, blowtorches, washing tanks, or sandblasters. Sand the final finish and apply sealer once a vehicle has dried properly. Sand vehicle surfaces between coats of paint and/or primer in order to remove flaws and enhance adhesion for subsequent coats. Select paint according to company requirements and match colors of paint, following specified color charts. Select the correct spray gun system for the material being applied. Set up portable equipment such as ventilators, exhaust units, ladders, and scaffolding. **SKILLS—Operation and Control:** Controlling operations of equipment or systems. **GOE—Interest Area:** 13. Manufacturing. **Work Group:** 13.09. Hands-On Work, Assorted Materials. **Other Jobs in This Work Group:** Coil Winders, Tapers, and Finishers; Cutters and Trimmers, Hand; Fabric and Apparel Patternmakers; Glass Blowers, Molders, Benders, and Finishers; Grinding and Polishing Workers, Hand; Mold Makers, Hand; Molding and Casting Workers; Painting, Coating, and Decorating Workers; Sewers, Hand. **PERSONALITY TYPE:** Realistic. Realistic occupations frequently involve work activities that include practical, hands-on problems and solutions. These occupations often deal with plants, animals, and real-world materials like wood, tools, and machinery. Many of the occupations require working outside and do not involve a lot of paperwork or working closely with others.

EDUCATION/TRAINING PROGRAM(S)—Auto Body/Collision and Repair Technology/Technician. **RELATED KNOWLEDGE/COURSES—Design:** Knowledge of design techniques, tools, and principles involved in production of precision technical plans, blueprints, drawings, and models. **Mechanical Devices:** Knowledge of machines and tools, including their designs, uses, repair, and maintenance. **Fine Arts:** Knowledge of the theory and techniques required to compose, produce, and perform works of music, dance, the visual arts, drama, and sculpture. **Chemistry:** Knowledge of the chemical composition, structure, and properties of substances and of the chemical processes and transformations that they undergo. This includes uses of chemicals and their danger signs, production techniques, and disposal methods.

Paralegals and Legal Assistants

- Education/Training Required: Associate degree
- Annual Earnings: $39,130
- Growth: 28.7%
- Annual Job Openings: 29,000
- Self-Employed: 2.3%
- Part-Time: 10.8%

Assist lawyers by researching legal precedent, investigating facts, or preparing legal documents. Conduct research to support a legal proceeding, to formulate a defense, or to initiate legal action. Prepare legal documents, including briefs, pleadings, appeals, wills, contracts, and real estate closing statements. Prepare affidavits or other documents, maintain document file, and file pleadings with court clerk. Gather and analyze research data, such as statutes; decisions; and legal articles, codes, and documents. Investigate facts and law of cases to determine causes of action and to prepare cases. Call upon witnesses to testify at hearing. Direct and coordinate law office activity, including delivery of subpoenas. Arbitrate disputes between parties and assist in real estate closing process. Keep and monitor legal volumes to ensure that law library is up-to-date. Appraise and inventory real and personal property for estate planning. **SKILLS—Time Management:** Managing one's own time and the time of others. **Active Listening:** Giving full attention to what other people are saying, taking time to understand the points being made, asking questions as appropriate, and not interrupting at inappropriate times. **Writing:** Communicating effectively in writing as appropriate for the needs of the audience. **Instructing:** Teaching others how to do something. **Speaking:** Talking to others to convey information effectively. **Social Perceptiveness:** Being aware of others' reactions and understanding why they react as they do. **Reading Comprehension:** Understanding written sentences and paragraphs in work-related documents. **Service Orientation:** Actively looking for ways to help people. **GOE—Interest Area:** 12. Law and Public Safety. **Work Group:** 12.03. Legal Support. **Other Jobs in This Work Group:** Law Clerks; Title Examiners and Abstractors; Title

Searchers. **PERSONALITY TYPE:** Enterprising. Enterprising occupations frequently involve starting up and carrying out projects. These occupations can involve leading people and making many decisions. They sometimes require risk taking and often deal with business.

EDUCATION/TRAINING PROGRAM(S)—Legal Assistant/Paralegal. **RELATED KNOWLEDGE/ COURSES**—**Clerical Practices:** Knowledge of administrative and clerical procedures and systems such as word processing, managing files and records, stenography and transcription, designing forms, and other office procedures and terminology. **Law and Government:** Knowledge of laws, legal codes, court procedures, precedents, government regulations, executive orders, agency rules, and the democratic political process. **Customer and Personal Service:** Knowledge of principles and processes for providing customer and personal services. This includes customer needs assessment, meeting quality standards for services, and evaluation of customer satisfaction. **Computers and Electronics:** Knowledge of circuit boards, processors, chips, electronic equipment, and computer hardware and software, including applications and programming. **English Language:** Knowledge of the structure and content of the English language, including the meaning and spelling of words, rules of composition, and grammar. **Personnel and Human Resources:** Knowledge of principles and procedures for personnel recruitment, selection, training, compensation and benefits, labor relations and negotiation, and personnel information systems.

Personal and Home Care Aides

- Education/Training Required: Short-term on-the-job training
- Annual Earnings: $16,900
- Growth: 40.5%
- Annual Job Openings: 154,000
- Self-Employed: 7.1%
- Part-Time: 34.0%

Assist elderly or disabled adults with daily living activities at the person's home or in a daytime non-residential facility. Duties performed at a place of residence may include keeping house (making beds, doing laundry, washing dishes) and preparing meals. May provide meals and supervised activities at non-residential care facilities. May advise families, the elderly, and disabled on such things as nutrition, cleanliness, and household utilities. Perform healthcare related tasks, such as monitoring vital signs and medication, under the direction of registered nurses and physiotherapists. Administer bedside and personal care, such as ambulation and personal hygiene assistance. Prepare and maintain records of client progress and services performed, reporting changes in client condition to manager or supervisor. Perform housekeeping duties, such as cooking, cleaning, washing clothes and dishes, and running errands. Care for individuals and families during periods of incapacitation, family disruption, or convalescence, providing companionship, personal care, and help in adjusting to new lifestyles. Instruct and advise clients on issues such as household cleanliness, utilities, hygiene, nutrition, and infant care. Plan, shop for, and prepare meals, including special diets, and assist families in planning, shopping for, and preparing nutritious meals. Participate in case reviews, consulting with the team caring for the client, to evaluate the client's needs and plan for continuing services. Transport clients to locations outside the home, such as to physicians' offices or on outings, using a motor vehicle. Train family members to provide bedside care. Provide clients with communication assistance, typing their correspondence and obtaining information for them. **SKILLS**—**Social Perceptiveness:** Being aware of others' reactions and understanding why they react as they do. **Persuasion:** Persuading others to change their minds or behavior. **Service Orientation:** Actively looking for ways to help people. **Learning Strategies:** Selecting and using training/instructional methods and procedures appropriate for the situation when learning or teaching new things. **Coordination:** Adjusting actions in relation to others' actions. **Active Listening:** Giving full attention to what other people are saying, taking time to understand the points being made, asking questions as appropriate, and not interrupting at inappropriate times. **Instructing:** Teaching others how to do something. **Critical**

Thinking: Using logic and reasoning to identify the strengths and weaknesses of alternative solutions, conclusions, or approaches to problems. **GOE—Interest Area:** 10. Human Service. **Work Group:** 10.03. Child/Personal Care and Services. **Other Jobs in This Work Group:** Child Care Workers; Funeral Attendants; Nannies. **PERSONALITY TYPE:** Social. Social occupations frequently involve working with, communicating with, and teaching people. These occupations often involve helping or providing service to others.

EDUCATION/TRAINING PROGRAM(S)—No data available. **RELATED KNOWLEDGE/COURSES—Customer and Personal Service:** Knowledge of principles and processes for providing customer and personal services. This includes customer needs assessment, meeting quality standards for services, and evaluation of customer satisfaction. **Medicine and Dentistry:** Knowledge of the information and techniques needed to diagnose and treat human injuries, diseases, and deformities. This includes symptoms, treatment alternatives, drug properties and interactions, and preventive health-care measures. **Therapy and Counseling:** Knowledge of principles, methods, and procedures for diagnosis, treatment, and rehabilitation of physical and mental dysfunctions and for career counseling and guidance.

Pest Control Workers

- ◎ Education/Training Required: Moderate-term on-the-job training
- ◎ Annual Earnings: $26,220
- ◎ Growth: 17.0%
- ◎ Annual Job Openings: 11,000
- ◎ Self-Employed: 9.1%
- ◎ Part-Time: 6.1%

Spray or release chemical solutions or toxic gases and set traps to kill pests and vermin, such as mice, termites, and roaches, that infest buildings and surrounding areas. Spray or dust chemical solutions, powders, or gases into rooms; onto clothing, furnishings, or wood; and over marshlands, ditches, and catch-basins. Set mechanical traps and place poisonous paste or bait in sewers, burrows, and ditches. Inspect premises to identify infestation source and extent of damage to property, wall and roof porosity, and access to infested locations. Cut or bore openings in building or surrounding concrete, access infested areas, insert nozzle, and inject pesticide to impregnate ground. Study preliminary reports and diagrams of infested area and determine treatment type required to eliminate and prevent recurrence of infestation. Direct and/or assist other workers in treatment and extermination processes to eliminate and control rodents, insects, and weeds. Measure area dimensions requiring treatment, using rule; calculate fumigant requirements; and estimate cost for service. Clean and remove blockages from infested areas to facilitate spraying procedure and provide drainage, using broom, mop, shovel, and rake. Position and fasten edges of tarpaulins over building and tape vents to ensure air-tight environment and check for leaks. Post warning signs and lock building doors to secure area to be fumigated. Drive truck equipped with power-spraying equipment. Record work activities performed. Clean work site after completion of job. Dig up and burnweeds or spray them with herbicides. **SKILLS—Mathematics:** Using mathematics to solve problems. **Operation and Control:** Controlling operations of equipment or systems. **Management of Personnel Resources:** Motivating, developing, and directing people as they work, identifying the best people for the job. **Operation Monitoring:** Watching gauges, dials, or other indicators to make sure a machine is working properly. **Judgment and Decision Making:** Considering the relative costs and benefits of potential actions to choose the most appropriate one. **GOE—Interest Area:** 01. Agriculture and Natural Resources. **Work Group:** 01.05. Nursery, Groundskeeping, and Pest Control. **Other Jobs in This Work Group:** Landscaping and Groundskeeping Workers; Nursery Workers; Pesticide Handlers, Sprayers, and Applicators, Vegetation; Tree Trimmers and Pruners. **PERSONALITY TYPE:** Realistic. Realistic occupations frequently involve work activities that include practical, hands-on problems and solutions. These occupations often deal with plants, animals, and real-world materials like wood, tools, and machinery. Many of the occupations require working outside and do not involve a lot of paperwork or working closely with others.

P

EDUCATION/TRAINING PROGRAM(S)—Agricultural/Farm Supplies Retailing and Wholesaling. **RELATED KNOWLEDGE/COURSES—Chemistry:** Knowledge of the chemical composition, structure, and properties of substances and of the chemical processes and transformations that they undergo. This includes uses of chemicals and their danger signs, production techniques, and disposal methods. **Mechanical Devices:** Knowledge of machines and tools, including their designs, uses, repair, and maintenance. **Biology:** Knowledge of plant and animal organisms and their tissues, cells, functions, interdependencies, and interactions with each other and the environment.

Pharmacy Technicians

- Education/Training Required: Moderate-term on-the-job training
- Annual Earnings: $23,650
- Growth: 28.8%
- Annual Job Openings: 39,000
- Self-Employed: 0%
- Part-Time: 23.0%

Prepare medications under the direction of a pharmacist. May measure, mix, count out, label, and record amounts and dosages of medications. Receive written prescription or refill requests and verify that information is complete and accurate. Maintain proper storage and security conditions for drugs. Answer telephones, responding to questions or requests. Fill bottles with prescribed medications and type and affix labels. Assist customers by answering simple questions, locating items, or referring them to the pharmacist for medication information. Price and file prescriptions that have been filled. Clean and help maintain equipment and work areas and sterilize glassware according to prescribed methods. Establish and maintain patient profiles, including lists of medications taken by individual patients. Order, label, and count stock of medications, chemicals, and supplies and enter inventory data into computer. Receive and store incoming supplies, verify quantities against invoices, and inform supervisors of stock needs and shortages. Transfer medication from vials to the appropriate number of sterile, disposable syringes, using aseptic techniques. Add measured drugs or nutrients to intravenous solutions under sterile conditions to prepare intravenous (IV) packs under pharmacist supervision. Supply and monitor robotic machines that dispense medicine into containers and label the containers. Prepare and process medical insurance claim forms and records. Mix pharmaceutical preparations according to written prescriptions. Operate cash registers to accept payment from customers. Compute charges for medication and equipment dispensed to hospital patients and enter data in computer. Deliver medications and pharmaceutical supplies to patients, nursing stations, or surgery. Price stock and mark items for sale. Maintain and merchandise home health-care products and services. **SKILLS—Instructing:** Teaching others how to do something. **Service Orientation:** Actively looking for ways to help people. **Active Listening:** Giving full attention to what other people are saying, taking time to understand the points being made, asking questions as appropriate, and not interrupting at inappropriate times. **Active Learning:** Understanding the implications of new information for both current and future problem-solving and decision-making. **Speaking:** Talking to others to convey information effectively. **Critical Thinking:** Using logic and reasoning to identify the strengths and weaknesses of alternative solutions, conclusions, or approaches to problems. **Mathematics:** Using mathematics to solve problems. **Troubleshooting:** Determining causes of operating errors and deciding what to do about them. **GOE— Interest Area:** 08. Health Science. **Work Group:** 08.02. Medicine and Surgery. **Other Jobs in This Work Group:** Anesthesiologists; Family and General Practitioners; Internists, General; Medical Assistants; Medical Transcriptionists; Obstetricians and Gynecologists; Pediatricians, General; Pharmacists; Pharmacy Aides; Physician Assistants; Psychiatrists; Registered Nurses; Surgeons; Surgical Technologists. **PERSONALITY TYPE:** Conventional. Conventional occupations frequently involve following set procedures and routines. These occupations can include working with data and details more than with ideas. Usually there is a clear line of authority to follow.

EDUCATION/TRAINING PROGRAM(S)—Pharmacy Technician/Assistant. **RELATED KNOWLEDGE/COURSES—Customer and Personal Service:** Knowledge of principles and processes for providing customer and personal services. This includes customer needs assessment, meeting quality standards for services, and evaluation of customer satisfaction. **Chemistry:** Knowledge of the chemical composition, structure, and properties of substances and of the chemical processes and transformations that they undergo. This includes uses of chemicals and their danger signs, production techniques, and disposal methods. **Medicine and Dentistry:** Knowledge of the information and techniques needed to diagnose and treat human injuries, diseases, and deformities. This includes symptoms, treatment alternatives, drug properties and interactions, and preventive health-care measures. **Mathematics:** Knowledge of arithmetic, algebra, geometry, calculus, and statistics and their applications. **Therapy and Counseling:** Knowledge of principles, methods, and procedures for diagnosis, treatment, and rehabilitation of physical and mental dysfunctions and for career counseling and guidance. **Clerical Practices:** Knowledge of administrative and clerical procedures and systems such as word processing, managing files and records, stenography and transcription, designing forms, and other office procedures and terminology.

Photographers, Scientific

- ◎ Education/Training Required: Long-term on-the-job training
- ◎ Annual Earnings: $26,080
- ◎ Growth: 13.6%
- ◎ Annual Job Openings: 18,000
- ◎ Self-Employed: 52.5%
- ◎ Part-Time: 24.0%

Photograph variety of subject material to illustrate or record scientific/medical data or phenomena, utilizing knowledge of scientific procedures and photographic technology and techniques. Photographs variety of subject material to illustrate or record scientific or medical data or phenomena related to an area of interest. Sights and focuses camera to take picture of subject material to illustrate or record scientific or medical data or phenomena. Plans methods and procedures for photographing subject material and setup of required equipment. Observes and arranges subject material to desired position. Engages in research to develop new photographic procedures, materials, and scientific data. Sets up, mounts, or installs photographic equipment and cameras. Removes exposed film and develops film, using chemicals, touch-up tools, and equipment. **SKILLS—Science:** Using scientific rules and methods to solve problems. **Reading Comprehension:** Understanding written sentences and paragraphs in work-related documents. **Equipment Selection:** Determining the kind of tools and equipment needed to do a job. **Technology Design:** Generating or adapting equipment and technology to serve user needs. **Operation and Control:** Controlling operations of equipment or systems. **Management of Material Resources:** Obtaining and seeing to the appropriate use of equipment, facilities, and materials needed to do certain work. **Active Learning:** Understanding the implications of new information for both current and future problem-solving and decision-making. **Writing:** Communicating effectively in writing as appropriate for the needs of the audience. **GOE—Interest Area:** 15. Scientific Research, Engineering, and Mathematics. **Work Group:** 15.05. Physical Science Laboratory Technology. **Other Jobs in This Work Group:** Chemical Technicians; Nuclear Equipment Operation Technicians. **PERSONALITY TYPE:** Artistic. Artistic occupations frequently involve working with forms, designs, and patterns. These occupations often require self-expression, and the work can be done without following a clear set of rules.

EDUCATION/TRAINING PROGRAM(S)— Art/Art Studies, General; Commercial Photography; Film/Video and Photographic Arts, Other; Photography; Photojournalism; Visual and Performing Arts, General. **RELATED KNOWLEDGE/COURSES—Chemistry:** Knowledge of the chemical composition, structure, and properties of substances and of the chemical processes and transformations that they undergo. This includes uses of chemicals and their danger signs, production techniques, and disposal methods. **Fine Arts:** Knowledge of the theory and techniques required to compose, produce, and perform works of music, dance, the visual arts, drama, and sculpture. **Physics:** Knowledge and prediction of physical principles and laws and their interrelationships and applications to understanding fluid, material, and atmospheric dynamics and mechanical,

P

electrical, atomic, and subatomic structures and processes. **Engineering and Technology:** Knowledge of the practical application of engineering science and technology. This includes applying principles, techniques, procedures, and equipment to the design and production of various goods and services. **Medicine and Dentistry:** Knowledge of the information and techniques needed to diagnose and treat human injuries, diseases, and deformities. This includes symptoms, treatment alternatives, drug properties and interactions, and preventive health-care measures. **Communications and Media:** Knowledge of media production, communication, and dissemination techniques and methods. This includes alternative ways to inform and entertain via written, oral, and visual media.

Physical Therapist Assistants

- ◎ Education/Training Required: Associate degree
- ◎ Annual Earnings: $37,890
- ◎ Growth: 44.6%
- ◎ Annual Job Openings: 10,000
- ◎ Self-Employed: 0.4%
- ◎ Part-Time: 22.8%

Assist physical therapists in providing physical therapy treatments and procedures. May, in accordance with state laws, assist in the development of treatment plans, carry out routine functions, document the progress of treatment, and modify specific treatments in accordance with patient status and within the scope of treatment plans established by a physical therapist. Generally requires formal training. Instruct, motivate, safeguard, and assist patients as they practice exercises and functional activities. Confer with physical therapy staff and others to discuss and evaluate patient information for planning, modifying, and coordinating treatment. Administer active and passive manual therapeutic exercises; therapeutic massage; and heat, light, sound, water, and electrical modality treatments, such as ultrasound. Observe patients during treatments to compile and evaluate

data on patients' responses and progress and report to physical therapist. Measure patients' range-of-joint motion, body parts, and vital signs to determine effects of treatments or for patient evaluations. Secure patients into or onto therapy equipment. Fit patients for orthopedic braces, prostheses, and supportive devices such as crutches. Train patients in the use of orthopedic braces, prostheses, and supportive devices. Transport patients to and from treatment areas, lifting and transferring them according to positioning requirements. Monitor operation of equipment and record use of equipment and administration of treatment. Clean work area and check and store equipment after treatment. Assist patients in dressing, undressing, and putting on and removing supportive devices, such as braces, splints, and slings. Administer traction to relieve neck and back pain, using intermittent and static traction equipment. Perform clerical duties, such as taking inventory, ordering supplies, answering telephone, taking messages, and filling out forms. Prepare treatment areas and electrotherapy equipment for use by physiotherapists. Perform postural drainage, percussions, and vibrations and teach deep breathing exercises to treat respiratory conditions. **SKILLS—Social Perceptiveness:** Being aware of others' reactions and understanding why they react as they do. **Service Orientation:** Actively looking for ways to help people. **Instructing:** Teaching others how to do something. **Time Management:** Managing one's own time and the time of others. **Learning Strategies:** Selecting and using training/instructional methods and procedures appropriate for the situation when learning or teaching new things. **Writing:** Communicating effectively in writing as appropriate for the needs of the audience. **Speaking:** Talking to others to convey information effectively. **Active Learning:** Understanding the implications of new information for both current and future problem-solving and decision-making. **GOE—Interest Area:** 08. Health Science. **Work Group:** 08.07. Medical Therapy. **Other Jobs in This Work Group:** Audiologists; Massage Therapists; Occupational Therapist Aides; Occupational Therapist Assistants; Occupational Therapists; Physical Therapist Aides; Physical Therapists; Radiation Therapists; Recreational Therapists; Respiratory Therapists; Respiratory Therapy Technicians; Speech-Language Pathologists. **PERSONALITY TYPE:** Social. Social occupations frequently involve working with, communicating with, and teaching people. These occupations often involve helping or providing service to others.

EDUCATION/TRAINING PROGRAM(S)—Physical Therapist Assistant. RELATED KNOWLEDGE/COURSES—Psychology: Knowledge of human behavior and performance; individual differences in ability, personality, and interests; learning and motivation; psychological research methods; and the assessment and treatment of behavioral and affective disorders. Therapy and Counseling: Knowledge of principles, methods, and procedures for diagnosis, treatment, and rehabilitation of physical and mental dysfunctions and for career counseling and guidance. Medicine and Dentistry: Knowledge of the information and techniques needed to diagnose and treat human injuries, diseases, and deformities. This includes symptoms, treatment alternatives, drug properties and interactions, and preventive health-care measures. Education and Training: Knowledge of principles and methods for curriculum and training design, teaching and instruction for individuals and groups, and the measurement of training effects. Customer and Personal Service: Knowledge of principles and processes for providing customer and personal services. This includes customer needs assessment, meeting quality standards for services, and evaluation of customer satisfaction. Sociology and Anthropology: Knowledge of group behavior and dynamics, societal trends and influences, human migrations, ethnicity, and cultures and their history and origins.

Pipe Fitters

- ◎ Education/Training Required: Long-term on-the-job training
- ◎ Annual Earnings: $41,290
- ◎ Growth: 18.7%
- ◎ Annual Job Openings: 56,000
- ◎ Self-Employed: 10.3%
- ◎ Part-Time: 3.4%

Lay out, assemble, install, and maintain pipe systems, pipe supports, and related hydraulic and pneumatic equipment for steam, hot water, heating, cooling, lubricating, sprinkling, and industrial production and processing systems. Cut, thread, and hammer pipe to specifications, using tools such as saws, cutting torches, and pipe threaders and benders. Assemble and secure pipes, tubes, fittings, and related equipment according to specifications by welding, brazing, cementing, soldering, and threading joints. Attach pipes to walls, structures, and fixtures, such as radiators or tanks, using brackets, clamps, tools, or welding equipment. Inspect, examine, and test installed systems and pipe lines, using pressure gauge, hydrostatic testing, observation, or other methods. Measure and mark pipes for cutting and threading. Lay out full-scale drawings of pipe systems, supports, and related equipment, following blueprints. Plan pipe system layout, installation, or repair according to specifications. Select pipe sizes and types and related materials, such as supports, hangers, and hydraulic cylinders, according to specifications. Cut and bore holes in structures, such as bulkheads, decks, walls, and mains, prior to pipe installation, using hand and power tools. Modify, clean, and maintain pipe systems, units, fittings, and related machines and equipment, following specifications and using hand and power tools. Install automatic controls used to regulate pipe systems. Turn valves to shut off steam, water, or other gases or liquids from pipe sections, using valve keys or wrenches. Remove and replace worn components. Prepare cost estimates for clients. Inspect work sites for obstructions and to ensure that holes will not cause structural weakness. Operate motorized pumps to remove water from flooded manholes, basements, or facility floors. SKILLS—Installation: Installing equipment, machines, wiring, or programs to meet specifications. Repairing: Repairing machines or systems by using the needed tools. Management of Personnel Resources: Motivating, developing, and directing people as they work, identifying the best people for the job. Coordination: Adjusting actions in relation to others' actions. Systems Analysis: Determining how a system should work and how changes in conditions, operations, and the environment will affect outcomes. Persuasion: Persuading others to change their minds or behavior. Service Orientation: Actively looking for ways to help people. Equipment Maintenance: Performing routine maintenance on equipment and determining when and what kind of maintenance is needed. GOE—

Interest Area: 02. Architecture and Construction. Work Group: 02.04. Construction Crafts. Other Jobs in This Work Group: Boat Builders and Shipwrights; Boilermakers; Brattice Builders; Brickmasons and Blockmasons; Carpet Installers; Ceiling Tile Installers; Cement Masons and Concrete Finishers; Commercial Divers; Construction Carpenters; Crane and Tower Operators; Dragline Operators; Drywall Installers; Electricians; Fence Erectors; Floor Layers, Except Carpet, Wood, and Hard Tiles; Floor Sanders and Finishers; Glaziers; Grader, Bulldozer, and Scraper Operators; Hazardous Materials Removal Workers; Insulation Workers, Floor, Ceiling, and Wall; Insulation Workers, Mechanical; Manufactured Building and Mobile Home Installers; Operating Engineers; Painters, Construction and Maintenance; Paperhangers; Paving, Surfacing, and Tamping Equipment Operators; Pile-Driver Operators; Pipelayers; Pipelaying Fitters; Plasterers and Stucco Masons; Plumbers; Rail-Track Laying and Maintenance Equipment Operators; Refractory Materials Repairers, Except Brickmasons; Reinforcing Iron and Rebar Workers; Riggers; Roofers; Rough Carpenters; Security and Fire Alarm Systems Installers; Segmental Pavers; Sheet Metal Workers; Ship Carpenters and Joiners; Stone Cutters and Carvers; Stonemasons; Structural Iron and Steel Workers; Tapers; Terrazzo Workers and Finishers; Tile and Marble Setters. **PERSONALITY TYPE:** Realistic. Realistic occupations frequently involve work activities that include practical, hands-on problems and solutions. These occupations often deal with plants, animals, and real-world materials like wood, tools, and machinery. Many of the occupations require working outside and do not involve a lot of paperwork or working closely with others.

EDUCATION/TRAINING PROGRAM(S)—Pipefitting/Pipefitter and Sprinkler Fitter; Plumbing and Related Water Supply Services, Other; Plumbing Technology/Plumber. **RELATED KNOWLEDGE/COURSES—Building and Construction:** Knowledge of the materials, methods, and tools involved in the construction or repair of houses, buildings, or other structures such as highways and roads. **Design:** Knowledge of design techniques, tools, and principles involved in production of precision technical plans, blueprints, drawings, and models. **Engineering and Technology:** Knowledge of the practical application of engineering science and technology. This includes applying principles, techniques, procedures, and equipment to the design and production of various goods and services. **Mechanical Devices:** Knowledge of machines and tools, including their designs, uses, repair, and maintenance. **Economics and Accounting:** Knowledge of economic and accounting principles and practices, the financial markets, banking, and the analysis and reporting of financial data. **Transportation:** Knowledge of principles and methods for moving people or goods by air, rail, sea, or road, including the relative costs and benefits.

Pipelaying Fitters

- Education/Training Required: Moderate-term on-the-job training
- Annual Earnings: $41,290
- Growth: 18.7%
- Annual Job Openings: 56,000
- Self-Employed: 10.3%
- Part-Time: 3.4%

Align pipeline section in preparation of welding. Signal tractor driver for placement of pipeline sections in proper alignment. Insert steel spacer. Correct misalignments of pipe, using a sledgehammer. Guide pipe into trench and signal hoist operator to move pipe until alignment is achieved so that pipes can be welded together. Insert spacers between pipe ends. Inspect joints to ensure uniform spacing and proper alignment of pipe surfaces. **SKILLS—Installation:** Installing equipment, machines, wiring, or programs to meet specifications. **Equipment Maintenance:** Performing routine maintenance on equipment and determining when and what kind of maintenance is needed. **Repairing:** Repairing machines or systems by using the needed tools. **GOE—Interest Area:** 02. Architecture and Construction. **Work Group:** 02.04. Construction Crafts. **Other Jobs in This Work Group:** Boat Builders and Shipwrights; Boilermakers; Brattice Builders; Brickmasons and Blockmasons; Carpet Installers; Ceiling Tile Installers; Cement Masons and Concrete Finishers; Commercial Divers; Construction

Carpenters; Crane and Tower Operators; Dragline Operators; Drywall Installers; Electricians; Fence Erectors; Floor Layers, Except Carpet, Wood, and Hard Tiles; Floor Sanders and Finishers; Glaziers; Grader, Bulldozer, and Scraper Operators; Hazardous Materials Removal Workers; Insulation Workers, Floor, Ceiling, and Wall; Insulation Workers, Mechanical; Manufactured Building and Mobile Home Installers; Operating Engineers; Painters, Construction and Maintenance; Paperhangers; Paving, Surfacing, and Tamping Equipment Operators; Pile-Driver Operators; Pipe Fitters; Pipelayers; Plasterers and Stucco Masons; Plumbers; Rail-Track Laying and Maintenance Equipment Operators; Refractory Materials Repairers, Except Brickmasons; Reinforcing Iron and Rebar Workers; Riggers; Roofers; Rough Carpenters; Security and Fire Alarm Systems Installers; Segmental Pavers; Sheet Metal Workers; Ship Carpenters and Joiners; Stone Cutters and Carvers; Stonemasons; Structural Iron and Steel Workers; Tapers; Terrazzo Workers and Finishers; Tile and Marble Setters. **PERSONALITY TYPE:** Realistic. Realistic occupations frequently involve work activities that include practical, hands-on problems and solutions. These occupations often deal with plants, animals, and real-world materials like wood, tools, and machinery. Many of the occupations require working outside and do not involve a lot of paperwork or working closely with others.

EDUCATION/TRAINING PROGRAM(S)—Pipefitting/Pipefitter and Sprinkler Fitter; Plumbing and Related Water Supply Services, Other; Plumbing Technology/Plumber. **RELATED KNOWLEDGE/ COURSES—Mechanical Devices:** Knowledge of machines and tools, including their designs, uses, repair, and maintenance. **Building and Construction:** Knowledge of the materials, methods, and tools involved in the construction or repair of houses, buildings, or other structures such as highways and roads.

Plasterers and Stucco Masons

- Education/Training Required: Long-term on-the-job training
- Annual Earnings: $32,440
- Growth: 13.5%
- Annual Job Openings: 8,000
- Self-Employed: 9.6%
- Part-Time: 7.2%

Apply interior or exterior plaster, cement, stucco, or similar materials. May also set ornamental plaster. Apply coats of plaster or stucco to walls, ceilings, or partitions of buildings, using trowels, brushes, or spray guns. Apply weatherproof decorative coverings to exterior surfaces of buildings, such as troweling or spraying on coats of stucco. Clean and prepare surfaces for applications of plaster, cement, stucco, or similar materials, such as by drywall taping. Cure freshly plastered surfaces. Install guidewires on exterior surfaces of buildings to indicate thickness of plaster or stucco and nail wire mesh, lath, or similar materials to the outside surface to hold stucco in place. Mix mortar and plaster to desired consistency or direct workers who perform mixing. Mold and install ornamental plaster pieces, panels, and trim. Rough the undercoat surface with a scratcher so the finish coat will adhere. Spray acoustic materials or texture finish over walls and ceilings. Apply insulation to building exteriors by installing prefabricated insulation systems over existing walls or by covering the outer wall with insulation board, reinforcing mesh, and a base coat. Create decorative textures in finish coat, using brushes or trowels, sand, pebbles, or stones. **SKILLS—Coordination:** Adjusting actions in relation to others' actions. **Installation:** Installing equipment, machines, wiring, or programs to meet specifications. **Management of Personnel Resources:** Motivating, developing, and directing people as they work, identifying the best people for the job. **GOE—Interest Area:** 02. Architecture and Construction. **Work Group:** 02.04. Construction Crafts. **Other Jobs in This Work Group:** Boat Builders and Shipwrights; Boilermakers; Brattice Builders; Brickmasons and Blockmasons; Carpet Installers; Ceiling Tile Installers; Cement Masons and Concrete Finishers;

Commercial Divers; Construction Carpenters; Crane and Tower Operators; Dragline Operators; Drywall Installers; Electricians; Fence Erectors; Floor Layers, Except Carpet, Wood, and Hard Tiles; Floor Sanders and Finishers; Glaziers; Grader, Bulldozer, and Scraper Operators; Hazardous Materials Removal Workers; Insulation Workers, Floor, Ceiling, and Wall; Insulation Workers, Mechanical; Manufactured Building and Mobile Home Installers; Operating Engineers; Painters, Construction and Maintenance; Paperhangers; Paving, Surfacing, and Tamping Equipment Operators; Pile-Driver Operators; Pipe Fitters; Pipelayers; Pipelaying Fitters; Plumbers; Rail-Track Laying and Maintenance Equipment Operators; Refractory Materials Repairers, Except Brickmasons; Reinforcing Iron and Rebar Workers; Riggers; Roofers; Rough Carpenters; Security and Fire Alarm Systems Installers; Segmental Pavers; Sheet Metal Workers; Ship Carpenters and Joiners; Stone Cutters and Carvers; Stonemasons; Structural Iron and Steel Workers; Tapers; Terrazzo Workers and Finishers; Tile and Marble Setters. **PERSONALITY TYPE:** Realistic. Realistic occupations frequently involve work activities that include practical, hands-on problems and solutions. These occupations often deal with plants, animals, and real-world materials like wood, tools, and machinery. Many of the occupations require working outside and do not involve a lot of paperwork or working closely with others.

EDUCATION/TRAINING PROGRAM(S)—Construction Trades, Other. **RELATED KNOWLEDGE/COURSES—Building and Construction:** Knowledge of the materials, methods, and tools involved in the construction or repair of houses, buildings, or other structures such as highways and roads. **Design:** Knowledge of design techniques, tools, and principles involved in production of precision technical plans, blueprints, drawings, and models. **Engineering and Technology:** Knowledge of the practical application of engineering science and technology. This includes applying principles, techniques, procedures, and equipment to the design and production of various goods and services.

Plumbers

- Education/Training Required: Long-term on-the-job training
- Annual Earnings: $41,290
- Growth: 18.7%
- Annual Job Openings: 56,000
- Self-Employed: 10.3%
- Part-Time: 3.4%

Assemble, install, and repair pipes, fittings, and fixtures of heating, water, and drainage systems according to specifications and plumbing codes. Assemble pipe sections, tubing, and fittings, using couplings; clamps; screws; bolts; cement; plastic solvent; caulking; or soldering, brazing, and welding equipment. Fill pipes or plumbing fixtures with water or air and observe pressure gauges to detect and locate leaks. Review blueprints and building codes and specifications to determine work details and procedures. Prepare written work cost estimates and negotiate contracts. Study building plans and inspect structures to assess material and equipment needs, to establish the sequence of pipe installations, and to plan installation around obstructions such as electrical wiring. Keep records of assignments and produce detailed work reports. Perform complex calculations and planning for special or very large jobs. Locate and mark the position of pipe installations, connections, passage holes, and fixtures in structures, using measuring instruments such as rulers and levels. Measure, cut, thread, and bend pipe to required angle, using hand and power tools or machines such as pipe cutters, pipe-threading machines, and pipe-bending machines. Install pipe assemblies, fittings, valves, appliances such as dishwashers and water heaters, and fixtures such as sinks and toilets, using hand and power tools. Cut openings in structures to accommodate pipes and pipe fittings, using hand and power tools. Hang steel supports from ceiling joists to hold pipes in place. Repair and maintain plumbing, replacing defective washers, replacing or mending broken pipes, and opening clogged drains. Direct workers engaged in pipe cutting and preassembly and installation of plumbing systems and components. Install underground storm, sanitary, and water piping systems and extend piping to connect fixtures and plumbing to these systems. Clear away debris in a renovation. Install oxygen and medical gas in hospitals. Use specialized techniques, equipment, or materials, such as performing computer-assisted welding of small pipes or working with the special piping used in microchip fabrication. **SKILLS—Installation:** Installing equipment, machines, wiring, or programs to meet specifications. **Repairing:** Repairing machines or systems by using the needed tools. **Troubleshooting:** Determining causes of operating errors and deciding what to do about them. **Management of Material Resources:** Obtaining and seeing to the appropriate use of equipment, facilities, and materials needed to do certain work. **Equipment Selection:** Determining the kind of tools and equipment needed to do a job. **Management of Financial Resources:** Determining how money will be spent to get the work done and accounting for these expenditures. **Coordination:** Adjusting actions in relation to others' actions. **Management of Personnel Resources:** Motivating, developing, and directing people as they work, identifying the best people for the job. **GOE—Interest Area:** 02. Architecture and Construction. **Work Group:** 02.04. Construction Crafts. **Other Jobs in This Work Group:** Boat Builders and Shipwrights; Boilermakers; Brattice Builders; Brickmasons and Blockmasons; Carpet Installers; Ceiling Tile Installers; Cement Masons and Concrete Finishers; Commercial Divers; Construction Carpenters; Crane and Tower Operators; Dragline Operators; Drywall Installers; Electricians; Fence Erectors; Floor Layers, Except Carpet, Wood, and Hard Tiles; Floor Sanders and Finishers; Glaziers; Grader, Bulldozer, and Scraper Operators; Hazardous Materials Removal Workers; Insulation Workers, Floor, Ceiling, and Wall; Insulation Workers, Mechanical; Manufactured Building and Mobile Home Installers; Operating Engineers; Painters, Construction and Maintenance; Paperhangers; Paving, Surfacing, and Tamping Equipment Operators; Pile-Driver Operators; Pipe Fitters; Pipelayers; Pipelaying Fitters; Plasterers and Stucco Masons; Rail-Track Laying and Maintenance Equipment Operators; Refractory Materials Repairers, Except Brickmasons; Reinforcing Iron and Rebar Workers; Riggers; Roofers; Rough Carpenters; Security and Fire Alarm Systems Installers; Segmental Pavers; Sheet Metal Workers; Ship Carpenters and Joiners; Stone Cutters and Carvers; Stonemasons; Structural Iron and Steel Workers; Tapers; Terrazzo Workers and Finishers; Tile and Marble Setters. **PERSONALITY TYPE:** Realistic. Realistic occupations frequently involve work activities that include practical, hands-on problems and solutions. These occupations often deal with plants, animals, and real-world materials like wood, tools, and machinery. Many of the occupations require working outside and do not involve a lot of paperwork or working closely with others.

EDUCATION/TRAINING PROGRAM(S)— Pipefitting/Pipefitter and Sprinkler Fitter; Plumbing and Related Water Supply Services, Other; Plumbing Technology/Plumber. **RELATED KNOWLEDGE/ COURSES—Physics:** Knowledge and prediction of physical principles and laws and their interrelationships and applications to understanding fluid, material, and atmospheric dynamics and mechanical, electrical, atomic, and subatomic structures and processes. **Building and Construction:** Knowledge of the materials, methods, and tools involved in the construction or repair of houses, buildings, or other structures such as highways and roads. **Mechanical Devices:** Knowledge of machines and tools, including their designs, uses, repair, and maintenance. **Chemistry:** Knowledge of the chemical composition, structure, and properties of substances and of the chemical processes and transformations that they undergo. This includes uses of chemicals and their danger signs, production techniques, and disposal methods. **Design:** Knowledge of design techniques, tools, and principles involved in production of precision technical plans, blueprints, drawings, and models. **Sales and Marketing:** Knowledge of principles and methods for showing, promoting, and selling products or services. This includes marketing strategy and tactics, product demonstrations, sales techniques, and sales control systems.

Police Detectives

- Education/Training Required: Work experience in a related occupation
- Annual Earnings: $53,990
- Growth: 22.4%
- Annual Job Openings: 11,000
- Self-Employed: 0%
- Part-Time: 0.5%

Conduct investigations to prevent crimes or solve criminal cases. Examine crime scenes to obtain clues and evidence, such as loose hairs, fibers, clothing, or weapons. Secure deceased body and obtain evidence from it, preventing bystanders from tampering with it prior to medical examiner's arrival. Obtain evidence from suspects. Provide testimony as a witness in court. Analyze completed police reports to determine what additional information and investigative work is needed. Prepare charges, responses to charges, or information for court cases according to formalized procedures. Note, mark, and photograph location of objects found, such as footprints, tire tracks, bullets, and bloodstains, and take measurements of the scene. Obtain facts or statements from complainants, witnesses, and accused persons and record interviews, using recording device. Obtain summary of incident from officer in charge at crime scene, taking care to avoid disturbing evidence. Examine records and governmental agency files to find identifying data about suspects. Prepare and serve search and arrest warrants. Block or rope off scene and check perimeter to ensure that entire scene is secured. Summon medical help for injured individuals and alert medical personnel to take statements from them. Provide information to lab personnel concerning the source of an item of evidence and tests to be performed. Monitor conditions of victims who are unconscious so that arrangements can be made to take statements if consciousness is regained. Secure persons at scene, keeping witnesses from conversing or leaving the scene before investigators arrive. Preserve, process, and analyze items of evidence obtained from crime scenes and suspects, placing them in proper containers and destroying evidence no longer needed. Record progress of investigation, maintain informational files on suspects, and submit reports to commanding officer or magistrate to authorize warrants. Take photographs from all angles of relevant parts of a crime scene, including entrance and exit routes and streets and intersections. Organize scene search, assigning specific tasks and areas of search to individual officers and obtaining adequate lighting as necessary. **SKILLS—Persuasion:** Persuading others to change their minds or behavior. **Negotiation:** Bringing others together and trying to reconcile differences. **Social Perceptiveness:** Being aware of others' reactions and understanding why they react as they do. **Coordination:** Adjusting actions in relation to others' actions. **Service Orientation:** Actively looking for ways to help people. **Active Listening:** Giving full attention to what other people are saying, taking time to understand the points being made, asking questions as appropriate, and not interrupting at inappropriate times. **Speaking:** Talking to others to convey information effectively. **Critical Thinking:** Using logic and reasoning to identify the strengths and weaknesses of alternative solutions, conclusions, or approaches to problems. **Learning Strategies:** Selecting and using training/instructional methods and procedures appropriate for the situation when learning or teaching new things. **Time Management:** Managing one's own time and the time of others. **GOE—Interest Area:** 12. Law and Public Safety. **Work Group:** 12.04. Law Enforcement and Public Safety. **Other Jobs in This Work Group:** Bailiffs; Correctional Officers and Jailers; Criminal Investigators and Special Agents; Fire Investigators; Forensic Science Technicians; Highway Patrol Pilots; Parking Enforcement Workers; Police Identification and Records Officers; Police Patrol Officers; Sheriffs and Deputy Sheriffs; Transit and Railroad Police. **PERSONALITY TYPE:** Enterprising. Enterprising occupations frequently involve starting up and carrying out projects. These occupations can involve leading people and making many decisions. They sometimes require risk taking and often deal with business.

EDUCATION/TRAINING PROGRAM(S)— Criminal Justice/Police Science; Criminalistics and Criminal Science. **RELATED KNOWLEDGE/ COURSES—Public Safety and Security:** Knowledge of relevant equipment, policies, procedures, and strategies to promote effective local, state, or national security operations for the protection of people, data, property, and institutions. **Law and Government:**

Knowledge of laws, legal codes, court procedures, precedents, government regulations, executive orders, agency rules, and the democratic political process. **Psychology:** Knowledge of human behavior and performance; individual differences in ability, personality, and interests; learning and motivation; psychological research methods; and the assessment and treatment of behavioral and affective disorders. **Customer and Personal Service:** Knowledge of principles and processes for providing customer and personal services. This includes customer needs assessment, meeting quality standards for services, and evaluation of customer satisfaction. **Education and Training:** Knowledge of principles and methods for curriculum and training design, teaching and instruction for individuals and groups, and the measurement of training effects. **Therapy and Counseling:** Knowledge of principles, methods, and procedures for diagnosis, treatment, and rehabilitation of physical and mental dysfunctions and for career counseling and guidance.

Police Identification and Records Officers

- Education/Training Required: Work experience in a related occupation
- Annual Earnings: $53,990
- Growth: 22.4%
- Annual Job Openings: 11,000
- Self-Employed: 0%
- Part-Time: 0.5%

Collect evidence at crime scene, classify and identify fingerprints, and photograph evidence for use in criminal and civil cases. Photograph crime or accident scenes for evidence records. Testify in court and present evidence. Dust selected areas of crime scene and lift latent fingerprints, adhering to proper preservation procedures. Look for trace evidence, such as fingerprints, hairs, fibers, or shoe impressions, using alternative light sources when necessary. Analyze and process evidence at crime scenes and in the laboratory, wearing protective equipment and using powders and chemicals. Package, store, and retrieve evidence. Serve as technical advisor and coordinate with other law enforcement workers to exchange information on crime-scene collection activities. Perform emergency work during off-hours. Submit evidence to supervisors. Process film and prints from crime or accident scenes. Identify, classify, and file fingerprints, using systems such as the Henry Classification system. **SKILLS—Persuasion:** Persuading others to change their minds or behavior. **Negotiation:** Bringing others together and trying to reconcile differences. **Service Orientation:** Actively looking for ways to help people. **Judgment and Decision Making:** Considering the relative costs and benefits of potential actions to choose the most appropriate one. **Social Perceptiveness:** Being aware of others' reactions and understanding why they react as they do. **Critical Thinking:** Using logic and reasoning to identify the strengths and weaknesses of alternative solutions, conclusions, or approaches to problems. **Time Management:** Managing one's own time and the time of others. **Learning Strategies:** Selecting and using training/instructional methods and procedures appropriate for the situation when learning or teaching new things. **GOE—Interest Area:** 12. Law and Public Safety. **Work Group:** 12.04. Law Enforcement and Public Safety. **Other Jobs in This Work Group:** Bailiffs; Correctional Officers and Jailers; Criminal Investigators and Special Agents; Fire Investigators; Forensic Science Technicians; Highway Patrol Pilots; Parking Enforcement Workers; Police Detectives; Police Patrol Officers; Sheriffs and Deputy Sheriffs; Transit and Railroad Police. **PERSONALITY TYPE:** Conventional. Conventional occupations frequently involve following set procedures and routines. These occupations can include working with data and details more than with ideas. Usually there is a clear line of authority to follow.

EDUCATION/TRAINING PROGRAM(S)— Criminal Justice/Police Science; Criminalistics and Criminal Science. **RELATED KNOWLEDGE/ COURSES—Law and Government:** Knowledge of laws, legal codes, court procedures, precedents, government regulations, executive orders, agency rules, and the democratic political process. **Customer and Personal Service:** Knowledge of principles and processes for providing customer and personal services. This includes customer needs assessment, meeting quality standards for services, and evaluation of customer satisfaction. **Public Safety and Security:** Knowledge of relevant equipment, policies, procedures, and strategies to promote effective local, state, or national security operations for the protection of people, data, property, and institutions. **Telecommunications:** Knowledge of transmission, broadcasting, switching, control, and operation of telecommunications systems. **Psychology:** Knowledge of human behavior and performance; individual differences in ability, personality, and interests; learning and motivation; psychological research methods; and the assessment and treatment of behavioral and affective disorders. **Computers and Electronics:** Knowledge of circuit boards, processors, chips, electronic equipment, and computer hardware and software, including applications and programming.

Police Patrol Officers

- ◎ Education/Training Required: Long-term on-the-job training
- ◎ Annual Earnings: $45,210
- ◎ Growth: 24.7%
- ◎ Annual Job Openings: 67,000
- ◎ Self-Employed: 0%
- ◎ Part-Time: 1.4%

Patrol assigned area to enforce laws and ordinances, regulate traffic, control crowds, prevent crime, and arrest violators. Provide for public safety by maintaining order, responding to emergencies, protecting people and property, enforcing motor vehicle and criminal laws, and promoting good community relations. Identify, pursue, and arrest suspects and perpetrators of criminal acts. Record facts to prepare reports that document incidents and activities. Review facts of incidents to determine if criminal act or statute violation was involved. Render aid to accident victims and other persons requiring first aid for physical injuries. Testify in court to present evidence or act as witness in traffic and criminal cases. Evaluate complaint and emergency-request information to determine response requirements. Patrol specific area on foot, horseback, or motorized conveyance, responding promptly to calls for assistance. Monitor, note, report, and investigate suspicious persons and situations, safety hazards, and unusual or illegal activity in patrol area. Investigate

traffic accidents and other accidents to determine causes and to determine whether a crime has been committed. Photograph or draw diagrams of crime or accident scenes and interview principals and eyewitnesses. Monitor traffic to ensure motorists observe traffic regulations and exhibit safe driving procedures. Relay complaint and emergency-request information to appropriate agency dispatchers. Issue citations or warnings to violators of motor vehicle ordinances. Direct traffic flow and reroute traffic in case of emergencies. Inform citizens of community services and recommend options to facilitate longer-term problem resolution. Provide road information to assist motorists. Process prisoners and prepare and maintain records of prisoner bookings and prisoner status during booking and pre-trial process. **SKILLS—Negotiation:** Bringing others together and trying to reconcile differences. **Persuasion:** Persuading others to change their minds or behavior. **Social Perceptiveness:** Being aware of others' reactions and understanding why they react as they do. **Judgment and Decision Making:** Considering the relative costs and benefits of potential actions to choose the most appropriate one. **Service Orientation:** Actively looking for ways to help people. **Active Listening:** Giving full attention to what other people are saying, taking time to understand the points being made, asking questions as appropriate, and not interrupting at inappropriate times. **Critical Thinking:** Using logic and reasoning to identify the strengths and weaknesses of alternative solutions, conclusions, or approaches to problems. **Coordination:** Adjusting actions in relation to others' actions. **GOE—Interest Area:** 12. Law and Public Safety. **Work Group:** 12.04. Law Enforcement and Public Safety. **Other Jobs in This Work Group:** Bailiffs; Correctional Officers and Jailers; Criminal Investigators and Special Agents; Fire Investigators; Forensic Science Technicians; Highway Patrol Pilots; Parking Enforcement Workers; Police Detectives; Police Identification and Records Officers; Sheriffs and Deputy Sheriffs; Transit and Railroad Police. **PERSONALITY TYPE:** Social. Social occupations frequently involve working with, communicating with, and teaching people. These occupations often involve helping or providing service to others.

EDUCATION/TRAINING PROGRAM(S)— Criminal Justice/Police Science; Criminalistics and Criminal Science. **RELATED KNOWLEDGE/**

COURSES—**Public Safety and Security:** Knowledge of relevant equipment, policies, procedures, and strategies to promote effective local, state, or national security operations for the protection of people, data, property, and institutions. **Law and Government:** Knowledge of laws, legal codes, court procedures, precedents, government regulations, executive orders, agency rules, and the democratic political process. **Customer and Personal Service:** Knowledge of principles and processes for providing customer and personal services. This includes customer needs assessment, meeting quality standards for services, and evaluation of customer satisfaction. **Psychology:** Knowledge of human behavior and performance; individual differences in ability, personality, and interests; learning and motivation; psychological research methods; and the assessment and treatment of behavioral and affective disorders. **Telecommunications:** Knowledge of transmission, broadcasting, switching, control, and operation of telecommunications systems. **Sociology and Anthropology:** Knowledge of group behavior and dynamics, societal trends and influences, human migrations, ethnicity, and cultures and their history and origins. **Therapy and Counseling:** Knowledge of principles, methods, and procedures for diagnosis, treatment, and rehabilitation of physical and mental dysfunctions and for career counseling and guidance.

Police, Fire, and Ambulance Dispatchers

- Education/Training Required: Moderate-term on-the-job training
- Annual Earnings: $28,930
- Growth: 12.7%
- Annual Job Openings: 15,000
- Self-Employed: 0.6%
- Part-Time: 8.5%

Receive complaints from public concerning crimes and police emergencies. Broadcast orders to police patrol units in vicinity of complaint to investigate. Operate radio, telephone, or computer equipment to receive reports of fires and medical emergencies and relay information or orders to proper officials. Deter-mine response requirements and relative priorities of situations and dispatch units in accordance with established procedures. Record details of calls, dispatches, and messages. Question callers to determine their locations and the nature of their problems in order to determine type of response needed. Enter, update, and retrieve information from teletype networks and computerized data systems regarding such things as wanted persons, stolen property, vehicle registration, and stolen vehicles. Scan status charts and computer screens and contact emergency response field units in order to determine emergency units available for dispatch. Relay information and messages to and from emergency sites, to law enforcement agencies, and to all other individuals or groups requiring notification. Receive incoming telephone or alarm system calls regarding emergency and non-emergency police and fire service, emergency ambulance service, information, and after-hours calls for departments within a city. Maintain access to and security of highly sensitive materials. Observe alarm registers and scan maps in order to determine whether a specific emergency is in the dispatch service area. Maintain files of information relating to emergency calls such as personnel rosters and emergency call-out and pager files. Monitor various radio frequencies such as those used by public works departments, school security, and civil defense in order to keep apprised of developing situations. Learn material and pass required tests for certification. Read and effectively interpret small-scale maps and information from a computer screen in order to determine locations and provide directions. Answer routine inquiries and refer calls not requiring dispatches to appropriate departments and agencies. Provide emergency medical instructions to callers. Monitor alarm systems to detect emergencies such as fires and illegal entry into establishments. Test and adjust communication and alarm systems and report malfunctions to maintenance units. Operate and maintain mobile dispatch vehicles and equipment. SKILLS—**Active Listening:** Giving full attention to what other people are saying, taking time to understand the points being made, asking questions as appropriate, and not interrupting at inappropriate times. **Speaking:** Talking to others to convey information effectively. **Social Perceptiveness:** Being aware of others' reactions and understanding why they react as they do. **Critical**

Thinking: Using logic and reasoning to identify the strengths and weaknesses of alternative solutions, conclusions, or approaches to problems. **Judgment and Decision Making:** Considering the relative costs and benefits of potential actions to choose the most appropriate one. **Service Orientation:** Actively looking for ways to help people. **Active Learning:** Understanding the implications of new information for both current and future problem-solving and decision-making. **Learning Strategies:** Selecting and using training/instructional methods and procedures appropriate for the situation when learning or teaching new things. **Coordination:** Adjusting actions in relation to others' actions. **GOE—Interest Area:** 03. Arts and Communication. **Work Group:** 03.10. Communications Technology. **Other Jobs in This Work Group:** Air Traffic Controllers; Airfield Operations Specialists; Central Office Operators; Directory Assistance Operators; Dispatchers, Except Police, Fire, and Ambulance. **PERSONALITY TYPE:** Social. Social occupations frequently involve working with, communicating with, and teaching people. These occupations often involve helping or providing service to others.

EDUCATION/TRAINING PROGRAM(S)—No data available. **RELATED KNOWLEDGE/COURSES—Customer and Personal Service:** Knowledge of principles and processes for providing customer and personal services. This includes customer needs assessment, meeting quality standards for services, and evaluation of customer satisfaction. **Telecommunications:** Knowledge of transmission, broadcasting, switching, control, and operation of telecommunications systems. **Clerical Practices:** Knowledge of administrative and clerical procedures and systems such as word processing, managing files and records, stenography and transcription, designing forms, and other office procedures and terminology. **Public Safety and Security:** Knowledge of relevant equipment, policies, procedures, and strategies to promote effective local, state, or national security operations for the protection of people, data, property, and institutions. **Law and Government:** Knowledge of laws, legal codes, court procedures, precedents, government regulations, executive orders, agency rules, and the democratic political process. **Computers and Electronics:** Knowledge of circuit boards, processors, chips, electronic equipment, and computer hardware and software, including applications and programming.

Postal Service Mail Carriers

- Education/Training Required: Short-term on-the-job training
- Annual Earnings: $44,450
- Growth: –0.5%
- Annual Job Openings: 20,000
- Self-Employed: 0%
- Part-Time: 6.5%

Sort mail for delivery. Deliver mail on established route by vehicle or on foot. Bundle mail in preparation for delivery or transportation to relay boxes. Deliver mail to residences and business establishments along specified routes by walking and/or driving, using a combination of satchels, carts, cars, and small trucks. Enter change-of-address orders into computers that process forwarding-address stickers. Hold mail for customers who are away from delivery locations. Leave notices telling patrons where to collect mail that could not be delivered. Maintain accurate records of deliveries. Meet schedules for the collection and return of mail. Record address changes and redirect mail for those addresses. Return incorrectly addressed mail to senders. Return to the post office with mail collected from homes, businesses, and public mailboxes. Sign for cash-on-delivery and registered mail before leaving the post office. Sort mail for delivery, arranging it in delivery sequence. Travel to post offices to pick up the mail for routes and/or pick up mail from postal relay boxes. Turn in money and receipts collected along mail routes. Answer customers' questions about postal services and regulations. Complete forms that notify publishers of address changes. Obtain signed receipts for registered, certified, and insured mail; collect associated charges; and complete any necessary paperwork. Provide customers with change-of-address cards and other forms. Register, certify, and insure parcels and letters. Report any unusual circumstances concerning mail delivery, including the condition of street letter boxes. Sell stamps and money orders. **SKILLS—**None met the criteria. **GOE—Interest Area:** 16. Transportation, Distribution, and Logistics. **Work Group:** 16.06. Other Services Requiring Driving. **Other Jobs in This Work Group:** Ambulance Drivers and Attendants, Except Emergency Medical Technicians; Bus Drivers, School; Bus Drivers, Transit and Intercity; Couriers and Messengers; Driver/Sales Workers; Parking Lot Attendants; Taxi Drivers and Chauffeurs. **PERSONALITY TYPE:** Conventional. Conventional occupations frequently involve following set procedures and routines. These occupations can include working with data and details more than with ideas. Usually there is a clear line of authority to follow.

EDUCATION/TRAINING PROGRAM(S)—General Office Occupations and Clerical Services. **RELATED KNOWLEDGE/COURSES—Transportation:** Knowledge of principles and methods for moving people or goods by air, rail, sea, or road, including the relative costs and benefits. **Geography:** Knowledge of principles and methods for describing the features of land, sea, and air masses, including their physical characteristics; locations; interrelationships; and distribution of plant, animal, and human life.

Precision Devices Inspectors and Testers

- Education/Training Required: Moderate-term on-the-job training
- Annual Earnings: $28,410
- Growth: 4.7%
- Annual Job Openings: 87,000
- Self-Employed: 1.2%
- Part-Time: 5.0%

Verify accuracy of and adjust precision devices, such as meters and gauges, testing instruments, and clock and watch mechanisms, to ensure operation of device is in accordance with design specifications. Inspects materials, products, and work in progress for conformance to specifications and adjusts process or assembly equipment to meet standards. Reads dials and meters to verify functioning of equipment according to specifications. Tests and measures finished products, components, or assemblies for functioning, operation,

accuracy, or assembly to verify adherence to functional specifications. Marks items for acceptance or rejection, records test results and inspection data, and compares findings with specifications to ensure conformance to standards. Completes necessary procedures to satisfy licensing requirements. Computes and/or calculates data and other information. Confers with vendors and others regarding inspection results and recommends corrective procedures. Disassembles defective parts and components. Estimates operational data to meet acceptable standards. Operates or tends machinery and equipment and uses hand tools. Discards or rejects products, materials, and equipment not meeting specifications. Analyzes and interprets blueprints, sample data, and other materials to determine, change, or measure specifications or inspection and testing procedures. Fabricates, installs, positions, or connects components, parts, finished products, or instruments for testing or operational purposes. Cleans and maintains test equipment and instruments and certifies that precision instruments meet standards. **SKILLS—Quality Control Analysis:** Conducting tests and inspections of products, services, or processes to evaluate quality or performance. **Operation Monitoring:** Watching gauges, dials, or other indicators to make sure a machine is working properly. **Technology Design:** Generating or adapting equipment and technology to serve user needs. **Installation:** Installing equipment, machines, wiring, or programs to meet specifications. **Science:** Using scientific rules and methods to solve problems. **Troubleshooting:** Determining causes of operating errors and deciding what to do about them. **Equipment Maintenance:** Performing routine maintenance on equipment and determining when and what kind of maintenance is needed. **Operation and Control:** Controlling operations of equipment or systems. **GOE—Interest Area:** 13. Manufacturing. **Work Group:** 13.07. Production Quality Control. **Other Jobs in This Work Group:** Electrical and Electronic Inspectors and Testers; Graders and Sorters, Agricultural Products; Materials Inspectors; Production Inspectors, Testers, Graders, Sorters, Samplers, Weighers. **PERSONALITY TYPE:** Realistic. Realistic occupations frequently involve work activities that include practical, hands-on problems and solutions. These occupations often deal with plants, animals, and real-world materials like wood, tools, and machinery. Many of the occupations require working outside and do not involve a lot of paperwork or working closely with others.

EDUCATION/TRAINING PROGRAM(S)— Quality Control Technology/Technician. **RELATED KNOWLEDGE/COURSES—Design:** Knowledge of design techniques, tools, and principles involved in production of precision technical plans, blueprints, drawings, and models. **Mechanical Devices:** Knowledge of machines and tools, including their designs, uses, repair, and maintenance. **Production and Processing:** Knowledge of raw materials, production processes, quality control, costs, and other techniques for maximizing the effective manufacture and distribution of goods. **Mathematics:** Knowledge of arithmetic, algebra, geometry, calculus, and statistics and their applications. **Engineering and Technology:** Knowledge of the practical application of engineering science and technology. This includes applying principles, techniques, procedures, and equipment to the design and production of various goods and services. **Physics:** Knowledge and prediction of physical principles and laws and their interrelationships and applications to understanding fluid, material, and atmospheric dynamics and mechanical, electrical, atomic, and subatomic structures and processes.

Pressure Vessel Inspectors

- ◎ Education/Training Required: Long-term on-the-job training
- ◎ Annual Earnings: $47,390
- ◎ Growth: 9.8%
- ◎ Annual Job Openings: 20,000
- ◎ Self-Employed: 0.9%
- ◎ Part-Time: 5.3%

Inspect pressure vessel equipment for conformance with safety laws and standards regulating their design, fabrication, installation, repair, and operation. Inspects drawings, designs, and specifications for piping, boilers, and other vessels. Performs standard tests to verify condition of equipment and calibration of meters and gauges, using test equipment and hand tools. Inspects gas mains to determine that rate of flow, pressure, location, construction, or installation conform to standards. Evaluates factors such as materials

used, safety devices, regulators, construction quality, riveting, welding, pitting, corrosion, cracking, and safety valve operation. Calculates allowable limits of pressure, strength, and stresses. Examines permits and inspection records to determine that inspection schedule and remedial actions conform to procedures and regulations. Keeps records and prepares reports of inspections and investigations for administrative or legal authorities. Investigates accidents to determine causes and to develop methods of preventing recurrences. Confers with engineers, manufacturers, contractors, owners, and operators concerning problems in construction, operation, and repair. Witnesses acceptance and installation tests. Recommends or orders actions to correct violations of legal requirements or to eliminate unsafe conditions. **SKILLS—Quality Control Analysis:** Conducting tests and inspections of products, services, or processes to evaluate quality or performance. **Operation Monitoring:** Watching gauges, dials, or other indicators to make sure a machine is working properly. **Mathematics:** Using mathematics to solve problems. **Science:** Using scientific rules and methods to solve problems. **Operations Analysis:** Analyzing needs and product requirements to create a design. **Systems Evaluation:** Identifying measures or indicators of system performance and the actions needed to improve or correct performance relative to the goals of the system. **Writing:** Communicating effectively in writing as appropriate for the needs of the audience. **Systems Analysis:** Determining how a system should work and how changes in conditions, operations, and the environment will affect outcomes. **GOE—Interest Area:** 07. Government and Public Administration. **Work Group:** 07.03. Regulations Enforcement. **Other Jobs in This Work Group:** Agricultural Inspectors; Aviation Inspectors; Child Support, Missing Persons, and Unemployment Insurance Fraud Investigators; Environmental Compliance Inspectors; Equal Opportunity Representatives and Officers; Financial Examiners; Fire Inspectors; Fish and Game Wardens; Forest Fire Inspectors and Prevention Specialists; Government Property Inspectors and Investigators; Immigration and Customs Inspectors; Licensing Examiners and Inspectors; Marine Cargo Inspectors; Mechanical Inspectors; Motor Vehicle Inspectors; Nuclear Monitoring Technicians; Occupational Health and Safety Specialists; Railroad Inspectors; Tax Examiners, Collectors, and Revenue Agents. **PERSONALITY TYPE:** Realistic. Realistic occupations frequently involve work activities that include practical, hands-on problems and solutions. These occupations often deal with plants, animals, and real-world materials like wood, tools, and machinery. Many of the occupations require working outside and do not involve a lot of paperwork or working closely with others.

EDUCATION/TRAINING PROGRAM(S)—No data available. **RELATED KNOWLEDGE/COURS- ES**—**Physics:** Knowledge and prediction of physical principles and laws and their interrelationships and applications to understanding fluid, material, and atmospheric dynamics and mechanical, electrical, atomic, and subatomic structures and processes. **Public Safety and Security:** Knowledge of relevant equipment, policies, procedures, and strategies to promote effective local, state, or national security operations for the protection of people, data, property, and institutions. **Mechanical Devices:** Knowledge of machines and tools, including their designs, uses, repair, and maintenance. **Engineering and Technology:** Knowledge of the practical application of engineering science and technology. This includes applying principles, techniques, procedures, and equipment to the design and production of various goods and services. **Law and Government:** Knowledge of laws, legal codes, court procedures, precedents, government regulations, executive orders, agency rules, and the democratic political process. **Design:** Knowledge of design techniques, tools, and principles involved in production of precision technical plans, blueprints, drawings, and models.

Private Detectives and Investigators

- ◎ Education/Training Required: Work experience in a related occupation
- ◎ Annual Earnings: $32,110
- ◎ Growth: 25.3%
- ◎ Annual Job Openings: 9,000
- ◎ Self-Employed: 34.7%
- ◎ Part-Time: 7.8%

Detect occurrences of unlawful acts or infractions of rules in private establishment or seek, examine, and compile information for client. Apprehend suspects and release them to law enforcement authorities or security personnel. Conduct background investigations of individuals, such as pre-employment checks, to obtain information about an individual's character, financial status, or personal history. Conduct private investigations on a paid basis. Confer with establishment officials, security departments, police, or postal officials to identify problems, provide information, and receive instructions. Monitor industrial or commercial properties to enforce conformance to establishment rules and to protect people or property. Observe and document activities of individuals in order to detect unlawful acts or to obtain evidence for cases, using binoculars and still or video cameras. Obtain and analyze information on suspects, crimes, and disturbances in order to solve cases, to identify criminal activity, and to gather information for court cases. Perform undercover operations such as evaluating the performance and honesty of employees by posing as customers or employees. Question persons to obtain evidence for cases of divorce, child custody, or missing persons or information about individuals' character or financial status. Search computer databases, credit reports, public records, tax and legal filings, and other resources in order to locate persons or to compile information for investigations. Write reports and case summaries to document investigations. Alert appropriate personnel to suspects' locations. Count cash and review transactions, sales checks, and register tapes in order to verify amounts and to identify shortages. Expose fraudulent insurance claims or stolen funds. Investigate companies' financial standings or locate funds stolen by embezzlers, using accounting skills. Testify at hearings and court trials to present evidence. Warn troublemakers causing problems on establishment premises and eject them from premises when necessary. **SKILLS**—**Systems Evaluation:** Identifying measures or indicators of system performance and the actions needed to improve or correct performance relative to the goals of the system. **Persuasion:** Persuading others to change their minds or behavior. **Systems Analysis:** Determining how a system should work and how changes in conditions, operations, and the environment will affect outcomes. **Active Listen-**

ing: Giving full attention to what other people are saying, taking time to understand the points being made, asking questions as appropriate, and not interrupting at inappropriate times. **Critical Thinking:** Using logic and reasoning to identify the strengths and weaknesses of alternative solutions, conclusions, or approaches to problems. **Social Perceptiveness:** Being aware of others' reactions and understanding why they react as they do. **Writing:** Communicating effectively in writing as appropriate for the needs of the audience. **Speaking:** Talking to others to convey information effectively. **GOE—Interest Area:** 12. Law and Public Safety. **Work Group:** 12.05. Safety and Security. **Other Jobs in This Work Group:** Animal Control Workers; Crossing Guards; Gaming Surveillance Officers and Gaming Investigators; Lifeguards, Ski Patrol, and Other Recreational Protective Service Workers; Security Guards. **PERSONALITY TYPE:** Enterprising. Enterprising occupations frequently involve starting up and carrying out projects. These occupations can involve leading people and making many decisions. They sometimes require risk taking and often deal with business.

EDUCATION/TRAINING PROGRAM(S)— Criminal Justice/Police Science. **RELATED KNOWLEDGE/COURSES—Public Safety and Security:** Knowledge of relevant equipment, policies, procedures, and strategies to promote effective local, state, or national security operations for the protection of people, data, property, and institutions. **Psychology:** Knowledge of human behavior and performance; individual differences in ability, personality, and interests; learning and motivation; psychological research methods; and the assessment and treatment of behavioral and affective disorders. **Telecommunications:** Knowledge of transmission, broadcasting, switching, control, and operation of telecommunications systems. **Law and Government:** Knowledge of laws, legal codes, court procedures, precedents, government regulations, executive orders, agency rules, and the democratic political process. **Medicine and Dentistry:** Knowledge of the information and techniques needed to diagnose and treat human injuries, diseases, and deformities. This includes symptoms, treatment alternatives, drug properties and interactions, and preventive health-care measures. **Therapy and Counseling:** Knowledge of principles, methods, and procedures for diagnosis,

treatment, and rehabilitation of physical and mental dysfunctions and for career counseling and guidance.

Production Inspectors, Testers, Graders, Sorters, Samplers, Weighers

- Education/Training Required: Short-term on-the-job training
- Annual Earnings: $28,410
- Growth: 4.7%
- Annual Job Openings: 87,000
- Self-Employed: 1.2%
- Part-Time: 5.0%

Inspect, test, grade, sort, sample, or weigh nonagricultural raw materials or processed, machined, fabricated, or assembled parts or products. Work may be performed before, during, or after processing. Grades, classifies, and sorts products according to size, weight, color, or other specifications. Marks, affixes, or stamps product or container to identify defects or denote grade or size information. Records inspection or test data, such as weight, temperature, grade, or moisture content and number inspected or graded. Collects or selects samples for testing or for use as model. Discards or routes defective products or contaminants for rework or reuse. Notifies supervisor or specified personnel of deviations from specifications, machine malfunctions, or need for equipment maintenance. Reads work order to determine inspection criteria and to verify identification numbers and product type. Uses or operates product to test functional performance. Computes percentages or averages, using formulas and calculator, and prepares reports of inspection or test findings. Sets controls, starts machine, and observes machine that automatically sorts or inspects products. Counts number of product tested or inspected and stacks or arranges for further processing, shipping, or packing. Cleans, trims, makes adjustments, or repairs product or processing equipment to correct defects found during inspection. Transports inspected or tested products to other work stations, using handtruck or lift truck. Wraps and packages product for shipment or delivery. Weighs materials, products, containers, or samples to verify packaging weight, to determine percentage of each ingredient, or to determine sorting. Compares color, shape, texture, or grade of product or material with color chart, template, or sample to verify conformance to standards. Tests samples, materials, or products, using test equipment such as thermometer, voltmeter, moisture meter, or tensiometer, for conformance to specifications. Measures dimensions of product, using measuring instruments, such as rulers, calipers, gauges, or micrometers, to verify conformance to specifications. Examines product or monitors processing of product, using any or all of five senses, to determine defects or grade. **SKILLS—Quality Control Analysis:** Conducting tests and inspections of products, services, or processes to evaluate quality or performance. **Operation Monitoring:** Watching gauges, dials, or other indicators to make sure a machine is working properly. **Operation and Control:** Controlling operations of equipment or systems. **Repairing:** Repairing machines or systems by using the needed tools. **Management of Material Resources:** Obtaining and seeing to the appropriate use of equipment, facilities, and materials needed to do certain work. **Troubleshooting:** Determining causes of operating errors and deciding what to do about them. **Equipment Maintenance:** Performing routine maintenance on equipment and determining when and what kind of maintenance is needed. **GOE—Interest Area:** 13. Manufacturing. **Work Group:** 13.07. Production Quality Control. **Other Jobs in This Work Group:** Electrical and Electronic Inspectors and Testers; Graders and Sorters, Agricultural Products; Materials Inspectors; Precision Devices Inspectors and Testers. **PERSONALITY TYPE:** Realistic. Realistic occupations frequently involve work activities that include practical, hands-on problems and solutions. These occupations often deal with plants, animals, and real-world materials like wood, tools, and machinery. Many of the occupations require working outside and do not involve a lot of paperwork or working closely with others.

EDUCATION/TRAINING PROGRAM(S)— Quality Control Technology/Technician. **RELATED KNOWLEDGE/COURSES—Production and Processing:** Knowledge of raw materials, production processes, quality control, costs, and other techniques for maximizing the effective manufacture and distribution of goods. **Engineering and Technology:** Knowledge of the practical application of engineering science and technology. This includes applying principles, techniques, procedures, and equipment to the design and production of various goods and services. **Mechanical Devices:** Knowledge of machines and tools, including their designs, uses, repair, and maintenance.

Production, Planning, and Expediting Clerks

- Education/Training Required: Short-term on-the-job training
- Annual Earnings: $36,340
- Growth: 14.1%
- Annual Job Openings: 51,000
- Self-Employed: 0.4%
- Part-Time: 9.3%

Coordinate and expedite the flow of work and materials within or between departments of an establishment according to production schedule. Duties include reviewing and distributing production, work, and shipment schedules; conferring with department supervisors to determine progress of work and completion dates; and compiling reports on progress of work, inventory levels, costs, and production problems. Arrange for delivery, assembly, and distribution of supplies and parts in order to expedite flow of materials and meet production schedules. Calculate figures such as required amounts of labor and materials, manufacturing costs, and wages, using pricing schedules, adding machines, calculators, or computers. Compile and prepare documentation related to production sequences; transportation; personnel schedules; and purchase, maintenance, and repair orders. Compile information such as production rates and progress, materials inventories, materials used, and customer information so that status reports can be completed. Confer with establishment personnel, vendors, and customers to coordinate production and shipping activities and to resolve complaints or eliminate delays. Contact suppliers to verify shipment details. Examine documents, materials, and products and monitor work processes in order to assess completeness, accuracy, and conformance to standards and specifications. Requisition and maintain inventories of materials and supplies necessary to meet production demands. Review documents such as production schedules, work orders, and staffing tables to determine personnel and materials requirements and material priorities. Revise production schedules when required due to design changes, labor or material shortages, backlogs, or other interruptions, collaborating with management, marketing, sales, production, and engineering. Confer with department supervisors and other personnel to assess progress and discuss needed changes. Distribute production schedules and work orders to departments. Establish and prepare product construction directions and locations and information on required tools, materials, and equipment, numbers of workers needed, and cost projections. Maintain files such as maintenance records, bills of lading, and cost reports. Plan production commitments and timetables for business units, specific programs, and/or jobs, using sales forecasts. Provide documentation and information to account for delays, difficulties, and changes to cost estimates. Record production data, including volume produced, consumption of raw materials, and quality control measures. **SKILLS—Management of Material Resources:** Obtaining and seeing to the appropriate use of equipment, facilities, and materials needed to do certain work. **Management of Personnel Resources:** Motivating, developing, and directing people as they work, identifying the best people for the job. **Systems Analysis:** Determining how a system should work and how changes in conditions, operations, and the environment will affect outcomes. **Management of Financial Resources:** Determining how money will be spent to get the work done and accounting for these expenditures. **Systems Evaluation:** Identifying measures or indicators of system performance and the actions needed to improve or correct performance relative to the goals of the system. **Time Management:** Managing one's own time and the time of others. **Service Orientation:** Actively looking for ways to help people. **Writing:** Communicating effectively in writing as appropriate for the needs of the audience. **GOE— Interest Area:** 04. Business and Administration. **Work Group:** 04.07. Records and Materials Processing.

Other Jobs in This Work Group: Correspondence Clerks; File Clerks; Human Resources Assistants, Except Payroll and Timekeeping; Mail Clerks, Except Mail Machine Operators and Postal Service; Marking Clerks; Meter Readers, Utilities; Office Clerks, General; Order Fillers, Wholesale and Retail Sales; Postal Service Clerks; Postal Service Mail Sorters, Processors, and Processing Machine Operators; Procurement Clerks; Shipping, Receiving, and Traffic Clerks; Stock Clerks, Sales Floor; Stock Clerks—Stockroom, Warehouse, or Storage Yard; Weighers, Measurers, Checkers, and Samplers, Recordkeeping. **PERSONALITY TYPE:** Conventional. Conventional occupations frequently involve following set procedures and routines. These occupations can include working with data and details more than with ideas. Usually there is a clear line of authority to follow.

EDUCATION/TRAINING PROGRAM(S)—Parts, Warehousing, and Inventory Management Operations. **RELATED KNOWLEDGE/COURSES— Clerical Practices:** Knowledge of administrative and clerical procedures and systems such as word processing, managing files and records, stenography and transcription, designing forms, and other office procedures and terminology. **Production and Processing:** Knowledge of raw materials, production processes, quality control, costs, and other techniques for maximizing the effective manufacture and distribution of goods. **Economics and Accounting:** Knowledge of economic and accounting principles and practices, the financial markets, banking, and the analysis and reporting of financial data. **Mathematics:** Knowledge of arithmetic, algebra, geometry, calculus, and statistics and their applications. **Computers and Electronics:** Knowledge of circuit boards, processors, chips, electronic equipment, and computer hardware and software, including applications and programming. **Administration and Management:** Knowledge of business and management principles involved in strategic planning, resource allocation, human resources modeling, leadership technique, production methods, and coordination of people and resources.

Professional Photographers

- Education/Training Required: Long-term on-the-job training
- Annual Earnings: $26,080
- Growth: 13.6%
- Annual Job Openings: 18,000
- Self-Employed: 52.5%
- Part-Time: 24.0%

Photograph subjects or newsworthy events, using still cameras, color or black-and-white film, and variety of photographic accessories. Frames subject matter and background in lens to capture desired image. Focuses camera and adjusts settings based on lighting, subject material, distance, and film speed. Selects and assembles equipment and required background properties according to subject, materials, and conditions. Directs activities of workers assisting in setting up photograph. Arranges subject material in desired position. Estimates or measures light level, distance, and number of exposures needed, using measuring devices and formulas. **SKILLS—Equipment Selection:** Determining the kind of tools and equipment needed to do a job. **Management of Material Resources:** Obtaining and seeing to the appropriate use of equipment, facilities, and materials needed to do certain work. **Technology Design:** Generating or adapting equipment and technology to serve user needs. **Operation and Control:** Controlling operations of equipment or systems. **Systems Analysis:** Determining how a system should work and how changes in conditions, operations, and the environment will affect outcomes. **Management of Personnel Resources:** Motivating, developing, and directing people as they work, identifying the best people for the job. **Social Perceptiveness:** Being aware of others' reactions and understanding why they react as they do. **GOE—Interest Area:** 03. Arts and Communication. **Work Group:** 03.09. Media Technology. **Other Jobs in This Work Group:** Audio and Video Equipment Technicians; Broadcast Technicians; Camera Operators, Television, Video, and Motion Picture; Film and Video Editors; Multi-Media Artists and Animators; Photographic Hand Developers; Photographic Reproduction Technicians; Photographic Retouchers and Restorers; Radio Operators; Sound Engineering Technicians. **PERSONALITY TYPE:** Artistic. Artistic occupations frequently involve working with forms, designs, and patterns. These occupations often require self-expression, and the work can be done without following a clear set of rules.

EDUCATION/TRAINING PROGRAM(S)— Art/Art Studies, General; Commercial Photography; Film/Video and Photographic Arts, Other; Photography; Photojournalism; Visual and Performing Arts, General. **RELATED KNOWLEDGE/COURSES— Fine Arts:** Knowledge of the theory and techniques required to compose, produce, and perform works of music, dance, the visual arts, drama, and sculpture. **Communications and Media:** Knowledge of media production, communication, and dissemination techniques and methods. This includes alternative ways to inform and entertain via written, oral, and visual media. **Chemistry:** Knowledge of the chemical composition, structure, and properties of substances and of the chemical processes and transformations that they undergo. This includes uses of chemicals and their danger signs, production techniques, and disposal methods. **Geography:** Knowledge of principles and methods for describing the features of land, sea, and air masses, including their physical characteristics; locations; interrelationships; and distribution of plant, animal, and human life. **Physics:** Knowledge and prediction of physical principles and laws and their interrelationships and applications to understanding fluid, material, and atmospheric dynamics and mechanical, electrical, atomic, and subatomic structures and processes. **Transportation:** Knowledge of principles and methods for moving people or goods by air, rail, sea, or road, including the relative costs and benefits.

Public Transportation Inspectors

- Education/Training Required: Work experience in a related occupation
- Annual Earnings: $50,380
- Growth: 7.7%
- Annual Job Openings: 5,000
- Self-Employed: 0.4%
- Part-Time: 3.2%

Monitor operation of public transportation systems to ensure good service and compliance with regulations. Investigate accidents, equipment failures, and complaints. Observes employees performing assigned duties to note their deportment, treatment of passengers, and adherence to company regulations and schedules. Observes and records time required to load and unload passengers or freight volume of traffic on vehicle and at stops. Investigates schedule delays, accidents, and complaints. Inspects company vehicles and other property for evidence of abuse, damage, and mechanical malfunction and directs repair. Determines need for changes in service, such as additional vehicles, route changes, and revised schedules to improve service and efficiency. Drives automobile along route to detect conditions hazardous to equipment and passengers and negotiates with local governments to eliminate hazards. Submits written reports to management with recommendations for improving service. Reports disruptions to service. Assists in dispatching equipment when necessary. Recommends promotions and disciplinary actions involving transportation personnel. **SKILLS—Operations Analysis:** Analyzing needs and product requirements to create a design. **Writing:** Communicating effectively in writing as appropriate for the needs of the audience. **Systems Evaluation:** Identifying measures or indicators of system performance and the actions needed to improve or correct performance relative to the goals of the system. **Management of Personnel Resources:** Motivating, developing, and directing people as they work, identifying the best people for the job. **Monitoring:** Monitoring or assessing your performance or that of other individuals or organizations to make improvements or take corrective action. **Speaking:** Talking to others to convey information effectively. **Systems Analysis:** Determining how a system should work and how changes in conditions, operations, and the environment will affect outcomes. **Negotiation:** Bringing others together and trying to reconcile differences. **GOE—Interest Area:** 16. Transportation, Distribution, and Logistics. **Work Group:** 16.07. Transportation Support Work. **Other Jobs in This Work Group:** Bridge and Lock Tenders; Cargo and Freight Agents; Cleaners of Vehicles and Equipment; Freight Inspectors; Railroad Yard Workers; Stevedores, Except Equipment Operators; Traffic Technicians; Train Crew Members. **PERSONALITY TYPE:** Enterprising. Enterprising occupations frequently involve starting up and carrying out projects. These occupations can involve leading people and making many decisions. They sometimes require risk taking and often deal with business.

EDUCATION/TRAINING PROGRAM(S)—No data available. **RELATED KNOWLEDGE/COURSES—Transportation:** Knowledge of principles and methods for moving people or goods by air, rail, sea, or road, including the relative costs and benefits. **Personnel and Human Resources:** Knowledge of principles and procedures for personnel recruitment, selection, training, compensation and benefits, labor relations and negotiation, and personnel information systems. **Public Safety and Security:** Knowledge of relevant equipment, policies, procedures, and strategies to promote effective local, state, or national security operations for the protection of people, data, property, and institutions. **Law and Government:** Knowledge of laws, legal codes, court procedures, precedents, government regulations, executive orders, agency rules, and the democratic political process. **Geography:** Knowledge of principles and methods for describing the features of land, sea, and air masses, including their physical characteristics; locations; interrelationships; and distribution of plant, animal, and human life. **Administration and Management:** Knowledge of business and management principles involved in strategic planning, resource allocation, human resources modeling, leadership technique, production methods, and coordination of people and resources.

Radiation Therapists

- ◉ Education/Training Required: Associate degree
- ◉ Annual Earnings: $57,700
- ◉ Growth: 31.6%
- ◉ Annual Job Openings: 1,000
- ◉ Self-Employed: 0%
- ◉ Part-Time: 14.2%

Provide radiation therapy to patients as prescribed by a radiologist according to established practices and standards. Duties may include reviewing prescription and diagnosis; acting as liaison with physician and supportive care personnel; preparing equipment such as immobilization, treatment, and protection devices; and maintaining records, reports, and files. May assist in dosimetry procedures and tumor localization. Administer prescribed doses of radiation to specific body parts, using radiation therapy equipment according to established practices and standards. Position patients for treatment with accuracy according to prescription. Enter data into computer and set controls to operate and adjust equipment and regulate dosage. Follow principles of radiation protection for patient, self, and others. Maintain records, reports, and files as required, including such information as radiation dosages, equipment settings, and patients' reactions. Review prescription, diagnosis, patient chart, and identification. Conduct most treatment sessions independently in accordance with the long-term treatment plan and under the general direction of the patient's physician. Check radiation therapy equipment to ensure proper operation. Observe and reassure patients during treatment and report unusual reactions to physician or turn equipment off if unexpected adverse reactions occur. Check for side effects such as skin irritation, nausea, and hair loss to assess patients' reaction to treatment. Educate, prepare, and reassure patients and their families by answering questions, providing physical assistance, and reinforcing physicians' advice regarding treatment reactions and post-treatment care. Calculate actual treatment dosages delivered during each session. Prepare and construct equipment, such as immobilization, treatment, and protection devices. Photograph treated area of patient and process film.

Help physicians, radiation oncologists, and clinical physicists to prepare physical and technical aspects of radiation treatment plans, using information about patient condition and anatomy. Train and supervise student or subordinate radiotherapy technologists. Act as liaison with physicist and supportive-care personnel. Provide assistance to other health-care personnel during dosimetry procedures and tumor localization. Implement appropriate follow-up care plans. Store, sterilize, or prepare the special applicators containing the radioactive substance implanted by the physician. Assist in the preparation of sealed radioactive materials, such as cobalt, radium, cesium, and isotopes, for use in radiation treatments. **SKILLS—Operation Monitoring:** Watching gauges, dials, or other indicators to make sure a machine is working properly. **Technology Design:** Generating or adapting equipment and technology to serve user needs. **Operation and Control:** Controlling operations of equipment or systems. **Time Management:** Managing one's own time and the time of others. **Management of Personnel Resources:** Motivating, developing, and directing people as they work, identifying the best people for the job. **Instructing:** Teaching others how to do something. **Service Orientation:** Actively looking for ways to help people. **Social Perceptiveness:** Being aware of others' reactions and understanding why they react as they do. **GOE—Interest Area:** 08. Health Science. **Work Group:** 08.07. Medical Therapy. **Other Jobs in This Work Group:** Audiologists; Massage Therapists; Occupational Therapist Aides; Occupational Therapist Assistants; Occupational Therapists; Physical Therapist Aides; Physical Therapist Assistants; Physical Therapists; Recreational Therapists; Respiratory Therapists; Respiratory Therapy Technicians; Speech-Language Pathologists. **PERSONALITY TYPE:** Social. Social occupations frequently involve working with, communicating with, and teaching people. These occupations often involve helping or providing service to others.

EDUCATION/TRAINING PROGRAM(S)—Medical Radiologic Technology/Science—Radiation Therapist. **RELATED KNOWLEDGE/ COURSES—Medicine and Dentistry:** Knowledge of the information and techniques needed to diagnose and treat human injuries, diseases, and deformities.

This includes symptoms, treatment alternatives, drug properties and interactions, and preventive health-care measures. **Customer and Personal Service:** Knowledge of principles and processes for providing customer and personal services. This includes customer needs assessment, meeting quality standards for services, and evaluation of customer satisfaction. **Psychology:** Knowledge of human behavior and performance; individual differences in ability, personality, and interests; learning and motivation; psychological research methods; and the assessment and treatment of behavioral and affective disorders. **Biology:** Knowledge of plant and animal organisms and their tissues, cells, functions, interdependencies, and interactions with each other and the environment. **Physics:** Knowledge and prediction of physical principles and laws and their interrelationships and applications to understanding fluid, material, and atmospheric dynamics and mechanical, electrical, atomic, and subatomic structures and processes. **Therapy and Counseling:** Knowledge of principles, methods, and procedures for diagnosis, treatment, and rehabilitation of physical and mental dysfunctions and for career counseling and guidance.

Radiologic Technicians

◎ Education/Training Required: Associate degree
◎ Annual Earnings: $43,350
◎ Growth: 22.9%
◎ Annual Job Openings: 21,000
◎ Self-Employed: 0.2%
◎ Part-Time: 17.5%

Maintain and use equipment and supplies necessary to demonstrate portions of the human body on X-ray film or fluoroscopic screen for diagnostic purposes. Use beam-restrictive devices and patient-shielding techniques to minimize radiation exposure to patient and staff. Position X-ray equipment and adjust controls to set exposure factors, such as time and distance. Position patient on examining table and set up and adjust equipment to obtain optimum view of specific body area as requested by physician. Determine patients' X-ray needs by reading requests or instruc-

tions from physicians. Make exposures necessary for the requested procedures, rejecting and repeating work that does not meet established standards. Process exposed radiographs, using film processors or computer-generated methods. Explain procedures to patients to reduce anxieties and obtain cooperation. Perform procedures such as linear tomography; mammography; sonograms; joint and cyst aspirations; routine contrast studies; routine fluoroscopy; and examinations of the head, trunk, and extremities under supervision of physician. Prepare and set up X-ray room for patient. Assure that sterile supplies, contrast materials, catheters, and other required equipment are present and in working order, requisitioning materials as necessary. Maintain records of patients examined, examinations performed, views taken, and technical factors used. Provide assistance to physicians or other technologists in the performance of more-complex procedures. Monitor equipment operation and report malfunctioning equipment to supervisor. Provide students and other technologists with suggestions of additional views, alternate positioning, or improved techniques to ensure that the images produced are of the highest quality. Coordinate work of other technicians or technologists when procedures require more than one person. Assist with on-the-job training of new employees and students and provide input to supervisors regarding training performance. Maintain a current file of examination protocols. Operate mobile X-ray equipment in operating room, in emergency room, or at patient's bedside. Provide assistance in radiopharmaceutical administration, monitoring patients' vital signs and notifying the radiologist of any relevant changes. **SKILLS—Service Orientation:** Actively looking for ways to help people. **Science:** Using scientific rules and methods to solve problems. **Negotiation:** Bringing others together and trying to reconcile differences. **Instructing:** Teaching others how to do something. **Active Listening:** Giving full attention to what other people are saying, taking time to understand the points being made, asking questions as appropriate, and not interrupting at inappropriate times. **Social Perceptiveness:** Being aware of others' reactions and understanding why they react as they do. **Equipment Selection:** Determining the kind of tools and equipment needed to do a job. **Operation Monitoring:** Watching gauges, dials, or other indicators to make sure a machine is working properly. **GOE— Interest Area:** 08. Health Science. **Work Group:** 08.06. Medical Technology. **Other Jobs in This Work Group:** Biological Technicians; Cardiovascular Technologists and Technicians; Diagnostic Medical Sonographers; Medical and Clinical Laboratory Technicians; Medical and Clinical Laboratory Technologists; Medical Equipment Preparers; Medical Records and Health Information Technicians; Nuclear Medicine Technologists; Opticians, Dispensing; Orthotists and Prosthetists; Radiologic Technologists. **PERSONALITY TYPE:** Realistic. Realistic occupations frequently involve work activities that include practical, hands-on problems and solutions. These occupations often deal with plants, animals, and real-world materials like wood, tools, and machinery. Many of the occupations require working outside and do not involve a lot of paperwork or working closely with others.

EDUCATION/TRAINING PROGRAM(S)— Allied Health Diagnostic, Intervention, and Treatment Professions, Other; Medical Radiologic Technology/ Science—Radiation Therapist; Radiologic Technology/Science—Radiographer. **RELATED KNOWLEDGE/COURSES—Clerical Practices:** Knowledge of administrative and clerical procedures and systems such as word processing, managing files and records, stenography and transcription, designing forms, and other office procedures and terminology. **Psychology:** Knowledge of human behavior and performance; individual differences in ability, personality, and interests; learning and motivation; psychological research methods; and the assessment and treatment of behavioral and affective disorders. **Medicine and Dentistry:** Knowledge of the information and techniques needed to diagnose and treat human injuries, diseases, and deformities. This includes symptoms, treatment alternatives, drug properties and interactions, and preventive health-care measures. **Customer and Personal Service:** Knowledge of principles and processes for providing customer and personal services. This includes customer needs assessment, meeting quality standards for services, and evaluation of customer satisfaction. **Physics:** Knowledge and prediction of physical principles and laws and their interrelationships and applications to understanding fluid, material, and atmospheric dynamics and mechanical, electrical,

atomic, and subatomic structures and processes. **English Language:** Knowledge of the structure and content of the English language, including the meaning and spelling of words, rules of composition, and grammar.

Radiologic Technologists

- Education/Training Required: Associate degree
- Annual Earnings: $43,350
- Growth: 22.9%
- Annual Job Openings: 21,000
- Self-Employed: 0.2%
- Part-Time: 17.5%

Take X rays and CAT scans or administer nonradioactive materials into patient's bloodstream for diagnostic purposes. Includes technologists who specialize in other modalities, such as computed tomography, ultrasound, and magnetic resonance. Review and evaluate developed X rays, videotape, or computergenerated information to determine if images are satisfactory for diagnostic purposes. Use radiation safety measures and protection devices to comply with government regulations and to ensure safety of patients and staff. Explain procedures and observe patients to ensure safety and comfort during scan. Operate or oversee operation of radiologic and magnetic imaging equipment to produce images of the body for diagnostic purposes. Position and immobilize patient on examining table. Position imaging equipment and adjust controls to set exposure time and distance, according to specification of examination. Key commands and data into computer to document and specify scan sequences, adjust transmitters and receivers, or photograph certain images. Monitor video display of area being scanned and adjust density or contrast to improve picture quality. Monitor patients' conditions and reactions, reporting abnormal signs to physician. Set up examination rooms, ensuring that all necessary equipment is ready. Prepare and administer oral or injected contrast media to patients. Take thorough and accurate patient medical histories. Remove and process film. Record, process, and maintain patient data and treatment records and prepare reports. Coordinate work with clerical personnel and other technologists. Demonstrate new equipment, procedures, and techniques to staff and provide technical assistance. Provide assistance with such tasks as dressing and changing to seriously ill, injured, or disabled patients. Move ultrasound scanner over patient's body and watch pattern produced on video screen. Measure thickness of section to be radiographed, using instruments similar to measuring tapes. Operate fluoroscope to aid physician to view and guide wire or catheter through blood vessels to area of interest. Assign duties to radiologic staff to maintain patient flows and achieve production goals. Collaborate with other medical team members, such as physicians and nurses, to conduct angiography or special vascular procedures. Perform administrative duties such as developing departmental operating budget, coordinating purchases of supplies and equipment, and preparing work schedules. **SKILLS—Instructing:** Teaching others how to do something. **Social Perceptiveness:** Being aware of others' reactions and understanding why they react as they do. **Service Orientation:** Actively looking for ways to help people. **Reading Comprehension:** Understanding written sentences and paragraphs in work-related documents. **Operation Monitoring:** Watching gauges, dials, or other indicators to make sure a machine is working properly. **Active Listening:** Giving full attention to what other people are saying, taking time to understand the points being made, asking questions as appropriate, and not interrupting at inappropriate times. **Speaking:** Talking to others to convey information effectively. **Critical Thinking:** Using logic and reasoning to identify the strengths and weaknesses of alternative solutions, conclusions, or approaches to problems. **Learning Strategies:** Selecting and using training/instructional methods and procedures appropriate for the situation when learning or teaching new things. **Coordination:** Adjusting actions in relation to others' actions. **GOE—Interest Area:** 08. Health Science. **Work Group:** 08.06. Medical Technology. **Other Jobs in This Work Group:** Biological Technicians; Cardiovascular Technologists and Technicians; Diagnostic Medical Sonographers; Medical and Clinical Laboratory Technicians; Medical and Clinical Laboratory Technologists; Medical Equipment Preparers; Medical Records and Health Information Technicians; Nuclear Medicine Technologists; Opticians,

Dispensing; Orthotists and Prosthetists; Radiologic Technicians. **PERSONALITY TYPE:** Realistic. Realistic occupations frequently involve work activities that include practical, hands-on problems and solutions. These occupations often deal with plants, animals, and real-world materials like wood, tools, and machinery. Many of the occupations require working outside and do not involve a lot of paperwork or working closely with others.

EDUCATION/TRAINING PROGRAM(S)— Allied Health Diagnostic, Intervention, and Treatment Professions, Other; Medical Radiologic Technology/Science—Radiation Therapist; Radiologic Technology/Science—Radiographer. **RELATED KNOWLEDGE/COURSES—Medicine and Dentistry:** Knowledge of the information and techniques needed to diagnose and treat human injuries, diseases, and deformities. This includes symptoms, treatment alternatives, drug properties and interactions, and preventive health-care measures. **Customer and Personal Service:** Knowledge of principles and processes for providing customer and personal services. This includes customer needs assessment, meeting quality standards for services, and evaluation of customer satisfaction. **Psychology:** Knowledge of human behavior and performance; individual differences in ability, personality, and interests; learning and motivation; psychological research methods; and the assessment and treatment of behavioral and affective disorders. **Physics:** Knowledge and prediction of physical principles and laws and their interrelationships and applications to understanding fluid, material, and atmospheric dynamics and mechanical, electrical, atomic, and subatomic structures and processes. **Biology:** Knowledge of plant and animal organisms and their tissues, cells, functions, interdependencies, and interactions with each other and the environment. **Chemistry:** Knowledge of the chemical composition, structure, and properties of substances and of the chemical processes and transformations that they undergo. This includes uses of chemicals and their danger signs, production techniques, and disposal methods.

Railroad Inspectors

- Education/Training Required: Work experience in a related occupation
- Annual Earnings: $50,380
- Growth: 7.7%
- Annual Job Openings: 5,000
- Self-Employed: 0.4%
- Part-Time: 3.2%

Inspect railroad equipment, roadbed, and track to ensure safe transport of people or cargo. Fills paint container on rail-detector car used to mark section of defective rail with paint. Directs crews to repair or replace defective equipment or to re-ballast roadbed. Places lanterns or flags in front and rear of train to signal that inspection is being performed. Seals leaks found during inspection that can be sealed with caulking compound. Replaces defective brake rod pins and tightens safety appliances. Notifies train dispatcher of railcar to be moved to shop for repair. Makes minor repairs. Packs brake bearings with grease. Inspects signals and track wiring to determine continuity of electrical connections. Examines roadbed, switches, fishplates, rails, and ties to detect damage or wear. Examines locomotives and cars to detect damage or structural defects. Inspects and tests completed work. Operates switches to determine working conditions. Tests and synchronizes rail-flaw-detection machine, using circuit tester and hand tools, and reloads machine with paper and ink. Starts machine and signals worker to operate rail-detector car. Prepares reports on repairs made and equipment, railcars, or roadbed needing repairs. Tags railcars needing immediate repair. **SKILLS—Repairing:** Repairing machines or systems by using the needed tools. **Troubleshooting:** Determining causes of operating errors and deciding what to do about them. **Operation Monitoring:** Watching gauges, dials, or other indicators to make sure a machine is working properly. **Equipment Maintenance:** Performing routine maintenance on equipment and determining when and what kind of maintenance is needed. **Quality Control Analysis:** Conducting tests and inspections of products, services, or processes to evaluate quality or performance. **Management of Personnel Resources:** Motivating, developing, and directing people as they work, identifying the best people for the job. **Systems Analysis:** Determining how a system should work and how changes in conditions, operations, and the environment will affect outcomes. **Science:** Using scientific rules and methods to solve problems. **Time Management:** Managing one's own time and the time of others. **GOE—Interest Area:** 07. Government and Public Administration. **Work Group:** 07.03. Regulations Enforcement. **Other Jobs in This Work Group:** Agricultural Inspectors; Aviation Inspectors; Child Support, Missing Persons, and Unemployment Insurance Fraud Investigators; Environmental Compliance Inspectors; Equal Opportunity Representatives and Officers; Financial Examiners; Fire Inspectors; Fish and Game Wardens; Forest Fire Inspectors and Prevention Specialists; Government Property Inspectors and Investigators; Immigration and Customs Inspectors; Licensing Examiners and Inspectors; Marine Cargo Inspectors; Mechanical Inspectors; Motor Vehicle Inspectors; Nuclear Monitoring Technicians; Occupational Health and Safety Specialists; Pressure Vessel Inspectors; Tax Examiners, Collectors, and Revenue Agents. **PERSONALITY TYPE:** Realistic. Realistic occupations frequently involve work activities that include practical, hands-on problems and solutions. These occupations often deal with plants, animals, and real-world materials like wood, tools, and machinery. Many of the occupations require working outside and do not involve a lot of paperwork or working closely with others.

EDUCATION/TRAINING PROGRAM(S)—No data available. **RELATED KNOWLEDGE/COURSES—Transportation:** Knowledge of principles and methods for moving people or goods by air, rail, sea, or road, including the relative costs and benefits. **Public Safety and Security:** Knowledge of relevant equipment, policies, procedures, and strategies to promote effective local, state, or national security operations for the protection of people, data, property, and institutions. **Mechanical Devices:** Knowledge of machines and tools, including their designs, uses, repair, and maintenance. **Engineering and Technology:** Knowledge of the practical application of engineering science and technology. This includes applying principles, techniques, procedures, and equipment to the design and production of various goods and services. **Building and Construction:** Knowledge of the materials, methods, and tools involved in the construction or repair of houses, buildings, or other structures such as highways and roads. **Geography:** Knowledge of principles and methods for describing the features of land, sea, and air masses, including their physical characteristics; locations; interrelationships; and distribution of plant, animal, and human life.

Real Estate Brokers

- Education/Training Required: Work experience in a related occupation
- Annual Earnings: $58,720
- Growth: 2.4%
- Annual Job Openings: 11,000
- Self-Employed: 59.1%
- Part-Time: 14.8%

Operate real estate office or work for commercial real estate firm, overseeing real estate transactions. Other duties usually include selling real estate or renting properties and arranging loans. Sell, for a fee, real estate owned by others. Obtain agreements from property owners to place properties for sale with real estate firms. Monitor fulfillment of purchase contract terms to ensure that they are handled in a timely manner. Compare a property with similar properties that have recently sold in order to determine its competitive market price. Act as an intermediary in negotiations between buyers and sellers over property prices and settlement details and during the closing of sales. Generate lists of properties for sale, their locations and descriptions, and available financing options, using computers. Maintain knowledge of real estate law; local economies; fair housing laws; and types of available mortgages, financing options, and government programs. Check work completed by loan officers, attorneys, and other professionals to ensure that it is performed properly. Arrange for financing of property purchases. Appraise property values, assessing income potential when relevant. Maintain awareness of current income tax regulations, local zoning, building and tax laws, and growth possibilities of the area where a property is located. Manage and operate real estate offices, handling associated business details. Supervise agents who handle real estate transactions. Rent properties or manage rental properties. Arrange for title

searches of properties being sold. Give buyers virtual tours of properties in which they are interested, using computers. Review property details to ensure that environmental regulations are met. Develop, sell, or lease property used for industry or manufacturing. **SKILLS—Negotiation:** Bringing others together and trying to reconcile differences. **Management of Financial Resources:** Determining how money will be spent to get the work done and accounting for these expenditures. **Persuasion:** Persuading others to change their minds or behavior. **Service Orientation:** Actively looking for ways to help people. **Active Listening:** Giving full attention to what other people are saying, taking time to understand the points being made, asking questions as appropriate, and not interrupting at inappropriate times. **Judgment and Decision Making:** Considering the relative costs and benefits of potential actions to choose the most appropriate one. **Mathematics:** Using mathematics to solve problems. **Complex Problem Solving:** Identifying complex problems and reviewing related information to develop and evaluate options and implement solutions. **GOE—Interest Area:** 14. Retail and Wholesale Sales and Service. **Work Group:** 14.03. General Sales. **Other Jobs in This Work Group:** Parts Salespersons; Real Estate Sales Agents; Retail Salespersons; Sales Representatives, Wholesale and Manufacturing, Except Technical and Scientific Products; Service Station Attendants. **PERSONALITY TYPE:** No data available.

EDUCATION/TRAINING PROGRAM(S)—Real Estate. **RELATED KNOWLEDGE/COURSES—Sales and Marketing:** Knowledge of principles and methods for showing, promoting, and selling products or services. This includes marketing strategy and tactics, product demonstrations, sales techniques, and sales control systems. **Customer and Personal Service:** Knowledge of principles and processes for providing customer and personal services. This includes customer needs assessment, meeting quality standards for services, and evaluation of customer satisfaction. **Law and Government:** Knowledge of laws, legal codes, court procedures, precedents, government regulations, executive orders, agency rules, and the democratic political process. **Personnel and Human Resources:** Knowledge of principles and procedures for personnel recruitment, selection, training, compensation and benefits, labor relations and negotiation, and personnel information systems. **Building and Construction:** Knowledge of the materials, methods, and tools involved in the construction or repair of houses, buildings, or other structures such as highways and roads. **Administration and Management:** Knowledge of business and management principles involved in strategic planning, resource allocation, human resources modeling, leadership technique, production methods, and coordination of people and resources.

Real Estate Sales Agents

- ◎ Education/Training Required: Postsecondary vocational training
- ◎ Annual Earnings: $35,670
- ◎ Growth: 5.7%
- ◎ Annual Job Openings: 34,000
- ◎ Self-Employed: 59.0%
- ◎ Part-Time: 14.8%

Rent, buy, or sell property for clients. Perform duties such as studying property listings, interviewing prospective clients, accompanying clients to property site, discussing conditions of sale, and drawing up real estate contracts. Includes agents who represent buyer. Present purchase offers to sellers for consideration. Confer with escrow companies, lenders, home inspectors, and pest control operators to ensure that terms and conditions of purchase agreements are met before closing dates. Interview clients to determine what kinds of properties they are seeking. Prepare documents such as representation contracts, purchase agreements, closing statements, deeds, and leases. Coordinate property closings, overseeing signing of documents and disbursement of funds. Act as an intermediary in negotiations between buyers and sellers, generally representing one or the other. Promote sales of properties through advertisements, open houses, and participation in multiple listing services. Compare a property with similar properties that have recently sold in order to determine its competitive market price. Coordinate appointments to show homes to prospective buyers. Generate lists of properties that are compatible with buyers' needs and financial resources. Display commercial, industrial, agricultural, and residential properties to clients and explain their features.

Arrange for title searches to determine whether clients have clear property titles. Review plans for new construction with clients, enumerating and recommending available options and features. Answer clients' questions regarding construction work, financing, maintenance, repairs, and appraisals. Inspect condition of premises and arrange for necessary maintenance or notify owners of maintenance needs. Accompany buyers during visits to and inspections of property, advising them on the suitability and value of the homes they are visiting. Advise sellers on how to make homes more appealing to potential buyers. Arrange meetings between buyers and sellers when details of transactions need to be negotiated. Advise clients on market conditions, prices, mortgages, legal requirements, and related matters. Evaluate mortgage options to help clients obtain financing at the best prevailing rates and terms. Review property listings, trade journals, and relevant literature and attend conventions, seminars, and staff and association meetings in order to remain knowledgeable about real estate markets. **SKILLS—Negotiation:** Bringing others together and trying to reconcile differences. **Coordination:** Adjusting actions in relation to others' actions. **Service Orientation:** Actively looking for ways to help people. **Time Management:** Managing one's own time and the time of others. **Social Perceptiveness:** Being aware of others' reactions and understanding why they react as they do. **Speaking:** Talking to others to convey information effectively. **Active Listening:** Giving full attention to what other people are saying, taking time to understand the points being made, asking questions as appropriate, and not interrupting at inappropriate times. **Writing:** Communicating effectively in writing as appropriate for the needs of the audience. **Management of Financial Resources:** Determining how money will be spent to get the work done and accounting for these expenditures. **GOE—Interest Area:** 14. Retail and Wholesale Sales and Service. **Work Group:** 14.03. General Sales. **Other Jobs in This Work Group:** Parts Salespersons; Real Estate Brokers; Retail Salespersons; Sales Representatives, Wholesale and Manufacturing, Except Technical and Scientific Products; Service Station Attendants. **PERSONALITY TYPE:** Enterprising. Enterprising occupations frequently involve starting up and carrying out projects. These occupations can involve leading people and making many decisions. They sometimes require risk taking and often deal with business.

EDUCATION/TRAINING PROGRAM(S)—Real Estate. **RELATED KNOWLEDGE/COURSES—Sales and Marketing:** Knowledge of principles and methods for showing, promoting, and selling products or services. This includes marketing strategy and tactics, product demonstrations, sales techniques, and sales control systems. **Customer and Personal Service:** Knowledge of principles and processes for providing customer and personal services. This includes customer needs assessment, meeting quality standards for services, and evaluation of customer satisfaction. **Clerical Practices:** Knowledge of administrative and clerical procedures and systems such as word processing, managing files and records, stenography and transcription, designing forms, and other office procedures and terminology. **Law and Government:** Knowledge of laws, legal codes, court procedures, precedents, government regulations, executive orders, agency rules, and the democratic political process. **Economics and Accounting:** Knowledge of economic and accounting principles and practices, the financial markets, banking, and the analysis and reporting of financial data. **Administration and Management:** Knowledge of business and management principles involved in strategic planning, resource allocation, human resources modeling, leadership technique, production methods, and coordination of people and resources.

Receptionists and Information Clerks

- ◎ Education/Training Required: Short-term on-the-job training
- ◎ Annual Earnings: $21,830
- ◎ Growth: 29.5%
- ◎ Annual Job Openings: 296,000
- ◎ Self-Employed: 1.2%
- ◎ Part-Time: 31.5%

Answer inquiries and obtain information for general public, customers, visitors, and other interested parties. Provide information regarding activities conducted at establishment and location of departments, offices, and employees within organization. Operate telephone switchboard to answer, screen, and forward calls, providing information, taking messages, and scheduling appointments. Receive payment and record receipts for services. Perform administrative support tasks such as proofreading, transcribing handwritten information, and operating calculators or computers to work with pay records, invoices, balance sheets, and other documents. Greet persons entering establishment, determine nature and purpose of visit, and direct or escort them to specific destinations. Hear and resolve complaints from customers and public. File and maintain records. Transmit information or documents to customers, using computer, mail, or facsimile machine. Schedule appointments and maintain and update appointment calendars. Analyze data to determine answers to questions from customers or members of the public. Provide information about establishment such as location of departments or offices, employees within the organization, or services provided. Keep a current record of staff members' whereabouts and availability. Collect, sort, distribute, and prepare mail, messages, and courier deliveries. Calculate and quote rates for tours, stocks, insurance policies, and other products and services. Take orders for merchandise or materials and send them to the proper departments to be filled. Process and prepare memos, correspondence, travel vouchers, or other documents. Schedule space and equipment for special programs and prepare lists of participants. Enroll individuals to participate in programs and notify them of their acceptance. **SKILLS—Service Orientation:** Actively looking for ways to help people. **Social Perceptiveness:** Being aware of others' reactions and understanding why they react as they do. **Active Listening:** Giving full attention to what other people are saying, taking time to understand the points being made, asking questions as appropriate, and not interrupting at inappropriate times. **Writing:** Communicating effectively in writing as appropriate for the needs of the audience. **Reading Comprehension:** Understanding written sentences and paragraphs in work-related documents. **Speaking:** Talking to others to convey information effectively. **Critical Thinking:** Using logic and reasoning to identify the strengths and weaknesses of alternative solutions, conclusions, or approaches to problems.

Learning Strategies: Selecting and using training/instructional methods and procedures appropriate for the situation when learning or teaching new things. **GOE—Interest Area:** 14. Retail and Wholesale Sales and Service. **Work Group:** 14.06. Customer Service. **Other Jobs in This Work Group:** Adjustment Clerks; Cashiers; Counter and Rental Clerks; Customer Service Representatives, Utilities; Gaming Change Persons and Booth Cashiers; Order Clerks. **PERSONALITY TYPE:** Conventional. Conventional occupations frequently involve following set procedures and routines. These occupations can include working with data and details more than with ideas. Usually there is a clear line of authority to follow.

EDUCATION/TRAINING PROGRAM(S)—General Office Occupations and Clerical Services; Health Unit Coordinator/Ward Clerk; Medical Reception/Receptionist; Receptionist. **RELATED KNOWLEDGE/COURSES—Customer and Personal Service:** Knowledge of principles and processes for providing customer and personal services. This includes customer needs assessment, meeting quality standards for services, and evaluation of customer satisfaction. **Clerical Practices:** Knowledge of administrative and clerical procedures and systems such as word processing, managing files and records, stenography and transcription, designing forms, and other office procedures and terminology. **Computers and Electronics:** Knowledge of circuit boards, processors, chips, electronic equipment, and computer hardware and software, including applications and programming. **Transportation:** Knowledge of principles and methods for moving people or goods by air, rail, sea, or road, including the relative costs and benefits. **Administration and Management:** Knowledge of business and management principles involved in strategic planning, resource allocation, human resources modeling, leadership technique, production methods, and coordination of people and resources. **English Language:** Knowledge of the structure and content of the English language, including the meaning and spelling of words, rules of composition, and grammar.

Recreational Vehicle Service Technicians

- Education/Training Required: Long-term on-the-job training
- Annual Earnings: $28,980
- Growth: 21.8%
- Annual Job Openings: 4,000
- Self-Employed: 1.2%
- Part-Time: 14.2%

Diagnose, inspect, adjust, repair, or overhaul recreational vehicles, including travel trailers. May specialize in maintaining gas, electrical, hydraulic, plumbing, or chassis/towing systems as well as repairing generators, appliances, and interior components. Confer with customers, read work orders, and examine vehicles needing repair in order to determine the nature and extent of damage. Connect electrical systems to outside power sources and activate switches to test the operation of appliances and light fixtures. Connect water hoses to inlet pipes of plumbing systems and test operation of toilets and sinks. Examine or test operation of parts or systems that have been repaired to ensure completeness of repairs. Inspect recreational vehicles to diagnose problems and then perform necessary adjustment, repair, or overhaul. List parts needed, estimate costs, and plan work procedures, using parts lists, technical manuals, and diagrams. Locate and repair frayed wiring, broken connections, or incorrect wiring, using ohmmeters, soldering irons, tape, and hand tools. Remove damaged exterior panels and repair and replace structural frame members. Repair leaks with caulking compound or replace pipes, using pipe wrenches. Repair plumbing and propane gas lines, using caulking compounds and plastic or copper pipe. Open and close doors, windows, and drawers to test their operation, trimming edges to fit as necessary. Refinish wood surfaces on cabinets, doors, moldings, and floors, using power sanders, putty, spray equipment, brushes, paints, or varnishes. Reset hardware, using chisels, mallets, and screwdrivers. Seal open sides of modular units to prepare them for shipment, using polyethylene sheets, nails, and hammers. **SKILLS—Installation:** Installing equipment, machines, wiring, or programs to meet specifications. **Repairing:** Repairing machines or systems by using the needed tools. **Troubleshooting:** Determining causes of operating errors and deciding what to do about them. **Equipment Maintenance:** Performing routine maintenance on equipment and determining when and what kind of maintenance is needed. **Quality Control Analysis:** Conducting tests and inspections of products, services, or processes to evaluate quality or performance. **Systems Evaluation:** Identifying measures or indicators of system performance and the actions needed to improve or correct performance relative to the goals of the system. **Equipment Selection:** Determining the kind of tools and equipment needed to do a job. **Technology Design:** Generating or adapting equipment and technology to serve user needs. **Management of Material Resources:** Obtaining and seeing to the appropriate use of equipment, facilities, and materials needed to do certain work. **GOE—Interest Area:** 13. Manufacturing. **Work Group:** 13.14. Vehicle and Facility Mechanical Work. **Other Jobs in This Work Group:** Aircraft Body and Bonded Structure Repairers; Aircraft Engine Specialists; Aircraft Rigging Assemblers; Aircraft Structure Assemblers, Precision; Aircraft Systems Assemblers, Precision; Airframe-and-Power-Plant Mechanics; Automotive Body and Related Repairers; Automotive Glass Installers and Repairers; Automotive Master Mechanics; Automotive Specialty Technicians; Bus and Truck Mechanics and Diesel Engine Specialists; Farm Equipment Mechanics; Fiberglass Laminators and Fabricators; Mobile Heavy Equipment Mechanics, Except Engines; Motorboat Mechanics; Motorcycle Mechanics; Outdoor Power Equipment and Other Small Engine Mechanics; Rail Car Repairers; Tire Repairers and Changers. **PERSONALITY TYPE:** Realistic. Realistic occupations frequently involve work activities that include practical, hands-on problems and solutions. These occupations often deal with plants, animals, and real-world materials like wood, tools, and machinery. Many of the occupations require working outside and do not involve a lot of paperwork or working closely with others.

EDUCATION/TRAINING PROGRAM(S)—Vehicle Maintenance and Repair Technologies, Other. **RELATED KNOWLEDGE/COURSES**—**Building and Construction:** Knowledge of the materials, methods, and tools involved in the construction or repair of houses, buildings, or other structures such as highways and roads. **Mechanical Devices:** Knowledge of machines and tools, including their designs, uses, repair, and maintenance. **Design:** Knowledge of design techniques, tools, and principles involved in production of precision technical plans, blueprints, drawings, and models. **Engineering and Technology:** Knowledge of the practical application of engineering science and technology. This includes applying principles, techniques, procedures, and equipment to the design and production of various goods and services. **Physics:** Knowledge and prediction of physical principles and laws and their interrelationships and applications to understanding fluid, material, and atmospheric dynamics and mechanical, electrical, atomic, and subatomic structures and processes.

Refractory Materials Repairers, Except Brickmasons

- Education/Training Required: Short-term on-the-job training
- Annual Earnings: $37,640
- Growth: 16.3%
- Annual Job Openings: 155,000
- Self-Employed: 6.1%
- Part-Time: 2.1%

Build or repair furnaces, kilns, cupolas, boilers, converters, ladles, soaking pits, ovens, etc., using refractory materials. Bolt sections of wooden molds together, using wrenches, and line molds with paper to prevent clay from sticking to molds. Chip slag from linings of ladles or remove linings when beyond repair, using hammers and chisels. Disassemble molds and cut, chip, and smooth clay structures such as floaters, drawbars, and L-blocks. Drill holes in furnace walls, bolt overlapping layers of plastic to walls, and hammer surfaces to compress layers into solid sheets. Dry and bake new linings by placing inverted linings over burners, by building fires in ladles, or by using blowtorches. Dump and tamp clay in molds, using tamping tools. Fasten stopper heads to rods with metal pins to assemble refractory stoppers used to plug pouring nozzles of steel ladles. Install clay structures in melting tanks and drawing kilns to control the flow and temperature of molten glass, using hoists and hand tools. Measure furnace walls to determine dimensions and then cut required number of sheets from plastic block, using saws. Mix specified amounts of sand, clay, mortar powder, and water to form refractory clay or mortar, using shovels or mixing machines. Reline or repair ladles and pouring spouts with refractory clay, using trowels. Remove worn or damaged plastic block refractory linings of furnaces, using hand tools. Spread mortar on stopper heads and rods, using trowels, and slide brick sleeves over rods to form refractory jackets. Tighten locknuts holding refractory stopper assemblies together, spread mortar on jackets to seal sleeve joints, and dry mortar in ovens. Climb scaffolding, carrying hoses, and spray surfaces of cupolas with refractory mixtures, using spray equipment. Install preformed metal scaffolding in interiors of cupolas, using hand tools. Transfer clay structures to curing ovens, melting tanks, and drawing kilns, using forklifts. **SKILLS— Repairing:** Repairing machines or systems by using the needed tools. **Installation:** Installing equipment, machines, wiring, or programs to meet specifications. **Operation and Control:** Controlling operations of equipment or systems. **Equipment Maintenance:** Performing routine maintenance on equipment and determining when and what kind of maintenance is needed. **Troubleshooting:** Determining causes of operating errors and deciding what to do about them. **Science:** Using scientific rules and methods to solve problems. **Equipment Selection:** Determining the kind of tools and equipment needed to do a job. **Operation Monitoring:** Watching gauges, dials, or other indicators to make sure a machine is working properly. **GOE—Interest Area:** 02. Architecture and Construction. **Work Group:** 02.04. Construction Crafts. **Other Jobs in This Work Group:** Boat Builders and Shipwrights; Boilermakers; Brattice Builders; Brickmasons and Blockmasons; Carpet Installers; Ceiling Tile Installers; Cement Masons and Concrete Finishers; Commercial Divers; Construction Carpenters; Crane and Tower Operators; Dragline Operators; Drywall Installers; Electricians; Fence Erectors; Floor Layers, Except Carpet, Wood, and Hard Tiles; Floor Sanders and Finishers; Glaziers; Grader, Bulldozer, and Scraper Operators; Hazardous Materials Removal Workers; Insulation Workers, Floor, Ceiling, and Wall; Insulation Workers, Mechanical; Manufactured Building and Mobile Home Installers; Operating Engineers; Painters, Construction and Maintenance; Paperhangers; Paving, Surfacing, and Tamping Equipment Operators; Pile-Driver Operators; Pipe Fitters; Pipelayers; Pipelaying Fitters; Plasterers and Stucco Masons; Plumbers; Rail-Track Laying and Maintenance Equipment Operators; Reinforcing Iron and Rebar Workers; Riggers; Roofers; Rough Carpenters; Security and Fire Alarm Systems Installers; Segmental Pavers; Sheet Metal Workers; Ship Carpenters and Joiners; Stone Cutters and Carvers; Stonemasons; Structural Iron and Steel Workers; Tapers; Terrazzo Workers and Finishers; Tile and Marble Setters. **PERSONALITY TYPE: Realistic.** Realistic occupations frequently involve work activities that include practical, hands-on problems and solutions. These occupations often deal with plants, animals, and real-world materials like wood, tools, and machinery. Many of the occupations require working outside and do not involve a lot of paperwork or working closely with others.

EDUCATION/TRAINING PROGRAM(S)— Industrial Mechanics and Maintenance Technology. **RELATED KNOWLEDGE/COURSES—Building and Construction:** Knowledge of the materials, methods, and tools involved in the construction or repair of houses, buildings, or other structures such as highways and roads. **Mechanical Devices:** Knowledge of machines and tools, including their designs, uses, repair, and maintenance. **Production and Processing:** Knowledge of raw materials, production processes, quality control, costs, and other techniques for maximizing the effective manufacture and distribution of goods. **Engineering and Technology:** Knowledge of the practical application of engineering science and technology. This includes applying principles, techniques, procedures, and equipment to the design and production of various goods and services. **Chemistry:** Knowledge of the chemical composition, structure, and properties of substances and of the chemical processes and transformations that they undergo. This includes uses of chemicals and their danger signs, production techniques, and disposal methods. **Fine Arts:** Knowledge of the theory and techniques required to compose, produce, and perform works of music, dance, the visual arts, drama, and sculpture.

Refrigeration Mechanics

- Education/Training Required: Long-term on-the-job training
- Annual Earnings: $36,260
- Growth: 31.8%
- Annual Job Openings: 35,000
- Self-Employed: 15.4%
- Part-Time: 3.1%

Install and repair industrial and commercial refrigerating systems. Braze or solder parts to repair defective joints and leaks. Observe and test system operation, using gauges and instruments. Test lines, components, and connections for leaks. Dismantle malfunctioning systems and test components, using electrical, mechanical, and pneumatic testing equipment. Adjust or replace worn or defective mechanisms and parts, and reassemble repaired systems. Read blueprints to determine location, size, capacity, and type of components needed to build refrigeration system. Supervise and instruct assistants. Install wiring to connect components to an electric power source. Perform mechanical overhauls and refrigerant reclaiming. Cut, bend, thread, and connect pipe to functional components and water, power, or refrigeration system. Adjust valves according to specifications and charge system with proper type of refrigerant by pumping the specified gas or fluid into the system. Estimate, order, pick up, deliver, and install materials and supplies needed to maintain equipment in good working condition. Install expansion and control valves, using acetylene torches and wrenches. Mount compressor, condenser, and other components in specified locations on frames, using hand tools and acetylene welding equipment. Keep records of repairs and replacements made and causes of malfunctions. Lay out reference points for installation of structural and functional components, using measuring instruments. Schedule work with customers and initiate work orders, house requisitions, and orders from stock. Fabricate and assemble structural and functional components of refrigeration system, using hand tools, power tools, and welding equipment. Lift and align components into position, using hoist or block and tackle. Drill holes and install mounting brackets and hangers into floor and walls of building. Insulate shells and cabinets of systems. **SKILLS—Installation:** Installing equipment, machines, wiring, or programs to meet specifications. **Repairing:** Repairing machines or systems by using the needed tools. **Equipment Maintenance:** Performing routine maintenance on equipment and determining when and what kind of maintenance is needed. **Operation Monitoring:** Watching gauges, dials, or other indicators to make sure a machine is working properly. **Troubleshooting:** Determining causes of operating errors and deciding what to do about them. **Systems Analysis:** Determining how a system should work and how changes in conditions, operations, and the environment will affect outcomes. **Systems Evaluation:** Identifying measures or indicators of system performance and the actions needed to improve or correct performance relative to the goals of the system. **Science:** Using scientific rules and methods to solve problems. **GOE—Interest Area:** 02. Architecture and Construction. **Work Group:** 02.05. Systems and Equipment Installation, Maintenance, and Repair. **Other Jobs in This Work Group:** Central Office and PBX Installers and Repairers; Communication Equipment Mechanics, Installers, and Repairers; Electric Meter Installers and Repairers; Electrical and Electronics Repairers, Powerhouse, Substation, and Relay; Electrical Power-Line Installers and Repairers; Elevator Installers and Repairers; Frame Wirers, Central Office; Heating and Air Conditioning Mechanics; Home Appliance Installers; Maintenance and Repair Workers, General; Meter Mechanics; Station Installers and Repairers, Telephone; Telecommunications Facility Examiners; Telecommunications Line Installers and Repairers. **PERSONALITY TYPE:** Realistic. Realistic occupations frequently involve work activities that include practical, hands-on problems and solutions. These occupations often deal with plants, animals, and real-world materials like wood, tools, and machinery. Many of the occupations require working outside and do not involve a lot of paperwork or working closely with others.

EDUCATION/TRAINING PROGRAM(S)— Heating, Air Conditioning, and Refrigeration Technology/Technician (ACH/ACR/ACHR/HRAC/

HVAC/AC Technology); Heating, Air Conditioning, Ventilation, and Refrigeration Maintenance Technology/Technician (HAC, HACR, HVAC, HVACR); Solar Energy Technology/Technician. **RELATED KNOWLEDGE/COURSES—Building and Construction:** Knowledge of the materials, methods, and tools involved in the construction or repair of houses, buildings, or other structures such as highways and roads. **Mechanical Devices:** Knowledge of machines and tools, including their designs, uses, repair, and maintenance. **Engineering and Technology:** Knowledge of the practical application of engineering science and technology. This includes applying principles, techniques, procedures, and equipment to the design and production of various goods and services. **Customer and Personal Service:** Knowledge of principles and processes for providing customer and personal services. This includes customer needs assessment, meeting quality standards for services, and evaluation of customer satisfaction. **Physics:** Knowledge and prediction of physical principles and laws and their interrelationships and applications to understanding fluid, material, and atmospheric dynamics and mechanical, electrical, atomic, and subatomic structures and processes. **Design:** Knowledge of design techniques, tools, and principles involved in production of precision technical plans, blueprints, drawings, and models.

Refuse and Recyclable Material Collectors

- ◎ Education/Training Required: Short-term on-the-job training
- ◎ Annual Earnings: $25,760
- ◎ Growth: 17.6%
- ◎ Annual Job Openings: 42,000
- ◎ Self-Employed: 1.8%
- ◎ Part-Time: 12.1%

Collect and dump refuse or recyclable materials from containers into truck. May drive truck. Inspect trucks prior to beginning routes to ensure safe operating condition. Refuel trucks and add other necessary fluids, such as oil. Fill out any needed reports for defective equipment. Drive to disposal sites to empty trucks that have been filled. Drive trucks along established routes through residential streets and alleys or through business and industrial areas. Operate equipment that compresses the collected refuse. Operate automated or semi-automated hoisting devices that raise refuse bins and dump contents into openings in truck bodies. Dismount garbage trucks to collect garbage and remount trucks to ride to the next collection point. Communicate with dispatchers concerning delays, unsafe sites, accidents, equipment breakdowns, and other maintenance problems. Keep informed of road and weather conditions to determine how routes will be affected. Tag garbage or recycling containers to inform customers of problems such as excess garbage or inclusion of items that are not permitted. Clean trucks and compactor bodies after routes have been completed. Sort items set out for recycling and throw materials into designated truck compartments. Organize schedules for refuse collection. **SKILLS—Equipment Maintenance:** Performing routine maintenance on equipment and determining when and what kind of maintenance is needed. **Operation Monitoring:** Watching gauges, dials, or other indicators to make sure a machine is working properly. **Operation and Control:** Controlling operations of equipment or systems. **Social Perceptiveness:** Being aware of others' reactions and understanding why they react as they do. **Coordination:** Adjusting actions in relation to others' actions. **Repairing:** Repairing machines or systems by using the needed tools. **Troubleshooting:** Determining causes of operating errors and deciding what to do about them. **Learning Strategies:** Selecting and using training/instructional methods and procedures appropriate for the situation when learning or teaching new things. **GOE—Interest Area:** 13. Manufacturing. **Work Group:** 13.17. Loading, Moving, Hoisting, and Conveying. **Other Jobs in This Work Group:** Conveyor Operators and Tenders; Freight, Stock, and Material Movers, Hand; Hoist and Winch Operators; Industrial Truck and Tractor Operators; Irradiated-Fuel Handlers; Machine Feeders and Offbearers; Packers and Packagers, Hand; Pump Operators, Except Wellhead Pumpers; Tank Car, Truck, and Ship Loaders. **PERSONALITY TYPE:** Realistic. Realistic occupations frequently involve work activities that include practical, hands-on problems and solutions. These occupations often deal with plants, animals, and real-world materials like wood, tools, and machinery. Many of the occupations require working outside and do not involve a lot of paperwork or working closely with others.

EDUCATION/TRAINING PROGRAM(S)—No data available. **RELATED KNOWLEDGE/COURSES—Transportation:** Knowledge of principles and methods for moving people or goods by air, rail, sea, or road, including the relative costs and benefits. **Customer and Personal Service:** Knowledge of principles and processes for providing customer and personal services. This includes customer needs assessment, meeting quality standards for services, and evaluation of customer satisfaction. **Public Safety and Security:** Knowledge of relevant equipment, policies, procedures, and strategies to promote effective local, state, or national security operations for the protection of people, data, property, and institutions. **Education and Training:** Knowledge of principles and methods for curriculum and training design, teaching and instruction for individuals and groups, and the measurement of training effects. **Production and Processing:** Knowledge of raw materials, production processes, quality control, costs, and other techniques for maximizing the effective manufacture and distribution of goods. **Mechanical Devices:** Knowledge of machines and tools, including their designs, uses, repair, and maintenance.

Registered Nurses

- Education/Training Required: Associate degree
- Annual Earnings: $52,330
- Growth: 27.3%
- Annual Job Openings: 215,000
- Self-Employed: 1.2%
- Part-Time: 22.0%

Assess patient health problems and needs, develop and implement nursing care plans, and maintain medical records. Administer nursing care to ill, injured, convalescent, or disabled patients. May advise patients on health maintenance and disease prevention or provide case management. Licensing or registration required. Includes advance practice nurses such as nurse practitioners, clinical nurse specialists, certified nurse midwives, and certified registered nurse anesthetists. Advanced practice nursing is practiced by RNs who have specialized formal, post-basic education and who function in highly autonomous and specialized roles. Maintain accurate, detailed reports and records. Monitor, record, and report symptoms and changes in patients' conditions. Record patients' medical information and vital signs. Modify patient treatment plans as indicated by patients' responses and conditions. Consult and coordinate with health-care team members to assess, plan, implement, and evaluate patient care plans. Order, interpret, and evaluate diagnostic tests to identify and assess patient's condition. Monitor all aspects of patient care, including diet and physical activity. Direct and supervise less-skilled nursing/health-care personnel or supervise a particular unit on one shift. Prepare patients for, and assist with, examinations and treatments. Observe nurses and visit patients to ensure that proper nursing care is provided. Assess the needs of individuals, families, and/or communities, including assessment of individuals' home and/or work environments, to identify potential health or safety problems. Instruct individuals, families, and other groups on topics such as health education, disease prevention, and childbirth and develop health improvement programs. Prepare rooms, sterile instruments, equipment, and supplies, and ensure that stock of supplies is maintained. Inform physician of patient's condition during anesthesia. Deliver infants and provide prenatal and postpartum care and treatment under obstetrician's supervision. Administer local, inhalation, intravenous, and other anesthetics. Provide health care, first aid, immunizations, and assistance in convalescence and rehabilitation in locations such as schools, hospitals, and industry. Perform physical examinations, make tentative diagnoses, and treat patients en route to hospitals or at disaster site triage centers. Conduct specified laboratory tests. Hand items to surgeons during operations. Prescribe or recommend drugs, medical devices, or other forms of treatment, such as physical therapy, inhalation therapy, or related therapeutic procedures. Direct and coordinate infection control programs, advising and consulting with specified personnel about necessary precautions. **SKILLS—Social Perceptive-**

R

ness: Being aware of others' reactions and understanding why they react as they do. **Service Orientation:** Actively looking for ways to help people. **Instructing:** Teaching others how to do something. **Time Management:** Managing one's own time and the time of others. **Learning Strategies:** Selecting and using training/instructional methods and procedures appropriate for the situation when learning or teaching new things. **Critical Thinking:** Using logic and reasoning to identify the strengths and weaknesses of alternative solutions, conclusions, or approaches to problems. **Coordination:** Adjusting actions in relation to others' actions. **Active Learning:** Understanding the implications of new information for both current and future problem-solving and decision-making. **Monitoring:** Monitoring or assessing your performance or that of other individuals or organizations to make improvements or take corrective action. **Negotiation:** Bringing others together and trying to reconcile differences. **GOE—Interest Area:** 08. Health Science. **Work Group:** 08.02. Medicine and Surgery. **Other Jobs in This Work Group:** Anesthesiologists; Family and General Practitioners; Internists, General; Medical Assistants; Medical Transcriptionists; Obstetricians and Gynecologists; Pediatricians, General; Pharmacists; Pharmacy Aides; Pharmacy Technicians; Physician Assistants; Psychiatrists; Surgeons; Surgical Technologists. **PERSONALITY TYPE:** Social. Social occupations frequently involve working with, communicating with, and teaching people. These occupations often involve helping or providing service to others.

EDUCATION/TRAINING PROGRAM(S)—Adult Health Nurse/Nursing; Clinical Nurse Specialist; Critical Care Nursing; Family Practice Nurse/Nurse Practitioner; Maternal/Child Health and Neonatal Nurse/Nursing; Nurse Anesthetist; Nurse Midwife/Nursing Midwifery; Nursing—Registered Nurse Training (RN, ASN, BSN, MSN); Nursing Science (MS, PhD); Nursing, Other; Occupational and Environmental Health Nursing; Pediatric Nurse/Nursing; Perioperative/Operating Room and Surgical Nurse/Nursing; Psychiatric/Mental Health Nurse/Nursing; Public Health/Community Nurse/Nursing. **RELATED KNOWLEDGE/COURSES**—**Psychology:** Knowledge of human behavior and performance; individual differences in ability, personality, and interests; learning and motivation; psychological

research methods; and the assessment and treatment of behavioral and affective disorders. **Medicine and Dentistry:** Knowledge of the information and techniques needed to diagnose and treat human injuries, diseases, and deformities. This includes symptoms, treatment alternatives, drug properties and interactions, and preventive health-care measures. **Customer and Personal Service:** Knowledge of principles and processes for providing customer and personal services. This includes customer needs assessment, meeting quality standards for services, and evaluation of customer satisfaction. **Therapy and Counseling:** Knowledge of principles, methods, and procedures for diagnosis, treatment, and rehabilitation of physical and mental dysfunctions and for career counseling and guidance. **Sociology and Anthropology:** Knowledge of group behavior and dynamics, societal trends and influences, human migrations, ethnicity, and cultures and their history and origins. **Biology:** Knowledge of plant and animal organisms and their tissues, cells, functions, interdependencies, and interactions with each other and the environment.

Reservation and Transportation Ticket Agents

- ◉ Education/Training Required: Short-term on-the-job training
- ◉ Annual Earnings: $27,750
- ◉ Growth: 12.2%
- ◉ Annual Job Openings: 35,000
- ◉ Self-Employed: 1.1%
- ◉ Part-Time: 15.7%

Make and confirm reservations for passengers and sell tickets for transportation agencies such as airlines, bus companies, railroads, and steamship lines. May check baggage and direct passengers to designated concourse, pier, or track. Arranges reservations and routing for passengers at request of ticket agent. Examines passenger ticket or pass to direct passenger to specified area for loading. Plans route and computes ticket cost, using schedules, rate books, and computer.

Reads coded data on tickets to ascertain destination, marks tickets, and assigns boarding pass. Assists passengers requiring special assistance to board or depart conveyance. Informs travel agents in other locations of space reserved or available. Sells travel insurance. Announces arrival and departure information, using public-address system. Telephones customer or ticket agent to advise of changes with travel conveyance or to confirm reservation. Sells and assembles tickets for transmittal or mailing to customers. Answers inquiries made to travel agencies or transportation firms, such as airlines, bus companies, railroad companies, and steamship lines. Checks baggage and directs passenger to designated location for loading. Assigns specified space to customers and maintains computerized inventory of passenger space available. Determines whether space is available on travel dates requested by customer. **SKILLS—Service Orientation:** Actively looking for ways to help people. **Active Listening:** Giving full attention to what other people are saying, taking time to understand the points being made, asking questions as appropriate, and not interrupting at inappropriate times. **Speaking:** Talking to others to convey information effectively. **GOE—Interest Area:** 09. Hospitality, Tourism, and Recreation. **Work Group:** 09.03. Hospitality and Travel Services. **Other Jobs in This Work Group:** Baggage Porters and Bellhops; Concierges; Flight Attendants; Hotel, Motel, and Resort Desk Clerks; Janitors and Cleaners, Except Maids and Housekeeping Cleaners; Maids and Housekeeping Cleaners; Tour Guides and Escorts; Transportation Attendants, Except Flight Attendants and Baggage Porters; Travel Agents; Travel Clerks; Travel Guides. **PERSONALITY TYPE:** Conventional. Conventional occupations frequently involve following set procedures and routines. These occupations can include working with data and details more than with ideas. Usually there is a clear line of authority to follow.

EDUCATION/TRAINING PROGRAM(S)—Selling Skills and Sales Operations; Tourism and Travel Services Marketing Operations; Tourism Promotion Operations. **RELATED KNOWLEDGE/COURSES—Geography:** Knowledge of principles and methods for describing the features of land, sea, and air masses, including their physical characteristics; locations; interrelationships; and distribution of plant, animal, and human life. **Transportation:** Knowledge of

principles and methods for moving people or goods by air, rail, sea, or road, including the relative costs and benefits. **Clerical Practices:** Knowledge of administrative and clerical procedures and systems such as word processing, managing files and records, stenography and transcription, designing forms, and other office procedures and terminology. **Sales and Marketing:** Knowledge of principles and methods for showing, promoting, and selling products or services. This includes marketing strategy and tactics, product demonstrations, sales techniques, and sales control systems. **Computers and Electronics:** Knowledge of circuit boards, processors, chips, electronic equipment, and computer hardware and software, including applications and programming. **Telecommunications:** Knowledge of transmission, broadcasting, switching, control, and operation of telecommunications systems.

Residential Advisors

- ◎ Education/Training Required: Moderate-term on-the-job training
- ◎ Annual Earnings: $21,430
- ◎ Growth: 33.6%
- ◎ Annual Job Openings: 12,000
- ◎ Self-Employed: 0.7%
- ◎ Part-Time: 22.0%

Coordinate activities for residents of boarding schools, college fraternities or sororities, college dormitories, or similar establishments. Order supplies and determine need for maintenance, repairs, and furnishings. May maintain household records and assign rooms. May refer residents to counseling resources if needed. Enforce rules and regulations to ensure the smooth and orderly operation of dormitory programs. Provide emergency first aid and summon medical assistance when necessary. Mediate interpersonal problems between residents. Administer, coordinate, or recommend disciplinary and corrective actions. Communicate with other staff to resolve problems with individual students. Counsel students in the handling of issues such as family, financial, and educational problems. Make regular rounds to ensure that residents and areas are safe and secure. Observe students in order to detect and report unusual behavior.

Determine the need for facility maintenance and repair; notify appropriate personnel. Collaborate with counselors to develop counseling programs that address the needs of individual students. Develop program plans for individuals or assist in plan development. Hold regular meetings with each assigned unit. Direct and participate in on- and off-campus recreational activities for residents of institutions, boarding schools, fraternities or sororities, children's homes, or similar establishments. Assign rooms to students. Provide requested information on students' progress and the development of case plans. Confer with medical personnel to better understand the backgrounds and needs of individual residents. Answer telephones and route calls or deliver messages. Supervise participants in work-study programs. Process contract cancellations for students who are unable to follow residence hall policies and procedures. Sort and distribute mail. Supervise the activities of housekeeping personnel. Order supplies for facilities. Supervise students' housekeeping work to ensure that it is done properly. **SKILLS—Social Perceptiveness:** Being aware of others' reactions and understanding why they react as they do. **Monitoring:** Monitoring or assessing your performance or that of other individuals or organizations to make improvements or take corrective action. **Management of Personnel Resources:** Motivating, developing, and directing people as they work, identifying the best people for the job. **Service Orientation:** Actively looking for ways to help people. **Persuasion:** Persuading others to change their minds or behavior. **Time Management:** Managing one's own time and the time of others. **Negotiation:** Bringing others together and trying to reconcile differences. **Active Listening:** Giving full attention to what other people are saying, taking time to understand the points being made, asking questions as appropriate, and not interrupting at inappropriate times. **Learning Strategies:** Selecting and using training/instructional methods and procedures appropriate for the situation when learning or teaching new things. **GOE—Interest Area:** 10. Human Service. **Work Group:** 10.01. Counseling and Social Work. **Other Jobs in This Work Group:** Child, Family, and School Social Workers; Clinical Psychologists; Counseling Psychologists; Marriage and Family Therapists; Medical and Public Health Social Workers; Mental Health and Substance Abuse Social Workers; Mental Health Counselors; Probation Officers and Correctional Treatment Specialists; Rehabilitation Counselors; Social and Human Service Assistants; Substance Abuse and Behavioral Disorder Counselors. **PERSONALITY TYPE:** Social. Social occupations frequently involve working with, communicating with, and teaching people. These occupations often involve helping or providing service to others.

EDUCATION/TRAINING PROGRAM(S)— Hotel/Motel Administration/Management. **RELATED KNOWLEDGE/COURSES—Therapy and Counseling:** Knowledge of principles, methods, and procedures for diagnosis, treatment, and rehabilitation of physical and mental dysfunctions and for career counseling and guidance. **Psychology:** Knowledge of human behavior and performance; individual differences in ability, personality, and interests; learning and motivation; psychological research methods; and the assessment and treatment of behavioral and affective disorders. **Philosophy and Theology:** Knowledge of different philosophical systems and religions. This includes their basic principles, values, ethics, ways of thinking, customs, and practices and their impact on human culture. **Sociology and Anthropology:** Knowledge of group behavior and dynamics, societal trends and influences, human migrations, ethnicity, and cultures and their history and origins. **Customer and Personal Service:** Knowledge of principles and processes for providing customer and personal services. This includes customer needs assessment, meeting quality standards for services, and evaluation of customer satisfaction. **Personnel and Human Resources:** Knowledge of principles and procedures for personnel recruitment, selection, training, compensation and benefits, labor relations and negotiation, and personnel information systems.

Respiratory Therapists

- Education/Training Required: Associate degree
- Annual Earnings: $43,140
- Growth: 34.8%
- Annual Job Openings: 10,000
- Self-Employed: 0%
- Part-Time: 15.5%

Assess, treat, and care for patients with breathing disorders. Assume primary responsibility for all respiratory care modalities, including the supervision of respiratory therapy technicians. Initiate and conduct therapeutic procedures; maintain patient records; and select, assemble, check, and operate equipment. Set up and operate devices such as mechanical ventilators, therapeutic gas administration apparatus, environmental control systems, and aerosol generators, following specified parameters of treatment. Provide emergency care, including artificial respiration, external cardiac massage, and assistance with cardiopulmonary resuscitation. Determine requirements for treatment, such as type, method and duration of therapy; precautions to be taken; and medication and dosages, compatible with physicians' orders. Monitor patient's physiological responses to therapy, such as vital signs, arterial blood gases, and blood chemistry changes, and consult with physician if adverse reactions occur. Read prescription, measure arterial blood gases, and review patient information to assess patient condition. Work as part of a team of physicians, nurses, and other health-care professionals to manage patient care. Enforce safety rules and ensure careful adherence to physicians' orders. Maintain charts that contain patients' pertinent identification and therapy information. Inspect, clean, test, and maintain respiratory therapy equipment to ensure equipment is functioning safely and efficiently, ordering repairs when necessary. Educate patients and their families about their conditions and teach appropriate disease management techniques, such as breathing exercises and the use of medications and respiratory equipment. Explain treatment procedures to patients to gain cooperation and allay fears. Relay blood analysis results to a physician. Perform pulmonary function and adjust equipment to obtain optimum results in therapy. Perform bronchopulmonary drainage and assist or instruct patients in performance of breathing exercises. Demonstrate respiratory care procedures to trainees and other health-care personnel. Teach, train, supervise, and utilize the assistance of students, respiratory therapy technicians, and assistants. Use a variety of testing techniques to assist doctors in cardiac and pulmonary research and to diagnose disorders. Make emergency visits to resolve equipment problems. Conduct tests such as electrocardiograms, stress testing, and lung capacity tests to evaluate patients' cardiopulmonary functions. **SKILLS—Instructing:** Teaching others how to do something. **Science:** Using scientific rules and methods to solve problems. **Active Learning:** Understanding the implications of new information for both current and future problem-solving and decision-making. **Service Orientation:** Actively looking for ways to help people. **Reading Comprehension:** Understanding written sentences and paragraphs in work-related documents. **Time Management:** Managing one's own time and the time of others. **Troubleshooting:** Determining causes of operating errors and deciding what to do about them. **Mathematics:** Using mathematics to solve problems. **GOE—Interest Area:** 08. Health Science. **Work Group:** 08.07. Medical Therapy. **Other Jobs in This Work Group:** Audiologists; Massage Therapists; Occupational Therapist Aides; Occupational Therapist Assistants; Occupational Therapists; Physical Therapist Aides; Physical Therapist Assistants; Physical Therapists; Radiation Therapists; Recreational Therapists; Respiratory Therapy Technicians; Speech-Language Pathologists. **PERSONALITY TYPE:** Investigative. Investigative occupations frequently involve working with ideas and require an extensive amount of thinking. These occupations can involve searching for facts and figuring out problems mentally.

EDUCATION/TRAINING PROGRAM(S)—Respiratory Care Therapy/Therapist. **RELATED KNOWLEDGE/COURSES—Medicine and Dentistry:** Knowledge of the information and techniques needed to diagnose and treat human injuries, diseases, and deformities. This includes symptoms, treatment alternatives, drug properties and interactions, and preventive health-care measures. **Customer and Personal Service:** Knowledge of principles and processes for providing customer and personal services. This includes customer needs assessment, meeting quality standards for services, and evaluation of customer satisfaction. **Psychology:** Knowledge of human behavior and performance; individual differences in ability, personality, and interests; learning and motivation; psychological research methods; and the assessment and treatment of behavioral and affective disorders. **Biology:** Knowledge of plant and animal organisms and their tissues, cells, functions, interdependencies, and interactions with each other and the environment.

Education and Training: Knowledge of principles and methods for curriculum and training design, teaching and instruction for individuals and groups, and the measurement of training effects. **Chemistry:** Knowledge of the chemical composition, structure, and properties of substances and of the chemical processes and transformations that they undergo. This includes uses of chemicals and their danger signs, production techniques, and disposal methods.

Respiratory Therapy Technicians

- Education/Training Required: Postsecondary vocational training
- Annual Earnings: $36,740
- Growth: 34.2%
- Annual Job Openings: 5,000
- Self-Employed: 0%
- Part-Time: 23.0%

Provide specific, well-defined respiratory care procedures under the direction of respiratory therapists and physicians. Use ventilators and various oxygen devices and aerosol and breathing treatments in the provision of respiratory therapy. Work with patients in areas such as the emergency room, neonatal/pediatric intensive care, and surgical intensive care, treating conditions including emphysema, chronic bronchitis, asthma, cystic fibrosis, and pneumonia. Read and evaluate physicians' orders and patients' chart information to determine patients' condition and treatment protocols. Keep records of patients' therapy, completing all necessary forms. Set equipment controls to regulate the flow of oxygen, gases, mists, or aerosols. Provide respiratory care involving the application of well-defined therapeutic techniques under the supervision of a respiratory therapist and a physician. Assess patients' response to treatments and modify treatments according to protocol if necessary. Prepare and test devices such as mechanical ventilators, therapeutic gas administration apparatus, environmental control systems, aerosol generators, and EKG machines. Monitor patients during treatment and report any unusual reactions to the respiratory therapist. Explain treatment procedures to patients. Clean, sterilize, check, and maintain respiratory therapy equipment. Perform diagnostic procedures to assess the severity of respiratory dysfunction in patients. Follow and enforce safety rules applying to equipment. Administer breathing and oxygen procedures such as intermittent positive pressure breathing treatments, ultrasonic nebulizer treatments, and incentive spirometer treatments. Recommend and review bedside procedures, X rays, and laboratory tests. Interview and examine patients to collect clinical data. Teach patients how to use respiratory equipment at home. Teach or oversee other workers who provide respiratory care services. **SKILLS—Troubleshooting:** Determining causes of operating errors and deciding what to do about them. **Operation Monitoring:** Watching gauges, dials, or other indicators to make sure a machine is working properly. **Time Management:** Managing one's own time and the time of others. **Social Perceptiveness:** Being aware of others' reactions and understanding why they react as they do. **Operation and Control:** Controlling operations of equipment or systems. **Learning Strategies:** Selecting and using training/instructional methods and procedures appropriate for the situation when learning or teaching new things. **Instructing:** Teaching others how to do something. **Equipment Maintenance:** Performing routine maintenance on equipment and determining when and what kind of maintenance is needed. **GOE—Interest Area:** 08. Health Science. **Work Group:** 08.07. Medical Therapy. **Other Jobs in This Work Group:** Audiologists; Massage Therapists; Occupational Therapist Aides; Occupational Therapist Assistants; Occupational Therapists; Physical Therapist Aides; Physical Therapist Assistants; Physical Therapists; Radiation Therapists; Recreational Therapists; Respiratory Therapists; Speech-Language Pathologists. **PERSONALITY TYPE:** No data available.

EDUCATION/TRAINING PROGRAM(S)—Respiratory Care Therapy/Therapist; Respiratory Therapy Technician/Assistant. **RELATED KNOWLEDGE/COURSES—Medicine and Dentistry:** Knowledge of the information and techniques needed to diagnose and treat human injuries, diseases, and deformities. This includes symptoms, treatment alternatives, drug properties and interactions, and preventive health-care measures. **Psychology:** Knowledge of human behavior and performance; individual differences in ability, personality, and interests; learning and motivation; psychological research methods; and the assessment and treatment of behavioral and affective disorders. **Customer and Personal Service:** Knowledge of principles and processes for providing customer and personal services. This includes customer needs assessment, meeting quality standards for services, and evaluation of customer satisfaction. **Chemistry:** Knowledge of the chemical composition, structure, and properties of substances and of the chemical processes and transformations that they undergo. This includes uses of chemicals and their danger signs, production techniques, and disposal methods. **Physics:** Knowledge and prediction of physical principles and laws and their interrelationships and applications to understanding fluid, material, and atmospheric dynamics and mechanical, electrical, atomic, and subatomic structures and processes. **Biology:** Knowledge of plant and animal organisms and their tissues, cells, functions, interdependencies, and interactions with each other and the environment.

Retail Salespersons

- Education/Training Required: Short-term on-the-job training
- Annual Earnings: $18,680
- Growth: 14.6%
- Annual Job Openings: 1,014,000
- Self-Employed: 4.3%
- Part-Time: 32.6%

Sell merchandise such as furniture, motor vehicles, appliances, or apparel in a retail establishment. Greet customers and ascertain what each customer wants or needs. Open and close cash registers, performing tasks such as counting money; separating charge slips, coupons, and vouchers; balancing cash drawers; and making deposits. Maintain knowledge of current sales and promotions, policies regarding payment and exchanges, and security practices. Compute sales prices and total purchases and receive and process cash or credit payment. Maintain records related to sales. Watch for and recognize security risks and thefts and know how to prevent or handle these situations. Recommend, select, and help locate or obtain merchan-

dise based on customer needs and desires. Answer questions regarding the store and its merchandise. Describe merchandise and explain use, operation, and care of merchandise to customers. Ticket, arrange, and display merchandise to promote sales. Prepare sales slips or sales contracts. Place special orders or call other stores to find desired items. Demonstrate use or operation of merchandise. Clean shelves, counters, and tables. Exchange merchandise for customers and accept returns. Bag or package purchases and wrap gifts. Help customers try on or fit merchandise. Inventory stock and requisition new stock. Prepare merchandise for purchase or rental. Sell or arrange for delivery, insurance, financing, or service contracts for merchandise. Estimate and quote trade-in allowances. **SKILLS—Social Perceptiveness:** Being aware of others' reactions and understanding why they react as they do. **Writing:** Communicating effectively in writing as appropriate for the needs of the audience. **Speaking:** Talking to others to convey information effectively. **Critical Thinking:** Using logic and reasoning to identify the strengths and weaknesses of alternative solutions, conclusions, or approaches to problems. **Negotiation:** Bringing others together and trying to reconcile differences. **Instructing:** Teaching others how to do something. **Management of Personnel Resources:** Motivating, developing, and directing people as they work, identifying the best people for the job. **GOE—Interest Area:** 14. Retail and Wholesale Sales and Service. **Work Group:** 14.03. General Sales. **Other Jobs in This Work Group:** Parts Salespersons; Real Estate Brokers; Real Estate Sales Agents; Sales Representatives, Wholesale and Manufacturing, Except Technical and Scientific Products; Service Station Attendants. **PERSONALITY TYPE:** Enterprising. Enterprising occupations frequently involve starting up and carrying out projects. These occupations can involve leading people and making many decisions. They sometimes require risk taking and often deal with business.

EDUCATION/TRAINING PROGRAM(S)—Floriculture/Floristry Operations and Management; Retailing and Retail Operations; Sales, Distribution, and Marketing Operations, General; Selling Skills and Sales Operations. **RELATED KNOWLEDGE/ COURSES—Sales and Marketing:** Knowledge of principles and methods for showing, promoting, and selling products or services. This includes marketing strategy and tactics, product demonstrations, sales techniques, and sales control systems. **Customer and Personal Service:** Knowledge of principles and processes for providing customer and personal services. This includes customer needs assessment, meeting quality standards for services, and evaluation of customer satisfaction. **Administration and Management:** Knowledge of business and management principles involved in strategic planning, resource allocation, human resources modeling, leadership technique, production methods, and coordination of people and resources. **Education and Training:** Knowledge of principles and methods for curriculum and training design, teaching and instruction for individuals and groups, and the measurement of training effects. **Personnel and Human Resources:** Knowledge of principles and procedures for personnel recruitment, selection, training, compensation and benefits, labor relations and negotiation, and personnel information systems. **Clerical Practices:** Knowledge of administrative and clerical procedures and systems such as word processing, managing files and records, stenography and transcription, designing forms, and other office procedures and terminology.

Riggers

- ◎ Education/Training Required: Short-term on-the-job training
- ◎ Annual Earnings: $35,330
- ◎ Growth: 14.3%
- ◎ Annual Job Openings: 3,000
- ◎ Self-Employed: 0%
- ◎ Part-Time: 1.4%

Set up or repair rigging for construction projects, manufacturing plants, logging yards, and ships and shipyards or for the entertainment industry. Align, level, and anchor machinery. Attach loads to rigging to provide support or prepare them for moving, using hand and power tools. Attach pulleys and blocks to fixed overhead structures such as beams, ceilings, and gin pole booms, using bolts and clamps. Control movement of heavy equipment through narrow openings or confined spaces, using chainfalls, gin poles, gal-

lows frames, and other equipment. Dismantle and store rigging equipment after use. Fabricate, set up, and repair rigging, supporting structures, hoists, and pulling gear, using hand and power tools. Manipulate rigging lines, hoists, and pulling gear to move or support materials such as heavy equipment, ships, or theatrical sets. Select gear such as cables, pulleys, and winches according to load weights and sizes, facilities, and work schedules. Signal or verbally direct workers engaged in hoisting and moving loads in order to ensure safety of workers and materials. Test rigging to ensure safety and reliability. Tilt, dip, and turn suspended loads to maneuver over, under, and/or around obstacles, using multi-point suspension techniques. Clean and dress machine surfaces and component parts. Install ground rigging for yarding lines, attaching chokers to logs and then to the lines. **SKILLS— Technology Design:** Generating or adapting equipment and technology to serve user needs. **Repairing:** Repairing machines or systems by using the needed tools. **Science:** Using scientific rules and methods to solve problems. **Coordination:** Adjusting actions in relation to others' actions. **Operation Monitoring:** Watching gauges, dials, or other indicators to make sure a machine is working properly. **Installation:** Installing equipment, machines, wiring, or programs to meet specifications. **Operation and Control:** Controlling operations of equipment or systems. **Management of Material Resources:** Obtaining and seeing to the appropriate use of equipment, facilities, and materials needed to do certain work. **Management of Personnel Resources:** Motivating, developing, and directing people as they work, identifying the best people for the job. **GOE—Interest Area:** 02. Architecture and Construction. **Work Group:** 02.04. Construction Crafts. **Other Jobs in This Work Group:** Boat Builders and Shipwrights; Boilermakers; Brattice Builders; Brickmasons and Blockmasons; Carpet Installers; Ceiling Tile Installers; Cement Masons and Concrete Finishers; Commercial Divers; Construction Carpenters; Crane and Tower Operators; Dragline Operators; Drywall Installers; Electricians; Fence Erectors; Floor Layers, Except Carpet, Wood, and Hard Tiles; Floor Sanders and Finishers; Glaziers; Grader, Bulldozer, and Scraper Operators; Hazardous Materials Removal Workers; Insulation Workers, Floor, Ceiling, and Wall; Insulation Workers, Mechanical;

Manufactured Building and Mobile Home Installers; Operating Engineers; Painters, Construction and Maintenance; Paperhangers; Paving, Surfacing, and Tamping Equipment Operators; Pile-Driver Operators; Pipe Fitters; Pipelayers; Pipelaying Fitters; Plasterers and Stucco Masons; Plumbers; Rail-Track Laying and Maintenance Equipment Operators; Refractory Materials Repairers, Except Brickmasons; Reinforcing Iron and Rebar Workers; Roofers; Rough Carpenters; Security and Fire Alarm Systems Installers; Segmental Pavers; Sheet Metal Workers; Ship Carpenters and Joiners; Stone Cutters and Carvers; Stonemasons; Structural Iron and Steel Workers; Tapers; Terrazzo Workers and Finishers; Tile and Marble Setters. **PERSONALITY TYPE:** Realistic. Realistic occupations frequently involve work activities that include practical, hands-on problems and solutions. They often deal with plants, animals, and real-world materials like wood, tools, and machinery. Many of the occupations require working outside and do not involve a lot of paperwork or working closely with others.

EDUCATION/TRAINING PROGRAM(S)—Construction/Heavy Equipment/Earthmoving Equipment Operation. **RELATED KNOWLEDGE/COURSES—Public Safety and Security:** Knowledge of relevant equipment, policies, procedures, and strategies to promote effective local, state, or national security operations for the protection of people, data, property, and institutions. **Mechanical Devices:** Knowledge of machines and tools, including their designs, uses, repair, and maintenance. **Engineering and Technology:** Knowledge of the practical application of engineering science and technology. This includes applying principles, techniques, procedures, and equipment to the design and production of various goods and services. **Building and Construction:** Knowledge of the materials, methods, and tools involved in the construction or repair of houses, buildings, or other structures such as highways and roads. **Physics:** Knowledge and prediction of physical principles and laws and their interrelationships and applications to understanding fluid, material, and atmospheric dynamics and mechanical, electrical, atomic, and subatomic structures and processes.

Roofers

- Education/Training Required: Moderate-term on-the-job training
- Annual Earnings: $30,840
- Growth: 18.6%
- Annual Job Openings: 38,000
- Self-Employed: 31.9%
- Part-Time: 10.0%

Cover roofs of structures with shingles, slate, asphalt, aluminum, wood, and related materials. May spray roofs, sidings, and walls with material to bind, seal, insulate, or soundproof sections of structures. Align roofing materials with edges of roofs. Apply alternate layers of hot asphalt or tar and roofing paper to roofs, according to specification. Apply gravel or pebbles over top layers of roofs, using rakes or stiff-bristled brooms. Apply plastic coatings and membranes, fiberglass, or felt over sloped roofs before applying shingles. Cement or nail flashing-strips of metal or shingle over joints to make them watertight. Cover exposed nailheads with roofing cement or caulking to prevent water leakage and rust. Cover roofs and exterior walls of structures with slate, asphalt, aluminum, wood, gravel, gypsum, and/or related materials, using brushes, knives, punches, hammers, and other tools. Cut felt, shingles, and strips of flashing and fit them into angles formed by walls, vents, and intersecting roof surfaces. Cut roofing paper to size, using knives, and nail or staple roofing paper to roofs in overlapping strips to form bases for other materials. Glaze top layers to make a smooth finish or embed gravel in the bitumen for rough surfaces. Inspect problem roofs to determine the best procedures for repairing them. Install partially overlapping layers of material over roof insulation surfaces, determining distance of roofing material overlap by using chalklines, gauges on shingling hatchets, or lines on shingles. Install vapor barriers and/or layers of insulation on the roof decks of flat roofs and seal the seams. Install, repair, or replace single-ply roofing systems, using waterproof sheet materials such as modified plastics, elastomeric, or other asphaltic compositions. Mop or pour hot asphalt or tar onto roof bases. Clean and maintain equipment. Hammer and chisel away rough spots or remove them with rubbing bricks to prepare surfaces for waterproofing. Punch holes in slate, tile, terra cotta, or wooden shingles, using punches and hammers. Remove snow, water, or debris from roofs prior to applying roofing materials. Set up scaffolding to provide safe access to roofs. Spray roofs, sidings, and walls with material to bind, seal, insulate, or sound-proof sections of structures, using spray guns, air compressors, and heaters. **SKILLS—Repairing:** Repairing machines or systems by using the needed tools. **Installation:** Installing equipment, machines, wiring, or programs to meet specifications. **Coordination:** Adjusting actions in relation to others' actions. **Equipment Selection:** Determining the kind of tools and equipment needed to do a job. **Operation and Control:** Controlling operations of equipment or systems. **GOE—Interest Area:** 02. Architecture and Construction. **Work Group:** 02.04. Construction Crafts. **Other Jobs in This Work Group:** Boat Builders and Shipwrights; Boilermakers; Brattice Builders; Brickmasons and Blockmasons; Carpet Installers; Ceiling Tile Installers; Cement Masons and Concrete Finishers; Commercial Divers; Construction Carpenters; Crane and Tower Operators; Dragline Operators; Drywall Installers; Electricians; Fence Erectors; Floor Layers, Except Carpet, Wood, and Hard Tiles; Floor Sanders and Finishers; Glaziers; Grader, Bulldozer, and Scraper Operators; Hazardous Materials Removal Workers; Insulation Workers, Floor, Ceiling, and Wall; Insulation Workers, Mechanical; Manufactured Building and Mobile Home Installers; Operating Engineers; Painters, Construction and Maintenance; Paperhangers; Paving, Surfacing, and Tamping Equipment Operators; Pile-Driver Operators; Pipe Fitters; Pipelayers; Pipelaying Fitters; Plasterers and Stucco Masons; Plumbers; Rail-Track Laying and Maintenance Equipment Operators; Refractory Materials Repairers, Except Brickmasons; Reinforcing Iron and Rebar Workers; Riggers; Rough Carpenters; Security and Fire Alarm Systems Installers; Segmental Pavers; Sheet Metal Workers; Ship Carpenters and Joiners; Stone Cutters and Carvers; Stonemasons; Structural Iron and Steel Workers; Tapers; Terrazzo Workers and Finishers; Tile and Marble Setters. **PERSONALITY TYPE:** Realistic. Realistic occupations frequently involve work activities that include practical, hands-on problems and solutions. These occupations often deal with plants, animals, and real-world materials like wood,

tools, and machinery. Many of the occupations require working outside and do not involve a lot of paperwork or working closely with others.

EDUCATION/TRAINING PROGRAM(S)— Roofer. **RELATED KNOWLEDGE/COURSES— Building and Construction:** Knowledge of the materials, methods, and tools involved in the construction or repair of houses, buildings, or other structures such as highways and roads. **Mechanical Devices:** Knowledge of machines and tools, including their designs, uses, repair, and maintenance.

Rough Carpenters

- Education/Training Required: Moderate-term on-the-job training
- Annual Earnings: $34,900
- Growth: 10.1%
- Annual Job Openings: 193,000
- Self-Employed: 29.7%
- Part-Time: 5.3%

Build rough wooden structures, such as concrete forms; scaffolds; tunnel, bridge, or sewer supports; billboard signs; and temporary frame shelters according to sketches, blueprints, or oral instructions. Study blueprints and diagrams to determine dimensions of structure or form to be constructed. Measure materials or distances, using square, measuring tape, or rule to lay out work. Cut or saw boards, timbers, or plywood to required size, using handsaw, power saw, or woodworking machine. Assemble and fasten material together to construct wood or metal framework of structure, using bolts, nails, or screws. Anchor and brace forms and other structures in place, using nails, bolts, anchor rods, steel cables, planks, wedges, and timbers. Mark cutting lines on materials, using pencil and scriber. Erect forms, framework, scaffolds, hoists, roof supports, or chutes, using hand tools, plumb rule, and level. Install rough door and window frames, subflooring, fixtures, or temporary supports in structures undergoing construction or repair. Examine structural timbers and supports to detect decay and replace timbers as required, using hand tools, nuts, and bolts. Bore boltholes in timber, masonry, or concrete walls, using power drill. Fabricate parts, using woodworking and metalworking machines. **SKILLS—Repairing:** Repairing machines or systems by using the needed tools. **Installation:** Installing equipment, machines, wiring, or programs to meet specifications. **Management of Personnel Resources:** Motivating, developing, and directing people as they work, identifying the best people for the job. **Equipment Selection:** Determining the kind of tools and equipment needed to do a job. **Mathematics:** Using mathematics to solve problems. **Coordination:** Adjusting actions in relation to others' actions. **Technology Design:** Generating or adapting equipment and technology to serve user needs. **Equipment Maintenance:** Performing routine maintenance on equipment and determining when and what kind of maintenance is needed. **GOE—Interest Area:** 02. Architecture and Construction. **Work Group:** 02.04. Construction Crafts. **Other Jobs in This Work Group:** Boat Builders and Shipwrights; Boilermakers; Brattice Builders; Brickmasons and Blockmasons; Carpet Installers; Ceiling Tile Installers; Cement Masons and Concrete Finishers; Commercial Divers; Construction Carpenters; Crane and Tower Operators; Dragline Operators; Drywall Installers; Electricians; Fence Erectors; Floor Layers, Except Carpet, Wood, and Hard Tiles; Floor Sanders and Finishers; Glaziers; Grader, Bulldozer, and Scraper Operators; Hazardous Materials Removal Workers; Insulation Workers, Floor, Ceiling, and Wall; Insulation Workers, Mechanical; Manufactured Building and Mobile Home Installers; Operating Engineers; Painters, Construction and Maintenance; Paperhangers; Paving, Surfacing, and Tamping Equipment Operators; Pile-Driver Operators; Pipe Fitters; Pipelayers; Pipelaying Fitters; Plasterers and Stucco Masons; Plumbers; Rail-Track Laying and Maintenance Equipment Operators; Refractory Materials Repairers, Except Brickmasons; Reinforcing Iron and Rebar Workers; Riggers; Roofers; Security and Fire Alarm Systems Installers; Segmental Pavers; Sheet Metal Workers; Ship Carpenters and Joiners; Stone Cutters and Carvers; Stonemasons; Structural Iron and Steel Workers; Tapers; Terrazzo Workers and Finishers; Tile and Marble Setters. **PERSONALITY TYPE:** Realistic. Realistic occupations frequently involve work activities that include practical, hands-on problems and solutions. These occupations often deal with plants, animals, and real-world materials like wood, tools, and machinery. Many of the occupations require working outside and do not involve a lot of paperwork or working closely with others.

EDUCATION/TRAINING PROGRAM(S)—Carpentry/Carpenter. **RELATED KNOWLEDGE/ COURSES—Building and Construction:** Knowledge of the materials, methods, and tools involved in the construction or repair of houses, buildings, or other structures such as highways and roads. **Design:** Knowledge of design techniques, tools, and principles involved in production of precision technical plans, blueprints, drawings, and models. **Engineering and Technology:** Knowledge of the practical application of engineering science and technology. This includes applying principles, techniques, procedures, and equipment to the design and production of various goods and services. **Mechanical Devices:** Knowledge of machines and tools, including their designs, uses, repair, and maintenance. **Production and Processing:** Knowledge of raw materials, production processes, quality control, costs, and other techniques for maximizing the effective manufacture and distribution of goods. **Public Safety and Security:** Knowledge of relevant equipment, policies, procedures, and strategies to promote effective local, state, or national security operations for the protection of people, data, property, and institutions.

Sales Representatives, Agricultural

- Education/Training Required: Moderate-term on-the-job training
- Annual Earnings: $58,580
- Growth: 19.3%
- Annual Job Openings: 44,000
- Self-Employed: 4.6%
- Part-Time: 8.1%

Sell agricultural products and services, such as animal feeds; farm and garden equipment; and dairy, poultry, and veterinarian supplies. Solicits orders from customers in person or by phone. Demonstrates use of agricultural equipment or machines. Recommends changes in customer use of agricultural products to improve production. Prepares reports of business transactions. Informs customer of estimated delivery schedule, service contracts, warranty, or other information pertaining to purchased products. Displays or shows customer agricultural-related products. Compiles lists of prospective customers for use as sales leads. Prepares sales contracts for orders obtained. Consults with customer regarding installation, setup, or layout of agricultural equipment and machines. Quotes prices and credit terms. **SKILLS—Persuasion:** Persuading others to change their minds or behavior. **Negotiation:** Bringing others together and trying to reconcile differences. **Speaking:** Talking to others to convey information effectively. **Active Listening:** Giving full attention to what other people are saying, taking time to understand the points being made, asking questions as appropriate, and not interrupting at inappropriate times. **Writing:** Communicating effectively in writing as appropriate for the needs of the audience. **Mathematics:** Using mathematics to solve problems. **Instructing:** Teaching others how to do something. **GOE—Interest Area:** 14. Retail and Wholesale Sales and Service. **Work Group:** 14.02. Technical Sales. **Other Jobs in This Work Group:** Sales Engineers; Sales Representatives, Chemical and Pharmaceutical; Sales Representatives, Electrical/Electronic; Sales Representatives, Instruments; Sales Representatives, Mechanical Equipment and Supplies; Sales Representatives, Medical. **PERSONALITY TYPE:** Enterprising. Enterprising occupations frequently involve starting up and carrying out projects. These occupations can involve leading people and making many decisions. They sometimes require risk taking and often deal with business.

EDUCATION/TRAINING PROGRAM(S)—Business, Management, Marketing, and Related Support Services, Other; Selling Skills and Sales Operations. **RELATED KNOWLEDGE/COURSES—Sales and Marketing:** Knowledge of principles and methods for showing, promoting, and selling products or services. This includes marketing strategy and tactics, product demonstrations, sales techniques, and sales control systems. **Economics and Accounting:** Knowledge of economic and accounting principles and practices, the financial markets, banking, and the analysis and

reporting of financial data. **Mathematics:** Knowledge of arithmetic, algebra, geometry, calculus, and statistics and their applications. **Food Production:** Knowledge of techniques and equipment for planting, growing, and harvesting food products (both plant and animal) for consumption, including storage/handling techniques. **Telecommunications:** Knowledge of transmission, broadcasting, switching, control, and operation of telecommunications systems. **Communications and Media:** Knowledge of media production, communication, and dissemination techniques and methods. This includes alternative ways to inform and entertain via written, oral, and visual media.

Sales Representatives, Chemical and Pharmaceutical

- Education/Training Required: Moderate-term on-the-job training
- Annual Earnings: $58,580
- Growth: 19.3%
- Annual Job Openings: 44,000
- Self-Employed: 4.6%
- Part-Time: 8.1%

Sell chemical or pharmaceutical products or services, such as acids, industrial chemicals, agricultural chemicals, medicines, drugs, and water treatment supplies. Promotes and sells pharmaceutical and chemical products to potential customers. Explains water-treatment package benefits to customer and sells chemicals to treat and resolve water process problems. Estimates and advises customer of service costs to correct water-treatment process problems. Discusses characteristics and clinical studies pertaining to pharmaceutical products with physicians, dentists, hospitals, and retail/wholesale establishments. Distributes drug samples to customer and takes orders for pharmaceutical supply items from customer. Inspects, tests, and observes chemical changes in water system equipment, utilizing test kit, reference manual, and knowledge of chemical treatment. **SKILLS—Science:** Using scientific rules and methods to solve problems. **Persuasion:**

Persuading others to change their minds or behavior. **Speaking:** Talking to others to convey information effectively. **Social Perceptiveness:** Being aware of others' reactions and understanding why they react as they do. **Active Listening:** Giving full attention to what other people are saying, taking time to understand the points being made, asking questions as appropriate, and not interrupting at inappropriate times. **Negotiation:** Bringing others together and trying to reconcile differences. **GOE—Interest Area:** 14. Retail and Wholesale Sales and Service. **Work Group:** 14.02. Technical Sales. **Other Jobs in This Work Group:** Sales Engineers; Sales Representatives, Agricultural; Sales Representatives, Electrical/Electronic; Sales Representatives, Instruments; Sales Representatives, Mechanical Equipment and Supplies; Sales Representatives, Medical. **PERSONALITY TYPE:** Enterprising. Enterprising occupations frequently involve starting up and carrying out projects. These occupations can involve leading people and making many decisions. They sometimes require risk taking and often deal with business.

EDUCATION/TRAINING PROGRAM(S)—Business, Management, Marketing, and Related Support Services, Other; Selling Skills and Sales Operations. **RELATED KNOWLEDGE/COURSES**—**Sales and Marketing:** Knowledge of principles and methods for showing, promoting, and selling products or services. This includes marketing strategy and tactics, product demonstrations, sales techniques, and sales control systems. **Chemistry:** Knowledge of the chemical composition, structure, and properties of substances and of the chemical processes and transformations that they undergo. This includes uses of chemicals and their danger signs, production techniques, and disposal methods. **Biology:** Knowledge of plant and animal organisms and their tissues, cells, functions, interdependencies, and interactions with each other and the environment. **Medicine and Dentistry:** Knowledge of the information and techniques needed to diagnose and treat human injuries, diseases, and deformities. This includes symptoms, treatment alternatives, drug properties and interactions, and preventive health-care measures. **Mathematics:** Knowledge of arithmetic, algebra, geometry, calculus, and statistics and their applications. **Economics and Accounting:** Knowledge of economic and accounting principles and practices,

the financial markets, banking, and the analysis and reporting of financial data.

Sales Representatives, Electrical/Electronic

- ◎ Education/Training Required: Moderate-term on-the-job training
- ◎ Annual Earnings: $58,580
- ◎ Growth: 19.3%
- ◎ Annual Job Openings: 44,000
- ◎ Self-Employed: 4.6%
- ◎ Part-Time: 8.1%

Sell electrical, electronic, or related products or services, such as communication equipment, radiographic-inspection equipment and services, ultrasonic equipment, electronics parts, computers, and EDP systems. Analyzes communication needs of customer and consults with staff engineers regarding technical problems. Trains establishment personnel in equipment use, utilizing knowledge of electronics and product sold. Recommends equipment to meet customer requirements, considering salable features such as flexibility, cost, capacity, and economy of operation. Negotiates terms of sale and services with customer. Sells electrical or electronic equipment such as computers, data-processing, and radiographic equipment to businesses and industrial establishments. **SKILLS**— **Persuasion:** Persuading others to change their minds or behavior. **Negotiation:** Bringing others together and trying to reconcile differences. **Instructing:** Teaching others how to do something. **Operations Analysis:** Analyzing needs and product requirements to create a design. **Active Listening:** Giving full attention to what other people are saying, taking time to understand the points being made, asking questions as appropriate, and not interrupting at inappropriate times. **Equipment Selection:** Determining the kind of tools and equipment needed to do a job. **Speaking:** Talking to others to convey information effectively. **Technology Design:** Generating or adapting equipment and technology to serve user needs. **GOE—Interest Area:** 14. Retail and Wholesale Sales and Service. **Work Group:** 14.02. Technical Sales. **Other Jobs in This Work**

Group: Sales Engineers; Sales Representatives, Agricultural; Sales Representatives, Chemical and Pharmaceutical; Sales Representatives, Instruments; Sales Representatives, Mechanical Equipment and Supplies; Sales Representatives, Medical. **PERSONALITY TYPE:** Enterprising. Enterprising occupations frequently involve starting up and carrying out projects. These occupations can involve leading people and making many decisions. They sometimes require risk taking and often deal with business.

EDUCATION/TRAINING PROGRAM(S)—Business, Management, Marketing, and Related Support Services, Other; Selling Skills and Sales Operations. **RELATED KNOWLEDGE/COURSES**—**Sales and Marketing:** Knowledge of principles and methods for showing, promoting, and selling products or services. This includes marketing strategy and tactics, product demonstrations, sales techniques, and sales control systems. **Computers and Electronics:** Knowledge of circuit boards, processors, chips, electronic equipment, and computer hardware and software, including applications and programming. **Economics and Accounting:** Knowledge of economic and accounting principles and practices, the financial markets, banking, and the analysis and reporting of financial data. **Education and Training:** Knowledge of principles and methods for curriculum and training design, teaching and instruction for individuals and groups, and the measurement of training effects. **Telecommunications:** Knowledge of transmission, broadcasting, switching, control, and operation of telecommunications systems. **Mathematics:** Knowledge of arithmetic, algebra, geometry, calculus, and statistics and their applications.

Sales Representatives, Instruments

- ◎ Education/Training Required: Moderate-term on-the-job training
- ◎ Annual Earnings: $58,580
- ◎ Growth: 19.3%
- ◎ Annual Job Openings: 44,000
- ◎ Self-Employed: 4.6%
- ◎ Part-Time: 8.1%

Sell precision instruments, such as dynamometers; spring scales; and laboratory, navigation, and surveying instruments. Assists customer with product selection, utilizing knowledge of engineering specifications and catalog resources. Evaluates customer needs and emphasizes product features based on technical knowledge of product capabilities and limitations. Sells weighing and other precision instruments, such as spring scales; dynamometers; and laboratory, navigational, and surveying instruments to customer. **SKILLS**—**Persuasion:** Persuading others to change their minds or behavior. **Active Listening:** Giving full attention to what other people are saying, taking time to understand the points being made, asking questions as appropriate, and not interrupting at inappropriate times. **Service Orientation:** Actively looking for ways to help people. **Speaking:** Talking to others to convey information effectively. **GOE—Interest Area:** 14. Retail and Wholesale Sales and Service. **Work Group:** 14.02. Technical Sales. **Other Jobs in This Work Group:** Sales Engineers; Sales Representatives, Agricultural; Sales Representatives, Chemical and Pharmaceutical; Sales Representatives, Electrical/Electronic; Sales Representatives, Mechanical Equipment and Supplies; Sales Representatives, Medical. **PERSONALITY TYPE:** Enterprising. Enterprising occupations frequently involve starting up and carrying out projects. These occupations can involve leading people and making many decisions. They sometimes require risk taking and often deal with business.

EDUCATION/TRAINING PROGRAM(S)—Business, Management, Marketing, and Related Support Services, Other; Selling Skills and Sales Operations. **RELATED KNOWLEDGE/COURSES**—**Sales and Marketing:** Knowledge of principles and methods for showing, promoting, and selling products or services. This includes marketing strategy and tactics, product demonstrations, sales techniques, and sales control systems. **Engineering and Technology:** Knowledge of the practical application of engineering science and technology. This includes applying principles, techniques, procedures, and equipment to the design and production of various goods and services.

Sales Representatives, Mechanical Equipment and Supplies

- Education/Training Required: Moderate-term on-the-job training
- Annual Earnings: $58,580
- Growth: 19.3%
- Annual Job Openings: 44,000
- Self-Employed: 4.6%
- Part-Time: 8.1%

Sell mechanical equipment, machinery, materials, and supplies, such as aircraft and railroad equipment and parts, construction machinery, material-handling equipment, industrial machinery, and welding equipment. Recommends and sells textile, industrial, construction, railroad, and oil field machinery, equipment, materials, supplies, and services, utilizing knowledge of machine operations. Computes installation or production costs, estimates savings, and prepares and submits bid specifications to customer for review and approval. Submits orders for product and follows up on order to verify that material list is accurate and delivery schedule meets project deadline. Appraises equipment and verifies customer credit rating to establish trade-in value and contract terms. Reviews existing machinery/equipment placement and diagrams proposal to illustrate efficient space utilization, using standard measuring devices and templates. Attends sales and trade meetings and reads related publications to obtain current market condition information, business trends, and industry developments. Inspects establishment premises to verify installation feasibility and obtains building blueprints and elevator specifications to submit to engineering department for bid. Demonstrates and explains use of installed equipment and production processes. Arranges for installation and test-operation of machinery and recommends solutions to product-related problems. Contacts current and potential customers, visits establishments to evaluate needs, and promotes sale of products and services. **SKILLS—Operations Analysis:** Analyzing needs and product requirements to create a design. **Persuasion:** Persuading others to change their minds or behavior. **Negotiation:** Bringing others together and trying to reconcile differences. **Equipment Selection:** Determining the kind of tools and equipment needed to do a job. **Active Listening:** Giving full attention to what other people are saying, taking time to understand the points being made, asking questions as appropriate, and not interrupting at inappropriate times. **Instructing:** Teaching others how to do something. **Speaking:** Talking to others to convey information effectively. **Reading Comprehension:** Understanding written sentences and paragraphs in work-related documents. **GOE—Interest Area:** 14. Retail and Wholesale Sales and Service. **Work Group:** 14.02. Technical Sales. **Other Jobs in This Work Group:** Sales Engineers; Sales Representatives, Agricultural; Sales Representatives, Chemical and Pharmaceutical; Sales Representatives, Electrical/Electronic; Sales Representatives, Instruments; Sales Representatives, Medical. **PERSONALITY TYPE:** Enterprising. Enterprising occupations frequently involve starting up and carrying out projects. These occupations can involve leading people and making many decisions. They sometimes require risk taking and often deal with business.

EDUCATION/TRAINING PROGRAM(S)—Business, Management, Marketing, and Related Support Services, Other; Selling Skills and Sales Operations. **RELATED KNOWLEDGE/COURSES—Sales and Marketing:** Knowledge of principles and methods for showing, promoting, and selling products or services. This includes marketing strategy and tactics, product demonstrations, sales techniques, and sales control systems. **Mathematics:** Knowledge of arithmetic, algebra, geometry, calculus, and statistics and their applications. **Economics and Accounting:** Knowledge of economic and accounting principles and practices, the financial markets, banking, and the analysis and reporting of financial data. **Design:** Knowledge of design techniques, tools, and principles involved in production of precision technical plans, blueprints, drawings, and models. **Telecommunications:** Knowledge of transmission, broadcasting, switching, control, and operation of telecommunications systems. **Engineering and Technology:** Knowledge of the practical application of engineering science and technology. This includes applying principles, techniques, procedures, and equipment to the design and production of various goods and services.

Sales Representatives, Medical

- Education/Training Required: Moderate-term on-the-job training
- Annual Earnings: $58,580
- Growth: 19.3%
- Annual Job Openings: 44,000
- Self-Employed: 4.6%
- Part-Time: 8.1%

Sell medical equipment, products, and services. Does not include pharmaceutical sales representatives. Promotes sale of medical and dental equipment, supplies, and services to doctors, dentists, hospitals, medical schools, and retail establishments. Writes specifications to order custom-made surgical appliances, using customer measurements and physician prescriptions. Advises customer regarding office layout, legal and insurance regulations, cost analysis, and collection methods. Designs and fabricates custom-made medical appliances. Selects surgical appliances from stock and fits and sells appliance to customer. Studies data describing new products to accurately recommend purchase of equipment and supplies. **SKILLS—Technology Design:** Generating or adapting equipment and technology to serve user needs. **Persuasion:** Persuading others to change their minds or behavior. **Negotiation:** Bringing others together and trying to reconcile differences. **Operations Analysis:** Analyzing needs and product requirements to create a design. **Active Listening:** Giving full attention to what other people are saying, taking time to understand the points being made, asking questions as appropriate, and not interrupting at inappropriate times. **Writing:** Communicating effectively in writing as appropriate for the needs of the audience. **Speaking:** Talking to others to convey information effectively. **Service Orientation:** Actively looking for ways to help people. **Equipment Selection:** Determining the kind of tools and equipment needed to do a job. **GOE—Interest Area:** 14.

Retail and Wholesale Sales and Service. **Work Group:** 14.02. Technical Sales. **Other Jobs in This Work Group:** Sales Engineers; Sales Representatives, Agricultural; Sales Representatives, Chemical and Pharmaceutical; Sales Representatives, Electrical/Electronic; Sales Representatives, Instruments; Sales Representatives, Mechanical Equipment and Supplies. **PERSONALITY TYPE:** Enterprising. Enterprising occupations frequently involve starting up and carrying out projects. These occupations can involve leading people and making many decisions. They sometimes require risk taking and often deal with business.

EDUCATION/TRAINING PROGRAM(S)—Business, Management, Marketing, and Related Support Services, Other; Selling Skills and Sales Operations. **RELATED KNOWLEDGE/COURSES—Sales and Marketing:** Knowledge of principles and methods for showing, promoting, and selling products or services. This includes marketing strategy and tactics, product demonstrations, sales techniques, and sales control systems. **Design:** Knowledge of design techniques, tools, and principles involved in production of precision technical plans, blueprints, drawings, and models. **Mathematics:** Knowledge of arithmetic, algebra, geometry, calculus, and statistics and their applications. **Economics and Accounting:** Knowledge of economic and accounting principles and practices, the financial markets, banking, and the analysis and reporting of financial data. **Engineering and Technology:** Knowledge of the practical application of engineering science and technology. This includes applying principles, techniques, procedures, and equipment to the design and production of various goods and services. **Medicine and Dentistry:** Knowledge of the information and techniques needed to diagnose and treat human injuries, diseases, and deformities. This includes symptoms, treatment alternatives, drug properties and interactions, and preventive health-care measures.

Sales Representatives, Wholesale and Manufacturing, Except Technical and Scientific Products

- Education/Training Required: Moderate-term on-the-job training
- Annual Earnings: $45,400
- Growth: 19.1%
- Annual Job Openings: 160,000
- Self-Employed: 4.6%
- Part-Time: 8.1%

Sell goods for wholesalers or manufacturers to businesses or groups of individuals. Work requires substantial knowledge of items sold. Answer customers' questions about products, prices, availability, product uses, and credit terms. Arrange and direct delivery and installation of products and equipment. Contact regular and prospective customers to demonstrate products, explain product features, and solicit orders. Estimate or quote prices, credit or contract terms, warranties, and delivery dates. Forward orders to manufacturers. Identify prospective customers by using business directories, following leads from existing clients, participating in organizations and clubs, and attending trade shows and conferences. Monitor market conditions; product innovations; and competitors' products, prices, and sales. Negotiate details of contracts and payments and prepare sales contracts and order forms. Prepare drawings, estimates, and bids that meet specific customer needs. Provide customers with product samples and catalogs. Recommend products to customers based on customers' needs and interests. Buy products from manufacturers or brokerage firms and distribute them to wholesale and retail clients. Check stock levels and reorder merchandise as necessary. Consult with clients after sales or contract signings in order to resolve problems and to provide ongoing support. Negotiate with retail merchants to improve product exposure such as shelf positioning and advertising. Obtain credit information about prospective customers. Perform administrative duties,

such as preparing sales budgets and reports, keeping sales records, and filing expense account reports. Plan, assemble, and stock product displays in retail stores or make recommendations to retailers regarding product displays, promotional programs, and advertising. Train customers' employees to operate and maintain new equipment. **SKILLS—Management of Material Resources:** Obtaining and seeing to the appropriate use of equipment, facilities, and materials needed to do certain work. **Negotiation:** Bringing others together and trying to reconcile differences. **Persuasion:** Persuading others to change their minds or behavior. **Service Orientation:** Actively looking for ways to help people. **Speaking:** Talking to others to convey information effectively. **Social Perceptiveness:** Being aware of others' reactions and understanding why they react as they do. **Writing:** Communicating effectively in writing as appropriate for the needs of the audience. **Instructing:** Teaching others how to do something. **Operations Analysis:** Analyzing needs and product requirements to create a design. **Systems Evaluation:** Identifying measures or indicators of system performance and the actions needed to improve or correct performance relative to the goals of the system. **GOE—Interest Area:** 14. Retail and Wholesale Sales and Service. **Work Group:** 14.03. General Sales. **Other Jobs in This Work Group:** Parts Salespersons; Real Estate Brokers; Real Estate Sales Agents; Retail Salespersons; Service Station Attendants. **PERSONALITY TYPE:** Enterprising. Enterprising occupations frequently involve starting up and carrying out projects. These occupations can involve leading people and making many decisions. They sometimes require risk taking and often deal with business.

EDUCATION/TRAINING PROGRAM(S)—Apparel and Accessories Marketing Operations; Business, Management, Marketing, and Related Support Services, Other; Fashion Merchandising; General Merchandising, Sales, and Related Marketing Operations, Other; Sales, Distribution, and Marketing Operations, General; Special Products Marketing Operations; Specialized Merchandising, Sales, and Related Marketing Operations, Other. **RELATED KNOWLEDGE/COURSES—Sales and Marketing:** Knowledge of principles and methods for showing, promoting, and selling products or services. This includes marketing strategy and tactics, product demonstrations, sales techniques, and sales control systems. **Communications and Media:** Knowledge of media production, communication, and dissemination techniques and methods. This includes alternative ways to inform and entertain via written, oral, and visual media. **Customer and Personal Service:** Knowledge of principles and processes for providing customer and personal services. This includes customer needs assessment, meeting quality standards for services, and evaluation of customer satisfaction. **Transportation:** Knowledge of principles and methods for moving people or goods by air, rail, sea, or road, including the relative costs and benefits. **Economics and Accounting:** Knowledge of economic and accounting principles and practices, the financial markets, banking, and the analysis and reporting of financial data. **Psychology:** Knowledge of human behavior and performance; individual differences in ability, personality, and interests; learning and motivation; psychological research methods; and the assessment and treatment of behavioral and affective disorders.

Sculptors

- Education/Training Required: Long-term on-the-job training
- Annual Earnings: $38,060
- Growth: 16.5%
- Annual Job Openings: 4,000
- Self-Employed: 55.5%
- Part-Time: 23.1%

Design and construct three-dimensional art works, using materials such as stone, wood, plaster, and metal and employing various manual and tool techniques. Carves objects from stone, concrete, plaster, wood, or other material, using abrasives and tools such as chisels, gouges, and mall. Models substances such as clay or wax, using fingers and small hand tools to form objects. Cuts, bends, laminates, arranges, and fastens individual or mixed raw and manufactured materials and products to form works of art. Constructs artistic forms from metal or stone, using metalworking, welding, or masonry tools and equipment. **SKILLS—** None met the criteria. **GOE—Interest Area:** 03. Arts and Communication. **Work Group:** 03.04. Studio

Art. **Other Jobs in This Work Group:** Cartoonists; Craft Artists; Painters and Illustrators; Potters; Sketch Artists. **PERSONALITY TYPE:** Artistic. Artistic occupations frequently involve working with forms, designs, and patterns. These occupations often require self-expression, and the work can be done without following a clear set of rules.

EDUCATION/TRAINING PROGRAM(S)— Art/Art Studies, General; Ceramic Arts and Ceramics; Fine Arts and Art Studies, Other; Fine/Studio Arts, General; Sculpture; Visual and Performing Arts, General. **RELATED KNOWLEDGE/COURSES—Fine Arts:** Knowledge of the theory and techniques required to compose, produce, and perform works of music, dance, the visual arts, drama, and sculpture. **Design:** Knowledge of design techniques, tools, and principles involved in production of precision technical plans, blueprints, drawings, and models. **Engineering and Technology:** Knowledge of the practical application of engineering science and technology. This includes applying principles, techniques, procedures, and equipment to the design and production of various goods and services. **Building and Construction:** Knowledge of the materials, methods, and tools involved in the construction or repair of houses, buildings, or other structures such as highways and roads.

Security and Fire Alarm Systems Installers

- Education/Training Required: Postsecondary vocational training
- Annual Earnings: $33,410
- Growth: 30.2%
- Annual Job Openings: 5,000
- Self-Employed: 6.8%
- Part-Time: 2.8%

Install, program, maintain, and repair security and fire alarm wiring and equipment. Ensure that work is in accordance with relevant codes. Adjust sensitivity of units based on room structures and manufacturers' recommendations, using programming keypads. Consult with clients to assess risks and to determine security requirements. Drill holes for wiring in wall studs, joists, ceilings, and floors. Examine systems to locate problems such as loose connections or broken insulation. Feed cables through access holes, roof spaces, and cavity walls to reach fixture outlets; then position and terminate cables, wires, and strapping. Inspect installation sites and study work orders, building plans, and installation manuals in order to determine materials requirements and installation procedures. Install, maintain, or repair security systems, alarm devices, and related equipment, following blueprints of electrical layouts and building plans. Mount and fasten control panels, door and window contacts, sensors, and video cameras and attach electrical and telephone wiring in order to connect components. Mount raceways and conduits and fasten wires to wood framing, using staplers. Test and repair circuits and sensors, following wiring and system specifications. Test backup batteries, keypad programming, sirens, and all security features in order to ensure proper functioning and to diagnose malfunctions. Demonstrate systems for customers and explain details such as the causes and consequences of false alarms. Keep informed of new products and developments. Order replacement parts. Prepare documents such as invoices and warranties. Provide customers with cost estimates for equipment installation. **SKILLS**—No data available. **GOE—Interest Area:** 02. Architecture and Construction. **Work Group:** 02.04. Construction Crafts. **Other Jobs in This Work Group:** Boat Builders and Shipwrights; Boilermakers; Brattice Builders; Brickmasons and Blockmasons; Carpet Installers; Ceiling Tile Installers; Cement Masons and Concrete Finishers; Commercial Divers; Construction Carpenters; Crane and Tower Operators; Dragline Operators; Drywall Installers; Electricians; Fence Erectors; Floor Layers, Except Carpet, Wood, and Hard Tiles; Floor Sanders and Finishers; Glaziers; Grader, Bulldozer, and Scraper Operators; Hazardous Materials Removal Workers; Insulation Workers, Floor, Ceiling, and Wall; Insulation Workers, Mechanical; Manufactured Building and Mobile Home Installers; Operating Engineers; Painters, Construction and Maintenance; Paperhangers; Paving, Surfacing, and Tamping Equipment Operators; Pile-Driver Operators; Pipe Fitters; Pipelayers; Pipelaying Fitters; Plasterers and Stucco Masons; Plumbers; Rail-Track Laying and Maintenance Equipment Operators;

Refractory Materials Repairers, Except Brickmasons; Reinforcing Iron and Rebar Workers; Riggers; Roofers; Rough Carpenters; Segmental Pavers; Sheet Metal Workers; Ship Carpenters and Joiners; Stone Cutters and Carvers; Stonemasons; Structural Iron and Steel Workers; Tapers; Terrazzo Workers and Finishers; Tile and Marble Setters. **PERSONALITY TYPE:** No data available.

EDUCATION/TRAINING PROGRAM(S)—Electrician; Security System Installation, Repair, and Inspection Technology/Technician. **RELATED KNOWLEDGE/COURSES**—No data available.

Security Guards

- Education/Training Required: Short-term on-the-job training
- Annual Earnings: $20,320
- Growth: 31.9%
- Annual Job Openings: 228,000
- Self-Employed: 0.9%
- Part-Time: 15.1%

Guard, patrol, or monitor premises to prevent theft, violence, or infractions of rules. Patrol industrial and commercial premises to prevent and detect signs of intrusion and ensure security of doors, windows, and gates. Answer alarms and investigate disturbances. Monitor and authorize entrance and departure of employees, visitors, and other persons to guard against theft and maintain security of premises. Write reports of daily activities and irregularities, such as equipment or property damage, theft, presence of unauthorized persons, or unusual occurrences. Call police or fire departments in cases of emergency, such as fire or presence of unauthorized persons. Circulate among visitors, patrons, and employees to preserve order and protect property. Answer telephone calls to take messages, answer questions, and provide information during non-business hours or when switchboard is closed. Warn persons of rule infractions or violations and apprehend or evict violators from premises, using force when necessary. Operate detecting devices to screen individuals and prevent passage of prohibited articles into restricted areas. Escort or drive motor vehicle to transport individuals to specified locations and to provide personal protection. Inspect and adjust security systems, equipment, and machinery to ensure operational use and to detect evidence of tampering. Drive and guard armored vehicle to transport money and valuables to prevent theft and ensure safe delivery. **SKILLS—Social Perceptiveness:** Being aware of others' reactions and understanding why they react as they do. **Negotiation:** Bringing others together and trying to reconcile differences. **Learning Strategies:** Selecting and using training/instructional methods and procedures appropriate for the situation when learning or teaching new things. **Speaking:** Talking to others to convey information effectively. **Active Listening:** Giving full attention to what other people are saying, taking time to understand the points being made, asking questions as appropriate, and not interrupting at inappropriate times. **Time Management:** Managing one's own time and the time of others. **Writing:** Communicating effectively in writing as appropriate for the needs of the audience. **Monitoring:** Monitoring or assessing your performance or that of other individuals or organizations to make improvements or take corrective action. **GOE—Interest Area:** 12. Law and Public Safety. **Work Group:** 12.05. Safety and Security. **Other Jobs in This Work Group:** Animal Control Workers; Crossing Guards; Gaming Surveillance Officers and Gaming Investigators; Lifeguards, Ski Patrol, and Other Recreational Protective Service Workers; Private Detectives and Investigators. **PERSONALITY TYPE:** Social. Social occupations frequently involve working with, communicating with, and teaching people. These occupations often involve helping or providing service to others.

EDUCATION/TRAINING PROGRAM(S)—Securities Services Administration/Management; Security and Loss Prevention Services. **RELATED KNOWLEDGE/COURSES—Public Safety and Security:** Knowledge of relevant equipment, policies, procedures, and strategies to promote effective local, state, or national security operations for the protection of people, data, property, and institutions. **Customer and Personal Service:** Knowledge of principles and processes for providing customer and personal services. This includes customer needs assessment, meeting quality standards for services, and evaluation of customer satisfaction. **Law and Government:** Knowledge

of laws, legal codes, court procedures, precedents, government regulations, executive orders, agency rules, and the democratic political process. **Clerical Practices:** Knowledge of administrative and clerical procedures and systems such as word processing, managing files and records, stenography and transcription, designing forms, and other office procedures and terminology. **Telecommunications:** Knowledge of transmission, broadcasting, switching, control, and operation of telecommunications systems. **Transportation:** Knowledge of principles and methods for moving people or goods by air, rail, sea, or road, including the relative costs and benefits.

Self-Enrichment Education Teachers

- Education/Training Required: Work experience in a related occupation
- Annual Earnings: $30,880
- Growth: 40.1%
- Annual Job Openings: 39,000
- Self-Employed: 19.9%
- Part-Time: 41.0%

Teach or instruct courses other than those that normally lead to an occupational objective or degree. Courses may include self-improvement, nonvocational, and nonacademic subjects. Teaching may or may not take place in a traditional educational institution. Conduct classes, workshops, and demonstrations and provide individual instruction to teach topics and skills such as cooking, dancing, writing, physical fitness, photography, personal finance, and flying. Instruct students individually and in groups, using various teaching methods such as lectures, discussions, and demonstrations. Adapt teaching methods and instructional materials to meet students' varying needs and interests. Assign and grade class work and homework. Confer with other teachers and professionals to plan and schedule lessons promoting learning and development. Enforce policies and rules governing students. Establish clear objectives for all lessons, units, and projects and communicate those objectives to students. Instruct and monitor students in use and care of equipment and materials in order to prevent injury and damage. Maintain accurate and complete student records as required by administrative policy. Meet with other instructors to discuss individual students and their progress. Monitor students' performance in order to make suggestions for improvement and to ensure that they satisfy course standards, training requirements, and objectives. Observe students to determine qualifications, limitations, abilities, interests, and other individual characteristics. Plan and conduct activities for a balanced program of instruction, demonstration, and work time that provides students with opportunities to observe, question, and investigate. Plan and supervise class projects, field trips, visits by guest speakers, contests, or other experiential activities and guide students in learning from those activities. Prepare and administer written, oral, and performance tests and issue grades in accordance with performance. Prepare and implement remedial programs for students requiring extra help. Prepare instructional program objectives, outlines, and lesson plans. Prepare materials and classrooms for class activities. Prepare students for further development by encouraging them to explore learning opportunities and to persevere with challenging tasks. Review instructional content, methods, and student evaluations in order to assess strengths and weaknesses and to develop recommendations for course revision, development, or elimination. **SKILLS—Instructing:** Teaching others how to do something. **Writing:** Communicating effectively in writing as appropriate for the needs of the audience. **Speaking:** Talking to others to convey information effectively. **Learning Strategies:** Selecting and using training/instructional methods and procedures appropriate for the situation when learning or teaching new things. **Service Orientation:** Actively looking for ways to help people. **Systems Evaluation:** Identifying measures or indicators of system performance and the actions needed to improve or correct performance relative to the goals of the system. **Reading Comprehension:** Understanding written sentences and paragraphs in work-related documents. **Active Listening:** Giving full attention to what other people are saying, taking time to understand the points being made, asking questions as appropriate, and not interrupting at inappropriate times. **GOE—Interest Area:** 05. Education and Training. **Work Group:** 05.03. Postsecondary and

Adult Teaching and Instructing. **Other Jobs in This Work Group:** Adult Literacy, Remedial Education, and GED Teachers and Instructors; Agricultural Sciences Teachers, Postsecondary; Anthropology and Archeology Teachers, Postsecondary; Architecture Teachers, Postsecondary; Area, Ethnic, and Cultural Studies Teachers, Postsecondary; Art, Drama, and Music Teachers, Postsecondary; Atmospheric, Earth, Marine, and Space Sciences Teachers, Postsecondary; Biological Science Teachers, Postsecondary; Business Teachers, Postsecondary; Chemistry Teachers, Postsecondary; Communications Teachers, Postsecondary; Computer Science Teachers, Postsecondary; Criminal Justice and Law Enforcement Teachers, Postsecondary; Economics Teachers, Postsecondary; Education Teachers, Postsecondary; Engineering Teachers, Postsecondary; English Language and Literature Teachers, Postsecondary; Environmental Science Teachers, Postsecondary; Farm and Home Management Advisors; Foreign Language and Literature Teachers, Postsecondary; Forestry and Conservation Science Teachers, Postsecondary; Geography Teachers, Postsecondary; Graduate Teaching Assistants; Health Specialties Teachers, Postsecondary; History Teachers, Postsecondary; Home Economics Teachers, Postsecondary; Law Teachers, Postsecondary; Library Science Teachers, Postsecondary; Mathematical Science Teachers, Postsecondary; Nursing Instructors and Teachers, Postsecondary; Philosophy and Religion Teachers, Postsecondary; Physics Teachers, Postsecondary; Political Science Teachers, Postsecondary; Psychology Teachers, Postsecondary; Recreation and Fitness Studies Teachers, Postsecondary; Social Work Teachers, Postsecondary; Sociology Teachers, Postsecondary; Vocational Education Teachers, Postsecondary. **PERSONALITY TYPE:** Social. Social occupations frequently involve working with, communicating with, and teaching people. These occupations often involve helping or providing service to others.

EDUCATION/TRAINING PROGRAM(S)—Adult and Continuing Education and Teaching. **RELATED KNOWLEDGE/COURSES—Education and Training:** Knowledge of principles and methods for curriculum and training design, teaching and instruction for individuals and groups, and the measurement of training effects. **English Language:** Knowledge of the structure and content of the English language, including the meaning and spelling of words, rules of composition, and grammar. **Economics and Accounting:** Knowledge of economic and accounting principles and practices, the financial markets, banking, and the analysis and reporting of financial data. **History and Archeology:** Knowledge of historical events and their causes, indicators, and effects on civilizations and cultures. **Philosophy and Theology:** Knowledge of different philosophical systems and religions. This includes their basic principles, values, ethics, ways of thinking, customs, and practices and their impact on human culture. **Sociology and Anthropology:** Knowledge of group behavior and dynamics, societal trends and influences, human migrations, ethnicity, and cultures and their history and origins.

Sheet Metal Workers

- Education/Training Required: Moderate-term on-the-job training
- Annual Earnings: $35,560
- Growth: 19.8%
- Annual Job Openings: 30,000
- Self-Employed: 3.1%
- Part-Time: 2.7%

Fabricate, assemble, install, and repair sheet metal products and equipment, such as ducts, control boxes, drainpipes, and furnace casings. Work may involve any of the following: setting up and operating fabricating machines to cut, bend, and straighten sheet metal; shaping metal over anvils, blocks, or forms, using hammer; operating soldering and welding equipment to join sheet metal parts; and inspecting, assembling, and smoothing seams and joints of burred surfaces. Determine project requirements, including scope, assembly sequences, and required methods and materials, according to blueprints, drawings, and written or verbal instructions. Lay out, measure, and mark dimensions and reference lines on material such as roofing panels according to drawings or templates, using calculators, scribes, dividers, squares, and rulers. Maneuver completed units into position for installation and anchor the units. Convert blueprints into shop drawings to be followed in the construction and assembly of sheet metal products.

Install assemblies such as flashing, pipes, tubes, heating and air conditioning ducts, furnace casings, rain gutters, and downspouts in supportive frameworks. Select gauges and types of sheet metal or non-metallic material according to product specifications. Drill and punch holes in metal for screws, bolts, and rivets. Fasten seams and joints together with welds, bolts, cement, rivets, solder, caulks, metal drive clips, and bonds in order to assemble components into products or to repair sheet metal items. Fabricate or alter parts at construction sites, using shears, hammers, punches, and drills. Trim, file, grind, deburr, buff, and smooth surfaces, seams, and joints of assembled parts, using hand tools and portable power tools. Finish parts, using hacksaws and hand, rotary, or squaring shears. Maintain equipment, making repairs and modifications when necessary. Shape metal material over anvils, blocks, or other forms, using hand tools. Transport prefabricated parts to construction sites for assembly and installation. Develop and lay out patterns that use materials most efficiently, using computerized metalworking equipment to experiment with different layouts. Inspect individual parts, assemblies, and installations for conformance to specifications and building codes, using measuring instruments such as calipers, scales, and micrometers. Secure metal roof panels in place and then interlock and fasten grooved panel edges. **SKILLS—Installation:** Installing equipment, machines, wiring, or programs to meet specifications. **Equipment Maintenance:** Performing routine maintenance on equipment and determining when and what kind of maintenance is needed. **Repairing:** Repairing machines or systems by using the needed tools. **Coordination:** Adjusting actions in relation to others' actions. **Mathematics:** Using mathematics to solve problems. **Technology Design:** Generating or adapting equipment and technology to serve user needs. **Troubleshooting:** Determining causes of operating errors and deciding what to do about them. **Instructing:** Teaching others how to do something. **GOE—Interest Area:** 02. Architecture and Construction. **Work Group:** 02.04. Construction Crafts. **Other Jobs in This Work Group:** Boat Builders and Shipwrights; Boilermakers; Brattice Builders; Brickmasons and Blockmasons; Carpet Installers; Ceiling Tile Installers; Cement Masons and Concrete Finishers; Commercial Divers; Construction Carpenters; Crane and Tower Operators; Dragline Operators; Drywall Installers; Electricians; Fence Erectors; Floor Layers, Except Carpet, Wood, and Hard Tiles; Floor Sanders and Finishers; Glaziers; Grader, Bulldozer, and Scraper Operators; Hazardous Materials Removal Workers; Insulation Workers, Floor, Ceiling, and Wall; Insulation Workers, Mechanical; Manufactured Building and Mobile Home Installers; Operating Engineers; Painters, Construction and Maintenance; Paperhangers; Paving, Surfacing, and Tamping Equipment Operators; Pile-Driver Operators; Pipe Fitters; Pipelayers; Pipelaying Fitters; Plasterers and Stucco Masons; Plumbers; Rail-Track Laying and Maintenance Equipment Operators; Refractory Materials Repairers, Except Brickmasons; Reinforcing Iron and Rebar Workers; Riggers; Roofers; Rough Carpenters; Security and Fire Alarm Systems Installers; Segmental Pavers; Ship Carpenters and Joiners; Stone Cutters and Carvers; Stonemasons; Structural Iron and Steel Workers; Tapers; Terrazzo Workers and Finishers; Tile and Marble Setters. **PERSONALITY TYPE:** Realistic. Realistic occupations frequently involve work activities that include practical, hands-on problems and solutions. These occupations often deal with plants, animals, and real-world materials like wood, tools, and machinery. Many of the occupations require working outside and do not involve a lot of paperwork or working closely with others.

EDUCATION/TRAINING PROGRAM(S)—Sheet Metal Technology/Sheetworking. **RELATED KNOWLEDGE/COURSES—Building and Construction:** Knowledge of the materials, methods, and tools involved in the construction or repair of houses, buildings, or other structures such as highways and roads. **Mechanical Devices:** Knowledge of machines and tools, including their designs, uses, repair, and maintenance. **Design:** Knowledge of design techniques, tools, and principles involved in production of precision technical plans, blueprints, drawings, and models. **Production and Processing:** Knowledge of raw materials, production processes, quality control, costs, and other techniques for maximizing the effective manufacture and distribution of goods. **Physics:** Knowledge and prediction of physical principles and laws and their interrelationships and applications to understanding fluid, material, and atmospheric dynamics and mechanical, electrical, atomic, and sub-

atomic structures and processes. **Mathematics:** Knowledge of arithmetic, algebra, geometry, calculus, and statistics and their applications.

Sheriffs and Deputy Sheriffs

- Education/Training Required: Long-term on-the-job training
- Annual Earnings: $45,210
- Growth: 24.7%
- Annual Job Openings: 67,000
- Self-Employed: 0%
- Part-Time: 1.4%

Enforce law and order in rural or unincorporated districts or serve legal processes of courts. May patrol courthouse, guard court or grand jury, or escort defendants. Drive vehicles or patrol specific areas to detect law violators, issue citations, and make arrests. Execute arrest warrants, locating and taking persons into custody. Investigate illegal or suspicious activities. Notify patrol units to take violators into custody or to provide needed assistance or medical aid. Question individuals entering secured areas to determine their business, directing and rerouting individuals as necessary. Record daily activities and submit logs and other related reports and paperwork to appropriate authorities. Serve statements of claims, subpoenas, summonses, jury summonses, orders to pay alimony, and other court orders. Take control of accident scenes to maintain traffic flow, to assist accident victims, and to investigate causes. Verify that the proper legal charges have been made against law offenders. Patrol and guard courthouses, grand jury rooms, or assigned areas in order to provide security, enforce laws, maintain order, and arrest violators. Locate and confiscate real or personal property as directed by court order. Manage jail operations and tend to jail inmates. Place people in protective custody. Transport or escort prisoners and defendants en route to courtrooms, prisons or jails, attorneys' offices, or medical facilities. **SKILLS— Social Perceptiveness:** Being aware of others' reactions and understanding why they react as they do. **Service Orientation:** Actively looking for ways to help people.

Active Listening: Giving full attention to what other people are saying, taking time to understand the points being made, asking questions as appropriate, and not interrupting at inappropriate times. Speaking: Talking to others to convey information effectively. Judgment and Decision Making: Considering the relative costs and benefits of potential actions to choose the most appropriate one. Coordination: Adjusting actions in relation to others' actions. Writing: Communicating effectively in writing as appropriate for the needs of the audience. Critical Thinking: Using logic and reasoning to identify the strengths and weaknesses of alternative solutions, conclusions, or approaches to problems. GOE—Interest Area: 12. Law and Public Safety. Work Group: 12.04. Law Enforcement and Public Safety. Other Jobs in This Work Group: Bailiffs; Correctional Officers and Jailers; Criminal Investigators and Special Agents; Fire Investigators; Forensic Science Technicians; Highway Patrol Pilots; Parking Enforcement Workers; Police Detectives; Police Identification and Records Officers; Police Patrol Officers; Transit and Railroad Police. PERSONALITY TYPE: Social. Social occupations frequently involve working with, communicating with, and teaching people. These occupations often involve helping or providing service to others.

EDUCATION/TRAINING PROGRAM(S)— Criminal Justice/Police Science; Criminalistics and Criminal Science. RELATED KNOWLEDGE/ COURSES—Public Safety and Security: Knowledge of relevant equipment, policies, procedures, and strategies to promote effective local, state, or national security operations for the protection of people, data, property, and institutions. Law and Government: Knowledge of laws, legal codes, court procedures, precedents, government regulations, executive orders, agency rules, and the democratic political process. Psychology: Knowledge of human behavior and performance; individual differences in ability, personality, and interests; learning and motivation; psychological research methods; and the assessment and treatment of behavioral and affective disorders. Geography: Knowledge of principles and methods for describing the features of land, sea, and air masses, including their physical characteristics; locations; interrelationships; and distribution of plant, animal, and human life. Sociology and Anthropology: Knowledge of group

behavior and dynamics, societal trends and influences, human migrations, ethnicity, and cultures and their history and origins. Clerical Practices: Knowledge of administrative and clerical procedures and systems such as word processing, managing files and records, stenography and transcription, designing forms, and other office procedures and terminology. Telecommunications: Knowledge of transmission, broadcasting, switching, control, and operation of telecommunications systems.

Ship Carpenters and Joiners

- Education/Training Required: Moderate-term on-the-job training
- Annual Earnings: $34,900
- Growth: 10.1%
- Annual Job Openings: 193,000
- Self-Employed: 29.7%
- Part-Time: 5.3%

Fabricate, assemble, install, or repair wooden furnishings in ships or boats. Reads blueprints to determine dimensions of furnishings in ships or boats. Shapes and laminates wood to form parts of ship, using steam chambers, clamps, glue, and jigs. Repairs structural woodwork and replaces defective parts and equipment, using hand tools and power tools. Shapes irregular parts and trims excess material from bulkhead and furnishings to ensure fit meets specifications. Constructs floors, doors, and partitions, using woodworking machines, hand tools, and power tools. Cuts wood or glass to specified dimensions, using hand tools and power tools. Assembles and installs hardware, gaskets, floors, furnishings, or insulation, using adhesive, hand tools, and power tools. Transfers dimensions or measurements of wood parts or bulkhead on plywood, using measuring instruments and marking devices. Greases gears and other moving parts of machines on ship. SKILLS—Installation: Installing equipment, machines, wiring, or programs to meet specifications. Repairing: Repairing machines or systems by using the needed tools. Equipment Maintenance: Performing routine maintenance on equipment and determining when and what kind of maintenance is needed. **Operations Analysis:** Analyzing needs and product requirements to create a design. **Systems Analysis:** Determining how a system should work and how changes in conditions, operations, and the environment will affect outcomes. **GOE—Interest Area:** 02. Architecture and Construction. **Work Group:** 02.04. Construction Crafts. **Other Jobs in This Work Group:** Boat Builders and Shipwrights; Boilermakers; Brattice Builders; Brickmasons and Blockmasons; Carpet Installers; Ceiling Tile Installers; Cement Masons and Concrete Finishers; Commercial Divers; Construction Carpenters; Crane and Tower Operators; Dragline Operators; Drywall Installers; Electricians; Fence Erectors; Floor Layers, Except Carpet, Wood, and Hard Tiles; Floor Sanders and Finishers; Glaziers; Grader, Bulldozer, and Scraper Operators; Hazardous Materials Removal Workers; Insulation Workers, Floor, Ceiling, and Wall; Insulation Workers, Mechanical; Manufactured Building and Mobile Home Installers; Operating Engineers; Painters, Construction and Maintenance; Paperhangers; Paving, Surfacing, and Tamping Equipment Operators; Pile-Driver Operators; Pipe Fitters; Pipelayers; Pipelaying Fitters; Plasterers and Stucco Masons; Plumbers; Rail-Track Laying and Maintenance Equipment Operators; Refractory Materials Repairers, Except Brickmasons; Reinforcing Iron and Rebar Workers; Riggers; Roofers; Rough Carpenters; Security and Fire Alarm Systems Installers; Segmental Pavers; Sheet Metal Workers; Stone Cutters and Carvers; Stonemasons; Structural Iron and Steel Workers; Tapers; Terrazzo Workers and Finishers; Tile and Marble Setters. **PERSONALITY TYPE:** Realistic. Realistic occupations frequently involve work activities that include practical, hands-on problems and solutions. These occupations often deal with plants, animals, and real-world materials like wood, tools, and machinery. Many of the occupations require working outside and do not involve a lot of paperwork or working closely with others.

EDUCATION/TRAINING PROGRAM(S)—Carpentry/Carpenter. **RELATED KNOWLEDGE/ COURSES**—**Building and Construction:** Knowledge of the materials, methods, and tools involved in the construction or repair of houses, buildings, or other structures such as highways and roads. **Design:** Knowledge of design techniques, tools, and principles involved in production of precision technical plans, blueprints, drawings, and models. **Engineering and Technology:** Knowledge of the practical application of engineering science and technology. This includes applying principles, techniques, procedures, and equipment to the design and production of various goods and services. **Mechanical Devices:** Knowledge of machines and tools, including their designs, uses, repair, and maintenance.

Sketch Artists

- Education/Training Required: Long-term on-the-job training
- Annual Earnings: $38,060
- Growth: 16.5%
- Annual Job Openings: 4,000
- Self-Employed: 55.5%
- Part-Time: 23.1%

Sketch likenesses of subjects according to observation or descriptions either to assist law enforcement agencies in identifying suspects, to depict courtroom scenes, or for entertainment purposes of patrons, using mediums such as pencil, charcoal, and pastels. Draws sketch, profile, or likeness of posed subject or photograph, using pencil, charcoal, pastels, or other medium. Assembles and arranges outlines of features to form composite image according to information provided by witness or victim. Alters copy of composite image until witness or victim is satisfied that composite is best possible representation of suspect. Poses subject to accentuate most pleasing features or profile. Classifies and codes components of image, using established system, to help identify suspect. Prepares series of simple line drawings conforming to description of suspect and presents drawings to informant for selection of sketch. Interviews crime victims and witnesses to obtain descriptive information concerning physical build, sex, nationality, and facial features of unidentified suspect. Measures distances and develops sketches of crime scene from photograph and measurements. Searches police photograph records, using classification and coding system to determine if existing photograph of suspects is available. Operates photocopy or similar machine to reproduce composite image.

SKILLS—**Active Listening:** Giving full attention to what other people are saying, taking time to understand the points being made, asking questions as appropriate, and not interrupting at inappropriate times. **Social Perceptiveness:** Being aware of others' reactions and understanding why they react as they do. **Speaking:** Talking to others to convey information effectively. **GOE—Interest Area:** 03. Arts and Communication. **Work Group:** 03.04. Studio Art. **Other Jobs in This Work Group:** Cartoonists; Craft Artists; Painters and Illustrators; Potters; Sculptors. **PERSONALITY TYPE:** Artistic. Artistic occupations frequently involve working with forms, designs, and patterns. These occupations often require self-expression, and the work can be done without following a clear set of rules.

EDUCATION/TRAINING PROGRAM(S)— Art/Art Studies, General; Drawing; Fine Arts and Art Studies, Other; Fine/Studio Arts, General; Medical Illustration/Medical Illustrator; Visual and Performing Arts, General. **RELATED KNOWLEDGE/COURSES—Fine Arts:** Knowledge of the theory and techniques required to compose, produce, and perform works of music, dance, the visual arts, drama, and sculpture. **Design:** Knowledge of design techniques, tools, and principles involved in production of precision technical plans, blueprints, drawings, and models.

Slaughterers and Meat Packers

- ◎ Education/Training Required: Moderate-term on-the-job training
- ◎ Annual Earnings: $20,860
- ◎ Growth: 18.1%
- ◎ Annual Job Openings: 23,000
- ◎ Self-Employed: 1.0%
- ◎ Part-Time: 7.0%

Work in slaughtering, meat-packing, or wholesale establishments performing precision functions involving the preparation of meat. Work may include specialized slaughtering tasks, cutting standard or premium cuts of meat for marketing, making sausage, or wrapping meats. Cut, trim, skin, sort, and wash viscera of slaughtered animals to separate edible portions from offal. Grind meat into hamburger and into trimmings used to prepare sausages, luncheon meats, and other meat products. Remove bones and cut meat into standard cuts in preparation for marketing. Saw, split, or scribe carcasses into smaller portions to facilitate handling. Sever jugular veins to drain blood and facilitate slaughtering. Shackle hind legs of animals to raise them for slaughtering or skinning. Shave or singe and defeather carcasses and wash them in preparation for further processing or packaging. Skin sections of animals or whole animals. Slit open, eviscerate, and trim carcasses of slaughtered animals. Stun animals prior to slaughtering. Trim head meat and sever or remove parts of animals' heads or skulls. Trim, clean, and/or cure animal hides. Wrap dressed carcasses and/or meat cuts. Tend assembly lines, performing a few of the many cuts needed to process a carcass. Slaughter animals in accordance with religious law and determine that carcasses meet specified religious standards. SKILLS—None met the criteria. **GOE—Interest Area:** 13. Manufacturing. **Work Group:** 13.03. Production Work, Assorted Materials Processing. **Other Jobs in This Work Group:** Bakers, Manufacturing; Cementing and Gluing Machine Operators and Tenders; Chemical Equipment Controllers and Operators; Chemical Equipment Tenders; Cleaning, Washing, and Metal Pickling Equipment Operators and Tenders; Coating, Painting, and Spraying Machine Operators and Tenders; Combination Machine Tool Operators and Tenders, Metal and Plastic; Cooling and Freezing Equipment Operators and Tenders; Cutting and Slicing Machine Operators and Tenders; Electrolytic Plating and Coating Machine Operators and Tenders, Metal and Plastic; Extruding and Forming Machine Operators and Tenders, Synthetic or Glass Fibers; Extruding, Forming, Pressing, and Compacting Machine Operators and Tenders; Food and Tobacco Roasting, Baking, and Drying Machine Operators and Tenders; Food Batchmakers; Food Cooking Machine Operators and Tenders; Furnace, Kiln, Oven, Drier, and Kettle Operators and Tenders; Heat Treating, Annealing, and Tempering Machine Operators and Tenders, Metal and Plastic; Heaters, Metal and Plastic; Meat, Poultry, and Fish Cutters and Trimmers; Metal-Refining Furnace Operators and Tenders; Mixing and Blending Machine Set-

S

ters, Operators, and Tenders; Nonelectrolytic Plating and Coating Machine Operators and Tenders, Metal and Plastic; Packaging and Filling Machine Operators and Tenders; Plastic Molding and Casting Machine Operators and Tenders; Pourers and Casters, Metal; Pressing Machine Operators and Tenders—Textile, Garment, and Related Materials; Production Helpers; Production Laborers; Sawing Machine Operators and Tenders; Separating, Filtering, Clarifying, Precipitating, and Still Machine Setters, Operators, and Tenders; Sewing Machine Operators, Garment; Sewing Machine Operators, Non-Garment; Shoe Machine Operators and Tenders; Stone Sawyers; Team Assemblers; Textile Bleaching and Dyeing Machine Operators and Tenders; Tire Builders; Woodworking Machine Operators and Tenders, Except Sawing. **PERSONALITY TYPE:** Realistic. Realistic occupations frequently involve work activities that include practical, hands-on problems and solutions. These occupations often deal with plants, animals, and real-world materials like wood, tools, and machinery. Many of the occupations require working outside and do not involve a lot of paperwork or working closely with others.

EDUCATION/TRAINING PROGRAM(S)—Meat Cutting/Meat Cutter. **RELATED KNOWLEDGE/ COURSES**—**Food Production:** Knowledge of techniques and equipment for planting, growing, and harvesting food products (both plant and animal) for consumption, including storage/handling techniques. **Biology:** Knowledge of plant and animal organisms and their tissues, cells, functions, interdependencies, and interactions with each other and the environment. **Philosophy and Theology:** Knowledge of different philosophical systems and religions. This includes their basic principles, values, ethics, ways of thinking, customs, and practices and their impact on human culture. **Public Safety and Security:** Knowledge of relevant equipment, policies, procedures, and strategies to promote effective local, state, or national security operations for the protection of people, data, property, and institutions. **Production and Processing:** Knowledge of raw materials, production processes, quality control, costs, and other techniques for maximizing the effective manufacture and distribution of goods. **Law and Government:** Knowledge of laws, legal codes, court procedures, precedents, government regu-

lations, executive orders, agency rules, and the democratic political process.

Social and Human Service Assistants

- Education/Training Required: Moderate-term on-the-job training
- Annual Earnings: $24,270
- Growth: 48.7%
- Annual Job Openings: 63,000
- Self-Employed: 0.2%
- Part-Time: 10.6%

Assist professionals from a wide variety of fields, such as psychology, rehabilitation, or social work, to provide client services, as well as support for families. May assist clients in identifying available benefits and social and community services and help clients obtain them. May assist social workers with developing, organizing, and conducting programs to prevent and resolve problems relevant to substance abuse, human relationships, rehabilitation, or adult day care. Provide information on and refer individuals to public or private agencies and community services for assistance. Keep records and prepare reports for owner or management concerning visits with clients. Visit individuals in homes or attend group meetings to provide information on agency services, requirements, and procedures. Advise clients regarding food stamps, child care, food, money management, sanitation, and housekeeping. Submit to and review reports and problems with superior. Oversee day-to-day group activities of residents in institution. Interview individuals and family members to compile information on social, educational, criminal, institutional, or drug history. Meet with youth groups to acquaint them with consequences of delinquent acts. Transport and accompany clients to shopping area and to appointments, using automobile. Explain rules established by owner or management, such as sanitation and maintenance requirements and parking regulations. Observe and discuss meal preparation and suggest alternate methods of food preparation. Demonstrate use and care of equipment for tenant use. Consult with supervisor concerning programs for individual families. Monitor free, supplementary meal program to ensure cleanliness of facility and that eligibility guidelines are met for persons receiving meals. Observe clients' food selections and recommend alternate economical and nutritional food choices. Inform tenants of facilities such as laundries and playgrounds. Care for children in client's home during client's appointments. Assist in locating housing for displaced individuals. Assist clients with preparation of forms, such as tax or rent forms. Assist in planning of food budget, utilizing charts and sample budgets. **SKILLS—Social Perceptiveness:** Being aware of others' reactions and understanding why they react as they do. **Service Orientation:** Actively looking for ways to help people. **Management of Financial Resources:** Determining how money will be spent to get the work done and accounting for these expenditures. **Learning Strategies:** Selecting and using training/instructional methods and procedures appropriate for the situation when learning or teaching new things. **Time Management:** Managing one's own time and the time of others. **Instructing:** Teaching others how to do something. **Active Listening:** Giving full attention to what other people are saying, taking time to understand the points being made, asking questions as appropriate, and not interrupting at inappropriate times. **Speaking:** Talking to others to convey information effectively. **GOE—Interest Area:** 10. Human Service. **Work Group:** 10.01. Counseling and Social Work. **Other Jobs in This Work Group:** Child, Family, and School Social Workers; Clinical Psychologists; Counseling Psychologists; Marriage and Family Therapists; Medical and Public Health Social Workers; Mental Health and Substance Abuse Social Workers; Mental Health Counselors; Probation Officers and Correctional Treatment Specialists; Rehabilitation Counselors; Residential Advisors; Substance Abuse and Behavioral Disorder Counselors. **PERSONALITY TYPE:** Social. Social occupations frequently involve working with, communicating with, and teaching people. These occupations often involve helping or providing service to others.

EDUCATION/TRAINING PROGRAM(S)—Mental and Social Health Services and Allied Professions, Other. **RELATED KNOWLEDGE/COURSES—Therapy and Counseling:** Knowledge of principles, methods, and procedures for diagnosis, treatment, and rehabilitation of physical and mental dysfunctions and for career counseling and guidance. **Psychology:** Knowledge of human behavior and performance; individual differences in ability, personality, and interests; learning and motivation; psychological research methods; and the assessment and treatment of behavioral and affective disorders. **Customer and Personal Service:** Knowledge of principles and processes for providing customer and personal services. This includes customer needs assessment, meeting quality standards for services, and evaluation of customer satisfaction. **Clerical Practices:** Knowledge of administrative and clerical procedures and systems such as word processing, managing files and records, stenography and transcription, designing forms, and other office procedures and terminology. **Sociology and Anthropology:** Knowledge of group behavior and dynamics, societal trends and influences, human migrations, ethnicity, and cultures and their history and origins. **Philosophy and Theology:** Knowledge of different philosophical systems and religions. This includes their basic principles, values, ethics, ways of thinking, customs, and practices and their impact on human culture.

Social Science Research Assistants

- Education/Training Required: Associate degree
- Annual Earnings: $34,360
- Growth: 17.5%
- Annual Job Openings: 18,000
- Self-Employed: 1.1%
- Part-Time: 20.2%

Assist social scientists in laboratory, survey, and other social research. May perform publication activities, laboratory analysis, quality control, or data management. Normally these individuals work under the direct supervision of a social scientist and assist in those activities which are more routine. Perform descriptive and multivariate statistical analyses of data, using computer software. Recruit and schedule research participants. Administer standardized tests to research subjects and/or interview them in order to collect research data. Code data in preparation for computer entry. Conduct Internet-based and library research. Develop and implement research quality control procedures. Edit and submit protocols and other required research documentation. Obtain informed consent of research subjects and/or their guardians. Prepare tables, graphs, fact sheets, and written reports summarizing research results. Prepare, manipulate, and manage extensive databases. Provide assistance in the design of survey instruments such as questionnaires. Screen potential subjects in order to determine their suitability as study participants. Track research participants and perform any necessary follow-up tasks. Verify the accuracy and validity of data entered in databases; correct any errors. Allocate and manage laboratory space and resources. Design and create special programs for tasks such as statistical analysis and data entry and cleaning. Perform data entry and other clerical work as required for project completion. Perform needs assessments and/or consult with clients in order to determine the types of research and information that are required. Present research findings to groups of people. Provide assistance with the preparation of project-related reports, manuscripts, and presentations. Supervise the work of survey interviewers. Track laboratory supplies and expenses such as participant reimbursement. Collect specimens such as blood samples as required by research projects. **SKILLS**—No data available. **GOE—Interest Area:** 15. Scientific Research, Engineering, and Mathematics. **Work Group:** 15.06. Mathematics and Data Analysis. **Other Jobs in This Work Group:** Actuaries; Mathematical Technicians; Mathematicians; Statistical Assistants; Statisticians. **PERSONALITY TYPE:** No data available.

EDUCATION/TRAINING PROGRAM(S)— Social Sciences, General. **RELATED KNOWLEDGE/COURSES**—No data available.

Solderers

- Education/Training Required: Short-term on-the-job training
- Annual Earnings: $30,620
- Growth: 17.0%
- Annual Job Openings: 71,000
- Self-Employed: 5.6%
- Part-Time: 2.1%

Solder together components to assemble fabricated metal products, using soldering iron. Melts and applies solder along adjoining edges of workpieces to solder joints, using soldering iron, gas torch, or electric-ultrasonic equipment. Grinds, cuts, buffs, or bends edges of workpieces to be joined to ensure snug fit, using power grinder and hand tools. Removes workpieces from molten solder and holds parts together until color indicates that solder has set. Cleans workpieces, using chemical solution, file, wire brush, or grinder. Cleans tip of soldering iron, using chemical solution or cleaning compound. Melts and separates soldered joints to repair misaligned or damaged assemblies, using soldering equipment. Applies flux to workpiece surfaces in preparation for soldering. Heats soldering iron or workpiece to specified temperature for soldering, using gas flame or electric current. Dips workpieces into molten solder or places solder strip between seams and heats seam with iron to band items together. Aligns and clamps workpieces together, using rule, square, or hand tools, or positions items in fixtures, jigs, or vise. Melts and applies solder to fill holes, indentations, and seams of fabricated metal products, using soldering equipment. **SKILLS—Operation and Control:** Controlling operations of equipment or systems. **Equipment Maintenance:** Performing routine maintenance on equipment and determining when and what kind of maintenance is needed. **Equipment Selection:** Determining the kind of tools and equipment needed to do a job. **Installation:** Installing equipment, machines, wiring, or programs to meet specifications. **Operation Monitoring:** Watching gauges, dials, or other indicators to make sure a machine is working properly. **Repairing:** Repairing machines or systems by using the needed tools. **GOE—Interest Area:** 13. Manufacturing. **Work**

Group: 13.04. Welding, Brazing, and Soldering. **Other Jobs in This Work Group:** Brazers; Fitters, Structural Metal—Precision; Metal Fabricators, Structural Metal Products; Soldering and Brazing Machine Operators and Tenders; Welder-Fitters; Welders and Cutters; Welders, Production; Welding Machine Operators and Tenders; Welding Machine Setters and Set-Up Operators. **PERSONALITY TYPE:** Realistic. Realistic occupations frequently involve work activities that include practical, hands-on problems and solutions. These occupations often deal with plants, animals, and real-world materials like wood, tools, and machinery. Many of the occupations require working outside and do not involve a lot of paperwork or working closely with others.

EDUCATION/TRAINING PROGRAM(S)— Welding Technology/Welder. **RELATED KNOWLEDGE/COURSES—Building and Construction:** Knowledge of the materials, methods, and tools involved in the construction or repair of houses, buildings, or other structures such as highways and roads. **Mechanical Devices:** Knowledge of machines and tools, including their designs, uses, repair, and maintenance. **Production and Processing:** Knowledge of raw materials, production processes, quality control, costs, and other techniques for maximizing the effective manufacture and distribution of goods.

Sound Engineering Technicians

- Education/Training Required: Postsecondary vocational training
- Annual Earnings: $38,110
- Growth: 25.5%
- Annual Job Openings: 2,000
- Self-Employed: 8.6%
- Part-Time: 12.5%

Operate machines and equipment to record, synchronize, mix, or reproduce music, voices, or sound effects in sporting arenas, theater productions, recording studios, or movie and video productions. Confer with producers, performers, and others in order to determine and achieve the desired sound for a production such as a musical recording or a film. Mix and edit voices, music, and taped sound effects for live performances and for prerecorded events, using sound mixing boards. Record speech, music, and other sounds on recording media, using recording equipment. Regulate volume level and sound quality during recording sessions, using control consoles. Reproduce and duplicate sound recordings from original recording media, using sound editing and duplication equipment. Separate instruments, vocals, and other sounds and then combine sounds later during the mixing or post-production stage. Set up, test, and adjust recording equipment for recording sessions and live performances; tear down equipment after event completion. Synchronize and equalize prerecorded dialogue, music, and sound effects with visual action of motion pictures or television productions, using control consoles. Create musical instrument digital interface programs for music projects, commercials, or film post-production. Keep logs of recordings. Prepare for recording sessions by performing activities such as selecting and setting up microphones. Report equipment problems and ensure that required repairs are made. **SKILLS— Operation and Control:** Controlling operations of equipment or systems. **Operation Monitoring:** Watching gauges, dials, or other indicators to make sure a machine is working properly. **Equipment Maintenance:** Performing routine maintenance on equipment and determining when and what kind of maintenance is needed. **Management of Personnel Resources:** Motivating, developing, and directing people as they work, identifying the best people for the job. **Equipment Selection:** Determining the kind of tools and equipment needed to do a job. **Troubleshooting:** Determining causes of operating errors and deciding what to do about them. **Management of Material Resources:** Obtaining and seeing to the appropriate use of equipment, facilities, and materials needed to do certain work. **Quality Control Analysis:** Conducting tests and inspections of products, services, or processes to evaluate quality or performance. **GOE—Interest Area:** 03. Arts and Communication. **Work Group:** 03.09. Media Technology. **Other Jobs in This Work Group:** Audio and Video Equipment Technicians; Broadcast Technicians; Camera Operators, Television, Video, and Motion Picture; Film and

Video Editors; Multi-Media Artists and Animators; Photographic Hand Developers; Photographic Reproduction Technicians; Photographic Retouchers and Restorers; Professional Photographers; Radio Operators. **PERSONALITY TYPE:** Realistic. Realistic occupations frequently involve work activities that include practical, hands-on problems and solutions. These occupations often deal with plants, animals, and real-world materials like wood, tools, and machinery. Many of the occupations require working outside and do not involve a lot of paperwork or working closely with others.

EDUCATION/TRAINING PROGRAM(S)— Communications Technology/Technician; Recording Arts Technology/Technician. **RELATED KNOWLEDGE/COURSES—Computers and Electronics:** Knowledge of circuit boards, processors, chips, electronic equipment, and computer hardware and software, including applications and programming. **Engineering and Technology:** Knowledge of the practical application of engineering science and technology. This includes applying principles, techniques, procedures, and equipment to the design and production of various goods and services. **Telecommunications:** Knowledge of transmission, broadcasting, switching, control, and operation of telecommunications systems. **Communications and Media:** Knowledge of media production, communication, and dissemination techniques and methods. This includes alternative ways to inform and entertain via written, oral, and visual media. **Administration and Management:** Knowledge of business and management principles involved in strategic planning, resource allocation, human resources modeling, leadership technique, production methods, and coordination of people and resources. **Fine Arts:** Knowledge of the theory and techniques required to compose, produce, and perform works of music, dance, the visual arts, drama, and sculpture.

Statement Clerks

- Education/Training Required: Short-term on-the-job training
- Annual Earnings: $27,040
- Growth: 7.9%
- Annual Job Openings: 78,000
- Self-Employed: 2.2%
- Part-Time: 16.1%

Prepare and distribute bank statements to customers, answer inquiries, and reconcile discrepancies in records and accounts. Compare previously prepared bank statements with canceled checks and reconcile discrepancies. Encode and cancel checks, using bank machines. Load machines with statements, cancelled checks, and envelopes in order to prepare statements for distribution to customers or stuff envelopes by hand. Maintain files of canceled checks and customers' signatures. Match statements with batches of canceled checks by account numbers. Monitor equipment in order to ensure proper operation. Retrieve checks returned to customers in error, adjusting customer accounts and answering inquiries about errors as necessary. Route statements for mailing or over-the-counter delivery to customers. Verify signatures and required information on checks. Weigh envelopes containing statements in order to determine correct postage and affix postage, using stamps or metering equipment. Fix minor problems, such as equipment jams, and notify repair personnel of major equipment problems. Post stop-payment notices in order to prevent payment of protested checks. Take orders for imprinted checks. **SKILLS—Active Listening:** Giving full attention to what other people are saying, taking time to understand the points being made, asking questions as appropriate, and not interrupting at inappropriate times. **Reading Comprehension:** Understanding written sentences and paragraphs in work-related documents. **GOE—Interest Area:** 04. Business and Administration. **Work Group:** 04.06. Mathematical Clerical Support. **Other Jobs in This Work Group:** Billing, Cost, and Rate Clerks; Bookkeeping, Accounting, and Auditing Clerks; Brokerage Clerks; Payroll and Timekeeping Clerks; Tax Preparers. **PERSONALITY TYPE:** Conventional. Conventional occupations frequently involve following set procedures and routines. These occupations can include working with data and details more than with ideas. Usually there is a clear line of authority to follow.

EDUCATION/TRAINING PROGRAM(S)— Accounting Technology/Technician and Bookkeeping. **RELATED KNOWLEDGE/COURSES—Clerical Practices:** Knowledge of administrative and clerical procedures and systems such as word processing, managing files and records, stenography and transcription, designing forms, and other office procedures and terminology. **Economics and Accounting:** Knowledge of economic and accounting principles and practices, the financial markets, banking, and the analysis and reporting of financial data. **Computers and Electronics:** Knowledge of circuit boards, processors, chips, electronic equipment, and computer hardware and software, including applications and programming. **Telecommunications:** Knowledge of transmission, broadcasting, switching, control, and operation of telecommunications systems.

Station Installers and Repairers, Telephone

- Education/Training Required: Postsecondary vocational training
- Annual Earnings: $49,840
- Growth: –0.6%
- Annual Job Openings: 23,000
- Self-Employed: 4.6%
- Part-Time: 1.7%

Install and repair telephone station equipment, such as telephones, coin collectors, telephone booths, and switching-key equipment. Installs communication equipment, such as intercommunication systems and related apparatus, using schematic diagrams, testing devices, and hand tools. Assembles telephone equipment, mounts brackets, and connects wire leads, using hand tools and following installation diagrams or work order. Analyzes equipment operation, using testing devices to locate and diagnose nature of malfunction and ascertain needed repairs. Operates and tests equipment to ensure elimination of malfunction. Climbs poles to install or repair outside service lines. Disas-

sembles components and replaces, cleans, adjusts, and repairs parts, wires, switches, relays, circuits, or signaling units, using hand tools. Repairs cables, lays out plans for new equipment, and estimates material required. **SKILLS—Troubleshooting:** Determining causes of operating errors and deciding what to do about them. **Installation:** Installing equipment, machines, wiring, or programs to meet specifications. **Repairing:** Repairing machines or systems by using the needed tools. **Equipment Maintenance:** Performing routine maintenance on equipment and determining when and what kind of maintenance is needed. **Quality Control Analysis:** Conducting tests and inspections of products, services, or processes to evaluate quality or performance. **Operation Monitoring:** Watching gauges, dials, or other indicators to make sure a machine is working properly. **Operation and Control:** Controlling operations of equipment or systems. **Technology Design:** Generating or adapting equipment and technology to serve user needs. **GOE—Interest Area:** 02. Architecture and Construction. **Work Group:** 02.05. Systems and Equipment Installation, Maintenance, and Repair. **Other Jobs in This Work Group:** Central Office and PBX Installers and Repairers; Communication Equipment Mechanics, Installers, and Repairers; Electric Meter Installers and Repairers; Electrical and Electronics Repairers, Powerhouse, Substation, and Relay; Electrical Power-Line Installers and Repairers; Elevator Installers and Repairers; Frame Wirers, Central Office; Heating and Air Conditioning Mechanics; Home Appliance Installers; Maintenance and Repair Workers, General; Meter Mechanics; Refrigeration Mechanics; Telecommunications Facility Examiners; Telecommunications Line Installers and Repairers. **PERSONALITY TYPE:** Realistic. Realistic occupations frequently involve work activities that include practical, hands-on problems and solutions. These occupations often deal with plants, animals, and real-world materials like wood, tools, and machinery. Many of the occupations require working outside and do not involve a lot of paperwork or working closely with others.

EDUCATION/TRAINING PROGRAM(S)— Communications Systems Installation and Repair Technology. **RELATED KNOWLEDGE/COURSES—Telecommunications:** Knowledge of transmission, broadcasting, switching, control, and operation of telecommunications systems. **Computers and Electronics:** Knowledge of circuit boards, processors, chips, electronic equipment, and computer hardware and software, including applications and programming. **Mechanical Devices:** Knowledge of machines and tools, including their designs, uses, repair, and maintenance. **Engineering and Technology:** Knowledge of the practical application of engineering science and technology. This includes applying principles, techniques, procedures, and equipment to the design and production of various goods and services. **Design:** Knowledge of design techniques, tools, and principles involved in production of precision technical plans, blueprints, drawings, and models. **Geography:** Knowledge of principles and methods for describing the features of land, sea, and air masses, including their physical characteristics; locations; interrelationships; and distribution of plant, animal, and human life.

Storage and Distribution Managers

- ◎ Education/Training Required: Work experience in a related occupation
- ◎ Annual Earnings: $66,600
- ◎ Growth: 19.7%
- ◎ Annual Job Openings: 13,000
- ◎ Self-Employed: 1.1%
- ◎ Part-Time: 2.4%

Plan, direct, and coordinate the storage and distribution operations within an organization or the activities of organizations that are engaged in storing and distributing materials and products. Supervise the activities of workers engaged in receiving, storing, testing, and shipping products or materials. Plan, develop, and implement warehouse safety and security programs and activities. Review invoices, work orders, consumption reports, and demand forecasts in order to estimate peak delivery periods and to issue work assignments. Schedule and monitor air or surface pickup, delivery, or distribution of products or materials. Interview, select, and train warehouse and supervisory personnel. Confer with department heads to coordinate warehouse activities, such as production, sales,

records control, and purchasing. Respond to customers' or shippers' questions and complaints regarding storage and distribution services. Inspect physical conditions of warehouses, vehicle fleets, and equipment and order testing, maintenance, repair, or replacement as necessary. Develop and document standard and emergency operating procedures for receiving, handling, storing, shipping, or salvaging products or materials. Examine products or materials in order to estimate quantities or weight and type of container required for storage or transport. Negotiate with carriers, warehouse operators, and insurance company representatives for services and preferential rates. Issue shipping instructions and provide routing information to ensure that delivery times and locations are coordinated. Examine invoices and shipping manifests for conformity to tariff and customs regulations. Prepare and manage departmental budgets. Prepare or direct preparation of correspondence; reports; and operations, maintenance, and safety manuals. Arrange for necessary shipping documentation and contact customs officials in order to effect release of shipments. Advise sales and billing departments of transportation charges for customers' accounts. Evaluate freight costs and the inventory costs associated with transit times in order to ensure that costs are appropriate. Participate in setting transportation and service rates. Track and trace goods while they are en route to their destinations, expediting orders when necessary. **SKILLS— Management of Personnel Resources:** Motivating, developing, and directing people as they work, identifying the best people for the job. **Operations Analysis:** Analyzing needs and product requirements to create a design. **Monitoring:** Monitoring or assessing your performance or that of other individuals or organizations to make improvements or take corrective action. **Management of Material Resources:** Obtaining and seeing to the appropriate use of equipment, facilities, and materials needed to do certain work. **Persuasion:** Persuading others to change their minds or behavior. **Service Orientation:** Actively looking for ways to help people. **Social Perceptiveness:** Being aware of others' reactions and understanding why they react as they do. **Systems Analysis:** Determining how a system should work and how changes in conditions, operations, and the environment will affect outcomes. **GOE—Interest Area:** 16. Transportation, Distribution, and Logistics.

Work Group: 16.01. Managerial Work in Transportation. **Other Jobs in This Work Group:** Aircraft Cargo Handling Supervisors; First-Line Supervisors/Managers of Transportation and Material-Moving Machine and Vehicle Operators; Postmasters and Mail Superintendents; Railroad Conductors and Yardmasters; Transportation Managers. **PERSONALITY TYPE:** Enterprising. Enterprising occupations frequently involve starting up and carrying out projects. These occupations can involve leading people and making many decisions. They sometimes require risk taking and often deal with business.

EDUCATION/TRAINING PROGRAM(S)—Aeronautics/Aviation/Aerospace Science and Technology, General; Aviation/Airway Management and Operations; Business Administration and Management, General; Business/Commerce, General; Logistics and Materials Management; Public Administration. RELATED KNOWLEDGE/COURSES—**Customer and Personal Service:** Knowledge of principles and processes for providing customer and personal services. This includes customer needs assessment, meeting quality standards for services, and evaluation of customer satisfaction. **Administration and Management:** Knowledge of business and management principles involved in strategic planning, resource allocation, human resources modeling, leadership technique, production methods, and coordination of people and resources. **Sales and Marketing:** Knowledge of principles and methods for showing, promoting, and selling products or services. This includes marketing strategy and tactics, product demonstrations, sales techniques, and sales control systems. **Personnel and Human Resources:** Knowledge of principles and procedures for personnel recruitment, selection, training, compensation and benefits, labor relations and negotiation, and personnel information systems. **Education and Training:** Knowledge of principles and methods for curriculum and training design, teaching and instruction for individuals and groups, and the measurement of training effects. **Production and Processing:** Knowledge of raw materials, production processes, quality control, costs, and other techniques for maximizing the effective manufacture and distribution of goods.

Structural Iron and Steel Workers

- Education/Training Required: Long-term on-the-job training
- Annual Earnings: $42,430
- Growth: 15.9%
- Annual Job Openings: 9,000
- Self-Employed: 6.2%
- Part-Time: 1.8%

Raise, place, and unite iron or steel girders, columns, and other structural members to form completed structures or structural frameworks. May erect metal storage tanks and assemble prefabricated metal buildings. Assemble hoisting equipment and rigging, such as cables, pulleys, and hooks, to move heavy equipment and materials. Bolt aligned structural-steel members in position for permanent riveting, bolting, or welding into place. Connect columns, beams, and girders with bolts, following blueprints and instructions from supervisors. Drive drift pins through rivet holes in order to align rivet holes in structural-steel members with corresponding holes in previously placed members. Erect metal and precast concrete components for structures such as buildings, bridges, dams, towers, storage tanks, fences, and highway guardrails. Fasten structural-steel members to hoist cables, using chains, cables, or rope. Force structural-steel members into final positions, using turnbuckles, crowbars, jacks, and hand tools. Hoist steel beams, girders, and columns into place, using cranes, or signal hoisting equipment operators to lift and position structural-steel members. Pull, push, or pry structural-steel members into approximate positions for bolting into place. Ride on girders or other structural-steel members to position them or use rope to guide them into position. Unload and position prefabricated steel units for hoisting as needed. Verify vertical and horizontal alignment of structural-steel members, using plumb bobs, laser equipment, transits, and/or levels. Catch hot rivets in buckets and insert rivets in holes, using tongs. Cut, bend, and weld steel pieces, using metal shears, torches, and welding equipment. Dismantle structures and equipment. Fabricate metal parts such as steel frames, columns, beams, and girders, according to blueprints or instructions from supervisors. Hold rivets while riveters use air hammers to form heads on rivets. Insert sealing strips, wiring, insulating material, ladders, flanges, gauges, and valves, depending on types of structures being assembled. Place blocks under reinforcing bars used to reinforce floors. Read specifications and blueprints to determine the locations, quantities, and sizes of materials required. **SKILLS—Installation:** Installing equipment, machines, wiring, or programs to meet specifications. **Repairing:** Repairing machines or systems by using the needed tools. **Coordination:** Adjusting actions in relation to others' actions. **Management of Material Resources:** Obtaining and seeing to the appropriate use of equipment, facilities, and materials needed to do certain work. **Equipment Selection:** Determining the kind of tools and equipment needed to do a job. **Operation and Control:** Controlling operations of equipment or systems. **Technology Design:** Generating or adapting equipment and technology to serve user needs. **GOE—Interest Area:** 02. Architecture and Construction. **Work Group:** 02.04. Construction Crafts. **Other Jobs in This Work Group:** Boat Builders and Shipwrights; Boilermakers; Brattice Builders; Brickmasons and Blockmasons; Carpet Installers; Ceiling Tile Installers; Cement Masons and Concrete Finishers; Commercial Divers; Construction Carpenters; Crane and Tower Operators; Dragline Operators; Drywall Installers; Electricians; Fence Erectors; Floor Layers, Except Carpet, Wood, and Hard Tiles; Floor Sanders and Finishers; Glaziers; Grader, Bulldozer, and Scraper Operators; Hazardous Materials Removal Workers; Insulation Workers, Floor, Ceiling, and Wall; Insulation Workers, Mechanical; Manufactured Building and Mobile Home Installers; Operating Engineers; Painters, Construction and Maintenance; Paperhangers; Paving, Surfacing, and Tamping Equipment Operators; Pile-Driver Operators; Pipe Fitters; Pipelayers; Pipelaying Fitters; Plasterers and Stucco Masons; Plumbers; Rail-Track Laying and Maintenance Equipment Operators; Refractory Materials Repairers, Except Brickmasons; Reinforcing Iron and Rebar Workers; Riggers; Roofers; Rough Carpenters; Security and Fire Alarm Systems Installers; Segmental Pavers; Sheet Metal Workers; Ship Carpenters and Joiners; Stone Cutters and Carvers; Stonemasons; Tapers; Terrazzo Workers and Finishers; Tile and Marble Setters. **PERSONALITY**

TYPE: Realistic. Realistic occupations frequently involve work activities that include practical, hands-on problems and solutions. These occupations often deal with plants, animals, and real-world materials like wood, tools, and machinery. Many of the occupations require working outside and do not involve a lot of paperwork or working closely with others.

EDUCATION/TRAINING PROGRAM(S)— Construction Trades, Other; Metal Building Assembly/Assembler. **RELATED KNOWLEDGE/ COURSES—Building and Construction:** Knowledge of the materials, methods, and tools involved in the construction or repair of houses, buildings, or other structures such as highways and roads. **Mechanical Devices:** Knowledge of machines and tools, including their designs, uses, repair, and maintenance. **Public Safety and Security:** Knowledge of relevant equipment, policies, procedures, and strategies to promote effective local, state, or national security operations for the protection of people, data, property, and institutions. **Engineering and Technology:** Knowledge of the practical application of engineering science and technology. This includes applying principles, techniques, procedures, and equipment to the design and production of various goods and services. **Physics:** Knowledge and prediction of physical principles and laws and their interrelationships and applications to understanding fluid, material, and atmospheric dynamics and mechanical, electrical, atomic, and subatomic structures and processes. **Design:** Knowledge of design techniques, tools, and principles involved in production of precision technical plans, blueprints, drawings, and models.

Subway and Streetcar Operators

- Education/Training Required: Moderate-term on-the-job training
- Annual Earnings: $49,290
- Growth: 13.2%
- Annual Job Openings: 2,000
- Self-Employed: 0%
- Part-Time: 8.8%

Operate subway or elevated suburban train with no separate locomotive or electric-powered streetcar to transport passengers. May handle fares. Drive and control rail-guided public transportation, such as subways; elevated trains; and electric-powered streetcars, trams, or trolleys, in order to transport passengers. Make announcements to passengers, such as notifications of upcoming stops or schedule delays. Operate controls to open and close transit vehicle doors. Regulate vehicle speed and the time spent at each stop in order to maintain schedules. Report delays, mechanical problems, and emergencies to supervisors or dispatchers, using radios. Monitor lights indicating obstructions or other trains ahead and watch for car and truck traffic at crossings to stay alert to potential hazards. Attend meetings on driver and passenger safety in order to learn ways in which job performance might be affected. Collect fares from passengers and issue change and transfers. Complete reports, including shift summaries and incident or accident reports. Direct emergency evacuation procedures. Greet passengers; provide information; and answer questions concerning fares, schedules, transfers, and routings. Record transactions and coin receptor readings in order to verify the amount of money collected. **SKILLS—Operation and Control:** Controlling operations of equipment or systems. **Operation Monitoring:** Watching gauges, dials, or other indicators to make sure a machine is working properly. **GOE—Interest Area:** 16. Transportation, Distribution, and Logistics. **Work Group:** 16.04. Rail Vehicle Operation. **Other Jobs in This Work Group:** Locomotive Engineers; Locomotive Firers; Rail Yard Engineers, Dinkey Operators, and Hostlers. **PERSONALITY TYPE:** Realistic. Realistic occupations frequently involve work activities that include practical, hands-on problems and solutions. These occupations often deal with plants, animals, and real-world materials like wood, tools, and machinery. Many of the occupations require working outside and do not involve a lot of paperwork or working closely with others.

EDUCATION/TRAINING PROGRAM(S)— Truck and Bus Driver/Commercial Vehicle Operation. **RELATED KNOWLEDGE/COURSES—Transportation:** Knowledge of principles and methods for moving people or goods by air, rail, sea, or road, including the relative costs and benefits. **Geography:**

Knowledge of principles and methods for describing the features of land, sea, and air masses, including their physical characteristics; locations; interrelationships; and distribution of plant, animal, and human life. **Clerical Practices:** Knowledge of administrative and clerical procedures and systems such as word processing, managing files and records, stenography and transcription, designing forms, and other office procedures and terminology. **Customer and Personal Service:** Knowledge of principles and processes for providing customer and personal services. This includes customer needs assessment, meeting quality standards for services, and evaluation of customer satisfaction. **Telecommunications:** Knowledge of transmission, broadcasting, switching, control, and operation of telecommunications systems.

Surgical Technologists

- Education/Training Required: Postsecondary vocational training
- Annual Earnings: $34,010
- Growth: 27.9%
- Annual Job Openings: 13,000
- Self-Employed: 0%
- Part-Time: 23.0%

Assist in operations under the supervision of surgeons, registered nurses, or other surgical personnel. May help set up operating room; prepare and transport patients for surgery; adjust lights and equipment; pass instruments and other supplies to surgeons and surgeon's assistants; hold retractors; cut sutures; and help count sponges, needles, supplies, and instruments. Count sponges, needles, and instruments before and after operation. Hand instruments and supplies to surgeons and surgeons' assistants, hold retractors and cut sutures, and perform other tasks as directed by surgeon during operation. Scrub arms and hands and assist the surgical team to scrub and put on gloves, masks, and surgical clothing. Position patients on the operating table and cover them with sterile surgical drapes to prevent exposure. Provide technical assistance to surgeons, surgical nurses, and anesthesiologists. Wash and sterilize equipment, using germicides and sterilizers. Prepare, care for, and dispose of tissue specimens taken for laboratory analysis. Clean and restock the operating room, placing equipment and supplies and arranging instruments according to instruction. Prepare dressings or bandages and apply or assist with their application following surgery. Operate, assemble, adjust, or monitor sterilizers, lights, suction machines, and diagnostic equipment to ensure proper operation. Monitor and continually assess operating room conditions, including patient and surgical team needs. Observe patients' vital signs to assess physical condition. Maintain supply of fluids, such as plasma, saline, blood, and glucose, for use during operations. Maintain files and records of surgical procedures. **SKILLS—Instructing:** Teaching others how to do something. **Troubleshooting:** Determining causes of operating errors and deciding what to do about them. **Learning Strategies:** Selecting and using training/instructional methods and procedures appropriate for the situation when learning or teaching new things. **Equipment Selection:** Determining the kind of tools and equipment needed to do a job. **Social Perceptiveness:** Being aware of others' reactions and understanding why they react as they do. **Reading Comprehension:** Understanding written sentences and paragraphs in work-related documents. **Active Learning:** Understanding the implications of new information for both current and future problem-solving and decision-making. **Coordination:** Adjusting actions in relation to others' actions. **Service Orientation:** Actively looking for ways to help people. **Operation Monitoring:** Watching gauges, dials, or other indicators to make sure a machine is working properly. **GOE—Interest Area:** 08. Health Science. **Work Group:** 08.02. Medicine and Surgery. **Other Jobs in This Work Group:** Anesthesiologists; Family and General Practitioners; Internists, General; Medical Assistants; Medical Transcriptionists; Obstetricians and Gynecologists; Pediatricians, General; Pharmacists; Pharmacy Aides; Pharmacy Technicians; Physician Assistants; Psychiatrists; Registered Nurses; Surgeons. **PERSONALITY TYPE:** Realistic. Realistic occupations frequently involve work activities that include practical, hands-on problems and solutions. These occupations often deal with plants, animals, and real-world materials like wood, tools, and machinery. Many of the occupations require working outside and do not involve a lot of paperwork or working closely with others.

EDUCATION/TRAINING PROGRAM(S)— Pathology/Pathologist Assistant; Surgical Technology/Technologist. **RELATED KNOWLEDGE/ COURSES—Medicine and Dentistry:** Knowledge of the information and techniques needed to diagnose and treat human injuries, diseases, and deformities. This includes symptoms, treatment alternatives, drug properties and interactions, and preventive health-care measures. **Customer and Personal Service:** Knowledge of principles and processes for providing customer and personal services. This includes customer needs assessment, meeting quality standards for services, and evaluation of customer satisfaction. **Chemistry:** Knowledge of the chemical composition, structure, and properties of substances and of the chemical processes and transformations that they undergo. This includes uses of chemicals and their danger signs, production techniques, and disposal methods. **Psychology:** Knowledge of human behavior and performance; individual differences in ability, personality, and interests; learning and motivation; psychological research methods; and the assessment and treatment of behavioral and affective disorders. **Philosophy and Theology:** Knowledge of different philosophical systems and religions. This includes their basic principles, values, ethics, ways of thinking, customs, and practices and their impact on human culture. **Education and Training:** Knowledge of principles and methods for curriculum and training design, teaching and instruction for individuals and groups, and the measurement of training effects.

Surveying Technicians

◎ Education/Training Required: Long-term on-the-job training
◎ Annual Earnings: $30,380
◎ Growth: 23.1%
◎ Annual Job Openings: 10,000
◎ Self-Employed: 5.5%
◎ Part-Time: 7.0%

Adjust and operate surveying instruments, such as the theodolite and electronic distance-measuring equipment, and compile notes, make sketches, and enter data into computers. Adjust and operate surveying instruments such as prisms, theodolites, and electronic distance-measuring equipment. Compile information necessary to stake projects for construction, using engineering plans. Run rods for benches and cross-section elevations. Position and hold the vertical rods, or targets, that theodolite operators use for sighting in order to measure angles, distances, and elevations. Record survey measurements and descriptive data, using notes, drawings, sketches, and inked tracings. Perform calculations to determine earth curvature corrections, atmospheric impacts on measurements, traverse closures and adjustments, azimuths, level runs, and placement of markers. Conduct surveys to ascertain the locations of natural features and human-made structures on the Earth's surface, underground, and under water, using electronic distance-measuring equipment and other surveying instruments. Search for section corners, property irons, and survey points. Operate and manage land-information computer systems, performing tasks such as storing data, making inquiries, and producing plots and reports. Direct and supervise work of subordinate members of surveying parties. Set out and recover stakes, marks, and other monumentation. Lay out grids and determine horizontal and vertical controls. Compare survey computations with applicable standards in order to determine adequacy of data. Collect information needed to carry out new surveys, using source maps, previous survey data, photographs, computer records, and other relevant information. Prepare topographic and contour maps of land surveyed, including site features and other relevant information such as charts, drawings, and survey notes. Maintain equipment and vehicles used by surveying crews. Place and hold measuring tapes when electronic distance-measuring equipment is not used. Provide assistance in the development of methods and procedures for conducting field surveys. Perform manual labor, such as cutting brush for lines; carrying stakes, rebar, and other heavy items; and stacking rods. **SKILLS—Mathematics:** Using mathematics to solve problems. **Coordination:** Adjusting actions in relation to others' actions. **Troubleshooting:** Determining causes of operating errors and deciding what to do about them. **Instructing:** Teaching others how to do something. **Time Management:** Managing one's own time and the time of others. **Active Learning:** Understanding the impli-

cations of new information for both current and future problem-solving and decision-making. **Equipment Selection:** Determining the kind of tools and equipment needed to do a job. **Equipment Maintenance:** Performing routine maintenance on equipment and determining when and what kind of maintenance is needed. **GOE—Interest Area:** 15. Scientific Research, Engineering, and Mathematics. **Work Group:** 15.09. Engineering Technology. **Other Jobs in This Work Group:** Aerospace Engineering and Operations Technicians; Calibration and Instrumentation Technicians; Cartographers and Photogrammetrists; Civil Engineering Technicians; Electrical Engineering Technicians; Electro-Mechanical Technicians; Electronic Drafters; Electronics Engineering Technicians; Environmental Engineering Technicians; Mapping Technicians; Mechanical Drafters; Mechanical Engineering Technicians. **PERSONALITY TYPE:** Realistic. Realistic occupations frequently involve work activities that include practical, hands-on problems and solutions. These occupations often deal with plants, animals, and real-world materials like wood, tools, and machinery. Many of the occupations require working outside and do not involve a lot of paperwork or working closely with others.

EDUCATION/TRAINING PROGRAM(S)—Cartography; Surveying Technology/Surveying. **RELATED KNOWLEDGE/COURSES—Building and Construction:** Knowledge of the materials, methods, and tools involved in the construction or repair of houses, buildings, or other structures such as highways and roads. **Design:** Knowledge of design techniques, tools, and principles involved in production of precision technical plans, blueprints, drawings, and models. **Geography:** Knowledge of principles and methods for describing the features of land, sea, and air masses, including their physical characteristics; locations; interrelationships; and distribution of plant, animal, and human life. **Engineering and Technology:** Knowledge of the practical application of engineering science and technology. This includes applying principles, techniques, procedures, and equipment to the design and production of various goods and services. **Mathematics:** Knowledge of arithmetic, algebra, geometry, calculus, and statistics and their applications. **Computers and Electronics:** Knowledge of circuit boards, processors, chips, electronic equipment, and computer hardware and software, including applications and programming.

Talent Directors

- Education/Training Required: Long-term on-the-job training
- Annual Earnings: $52,840
- Growth: 18.3%
- Annual Job Openings: 10,000
- Self-Employed: 32.8%
- Part-Time: 9.1%

Audition and interview performers to select most appropriate talent for parts in stage, television, radio, or motion picture productions. Arrange for and/or design screen tests or auditions for prospective performers. Attend or view productions in order to maintain knowledge of available actors. Audition and interview performers in order to match their attributes to specific roles or to increase the pool of available acting talent. Contact agents and actors in order to provide notification of audition and performance opportunities and to set up audition times. Locate performers or extras for crowd and background scenes and stand-ins or photo doubles for actors by direct contact or through agents. Maintain talent files that include information such as performers' specialties, past performances, and availability. Negotiate contract agreements with performers, with agents, or between performers and agents or production companies. Prepare actors for auditions by providing scripts and information about roles and casting requirements. Read scripts and confer with producers in order to determine the types and numbers of performers required for a given production. Review performer information such as photos, resumes, voice tapes, videos, and union membership in order to decide whom to audition for parts. Select performers for roles or submit lists of suitable performers to producers or directors for final selection. Hire and supervise workers who help locate people with specified attributes and talents. Serve as liaisons between directors, actors, and agents. **SKILLS—Negotiation:** Bringing others together and trying to reconcile differences. **Management of Personnel Resources:** Motivating, developing, and directing people as they work, identifying the best people for the job. **Speaking:** Talking to others to convey information effectively. **Social Perceptiveness:** Being aware of others' reactions and understanding why they react as they do. **Persuasion:** Persuading others to change their minds or behavior. **Active Listening:** Giving full attention to what other people are saying, taking time to understand the points being made, asking questions as appropriate, and not interrupting at inappropriate times. **Writing:** Communicating effectively in writing as appropriate for the needs of the audience. **Reading Comprehension:** Understanding written sentences and paragraphs in work-related documents. **GOE—Interest Area:** 03. Arts and Communication. **Work Group:** 03.07. Music. **Other Jobs in This Work Group:** Composers; Music Arrangers and Orchestrators; Music Directors; Musicians, Instrumental; Singers. **PERSONALITY TYPE:** Artistic. Artistic occupations frequently involve working with forms, designs, and patterns. These occupations often require self-expression, and the work can be done without following a clear set of rules.

EDUCATION/TRAINING PROGRAM(S)—Cinematography and Film/Video Production; Directing and Theatrical Production; Drama and Dramatics/Theatre Arts, General; Dramatic/Theatre Arts and Stagecraft, Other; Film/Cinema Studies; Radio and Television; Theatre/Theatre Arts Management. **RELATED KNOWLEDGE/COURSES—Fine Arts:** Knowledge of the theory and techniques required to compose, produce, and perform works of music, dance, the visual arts, drama, and sculpture. **Sales and Marketing:** Knowledge of principles and methods for showing, promoting, and selling products or services. This includes marketing strategy and tactics, product demonstrations, sales techniques, and sales control systems. **Administration and Management:** Knowledge of business and management principles involved in strategic planning, resource allocation, human resources modeling, leadership technique, production methods, and coordination of people and resources. **Personnel and Human Resources:** Knowledge of principles and procedures for personnel recruitment, selection, training, compensation and benefits, labor relations and negotiation, and personnel information systems. **Communications and Media:** Knowledge of media production, communication, and dissemination techniques and methods. This includes alternative ways to inform and entertain via written, oral, and visual media. **Economics and Accounting:** Knowledge of economic and accounting principles and practices, the financial markets, banking, and the analysis and reporting of financial data.

Tapers

- Education/Training Required: Moderate-term on-the-job training
- Annual Earnings: $39,070
- Growth: 20.8%
- Annual Job Openings: 5,000
- Self-Employed: 19.1%
- Part-Time: 5.9%

Seal joints between plasterboard or other wallboard to prepare wall surface for painting or papering. Apply texturizing compounds and primers to walls and ceilings before final finishing, using trowels, brushes, rollers, or spray guns. Check adhesives to ensure that they will work and will remain durable. Countersink nails or screws below surfaces of walls before applying sealing compounds, using hammers or screwdrivers. Install metal molding at wall corners to secure wallboard. Mix sealing compounds by hand or with portable electric mixers. Press paper tape over joints to embed tape into sealing compound and to seal joints. Remove extra compound after surfaces have been covered sufficiently. Sand rough spots of dried cement between applications of compounds. Seal joints between plasterboard or other wallboard in order to prepare wall surfaces for painting or papering. Select the correct sealing compound or tape. Spread and smooth cementing material over tape, using trowels or floating machines to blend joints with wall surfaces. Spread sealing compound between boards or panels and over cracks, holes, and nail and screw heads, using trowels, broadknives, or spatulas. Use mechanical applicators that spread compounds and embed tape in one operation. Apply additional coats to fill in holes and make surfaces smooth. Sand or patch nicks or cracks in plasterboard or wallboard. **SKILLS**—None met the criteria. **GOE—Interest Area:** 02. Architec-

ture and Construction. **Work Group:** 02.04. Construction Crafts. **Other Jobs in This Work Group:** Boat Builders and Shipwrights; Boilermakers; Brattice Builders; Brickmasons and Blockmasons; Carpet Installers; Ceiling Tile Installers; Cement Masons and Concrete Finishers; Commercial Divers; Construction Carpenters; Crane and Tower Operators; Dragline Operators; Drywall Installers; Electricians; Fence Erectors; Floor Layers, Except Carpet, Wood, and Hard Tiles; Floor Sanders and Finishers; Glaziers; Grader, Bulldozer, and Scraper Operators; Hazardous Materials Removal Workers; Insulation Workers, Floor, Ceiling, and Wall; Insulation Workers, Mechanical; Manufactured Building and Mobile Home Installers; Operating Engineers; Painters, Construction and Maintenance; Paperhangers; Paving, Surfacing, and Tamping Equipment Operators; Pile-Driver Operators; Pipe Fitters; Pipelayers; Pipelaying Fitters; Plasterers and Stucco Masons; Plumbers; Rail-Track Laying and Maintenance Equipment Operators; Refractory Materials Repairers, Except Brickmasons; Reinforcing Iron and Rebar Workers; Riggers; Roofers; Rough Carpenters; Security and Fire Alarm Systems Installers; Segmental Pavers; Sheet Metal Workers; Ship Carpenters and Joiners; Stone Cutters and Carvers; Stonemasons; Structural Iron and Steel Workers; Terrazzo Workers and Finishers; Tile and Marble Setters. **PERSONALITY TYPE:** Realistic. Realistic occupations frequently involve work activities that include practical, hands-on problems and solutions. These occupations often deal with plants, animals, and real-world materials like wood, tools, and machinery. Many of the occupations require working outside and do not involve a lot of paperwork or working closely with others.

EDUCATION/TRAINING PROGRAM(S)—Construction Trades, Other. **RELATED KNOWLEDGE/COURSES—Building and Construction:** Knowledge of the materials, methods, and tools involved in the construction or repair of houses, buildings, or other structures such as highways and roads. **Sales and Marketing:** Knowledge of principles and methods for showing, promoting, and selling products or services. This includes marketing strategy and tactics, product demonstrations, sales techniques, and sales control systems.

Tax Preparers

- ⦿ Education/Training Required: Moderate-term on-the-job training
- ⦿ Annual Earnings: $27,730
- ⦿ Growth: 23.2%
- ⦿ Annual Job Openings: 11,000
- ⦿ Self-Employed: 26.2%
- ⦿ Part-Time: 20.3%

Prepare tax returns for individuals or small businesses, but do not have the background or responsibilities of an accredited or certified public accountant. Check data input or verify totals on forms prepared by others to detect errors in arithmetic, data entry, or procedures. Compute taxes owed or overpaid, using adding machines or personal computers, and complete entries on forms, following tax form instructions and tax tables. Interview clients to obtain additional information on taxable income and deductible expenses and allowances. Prepare or assist in preparing simple to complex tax returns for individuals or small businesses. Review financial records such as income statements and documentation of expenditures in order to determine forms needed to prepare tax returns. Use all appropriate adjustments, deductions, and credits to keep clients' taxes to a minimum. Calculate form preparation fees according to return complexity and processing time required. Consult tax law handbooks or bulletins in order to determine procedures for preparation of atypical returns. Furnish taxpayers with sufficient information and advice in order to ensure correct tax form completion. **SKILLS—Mathematics:** Using mathematics to solve problems. **Reading Comprehension:** Understanding written sentences and paragraphs in work-related documents. **Active Listening:** Giving full attention to what other people are saying, taking time to understand the points being made, asking questions as appropriate, and not interrupting at inappropriate times. **Speaking:** Talking to others to convey information effectively. **Active Learning:** Understanding the implications of new information for both current and future problem-solving and decision-making. **Judgment and Decision Making:** Considering the relative costs and benefits of potential actions to choose the most appropriate one. **Monitor-**

ing: Monitoring or assessing your performance or that of other individuals or organizations to make improvements or take corrective action. **GOE—Interest Area:** 04. Business and Administration. **Work Group:** 04.06. Mathematical Clerical Support. **Other Jobs in This Work Group:** Billing, Cost, and Rate Clerks; Bookkeeping, Accounting, and Auditing Clerks; Brokerage Clerks; Payroll and Timekeeping Clerks; Statement Clerks. **PERSONALITY TYPE:** Conventional. Conventional occupations frequently involve following set procedures and routines. These occupations can include working with data and details more than with ideas. Usually there is a clear line of authority to follow.

EDUCATION/TRAINING PROGRAM(S)— Accounting Technology/Technician and Bookkeeping; Taxation. **RELATED KNOWLEDGE/COURSES— Economics and Accounting:** Knowledge of economic and accounting principles and practices, the financial markets, banking, and the analysis and reporting of financial data. **Law and Government:** Knowledge of laws, legal codes, court procedures, precedents, government regulations, executive orders, agency rules, and the democratic political process. **Clerical Practices:** Knowledge of administrative and clerical procedures and systems such as word processing, managing files and records, stenography and transcription, designing forms, and other office procedures and terminology. **Mathematics:** Knowledge of arithmetic, algebra, geometry, calculus, and statistics and their applications.

Taxi Drivers and Chauffeurs

- ⦿ Education/Training Required: Short-term on-the-job training
- ⦿ Annual Earnings: $19,570
- ⦿ Growth: 21.7%
- ⦿ Annual Job Openings: 28,000
- ⦿ Self-Employed: 4.8%
- ⦿ Part-Time: 17.3%

Drive automobiles, vans, or limousines to transport passengers. May occasionally carry cargo. Test vehicle equipment such as lights, brakes, horns, and windshield wipers in order to ensure proper operation. Notify dispatchers or company mechanics of vehicle problems. Drive taxicabs, limousines, company cars, or privately owned vehicles in order to transport passengers. Follow regulations governing taxi operation and ensure that passengers follow safety regulations. Pick up passengers at prearranged locations, at taxi stands, or by cruising streets in high-traffic areas. Perform routine vehicle maintenance, such as regulating tire pressure and adding gasoline, oil, and water. Communicate with dispatchers by radio, telephone, or computer in order to exchange information and receive requests for passenger service. Record name, date, and taxi identification information on trip sheets, along with trip information such as time and place of pickup and drop-off and total fee. Complete accident reports when necessary. Provide passengers with assistance entering and exiting vehicles and help them with any luggage. Arrange to pick up particular customers or groups on a regular schedule. Vacuum and clean interiors and wash and polish exteriors of automobiles. Pick up or meet employers according to requests, appointments, or schedules. Operate vans with special equipment such as wheelchair lifts to transport people with special needs. Collect fares or vouchers from passengers and make change and/or issue receipts, as necessary. Determine fares based on trip distances and times, using taximeters and fee schedules, and announce fares to passengers. Perform minor vehicle repairs such as cleaning spark plugs or take vehicles to mechanics for servicing. Turn the taximeter on when passengers enter the cab and turn it off when they reach the final destination. Report to taxicab services or garages in order to receive vehicle assignments. Perform errands for customers or employers, such as delivering or picking up mail and packages. Provide passengers with information about the local area and points of interest and/or give advice on hotels and restaurants. **SKILLS—Service Orientation:** Actively looking for ways to help people. **Operation and Control:** Controlling operations of equipment or systems. **Installation:** Installing equipment, machines, wiring, or programs to meet specifications. **Equipment Maintenance:** Performing routine maintenance on equipment and determining when and what kind of maintenance is needed. **Social Perceptiveness:** Being

aware of others' reactions and understanding why they react as they do. **Learning Strategies:** Selecting and using training/instructional methods and procedures appropriate for the situation when learning or teaching new things. **Negotiation:** Bringing others together and trying to reconcile differences. **Coordination:** Adjusting actions in relation to others' actions. **Instructing:** Teaching others how to do something. **GOE—Interest Area:** 16. Transportation, Distribution, and Logistics. **Work Group:** 16.06. Other Services Requiring Driving. **Other Jobs in This Work Group:** Ambulance Drivers and Attendants, Except Emergency Medical Technicians; Bus Drivers, School; Bus Drivers, Transit and Intercity; Couriers and Messengers; Driver/Sales Workers; Parking Lot Attendants; Postal Service Mail Carriers. **PERSONALITY TYPE:** Realistic. Realistic occupations frequently involve work activities that include practical, hands-on problems and solutions. These occupations often deal with plants, animals, and real-world materials like wood, tools, and machinery. Many of the occupations require working outside and do not involve a lot of paperwork or working closely with others.

EDUCATION/TRAINING PROGRAM(S)— Truck and Bus Driver/Commercial Vehicle Operation. **RELATED KNOWLEDGE/COURSES—Transportation:** Knowledge of principles and methods for moving people or goods by air, rail, sea, or road, including the relative costs and benefits. **Economics and Accounting:** Knowledge of economic and accounting principles and practices, the financial markets, banking, and the analysis and reporting of financial data. **English Language:** Knowledge of the structure and content of the English language, including the meaning and spelling of words, rules of composition, and grammar. **Clerical Practices:** Knowledge of administrative and clerical procedures and systems such as word processing, managing files and records, stenography and transcription, designing forms, and other office procedures and terminology.

Teacher Assistants

- ⚲ Education/Training Required: Short-term on-the-job training
- ⚲ Annual Earnings: $19,410
- ⚲ Growth: 23.0%
- ⚲ Annual Job Openings: 259,000
- ⚲ Self-Employed: 0.3%
- ⚲ Part-Time: 41.1%

Perform duties that are instructional in nature or deliver direct services to students or parents. Serve in a position for which a teacher or another professional has ultimate responsibility for the design and implementation of educational programs and services. Discuss assigned duties with classroom teachers in order to coordinate instructional efforts. Prepare lesson materials, bulletin board displays, exhibits, equipment, and demonstrations. Present subject matter to students under the direction and guidance of teachers, using lectures, discussions, or supervised role-playing methods. Tutor and assist children individually or in small groups in order to help them master assignments and to reinforce learning concepts presented by teachers. Supervise students in classrooms, halls, cafeterias, school yards, and gymnasiums or on field trips. Conduct demonstrations to teach such skills as sports, dancing, and handicrafts. Distribute teaching materials such as textbooks, workbooks, papers, and pencils to students. Distribute tests and homework assignments and collect them when they are completed. Enforce administration policies and rules governing students. Grade homework and tests and compute and record results, using answer sheets or electronic marking devices. Instruct and monitor students in the use and care of equipment and materials in order to prevent injuries and damage. Observe students' performance and record relevant data to assess progress. Organize and label materials and display students' work in a manner appropriate for their eye levels and perceptual skills. Organize and supervise games and other recreational activities to promote physical, mental, and social development. Participate in teacher-parent conferences regarding students' progress or problems. Plan, prepare, and develop various teaching aids such as bibliographies, charts, and graphs. Prepare lesson outlines and plans in assigned subject areas and submit outlines to teachers for review. Provide extra assistance to students with special needs, such as non-English-speaking students or those with physical and mental disabilities. Take class attendance and maintain attendance records. Assist in bus loading and unloading. Assist librarians in school libraries. Attend staff meetings and serve on committees as required. Carry out therapeutic regimens such as behavior modification and personal development programs under the supervision of special education instructors, psychologists, or speech-language pathologists. **SKILLS—Learning Strategies:** Selecting and using training/instructional methods and procedures appropriate for the situation when learning or teaching new things. **Instructing:** Teaching others how to do something. **Service Orientation:** Actively looking for ways to help people. **Speaking:** Talking to others to convey information effectively. **Active Listening:** Giving full attention to what other people are saying, taking time to understand the points being made, asking questions as appropriate, and not interrupting at inappropriate times. **Social Perceptiveness:** Being aware of others' reactions and understanding why they react as they do. **Reading Comprehension:** Understanding written sentences and paragraphs in work-related documents. **Writing:** Communicating effectively in writing as appropriate for the needs of the audience. **GOE—Interest Area:** 05. Education and Training. **Work Group:** 05.02. Preschool, Elementary, and Secondary Teaching and Instructing. **Other Jobs in This Work Group:** Elementary School Teachers, Except Special Education; Kindergarten Teachers, Except Special Education; Middle School Teachers, Except Special and Vocational Education; Preschool Teachers, Except Special Education; Secondary School Teachers, Except Special and Vocational Education; Special Education Teachers, Middle School; Special Education Teachers, Preschool, Kindergarten, and Elementary School; Special Education Teachers, Secondary School; Vocational Education Teachers, Middle School; Vocational Education Teachers, Secondary School. **PERSONALITY TYPE:** Social. Social occupations frequently involve working with, communicating with, and teaching people. These occupations often involve helping or providing service to others.

EDUCATION/TRAINING PROGRAM(S)— Teacher Assistant/Aide; Teaching Assistants/Aides, Other. **RELATED KNOWLEDGE/COURSES— Education and Training:** Knowledge of principles and methods for curriculum and training design, teaching and instruction for individuals and groups, and the measurement of training effects. **English Language:** Knowledge of the structure and content of the English language, including the meaning and spelling of words, rules of composition, and grammar. **History and Archeology:** Knowledge of historical events and their causes, indicators, and effects on civilizations and cultures. **Psychology:** Knowledge of human behavior and performance; individual differences in ability, personality, and interests; learning and motivation; psychological research methods; and the assessment and treatment of behavioral and affective disorders. **Sociology and Anthropology:** Knowledge of group behavior and dynamics, societal trends and influences, human migrations, ethnicity, and cultures and their history and origins. **Clerical Practices:** Knowledge of administrative and clerical procedures and systems such as word processing, managing files and records, stenography and transcription, designing forms, and other office procedures and terminology.

Technical Directors/Managers

- Education/Training Required: Long-term on-the-job training
- Annual Earnings: $52,840
- Growth: 18.3%
- Annual Job Openings: 10,000
- Self-Employed: 32.8%
- Part-Time: 9.1%

Coordinate activities of technical departments, such as taping, editing, engineering, and maintenance, to produce radio or television programs. Direct technical aspects of newscasts and other productions, checking and switching between video sources and taking responsibility for the on-air product, including camera shots and graphics. Test equipment in order to ensure proper operation. Monitor broadcasts in order to ensure that programs conform to station or network policies and regulations. Observe pictures through monitors and direct camera and video staff concerning shading and composition. Act as liaisons between engineering and production departments. Supervise and assign duties to workers engaged in technical control and production of radio and television programs. Schedule use of studio and editing facilities for producers and engineering and maintenance staff. Confer with operations directors in order to formulate and maintain fair and attainable technical policies for programs. Operate equipment to produce programs or broadcast live programs from remote locations. Train workers in use of equipment such as switchers, cameras, monitors, microphones, and lights. Switch between video sources in a studio or on multi-camera remotes, using equipment such as switchers, video slide projectors, and video effects generators. Set up and execute video transitions and special effects such as fades, dissolves, cuts, keys, and supers, using computers to manipulate pictures as necessary. Collaborate with promotions directors to produce on-air station promotions. Discuss filter options, lens choices, and the visual effects of objects being filmed with photography directors and video operators. Follow instructions from production managers and directors during productions, such as commands for camera cuts, effects, graphics, and takes. **SKILLS—Operation Monitoring:** Watching gauges, dials, or other indicators to make sure a machine is working properly. **Time Management:** Managing one's own time and the time of others. **Operation and Control:** Controlling operations of equipment or systems. **Monitoring:** Monitoring or assessing your performance or that of other individuals or organizations to make improvements or take corrective action. **Coordination:** Adjusting actions in relation to others' actions. **Management of Personnel Resources:** Motivating, developing, and directing people as they work, identifying the best people for the job. **Troubleshooting:** Determining causes of operating errors and deciding what to do about them. **Instructing:** Teaching others how to do something. **Systems Analysis:** Determining how a system should work and how changes in conditions, operations, and the environment will affect outcomes. **GOE—Interest Area:** 03. Arts and Communication. **Work Group:** 03.01. Managerial Work in Arts and

Communication. **Other Jobs in This Work Group:** Agents and Business Managers of Artists, Performers, and Athletes; Art Directors; Producers; Program Directors; Public Relations Managers. **PERSONALITY TYPE:** Realistic. Realistic occupations frequently involve work activities that include practical, hands-on problems and solutions. These occupations often deal with plants, animals, and real-world materials like wood, tools, and machinery. Many of the occupations require working outside and do not involve a lot of paperwork or working closely with others.

EDUCATION/TRAINING PROGRAM(S)—Cinematography and Film/Video Production; Directing and Theatrical Production; Drama and Dramatics/Theatre Arts, General; Dramatic/Theatre Arts and Stagecraft, Other; Film/Cinema Studies; Radio and Television; Theatre/Theatre Arts Management. **RELATED KNOWLEDGE/COURSES**— **Communications and Media:** Knowledge of media production, communication, and dissemination techniques and methods. This includes alternative ways to inform and entertain via written, oral, and visual media. **Telecommunications:** Knowledge of transmission, broadcasting, switching, control, and operation of telecommunications systems. **Computers and Electronics:** Knowledge of circuit boards, processors, chips, electronic equipment, and computer hardware and software, including applications and programming. **Engineering and Technology:** Knowledge of the practical application of engineering science and technology. This includes applying principles, techniques, procedures, and equipment to the design and production of various goods and services. **Philosophy and Theology:** Knowledge of different philosophical systems and religions. This includes their basic principles, values, ethics, ways of thinking, customs, and practices and their impact on human culture. **Sales and Marketing:** Knowledge of principles and methods for showing, promoting, and selling products or services. This includes marketing strategy and tactics, product demonstrations, sales techniques, and sales control systems.

Telecommunications Facility Examiners

- Education/Training Required: Long-term on-the-job training
- Annual Earnings: $49,840
- Growth: –0.6%
- Annual Job Openings: 23,000
- Self-Employed: 4.6%
- Part-Time: 1.7%

Examine telephone transmission facilities to determine equipment requirements for providing subscribers with new or additional telephone services. Examines telephone transmission facilities to determine requirements for new or additional telephone services. Visits subscribers' premises to arrange for new installations, such as telephone booths and telephone poles. Designates cables available for use. Climbs telephone poles or stands on truck-mounted boom to examine terminal boxes for available connections. **SKILLS—Technology Design:** Generating or adapting equipment and technology to serve user needs. **Installation:** Installing equipment, machines, wiring, or programs to meet specifications. **GOE—Interest Area:** 02. Architecture and Construction. **Work Group:** 02.05. Systems and Equipment Installation, Maintenance, and Repair. **Other Jobs in This Work Group:** Central Office and PBX Installers and Repairers; Communication Equipment Mechanics, Installers, and Repairers; Electric Meter Installers and Repairers; Electrical and Electronics Repairers, Powerhouse, Substation, and Relay; Electrical Power-Line Installers and Repairers; Elevator Installers and Repairers; Frame Wirers, Central Office; Heating and Air Conditioning Mechanics; Home Appliance Installers; Maintenance and Repair Workers, General; Meter Mechanics; Refrigeration Mechanics; Station Installers and Repairers, Telephone; Telecommunications Line Installers and Repairers. **PERSONALITY TYPE:** Realistic. Realistic occupations frequently involve work activities that include practical, hands-on problems and solutions. These occupations often deal with plants, animals, and real-world materials like wood, tools, and machinery. Many of the occupations require working outside and do not involve a lot of paperwork or working closely with others.

EDUCATION/TRAINING PROGRAM(S)— Communications Systems Installation and Repair Technology. **RELATED KNOWLEDGE/COURSES—Telecommunications:** Knowledge of transmission, broadcasting, switching, control, and operation of telecommunications systems. **Computers and Electronics:** Knowledge of circuit boards, processors, chips, electronic equipment, and computer hardware and software, including applications and programming. **Engineering and Technology:** Knowledge of the practical application of engineering science and technology. This includes applying principles, techniques, procedures, and equipment to the design and production of various goods and services. **Geography:** Knowledge of principles and methods for describing the features of land, sea, and air masses, including their physical characteristics; locations; interrelationships; and distribution of plant, animal, and human life.

Telecommunications Line Installers and Repairers

- ◎ Education/Training Required: Long-term on-the-job training
- ◎ Annual Earnings: $40,330
- ◎ Growth: 18.8%
- ◎ Annual Job Openings: 13,000
- ◎ Self-Employed: 3.7%
- ◎ Part-Time: 1.4%

String and repair telephone and television cable, including fiber optics and other equipment for transmitting messages or television programming. Access specific areas to string lines and install terminal boxes, auxiliary equipment, and appliances, using bucket trucks or by climbing poles and ladders or entering tunnels, trenches, or crawl spaces. Inspect and test lines and cables, recording and analyzing test results to assess transmission characteristics and locate faults and malfunctions. Install equipment such as amplifiers and repeaters in order to maintain the strength of communications transmissions. Lay underground cable directly in trenches or string it through conduits running through trenches. Measure signal strength at utility poles, using electronic test equipment. Place insulation over conductors and seal splices with moisture-proof covering. Pull up cable by hand from large reels mounted on trucks; then pull lines through ducts by hand or with winches. Set up service for customers, installing, connecting, testing, and adjusting equipment. Splice cables, using hand tools, epoxy, or mechanical equipment. String cables between structures and lines from poles, towers, or trenches and pull lines to proper tension. Travel to customers' premises to install, maintain, and repair audio and visual electronic reception equipment and accessories. Use a variety of construction equipment to complete installations, including digger derricks, trenchers, and cable plows. Clean and maintain tools and test equipment. Compute impedance of wires from poles to houses in order to determine additional resistance needed for reducing signals to desired levels. Dig holes for power poles, using power augers or shovels; set poles in place with cranes; and hoist poles upright, using winches. Dig trenches for underground wires and cables. Explain cable service to subscribers after installation and collect any installation fees that are due. Fill and tamp holes, using cement, earth, and tamping devices. Participate in the construction and removal of telecommunication towers and associated support structures. **SKILLS—Installation:** Installing equipment, machines, wiring, or programs to meet specifications. **Repairing:** Repairing machines or systems by using the needed tools. **Troubleshooting:** Determining causes of operating errors and deciding what to do about them. **Equipment Maintenance:** Performing routine maintenance on equipment and determining when and what kind of maintenance is needed. **Operation Monitoring:** Watching gauges, dials, or other indicators to make sure a machine is working properly. **Systems Evaluation:** Identifying measures or indicators of system performance and the actions needed to improve or correct performance relative to the goals of the system. **Operation and Control:** Controlling operations of equipment or systems. **Mathematics:** Using mathematics to solve problems. **GOE—Interest Area:** 02. Architecture and Construction. **Work Group:** 02.05. Systems and Equipment Installation, Maintenance, and Repair. **Other Jobs in This Work Group:** Central Office and PBX Installers and Repairers; Communication Equipment Mechanics, Installers, and Repairers; Electric Meter Installers and Repairers; Electrical and Electronics Repairers, Powerhouse, Substation, and Relay; Electrical Power-Line Installers and Repairers; Elevator Installers and Repairers; Frame Wirers, Central Office; Heating and Air Conditioning Mechanics; Home Appliance Installers; Maintenance and Repair Workers, General; Meter Mechanics; Refrigeration Mechanics; Station Installers and Repairers, Telephone; Telecommunications Facility Examiners. **PERSONALITY TYPE:** Realistic. Realistic occupations frequently involve work activities that include practical, hands-on problems and solutions. These occupations often deal with plants, animals, and real-world materials like wood, tools, and machinery. Many of the occupations require working outside and do not involve a lot of paperwork or working closely with others.

EDUCATION/TRAINING PROGRAM(S)— Communications Systems Installation and Repair Technology. **RELATED KNOWLEDGE/COURS-ES—Telecommunications:** Knowledge of transmission, broadcasting, switching, control, and operation of telecommunications systems. **Computers and Electronics:** Knowledge of circuit boards, processors, chips, electronic equipment, and computer hardware and software, including applications and programming. **Mechanical Devices:** Knowledge of machines and tools, including their designs, uses, repair, and maintenance. **Physics:** Knowledge and prediction of physical principles and laws and their interrelationships and applications to understanding fluid, material, and atmospheric dynamics and mechanical, electrical, atomic, and subatomic structures and processes. **Sales and Marketing:** Knowledge of principles and methods for showing, promoting, and selling products or services. This includes marketing strategy and tactics, product demonstrations, sales techniques, and sales control systems. **Engineering and Technology:** Knowledge of the practical application of engineering science and technology. This includes applying principles, techniques, procedures, and equipment to the design and production of various goods and services.

Tile and Marble Setters

- ⦿ Education/Training Required: Long-term on-the-job training
- ⦿ Annual Earnings: $35,410
- ⦿ Growth: 26.5%
- ⦿ Annual Job Openings: 4,000
- ⦿ Self-Employed: 0%
- ⦿ Part-Time: 5.0%

Apply hard tile, marble, and wood tile to walls, floors, ceilings, and roof decks. Align and straighten tile, using levels, squares, and straightedges. Determine and implement the best layout to achieve a desired pattern. Cut and shape tile to fit around obstacles and into odd spaces and corners, using hand and power cutting tools. Finish and dress the joints and wipe excess grout from between tiles, using damp sponge. Apply mortar to tile back, position the tile, and press or tap with trowel handle to affix tile to base. Mix, apply, and spread plaster, concrete, mortar, cement, mastic, glue, or other adhesives to form a bed for the tiles, using brush, trowel, and screed. Prepare cost and labor estimates based on calculations of time and materials needed for project. Measure and mark surfaces to be tiled, following blueprints. Level concrete and allow to dry. Build underbeds and install anchor bolts, wires, and brackets. Prepare surfaces for tiling by attaching lath or waterproof paper or by applying a cement mortar coat onto a metal screen. Study blueprints and examine surface to be covered to determine amount of material needed. Cut, surface, polish, and install marble and granite and/or install pre-cast terrazzo, granite, or marble units. Install and anchor fixtures in designated positions, using hand tools. Cut tile backing to required size, using shears. Remove any old tile, grout, and adhesive, using chisels and scrapers, and clean the surface carefully. Lay and set mosaic tiles to create decorative wall, mural, and floor designs. Assist customers in selection of tile and grout. Remove and replace cracked or damaged tile. Measure and cut metal lath to size for walls and ceilings, using tin snips. Select and order tile and other items to be installed, such as bathroom accessories, walls, panels, and cabinets, according to specifications. Mix and apply mortar or cement to edges and ends of drain tiles to seal halves and joints. Spread mastic or other adhesive base on roof deck to form base for promenade tile, using serrated spreader. **SKILLS—Installation:** Installing equipment, machines, wiring, or programs to meet specifications. **Social Perceptiveness:** Being aware of others' reactions and understanding why they react as they do. **Management of Financial Resources:** Determining how money will be spent to get the work done and accounting for these expenditures. **Mathematics:** Using mathematics to solve problems. **Instructing:** Teaching others how to do something. **Coordination:** Adjusting actions in relation to others' actions. **Critical Thinking:** Using logic and reasoning to identify the strengths and weaknesses of alternative solutions, conclusions, or approaches to problems. **Complex Problem Solving:** Identifying complex problems and reviewing related information to develop and evaluate options and implement solutions. **GOE—Interest Area:** 02. Architecture and Construction. **Work Group:** 02.04. Construction Crafts. **Other Jobs in This Work Group:** Boat Builders and Shipwrights; Boilermakers; Brattice Builders; Brickmasons and Blockmasons; Carpet Installers; Ceiling Tile Installers; Cement Masons and Concrete Finishers; Commercial Divers; Construction Carpenters; Crane and Tower Operators; Dragline Operators; Drywall Installers; Electricians; Fence Erectors; Floor Layers, Except Carpet, Wood, and Hard Tiles; Floor Sanders and Finishers; Glaziers; Grader, Bulldozer, and Scraper Operators; Hazardous Materials Removal Workers; Insulation Workers, Floor, Ceiling, and Wall; Insulation Workers, Mechanical; Manufactured Building and Mobile Home Installers; Operating Engineers; Painters, Construction and Maintenance; Paperhangers; Paving, Surfacing, and Tamping Equipment Operators; Pile-Driver Operators; Pipe Fitters; Pipelayers; Pipelaying Fitters; Plasterers and Stucco Masons; Plumbers; Rail-Track Laying and Maintenance Equipment Operators; Refractory Materials Repairers, Except Brickmasons; Reinforcing Iron and Rebar Workers; Riggers; Roofers; Rough Carpenters; Security and Fire Alarm Systems Installers; Segmental Pavers; Sheet Metal Workers; Ship Carpenters and Joiners; Stone Cutters and Carvers; Stonemasons; Structural Iron and Steel Workers; Tapers; Terrazzo Workers and Finishers. **PERSONALITY TYPE:** Realistic. Realistic occupations frequently involve work activities that include practical, hands-on problems and solutions. These occupations often deal with plants, animals, and real-world materials like wood, tools, and machinery. Many of the occupations require working outside and do not involve a lot of paperwork or working closely with others.

EDUCATION/TRAINING PROGRAM(S)— Building/Construction Finishing, Management, and Inspection, Other. **RELATED KNOWLEDGE/ COURSES—Building and Construction:** Knowledge of the materials, methods, and tools involved in the construction or repair of houses, buildings, or other structures such as highways and roads. **Design:** Knowledge of design techniques, tools, and principles involved in production of precision technical plans, blueprints, drawings, and models. **Production and Processing:** Knowledge of raw materials, production processes, quality control, costs, and other techniques for maximizing the effective manufacture and distribution of goods. **Administration and Management:** Knowledge of business and management principles involved in strategic planning, resource allocation, human resources modeling, leadership technique, production methods, and coordination of people and resources. **Economics and Accounting:** Knowledge of economic and accounting principles and practices, the financial markets, banking, and the analysis and reporting of financial data. **Transportation:** Knowledge of principles and methods for moving people or goods by air, rail, sea, or road, including the relative costs and benefits.

Tractor-Trailer Truck Drivers

- Education/Training Required: Moderate-term on-the-job training
- Annual Earnings: $33,520
- Growth: 19.0%
- Annual Job Openings: 299,000
- Self-Employed: 13.1%
- Part-Time: 7.7%

Drive tractor-trailer truck to transport products, livestock, or materials to specified destinations. Drives tractor-trailer combination, applying knowledge of commercial driving regulations, to transport and deliver products, livestock, or materials, usually over long distance. Maneuvers truck into loading or unloading position, following signals from loading crew as needed. Drives truck to weigh station before and after loading and along route to document weight and conform to state regulations. Maintains driver log according to I.C.C. regulations. Inspects truck before and after trips and submits report indicating truck condition. Reads bill of lading to determine assignment. Fastens chain or binders to secure load on trailer during transit. Loads or unloads or assists in loading and unloading truck. Works as member of two-person team driving tractor with sleeper bunk behind cab. Services truck with oil, fuel, and radiator fluid to maintain tractor-trailer. Obtains customer's signature or collects payment for services. Inventories and inspects goods to be moved. Wraps goods, using pads, packing paper, and containers, and secures load to trailer wall, using straps. Gives directions to helper in packing and moving goods to trailer. **SKILLS—Operation and Control:** Controlling operations of equipment or systems. **Equipment Maintenance:** Performing routine maintenance on equipment and determining when and what kind of maintenance is needed. **Repairing:** Repairing machines or systems by using the needed tools. **Management of Material Resources:** Obtaining and seeing to the appropriate use of equipment, facilities, and materials needed to do certain work. **Troubleshooting:** Determining causes of operating errors and deciding what to do about them. **Operation Monitoring:** Watching gauges, dials, or other indicators to make sure a machine is working properly. **GOE—Interest Area:** 16. Transportation, Distribution, and Logistics. **Work Group:** 16.03. Truck Driving. **Other Jobs in This Work Group:** Truck Drivers, Heavy; Truck Drivers, Light or Delivery Services. **PERSONALITY TYPE:** Realistic. Realistic occupations frequently involve work activities that include practical, hands-on problems and solutions. These occupations often deal with plants, animals, and real-world materials like wood, tools, and machinery. Many of the occupations require working outside and do not involve a lot of paperwork or working closely with others.

EDUCATION/TRAINING PROGRAM(S)— Truck and Bus Driver/Commercial Vehicle Operation. **RELATED KNOWLEDGE/COURSES—Transportation:** Knowledge of principles and methods for moving people or goods by air, rail, sea, or road, including the relative costs and benefits. **Geography:** Knowledge of principles and methods for describing the features of land, sea, and air masses, including their physical characteristics; locations; interrelationships; and distribution of plant, animal, and human life. **Mechanical Devices:** Knowledge of machines and tools, including their designs, uses, repair, and maintenance. **Law and Government:** Knowledge of laws, legal codes, court procedures, precedents, government regulations, executive orders, agency rules, and the democratic political process. **Public Safety and Security:** Knowledge of relevant equipment, policies, procedures, and strategies to promote effective local, state, or national security operations for the protection of people, data, property, and institutions. **Telecommunications:** Knowledge of transmission, broadcasting, switching, control, and operation of telecommunications systems.

Transit and Railroad Police

- Education/Training Required: Long-term on-the-job training
- Annual Earnings: $45,430
- Growth: 15.9%
- Annual Job Openings: 1,000
- Self-Employed: 0%
- Part-Time: 1.4%

Protect and police railroad and transit property, employees, or passengers. Apprehend or remove trespassers or thieves from railroad property or coordinate with law enforcement agencies in apprehensions and removals. Direct and coordinate the daily activities and training of security staff. Direct security activities at derailments, fires, floods, and strikes involving railroad property. Examine credentials of unauthorized persons attempting to enter secured areas. Investigate or direct investigations of freight theft, suspicious damage or loss of passengers' valuables, and other crimes on railroad property. Patrol railroad yards, cars, stations, and other facilities in order to protect company property and shipments and to maintain order. Plan and implement special safety and preventive programs, such as fire and accident prevention. Prepare reports documenting investigation activities and results. Record and verify seal numbers from boxcars containing frequently pilfered items, such as cigarettes and liquor, in order to detect tampering. Seal empty boxcars by twisting nails in door hasps, using nail twisters. Interview neighbors, associates, and former employers of job applicants in order to verify personal references and to obtain work history data. **SKILLS—Management of Personnel Resources:** Motivating, developing, and directing people as they work, identifying the best people for the job. **Active Listening:** Giving full attention to what other people are saying, taking time to understand the points being made, asking questions as appropriate, and not interrupting at inappropriate times. **Speaking:** Talking to others to convey information effectively. **Social Perceptiveness:** Being aware of others' reactions and understanding why they react as they do. **Coordination:** Adjusting actions in relation to others' actions. **Writing:** Communicating effectively in writing as appropriate for the needs of the audience. **Systems Analysis:** Determining how a system should work and how changes in conditions, operations, and the environment will affect outcomes. **Learning Strategies:** Selecting and using training/instructional methods and procedures appropriate for the situation when learning or teaching new things. **GOE—Interest Area:** 12. Law and Public Safety. **Work Group:** 12.04. Law Enforcement and Public Safety. **Other Jobs in This Work Group:** Bailiffs; Correctional Officers and Jailers; Criminal Investigators and Special Agents; Fire Investigators; Forensic Science Technicians; Highway Patrol Pilots; Parking Enforcement Workers; Police Detectives; Police Identification and Records Officers; Police Patrol Officers; Sheriffs and Deputy Sheriffs. **PERSONALITY TYPE:** Enterprising. Enterprising occupations frequently involve starting up and carrying out projects. These occupations can involve leading people and making many decisions. They sometimes require risk taking and often deal with business.

EDUCATION/TRAINING PROGRAM(S)—Security and Loss Prevention Services; Security and Protective Services, Other. **RELATED KNOWLEDGE/ COURSES—Public Safety and Security:** Knowledge of relevant equipment, policies, procedures, and strategies to promote effective local, state, or national security operations for the protection of people, data, property, and institutions. **Law and Government:** Knowledge of laws, legal codes, court procedures, precedents, government regulations, executive orders, agency rules, and the democratic political process. **Transportation:** Knowledge of principles and methods for moving people or goods by air, rail, sea, or road, including the relative costs and benefits. **Administration and Management:** Knowledge of business and management principles involved in strategic planning, resource allocation, human resources modeling, leadership technique, production methods, and coordination of people and resources. **Personnel and Human Resources:** Knowledge of principles and procedures for personnel recruitment, selection, training, compensation and benefits, labor relations and negotiation, and personnel information systems. **Sociology and Anthropology:** Knowledge of group behavior and dynamics, societal trends and influences, human migrations, ethnicity, and cultures and their history and origins.

Transportation Managers

- Education/Training Required: Work experience in a related occupation
- Annual Earnings: $66,600
- Growth: 19.7%
- Annual Job Openings: 13,000
- Self-Employed: 1.1%
- Part-Time: 2.4%

Plan, direct, and coordinate the transportation operations within an organization or the activities of organizations that provide transportation services. Direct activities related to dispatching, routing, and tracking transportation vehicles, such as aircraft and railroad cars. Plan, organize, and manage the work of subordinate staff to ensure that the work is accomplished in a manner consistent with organizational requirements. Direct investigations to verify and resolve customer or shipper complaints. Serve as contact persons for all workers within assigned territories. Implement schedule and policy changes. Collaborate with other managers and staff members in order to formulate and implement policies, procedures, goals, and objectives. Monitor operations to ensure that staff members comply with administrative policies and procedures, safety rules, union contracts, and government regulations. Promote safe work activities by conducting safety audits, attending company safety meetings, and meeting with individual staff members. Develop criteria, application instructions, procedural manuals, and contracts for federal and state public transportation programs. Monitor spending to ensure that expenses are consistent with approved budgets. Direct and coordinate, through subordinates, activities of operations department in order to obtain use of equipment, facilities, and human resources. Direct activities of staff performing repairs and maintenance to equipment, vehicles, and facilities. Conduct investigations in cooperation with government agencies to determine causes of transportation accidents and to improve safety procedures. Analyze expenditures and other financial information in order to develop plans, policies, and budgets for increasing profits and improving services. Negotiate and authorize contracts with equipment and materials suppliers and monitor contract fulfillment. Supervise workers assigning tariff classifications and preparing billing. Set operations policies and standards, including determination of safety procedures for the handling of dangerous goods. Recommend or authorize capital expenditures for acquisition of new equipment or property in order to increase efficiency and services of operations department. Prepare management recommendations, such as proposed fee and tariff increases or schedule changes. **SKILLS— Negotiation:** Bringing others together and trying to reconcile differences. **Time Management:** Managing one's own time and the time of others. **Coordination:** Adjusting actions in relation to others' actions. **Instructing:** Teaching others how to do something. **Monitoring:** Monitoring or assessing your performance or that of other individuals or organizations to make improvements or take corrective action. **Critical Thinking:** Using logic and reasoning to identify the strengths and weaknesses of alternative solutions, con-

clusions, or approaches to problems. **Management of Financial Resources:** Determining how money will be spent to get the work done and accounting for these expenditures. **Active Learning:** Understanding the implications of new information for both current and future problem-solving and decision-making. **GOE— Interest Area:** 16. Transportation, Distribution, and Logistics. **Work Group:** 16.01. Managerial Work in Transportation. **Other Jobs in This Work Group:** Aircraft Cargo Handling Supervisors; First-Line Supervisors/Managers of Transportation and Material-Moving Machine and Vehicle Operators; Postmasters and Mail Superintendents; Railroad Conductors and Yardmasters; Storage and Distribution Managers. **PERSONALITY TYPE:** Enterprising. Enterprising occupations frequently involve starting up and carrying out projects. These occupations can involve leading people and making many decisions. They sometimes require risk taking and often deal with business.

EDUCATION/TRAINING PROGRAM(S)—Aeronautics/Aviation/Aerospace Science and Technology, General; Aviation/Airway Management and Operations; Business Administration and Management, General; Business/Commerce, General; Logistics and Materials Management; Public Administration. **RELATED KNOWLEDGE/COURSES—Transportation:** Knowledge of principles and methods for moving people or goods by air, rail, sea, or road, including the relative costs and benefits. **Customer and Personal Service:** Knowledge of principles and processes for providing customer and personal services. This includes customer needs assessment, meeting quality standards for services, and evaluation of customer satisfaction. **Clerical Practices:** Knowledge of administrative and clerical procedures and systems such as word processing, managing files and records, stenography and transcription, designing forms, and other office procedures and terminology. **Administration and Management:** Knowledge of business and management principles involved in strategic planning, resource allocation, human resources modeling, leadership technique, production methods, and coordination of people and resources. **Sales and Marketing:** Knowledge of principles and methods for showing, promoting, and selling products or services. This includes marketing strategy and tactics, product demonstrations, sales techniques, and sales control systems. **Psychology:** Knowledge of human behavior and performance; individual differences in ability, personality, and interests; learning and motivation; psychological research methods; and the assessment and treatment of behavioral and affective disorders.

Travel Clerks

- Education/Training Required: Short-term on-the-job training
- Annual Earnings: $27,750
- Growth: 12.2%
- Annual Job Openings: 35,000
- Self-Employed: 1.1%
- Part-Time: 15.7%

Provide tourists with travel information, such as points of interest, restaurants, rates, and emergency service. Duties include answering inquiries; offering suggestions; and providing literature pertaining to trips, excursions, sporting events, concerts, and plays. May make reservations, deliver tickets, arrange for visas, or contact individuals and groups to inform them of package tours. Provides customers with travel suggestions and information such as guides, directories, brochures, and maps. Contacts motel, hotel, resort, and travel operators by mail or telephone to obtain advertising literature. Studies maps, directories, routes, and rate tables to determine travel route and cost and availability of accommodations. Calculates estimated travel rates and expenses, using items such as rate tables and calculators. Informs client of travel dates, times, connections, baggage limits, medical and visa requirements, and emergency information. Obtains reservations for air, train, or car travel and hotel or other housing accommodations. Confirms travel arrangements and reservations. Assists client in preparing required documents and forms for travel, such as visas. Plans itinerary for travel and accommodations, using knowledge of routes, types of carriers, and regulations. Provides information concerning fares, availability of travel, and accommodations, either orally or by using guides, brochures, and maps. Confers with customers by telephone, writing, or in person to answer questions regarding services and determine travel preferences. **SKILLS—Service Orientation:** Actively looking for ways to help people. **Active Listening:** Giving full attention to what other people are saying, taking time to understand the points being made, asking questions as appropriate, and not interrupting at inappropriate times. **Speaking:** Talking to others to convey information effectively. **Social Perceptiveness:** Being aware of others' reactions and understanding why they react as they do. **GOE— Interest Area:** 09. Hospitality, Tourism, and Recreation. **Work Group:** 09.03. Hospitality and Travel Services. **Other Jobs in This Work Group:** Baggage Porters and Bellhops; Concierges; Flight Attendants; Hotel, Motel, and Resort Desk Clerks; Janitors and Cleaners, Except Maids and Housekeeping Cleaners; Maids and Housekeeping Cleaners; Reservation and Transportation Ticket Agents; Tour Guides and Escorts; Transportation Attendants, Except Flight Attendants and Baggage Porters; Travel Agents; Travel Guides. **PERSONALITY TYPE:** Conventional. Conventional occupations frequently involve following set procedures and routines. These occupations can include working with data and details more than with ideas. Usually there is a clear line of authority to follow.

EDUCATION/TRAINING PROGRAM(S)—Selling Skills and Sales Operations; Tourism and Travel Services Marketing Operations; Tourism Promotion Operations. **RELATED KNOWLEDGE/COURSES—Geography:** Knowledge of principles and methods for describing the features of land, sea, and air masses, including their physical characteristics; locations; interrelationships; and distribution of plant, animal, and human life. **Transportation:** Knowledge of principles and methods for moving people or goods by air, rail, sea, or road, including the relative costs and benefits. **Customer and Personal Service:** Knowledge of principles and processes for providing customer and personal services. This includes customer needs assessment, meeting quality standards for services, and evaluation of customer satisfaction. **Telecommunications:** Knowledge of transmission, broadcasting, switching, control, and operation of telecommunications systems.

Tree Trimmers and Pruners

- Education/Training Required: Short-term on-the-job training
- Annual Earnings: $26,150
- Growth: 18.6%
- Annual Job Openings: 11,000
- Self-Employed: 25.6%
- Part-Time: 15.3%

Cut away dead or excess branches from trees or shrubs to maintain right-of-way for roads, sidewalks, or utilities or to improve appearance, health, and value of tree. Prune or treat trees or shrubs, using handsaws, pruning hooks, shears, and clippers. May use truck-mounted lifts and power pruners. May fill cavities in trees to promote healing and prevent deterioration. Cable, brace, tie, bolt, stake, and guy trees and branches to provide support. Clean, sharpen, and lubricate tools and equipment. Clear sites, streets, and grounds of woody and herbaceous materials, such as tree stumps and fallen trees and limbs. Climb trees, using climbing hooks and belts, or climb ladders to gain access to work areas. Collect debris and refuse from tree trimming and removal operations into piles, using shovels, rakes, or other tools. Cut away dead and excess branches from trees or clear branches around power lines, using climbing equipment or buckets of extended truck booms and/or chainsaws, hooks, handsaws, shears, and clippers. Inspect trees to determine if they have diseases or pest problems. Load debris and refuse onto trucks and haul it away for disposal. Operate shredding and chipping equipment and feed limbs and brush into the machines. Spray trees to treat diseased or unhealthy trees, including mixing chemicals and calibrating spray equipment. Prune, cut down, fertilize, and spray trees as directed by tree surgeons. Remove broken limbs from wires, using hooked extension poles. Trim jagged stumps, using saws or pruning shears. Trim, top, and reshape trees to achieve attractive shapes or to remove low-hanging branches. Water, root-feed, and fertilize trees. Apply tar or other protective substances to cut surfaces to seal surfaces and to protect them from fungi and insects. Harvest tanbark by cutting rings and slits in bark and stripping bark from trees, using spuds or axes. Hoist tools and equipment to tree trimmers and lower branches with ropes or block and tackle. Install lightning protection on trees. Plan and develop budgets for tree work and estimate the monetary value of trees. Provide information to the public regarding trees, such as advice on tree care. Scrape decayed matter from cavities in trees and fill holes with cement to promote healing and to prevent further deterioration. Split logs or wooden blocks into bolts, pickets, posts, or stakes, using hand tools such as ax wedges, sledgehammers, and mallets. Supervise others engaged in tree-trimming work and train lower-level employees. **SKILLS—Operation and Control:** Controlling operations of equipment or systems. **GOE—Interest Area:** 01. Agriculture and Natural Resources. **Work Group:** 01.05. Nursery, Groundskeeping, and Pest Control. **Other Jobs in This Work Group:** Landscaping and Groundskeeping Workers; Nursery Workers; Pest Control Workers; Pesticide Handlers, Sprayers, and Applicators, Vegetation. **PERSONALITY TYPE:** Realistic. Realistic occupations frequently involve work activities that include practical, hands-on problems and solutions. These occupations often deal with plants, animals, and real-world materials like wood, tools, and machinery. Many of the occupations require working outside and do not involve a lot of paperwork or working closely with others.

EDUCATION/TRAINING PROGRAM(S)— Applied Horticulture/Horticultural Business Services, Other. **RELATED KNOWLEDGE/COURSES— Chemistry:** Knowledge of the chemical composition, structure, and properties of substances and of the chemical processes and transformations that they undergo. This includes uses of chemicals and their danger signs, production techniques, and disposal methods. **Biology:** Knowledge of plant and animal organisms and their tissues, cells, functions, interdependencies, and interactions with each other and the environment. **Mechanical Devices:** Knowledge of machines and tools, including their designs, uses, repair, and maintenance.

Truck Drivers, Heavy

- Education/Training Required: Short-term on-the-job training
- Annual Earnings: $33,520
- Growth: 19.0%
- Annual Job Openings: 299,000
- Self-Employed: 13.1%
- Part-Time: 7.7%

Drive truck with capacity of more than three tons to transport materials to specified destinations. Drives truck with capacity of more than three tons to transport and deliver cargo, materials, or damaged vehicle. Maintains radio or telephone contact with base or supervisor to receive instructions or be dispatched to new location. Maintains truck log according to state and federal regulations. Keeps record of materials and products transported. Position blocks and ties rope around items to secure cargo for transport. Cleans, inspects, and services vehicle. Operates equipment on vehicle to load, unload, or disperse cargo or materials. Obtains customer signature or collects payment for goods delivered and delivery charges. Assists in loading and unloading truck manually. **SKILLS—Equipment Maintenance:** Performing routine maintenance on equipment and determining when and what kind of maintenance is needed. **Repairing:** Repairing machines or systems by using the needed tools. **Operation Monitoring:** Watching gauges, dials, or other indicators to make sure a machine is working properly. **Operation and Control:** Controlling operations of equipment or systems. **GOE—Interest Area:** 16. Transportation, Distribution, and Logistics. **Work Group:** 16.03. Truck Driving. **Other Jobs in This Work Group:** Tractor-Trailer Truck Drivers; Truck Drivers, Light or Delivery Services. **PERSONALITY TYPE:** Realistic. Realistic occupations frequently involve work activities that include practical, hands-on problems and solutions. These occupations often deal with plants, animals, and real-world materials like wood, tools, and machinery. Many of the occupations require working outside and do not involve a lot of paperwork or working closely with others. **EDUCATION/TRAINING PROGRAM(S)—** Truck and Bus Driver/Commercial Vehicle Operation.

RELATED KNOWLEDGE/COURSES—Transportation: Knowledge of principles and methods for moving people or goods by air, rail, sea, or road, including the relative costs and benefits. **Geography:** Knowledge of principles and methods for describing the features of land, sea, and air masses, including their physical characteristics; locations; interrelationships; and distribution of plant, animal, and human life. **Telecommunications:** Knowledge of transmission, broadcasting, switching, control, and operation of telecommunications systems. **Mechanical Devices:** Knowledge of machines and tools, including their designs, uses, repair, and maintenance. **Public Safety and Security:** Knowledge of relevant equipment, policies, procedures, and strategies to promote effective local, state, or national security operations for the protection of people, data, property, and institutions. **Law and Government:** Knowledge of laws, legal codes, court procedures, precedents, government regulations, executive orders, agency rules, and the democratic political process.

Truck Drivers, Light or Delivery Services

- Education/Training Required: Short-term on-the-job training
- Annual Earnings: $24,540
- Growth: 23.2%
- Annual Job Openings: 219,000
- Self-Employed: 4.7%
- Part-Time: 17.3%

Drive a truck or van with a capacity of under 26,000 GVW, primarily to deliver or pick up merchandise or to deliver packages within a specified area. May require use of automatic routing or location software. May load and unload truck. Drive vehicles with capacities under three tons in order to transport materials to and from specified destinations such as railroad stations, plants, residences, and offices or within industrial yards. Inspect and maintain vehicle supplies and equipment, such as gas, oil, water, tires, lights, and brakes, in order to ensure that vehicles are in proper working condition. Load and unload trucks, vans, or automobiles. Obey traffic laws and follow established traffic and transportation procedures. Read maps and follow written and verbal geographic directions. Verify the contents of inventory loads against shipping papers. Maintain records such as vehicle logs, records of cargo, or billing statements in accordance with regulations. Perform emergency repairs such as changing tires or installing light bulbs, fuses, tire chains, and spark plugs. Present bills and receipts and collect payments for goods delivered or loaded. Report any mechanical problems encountered with vehicles. Report delays, accidents, or other traffic and transportation situations to bases or other vehicles, using telephones or mobile two-way radios. Turn in receipts and money received from deliveries. Drive trucks equipped with public address systems through city streets in order to broadcast announcements for advertising or publicity purposes. Sell and keep records of sales for products from truck inventory. Use and maintain the tools and equipment found on commercial vehicles, such as weighing and measuring devices. **SKILLS—Repairing:** Repairing machines or systems by using the needed tools. **Equipment Maintenance:** Performing routine maintenance on equipment and determining when and what kind of maintenance is needed. **Operation Monitoring:** Watching gauges, dials, or other indicators to make sure a machine is working properly. **Operation and Control:** Controlling operations of equipment or systems. **Troubleshooting:** Determining causes of operating errors and deciding what to do about them. **GOE—Interest Area:** 16. Transportation, Distribution, and Logistics. **Work Group:** 16.03. Truck Driving. **Other Jobs in This Work Group:** Tractor-Trailer Truck Drivers; Truck Drivers, Heavy. **PERSONALITY TYPE:** Realistic. Realistic occupations frequently involve work activities that include practical, hands-on problems and solutions. These occupations often deal with plants, animals, and real-world materials like wood, tools, and machinery. Many of the occupations require working outside and do not involve a lot of paperwork or working closely with others.

EDUCATION/TRAINING PROGRAM(S)— Truck and Bus Driver/Commercial Vehicle Operation. **RELATED KNOWLEDGE/COURSES—Transportation:** Knowledge of principles and methods for moving people or goods by air, rail, sea, or road,

including the relative costs and benefits. **Telecommunications:** Knowledge of transmission, broadcasting, switching, control, and operation of telecommunications systems. **Geography:** Knowledge of principles and methods for describing the features of land, sea, and air masses, including their physical characteristics; locations; interrelationships; and distribution of plant, animal, and human life. **Mechanical Devices:** Knowledge of machines and tools, including their designs, uses, repair, and maintenance. **Law and Government:** Knowledge of laws, legal codes, court procedures, precedents, government regulations, executive orders, agency rules, and the democratic political process. **Public Safety and Security:** Knowledge of relevant equipment, policies, procedures, and strategies to promote effective local, state, or national security operations for the protection of people, data, property, and institutions.

Valve and Regulator Repairers

- ◎ Education/Training Required: Moderate-term on-the-job training
- ◎ Annual Earnings: $43,710
- ◎ Growth: 12.0%
- ◎ Annual Job Openings: 5,000
- ◎ Self-Employed: 0.7%
- ◎ Part-Time: 2.0%

Test, repair, and adjust mechanical regulators and valves. Replaces, repairs, or adjusts defective valve or regulator parts and tightens attachments, using hand tools, power tools, and welder. Tests valves and regulators for leaks, temperature, and pressure settings, using precision testing equipment. Examines valves or mechanical control device parts for defects, dents, or loose attachments. Measures salvageable parts removed from mechanical control devices for conformance to standards or specifications, using gauges, micrometers, and calipers. Dips valves and regulators in molten lead to prevent leakage and paints valves, fittings, and other devices, using spray gun. Advises customers on proper installation of valves or regulators and related equipment. Records repair work, inventories parts, and orders new parts. Correlates testing data, performs technical calculations, and writes test reports to record data. Cleans corrosives and other deposits from serviceable parts, using solvents, wire brushes, or sandblaster. Lubricates wearing surfaces of mechanical parts, using oils or other lubricants. Disassembles mechanical control devices or valves, such as regulators, thermostats, or hydrants, using power tools, hand tools, and cutting torch. **SKILLS—Repairing:** Repairing machines or systems by using the needed tools. **Equipment Maintenance:** Performing routine maintenance on equipment and determining when and what kind of maintenance is needed. **Installation:** Installing equipment, machines, wiring, or programs to meet specifications. **Quality Control Analysis:** Conducting tests and inspections of products, services, or processes to evaluate quality or performance. **Troubleshooting:** Determining causes of operating errors and deciding what to do about them. **Mathematics:** Using mathematics to solve problems. **Writing:** Communicating effectively in writing as appropriate for the needs of the audience. **Science:** Using scientific rules and methods to solve problems. **Operation and Control:** Controlling operations of equipment or systems. **GOE— Interest Area:** 13. Manufacturing. **Work Group:** 13.13. Machinery Repair. **Other Jobs in This Work Group:** Bicycle Repairers; Gas Appliance Repairers; Hand and Portable Power Tool Repairers; Industrial Machinery Mechanics; Locksmiths and Safe Repairers; Maintenance Workers, Machinery; Mechanical Door Repairers; Millwrights; Signal and Track Switch Repairers. **PERSONALITY TYPE:** Realistic. Realistic occupations frequently involve work activities that include practical, hands-on problems and solutions. These occupations often deal with plants, animals, and real-world materials like wood, tools, and machinery. Many of the occupations require working outside and do not involve a lot of paperwork or working closely with others.

EDUCATION/TRAINING PROGRAM(S)— Electromechanical and Instrumentation and Maintenance Technologies/Technicians, Other. **RELATED KNOWLEDGE/COURSES—Mechanical Devices:** Knowledge of machines and tools, including their designs, uses, repair, and maintenance. **Physics:** Knowledge and prediction of physical principles and laws and their interrelationships and applications to understanding fluid, material, and atmospheric dynamics and mechanical, electrical, atomic, and subatomic structures and processes. **Engineering and Technology:** Knowledge of the practical application of engineering science and technology. This includes applying principles, techniques, procedures, and equipment to the design and production of various goods and services. **Mathematics:** Knowledge of arithmetic, algebra, geometry, calculus, and statistics and their applications. **Chemistry:** Knowledge of the chemical composition, structure, and properties of substances and of the chemical processes and transformations that they undergo. This includes uses of chemicals and their danger signs, production techniques, and disposal methods. **Building and Construction:** Knowledge of the materials, methods, and tools involved in the construction or repair of houses, buildings, or other structures such as highways and roads.

Veterinary Technologists and Technicians

- Education/Training Required: Associate degree
- Annual Earnings: $24,940
- Growth: 44.1%
- Annual Job Openings: 11,000
- Self-Employed: 0%
- Part-Time: 23.0%

Perform medical tests in a laboratory environment for use in the treatment and diagnosis of diseases in animals. Prepare vaccines and serums for prevention of diseases. Prepare tissue samples, take blood samples, and execute laboratory tests such as urinalysis and blood counts. Clean and sterilize instruments and materials and maintain equipment and machines. Administer anesthesia to animals, under the direction of a veterinarian, and monitor animals' responses to anesthetics so that dosages can be adjusted. Care for and monitor the condition of animals recovering from surgery. Prepare and administer medications, vaccines, serums, and treatments as prescribed by veterinarians. Perform laboratory tests on blood, urine, and feces, such as urinalyses and blood counts, to assist in the diagnosis and treatment of animal health problems. Administer emergency first aid, such as performing emergency resuscitation or other life-saving procedures. Collect, prepare, and label samples for laboratory testing, culture, or microscopic examination. Clean and sterilize instruments, equipment, and materials. Provide veterinarians with the correct equipment and instruments as needed. Fill prescriptions, measuring medications and labeling containers. Prepare animals for surgery, performing such tasks as shaving surgical areas. Take animals into treatment areas and assist with physical examinations by performing such duties as obtaining temperature, pulse, and respiration data. Observe the behavior and condition of animals and monitor their clinical symptoms. Take and develop diagnostic radiographs, using X-ray equipment. Maintain laboratory, research, and treatment records, as well as inventories of pharmaceuticals, equipment, and supplies. Give enemas and perform catheterizations, ear flushes, intravenous feedings, and gavages. Prepare treatment rooms for surgery. Maintain instruments, equipment, and machinery to ensure proper working condition. Perform dental work such as cleaning, polishing, and extracting teeth. Clean kennels, animal holding areas, surgery suites, examination rooms, and animal loading/unloading facilities to control the spread of disease. Provide information and counseling regarding issues such as animal health care, behavior problems, and nutrition. Provide assistance with animal euthanasia and the disposal of remains. Dress and suture wounds and apply splints and other protective devices. Perform a variety of office, clerical, and accounting duties, such as reception, billing, bookkeeping, and/or selling products. **SKILLS— Instructing:** Teaching others how to do something. **Social Perceptiveness:** Being aware of others' reactions and understanding why they react as they do. **Science:** Using scientific rules and methods to solve problems. **Operation Monitoring:** Watching gauges, dials, or other indicators to make sure a machine is working properly. **Active Learning:** Understanding the implications of new information for both current and future problem-solving and decision-making. **Time Management:** Managing one's own time and the time of others. **Reading Comprehension:** Understanding written sentences and paragraphs in work-related documents.

Active Listening: Giving full attention to what other people are saying, taking time to understand the points being made, asking questions as appropriate, and not interrupting at inappropriate times. **Equipment Maintenance:** Performing routine maintenance on equipment and determining when and what kind of maintenance is needed. **GOE—Interest Area:** 08. Health Science. **Work Group:** 08.05. Animal Care. **Other Jobs in This Work Group:** Animal Breeders; Animal Trainers; Nonfarm Animal Caretakers; Veterinarians; Veterinary Assistants and Laboratory Animal Caretakers. **PERSONALITY TYPE:** No data available.

EDUCATION/TRAINING PROGRAM(S)—Veterinary/Animal Health Technology/Technician and Veterinary Assistant. **RELATED KNOWLEDGE/ COURSES—Biology:** Knowledge of plant and animal organisms and their tissues, cells, functions, interdependencies, and interactions with each other and the environment. **Customer and Personal Service:** Knowledge of principles and processes for providing customer and personal services. This includes customer needs assessment, meeting quality standards for services, and evaluation of customer satisfaction. **Medicine and Dentistry:** Knowledge of the information and techniques needed to diagnose and treat human injuries, diseases, and deformities. This includes symptoms, treatment alternatives, drug properties and interactions, and preventive health-care measures. **Chemistry:** Knowledge of the chemical composition, structure, and properties of substances and of the chemical processes and transformations that they undergo. This includes uses of chemicals and their danger signs, production techniques, and disposal methods. **Sales and Marketing:** Knowledge of principles and methods for showing, promoting, and selling products or services. This includes marketing strategy and tactics, product demonstrations, sales techniques, and sales control systems. **Mathematics:** Knowledge of arithmetic, algebra, geometry, calculus, and statistics and their applications.

Vocational Education Teachers, Postsecondary

◎ Education/Training Required: Work experience in a related occupation
◎ Annual Earnings: $40,740
◎ Growth: 38.1%
◎ Annual Job Openings: 216,000
◎ Self-Employed: 0.3%
◎ Part-Time: 27.7%

Teach or instruct vocational or occupational subjects at the postsecondary level (but at less than the baccalaureate) to students who have graduated or left high school. Includes correspondence school instructors; industrial, commercial, and government training instructors; and adult education teachers and instructors who prepare persons to operate industrial machinery and equipment and transportation and communications equipment. Teaching may take place in public or private schools whose primary business is education or in a school associated with an organization whose primary business is other than education. Supervise and monitor students' use of tools and equipment. Observe and evaluate students' work to determine progress, provide feedback, and make suggestions for improvement. Present lectures and conduct discussions to increase students' knowledge and competence, using visual aids such as graphs, charts, videotapes, and slides. Administer oral, written, or performance tests in order to measure progress and to evaluate training effectiveness. Prepare reports and maintain records such as student grades, attendance rolls, and training activity details. Supervise independent or group projects, field placements, laboratory work, or other training. Determine training needs of students or workers. Provide individualized instruction and tutorial and/or remedial instruction. Conduct on-the-job training, classes, or training sessions to teach and demonstrate principles, techniques, procedures, and/or methods of designated subjects. Develop curricula and plan course content and methods of instruction. Prepare outlines of instructional programs and training schedules and establish course goals. Integrate academic and vocational curricula so that students can obtain a variety of skills. Develop teaching aids such as instructional software, multimedia visual aids, or study materials. Select and assemble books, materials, supplies, and equipment for training, courses, or projects. Advise students on course selection, career decisions, and other academic and vocational concerns. Participate in conferences, seminars, and training sessions to keep abreast of developments in the field and integrate relevant information into training programs. Serve on faculty and school committees concerned with budgeting, curriculum revision, and course and diploma requirements. Review enrollment applications and correspond with applicants to obtain additional information. Arrange for lectures by experts in designated fields. **SKILLS—Instructing:** Teaching others how to do something. **Learning Strategies:** Selecting and using training/instructional methods and procedures appropriate for the situation when learning or teaching new things. **Social Perceptiveness:** Being aware of others' reactions and understanding why they react as they do. **Service Orientation:** Actively looking for ways to help people. **Time Management:** Managing one's own time and the time of others. **Persuasion:** Persuading others to change their minds or behavior. **Speaking:** Talking to others to convey information effectively. **Negotiation:** Bringing others together and trying to reconcile differences. **GOE—Interest Area:** 05. Education and Training. **Work Group:** 05.03. Postsecondary and Adult Teaching and Instructing. **Other Jobs in This Work Group:** Adult Literacy, Remedial Education, and GED Teachers and Instructors; Agricultural Sciences Teachers, Postsecondary; Anthropology and Archeology Teachers, Postsecondary; Architecture Teachers, Postsecondary; Area, Ethnic, and Cultural Studies Teachers, Postsecondary; Art, Drama, and Music Teachers, Postsecondary; Atmospheric, Earth, Marine, and Space Sciences Teachers, Postsecondary; Biological Science Teachers, Postsecondary; Business Teachers, Postsecondary; Chemistry Teachers, Postsecondary; Communications Teachers, Postsecondary; Computer Science Teachers, Postsecondary; Criminal Justice and Law Enforcement Teachers, Postsecondary; Economics Teachers, Postsecondary; Education Teachers, Postsecondary; Engineering Teachers, Postsecondary; English Language and Literature Teachers, Postsecondary; Environmental Science Teachers, Postsecondary; Farm and Home Management Advisors; Foreign Language and

Literature Teachers, Postsecondary; Forestry and Conservation Science Teachers, Postsecondary; Geography Teachers, Postsecondary; Graduate Teaching Assistants; Health Specialties Teachers, Postsecondary; History Teachers, Postsecondary; Home Economics Teachers, Postsecondary; Law Teachers, Postsecondary; Library Science Teachers, Postsecondary; Mathematical Science Teachers, Postsecondary; Nursing Instructors and Teachers, Postsecondary; Philosophy and Religion Teachers, Postsecondary; Physics Teachers, Postsecondary; Political Science Teachers, Postsecondary; Psychology Teachers, Postsecondary; Recreation and Fitness Studies Teachers, Postsecondary; Self-Enrichment Education Teachers; Social Work Teachers, Postsecondary; Sociology Teachers, Postsecondary. **PERSONALITY TYPE:** Social. Social occupations frequently involve working with, communicating with, and teaching people. These occupations often involve helping or providing service to others.

EDUCATION/TRAINING PROGRAM(S)—Agricultural Teacher Education; Business Teacher Education; Health Occupations Teacher Education; Sales and Marketing Operations/Marketing and Distribution Teacher Education; Teacher Education and Professional Development, Specific Subject Areas, Other; Technical Teacher Education; Technology Teacher Education/Industrial Arts Teacher Education; Trade and Industrial Teacher Education. **RELATED KNOWLEDGE/COURSES**—Education and Training: Knowledge of principles and methods for curriculum and training design, teaching and instruction for individuals and groups, and the measurement of training effects. **Psychology:** Knowledge of human behavior and performance; individual differences in ability, personality, and interests; learning and motivation; psychological research methods; and the assessment and treatment of behavioral and affective disorders. **Computers and Electronics:** Knowledge of circuit boards, processors, chips, electronic equipment, and computer hardware and software, including applications and programming. **Customer and Personal Service:** Knowledge of principles and processes for providing customer and personal services. This includes customer needs assessment, meeting quality standards for services, and evaluation of customer satisfaction. **Clerical Practices:** Knowledge of administra-

tive and clerical procedures and systems such as word processing, managing files and records, stenography and transcription, designing forms, and other office procedures and terminology. **Sales and Marketing:** Knowledge of principles and methods for showing, promoting, and selling products or services. This includes marketing strategy and tactics, product demonstrations, sales techniques, and sales control systems.

Waiters and Waitresses

- ◎ Education/Training Required: Short-term on-the-job training
- ◎ Annual Earnings: $14,050
- ◎ Growth: 17.5%
- ◎ Annual Job Openings: 721,000
- ◎ Self-Employed: 0.3%
- ◎ Part-Time: 49.9%

Take orders and serve food and beverages to patrons at tables in dining establishment. Check patrons' identification in order to ensure that they meet minimum age requirements for consumption of alcoholic beverages. Collect payments from customers. Write patrons' food orders on order slips, memorize orders, or enter orders into computers for transmittal to kitchen staff. Take orders from patrons for food or beverages. Check with customers to ensure that they are enjoying their meals and take action to correct any problems. Serve food and/or beverages to patrons; prepare and serve specialty dishes at tables as required. Prepare checks that itemize and total meal costs and sales taxes. Remove dishes and glasses from tables or counters and take them to kitchen for cleaning. Present menus to patrons and answer questions about menu items, making recommendations upon request. Inform customers of daily specials. Clean tables and/or counters after patrons have finished dining. Prepare hot, cold, and mixed drinks for patrons and chill bottles of wine. Explain how various menu items are prepared, describing ingredients and cooking methods. Prepare tables for meals, including setting up items such as linens, silverware, and glassware. Perform food preparation duties such as preparing salads, appetizers, and cold dishes; portioning desserts; and brewing coffee. Stock service areas with supplies such as coffee, food, tableware, and linens. Garnish and decorate dishes in preparation for serving. Fill salt, pepper, sugar, cream, condiment, and napkin containers. Escort customers to their tables. Describe and recommend wines to customers. Bring wine selections to tables with appropriate glasses and pour the wines for customers. **SKILLS—Service Orientation:** Actively looking for ways to help people. **Persuasion:** Persuading others to change their minds or behavior. **Instructing:** Teaching others how to do something. **Social Perceptiveness:** Being aware of others' reactions and understanding why they react as they do. **Learning Strategies:** Selecting and using training/instructional methods and procedures appropriate for the situation when learning or teaching new things. **Negotiation:** Bringing others together and trying to reconcile differences. **Coordination:** Adjusting actions in relation to others' actions. **Speaking:** Talking to others to convey information effectively. **GOE—Interest Area:** 09. Hospitality, Tourism, and Recreation. **Work Group:** 09.05. Food and Beverage Service. **Other Jobs in This Work Group:** Bartenders; Combined Food Preparation and Serving Workers, Including Fast Food; Counter Attendants, Cafeteria, Food Concession, and Coffee Shop; Dining Room and Cafeteria Attendants and Bartender Helpers; Food Servers, Nonrestaurant; Hosts and Hostesses, Restaurant, Lounge, and Coffee Shop. **PERSONALITY TYPE:** Social. Social occupations frequently involve working with, communicating with, and teaching people. These occupations often involve helping or providing service to others.

EDUCATION/TRAINING PROGRAM(S)—Food Service, Waiter/Waitress, and Dining Room Management/Manager. **RELATED KNOWLEDGE/COURSES—Customer and Personal Service:** Knowledge of principles and processes for providing customer and personal services. This includes customer needs assessment, meeting quality standards for services, and evaluation of customer satisfaction. **Food Production:** Knowledge of techniques and equipment for planting, growing, and harvesting food products (both plant and animal) for consumption, including storage/handling techniques. **Sales and Marketing:** Knowledge of principles and methods for showing, promoting, and selling products or services. This includes marketing strategy and tactics, product

demonstrations, sales techniques, and sales control systems. **Psychology:** Knowledge of human behavior and performance; individual differences in ability, personality, and interests; learning and motivation; psychological research methods; and the assessment and treatment of behavioral and affective disorders. **Education and Training:** Knowledge of principles and methods for curriculum and training design, teaching and instruction for individuals and groups, and the measurement of training effects. **Public Safety and Security:** Knowledge of relevant equipment, policies, procedures, and strategies to promote effective local, state, or national security operations for the protection of people, data, property, and institutions.

Water and Liquid Waste Treatment Plant and System Operators

- Education/Training Required: Long-term on-the-job training
- Annual Earnings: $34,960
- Growth: 16.0%
- Annual Job Openings: 9,000
- Self-Employed: 0%
- Part-Time: 1.2%

Operate or control an entire process or system of machines, often through the use of control boards, to transfer or treat water or liquid waste. Add chemicals, such as ammonia, chlorine, and lime, to disinfect and deodorize water and other liquids. Operate and adjust controls on equipment to purify and clarify water, process or dispose of sewage, and generate power. Inspect equipment and monitor operating conditions, meters, and gauges to determine load requirements and detect malfunctions. Collect and test water and sewage samples, using test equipment and color analysis standards. Record operational data, personnel attendance, and meter and gauge readings on specified forms. Maintain, repair, and lubricate equipment, using hand tools and power tools. Clean and maintain tanks and filter beds, using hand tools and power tools. Direct and coordinate plant workers engaged in rou-

W

tine operations and maintenance activities. **SKILLS— Operation Monitoring:** Watching gauges, dials, or other indicators to make sure a machine is working properly. **Installation:** Installing equipment, machines, wiring, or programs to meet specifications. **Operation and Control:** Controlling operations of equipment or systems. **Troubleshooting:** Determining causes of operating errors and deciding what to do about them. **Management of Material Resources:** Obtaining and seeing to the appropriate use of equipment, facilities, and materials needed to do certain work. **Management of Personnel Resources:** Motivating, developing, and directing people as they work, identifying the best people for the job. **Operations Analysis:** Analyzing needs and product requirements to create a design. **Equipment Maintenance:** Performing routine maintenance on equipment and determining when and what kind of maintenance is needed. **GOE—Interest Area:** 13. Manufacturing. **Work Group:** 13.16. Utility Operation and Energy Distribution. **Other Jobs in This Work Group:** Auxiliary Equipment Operators, Power; Boiler Operators and Tenders, Low Pressure; Chemical Plant and System Operators; Gas Compressor Operators; Gas Distribution Plant Operators; Gas Processing Plant Operators; Gas Pumping Station Operators; Gaugers; Nuclear Power Reactor Operators; Petroleum Pump System Operators; Petroleum Refinery and Control Panel Operators; Power Distributors and Dispatchers; Power Generating Plant Operators, Except Auxiliary Equipment Operators; Ship Engineers; Stationary Engineers. **PERSONALITY TYPE:** Realistic. Realistic occupations frequently involve work activities that include practical, hands-on problems and solutions. These occupations often deal with plants, animals, and real-world materials like wood, tools, and machinery. Many of the occupations require working outside and do not involve a lot of paperwork or working closely with others.

EDUCATION/TRAINING PROGRAM(S)— Water Quality and Wastewater Treatment Management and Recycling Technology/Technician. **RELATED KNOWLEDGE/COURSES—Biology:** Knowledge of plant and animal organisms and their tissues, cells, functions, interdependencies, and interactions with each other and the environment. **Chemistry:** Knowledge of the chemical composition, structure, and properties of substances and of the

chemical processes and transformations that they undergo. This includes uses of chemicals and their danger signs, production techniques, and disposal methods. **Physics:** Knowledge and prediction of physical principles and laws and their interrelationships and applications to understanding fluid, material, and atmospheric dynamics and mechanical, electrical, atomic, and subatomic structures and processes. **Public Safety and Security:** Knowledge of relevant equipment, policies, procedures, and strategies to promote effective local, state, or national security operations for the protection of people, data, property, and institutions. **Mathematics:** Knowledge of arithmetic, algebra, geometry, calculus, and statistics and their applications. **Law and Government:** Knowledge of laws, legal codes, court procedures, precedents, government regulations, executive orders, agency rules, and the democratic political process.

Welder-Fitters

- Education/Training Required: Long-term on-the-job training
- Annual Earnings: $30,620
- Growth: 17.0%
- Annual Job Openings: 71,000
- Self-Employed: 5.6%
- Part-Time: 2.1%

Lay out, fit, and fabricate metal components to assemble structural forms such as machinery frames, bridge parts, and pressure vessels, using knowledge of welding techniques, metallurgy, and engineering requirements. Includes experimental welders who analyze engineering drawings and specifications to plan welding operations where procedural information is unavailable. Lays out, positions, and secures parts and assemblies according to specifications, using straightedge, combination square, calipers, and ruler. Tack-welds or welds components and assemblies, using electric, gas, arc, or other welding equipment. Cuts workpiece, using powered saws, hand shears, or chipping knife. Melts lead bar, wire, or scrap to add lead to joint or to extrude melted scrap into reusable form. Installs or repairs equipment such as lead pipes, valves, floors, and tank linings. Observes tests on welded surfaces, such as hydrostatic, X-ray, and dimension toler-ance, to evaluate weld quality and conformance to specifications. Inspects grooves, angles, or gap allowances, using micrometer, caliper, and precision measuring instruments. Removes rough spots from workpiece, using portable grinder, hand file, or scraper. Welds components in flat, vertical, or overhead posi-tions. Heats, forms, and dresses metal parts, using hand tools, torch, or arc-welding equipment. Ignites torch and adjusts valves, amperage, or voltage to obtain desired flame or arc. Analyzes engineering drawings and specifications to plan layout, assembly, and weld-ing operations. Develops templates and other work aids to hold and align parts. Determines required equipment and welding method, applying knowledge of metallurgy, geometry, and welding techniques. **SKILLS—Repairing:** Repairing machines or systems by using the needed tools. **Installation:** Installing equipment, machines, wiring, or programs to meet specifications. **Equipment Maintenance:** Performing routine maintenance on equipment and determining when and what kind of maintenance is needed. **Equip-ment Selection:** Determining the kind of tools and equipment needed to do a job. **Quality Control Analysis:** Conducting tests and inspections of prod-ucts, services, or processes to evaluate quality or per-formance. **Mathematics:** Using mathematics to solve problems. **Operation Monitoring:** Watching gauges, dials, or other indicators to make sure a machine is working properly. **GOE—Interest Area:** 13. Manufac-turing. **Work Group:** 13.04. Welding, Brazing, and Soldering. **Other Jobs in This Work Group:** Brazers; Fitters, Structural Metal—Precision; Metal Fabrica-tors, Structural Metal Products; Solderers; Soldering and Brazing Machine Operators and Tenders; Welders and Cutters; Welders, Production; Welding Machine Operators and Tenders; Welding Machine Setters and Set-Up Operators. **PERSONALITY TYPE:** Realistic. Realistic occupations frequently involve work activities that include practical, hands-on problems and solu-tions. These occupations often deal with plants, ani-mals, and real-world materials like wood, tools, and machinery. Many of the occupations require working outside and do not involve a lot of paperwork or work-ing closely with others.

EDUCATION/TRAINING PROGRAM(S)— Welding Technology/Welder. **RELATED KNOWL-**

EDGE/COURSES—Design: Knowledge of design techniques, tools, and principles involved in produc-tion of precision technical plans, blueprints, drawings, and models. **Building and Construction:** Knowledge of the materials, methods, and tools involved in the construction or repair of houses, buildings, or other structures such as highways and roads. **Mechanical Devices:** Knowledge of machines and tools, including their designs, uses, repair, and maintenance. **Produc-tion and Processing:** Knowledge of raw materials, pro-duction processes, quality control, costs, and other techniques for maximizing the effective manufacture and distribution of goods. **Engineering and Technol-ogy:** Knowledge of the practical application of engi-neering science and technology. This includes applying principles, techniques, procedures, and equipment to the design and production of various goods and serv-ices. **Physics:** Knowledge and prediction of physical principles and laws and their interrelationships and applications to understanding fluid, material, and atmospheric dynamics and mechanical, electrical, atomic, and subatomic structures and processes.

Welders and Cutters

- ◎ Education/Training Required: Long-term on-the-job training
- ◎ Annual Earnings: $30,620
- ◎ Growth: 17.0%
- ◎ Annual Job Openings: 71,000
- ◎ Self-Employed: 5.6%
- ◎ Part-Time: 2.1%

Use hand-welding and flame-cutting equipment to weld together metal components and parts or to cut, trim, or scarf metal objects to dimensions as specified by layouts, work orders, or blueprints. Welds metal parts or components together, using brazing, gas, or arc-welding equipment. Repairs broken or cracked parts, fills holes, and increases size of metal parts, using welding equipment. Welds in flat, horizontal, vertical, or overhead position. Cleans or degreases parts, using wire brush, portable grinder, or chemical bath. Inspects finished workpiece for conformance to speci-fications. Chips or grinds off excess weld, slag, or spat-ter, using hand scraper or power chipper, portable

W

grinder, or arc-cutting equipment. Positions workpieces and clamps together or assembles in jigs or fixtures. Preheats workpiece, using hand torch or heating furnace. Ignites torch or starts power supply and strikes arc. Reviews layouts, blueprints, diagrams, or work orders in preparation for welding or cutting metal components. Selects and inserts electrode or gas nozzle into holder and connects hoses and cables to obtain gas or specified amperage, voltage, or polarity. Connects and turns regulator valves to activate and adjust gas flow and pressure to obtain desired flame. Selects and installs torch, torch tip, filler rod, and flux according to welding chart specifications or type and thickness of metal. Guides electrodes or torch along weld line at specified speed and angle to weld, melt, cut, or trim metal. **SKILLS—Operation Monitoring:** Watching gauges, dials, or other indicators to make sure a machine is working properly. **Repairing:** Repairing machines or systems by using the needed tools. **Operation and Control:** Controlling operations of equipment or systems. **Equipment Maintenance:** Performing routine maintenance on equipment and determining when and what kind of maintenance is needed. **Installation:** Installing equipment, machines, wiring, or programs to meet specifications. **Quality Control Analysis:** Conducting tests and inspections of products, services, or processes to evaluate quality or performance. **GOE—Interest Area:** 13. Manufacturing. **Work Group:** 13.04. Welding, Brazing, and Soldering. **Other Jobs in This Work Group:** Brazers; Fitters, Structural Metal—Precision; Metal Fabricators, Structural Metal Products; Solderers; Soldering and Brazing Machine Operators and Tenders; Welder-Fitters; Welders, Production; Welding Machine Operators and Tenders; Welding Machine Setters and Set-Up Operators. **PERSONALITY TYPE:** Realistic. Realistic occupations frequently involve work activities that include practical, hands-on problems and solutions. These occupations often deal with plants, animals, and real-world materials like wood, tools, and machinery. Many of the occupations require working outside and do not involve a lot of paperwork or working closely with others.

EDUCATION/TRAINING PROGRAM(S)— Welding Technology/Welder. **RELATED KNOWLEDGE/COURSES—Building and Construction:** Knowledge of the materials, methods, and tools involved in the construction or repair of houses, buildings, or other structures such as highways and roads. **Mechanical Devices:** Knowledge of machines and tools, including their designs, uses, repair, and maintenance. **Design:** Knowledge of design techniques, tools, and principles involved in production of precision technical plans, blueprints, drawings, and models. **Production and Processing:** Knowledge of raw materials, production processes, quality control, costs, and other techniques for maximizing the effective manufacture and distribution of goods. **Physics:** Knowledge and prediction of physical principles and laws and their interrelationships and applications to understanding fluid, material, and atmospheric dynamics and mechanical, electrical, atomic, and subatomic structures and processes. **Chemistry:** Knowledge of the chemical composition, structure, and properties of substances and of the chemical processes and transformations that they undergo. This includes uses of chemicals and their danger signs, production techniques, and disposal methods.

Welders, Production

- ◎ Education/Training Required: Short-term on-the-job training
- ◎ Annual Earnings: $30,620
- ◎ Growth: 17.0%
- ◎ Annual Job Openings: 71,000
- ◎ Self-Employed: 5.6%
- ◎ Part-Time: 2.1%

Assemble and weld metal parts on production line, using welding equipment requiring only a limited knowledge of welding techniques. Welds or tack-welds metal parts together, using spot-welding gun or hand, electric, or gas welding equipment. Connects hoses from torch to tanks of oxygen and fuel gas and turns valves to release mixture. Ignites torch and regulates flow of gas and air to obtain desired temperature, size, and color of flame. Preheats workpieces preparatory to welding or bending, using torch. Fills cavities or corrects malformation in lead parts and hammers out bulges and bends in metal workpieces. Examines workpiece for defects and measures workpiece with straightedge or template to ensure conformance with specifications. Climbs ladders or works on scaffolds to disassemble structures. Signals crane operator to move large workpieces. Dismantles metal assemblies or cuts scrap metal, using thermal-cutting equipment such as flame-cutting torch or plasma-arc equipment. Positions and secures workpiece, using hoist, crane, wire and banding machine, or hand tools. Selects, positions, and secures torch, cutting tips, or welding rod according to type, thickness, area, and desired temperature of metal. Guides and directs flame or electrodes on or across workpiece to straighten, bend, melt, or build up metal. Fuses parts together, seals tension points, and adds metal to build up parts. **SKILLS— Operation Monitoring:** Watching gauges, dials, or other indicators to make sure a machine is working properly. **Operation and Control:** Controlling operations of equipment or systems. **Equipment Maintenance:** Performing routine maintenance on equipment and determining when and what kind of maintenance is needed. **Repairing:** Repairing machines or systems by using the needed tools. **Troubleshooting:** Determining causes of operating errors and deciding what to do about them. **Installation:** Installing equipment, machines, wiring, or programs to meet specifications. **Quality Control Analysis:** Conducting tests and inspections of products, services, or processes to evaluate quality or performance. **GOE—Interest Area:** 13. Manufacturing. **Work Group:** 13.04. Welding, Brazing, and Soldering. **Other Jobs in This Work Group:**

Brazers; Fitters, Structural Metal—Precision; Metal Fabricators, Structural Metal Products; Solderers; Soldering and Brazing Machine Operators and Tenders; Welder-Fitters; Welders and Cutters; Welding Machine Operators and Tenders; Welding Machine Setters and Set-Up Operators. **PERSONALITY TYPE:** Realistic. Realistic occupations frequently involve work activities that include practical, hands-on problems and solutions. These occupations often deal with plants, animals, and real-world materials like wood, tools, and machinery. Many of the occupations require working outside and do not involve a lot of paperwork or working closely with others.

EDUCATION/TRAINING PROGRAM(S)— Welding Technology/Welder. **RELATED KNOWL-EDGE/COURSES—Mechanical Devices:** Knowledge of machines and tools, including their designs, uses, repair, and maintenance. **Production and Processing:** Knowledge of raw materials, production processes, quality control, costs, and other techniques for maximizing the effective manufacture and distribution of goods. **Building and Construction:** Knowledge of the materials, methods, and tools involved in the construction or repair of houses, buildings, or other structures such as highways and roads. **Physics:** Knowledge and prediction of physical principles and laws and their interrelationships and applications to understanding fluid, material, and atmospheric dynamics and mechanical, electrical, atomic, and subatomic structures and processes.

Index

C

D

J–K

L